"The simplified yet deep level of detail, comprehensive coverage of material, and informative historical references make this book perfect for th~~~~~~ ~~~room... An easy read, with complex examples present~~~ ~historical references rarely found in such boo~

Praise for the Previous Edition

"The long-awaited second edition of Wesley Chun's *Core Python Programming* proves to be well worth the wait—its deep and broad coverage and useful exercises will help readers learn and practice good Python."
—Alex Martelli, author of *Python in a Nutshell* and editor of *Python Cookbook*

"There has been lot of good buzz around Wesley Chun's *Core Python Programming*. It turns out that all the buzz is well earned. I think this is the best book currently available for learning Python. I would recommend Chun's book over *Learning Python* (O'Reilly), *Programming Python* (O'Reilly), or *The Quick Python Book* (Manning)."
—David Mertz, Ph.D., IBM DeveloperWorks

"I have been doing a lot of research [on] Python for the past year and have seen a number of positive reviews of your book. The sentiment expressed confirms the opinion that *Core Python Programming* is now considered the standard introductory text."
—Richard Ozaki, Lockheed Martin

"Finally, a book good enough to be both a textbook and a reference on the Python language now exists."
—Michael Baxter, *Linux Journal*

"Very well written. It is the clearest, friendliest book I have come across yet for explaining Python, and putting it in a wider context. It does not presume a large amount of other experience. It does go into some important Python topics carefully and in depth. Unlike too many beginner books, it never condescends or tortures the reader with childish hide-and-seek prose games. [It] sticks to gaining a solid grasp of Python syntax and structure."
—http://python.org bookstore Web site

"[If] I could only own one Python book, it would be *Core Python Programming* by Wesley Chun. This book manages to cover more topics in more depth than *Learning Python* but includes it all in one book that also more than adequately covers the core language. [If] you are in the market for just one book about Python, I recommend this book. You will enjoy reading it, including its wry programmer's wit. More importantly, you will learn Python. Even more importantly, you will find it invaluable in helping you in your day-to-day Python programming life. Well done, Mr. Chun!"
— Ron Stephens, Python Learning Foundation

"I think the best language for beginners is Python, without a doubt. My favorite book is *Core Python Programming*."
— s003apr, MP3Car.com Forums

"Personally, I really like Python. It's simple to learn, completely intuitive, amazingly flexible, and pretty darned fast. Python has only just started to claim mindshare in the Windows world, but look for it to start gaining lots of support as people discover it. To learn Python, I'd start with *Core Python Programming* by Wesley Chun."
— Bill Boswell, MCSE, Microsoft Certified Professional Magazine Online

"If you learn well from books, I suggest *Core Python Programming*. It is by far the best I've found. I'm a Python newbie as well and in three months' time I've been able to implement Python in projects at work (automating MSOffice, SQL DB stuff, etc.)."
— ptonman, Dev Shed Forums

"Python is simply a beautiful language. It's easy to learn, it's cross-platform, and it works. It has achieved many of the technical goals that Java strives for. A one-sentence description of Python would be: 'All other languages appear to have evolved over time—but Python was designed.' And it was designed well. Unfortunately, there aren't a large number of books for Python. The best one I've run across so far is *Core Python Programming*."
— Chris Timmons, C. R. Timmons Consulting

"If you like the Prentice Hall Core series, another good full-blown treatment to consider would be *Core Python Programming*. It addresses in elaborate concrete detail many practical topics that get little, if any, coverage in other books."
— Mitchell L. Model, MLM Consulting

Core

PYTHON

Applications Programming

Third Edition

The Core Series

PRENTICE HALL

Visit informit.com/coreseries for a complete list of available publications.

The Core Series is designed to provide you – the experienced programmer – with the essential information you need to quickly learn and apply the latest, most important technologies.

Authors in The Core Series are seasoned professionals who have pioneered the use of these technologies to achieve tangible results in real-world settings. These experts:

• Share their practical experiences
• Support their instruction with real-world examples
• Provide an accelerated, highly effective path to learning the subject at hand

The resulting book is a no-nonsense tutorial and thorough reference that allows you to quickly produce robust, production-quality code.

Make sure to connect with us!
informit.com/socialconnect

ALWAYS LEARNING

PEARSON

Core

PYTHON

Applications Programming

Third Edition

Wesley J. Chun

PRENTICE
HALL

Upper Saddle River, NJ • Boston • Indianapolis • San Francisco
New York • Toronto • Montreal • London • Munich • Paris • Madrid
Capetown • Sydney • Tokyo • Singapore • Mexico City

Many of the designations used by manufacturers and sellers to distinguish their products are claimed as trademarks. Where those designations appear in this book, and the publisher was aware of a trademark claim, the designations have been printed with initial capital letters or in all capitals.

The author and publisher have taken care in the preparation of this book, but make no expressed or implied warranty of any kind and assume no responsibility for errors or omissions. No liability is assumed for incidental or consequential damages in connection with or arising out of the use of the information or programs contained herein.

The publisher offers excellent discounts on this book when ordered in quantity for bulk purchases or special sales, which may include electronic versions and/or custom covers and content particular to your business, training goals, marketing focus, and branding interests. For more information, please contact:

U.S. Corporate and Government Sales
(800) 382-3419
corpsales@pearsontechgroup.com

For sales outside the United States please contact:

International Sales
international@pearson.com

Visit us on the Web: informit.com/ph

Library of Congress Cataloging-in-Publication Data
Chun, Wesley.
    Core python applications programming / Wesley J. Chun. — 3rd ed.
        p.   cm.
    Rev. ed. of: Core Python programming / Wesley J. Chun. c2007.
    Includes index.
    ISBN 0-13-267820-9 (pbk. : alk. paper)
    1. Python (Computer program language) I. Chun, Wesley. Core Python
programming. II. Title.
    QA76.73.P98C48 2012
    005.1'17—dc23   2011052903

ISBN-13: 978-0-13-267820-9
ISBN-10:   0-13-267820-9

Text printed in the United States on recycled paper at Edwards Brothers Malloy in Ann Arbor, Michigan.
Second printing, June 2013

To my parents,
who taught me that everybody is different.

And to my wife,
who *lives* with someone who is different.

CONTENTS

Preface   **xv**

Acknowledgments   **xxvii**

About the Author   **xxxi**

Part I General Application Topics   **1**

Chapter 1 Regular Expressions   **2**

1.1   Introduction/Motivation   3
1.2   Special Symbols and Characters   6
1.3   Regexes and Python   16
1.4   Some Regex Examples   36
1.5   A Longer Regex Example   41
1.6   Exercises   48

Chapter 2 Network Programming   **53**

2.1   Introduction   54
2.2   What Is Client/Server Architecture?   54
2.3   Sockets: Communication Endpoints   58
2.4   Network Programming in Python   61
2.5   *The SocketServer Module   79
2.6   *Introduction to the Twisted Framework   84
2.7   Related Modules   88
2.8   Exercises   89

Chapter 3 Internet Client Programming   **94**

3.1   What Are Internet Clients?   95
3.2   Transferring Files   96
3.3   Network News   104
3.4   E-Mail   114
3.5   In Practice   131
    3.5.1   E-Mail Composition   131
    3.5.2   E-Mail Parsing   134
    3.5.3   Web-Based Cloud E-Mail Services   135
    3.5.4   Best Practices: Security, Refactoring   136
    3.5.5   Yahoo! Mail   138
    3.5.6   Gmail   144
3.6   Related Modules   146
3.7   Exercises   148

Chapter 4 Multithreaded Programming   **156**

4.1   Introduction/Motivation   157
4.2   Threads and Processes   158
4.3   Threads and Python   160
4.4   The thread Module   164
4.5   The threading Module   169
4.6   Comparing Single vs. Multithreaded Execution   180
4.7   Multithreading in Practice   182
4.8   Producer-Consumer Problem and the Queue/queue Module   202
4.9   Alternative Considerations to Threads   206
4.10   Related Modules   209
4.11   Exercises   210

Chapter 5 GUI Programming   **213**

5.1   Introduction   214
5.2   Tkinter and Python Programming   216
5.3   Tkinter Examples   221
5.4   A Brief Tour of Other GUIs   236
5.5   Related Modules and Other GUIs   247
5.6   Exercises   250

Chapter 6 Database Programming   **253**

6.1   Introduction   254
6.2   The Python DB-API   259
6.3   ORMs   289
6.4   Non-Relational Databases   309
6.5   Related References   316
6.6   Exercises   319

Chapter 7 *Programming Microsoft Office   **324**

7.1   Introduction   325
7.2   COM Client Programming with Python   326
7.3   Introductory Examples   328
7.4   Intermediate Examples   338
7.5   Related Modules/Packages   357
7.6   Exercises   357

Chapter 8 Extending Python   **364**

8.1   Introduction/Motivation   365
8.2   Extending Python by Writing Extensions   368
8.3   Related Topics   384
8.4   Exercises   388

Part II Web Development   **389**

Chapter 9 Web Clients and Servers   **390**

9.1   Introduction   391
9.2   Python Web Client Tools   396
9.3   Web Clients   410
9.4   Web (HTTP) Servers   428
9.5   Related Modules   433
9.6   Exercises   436

Chapter 10 Web Programming: CGI and WSGI   **441**

10.1   Introduction   442
10.2   Helping Web Servers Process Client Data   442
10.3   Building CGI Applications   446
10.4   Using Unicode with CGI   464
10.5   Advanced CGI   466
10.6   Introduction to WSGI   478
10.7   Real-World Web Development   487
10.8   Related Modules   488
10.9   Exercises   490

Chapter 11 Web Frameworks: Django   **493**

11.1   Introduction   494
11.2   Web Frameworks   494
11.3   Introduction to Django   496
11.4   Projects and Apps   501
11.5   Your "Hello World" Application (A Blog)   507
11.6   Creating a Model to Add Database Service   509
11.7   The Python Application Shell   514
11.8   The Django Administration App   518
11.9   Creating the Blog's User Interface   527

11.10   Improving the Output   537
11.11   Working with User Input   542
11.12   Forms and Model Forms   546
11.13   More About Views   551
11.14   *Look-and-Feel Improvements   553
11.15   *Unit Testing   554
11.16   *An Intermediate Django App: The TweetApprover   564
11.17   Resources   597
11.18   Conclusion   597
11.19   Exercises   598

Chapter 12 Cloud Computing: Google App Engine   604

12.1   Introduction   605
12.2   What Is Cloud Computing?   605
12.3   The Sandbox and the App Engine SDK   612
12.4   Choosing an App Engine Framework   617
12.5   Python 2.7 Support   626
12.6   Comparisons to Django   628
12.7   Starting "Hello World"   628
12.8   Creating "Hello World" Manually (Zip File Users)   629
12.9   Uploading your Application to Google   629
12.10   Morphing "Hello World" into a Simple Blog   631
12.11   Adding Memcache Service   647
12.12   Static Files   651
12.13   Adding Users Service   652
12.14   Remote API Shell   654
12.15   Lightning Round (with Python Code)   656
12.16   Sending Instant Messages by Using XMPP   660
12.17   Processing Images   662
12.18   Task Queues (Unscheduled Tasks)   663
12.19   Profiling with Appstats   670
12.20   The URLfetch Service   672
12.21   Lightning Round (without Python Code)   673
12.22   Vendor Lock-In   675
12.23   Resources   676
12.24   Conclusion   679
12.25   Exercises   680

Chapter 13 Web Services   684

13.1   Introduction   685
13.2   The Yahoo! Finance Stock Quote Server   685
13.3   Microblogging with Twitter   690
13.4   Exercises   707

Part III Supplemental/Experimental   **713**

Chapter 14 Text Processing   **714**

14.1   Comma-Separated Values   715
14.2   JavaScript Object Notation   719
14.3   Extensible Markup Language   724
14.4   References   738
14.5   Related Modules   740
14.6   Exercises   740

Chapter 15 Miscellaneous   **743**

15.1   Jython   744
15.2   Google+   748
15.3   Exercises   759

Appendix A Answers to Selected Exercises   **763**

Appendix B Reference Tables   **768**

Appendix C Python 3: The Evolution of a Programming Language   **798**

C.1   Why Is Python Changing?   799
C.2   What Has Changed?   799
C.3   Migration Tools   805
C.4   Conclusion   806
C.5   References   806

Appendix D Python 3 Migration with 2.6+   **807**

D.1   Python 3: The Next Generation   807
D.2   Integers   809
D.3   Built-In Functions   812
D.4   Object-Oriented Programming: Two Different Class Objects   814
D.5   Strings   815
D.6   Exceptions   816
D.7   Other Transition Tools and Tips   817
D.8   Writing Code That is Compatible in Both Versions 2.x and 3.x   818
D.9   Conclusion   822

Index   **823**

PREFACE

Welcome to the Third Edition of *Core Python Applications Programming*!

We are delighted that you have engaged us to help you learn Python as quickly and as deeply as possible. The goal of the *Core Python* series of books is not to just teach developers the Python language; we want you you to develop enough of a personal knowledge base to be able to develop software in any application area.

In our other Core Python offerings, *Core Python Programming* and *Core Python Language Fundamentals*, we not only teach you the syntax of the Python language, but we also strive to give you in-depth knowledge of how Python works under the hood. We believe that armed with this knowledge, you will write more *effective* Python applications, whether you're a beginner to the language or a journeyman (or journeywoman!).

Upon completion of either or any other introductory Python books, you might be satisfied that you have learned Python and learned it well. By completing many of the exercises, you're probably even fairly confident in your newfound Python coding skills. Still, you might be left wondering, "Now what? What kinds of applications can I build with Python?" Perhaps you learned Python for a work project that's constrained to a very narrow focus. "What *else* can I build with Python?"

About this Book

In *Core Python Applications Programming*, you will take all the Python knowledge gained elsewhere and develop new skills, building up a toolset with which you'll be able to use Python for a variety of general applications. These advanced topics chapters are meant as intros or "quick dives" into a variety of distinct subjects. If you're moving toward the specific areas of application development covered by any of these chapters, you'll likely discover that they contain more than enough information to get you pointed in the right direction. Do *not* expect an in-depth treatment because that will detract from the breadth-oriented treatment that this book is designed to convey.

Like all other *Core Python* books, throughout this one, you will find many examples that you can try right in front of your computer. To hammer the concepts home, you will also find fun and challenging exercises at the end of every chapter. These easy and intermediate exercises are meant to test your learning and push your Python skills. There simply is no substitute for hands-on experience. We believe you should not only pick up Python programming skills but also be able to master them in as short a time period as possible.

Because the best way for you to extend your Python skills is through practice, you will find these exercises to be one of the greatest strengths of this book. They will test your knowledge of chapter topics and definitions as well as motivate you to code as much as possible. There is no substitute for improving your skills more effectively than by building applications. You will find easy, intermediate, and difficult problems to solve. It is also here that you might need to write one of those "large" applications that many readers wanted to see in the book, but rather than scripting them—which frankly doesn't do you all that much good—you gain by jumping right in and doing it yourself. Appendix A, "Answers to Selected Exercises," features answers to selected problems from each chapter. As with the second edition, you'll find useful reference tables collated in Appendix B, "Reference Tables."

I'd like to personally thank all readers for your feedback and encouragement. You're the reason why I go through the effort of writing these books. I encourage you to keep sending your feedback and help us make a *fourth* edition possible, and even better than its predecessors!

Who Should Read This Book?

This book is meant for anyone who already knows some Python but wants to know more and expand their application development skillset.

Python is used in many fields, including engineering, information technology, science, business, entertainment, and so on. This means that the list of Python users (and readers of this book) includes but is not limited to

- Software engineers

- Hardware design/CAD engineers

- QA/testing and automation framework developers

- IS/IT/system and network administrators

- Scientists and mathematicians

- Technical or project management staff

- Multimedia or audio/visual engineers

- SCM or release engineers

- Web masters and content management staff

- Customer/technical support engineers

- Database engineers and administrators

- Research and development engineers

- Software integration and professional services staff

- Collegiate and secondary educators

- Web service engineers

- Financial software engineers

- And many others!

Some of the most famous companies that use Python include Google, Yahoo!, NASA, Lucasfilm/Industrial Light and Magic, Red Hat, Zope, Disney, Pixar, and Dreamworks.

The Author and Python

I discovered Python over a decade ago at a company called Four11. At the time, the company had one major product, the Four11.com White Page directory service. Python was being used to design its next product: the Rocketmail Web-based e-mail service that would eventually evolve into what today is Yahoo! Mail.

It was fun learning Python and being on the original Yahoo! Mail engineering team. I helped re-design the address book and spell checker. At the time, Python also became part of a number of other Yahoo! sites, including People Search, Yellow Pages, and Maps and Driving Directions, just to name a few. In fact, I was the lead engineer for People Search.

Although Python was new to me then, it was fairly easy to pick up—much simpler than other languages I had learned in the past. The scarcity of textbooks at the time led me to use the Library Reference and Quick Reference Guide as my primary learning tools; it was also a driving motivation for the book you are reading right now.

Since my days at Yahoo!, I have been able to use Python in all sorts of interesting ways at the jobs that followed. In each case, I was able to harness the power of Python to solve the problems at hand, in a timely manner. I have also developed several Python courses and have used this book to teach those classes—truly eating my own dogfood.

Not only are the *Core Python* books great *learning* devices, but they're also among the best tools with which to *teach* Python. As an engineer, I know what it takes to learn, understand, and apply a new technology. As a professional instructor, I also know *what is needed to deliver the most effective sessions for clients*. These books provide the experience necessary to be able to give you real-world analogies and tips that you cannot get from someone who is "just a trainer" or "just a book author."

What to Expect of the Writing Style: Technical, Yet Easy Reading

Rather than being strictly a "beginners" book or a pure, hard-core computer science reference book, my instructional experience has taught me that an easy-to-read, yet technically oriented book serves the purpose the best, which is to get you up to speed on Python as quickly as possible so that you can apply it to your tasks *posthaste*. We will introduce concepts coupled with appropriate examples to expedite the learning process. At the end of each chapter you will find numerous exercises to reinforce some of the concepts and ideas acquired in your reading.

We are thrilled and humbled to be compared with Bruce Eckel's writing style (see the reviews to the first edition at the book's Web site, http://corepython.com). This is not a dry college textbook. Our goal is to have a conversation with you, as if you were attending one of my well-received Python training courses. As a lifelong student, I constantly put myself in my student's shoes and tell you what you need to hear in order to learn the concepts as quickly and as thoroughly as possible. You will find reading this book fast and easy, without losing sight of the technical details.

As an engineer, I know what I need to tell you in order to teach you a concept in Python. As a teacher, I can take technical details and boil them down into language that is easy to understand and grasp right away. You are getting the best of both worlds with my writing and teaching styles, but you will enjoy programming in Python even more.

Thus, you'll notice that even though I'm the sole author, I use the "third-person plural" writing structure; that is to say, I use verbiage such as "we" and "us" and "our," because in the grand scheme of this book, we're all in this together, working toward the goal of expanding the Python programming universe.

About This Third Edition

At the time the first edition of this book was published, Python was entering its second era with the release of version 2.0. Since then, the language has undergone significant improvements that have contributed to the overall continued success, acceptance, and growth in the use of the language. Deficiencies have been removed and new features added that bring a new level of power and sophistication to Python developers worldwide. The second edition of the book came out in 2006, at the height of Python's ascendance, during the time of its most popular release to date, 2.5.

The second edition was released to rave reviews and ended up outselling the first edition. Python itself had won numerous accolades since that time as well, including the following:

- Tiobe (www.tiobe.com)
  - Language of the Year (2007, 2010)

- LinuxJournal (linuxjournal.com)

  – Favorite Programming Language (2009–2011)

  – Favorite Scripting Language (2006–2008, 2010, 2011)

- LinuxQuestions.org Members Choice Awards

  – Language of the Year (2007–2010)

These awards and honors have helped propel Python even further. Now it's on its next generation with Python 3. Likewise, *Core Python Programming* is moving towards its "third generation," too, as I'm exceedingly pleased that Prentice Hall has asked me to develop this third edition. Because version 3.x is backward-incompatible with Python 1 and 2, it will take some time before it is universally adopted and integrated into industry. We are happy to guide you through this transition. The code in this edition will be presented in both Python 2 and 3 (as appropriate—not everything has been ported yet). We'll also discuss various tools and practices when porting.

The changes brought about in version 3.x continue the trend of iterating and improving the language, taking a larger step toward removing some of its last major flaws, and representing a bigger jump in the continuing evolution of the language. Similarly, the structure of the book is also making a rather significant transition. Due to its size and scope, *Core Python Programming* as it has existed wouldn't be able to handle all the new material introduced in this third edition.

Therefore, Prentice Hall and I have decided the best way of moving forward is to take that logical division represented by Parts I and II of the previous editions, representing the core language and advanced applications topics, respectively, and divide the book into two volumes at this juncture. You are holding in your hands (perhaps in eBook form) the second half of the third edition of *Core Python Programming*. The good news is that the first half is not required in order to make use of the rich amount of content in this volume. We only recommend that you have intermediate Python experience. If you've learned Python recently and are fairly comfortable with using it, or have existing Python skills and want to take it to the next level, then you've come to the right place!

As existing *Core Python Programming* readers already know, my primary focus is teaching you the core of the Python language in a comprehensive manner, much more than just its syntax (which you don't really need a book to learn, right?). Knowing more about how Python works under the hood—including the relationship between data objects and memory management—will make you a much more effective Python programmer right out of the gate. This is what Part I, and now *Core Python Language Fundamentals*, is all about.

As with all editions of this book, I will continue to update the book's Web site and my blog with updates, downloads, and other related articles to keep this publication as contemporary as possible, regardless to which new release of Python you have migrated.

For existing readers, the new topics we have added to this edition include:

- Web-based e-mail examples (Chapter 3)

- Using Tile/Ttk (Chapter 5)

- Using MongoDB (Chapter 6)

- More significant Outlook and PowerPoint examples (Chapter 7)

- Web server gateway interface (WSGI) (Chapter 10)

- Using Twitter (Chapter 13)

- Using Google+ (Chapter 15)

In addition, we are proud to introduce three brand new chapters to the book: Chapter 11, "Web Frameworks: Django," Chapter 12, "Cloud Computing: Google App Engine," and Chapter 14, "Text Processing." These represent new or ongoing areas of application development for which Python is used quite often. All existing chapters have been refreshed and updated to the latest versions of Python, possibly including new material. Take a look at the chapter guide that follows for more details on what to expect from every part of this volume.

Chapter Guide

This book is divided into three parts. The first part, which takes up about two-thirds of the text, gives you treatment of the "core" members of any application development toolset (with Python being the focus, of course). The second part concentrates on a variety of topics, all tied to Web programming. The book concludes with the supplemental section which provides experimental chapters that are under development and hopefully will grow into independent chapters in future editions.

All three parts provide a set of various advanced topics to show what you can build by using Python. We are certainly glad that we were at least able to provide you with a good introduction to many of the key areas of Python development including some of the topics mentioned previously.

Following is a more in-depth, chapter-by-chapter guide.

Part I: General Application Topics

Chapter 1—Regular Expressions

Regular expressions are a powerful tool that you can use for pattern matching, extracting, and search-and-replace functionality.

Chapter 2—Network Programming

So many applications today need to be network oriented. In this chapter, you learn to create clients and servers using TCP/IP and UDP/IP as well as get an introduction to SocketServer and Twisted.

Chapter 3—Internet Client Programming

Most Internet protocols in use today were developed using sockets. In Chapter 3, we explore some of those higher-level libraries that are used to build clients of these Internet protocols. In particular, we focus on file transfer (FTP), the Usenet news protocol (NNTP), and a variety of e-mail protocols (SMTP, POP3, IMAP4).

Chapter 4—Multithreaded Programming

Multithreaded programming is one way to improve the execution performance of many types of applications by introducing concurrency. This chapter ends the drought of written documentation on how to implement threads in Python by explaining the concepts and showing you how to correctly build a Python multithreaded application and what the best use cases are.

Chapter 5—GUI Programming

Based on the Tk graphical toolkit, Tkinter (renamed to tkinter in Python 3) is Python's default GUI development library. We introduce Tkinter to you by showing you how to build simple GUI applications. One of the best ways to learn is to copy, and by building on top of some of these applications, you will be on your way in no time. We conclude the chapter by taking a brief look at other graphical libraries, such as Tix, Pmw, wxPython, PyGTK, and Ttk/Tile.

Chapter 6—Database Programming

Python helps simplify database programming, as well. We first review basic concepts and then introduce you to the Python database application programmer's interface (DB-API). We then show you how you can connect to a relational database and perform queries and operations by using Python. If you prefer a hands-off approach that uses the Structured Query Language (SQL) and want to just work with objects without having to worry about the underlying database layer, we have object-relational managers (ORMs) just for that purpose. Finally, we introduce you to the world of non-relational databases, experimenting with MongoDB as our NoSQL example.

Chapter 7—Programming Microsoft Office

Like it or not, we live in a world where we will likely have to interact with Microsoft Windows-based PCs. It might be intermittent or something we have to deal with on a daily basis, but regardless of how much exposure we face, the power of Python can be used to make our lives easier. In this chapter, we explore COM Client programming by using Python to control and communicate with Office applications, such as Word, Excel, PowerPoint, and Outlook. Although experimental in the previous edition, we're glad we were able to add enough material to turn this into a standalone chapter.

Chapter 8—Extending Python

We mentioned earlier how powerful it is to be able to reuse code and extend the language. In pure Python, these extensions are modules and packages, but you can also develop lower-level code in C/C++, C#, or Java. Those extensions then can interface with Python in a seamless fashion. Writing your extensions in a lower-level programming language gives you added performance and some security (because the source code does not have to be revealed). This chapter walks you step-by-step through the extension building process using C.

Part II: Web Development

Chapter 9—Web Clients and Servers

Extending our discussion of client-server architecture in Chapter 2, we apply this concept to the Web. In this chapter, we not only look at clients, but also explore a variety of Web client tools, parsing Web content, and finally, we introduce you to customizing your own Web servers in Python.

Chapter 10—Web Programming: CGI and WSGI

The main job of Web servers is to take client requests and return results. But *how* do servers get that data? Because they're really only good at returning results, they generally do not have the capabilities or logic necessary to do so; the heavy lifting is done elsewhere. CGI gives servers the ability to spawn another program to do this processing and has historically been the solution, but it doesn't scale and is thus not really used in practice; however, its concepts still apply, regardless of what framework(s) you use, so we'll spend most of the chapter learning CGI. You will also learn how WSGI helps application developers by providing them a common programming interface. In addition, you'll see how WSGI helps framework developers who have to connect to Web servers on one side and application code on the other so that application developers can write code without having to worry about the execution platform.

Chapter 11—Web Frameworks: Django

Python features a host of Web frameworks with Django being one of the most popular. In this chapter, you get an introduction to this framework and learn how to write simple Web applications. With this knowledge, you can then explore other Web frameworks as you wish.

Chapter 12—Cloud Computing: Google App Engine

Cloud computing is taking the industry by storm. While the world is most familiar with infrastructure services like Amazon's AWS and online applications such as Gmail and Yahoo! Mail, platforms present a powerful alternative that take advantage of infrastructure without user involvement but give more flexibility than cloud software because you control the application and its code. In this chapter, you get a comprehensive introduction to the first platform service using Python, Google App Engine. With the knowledge gained here, you can then explore similar services in the same space.

Chapter 13—Web Services

In this chapter, we explore higher-level services on the Web (using HTTP). We look at an older service (Yahoo! Finance) and a newer one (Twitter). You learn how to interact with both of these services by using Python as well as knowledge you've gained from earlier chapters.

Part III: Supplemental/Experimental

Chapter 14—Text Processing

Our first supplemental chapter introduces you to text processing using Python. We first explore CSV, then JSON, and finally XML. In the last part of this chapter, we take our client/server knowledge from earlier in the book and combine it with XML to look at how you can create online remote procedure calls (RPC) services by using XML-RPC.

Chapter 15—Miscellaneous

This chapter consists of bonus material that we will likely develop into full, individual chapters in a future edition. Topics covered here include Java/Jython and Google+.

Conventions

All program output and source code are in monospaced font. Python keywords appear in **Bold-monospaced** font. Lines of output with three leading greater than signs (>>>) represent the Python interpreter prompt. A leading asterisk (*) in front of a chapter, section, or exercise, indicates that this is advanced and/or optional material.

 Represents Core Notes

 Represents Core Module

 Represents Core Tips

2.5 New features to Python are highlighted with this icon, with the number representing version(s) of Python in which the features first appeared.

Book Resources

We welcome any and all feedback—the good, the bad, and the ugly. If you have any comments, suggestions, kudos, complaints, bugs, questions, or anything at all, feel free to contact me at corepython@yahoo.com.

You will find errata, source code, updates, upcoming talks, Python training, downloads, and other information at the book's Web site located at: http://corepython.com. You can also participate in the community discussion around the "Core Python" books at their Google+ page, which is located at: http://plus.ly/corepython.

ACKNOWLEDGMENTS

Acknowledgments for the Third Edition

Reviewers and Contributors

Gloria Willadsen (lead reviewer)
Martin Omander (reviewer and also coauthor of Chapter 11, "Web Frameworks: Django," creator of the TweetApprover application, and coauthor of Section 15.2, "Google+," in Chapter 15, "Miscellaneous").
Darlene Wong
Bryce Verdier
Eric Walstad
Paul Bissex (coauthor of *Python Web Development with Django*)
Johan "proppy" Euphrosine
Anthony Vallone

Inspiration

My wife Faye, who has continued to amaze me by being able to run the household, take care of the kids and their schedule, feed us all, handle the finances, and be able to do this while I'm off on the road driving cloud adoption or under foot at home, writing books.

Editorial

Mark Taub (Editor-in-Chief)
Debra Williams Cauley (Acquisitions Editor)
John Fuller (Managing Editor)
Elizabeth Ryan (Project Editor)
Bob Russell, Octal Publishing, Inc. (Copy Editor)
Dianne Russell, Octal Publishing, Inc. (Production and Management Services)

Acknowledgments for the Second Edition

Reviewers and Contributors

Shannon -jj Behrens (lead reviewer)
Michael Santos (lead reviewer)
Rick Kwan
Lindell Aldermann (coauthor of the Unicode section in Chapter 6)
Wai-Yip Tung (coauthor of the Unicode example in Chapter 20)
Eric Foster-Johnson (coauthor of *Beginning Python*)
Alex Martelli (editor of *Python Cookbook* and author of *Python in a Nutshell*)
Larry Rosenstein
Jim Orosz
Krishna Srinivasan
Chuck Kung

Inspiration

My wonderful children and pet hamster.

Acknowledgments for the First Edition

Reviewers and Contributors

Guido van Rossum (creator of the Python language)
Dowson Tong
James C. Ahlstrom (coauthor of *Internet Programming with Python*)
S. Candelaria de Ram
Cay S. Horstmann (coauthor of *Core Java* and *Core JavaServer Faces*)
Michael Santos
Greg Ward (creator of `distutils` package and its documentation)
Vincent C. Rubino
Martijn Faassen
Emile van Sebille
Raymond Tsai
Albert L. Anders (coauthor of MT Programming chapter)
Fredrik Lundh (author of *Python Standard Library*)
Cameron Laird
Fred L. Drake, Jr. (coauthor of *Python & XML* and editor of the official Python documentation)
Jeremy Hylton
Steve Yoshimoto
Aahz Maruch (author of *Python for Dummies*)
Jeffrey E. F. Friedl (author of *Mastering Regular Expressions*)
Pieter Claerhout
Catriona (Kate) Johnston
David Ascher (coauthor of *Learning Python* and editor of *Python Cookbook*)
Reg Charney
Christian Tismer (creator of Stackless Python)
Jason Stillwell
and my students at UC Santa Cruz Extension

Inspiration

I would like to extend my great appreciation to James P. Prior, my high school programming teacher.

To Louise Moser and P. Michael Melliar-Smith (my graduate thesis advisors at The University of California, Santa Barbara), you have my deepest gratitude.)

Thanks to Alan Parsons, Eric Woolfson, Andrew Powell, Ian Bairnson, Stuart Elliott, David Paton, all other Project participants, and fellow Projectologists and Roadkillers (for all the music, support, and good times).

I would like to thank my family, friends, and the Lord above, who have kept me safe and sane during this crazy period of late nights and abandonment, on the road and off. I want to also give big thanks to all those who believed in me for the past two decades (you know who you are!)—I couldn't have done it without you.

Finally, I would like to thank you, my readers, and the Python community at large. I am excited at the prospect of teaching you Python and hope that you enjoy your travels with me on this, our third journey.

Wesley J. Chun
Silicon Valley, CA
(It's not so much a place as it is a state of sanity.)
October 2001; updated July 2006,
March 2009, March 2012

ABOUT THE AUTHOR

Wesley Chun was initiated into the world of computing during high school, using BASIC and 6502 assembly on Commodore systems. This was followed by Pascal on the Apple IIe, and then ForTran on punch cards. It was the last of these that made him a careful/cautious developer, because sending the deck out to the school district's mainframe and getting the results was a one-week round-trip process. Wesley also converted the journalism class from typewriters to Osborne 1 CP/M computers. He got his first paying job as a student-instructor teaching BASIC programming to fourth, fifth, and sixth graders and their parents.

After high school, Wesley went to University of California at Berkeley as a California Alumni Scholar. He graduated with an AB in applied math (computer science) and a minor in music (classical piano). While at Cal, he coded in Pascal, Logo, and C. He also took a tutoring course that featured videotape training and psychological counseling. One of his summer internships involved coding in a 4GL and writing a "Getting Started" user manual. He then continued his studies several years later at University of California, Santa Barbara, receiving an MS in computer science (distributed systems). While there, he also taught C programming. A paper based on his master's thesis was nominated for Best Paper at the 29th HICSS conference, and a later version appeared in the University of Singapore's *Journal of High Performance Computing*.

Wesley has been in the software industry since graduating and has continued to teach and write, publishing several books and delivering hundreds of conference talks and tutorials, plus Python courses, both to the public as well as private corporate training. Wesley's Python experience began with version 1.4 at a startup where he designed the Yahoo! Mail spellchecker and address book. He then became the lead engineer for Yahoo! People Search. After leaving Yahoo!, he wrote the first edition of this book and then traveled around the world. Since returning, he has used Python in a variety of ways, from local product search, anti-spam and antivirus e-mail appliances, and Facebook games/applications to something completely different: software for doctors to perform spinal fracture analysis.

In his spare time, Wesley enjoys piano, bowling, basketball, bicycling, ultimate frisbee, poker, traveling, and spending time with his family. He volunteers for Python users groups, the Tutor mailing list, and PyCon. He also maintains the Alan Parsons Project Monster Discography. If you think you're a fan but don't have "Freudiana," you had better find it! At the time of this writing, Wesley was a Developer Advocate at Google, representing its cloud products. He is based in Silicon Valley, and you can follow him at @wescpy or plus.ly/wescpy.

General Application Topics

CHAPTER 1

Regular Expressions

Some people, when confronted with a problem, think, "I know, I'll use regular expressions." Now they have two problems.
—Jamie "jwz" Zawinski, August 1997

In this chapter...

- Introduction/Motivation
- Special Symbols and Characters
- Regexes and Python
- Some Regex Examples
- A Longer Regex Example

1.1   Introduction/Motivation

Manipulating text or data is a big thing. If you don't believe me, look very carefully at what computers primarily do today. Word processing, "fill-out-form" Web pages, streams of information coming from a database dump, stock quote information, news feeds—the list goes on and on. Because we might not know the exact text or data that we have programmed our machines to process, it becomes advantageous to be able to express it in patterns that a machine can recognize and take action upon.

If I were running an e-mail archiving company, and you, as one of my customers, requested all of the e-mail that you sent and received last February, for example, it would be nice if I could set a computer program to collate and forward that information to you, rather than having a human being read through your e-mail and process your request manually. You would be horrified (and infuriated) that someone would be rummaging through your messages, even if that person were *supposed* to be looking only at time-stamp. Another example request might be to look for a subject line like "ILOVEYOU," indicating a virus-infected message, and remove those e-mail messages from your personal archive. So this begs the question of how we can program machines with the ability to look for patterns in text.

Regular expressions provide such an infrastructure for advanced text pattern matching, extraction, and/or search-and-replace functionality. To put it simply, a regular expression (a.k.a. a "*regex*" for short) is a string that use special symbols and characters to indicate pattern repetition or to represent multiple characters so that they can "match" a set of strings with similar characteristics described by the pattern (Figure 1-1). In other words, they enable matching of multiple strings—a regex pattern that matched only one string would be rather boring and ineffective, wouldn't you say?

Python supports regexes through the standard library re module. In this introductory subsection, we will give you a brief and concise introduction. Due to its brevity, only the most common aspects of regexes used in everyday Python programming will be covered. Your experience will, of course, vary. We highly recommend reading any of the official supporting documentation as well as external texts on this interesting subject. You will never look at strings in the same way again!

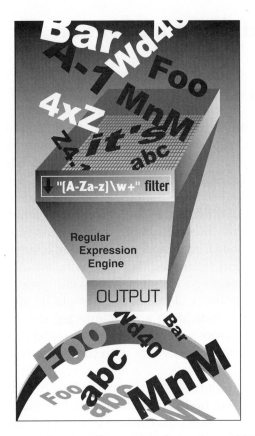

Figure 1-1 You can use regular expressions, such as the one here, which recognizes valid Python identifiers. [A-Za-z]\w+ means the first character should be alphabetic, that is, either A–Z or a–z, followed by at least one (+) alphanumeric character (\w). In our filter, notice how many strings go into the filter, but the only ones to come out are the ones we asked for via the regex. One example that did not make it was "4xZ" because it starts with a number.

 CORE NOTE: Searching vs. matching

Throughout this chapter, you will find references to searching and matching. When we are strictly discussing regular expressions with respect to patterns in strings, we will say "matching," referring to the term *pattern-matching*. In Python terminology, there are two main ways to accomplish pattern-matching: *searching*, that is, looking for a pattern match in any part of a string; and *matching*, that is, attempting to match a pattern to an entire string (starting from the beginning). Searches are accomplished by using the search() function or method, and matching is done with the match() function or method. In summary, we keep the term "matching" universal when referencing patterns, and we differentiate between "searching" and "matching" in terms of how Python accomplishes pattern-matching.

1.1.1   Your First Regular Expression

As we mentioned earlier, regexes are strings containing text and special characters that describe a pattern with which to recognize multiple strings. We also briefly discussed a regular expression *alphabet*. For general text, the alphabet used for regular expressions is the set of all uppercase and lowercase letters plus numeric digits. Specialized alphabets are also possible; for instance, you can have one consisting of only the characters "0" and "1." The set of all strings over this alphabet describes all binary strings, that is, "0," "1," "00," "01," "10," "11," "100," etc.

Let's look at the most basic of regular expressions now to show you that although regexes are sometimes considered an advanced topic, they can also be rather simplistic. Using the standard alphabet for general text, we present some simple regexes and the strings that their patterns describe. The following regular expressions are the most basic, "true vanilla," as it were. They simply consist of a string pattern that matches only one string: the string defined by the regular expression. We now present the regexes followed by the strings that match them:

Regex Pattern	String(s) Matched
foo	foo
Python	Python
abc123	abc123

The first regular expression pattern from the above chart is "foo." This pattern has no special symbols to match any other symbol other than those described, so the only string that matches this pattern is the string "foo." The same thing applies to "Python" and "abc123." The power of regular expressions comes in when special characters are used to define character sets, subgroup matching, and pattern repetition. It is these special symbols that allow a regex to match a set of strings rather than a single one.

1.2   Special Symbols and Characters

We will now introduce the most popular of the special characters and symbols, known as *metacharacters*, which give regular expressions their power and flexibility. You will find the most common of these symbols and characters in Table 1-1.

Table 1-1   Common Regular Expression Symbols and Special Characters

Notation	Description	Example Regex
Symbols		
`literal`	Match literal string value `literal`	`foo`
`re1|re2`	Match regular expressions *re1* or *re2*	`foo|bar`
`.`	Match *any character* (except `\n`)	`b.b`
`^`	Match *start of string*	`^Dear`
`$`	Match *end of string*	`/bin/*sh$`
`*`	Match *0 or more* occurrences of preceding regex	`[A-Za-z0-9]*`
`+`	Match *1 or more* occurrences of preceding regex	`[a-z]+\.com`
`?`	Match *0 or 1* occurrence(s) of preceding regex	`goo?`
`{N}`	Match *N* occurrences of preceding regex	`[0-9]{3}`
`{M,N}`	Match from *M* to *N* occurrences of preceding regex	`[0-9]{5,9}`
`[...]`	Match any single character from *character* class	`[aeiou]`
`[..x-y..]`	Match any single character in the *range from* x to y	`[0-9],[A-Za-z]`

Notation	Description	Example Regex
Symbols		
[^...]	*Do not match* any character from character class, including any ranges, if present	[^aeiou], [^A-Za-z0-9_]
(*|+|?|{})?	Apply "non-greedy" versions of above occurrence/repetition symbols (*, +, ?, {})	.*?[a-z]
(...)	Match enclosed regex and save as *subgroup*	([0-9]{3})?, f(oo|u)bar
Special Characters		
\d	Match any decimal *digit*, same as [0-9] (\D is inverse of \d: do not match any numeric digit)	data\d+.txt
\w	Match any *alphanumeric* character, same as [A-Za-z0-9_] (\W is inverse of \w)	[A-Za-z_]\w+
\s	Match *any whitespace* character, same as [\n\t\r\v\f] (\S is inverse of \s)	of\sthe
\b	Match any *word boundary* (\B is inverse of \b)	\bThe\b
N	Match saved *subgroup N* (see (...) above)	price: \16
c	Match any *special character c* verbatim (i.e., without its special meaning, literal)	\., \\, *
\A (\Z)	Match *start (end) of string* (also see ^ and $ above)	\ADear

(Continued)

Table 1-1   Common Regular Expression Symbols and Special Characters
(Continued)

Notation	Description	Example Regex
Extension Notation		
`(?iLmsux)`	Embed one or more special "flags" parameters within the regex itself (vs. via function/method)	`(?x)`, `(?im)`
`(?:...)`	Signifies a group whose match is *not* saved	`(?:\w+\.)*`
`(?P<name>...)`	Like a regular group match only identified with name rather than a numeric ID	`(?P<data>)`
`(?P=name)`	Matches text previously grouped by `(?P<name>)` in the same string	`(?P=data)`
`(?#...)`	Specifies a comment, all contents within ignored	`(?#comment)`
`(?=...)`	Matches if ... comes next without consuming input string; called *positive lookahead assertion*	`(?=.com)`
`(?!...)`	Matches if ... doesn't come next without consuming input; called *negative lookahead assertion*	`(?!.net)`
`(?<=...)`	Matches if ... comes prior without consuming input string; called *positive lookbehind assertion*	`(?<=800-)`
`(?<!...)`	Matches if ... doesn't come prior without consuming input; called *negative lookbehind assertion*	`(?<!192\.168\.)`
`(?(id/name)Y|N)`	Conditional match of regex *Y* if group with given *id* or name exists else *N*; `|N` is optional	`(?(1)y|x`

1.2.1 Matching More Than One Regex Pattern with Alternation (|)

The pipe symbol (|), a vertical bar on your keyboard, indicates an alternation operation. It is used to separate different regular expressions. For example, the following are some patterns that employ alternation, along with the strings they match:

Regex Pattern	Strings Matched
at|home	at, home
r2d2|c3po	r2d2, c3po
bat|bet|bit	bat, bet, bit

With this one symbol, we have just increased the flexibility of our regular expressions, enabling the matching of more than just one string. Alternation is also sometimes called *union* or *logical OR*.

1.2.2 Matching Any Single Character (.)

The dot or period (.) symbol matches any single character except for \n. (Python regexes have a compilation flag [S or DOTALL], which can override this to include \ns.) Whether letter, number, whitespace (not including "\n"), printable, non-printable, or a symbol, the dot can match them all.

Regex Pattern	Strings Matched
f.o	Any character between "f" and "o"; for example, fao, f9o, f#o, etc.
..	Any pair of characters
.end	Any character before the string end

Q: What if I want to match the dot or period character?

A: To specify a dot character explicitly, you must escape its functionality with a backslash, as in "\.".

1.2.3   Matching from the Beginning or End of Strings or Word Boundaries (^, $, \b, \B)

There are also symbols and related special characters to specify searching for patterns at the beginning and end of strings. To match a pattern starting from the beginning, you must use the carat symbol (^) or the special character \A (backslash-capital "A"). The latter is primarily for keyboards that do not have the carat symbol (for instance, an international keyboard). Similarly, the dollar sign ($) or \Z will match a pattern from the end of a string.

Patterns that use these symbols differ from most of the others we describe in this chapter because they dictate location or position. In the previous Core Note, we noted that a distinction is made between *matching* (attempting matches of entire strings starting at the beginning) and *searching* (attempting matches from anywhere within a string). With that said, here are some examples of "edge-bound" regex search patterns:

Regex Pattern	Strings Matched
^From	Any string that starts with From
/bin/tcsh$	Any string that ends with /bin/tcsh
^Subject: hi$	Any string consisting solely of the string Subject: hi

Again, if you want to match either (or both) of these characters verbatim, you must use an escaping backslash. For example, if you wanted to match any string that ended with a dollar sign, one possible regex solution would be the pattern .*\$$.

The special characters \b and \B pertain to word boundary matches. The difference between them is that \b will match a pattern to a word boundary, meaning that a pattern must be at the beginning of a word, whether there are any characters in front of it (word in the middle of a string) or not (word at the beginning of a line). And likewise, \B will match a pattern only if it appears starting in the middle of a word (i.e., not at a word boundary). Here are some examples:

Regex Pattern	Strings Matched
the	Any string containing the
\bthe	Any word that starts with the

Regex Pattern	Strings Matched
\bthe\b	Matches only the word the
\Bthe	Any string that contains but does not begin with the

1.2.4   Creating Character Classes ([ ])

Whereas the dot is good for allowing matches of any symbols, there might be occasions for which there are specific characters that you want to match. For this reason, the bracket symbols ([]) were invented. The regular expression will match any of the enclosed characters. Here are some examples:

Regex Pattern	Strings Matched
b[aeiu]t	bat, bet, bit, but
[cr][23][dp][o2]	A string of four characters: first is "c" or "r," then "2" or "3," followed by "d" or "p," and finally, either "o" or "2." For example, c2do, r3p2, r2d2, c3po, etc.

One side note regarding the regex [cr][23][dp][o2] — a more restrictive version of this regex would be required to allow only "r2d2" or "c3po" as valid strings. Because brackets merely imply logical OR functionality, it is not possible to use brackets to enforce such a requirement. The only solution is to use the pipe, as in r2d2|c3po.

For single-character regexes, though, the pipe and brackets are equivalent. For example, let's start with the regular expression "ab," which matches only the string with an "a" followed by a "b." If we wanted either a one-letter string, for instance, either "a" or a "b," we could use the regex [ab]. Because "a" and "b" are individual strings, we can also choose the regex a|b. However, if we wanted to match the string with the pattern "ab" followed by "cd," we cannot use the brackets because they work only for single characters. In this case, the only solution is ab|cd, similar to the r2d2/c3po problem just mentioned.

1.2.5   Denoting Ranges (-) and Negation (^)

In addition to single characters, the brackets also support ranges of characters. A hyphen between a pair of symbols enclosed in brackets is used to indicate a range of characters; for example A–Z, a–z, or 0–9 for uppercase letters, lowercase letters, and numeric digits, respectively. This is a lexicographic range, so you are not restricted to using just alphanumeric characters. Additionally, if a caret (^) is the first character immediately inside the open left bracket, this symbolizes a directive *not* to match any of the characters in the given character set.

Regex Pattern	Strings Matched
z.[0-9]	"z" followed by any character then followed by a single digit
[r-u][env-y] [us]	"r," "s," "t," or "u" followed by "e," "n," "v," "w," "x," or "y" followed by "u" or "s"
[^aeiou]	A non-vowel character (Exercise: why do we say "non-vowels" rather than "consonants"?)
[^\t\n]	Not a TAB or \n
["-a]	In an ASCII system, all characters that fall between '"' and "a," that is, between ordinals 34 and 97

1.2.6   Multiple Occurrence/Repetition Using Closure Operators (*, +, ?, {})

We will now introduce the most common regex notations, namely, the special symbols *, +, and ?, all of which can be used to match single, multiple, or no occurrences of string patterns. The asterisk or star operator (*) will match zero or more occurrences of the regex immediately to its left (in language and compiler theory, this operation is known as the *Kleene Closure*). The plus operator (+) will match one or more occurrences of a regex (known as *Positive Closure*), and the question mark operator (?) will match exactly 0 or 1 occurrences of a regex.

There are also brace operators ({}) with either a single value or a comma-separated pair of values. These indicate a match of exactly N occurrences (for {N}) or a range of occurrences; for example, {M, N} will match from M to N occurrences. These symbols can also be escaped by using the backslash character; * matches the asterisk, etc.

In the previous table, we notice the question mark is used more than once (overloaded), meaning either matching 0 or 1 occurrences, or its other meaning: if it follows any matching using the close operators, it will direct the regular expression engine to match as few repetitions as possible.

What does "as few repetitions as possible" mean? When pattern-matching is employed using the grouping operators, the regular expression engine will try to "absorb" as many characters as possible that match the pattern. This is known as being *greedy*. The question mark tells the engine to lay off and, if possible, take as few characters as possible in the current match, leaving the rest to match as many succeeding characters of the next pattern (if applicable). Toward the end of the chapter, we will show you a great example where non-greediness is required. For now, let's continue to look at the closure operators:

Regex Pattern	Strings Matched
[dn]ot?	"d" or "n," followed by an "o" and, at most, one "t" after that; thus, do, no, dot, not.
0?[1-9]	Any numeric digit, possibly prepended with a "0." For example, the set of numeric representations of the months January to September, whether single or double-digits.
[0-9]{15,16}	Fifteen or sixteen digits (for example, credit card numbers.
</?[^>]+>	Strings that match all valid (and invalid) HTML tags.
[KQRBNP][a-h][1-8]-[a-h][1-8]	Legal chess move in "long algebraic" notation (move only, no capture, check, etc.); that is, strings that start with any of "K," "Q," "R," "B," "N," or "P" followed by a hyphenated-pair of chess board grid locations from "a1" to "h8" (and everything in between), with the first coordinate indicating the former position, and the second being the new position.

1.2.7   Special Characters Representing Character Sets

We also mentioned that there are special characters that can represent character sets. Rather than using a range of "0–9," you can simply use \d to indicate the match of any decimal digit. Another special character, \w, can be used to denote the entire alphanumeric character class, serving as a shortcut for A-Za-z0-9_, and \s can be used for whitespace characters. Uppercase versions of these strings symbolize non-matches; for example, \D matches any non-decimal digit (same as [^0-9]), etc.

Using these shortcuts, we will present a few more complex examples:

Regex Pattern	Strings Matched
\w+-\d+	Alphanumeric string and number separated by a hyphen
[A-Za-z]\w*	Alphabetic first character; additional characters (if present) can be alphanumeric (almost equivalent to the set of valid Python identifiers [see exercises])
\d{3}-\d{3}-\d{4}	American-format telephone numbers with an area code prefix, as in 800-555-1212
\w+@\w+\.com	Simple e-mail addresses of the form *XXX@YYY.com*

1.2.8   Designating Groups with Parentheses (())

Now, we have achieved the goal of matching a string and discarding non-matches, but in some cases, we might also be more interested in the data that we did match. Not only do we want to know whether the entire string matched our criteria, but also whether we can extract any specific strings or substrings that were part of a successful match. The answer is yes. To accomplish this, surround any regex with a pair of parentheses.

A pair of parentheses (()) can accomplish either (or both) of the following when used with regular expressions:

- Grouping regular expressions
- Matching subgroups

One good example of why you would want to group regular expressions is when you have two different regexes with which you want to compare a string. Another reason is to group a regex in order to use a repetition operator on the entire regex (as opposed to an individual character or character class).

One side effect of using parentheses is that the substring that matched the pattern is saved for future use. These subgroups can be recalled for the same match or search, or extracted for post-processing. You will see some examples of pulling out subgroups at the end of Section 1.3.9.

Why are matches of subgroups important? The main reason is that there are times when you want to extract the patterns you match, in addition to making a match. For example, what if we decided to match the pattern \w+-\d+ but wanted save the alphabetic first part and the numeric second part individually? We might want to do this because with any successful match, we might want to see just what those strings were that matched our regex patterns.

If we add parentheses to both subpatterns such as (\w+)-(\d+), then we can access each of the matched subgroups individually. Subgrouping is preferred because the alternative is to write code to determine we have a match, then execute another separate routine (which we also had to create) to parse the entire match just to extract both parts. Why not let Python do it; it's a supported feature of the re module, so why reinvent the wheel?

Regex Pattern	Strings Matched
\d+(\.\d*)?	Strings representing simple floating-point numbers; that is, any number of digits followed optionally by a single decimal point and zero or more numeric digits, as in "0.004," "2," "75.," etc.
(Mr?s?\.)?[A-Z] [a-z]* [A-Za-z-]+	First name and last name, with a restricted first name (must start with uppercase; lowercase only for remaining letters, if any), the full name, prepended by an optional title of "Mr.," "Mrs.," "Ms.," or "M.," and a flexible last name, allowing for multiple words, dashes, and uppercase letters

1.2.9   Extension Notations

One final aspect of regular expressions we have not touched upon yet include the extension notations that begin with the question mark symbol (? . . .). We are not going to spend a lot of time on these as they are generally used more to provide flags, perform look-ahead (or look-behind), or check conditionally before determining a match. Also, although parentheses are used with these notations, only (?P<name>) represents a grouping for matches. All others do *not* create a group. However, you should still know what they are because they might be "the right tool for the job."

Regex Pattern	Notation Definition
(?:\w+\.)*	Strings that end with a dot, like "google.", "twitter.", "facebook.", but such matches are neither saved for use nor retrieval later.
(?#comment)	No matching here, just a comment.
(?=.com)	Only do a match if ".com" follows; do not consume any of the target string.
(?!.net)	Only do a match if ".net" does *not* follow.
(?<=800-)	Only do a match if string is preceded by "800-", presumably for phone numbers; again, do not consume the input string.
(?<!192\.168\.)	Only do a match if string is not preceded by "192.168.", presumably to filter out a group of Class C IP addresses.
(?(1)y|x)	If a matched group 1 (\1) exists, match against y; otherwise, match against x.

1.3   Regexes and Python

Now that we know all about regular expressions, we can examine how Python currently supports regular expressions through the re module, which was introduced way back in ancient history (Python 1.5), replacing the deprecated regex and regsub modules—both modules were removed from Python in version 2.5, and importing either module from that release on triggers an ImportError exception.

The re module supports the more powerful and regular Perl-style (Perl 5) regexes, allows multiple threads to share the same compiled regex objects, and supports named subgroups.

2.5

1.3.1   The re Module: Core Functions and Methods

The chart in Table 1-2 lists the more popular functions and methods from the re module. Many of these functions are also available as methods of compiled regular expression objects (regex objects and regex match objects. In this subsection, we will look at the two main functions/methods, match() and search(), as well as the compile() function. We will introduce several more in the next section, but for more information on all these and the others that we do not cover, we refer you to the Python documentation.

Table 1-2 Common Regular Expression Attributes

Function/Method	Description
re Module Function Only	
compile(pattern, flags=0)	Compile regex *pattern* with any optional *flags* and return a regex object
re Module Functions and Regex Object Methods	
match(pattern, string, flags=0)	Attempt to match *pattern* to *string* with optional *flags*; return match object on success, None on failure
search(pattern, string, flags=0)	Search for first occurrence of *pattern* within *string* with optional *flags*; return match object on success, None on failure
findall(pattern, string[, flags])[a]	Look for all (non-overlapping) occurrences of *pattern* in *string*; return a list of matches
finditer(pattern, string[, flags])[b]	Same as findall(), except returns an iterator instead of a list; for each match, the iterator returns a match object
split(pattern, string, max=0)[c]	Split *string* into a list according to regex *pattern* delimiter and return list of successful matches, splitting at most *max* times (split all occurrences is the default)

(Continued)

Table 1-2 Common Regular Expression Attributes *(Continued)*

Function/Method	Description
re *Module Functions and Regex Object Methods*	
sub*(pattern, repl, string, count=0)*c	Replace all occurrences of the regex *pattern* in *string* with *repl*, substituting all occurrences unless *count* provided (see also subn(), which, in addition, returns the number of substitutions made)
purge()	Purge cache of implicitly compiled regex patterns
Common Match Object Methods (see documentation for others)	
group*(num=0)*	Return entire match (or specific subgroup *num*)
groups *(default=None)*	Return all matching subgroups in a tuple (empty if there aren't any)
groupdict *(default=None)*	Return dict containing all matching named subgroups with the names as the keys (empty if there weren't any)
Common Module Attributes (flags for most regex functions)	
re.I, re.IGNORECASE	Case-insensitive matching
re.L, re.LOCALE	Matches via \w, \W, \b, \B, \s, \S depends on locale
re.M, re.MULTILINE	Respectively causes ∧ and $ to match the beginning and end of each line in target string rather than strictly the beginning and end of the entire string itself
re.S, re.DOTALL	The . normally matches any single character except \n; this flag says . should match them, too
re.X, re.VERBOSE	All whitespace plus # (and all text after it on a single line) are ignored unless in a character class or backslash-escaped, allowing comments and improving readability

a.   New in Python 1.5.2; *flags* parameter added in 2.4.
b.   New in Python 2.2; *flags* parameter added in 2.4.
c.   *flags* parameter added in version 2.7 and 3.1.

CORE NOTE: Regex compilation (to compile or not to compile?)

In the Execution Environment chapter of *Core Python Programming* or the forth-coming *Core Python Language Fundamentals*, we describe how Python code is eventually compiled into bytecode, which is then executed by the interpreter. In particular, we specified that calling eval() or exec (in version 2.x or exec() in version 3.x) with a code object rather than a string provides a performance improvement due to the fact that the compilation process does not have to be performed repeatedly. In other words, using precompiled code objects is faster than using strings because the interpreter will have to compile it into a code object (anyway) each time before execution.

The same concept applies to regexes—regular expression patterns must be compiled into *regex* objects before any pattern matching can occur. For regexes, which are compared many times during the course of execution, we highly recommend using precompilation because, again, regexes have to be compiled anyway, so doing it ahead of time is prudent for performance reasons. re.compile() provides this functionality.

The module functions do cache the compiled objects, though, so it's not as if every search() and match() with the same regex pattern requires compila-tion. Still, you save the cache lookups and do not have to make function calls with the same string, over and over. The number of compiled regex objects that are cached might vary between releases, and is undocumented. The purge() function can be used to clear this cache.

1.3.2   Compiling Regexes with compile()

Almost all of the re module functions we will be describing shortly are available as methods for regex objects. Remember, even though we recom-mend it, precompilation is not required. If you compile, you will use methods; if you don't, you will just use functions. The good news is that either way, the names are the same, whether a function or a method. (This is the reason why there are module functions and methods that are identi-cal; for example, search(), match(), etc., in case you were wondering.) Because it saves one small step for most of our examples, we will use strings, instead. We will throw in a few with compilation, though, just so you know how it is done.

Optional flags may be given as arguments for specialized compilation. These flags allow for case-insensitive matching, using system locale set-tings for matching alphanumeric characters, etc. Please see the entries in

Table 1-2 and the official documentation for more information on these flags (re.IGNORECASE, re.MULTILINE, re.DOTALL, re.VERBOSE, etc.). They can be combined by using the bitwise OR operator (|).

These flags are also available as a parameter to most re module functions. If you want to use these flags with the methods, they must already be integrated into the compiled regex objects, or you need to use the (?F) notation directly embedded in the regex itself, where F is one or more of i (for re.I/IGNORECASE), m (for re.M/MULTILINE), s (for re.S/DOTALL), etc. If more than one is desired, you place them together rather than using the bitwise OR operation; for example, (?im) for both re.IGNORECASE plus re.MULTILINE.

1.3.3   Match Objects and the group() and groups() Methods

When dealing with regular expressions, there is another object type in addition to the regex object: the *match object*. These are the objects returned on successful calls to match() or search(). Match objects have two primary methods, group() and groups().

group() either returns the entire match, or a specific subgroup, if requested. groups() simply returns a tuple consisting of only/all the subgroups. If there are no subgroups requested, then groups() returns an empty tuple while group() still returns the entire match.

Python regexes also allow for named matches, which are beyond the scope of this introductory section. We refer you to the complete re module documentation for a complete listing of the more advanced details we have omitted here.

1.3.4   Matching Strings with match()

match() is the first re module function and regex object (regex object) method we will look at. The match() function attempts to match the pattern to the string, starting at the beginning. If the match is successful, a match object is returned; if it is unsuccessful, None is returned. The group() method of a match object can be used to show the successful match. Here is an example of how to use match() [and group()]:

```
>>> m = re.match('foo', 'foo')   # pattern matches string
>>> if m is not None:            # show match if successful
...     m.group()
...
'foo'
```

The pattern "foo" matches exactly the string "foo." We can also confirm that m is an example of a match object from within the interactive interpreter:

```
>>> m                           # confirm match object returned
<re.MatchObject instance at 80ebf48>
```

Here is an example of a failed match for which None is returned:

```
>>> m = re.match('foo', 'bar')# pattern does not match string
>>> if m is not None: m.group() # (1-line version of if clause)
...
>>>
```

The preceding match fails, thus None is assigned to m, and no action is taken due to the way we constructed our if statement. For the remaining examples, we will try to leave out the if check for brevity, if possible, but in practice, it is a good idea to have it there to prevent AttributeError exceptions. (None is returned on failures, which does not have a group() attribute [method].)

A match will still succeed even if the string is longer than the pattern, as long as the pattern matches from the beginning of the string. For example, the pattern "foo" will find a match in the string "food on the table" because it matches the pattern from the beginning:

```
>>> m = re.match('foo', 'food on the table') # match succeeds
>>> m.group()
'foo'
```

As you can see, although the string is longer than the pattern, a successful match was made from the beginning of the string. The substring "foo" represents the match, which was extracted from the larger string.

We can even sometimes bypass saving the result altogether, taking advantage of Python's object-oriented nature:

```
>>> re.match('foo', 'food on the table').group()
'foo'
```

Note from a few paragraphs above that an AttributeError will be generated on a non-match.

1.3.5   Looking for a Pattern within a String with search() (Searching versus Matching)

The chances are greater that the pattern you seek is somewhere in the middle of a string, rather than at the beginning. This is where search() comes in handy. It works exactly in the same way as match, except that it searches for the first occurrence of the given regex pattern anywhere with its string argument. Again, a match object is returned on success; None is returned otherwise.

We will now illustrate the difference between match() and search(). Let's try a longer string match attempt. This time, let's try to match our string "foo" to "seafood":

```
>>> m = re.match('foo', 'seafood')     # no match
>>> if m is not None: m.group()
...
>>>
```

As you can see, there is no match here. match() attempts to match the pattern to the string from the beginning; that is, the "f" in the pattern is matched against the "s" in the string, which fails immediately. However, the string "foo" does appear (elsewhere) in "seafood," so how do we get Python to say "yes"? The answer is by using the search() function. Rather than attempting a *match*, search() looks for the first occurrence of the pattern within the string. search() evaluates a string strictly from left to right.

```
>>> m = re.search('foo', 'seafood')   # use search() instead
>>> if m is not None: m.group()
...
'foo'                    # search succeeds where match failed
>>>
```

Furthermore, both match() and search() take the optional flags parameter described earlier in Section 1.3.2. Lastly, we want to note that the equivalent regex object methods optionally take pos and endpos arguments to specify the search boundaries of the target string.

We will be using the match() and search() regex object methods and the group() and groups() match object methods for the remainder of this subsection, exhibiting a broad range of examples of how to use regular expressions with Python. We will be using almost all of the special characters and symbols that are part of the regular expression syntax.

1.3.6   Matching More than One String (|)

In Section 1.2, we used the pipe character in the regex bat|bet|bit. Here is how we would use that regex with Python:

```
>>> bt = 'bat|bet|bit'           # regex pattern: bat, bet, bit
>>> m = re.match(bt, 'bat')      # 'bat' is a match
>>> if m is not None: m.group()
...
```

```
'bat'
>>> m = re.match(bt, 'blt')          # no match for 'blt'
>>> if m is not None: m.group()
...
>>> m = re.match(bt, 'He bit me!') # does not match string
>>> if m is not None: m.group()
...
>>> m = re.search(bt, 'He bit me!') # found 'bit' via search
>>> if m is not None: m.group()
...
'bit'
```

1.3.7   Matching Any Single Character (.)

In the following examples, we show that a dot cannot match a \n or a non-character; that is, the empty string:

```
>>> anyend = '.end'
>>> m = re.match(anyend, 'bend')    # dot matches 'b'
>>> if m is not None: m.group()
...
'bend'
>>> m = re.match(anyend, 'end')     # no char to match
>>> if m is not None: m.group()
...
>>> m = re.match(anyend, '\nend')   # any char except \n
>>> if m is not None: m.group()
...
>>> m = re.search('.end', 'The end.')# matches ' ' in search
>>> if m is not None: m.group()
...
' end'
```

The following is an example of searching for a real dot (decimal point) in a regular expression, wherein we escape its functionality by using a backslash:

```
>>> patt314 = '3.14'            # regex dot
>>> pi_patt = '3\.14'          # literal dot (dec. point)
>>> m = re.match(pi_patt, '3.14') # exact match
>>> if m is not None: m.group()
...
'3.14'
>>> m = re.match(patt314, '3014') # dot matches '0'
>>> if m is not None: m.group()
...
'3014'
>>> m = re.match(patt314, '3.14') # dot matches '.'
>>> if m is not None: m.group()
...
'3.14'
```

1.3.8   Creating Character Classes ([])

Earlier, we had a long discussion about `[cr][23][dp][o2]` and how it differs from `r2d2|c3po"` In the following examples, we will show that `r2d2|c3po` is more restrictive than `[cr][23][dp][o2]`:

```
>>> m = re.match('[cr][23][dp][o2]', 'c3po')# matches 'c3po'
>>> if m is not None: m.group()
...
'c3po'
>>> m = re.match('[cr][23][dp][o2]', 'c2do')# matches 'c2do'
>>> if m is not None: m.group()
...
'c2do'
>>> m = re.match('r2d2|c3po', 'c2do')# does not match 'c2do'
>>> if m is not None: m.group()
...
>>> m = re.match('r2d2|c3po', 'r2d2')# matches 'r2d2'
>>> if m is not None: m.group()
...
'r2d2'
```

1.3.9   Repetition, Special Characters, and Grouping

The most common aspects of regexes involve the use of special characters, multiple occurrences of regex patterns, and using parentheses to group and extract submatch patterns. One particular regex we looked at related to simple e-mail addresses (\w+@\w+\.com). Perhaps we want to match more e-mail addresses than this regex allows. To support an additional hostname that precedes the domain, for example, www.xxx.com as opposed to accepting only xxx.com as the entire domain, we have to modify our existing regex. To indicate that the hostname is optional, we create a pattern that matches the hostname (followed by a dot), use the ? operator, indicating zero or one copy of this pattern, and insert the optional regex into our previous regex as follows: \w+@(\w+\.)?\w+\.com. As you can see from the following examples, either one or two names are now accepted before the .com:

```
>>> patt = '\w+@(\w+\.)?\w+\.com'
>>> re.match(patt, 'nobody@xxx.com').group()
'nobody@xxx.com'
>>> re.match(patt, 'nobody@www.xxx.com').group()
'nobody@www.xxx.com'
```

Furthermore, we can even extend our example to allow any number of intermediate subdomain names with the following pattern. Take special note of our slight change from using ? to *. : \w+@(\w+\.)*\w+\.com:

```
>>> patt = '\w+@(\w+\.)*\w+\.com'
>>> re.match(patt, 'nobody@www.xxx.yyy.zzz.com').group()
'nobody@www.xxx.yyy.zzz.com'
```

However, we must add the disclaimer that using solely alphanumeric characters does not match all the possible characters that might make up e-mail addresses. The preceding regex patterns would not match a domain such as xxx-yyy.com or other domains with \W characters.

Earlier, we discussed the merits of using parentheses to match and save subgroups for further processing rather than coding a separate routine to manually parse a string after a regex match had been determined. In particular, we discussed a simple regex pattern of an alphanumeric string and a number separated by a hyphen, \w+-\d+, and how adding subgrouping to form a new regex, (\w+)-(\d+), would do the job. Here is how the original regex works:

```
>>> m = re.match('\w\w\w-\d\d\d', 'abc-123')
>>> if m is not None: m.group()
...
'abc-123'

>>> m = re.match('\w\w\w-\d\d\d', 'abc-xyz')
>>> if m is not None: m.group()
...
>>>
```

In the preceding code, we created a regex to recognize three alphanumeric characters followed by three digits. Testing this regex on abc-123, we obtained positive results, whereas abc-xyz fails. We will now modify our regex as discussed before to be able to extract the alphanumeric string and number. Note how we can now use the group() method to access individual subgroups or the groups() method to obtain a tuple of all the subgroups matched:

```
>>> m = re.match('(\w\w\w)-(\d\d\d)', 'abc-123')
>>> m.group()                    # entire match
'abc-123'
>>> m.group(1)                   # subgroup 1
'abc'
>>> m.group(2)                   # subgroup 2
'123'
>>> m.groups()                   # all subgroups
('abc', '123')
```

As you can see, group() is used in the normal way to show the entire match, but it can also be used to grab individual subgroup matches. We can also use the groups() method to obtain a tuple of all the substring matches.

Here is a simpler example that shows different group permutations, which will hopefully make things even more clear:

```
>>> m = re.match('ab', 'ab')        # no subgroups
>>> m.group()                       # entire match
'ab'
>>> m.groups()                      # all subgroups
()
>>>
>>> m = re.match('(ab)', 'ab')      # one subgroup
>>> m.group()                       # entire match
'ab'
>>> m.group(1)                      # subgroup 1
'ab'
>>> m.groups()                      # all subgroups
('ab',)
>>>
>>> m = re.match('(a)(b)', 'ab')    # two subgroups
>>> m.group()                       # entire match
'ab'
>>> m.group(1)                      # subgroup 1
'a'
>>> m.group(2)                      # subgroup 2
'b'
>>> m.groups()                      # all subgroups
('a', 'b')
>>>
>>> m = re.match('(a(b))', 'ab')    # two subgroups
>>> m.group()                       # entire match
'ab'
>>> m.group(1)                      # subgroup 1
'ab'
>>> m.group(2)                      # subgroup 2
'b'
>>> m.groups()                      # all subgroups
('ab', 'b')
```

1.3.10   Matching from the Beginning and End of Strings and on Word Boundaries

The following examples highlight the positional regex operators. These apply more for searching than matching because match() always starts at the beginning of a string.

```
>>> m = re.search('^The', 'The end.')            # match
>>> if m is not None: m.group()
...
'The'
>>> m = re.search('^The', 'end. The')            # not at beginning
>>> if m is not None: m.group()
...
>>> m = re.search(r'\bthe', 'bite the dog') # at a boundary
>>> if m is not None: m.group()
...
'the'
>>> m = re.search(r'\bthe', 'bitethe dog')  # no boundary
>>> if m is not None: m.group()
...
>>> m = re.search(r'\Bthe', 'bitethe dog')  # no boundary
>>> if m is not None: m.group()
...
'the'
```

You will notice the appearance of raw strings here. You might want to take a look at the Core Note, "Using Python raw strings," toward the end of this chapter for clarification on why they are here. In general, it is a good idea to use raw strings with regular expressions.

There are four other re module functions and regex object methods that we think you should be aware of: findall(), sub(), subn(), and split().

1.3.11   Finding Every Occurrence with findall() and finditer()

findall() looks for all non-overlapping occurrences of a regex pattern in a string. It is similar to search() in that it performs a string search, but it differs from match() and search() in that findall() always returns a list. The list will be empty if no occurrences are found, but if successful, the list will consist of all matches found (grouped in left-to-right order of occurrence).

```
>>> re.findall('car', 'car')
['car']
>>> re.findall('car', 'scary')
['car']
>>> re.findall('car', 'carry the barcardi to the car')
['car', 'car', 'car']
```

Subgroup searches result in a more complex list returned, and that makes sense, because subgroups are a mechanism with which you can extract specific patterns from within your single regular expression, such as matching an area code that is part of a complete telephone number, or a login name that is part of an entire e-mail address.

For a single successful match, each subgroup match is a single element of the resulting list returned by findall(); for multiple successful matches, each subgroup match is a single element in a tuple, and such tuples (one for each successful match) are the elements of the resulting list. This part might sound confusing at first, but if you try different examples, it will help to clarify things.

2.2   The finditer() function, which was added back in Python 2.2, is a similar, more memory-friendly alternative to findall(). The main difference between it and its cousin, other than the return of an iterator versus a list (obviously), is that rather than returning matching strings, finditer() iterates over match objects. The following are the differences between the two with different groups in a single string:

```
>>> s = 'This and that.'
>>> re.findall(r'(th\w+) and (th\w+)', s, re.I)
[('This', 'that')]
>>> re.finditer(r'(th\w+) and (th\w+)', s,
...     re.I).next().groups()
('This', 'that')
>>> re.finditer(r'(th\w+) and (th\w+)', s,
...     re.I).next().group(1)
'This'
>>> re.finditer(r'(th\w+) and (th\w+)', s,
...     re.I).next().group(2)
'that'
>>> [g.groups() for g in re.finditer(r'(th\w+) and (th\w+)',
...     s, re.I)]
[('This', 'that')]
```

In the example that follows, we have multiple matches of a single group in a single string:

```
>>> re.findall(r'(th\w+)', s, re.I)
['This', 'that']
>>> it = re.finditer(r'(th\w+)', s, re.I)
>>> g = it.next()
>>> g.groups()
('This',)
>>> g.group(1)
'This'
>>> g = it.next()
>>> g.groups()
('that',)
>>> g.group(1)
'that'
>>> [g.group(1) for g in re.finditer(r'(th\w+)', s, re.I)]
['This', 'that']
```

Note all the additional work that we had to do using finditer() to get its output to match that of findall().

Finally, like match() and search(), the method versions of findall() and finditer() support the optional pos and endpos parameters that control the search boundaries of the target string, as described earlier in this chapter.

1.3.12 Searching and Replacing with sub() and subn()

There are two functions/methods for search-and-replace functionality: sub() and subn(). They are almost identical and replace all matched occurrences of the regex pattern in a string with some sort of replacement. The replacement is usually a string, but it can also be a function that returns a replacement string. subn() is exactly the same as sub(), but it also returns the total number of substitutions made—both the newly substituted string and the substitution count are returned as a 2-tuple.

```
>>> re.sub('X', 'Mr. Smith', 'attn: X\n\nDear X,\n')
'attn: Mr. Smith\012\012Dear Mr. Smith,\012'
>>>
>>> re.subn('X', 'Mr. Smith', 'attn: X\n\nDear X,\n')
('attn: Mr. Smith\012\012Dear Mr. Smith,\012', 2)
>>>
>>> print re.sub('X', 'Mr. Smith', 'attn: X\n\nDear X,\n')
attn: Mr. Smith

Dear Mr. Smith,

>>> re.sub('[ae]', 'X', 'abcdef')
'XbcdXf'
>>> re.subn('[ae]', 'X', 'abcdef')
('XbcdXf', 2)
```

As we saw in an earlier section, in addition to being able to pull out the matching group number using the match object's group() method, you can use \N, where N is the group number to use in the replacement string. Below, we're just converting the American style of date presentation, MM/DD/YY{,YY} to the format used by all other countries, DD/MM/YY{,YY}:

```
>>> re.sub(r'(\d{1,2})/(\d{1,2})/(\d{2}|\d{4})',
...       r'\2/\1/\3', '2/20/91') # Yes, Python is...
'20/2/91'
>>> re.sub(r'(\d{1,2})/(\d{1,2})/(\d{2}|\d{4})',
...       r'\2/\1/\3', '2/20/1991') # ... 20+ years old!
'20/2/1991'
```

1.3.13 Splitting (on Delimiting Pattern) with `split()`

The re module and regex object method `split()` work similarly to its string counterpart, but rather than splitting on a fixed string, they split a string based on a regex pattern, adding some significant power to string splitting capabilities. If you do not want the string split for every occurrence of the pattern, you can specify the maximum number of splits by setting a value (other than zero) to the max argument.

If the delimiter given is not a regular expression that uses special symbols to match multiple patterns, then `re.split()` works in exactly the same manner as `str.split()`, as illustrated in the example that follows (which splits on a single colon):

```
>>> re.split(':', 'str1:str2:str3')
['str1', 'str2', 'str3']
```

That's a simple example. What if we have a more complex example, such as a simple parser for a Web site like Google or Yahoo! Maps? Users can enter city and state, or city plus ZIP code, or all three? This requires more powerful processing than just a plain 'ol string split:

```
>>> import re
>>> DATA = (
...     'Mountain View, CA 94040',
...     'Sunnyvale, CA',
...     'Los Altos, 94023',
...     'Cupertino 95014',
...     'Palo Alto CA',
... )
>>> for datum in DATA:
...     print re.split(', |(?= (?:\d{5}|[A-Z]{2})) ', datum)
...
['Mountain View', 'CA', '94040']
['Sunnyvale', 'CA']
['Los Altos', '94023']
['Cupertino', '95014']
['Palo Alto', 'CA']
```

The preceding regex has a simple component, split on comma-space (", "). The harder part is the last regex, which previews some of the extension notations that you'll learn in the next subsection. In plain English, this is what it says: also split on a single space if that space is immediately followed by five digits (ZIP code) or two capital letters (US state abbreviation). This allows us to keep together city names that have spaces in them.

Naturally, this is just a simplistic regex that could be a starting point for an application that parses location information. It doesn't process (or fails) lowercase states or their full spellings, street addresses, country codes, ZIP+4 (nine-digit ZIP codes), latitude-longitude, multiple spaces, etc. It's just meant as a simple demonstration of `re.split()` doing something `str.split()` can't do.

As we just demonstrated, you benefit from much more power with a regular expression split; however, remember to always use the best tool for the job. If a string split is good enough, there's no need to bring in the additional complexity and performance impact of regexes.

1.3.14   Extension Notations (?...)

There are a variety of extension notations supported by Python regular expressions. Let's take a look at some of them now and provide some usage examples.

With the `(?iLmsux)` set of options, users can specify one or more flags directly into a regular expression rather than via `compile()` or other `re` module functions. Below are several examples that use `re.I/IGNORECASE`, with the last mixing in `re.M/MULTILINE`:

```
>>> re.findall(r'(?i)yes', 'yes? Yes. YES!!')
['yes', 'Yes', 'YES']
>>> re.findall(r'(?i)th\w+', 'The quickest way is through this
tunnel.')
['The', 'through', 'this']
>>> re.findall(r'(?im)(^th[\w ]+)', """
... This line is the first,
... another line,
... that line, it's the best
... """)
['This line is the first', 'that line']
```

For the previous examples, the case-insensitivity should be fairly straightforward. In the last example, by using "multiline" we can perform the search across multiple lines of the target string rather than treating the entire string as a single entity. Notice that the instances of "the" are skipped because they do not appear at the beginning of their respective lines.

The next pair demonstrates the use of `re.S/DOTALL`. This flag indicates that the dot (.) can be used to represent \n characters (whereas normally it represents all characters except \n):

```
>>> re.findall(r'th.+', '''
... The first line
... the second line
... the third line
```

```
... ''')
['the second line', 'the third line']
>>> re.findall(r'(?s)th.+', '''
... The first line
... the second line
... the third line
... ''')
['the second line\nthe third line\n']
```

The re.X/VERBOSE flag is quite interesting; it lets users create more human-readable regular expressions by suppressing whitespace characters within regexes (except those in character classes or those that are backslash-escaped). Furthermore, hash/comment/octothorpe symbols (#) can also be used to start a comment, also as long as they're not within a character class backslash-escaped:

```
>>> re.search(r'''(?x)
...      \((\d{3})\) # area code
...      [ ]         # space
...      (\d{3})     # prefix
...      -           # dash
...      (\d{4})     # endpoint number
... ''', '(800) 555-1212').groups()
('800', '555', '1212')
```

The (?:...) notation should be fairly popular; with it, you can group parts of a regex, but it does not save them for future retrieval or use. This comes in handy when you don't want superfluous matches that are saved and never used:

```
>>> re.findall(r'http://(?:\w+\.)*(\w+\.com)',
...      'http://google.com http://www.google.com http://
code.google.com')
['google.com', 'google.com', 'google.com']
>>> re.search(r'\((?P<areacode>\d{3})\) (?P<prefix>\d{3})-(?:\d{4})',
...      '(800) 555-1212').groupdict()
{'areacode': '800', 'prefix': '555'}
```

You can use the (?P<*name*>) and (?P=*name*) notations together. The former saves matches by using a name identifier rather than using increasing numbers, starting at one and going through *N*, which are then retrieved later by using \1, \2, ... \N. You can retrieve them in a similar manner using \g<name>:

```
>>> re.sub(r'\((?P<areacode>\d{3})\) (?P<prefix>\d{3})-(?:\d{4})',
...      '(\g<areacode>) \g<prefix>-xxxx', '(800) 555-1212')
'(800) 555-xxxx'
```

Using the latter, you can reuse patterns in the same regex without specifying the same pattern again later on in the (same) regex, such as in this example, which presumably lets you validate normalization of phone numbers. Here are the ugly and compressed versions followed by a good use of (?x) to make things (slightly) more readable:

```
>>> bool(re.match(r'\((?P<areacode>\d{3})\) (?P<prefix>\d{3})-
(?P<number>\d{4}) (?P=areacode)-(?P=prefix)-(?P=number)
1(?P=areacode)(?P=prefix)(?P=number)',
...        '(800) 555-1212 800-555-1212 18005551212'))
True
>>> bool(re.match(r'''(?x)
...
...     # match (800) 555-1212, save areacode, prefix, no.
...     \((?P<areacode>\d{3})\)[ ](?P<prefix>\d{3})-(?P<number>\d{4})
...
...     # space
...     [ ]
...
...     # match 800-555-1212
...     (?P=areacode)-(?P=prefix)-(?P=number)
...
...     # space
...     [ ]
...
...     # match 18005551212
...     1(?P=areacode)(?P=prefix)(?P=number)
...
... ''', '(800) 555-1212 800-555-1212 18005551212'))
True
```

You use the (?=...) and (?!...) notations to perform a lookahead in the target string without actually consuming those characters. The first is the positive lookahead assertion, while the latter is the negative. In the examples that follow, we are only interested in the first names of the persons who have a last name of "van Rossum," and the next example let's us ignore e-mail addresses that begin with "noreply" or "postmaster."

The third snippet is another demonstration of the difference between findall() and finditer(); we use the latter to build a list of e-mail addresses (in a more memory-friendly way by skipping the creation of the intermediary list that would be thrown away) using the same login names but on a different domain.

```
>>> re.findall(r'\w+(?= van Rossum)',
... '''
...     Guido van Rossum
...     Tim Peters
...     Alex Martelli
...     Just van Rossum
...     Raymond Hettinger
... ''')
['Guido', 'Just']
>>> re.findall(r'(?m)^\s+(?!noreply|postmaster)(\w+)',
```

```
...    '''
...        sales@phptr.com
...        postmaster@phptr.com
...        eng@phptr.com
...        noreply@phptr.com
...        admin@phptr.com
... ''')
['sales', 'eng', 'admin']
>>> ['%s@aw.com' % e.group(1) for e in \
re.finditer(r'(?m)^\s+(?!noreply|postmaster)(\w+)',
...    '''
...        sales@phptr.com
...        postmaster@phptr.com
...        eng@phptr.com
...        noreply@phptr.com
...        admin@phptr.com
... ''')]
['sales@aw.com', 'eng@aw.com', 'admin@aw.com']
```

The last examples demonstrate the use of conditional regular expression matching. Suppose that we have another specialized alphabet consisting only of the characters 'x' and 'y,' where we only want to restrict the string in such a way that two-letter strings must consist of one character followed by the other. In other words, you can't have both letters be the same; either it's an 'x' followed by a 'y' or vice versa:

```
>>> bool(re.search(r'(?:(x)|y)(?(1)y|x)', 'xy'))
True
>>> bool(re.search(r'(?:(x)|y)(?(1)y|x)', 'xx'))
False
```

1.3.15   Miscellaneous

There can be confusion between regular expression special characters and special ASCII symbols. We can use \n to represent a NEWLINE character, but we can use \d meaning a regular expression match of a single numeric digit.

Problems can occur if there is a symbol used by both ASCII and regular expressions, so in the following Core Note, we recommend the use of Python raw strings to prevent any problems. One more caution: the \w and \W alphanumeric character sets are affected by the re.L/LOCALE and Unicode (re.U/UNICODE) flags.

CORE NOTE: Using Python raw strings

You might have seen the use of raw strings in some of the previous examples. Regular expressions were a strong motivation for the advent of raw strings. The reason lies in the conflicts between ASCII characters and regular expression special characters. As a special symbol, \b represents the ASCII character for backspace, but \b is also a regular expression special symbol, meaning "match" on a word boundary. For the regex compiler to see the two characters \b as your string and not a (single) backspace, you need to escape the backslash in the string by using another backslash, resulting in \\b.

This can get messy, especially if you have a lot of special characters in your string, adding to the confusion. We were introduced to raw strings in the Sequences chapter of *Core Python Programming* or *Core Python Language Fundamentals*, and they can be (and are often) used to help keep regexes looking somewhat manageable. In fact, many Python programmers swear by these and only use raw strings when defining regular expressions.

Here are some examples of differentiating between the backspace \b and the regular expression \b, with and without raw strings:

```
>>> m = re.match('\bblow', 'blow') # backspace, no match
>>> if m: m.group()
...
>>> m = re.match('\\bblow', 'blow') # escaped \, now it works
>>> if m: m.group()
...
'blow'
>>> m = re.match(r'\bblow', 'blow') # use raw string instead
>>> if m: m.group()
...
'blow'
```

You might have recalled that we had no trouble using \d in our regular expressions without using raw strings. That is because there is no ASCII equivalent special character, so the regular expression compiler knew that you meant a decimal digit.

1.4   Some Regex Examples

Let's look at a few examples of some Python regex code that takes us a step closer to something that you would actually use in practice. Take, for example, the output from the POSIX (Unix-flavored systems like Linux, Mac OS X, etc.) who command, which lists all the users logged in to a system:

```
$ who
wesley          console      Jun 20 20:33
wesley          pts/9        Jun 22 01:38     (192.168.0.6)
wesley          pts/1        Jun 20 20:33     (:0.0)
wesley          pts/2        Jun 20 20:33     (:0.0)
wesley          pts/4        Jun 20 20:33     (:0.0)
wesley          pts/3        Jun 20 20:33     (:0.0)
wesley          pts/5        Jun 20 20:33     (:0.0)
wesley          pts/6        Jun 20 20:33     (:0.0)
wesley          pts/7        Jun 20 20:33     (:0.0)
wesley          pts/8        Jun 20 20:33     (:0.0)
```

Perhaps we want to save some user login information such as login name, the teletype at which the user logged in, when the user logged in, and from where. Using str.split() on the preceding example would not be effective because the spacing is erratic and inconsistent. The other problem is that there is a space between the month, day, and time for the login timestamps. We would probably want to keep these fields together.

You need some way to describe a pattern such as "split on two or more spaces." This is easily done with regular expressions. In no time, we whip up the regex pattern \s\s+, which means at least two whitespace characters.

Let's create a program called rewho.py that reads the output of the who command, presumably saved into a file called whodata.txt. Our rewho.py script initially looks something like this:

```
import re
f = open('whodata.txt', 'r')
for eachLine in f:
    print re.split(r'\s\s+', eachLine)
f.close()
```

The preceding code also uses raw strings (leading "r" or "R" in front of the opening quotes). The main idea is to avoid translating special string characters like \n, which is not a special regex pattern. For regex patterns that do have backslashes, you want them treated verbatim; otherwise, you'd have to double-backslash them to keep them safe.

We will now execute the who command, saving the output into whodata.txt, and then call rewho.py to take a look at the results:

```
$ who > whodata.txt
$ rewho.py
['wesley', 'console', 'Jun 20 20:33\012']
['wesley', 'pts/9', 'Jun 22 01:38\011(192.168.0.6)\012']
['wesley', 'pts/1', 'Jun 20 20:33\011(:0.0)\012']
['wesley', 'pts/2', 'Jun 20 20:33\011(:0.0)\012']
['wesley', 'pts/4', 'Jun 20 20:33\011(:0.0)\012']
['wesley', 'pts/3', 'Jun 20 20:33\011(:0.0)\012']
['wesley', 'pts/5', 'Jun 20 20:33\011(:0.0)\012']
['wesley', 'pts/6', 'Jun 20 20:33\011(:0.0)\012']
['wesley', 'pts/7', 'Jun 20 20:33\011(:0.0)\012']
['wesley', 'pts/8', 'Jun 20 20:33\011(:0.0)\012']
```

It was a good first try, but not quite correct. For one thing, we did not anticipate a single TAB (ASCII \011) as part of the output (which looked like at least two spaces, right?), and perhaps we aren't really keen on saving the \n (ASCII \012), which terminates each line. We are now going to fix those problems as well as improve the overall quality of our application by making a few more changes.

First, we would rather run the who command from within the script instead of doing it externally and saving the output to a whodata.txt file—doing this repeatedly gets tiring rather quickly. To accomplish invoking another program from within ours, we call upon the os.popen() command. Although os.popen() has now been made obsolete by the subprocess module, it's still simpler to use, and the main point is to illustrate the functionality of re.split().

We get rid of the trailing \ns (with str.rstrip()) and add the detection of a single TAB as an additional, alternative re.split() delimiter. Example 1-1 presents the final Python 2 version of our rewho.py script:

Example 1-1   Split Output of the POSIX who Command (rewho.py)

This script calls the who command and parses the input by splitting up its data along various types of whitespace characters.

```
1    #!/usr/bin/env python
2
3    import os
4    import re
5
6    f = os.popen('who', 'r')
7    for eachLine in f:
8        print re.split(r'\s\s+|\t', eachLine.rstrip())
9    f.close()
```

Example 1-2 presents rewho3.py, which is the Python 3 version with an additional twist. The main difference from the Python 2 version is the

3.x

2.5-2.6

`print()` function (vs. a statement). This entire line is italicized to indicate critical Python 2 versus 3 differences. The `with` statement, available as experimental in version 2.5, and official in version 2.6, works with objects built to support it.

Example 1-2   Python 3 Version of `rewho.py` Script (`rewho3.py`)

This Python 3 equivalent of `rewho.py` simply replaces the **print** statement with the `print()` function. When using the **with** statement (available starting in Python 2.5), keep in mind that the `file` (Python 2) or `io` (Python 3) object's context manager will automatically call `f.close()` for you.

```
1    #!/usr/bin/env python
2
3    import os
4    import re
5
6    with os.popen('who', 'r') as f:
7        for eachLine in f:
8            print(re.split(r'\s\s+|\t', eachLine.rstrip()))
```

Objects that have context managers implemented for them makes them eligible to be used with **with**. For more on the **with** statement and context management, please review the "Errors and Exceptions" chapter of *Core Python Programming* or *Core Python Language Fundamentals*. Don't forget for either version (`rewho.py` or `rewho3.py`) that the who command is only available on POSIX systems unless you're using Cygwin on a Windows-based computer. For PCs running Microsoft Windows, try `tasklist` instead, but there's an additional tweak you need to do. Keep reading to see a sample execution using *that* command.

Example 1-3 merges together both `rewho.py` and `rewho3.py` into `rewhoU.py`, with the name meaning "rewho universal." It runs under both Python 2 and 3 interpreters. We cheat and avoid the use of `print` or `print()` by using a less than fully-featured function that exists in both version 2.x and version 3.x: `distutils.log.warn()`. It's a one-string output function, so if your display is more complex than that, you'll need to merge it all into a single string, and then make the call. To indicate its use within our script, we'll name it `printf()`.

We also roll in the **with** statement here, too. This means that you need at least version 2.6 to run this. Well, that's not quite true. We mentioned earlier that it's experimental in version 2.5. This means that you need to include this additional statement if you wish to use it: `from __future__ import with_statement`. If you're still using version 2.4 or older, you have no access to this import and must run code such as that in Example 1-1.

Example 1-3   Universal Version of rewho.py Script (rewhoU.py)

This script runs under both Python 2 and 3 by proxying out the **print** statement and the print() function with a cheap substitute. It also includes the **with** statement available starting in Python 2.5.

```
1   #!/usr/bin/env python
2
3   import os
4   from distutils.log import warn as printf
5   import re
6
7   with os.popen('who', 'r') as f:
8       for eachLine in f:
9           printf(re.split(r'\s\s+|\t', eachLine.strip()))
```

The creation of rewhoU.py is one example of how you can create a universal script that helps avoid the need to maintain two versions of the same script for both Python 2 and 3.

Executing any of these scripts with the appropriate interpreter yields the corrected, cleaner output:

```
$ rewho.py
['wesley', 'console', 'Feb 22 14:12']
['wesley', 'ttys000', 'Feb 22 14:18']
['wesley', 'ttys001', 'Feb 22 14:49']
['wesley', 'ttys002', 'Feb 25 00:13', '(192.168.0.20)']
['wesley', 'ttys003', 'Feb 24 23:49', '(192.168.0.20)']
```

Also don't forget that the re.split() function also takes the optional flags parameter described earlier in this chapter.

A similar exercise can be achieved on Windows-based computers by using the tasklist command in place of who. Let's take a look at its output on the following page.

```
C:\WINDOWS\system32>tasklist
```

Image Name	PID	Session Name	Session#	Mem Usage
=====================	======	================	========	============
System Idle Process	0	Console	0	28 K
System	4	Console	0	240 K
smss.exe	708	Console	0	420 K
csrss.exe	764	Console	0	4,876 K
winlogon.exe	788	Console	0	3,268 K
services.exe	836	Console	0	3,932 K
. . .				

As you can see, the output contains different information than that of who, but the format is similar, so we can consider our previous solution by performing an re.split() on one or more spaces (no TAB issue here).

The problem is that the command name might have a space, and we (should) prefer to keep the entire command name together. The same is true of the memory usage, which is given by "NNN K," where NNN is the amount of memory K designates kilobytes. We want to keep this together, too, so we'd better split off of *at least* one space, right?

Nope, no can do. Notice that the process ID (PID) and Session Name columns are delimited only by a single space. This means that if we split off at least one space, the PID and Session Name would be kept together as a single result. If we copied one of the preceding scripts and call it `retasklist.py`, change the command from who to `tasklist /nh` (the /nh option suppresses the column headers), and use a regex of \s\s+, we get output that looks like this:

```
Z:\corepython\ch1>python retasklist.py
['']
['System Idle Process', '0 Console', '0', '28 K']
['System', '4 Console', '0', '240 K']
['smss.exe', '708 Console', '0', '420 K']
['csrss.exe', '764 Console', '0', '5,028 K']
['winlogon.exe', '788 Console', '0', '3,284 K']
['services.exe', '836 Console', '0', '3,924 K']
. . .
```

We have confirmed that although we've kept the command name and memory usage strings together, we've inadvertently put the PID and Session Name together. We have to discard our use of split and just do a regular expression match. Let's do that and filter out both the Session Name and Number because neither add value to our output. Example 1-4 shows the final version of our Python 2 `retasklist.py`:

Example 1-4   Processing the DOS `tasklist` Command Output (retasklist.py)

This script uses a regex and `findall()` to parse the output of the DOS `tasklist` command, displaying only the data that's interesting to us. Porting this script to Python 3 merely requires a switch to the `print()` function.

```
1   #!/usr/bin/env python
2
3   import os
4   import re
5
6   f = os.popen('tasklist /nh', 'r')
7   for eachLine in f:
8       print re.findall(
9           r'([\w.]+(?: [\w.]+)*)\s\s+(\d+) \w+\s\s+\d+\s\s+([\d,]+ K)',
10          eachLine.rstrip())
11  f.close()
```

If we run this script, we get our desired (truncated) output:

```
Z:\corepython\ch1>python retasklist.py
[]
[('System Idle Process', '0', '28 K')]
[('System', '4', '240 K')]
[('smss.exe', '708', '420 K')]
[('csrss.exe', '764', '5,016 K')]
[('winlogon.exe', '788', '3,284 K')]
[('services.exe', '836', '3,932 K')]
. . .
```

The meticulous regex used goes through all five columns of the output string, grouping together only those values that matter to us: the command name, its PID, and how much memory it takes. It uses many regex features that we've already read about in this chapter.

Naturally, all of the scripts we've done in this subsection merely display output to the user. In practice, you're likely to be processing this data, instead, saving it to a database, using the output to generate reports to management, etc.

1.5   A Longer Regex Example

We will now run through an in-depth example of the different ways to use regular expressions for string manipulation. The first step is to come up with some code that actually generates random (but not too random) data on which to operate. In Example 1-5, we present gendata.py, a script that generates a data set. Although this program simply displays the generated set of strings to standard output, this output could very well be redirected to a test file.

Example 1-5   Data Generator for Regex Exercises (gendata.py)

This script creates random data for regular expressions practice and outputs the generated data to the screen. To port this to Python 3, just convert **print** to a function, switch from xrange() back to range(), and change from using sys.maxint to sys.maxsize.

```
1    #!/usr/bin/env python
2
3    from random import randrange, choice
4    from string import ascii_lowercase as lc
5    from sys import maxint
6    from time import ctime
7
```

(Continued)

Example 1-5   Data Generator for Regex Exercises (`gendata.py`)
(Continued)

```
8    tlds = ('com', 'edu', 'net', 'org', 'gov')
9
10   for i in xrange(randrange(5, 11)):
11       dtint = randrange(maxint)      # pick date
12       dtstr = ctime(dtint)           # date string
13       llen = randrange(4, 8)         # login is shorter
14       login = ''.join(choice(lc) for j in range(llen))
15       dlen = randrange(llen, 13)     # domain is longer
16       dom = ''.join(choice(lc) for j in xrange(dlen))
17       print '%s::%s@%s.%s::%d-%d-%d' % (dtstr, login,
18           dom, choice(tlds), dtint, llen, dlen)
```

This script generates strings with three fields, delimited by a pair of colons, or a double-colon. The first field is a random (32-bit) integer, which is converted to a date. The next field is a randomly generated e-mail address, and the final field is a set of integers separated by a single dash (-).

Running this code, we get the following output (your mileage will definitely vary) and store it locally as the file `redata.txt`:

```
Thu Jul 22 19:21:19 2004::izsp@dicqdhytvhv.edu::1090549279-4-11
Sun Jul 13 22:42:11 2008::zqeu@dxaibjgkniy.com::1216014131-4-11
Sat May  5 16:36:23 1990::fclihw@alwdbzpsdg.edu::641950583-6-10
Thu Feb 15 17:46:04 2007::uzifzf@dpyivihw.gov::1171590364-6-8
Thu Jun 26 19:08:59 2036::ugxfugt@jkhuqhs.net::2098145339-7-7
Tue Apr 10 01:04:45 2012::zkwaq@rpxwmtikse.com::1334045085-5-10
```

You might or might not be able to tell, but the output from this program is ripe for regular expression processing. Following our line-by-line explanation, we will implement several regexes to operate on this data as well as leave plenty for the end-of-chapter exercises.

Line-by-Line Explanation

Lines 1–6

In our example script, we require the use of multiple modules. Although we caution against the use of **from-import** because of various reasons (e.g., it's easier to determine where a function comes from, possible local module conflict, etc.), we choose to import only specific attributes from these modules to help you focus on those attributes only as well as shortening each line of code.

Line 8

`tlds` is simply a set of higher-level domain names from which we will randomly pick for each randomly generated e-mail address.

Lines 10–12

Each time `gendata.py` executes, between 5 and 10 lines of output are generated. (Our script uses the `random.randrange()` function for all cases for which we desire a random integer.) For each line, we choose a random integer from the entire possible range (0 to $2^{31} - 1$ [`sys.maxint`]), and then convert that integer to a date by using `time.ctime()`. System time in Python and most POSIX-based computers is based on the number of seconds that have elapsed since the "epoch," which is midnight UTC/GMT on January 1, 1970. If we choose a 32-bit integer, that represents one moment in time from the epoch to the maximum possible time, 2^{32} seconds *after* the epoch.

Lines 13–16

The login name for the fake e-mail address should be between 4 and 7 characters in length (thus `randrange(4, 8)`). To put it together, we randomly choose between 4 and 7 random lowercase letters, concatenating each letter to our string, one at a time. The functionality of the `random.choice()` function is to accept a sequence, and then return a random element of that sequence. In our case, the sequence is the set of all 26 lowercase letters of the alphabet, `string.ascii_lowercase`.

We decided that the main domain name for the fake e-mail address should be no more than 12 characters in length, but at least as long as the login name. Again, we use random lowercase letters to put this name together, letter by letter.

Lines 17–18

The key component of our script puts together all of the random data into the output line. The date string comes first, followed by the delimiter. We then put together the random e-mail address by concatenating the login name, the "@" symbol, the domain name, and a randomly chosen high-level domain. After the final double-colon, we put together a random integer string using the original time chosen (for the date string), followed by the lengths of the login and domain names, all separated by a single hyphen.

1.5.1   Matching a String

For the following exercises, create both permissive and restrictive versions of your regexes. We recommend that you test these regexes in a short application that utilizes our sample `redata.txt`, presented earlier (or use your own generated data from running `gendata.py`). You will need to use it again when you do the exercises.

To test the regex before putting it into our little application, we will import the `re` module and assign one sample line from `redata.txt` to a string variable data. These statements are constant across both illustrated examples.

```
>>> import re
>>> data = 'Thu Feb 15 17:46:04 2007::uzifzf@dpyivihw.gov::1171590364-6-8'
```

In our first example, we will create a regular expression to extract (only) the days of the week from the timestamps from each line of the data file `redata.txt`. We will use the following regex:

"^Mon|^Tue|^Wed|^Thu|^Fri|^Sat|^Sun"

This example requires that the string start with ("^" regex operator) any of the seven strings listed. If we were to "translate" the above regex to English, it would read something like, "the string should start with "Mon," "Tue,"..., "Sat," or "Sun."

Alternatively, we can bypass all the caret operators with a single caret if we group the day strings like this:

"^(Mon|Tue|Wed|Thu|Fri|Sat|Sun)"

The parentheses around the set of strings mean that one of these strings must be encountered for a match to succeed. This is a "friendlier" version of the original regex we came up with, which did not have the parentheses. Using our modified regex, we can take advantage of the fact that we can access the matched string as a subgroup:

```
>>> patt = '^(Mon|Tue|Wed|Thu|Fri|Sat|Sun)'
>>> m = re.match(patt, data)
>>> m.group()                    # entire match
'Thu'
>>> m.group(1)                   # subgroup 1
'Thu'
>>> m.groups()                   # all subgroups
('Thu',)
```

This feature might not seem as revolutionary as we have made it out to be for this example, but it is definitely advantageous in the next example or anywhere you provide extra data as part of the regex to help in the string matching process, even though those characters might not be part of the string you are interested in.

Both of the above regexes are the most restrictive, specifically requiring a set number of strings. This might not work well in an internationalization environment, where localized days and abbreviations are used. A looser regex would be: ^\w{3}. This one requires only that a string begin with three consecutive alphanumeric characters. Again, to translate the regex into English, the caret indicates "begins with," the \w means any single alphanumeric character, and the {3} means that there should be 3 consecutive copies of the regex which the {3} embellishes. Again, if you want grouping, parentheses should be used, such as ^(\w{3}):

```
>>> patt = '^(\w{3})'
>>> m = re.match(patt, data)
>>> if m is not None: m.group()
...
'Thu'
>>> m.group(1)
'Thu'
```

Note that a regex of ^(\w){3} is not correct. When the {3} was inside the parentheses, the match for three consecutive alphanumeric characters was made first, and then represented as a group. But by moving the {3} outside, it is now equivalent to three consecutive single alphanumeric characters:

```
>>> patt = '^(\w){3}'
>>> m = re.match(patt, data)
>>> if m is not None: m.group()
...
'Thu'
>>> m.group(1)
'u'
```

The reason why only the "u" shows up when accessing subgroup 1 is that subgroup 1 was being continually replaced by the next character. In other words, m.group(1) started out as "T," then changed to "h," and then finally was replaced by "u." These are three individual (and overlapping) groups of a single alphanumeric character, as opposed to a single group consisting of three consecutive alphanumeric characters.

In our next (and final) example, we will create a regular expression to extract the numeric fields found at the end of each line of redata.txt.

1.5.2   Search versus Match... and Greediness, too

Before we create any regexes, however, we realize that these integer data items are at the end of the data strings. This means that we have a choice of using either search or match. Initiating a search makes more sense because we know exactly what we are looking for (a set of three integers), that what we seek is not at the beginning of the string, and that it does not make up the entire string. If we were to perform a match, we would have to create a regex to match the entire line and use subgroups to save the data we are interested in. To illustrate the differences, we will perform a search first, and then do a match to show you that searching is more appropriate.

Because we are looking for three integers delimited by hyphens, we create our regex to indicate as such: \d+-\d+-\d+. This regular expression means, "any number of digits (at least one, though) followed by a hyphen, then more digits, another hyphen, and finally, a final set of digits." We test our regex now by using search():

```
>>> patt = '\d+-\d+-\d+'
>>> re.search(patt, data).group()          # entire match
'1171590364-6-8'
```

A match attempt, however, would fail. Why? Because matches start at the beginning of the string, the numeric strings are at the end. We would have to create another regex to match the entire string. We can be lazy, though, by using .+ to indicate just an arbitrary set of characters followed by what we are really interested in:

```
patt = '.+\d+-\d+-\d+'
>>> re.match(patt, data).group()            # entire match
'Thu Feb 15 17:46:04 2007::uzifzf@dpyivihw.gov::1171590364-6-8'
```

This works great, but we really want the number fields at the end, not the entire string, so we have to use parentheses to group what we want:

```
>>> patt = '.+(\d+-\d+-\d+)'
>>> re.match(patt, data).group(1)           # subgroup 1
'4-6-8'
```

What happened? We should have extracted 1171590364-6-8, not just 4-6-8. Where is the rest of the first integer? The problem is that regular expressions are inherently greedy. This means that with wildcard patterns, regular expressions are evaluated in left-to-right order and try to "grab" as many characters as possible that match the pattern. In the preceding case, the .+ grabbed every single character from the beginning of the string, including most of the first integer field that we wanted. The \d+ needed only a single digit, so it got "4," whereas the .+ matched everything from the beginning of the string up to that first digit: "Thu Feb 15 17:46:04 2007::uzifzf@dpyivihw.gov::117159036," as indicated in Figure 1–2.

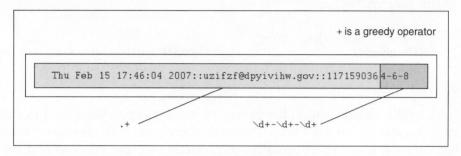

Figure 1-2 Why our match went awry: + is a greedy operator.

One solution is to use the "don't be greedy" operator: ?. You can use this operator after *, +, or ?. It directs the regular expression engine to match as few characters as possible. So if we place a ? after the .+, we obtain the desired result, as illustrated in Figure 1–3.

```
>>> patt = '.+?(\d+-\d+-\d+)'
>>> re.match(patt, data).group(1)          # subgroup 1
'1171590364-6-8'
```

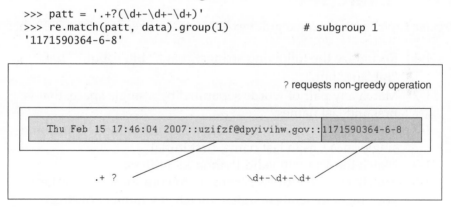

Figure 1-3 Solving the greedy problem: ? requests non-greediness.

Another solution, which is actually easier, is to recognize that "::" is our field separator. You can then just use the regular string strip('::') method to get all the parts, and then take another split on the dash with strip('-') to obtain the three integers you were originally seeking. Now, we did not choose this solution first because this is how we put the strings together to begin with using gendata.py!

One final example: suppose that we want to pull out only the middle integer of the three-integer field. Here is how we would do it (using a search so that we don't have to match the entire string): `-(\d+)-`. Trying out this pattern, we get:

```
>>> patt = '-(\d+)-'
>>> m = re.search(patt, data)
>>> m.group()                    # entire match
'-6-'
>>> m.group(1)                   # subgroup 1
'6'
```

We barely touched upon the power of regular expressions, and in this limited space we have not been able to do them justice. However, we hope that we have given an informative introduction so that you can add this powerful tool to your programming skills. We suggest that you refer to the documentation for more details on how to use regexes with Python. For a more complete immersion into the world of regular expressions, we recommend *Mastering Regular Expressions* by Jeffrey E. F. Friedl.

1.6   Exercises

Regular Expressions. Create regular expressions in Exercises 1-1 to1-12 that:

1-1.   Recognize the following strings: "bat," "bit," "but," "hat," "hit," or "hut."

1-2.   Match any pair of words separated by a single space, that is, first and last names.

1-3.   Match any word and single letter separated by a comma and single space, as in last name, first initial.

1-4.   Match the set of all valid Python identifiers.

1-5.   Match a street address according to your local format (keep your regex general enough to match any number of street words, including the type designation). For example, American street addresses use the format: 1180 Bordeaux Drive. Make your regex flexible enough to support multi-word street names such as: 3120 De la Cruz Boulevard.

1-6.   Match simple Web domain names that begin with "www." and end with a ".com" suffix; for example, www.yahoo.com. Extra Credit: If your regex also supports other high-level domain names, such as .edu, .net, etc. (for example, www.foothill.edu).

1-7.   Match the set of the string representations of all Python integers.

1-8.   Match the set of the string representations of all Python longs.

1-9.   Match the set of the string representations of all Python floats.

1-10. Match the set of the string representations of all Python complex numbers.

1-11. Match the set of all valid e-mail addresses (start with a loose regex, and then try to tighten it as much as you can, yet maintain correct functionality).

1-12. Match the set of all valid Web site addresses (URLs) (start with a loose regex, and then try to tighten it as much as you can, yet maintain correct functionality).

1-13. *type()*. The type() built-in function returns a type object, which is displayed as the following Pythonic-looking string:

```
>>> type(0)
<type 'int'>
>>> type(.34)
<type 'float'>
>>> type(dir)
<type 'builtin_function_or_method'>
```

Create a regex that would extract the actual type name from the string. Your function should take a string like this <type 'int'> and return int. (Ditto for all other types, such as 'float', 'builtin_function_or_method', etc.) Note: You are implementing the value that is stored in the __name__ attribute for classes and some built-in types.

1-14. *Processing Dates*. In Section 1.2, we gave you the regex pattern that matched the single or double-digit string representations of the months January to September (0?[1-9]). Create the regex that represents the remaining three months in the standard calendar.

1-15. *Processing Credit Card Numbers*. Also in Section 1.2, we gave you the regex pattern that matched credit card (CC) numbers ([0-9]{15,16}). However, this pattern does not allow for hyphens separating blocks of numbers. Create the regex that allows hyphens, but only in the correct locations. For example, 15-digit CC numbers have a pattern of 4-6-5, indicating four digits-hyphen-six digits-hyphen-five digits; and 16-digit CC numbers have a 4-4-4-4 pattern. Remember to "balloon" the size of the entire string correctly. Extra Credit: There is a standard algorithm for determining whether a CC number is valid. Write some code that not only recognizes a correctly formatted CC number, but also a valid one.

Playing with `gendata.py`. The next set of Exercises (1-16 through 1-27) deal specifically with the data that is generated by `gendata.py`. Before approaching Exercises 1-17 and 1-18, you might want to do 1-16 and all the regular expressions first.

1-16. Update the code for `gendata.py` so that the data is written directly to `redata.txt` rather than output to the screen.

1-17. Determine how many times each day of the week shows up for any incarnation of `redata.txt`. (Alternatively, you can also count how many times each month of the year was chosen.)

1-18. Ensure that there is no data corruption in `redata.txt` by confirming that the first integer of the integer field matches the timestamp given at the beginning of each output line.

Create Regular Expressions That:

1-19. Extract the complete timestamps from each line.

1-20. Extract the complete e-mail address from each line.

1-21. Extract only the months from the timestamps.

1-22. Extract only the years from the timestamps.

1-23. Extract only the time (HH:MM:SS) from the timestamps.

1-24. Extract only the login and domain names (both the main domain name and the high-level domain together) from the e-mail address.

1-25. Extract only the login and domain names (both the main domain name and the high-level domain) from the e-mail address.

1-26. Replace the e-mail address from each line of data with your e-mail address.

1-27. Extract the months, days, and years from the timestamps and output them in "Mon, Day, Year" format, iterating over each line only once.

Processing Telephone Numbers. For Exercises 1-28 and 1-29, recall the regular expression introduced in Section 1.2, which matched telephone numbers but allowed for an optional area code prefix: \d{3}-\d{3}-\d{4}. Update this regular expression so that:

1-28. Area codes (the first set of three-digits and the accompanying hyphen) are optional, that is, your regex should match both 800-555-1212 as well as just 555-1212.

1-29. Either parenthesized or hyphenated area codes are supported, not to mention optional; make your regex match 800-555-1212, 555-1212, and also (800) 555-1212.

Regex Utilities. The final set of exercises make useful utility scripts when processing online data:

1-30. *HTML Generation.* Given a list of links (and optional short description), whether user-provided on command-line, via input from another script, or from a database, generate a Web page (.html) that includes all links as hypertext anchors, which upon viewing in a Web browser, allows users to click those links and visit the corresponding site. If the short description is provided, use that as the hypertext instead of the URL.

1-31. *Tweet Scrub.* Sometimes all you want to see is the plain text of a tweet as posted to the Twitter service by users. Create a function that takes a tweet and an optional "meta" flag defaulted False, and then returns a string of the scrubbed tweet, removing all the extraneous information, such as an "RT" notation for "retweet", a leading ., and all "#hashtags". If the meta flag is True, then also return a dict containing the metadata. This can include a key "RT," whose value is a tuple of strings of users who retweeted the message, and/or a key "hashtags" with a tuple of the hashtags. If the values don't exist (empty tuples), then don't even bother creating a key-value entry for them.

1-32. *Amazon Screenscraper.* Create a script that helps you to keep track of your favorite books and how they're doing on Amazon (or any other online bookseller that tracks book rankings). For example, the Amazon link for any book is of the format, http://amazon.com/dp/ISBN (for example, http://amazon.com/dp/0132678209). You can then change the domain name to check out the equivalent rankings on Amazon sites in other countries, such as Germany (.de), France (.fr), Japan (.jp), China (.cn), and the UK (.co.uk). Use regular expressions or a markup parser, such as BeautifulSoup, lxml, or html5lib to parse the ranking, and then let the user pass in a command-line argument that specifies whether the output should be in plain text, perhaps for inclusion in an e-mail body, or formatted in HTML for Web consumption.

CHAPTER 2

Network Programming

So, IPv6. You all know that we are almost out of IPv4 address space. I am a little embarrassed about that because I was the guy who decided that 32-bit was enough for the Internet experiment. My only defense is that that choice was made in 1977, and I thought it was an experiment. The problem is the experiment didn't end, so here we are.
—Vint Cerf, January 2011[1]
(verbally at linux.conf.au conference)

In this chapter...

- Introduction
- What Is Client/Server Architecture?
- Sockets: Communication Endpoints
- Network Programming in Python

- *The SocketServer Module
- *Introduction to the Twisted Framework
- Related Modules

---

1. Dates back to 2004 via http://www.educause.edu/EDUCAUSE+Review/
   EDUCAUSEReviewMagazineVolume39/MusingsontheInternetPart2/
   157899

2.1   Introduction

In this section, we will take a brief look at network programming using sockets. But before we delve into that, we will present some background information on network programming, how sockets apply to Python, and then show you how to use some of Python's modules to build networked applications.

2.2   What Is Client/Server Architecture?

What is client/server architecture? It means different things to different people, depending on whom you ask as well as whether you are describing a software or a hardware system. In either case, the premise is simple: the *server*—a piece of hardware or software—provides a "service" that is needed by one or more *clients* (users of the service). Its sole purpose of existence is to wait for (client) requests, respond to those clients (provide the service), and then wait for more requests.

Clients, on the other hand, contact a server for a particular request, send over any necessary data, and then wait for the server to reply, either completing the request or indicating the cause of failure. The server runs indefinitely, continually processing requests; clients make a one-time request for service, receive that service, and thus conclude their transaction. A client might make additional requests at some later time, but these are considered separate transactions.

The most common notion of the client/server architecture today is illustrated in Figure 2-1, which depicts a user or client computer retrieving information from a server across the Internet. Although such a system is indeed an example of a client/server architecture, it isn't the only one. Furthermore, client/server architecture can be applied to computer hardware as well as software.

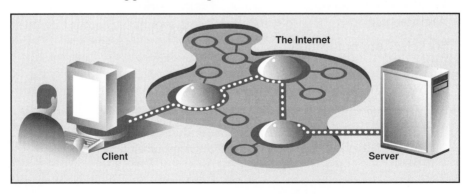

Figure 2-1   Typical conception of a client/server system on the Internet.

2.2.1   Hardware Client/Server Architecture

Print(er) servers are examples of hardware servers. They process incoming print jobs and send them to a printer (or some other printing device) attached to such a system. Such a computer is generally network-accessible and client computers would send it print requests.

Another example of a hardware server is a file server. These are typically computers with large, generalized storage capacity, which is remotely accessible to clients. Client computers mount the disks from the server computer as if the disk itself were on the local computer. One of the most popular network operating systems that support file servers is Sun Micro-systems' Network File System (NFS). If you are accessing a networked disk drive and cannot tell whether it is local or on the network, then the client/server system has done its job. The goal is for the user experience to be exactly the same as that of a local disk—the abstraction is normal disk access. It is up to the programmed implementation to make it behave in such a manner.

2.2.2   Software Client/Server Architecture

Software servers also run on a piece of hardware but do not have dedicated peripheral devices as hardware servers do (i.e., printers, disk drives, etc.). The primary services provided by software servers include program execution, data transfer retrieval, aggregation, update, or other types of programmed or data manipulation.

One of the more common software servers today is the Web server. Individuals or companies desiring to run their own Web server will get one or more computers, install the Web pages and or Web applications they wish to provide to users, and then start the Web server. The job of such a server is to accept client requests, send back Web pages to (Web) clients, that is, browsers on users' computers, and then wait for the next client request. These servers are started with the expectation of running forever. Although they do not achieve that goal, they go for as long as possible unless stopped by some external force such as being shut down, either explicitly or catastrophically (due to hardware failure).

Database servers are another kind of software server. They take client requests for either storage or retrieval, act upon that request, and then wait for more business. They are also designed to run forever.

The last type of software server we will discuss are windows servers. These servers can almost be considered hardware servers. They run on a computer with an attached display, such as a monitor of some sort. Windows clients are actually programs that require a windowing environment in which to execute. These are generally considered graphical user interface (GUI) applications. If they are executed without a window server, meaning, in a text-based environment such as a DOS window or a Unix shell, they are unable to start. Once a windows server is accessible, then things are fine.

Such an environment becomes even more interesting when networking comes into play. The usual display for a windows client is the server on the local computer, but it is possible in some networked windowing environments, such as the X Window system, to choose another computer's window server as a display. In such situations, you can be running a GUI program on one computer, but have it displayed at another!

2.2.3   Bank Tellers as Servers?

One way to imagine how client/server architecture works is to create in your mind the image of a bank teller who neither eats, sleeps, nor rests, serving one customer after another in a line that never seems to end (see Figure 2-2). The line might be long or it might be empty on occasion, but at any given moment, a customer might show up. Of course, such a teller was fantasy years ago, but automated teller machines (ATMs) seem to come close to such a model now.

The teller is, of course, the server that runs in an infinite loop. Each customer is a client with a need that must be addressed. Customers arrive and are handled by the teller in a first-come-first-served manner. Once a transaction has been completed, the client goes away while the server either serves the next customer or sits and waits until one comes along.

Why is all this important? The reason is that this style of execution is how client/server architecture works in a general sense. Now that you have the basic idea, let's adapt it to network programming, which follows the software client/server architecture model.

2.2.4   Client/Server Network Programming

Before a server can respond to client requests, some preliminary setup procedures must be performed to prepare it for the work that lies ahead. A *communication endpoint* is created which allows a server to listen for requests. One can liken our server to a company receptionist or switchboard operator who answers calls on the main corporate line. Once the phone number and equipment are installed and the operator arrives, the service can begin.

Figure 2-2 The bank teller in this diagram works "forever" serving client requests. The teller runs in an infinite loop receiving requests, servicing them, and then going back to serve or wait for another client. There might be a long line of clients, or there might be none at all, but in either case, a server's work is never done.

This process is the same in the networked world—once a communication endpoint has been established, our listening server can now enter its infinite loop, waiting for clients to connect, and responding to requests. Of course, to keep our corporate phone receptionist busy, we must not forget to put that phone number on company letterhead, in advertisements, or some sort of press release; otherwise, no one will ever call!

Similarly, potential clients must be made aware that this server exists to handle their needs—otherwise, the server will never get a single request. Imagine creating a brand new Web site. It might be the most super-duper, awesome, amazing, useful, and coolest Web site of all, but if the Web address or URL is never broadcast or advertised in any way, no one will ever know about it, and it will never see the any visitors.

Now you have a good idea as to how the server works. You have made it past the difficult part. The client-side stuff is much more simple than that on the server side. All the client has to do is to create its single communication endpoint, and then establish a connection to the server. The client can now make a request, which includes any necessary exchange of data. Once the request has been processed and the client has received the result or some sort of acknowledgement, communication is terminated.

2.3   Sockets: Communication Endpoints

In this subsection, you'll be introduced to sockets, get some background on their origins, learn about the various types of sockets, and finally, how they're used to allow processes running on different (or the same) computers to communicate with each other.

2.3.1   What Are Sockets?

Sockets are computer networking data structures that embody the concept of the "communication endpoint," described in the previous section. Networked applications must create sockets before any type of communication can commence. They can be likened to telephone jacks, without which, engaging in communication is impossible.

Sockets can trace their origins to the 1970s as part of the University of California, Berkeley version of Unix, known as BSD Unix. Therefore, you will sometimes hear these sockets referred to as *Berkeley sockets* or *BSD sockets*. Sockets were originally created for same-host applications where they would enable one running program (a.k.a. a process) to communicate with another running program. This is known as *interprocess communication,* or IPC. There are two types of sockets: file-based and network-oriented.

Unix sockets are the first family of sockets we are looking at and have a "family name" of AF_UNIX (a.k.a. AF_LOCAL, as specified in the POSIX1.g standard), which stands for *address family*: UNIX. Most popular platforms, including Python, use the term *address families* and the abbreviation *AF*; other perhaps older systems might refer to address families as *domains* or *protocol families* and use *PF* rather than AF. Similarly, AF_LOCAL (standardized in 2000–2001) is supposed to replace AF_UNIX; however, for backward-compatibility, many systems use both and just make them aliases to the same constant. Python itself still uses AF_UNIX.

Because both processes run on the same computer, these sockets are file-based, meaning that their underlying infrastructure is supported by the file system. This makes sense, because the file system is a shared constant between processes running on the same host.

The second type of socket is networked-based and has its own family name, AF_INET, or *address family*: Internet. Another address family, AF_INET6, is used for Internet Protocol version 6 (IPv6) addressing. There are other address families, all of which are either specialized, antiquated, seldom used, or remain unimplemented. Of all address families, AF_INET is now the most widely used.

Support for a special type of Linux socket was introduced in Python 2.5.
The AF_NETLINK family of (connectionless [see Section 2.3.3]) sockets **2.5**
allow for IPC between user and kernel-level code using the standard BSD
socket interface. It is seen as an elegant and less risky solution over previous
and more cumbersome solutions, such as adding new system calls, /proc
support, or "IOCTL"s to an operating system.

Another feature (new in version 2.6) for Linux is support for the Trans- **2.6**
parent Interprocess Communication (TIPC) protocol. TIPC is used to
allow clusters of computers to "talk" to each other without using IP-based
addressing. The Python support for TIPC comes in the form of the
AF_TIPC family.

Overall, Python supports only the AF_UNIX, AF_NETLINK, AF_TIPC,
and AF_INET{,6} families. Because of our focus on network programming,
we will be using AF_INET for most of the remainder of this chapter.

2.3.2   Socket Addresses: Host-Port Pairs

If a socket is like a telephone jack—a piece of infrastructure that enables
communication—then a hostname and port number are like an area code
and telephone number combination. Having the hardware and ability to
communicate doesn't do any good unless you know to whom and how
to "dial." An Internet address is comprised of a hostname and port number pair, which is required for networked communication. It goes without
saying that there should also be someone listening at the other end; otherwise, you get the familiar tones, followed by "I'm sorry, that number is
no longer in service. Please check the number and try your call again." You
have probably seen one networking analogy during Web surfing, for
example, "Unable to contact server. Server is not responding or is unreach-
able."

Valid port numbers range from 0–65535, although those less than 1024
are reserved for the system. If you are using a POSIX-compliant system
(e.g., Linux, Mac OS X, etc.), the list of reserved port numbers (along with
servers/protocols and socket types) is found in the /etc/services file. A
list of well-known port numbers is accessible at this Web site:

http://www.iana.org/assignments/port-numbers

2.3.3   Connection-Oriented Sockets vs. Connectionless

Connection-Oriented Sockets

Regardless of which address family you are using, there are two different styles of socket connections. The first type is connection-oriented. What this means is that a connection must be established before communication can occur, such as calling a friend using the telephone system. This type of communication is also referred to as a *virtual circuit* or *stream socket*.

Connection-oriented communication offers sequenced, reliable, and unduplicated delivery of data, without record boundaries. That basically means that each message may be broken up into multiple pieces, which are all guaranteed to arrive at their destination, put back together and in order, and delivered to the waiting application.

The primary protocol that implements such connection types is the *Transmission Control Protocol* (better known by its acronym, TCP). To create TCP sockets, one must use SOCK_STREAM as the socket type. The SOCK_STREAM name for a TCP socket is based on one of its denotations as stream socket. Because the networked version of these sockets (AF_INET) use the *Internet Protocol* (IP) to find hosts in the network, the entire system generally goes by the combined names of both protocols (TCP and IP), or TCP/IP. (Of course, you can also use TCP with local [non-networked AF_LOCAL/AF_UNIX] sockets, but obviously there's no IP usage there.)

Connectionless Sockets

In stark contrast to virtual circuits is the *datagram* type of socket, which is connectionless. This means that no connection is necessary before communication can begin. Here, there are no guarantees of sequencing, reliability, or non-duplication in the process of data delivery. Datagrams do preserve record boundaries, however, meaning that entire messages are sent rather than being broken into pieces first, such as with connection-oriented protocols.

Message delivery using datagrams can be compared to the postal service. Letters and packages might not arrive in the order they were sent. In fact, they might not arrive at all! To add to the complication, in the land of networking, *duplication* of messages is even possible.

So with all this negativity, why use datagrams at all? (There must be *some* advantage over using stream sockets.) Because of the guarantees provided by connection-oriented sockets, a good amount of overhead is required for their setup as well as in maintaining the virtual circuit connection. Datagrams do not have this overhead and thus are "less expensive." They usually provide better performance and might be suitable for some types of applications.

The primary protocol that implements such connection types is the *User Datagram Protocol* (better known by its acronym, UDP). To create UDP sockets, we must use SOCK_DGRAM as the socket type. The SOCK_DGRAM name for a UDP socket, as you can probably tell, comes from the word "datagram." Because these sockets also use the Internet Protocol to find hosts in the network, this system also has a more general name, going by the combined names of both of these protocols (UDP and IP), or UDP/IP.

2.4   Network Programming in Python

Now that you know all about client/server architecture, sockets, and networking, let's try to bring these concepts to Python. The primary module we will be using in this section is the `socket` module. Found within this module is the `socket()` function, which is used to create socket objects. Sockets also have their own set of methods, which enable socket-based network communication.

2.4.1   socket() Module Function

To create a socket, you must use the `socket.socket()` function, which has the general syntax:

```
socket(socket_family, socket_type, protocol=0)
```

The *socket_family* is either AF_UNIX or AF_INET, as explained earlier, and the *socket_type* is either SOCK_STREAM or SOCK_DGRAM, also explained earlier. The *protocol* is usually left out, defaulting to 0.

So to create a TCP/IP socket, you call `socket.socket()` like this:

```
tcpSock = socket.socket(socket.AF_INET, socket.SOCK_STREAM)
```

Likewise, to create a UDP/IP socket you perform:

```
udpSock = socket.socket(socket.AF_INET, socket.SOCK_DGRAM)
```

Because there are numerous `socket` module attributes, this is one of the exceptions where using **from** *module* **import** * is somewhat acceptable. If we applied **from** socket **import** *, we bring the socket attributes into our namespace, but our code is shortened considerably, as demonstrated in the following:

```
tcpSock = socket(AF_INET, SOCK_STREAM)
```

Once we have a socket object, all further interaction will occur using that socket object's methods.

2.4.2   Socket Object (Built-In) Methods

In Table 2-1, we present a list of the most common socket methods. In the next subsections, we will create both TCP and UDP clients and servers, using some of these methods. Although we focus on Internet sockets, these methods have similar meanings when using local/non-networked sockets.

Table 2-1   Common Socket Object Methods and Attributes

Name	Description
Server Socket Methods	
s.bind()	Bind address (hostname, port number pair) to socket
s.listen()	Set up and start TCP listener
s.accept()	Passively accept TCP client connection, waiting until connection arrives (blocking)
Client Socket Methods	
s.connect()	Actively initiate TCP server connection
s.connect_ex()	Extended version of connect(), where problems returned as error codes rather than an exception being thrown

Name	Description
General Socket Methods	
s.recv()	Receive TCP message
s.recv_into()[a]	Receive TCP message into specified buffer
s.send()	Transmit TCP message
s.sendall()	Transmit TCP message completely
s.recvfrom()	Receive UDP message
s.recvfrom_into()[a]	Receive UDP message into specified buffer
s.sendto()	Transmit UDP message
s.getpeername()	Remote address connected to socket (TCP)
s.getsockname()	Address of current socket
s.getsockopt()	Return value of given socket option
s.setsockopt()	Set value for given socket option
s.shutdown()	Shut down the connection
s.close()	Close socket
s.detach()[b]	Close socket without closing file descriptor, return the latter
s.ioctl()[c]	Control the mode of a socket (Windows only)
Blocking-Oriented Socket Methods	
s.setblocking()	Set blocking or non-blocking mode of socket
s.settimeout()[d]	Set timeout for blocking socket operations
s.gettimeout()[d]	Get timeout for blocking socket operations

(Continued)

Table 2-1   Common Socket Object Methods and Attributes *(Continued)*

Name	Description
File-Oriented Socket Methods	
s.fileno()	File descriptor of socket
s.makefile()	Create a file object associated with socket
Data Attributes	
s.family[a]	The socket family
s.type[a]	The socket type
s.proto[a]	The socket protocol

a. New in Python 2.5.
b. New in Python 3.2.
c. New in Python 2.6; Windows platform only. POSIX systems can use functl module functions.
d. New in Python 2.3.

 CORE TIP: Install clients and servers on different computers to run networked applications

In our multitude of examples in this chapter, you will often see code and output referring to host "localhost" or see an IP address of 127.0.0.1. Our examples are running the client(s) and server(s) on the same computer. We encourage the reader to change the hostnames and copy the code to different computers as it is much more fun developing and playing around with code that lets computers talk to one another across the network, and to see network programs that really do work!

2.4.3   Creating a TCP Server

We will first present some general pseudocode needed to create a generic TCP server, followed by a general description of what is going on. Keep in mind that this is only one way of designing your server. Once you become comfortable with server design, you will be able to modify the following pseudocode to operate the server however you want it to:

```
ss = socket()              # create server socket
ss.bind()                  # bind socket to address
ss.listen()                # listen for connections
inf_loop:                  # server infinite loop
    cs = ss.accept()       # accept client connection
    comm_loop:             # communication loop
        cs.recv()/cs.send() # dialog (receive/send)
    cs.close()             # close client socket
ss.close()                 # close server socket # (opt)
```

All sockets are created by using the socket.socket() function. Servers need to "sit on a port" and wait for requests, so they all must *bind* to a local address. Because TCP is a connection-oriented communication system, some infrastructure must be set up before a TCP server can begin operation. In particular, TCP servers must "listen" for (incoming) connections. Once this setup process is complete, a server can start its infinite loop.

A simple (single-threaded) server will then sit on an accept() call, waiting for a connection. By default, accept() is blocking, meaning that execution is suspended until a connection arrives. Sockets do support a non-blocking mode; refer to the documentation or operating systems textbooks for more details on why and how you would use non-blocking sockets.

Once a connection is accepted, a separate client socket is returned (by accept()) for the upcoming message interchange. Using the new client socket is similar to handing off a customer call to a service representative. When a client eventually does come in, the main switchboard operator takes the incoming call and patches it through, using another line to connect to the appropriate person to handle the client's needs.

This frees up the main line (the original server socket) so that the operator can resume waiting for new calls (client requests) while the customer and the service representative he is connected to carry on their own conversation. Likewise, when an incoming request arrives, a new communication port is created to converse directly with that client, again, leaving the main port free to accept new client connections.

 CORE TIP: Spawning threads to handle client requests

We do not implement this in our examples, but it is also fairly common to hand off a client request to a new thread or process to complete the client processing. The SocketServer module, a high-level socket communication module written on top of socket, supports both threaded and spawned process handling of client requests. Refer to the documentation to obtain more information about the SocketServer module as well as the exercises in Chapter 4, "Multithreaded Programming."

Once the temporary socket is created, communication can commence, and both client and server proceed to engage in a dialog of sending and receiving, using this new socket until the connection is terminated. This usually happens when one of the parties either closes its connection or sends an empty string to its counterpart.

In our code, after a client connection is closed, the server goes back to wait for another client connection. The final line of code, in which we close the server socket, is optional. It is never encountered because the server is supposed to run in an infinite loop. We leave this code in our example as a reminder to the reader that calling the close() method is recommended when implementing an intelligent exit scheme for the server—for example, when a handler detects some external condition whereby the server should be shut down. In those cases, a close() method call is warranted.

In Example 2-1, we present tsTserv.py, a TCP server program that takes the data string sent from a client and returns it timestamped (format: [timestamp]data) back to the client. ("tsTserv" stands for *t*imestamp TCP server. The other files are named in a similar manner.)

Example 2-1   TCP Timestamp Server (tsTserv.py)

This script creates a TCP server that accepts messages from clients and returns them with a timestamp prefix.

```
1    #!/usr/bin/env python
2
3    from socket import *
4    from time import ctime
5
6    HOST = ''
7    PORT = 21567
8    BUFSIZ = 1024
9    ADDR = (HOST, PORT)
10
11   tcpSerSock = socket(AF_INET, SOCK_STREAM)
12   tcpSerSock.bind(ADDR)
13   tcpSerSock.listen(5)
14
15   while True:
16       print 'waiting for connection...'
17       tcpCliSock, addr = tcpSerSock.accept()
18       print '...connected from:', addr
19
20       while True:
21           data = tcpCliSock.recv(BUFSIZ)
22           if not data:
23               break
24           tcpCliSock.send('[%s] %s' % (
25               ctime(), data))
26
27       tcpCliSock.close()
28   tcpSerSock.close()
```

Line-by-Line Explanation

Lines 1–4

After the Unix start-up line, we import `time.ctime()` and all the attributes from the `socket` module.

Lines 6–13

The `HOST` variable is blank, which is an indication to the `bind()` method that it can use any available address. We also choose a random port number, which does not appear to be used or reserved by the system. For our application, we set the buffer size to 1K. You can vary this size based on your networking capability and application needs. The argument for the `listen()` method is simply a maximum number of incoming connection requests to accept before connections are turned away or refused.

The TCP server socket (`tcpSerSock`) is allocated on line 11, followed by the calls to bind the socket to the server's address and to start the TCP listener.

Lines 15–28

Once we are inside the server's infinite loop, we (passively) wait for a connection. When one comes in, we enter the dialog loop where we wait for the client to send its message. If the message is blank, that means that the client has quit, so we would break from the dialog loop, close the client connection, and then go back to wait for another client. If we did get a message from the client, we format and return the same data but prepend it with the current timestamp. The final line is never executed; it is there as a reminder to the reader that a `close()` call should be made if a handler is written to allow for a more graceful exit, as we discussed earlier.

Now let's take a look at the Python 3 version (`tsTserv3.py`), as shown in Example 2-2:

Example 2-2   Python 3 TCP Timestamp Server (`tsTserv3.py`)

This script creates a TCP server that accepts messages from clients and returns them with a timestamp prefix.

```
1    #!/usr/bin/env python
2
3    from socket import *
4    from time import ctime
5
```

(Continued)

Example 2-2   Python 3 TCP Timestamp Server (`tsTserv3.py`) *(Continued)*

```
 6   HOST = ''
 7   PORT = 21567
 8   BUFSIZ = 1024
 9   ADDR = (HOST, PORT)
10
11   tcpSerSock = socket(AF_INET, SOCK_STREAM)
12   tcpSerSock.bind(ADDR)
13   tcpSerSock.listen(5)
14
15   while True:
16       print('waiting for connection...')
17       tcpCliSock, addr = tcpSerSock.accept()
18       print('...connected from:', addr)
19
20       while True:
21           data = tcpCliSock.recv(BUFSIZ)
22           if not data:
23               break
24           tcpCliSock.send('[%s] %s' % (
25               bytes(ctime(), 'utf-8'), data))
26
27       tcpCliSock.close()
28   tcpSerSock.close()
```

We've italicized the relevant changes in lines 16, 18, and 25, wherein **print** becomes a function, and we also transmit the strings as an ASCII bytes "string" rather than in Unicode. Later in this book, we'll discuss Python 2-to-Python 3 migration and how it's also possible to write code that runs unmodified by either version 2.x or 3.x interpreters.

Another pair of variations to support the IPv6, `tsTservV6.py` and `tsTserv3V6.py`, are not shown here, but you would only need to change the address family from `AF_INET` (IPv4) to `AF_INET6` (IPv6) when creating the socket. (In case you're not familiar with these terms, IPv4 describes the current Internet Protocol. The next generation is version 6, hence "IPv6.")

2.4.4   Creating a TCP Client

Creating a client is much simpler than a server. Similar to our description of the TCP server, we will present the pseudocode with explanations first, then show you the real thing.

```
cs = socket()               # create client socket
cs.connect()                # attempt server connection
comm_loop:                  # communication loop
    cs.send()/cs.recv()     # dialog (send/receive)
cs.close()                  # close client socket
```

As we noted earlier, all sockets are created by using `socket.socket()`. Once a client has a socket, however, it can immediately make a connection to a server by using the socket's `connect()` method. When the connection has been established, it can participate in a dialog with the server. Once the client has completed its transaction, it can close its socket, terminating the connection.

We present the code for `tsTclnt.py` in Example 2-3. This script connects to the server and prompts the user for line after line of data. The server returns this data timestamped, which is presented to the user by the client code.

Example 2-3   TCP Timestamp Client (`tsTclnt.py`)

This script creates a TCP client that prompts the user for messages to send to the server, receives them back from the server with a timestamp prefix, and then displays the results to the user.

```
1    #!/usr/bin/env python
2
3    from socket import *
4
5    HOST = 'localhost'
6    PORT = 21567
7    BUFSIZ = 1024
8    ADDR = (HOST, PORT)
9
10   tcpCliSock = socket(AF_INET, SOCK_STREAM)
11   tcpCliSock.connect(ADDR)
12
13   while True:
14       data = raw_input('> ')
15       if not data:
16           break
17       tcpCliSock.send(data)
18       data = tcpCliSock.recv(BUFSIZ)
19       if not data:
20           break
21       print data
22
23   tcpCliSock.close()
```

Line-by-Line Explanation

Lines 1–3

After the Unix startup line, we import all the attributes from the `socket` module.

Lines 5–11

The HOST and PORT variables refer to the server's hostname and port number. Because we are running our test (in this case) on the same computer, HOST contains the local hostname (change it accordingly if you are running your server on a different host). The port number PORT should be exactly the same as what you set for your server (otherwise, there won't be much communication). We also choose the same 1K buffer size.

The TCP client socket (tcpCliSock) is allocated in line 10, followed by (an active) call to connect to the server.

Lines 13–23

The client also has an infinite loop, but it is not meant to run forever like the server's loop. The client loop will exit on either of two conditions: the user enters no input (lines 14–16), or the server somehow quit and our call to the recv() method fails (lines 18–20). Otherwise, in a normal situation, the user enters in some string data, which is sent to the server for processing. The newly timestamped input string is then received and displayed to the screen.

Similar to what we did for the server, let's take a look at the Python 3 and IPv6 versions of the client (tsTclnt3.py), starting with the former as shown in Example 2-4:

Example 2-4   Python 3 TCP Timestamp Client (tsTclnt3.py)

This is the Python 3 equivalent to tsTclnt.py.

```
1    #!/usr/bin/env python
2
3    from socket import *
4
5    HOST = '127.0.0.1' # or 'localhost'
6    PORT = 21567
7    BUFSIZ = 1024
8    ADDR = (HOST, PORT)
9
10   tcpCliSock = socket(AF_INET, SOCK_STREAM)
11   tcpCliSock.connect(ADDR)
12
13   while True:
14       data = input('> ')
15       if not data:
16           break
17       tcpCliSock.send(data)
18       data = tcpCliSock.recv(BUFSIZ)
19       if not data:
20           break
21       print(data.decode('utf-8'))
22
23   tcpCliSock.close()
```

In addition to changing **print** to a function, we also have to decode the string that comes from the server. (With the help of distutils.log.warn(), it would be simple to convert the original script to run under both Python 2 and 3, just like rewhoU.py from Chapter 1, "Regular Expressions.") Finally, let's take a look at the (Python 2) IPv6 version (tsTclntV6.py), as shown in Example 2-5.

Example 2-5   IPv6 TCP Timestamp Client (tsTclntV6.py)

This is the IPv6 version of the TCP client from the previous two examples.

```
1   #!/usr/bin/env python
2
3   from socket import *
4
5   HOST = '::1'
6   PORT = 21567
7   BUFSIZ = 1024
8   ADDR = (HOST, PORT)
9
10  tcpCliSock = socket(AF_INET6, SOCK_STREAM)
11  tcpCliSock.connect(ADDR)
12
13  while True:
14      data = raw_input('> ')
15      if not data:
16          break
17      tcpCliSock.send(data)
18      data = tcpCliSock.recv(BUFSIZ)
19      if not data:
20          break
21      print data
22
23  tcpCliSock.close()
```

In this snippet, we needed to change the localhost to its IPv6 address of "::1" as well as request the AF_INET6 family of sockets. If you combine the changes from tsTclnt3.py and tsTclntV6.py, you should also be able to arrive at an IPv6 Python 3 version of the TCP client.

2.4.5   Executing Our TCP Server and Client(s)

Now let's run the server and client programs to see how they work. Should we run the server first or the client? Naturally, if we ran the client first, no connection would be possible because there is no server waiting to accept the request. The server is considered a passive partner because it has to establish itself first and passively wait for a connection. A client, on the other hand, is an active partner because it actively initiates a connection. In other words:

Start the server first (before any clients try to connect).

In our example, we use the same computer, but there is nothing to stop us from using another host for the server. If this is the case, just change the hostname. (It is rather exciting when you get your first networked application running the server and client from different machines!)

We now present the corresponding input and output from the client program, which exits with a simple Return (or Enter) keystroke with no data entered:

```
$ tsTclnt.py
> hi
[Sat Jun 17 17:27:21 2006] hi
> spanish inquisition
[Sat Jun 17 17:27:37 2006] spanish inquisition
>
$
```

The server's output is mainly diagnostic:

```
$ tsTserv.py
waiting for connection...
...connected from: ('127.0.0.1', 1040)
waiting for connection...
```

The ". . . connected from . . ." message was received when our client made its connection. The server went back to wait for new clients while we continued receiving "service." When we exited from the server, we had to break out of it, resulting in an exception. The best way to avoid such an error is to create a more graceful exit, as we have been discussing.

 CORE TIP: Exit gracefully and call the server `close()` method

One way to create this "friendly" exit in development is to put the server's **while** loop inside the **except** clause of a **try-except** statement and monitor for EOFError or KeyboardInterrupt exceptions so that you can close the server's socket in the **except** or **finally** clauses. In production, you'll want to be able to start up and shut down servers in a more automated fashion. In these cases, you'll want to set a flag to shut down service by using a thread or creating a special file or database entry.

The interesting thing about this simple networked application is that we are not only showing how our data takes a round trip from the client to the server and back to the client, but we also use the server as a sort of "time server," because the timestamp we receive is purely from the server.

2.4.6 Creating a UDP Server

UDP servers do not require as much setup as TCP servers because they are not connection-oriented. There is virtually no work that needs to be done other than just waiting for incoming connections.

```
ss = socket()                      # create server socket
ss.bind()                          # bind server socket
inf_loop:                          # server infinite loop
    cs = ss.recvfrom()/ss.sendto()# dialog (receive/send)
ss.close()                         # close server socket
```

As you can see from the pseudocode, there is nothing extra other than the usual create-the-socket and bind it to the local address (host/port pair). The infinite loop consists of receiving a message from a client, timestamping and returning the message, and then going back to wait for another message. Again, the `close()` call is optional and will not be reached due to the infinite loop, but it serves as a reminder that it should be part of the graceful or intelligent exit scheme we've been mentioning.

One other significant difference between UDP and TCP servers is that because datagram sockets are connectionless, there is no "handing off" of a client connection to a separate socket for succeeding communication. These servers just accept messages and perhaps reply.

You will find the code to `tsUserv.py` in Example 2-6, which is a UDP version of the TCP server presented earlier. It accepts a client message and returns it to the client with a timestamp.

Example 2-6   UDP Timestamp Server (`tsUserv.py`)

This script creates a UDP server that accepts messages from clients and returns them with a timestamp prefix.

```
1    #!/usr/bin/env python
2
3    from socket import *
4    from time import ctime
5
6    HOST = ''
7    PORT = 21567
8    BUFSIZ = 1024
9    ADDR = (HOST, PORT)
10
```

(Continued)

Example 2-6   UDP Timestamp Server (tsUserv.py) *(Continued)*

```
11   udpSerSock = socket(AF_INET, SOCK_DGRAM)
12   udpSerSock.bind(ADDR)
13
14   while True:
15       print 'waiting for message...'
16       data, addr = udpSerSock.recvfrom(BUFSIZ)
17       udpSerSock.sendto('[%s] %s' % (
18           ctime(), data), addr)
19       print '...received from and returned to:', addr
20
21   udpSerSock.close()
```

Line-by-Line Explanation

Lines 1–4

After the Unix startup line, we import time.ctime() and all the attributes from the socket module, just like the TCP server setup.

Lines 6–12

The HOST and PORT variables are the same as before, and for all the same reasons. The call socket() differs only in that we are now requesting a datagram/UDP socket type, but bind() is invoked in the same way as in the TCP server version. Again, because UDP is connectionless, no call to "listen for incoming connections" is made here.

Lines 14–21

Once we are inside the server's infinite loop, we (passively) wait for a message (a datagram). When one comes in, we process it (by adding a timestamp to it), then send it right back and go back to wait for another message. The socket close() method is there for show only, as indicated before.

2.4.7   Creating a UDP Client

Of the four clients highlighted here in this section, the UDP client is the shortest bit of code that we will look at. The pseudocode looks like this:

```
cs = socket()                    # create client socket
comm_loop:                       # communication loop
    cs.sendto()/cs.recvfrom()    # dialog (send/receive)
cs.close()                       # close client socket
```

Once a socket object is created, we enter the dialog loop, wherein we exchange messages with the server. When communication is complete, the socket is closed.

The real client code, tsUclnt.py, is presented in Example 2-7.

Example 2-7	UDP Timestamp Client (tsUclnt.py)

This script creates a UDP client that prompts the user for messages to send to the server, receives them back with a timestamp prefix, and then displays them back to the user.

```
1   #!/usr/bin/env python
2
3   from socket import *
4
5   HOST = 'localhost'
6   PORT = 21567
7   BUFSIZ = 1024
8   ADDR = (HOST, PORT)
9
10  udpCliSock = socket(AF_INET, SOCK_DGRAM)
11
12  while True:
13      data = raw_input('> ')
14      if not data:
15          break
16      udpCliSock.sendto(data, ADDR)
17      data, ADDR = udpCliSock.recvfrom(BUFSIZ)
18      if not data:
19          break
20      print data
21
22  udpCliSock.close()
```

Line-by-Line Explanation

Lines 1–3

After the Unix startup line, we import all the attributes from the socket module, again, just like in the TCP version of the client.

Lines 5–10

Because we are running the server on our local computer again, we use "localhost" and the same port number on the client side, not to mention the same 1K buffer. We allocate our socket object in the same way as the UDP server.

Lines 12–22

Our UDP client loop works in almost the exact manner as the TCP client. The only difference is that we do not have to establish a connection to the UDP server first; we simply send a message to it and await the reply. After the timestamped string is returned, we display it to the screen and go back for more. When the input is complete, we break out of the loop and close the socket.

Based on the TCP client/server examples, it should be pretty straightforward to create Python 3 and IPv6 equivalents for UDP.

2.4.8   Executing Our UDP Server and Client(s)

The UDP client behaves the same as the TCP client:

```
$ tsUclnt.py
> hi
[Sat Jun 17 19:55:36 2006] hi
> spam! spam! spam!
[Sat Jun 17 19:55:40 2006] spam! spam! spam!
>
$
```

Likewise for the server:

```
$ tsUserv.py
waiting for message...
...received from and returned to: ('127.0.0.1', 1025)
waiting for message...
```

In fact, we output the client's information because we can be receiving messages from multiple clients and sending replies, and such output helps by indicating where messages came from. With the TCP server, we know where messages come from because each client makes a connection. Note how the messages says "waiting for message," as opposed to "waiting for connection."

2.4.9   socket Module Attributes

In addition to the socket.socket() function that we are now familiar with, the socket module features many more attributes that are used in network application development. Some of the most popular ones are shown in Table 2-2.

Table 2-2   socket Module Attributes

Attribute Name	Description
Data Attributes	
AF_UNIX, AF_INET, AF_INET6,[a] AF_NETLINK,[b] AF_TIPC[c]	Socket address families supported by Python
SO_STREAM, SO_DGRAM	Socket types (TCP = stream, UDP = datagram)
has_ipv6[d]	Boolean flag indicating whether IPv6 is supported
Exceptions	
error	Socket-related error
herror[a]	Host and address-related error
gaierror[a]	Address-related error
timeout	Timeout expiration
Functions	
socket()	Create a socket object from the given address family, socket type, and protocol type (optional)
socketpair()[e]	Create a pair of socket objects from the given address family, socket type, and protocol type (optional)
create_connection()	Convenience function that takes an address (host, port) pair and returns the socket object
fromfd()	Create a socket object from an open file descriptor
ssl()	Initiates a Secure Socket Layer connection over socket; does *not* perform certificate validation
getaddrinfo()[a]	Gets address information as a sequence of 5-tuples
getnameinfo()	Given a socket address, returns (host, port) 2-tuple

(Continued)

Table 2-2   socket Module Attributes *(Continued)*

Attribute Name	Description
Functions	
getfqdn()[f]	Returns fully-qualified domain name
gethostname()	Returns current hostname
gethostbyname()	Maps a hostname to its IP address
gethostbyname_ex()	Extended version of gethostbyname() returning hostname, set of alias hostnames, and list of IP addresses
gethostbyaddr()	Maps an IP address to DNS information; returns same 3-tuple as gethostbyname_ex()
getprotobyname()	Maps a protocol name (e.g., 'tcp') to a number
getservbyname()/ getservbyport()	Maps a service name to a port number or vice versa; a protocol name is optional for either function
ntohl()/ntohs()	Converts integers from network to host byte order
htonl()/htons()	Converts integers from host to network byte order
inet_aton()/inet_ntoa()	Convert IP address octet string to 32-bit packed format or vice versa (for IPv4 addresses only)
inet_pton()/inet_ntop()	Convert IP address string to packed binary format or vice versa (for both IPv4 and IPv6 addresses)
getdefaulttimeout()/ setdefaulttimeout()	Return default socket timeout in seconds (float); set default socket timeout in seconds (float)

a. New in Python 2.2.
b. New in Python 2.5.
c. New in Python 2.6.
d. New in Python 2.3.
e. New in Python 2.4.
f. New in Python 2.0.

For more information, refer to the socket module documentation in the Python Library Reference.

2.5 ***The** SocketServer **Module**

SocketServer is a higher-level module in the standard library (renamed as socketserver in Python 3.x). Its goal is to simplify a lot of the boiler-plate code that is necessary to create networked clients and servers. In this module there are various classes created on your behalf, as shown in Table 2-3 below.

3.x

Table 2-3   SocketServer Module Classes

Class	Description
BaseServer	Contains core server functionality and hooks for mix-in classes; used only for derivation so you will not create instances of this class; use TCPServer or UDPServer instead
TCPServer/ UDPServer	Basic networked synchronous TCP/UDP server
UnixStreamServer/ UnixDatagramServer	Basic file-based synchronous TCP/UDP server
ForkingMixIn/Threading MixIn	Core forking or threading functionality; used only as mix-in classes with one of the server classes to achieve some asynchronicity; you will not instantiate this class directly
ForkingTCPServer/ ForkingUDPServer	Combination of ForkingMixIn and TCPServer/ UDPServer
ThreadingTCPServer/ ThreadingUDPServer	Combination of ThreadingMixIn and TCPServer/ UDPServer
BaseRequestHandler	Contains core functionality for handling service requests; used only for derivation so you will create subclasses of this class; use StreamRequest Handler or DatagramRequestHandler instead
StreamRequestHandler/ DatagramRequestHandler	Implement service handler for TCP/UDP servers

We will create a TCP client and server that duplicates the base TCP example shown earlier. You will notice the immediate similarities but should recognize how some of the dirty work is now taken care of so that you do not have to worry about that boilerplate code. These represent the simplest synchronous servers you can write. (To configure your server to run asynchronously, go to the exercises at the end of the chapter.)

In addition to hiding implementation details from you, another difference is that we are now writing our applications using classes. Doing things in an object-oriented way helps us organize our data and logically direct functionality to the right places. You will also notice that our applications are now *event-driven*, meaning that they only work when reacting to an occurrence of an *event* in our system.

Events include the sending and receiving of messages. In fact, you will see that our class definition only consists of an event handler for receiving a client message. All other functionality is taken from the SocketServer classes we use. GUI programming (see Chapter 5, "GUI Programming,") is also event-driven. You will notice the similarity immediately as the final line of our code is usually a server's infinite loop waiting for and responding to client service requests. It works almost the same as our infinite while loop in the original base TCP server earlier in this chapter.

In our original server loop, we block waiting for a request, service it when something comes in, and then go back to waiting. In the server loop here, instead of building your code in the server, you define a handler so that the server can just call your function when it receives an incoming request.

2.5.1   Creating a SocketServer TCP Server

In Example 2-8, we first import our server classes, and then define the same host constants as before. That is followed by our request handler class, and then startup. More details follow our code snippet.

> **Example 2-8**   SocketServer Timestamp TCP Server (tsTservSS.py)
>
> This script creates a timestamp TCP server by using SocketServer classes, TCPServer and StreamRequestHandler.

```
1    #!/usr/bin/env python
2
3    from SocketServer import (TCPServer as TCP,
4        StreamRequestHandler as SRH)
5    from time import ctime
6
```

```
 7   HOST = ''
 8   PORT = 21567
 9   ADDR = (HOST, PORT)
10
11   class MyRequestHandler(SRH):
12       def handle(self):
13           print '...connected from:', self.client_address
14           self.wfile.write('[%s] %s' % (ctime(),
15               self.rfile.readline()))
16
17   tcpServ = TCP(ADDR, MyRequestHandler)
18   print 'waiting for connection...'
19   tcpServ.serve_forever()
```

Line-by-Line Explanation

Lines 1–9

The initial stuff consists of importing the right classes from SocketServer. Note that we are using the multiline import feature introduced in Python 2.4. If you are using an earlier version of Python, then you will have to use the fully-qualified *module.attribute* names or put both attribute imports on the same line:

```
from SocketServer import TCPServer as TCP, StreamRequestHandler as SRH
```

Lines 11–15

The bulk of the work happens here. We derive our request handler MyRequest Handler as a subclass of SocketServer's StreamRequestHandler and override its handle() method, which is stubbed out in the Base Request class with no default action as:

```
def handle(self):
    pass
```

The handle() method is called when an incoming message is received from a client. The StreamRequestHandler class treats input and output sockets as file-like objects, so we will use readline() to get the client message and write() to send a string back to the client.

Accordingly, we need additional carriage return and NEWLINE characters in both the client and server code. Actually, you will *not* see it in the code because we are just reusing those which come from the client. Other than these minor differences, it should look just like our earlier server.

Lines 17–19

The final bits of code create the TCP server with the given host informa-tion and request handler class. We then have our entire infinite loop wait-ing for and servicing client requests.

2.5.2   Creating a SocketServer TCP Client

Our client, shown in Example 2-9, will naturally resemble our original client, much more so than the server, but it has to be tweaked a bit to work well with our new server.

Example 2-9   SocketServer Timestamp TCP Client (tsTclntSS.py)

This is a timestamp TCP client that knows how to speak to the file-like Socket Server class StreamRequestHandler objects.

```
1    #!/usr/bin/env python
2
3    from socket import *
4
5    HOST = 'localhost'
6    PORT = 21567
7    BUFSIZ = 1024
8    ADDR = (HOST, PORT)
9
10   while True:
11       tcpCliSock = socket(AF_INET, SOCK_STREAM)
12       tcpCliSock.connect(ADDR)
13       data = raw_input('> ')
14       if not data:
15           break
16       tcpCliSock.send('%s\r\n' % data)
17       data = tcpCliSock.recv(BUFSIZ)
18       if not data:
19           break
20       print data.strip()
21       tcpCliSock.close()
```

Line-by-Line Explanation

Lines 1–8

Nothing special here; this is an exact replica of our original client code.

Lines 10–21

The default behavior of the SocketServer request handlers is to accept a connection, get the request, and then close the connection. This makes it so that we cannot keep our connection throughout the execution of our application, so we need to create a new socket each time we send a message to the server.

This behavior makes the TCP server act more like a UDP server; however, this can be changed by overriding the appropriate methods in our request handler classes. We leave this as an exercise at the end of this chapter.

Other than the fact that our client is somewhat "inside-out" now (because we have to create a connection each time), the only other minor difference was previewed in the line-by-line explanation for the server code: the handler class we are using treats socket communication like a file, so we have to send line-termination characters (carriage return and NEWLINE) each way. The server just retains and reuses the ones we send here. When we get a message back from the server, we strip() them and just use the NEWLINE that is automatically provided by the **print** statement.

2.5.3   Executing our TCP Server and Client(s)

Here is the output of our SocketServer TCP client:

```
$ tsTclntSS.py
> 'Tis but a scratch.
[Tue Apr 18 20:55:49 2006] 'Tis but a scratch.
> Just a flesh wound.
[Tue Apr 18 20:55:56 2006] Just a flesh wound.
>
$
```

And here is the server's output:

```
$ tsTservSS.py
waiting for connection...
...connected from: ('127.0.0.1', 53476)
...connected from: ('127.0.0.1', 53477)
```

The output is similar to that of our original TCP client and servers; however, you will notice that we connected to the server twice.

2.6   *Introduction to the Twisted Framework

Twisted is a complete event-driven networking framework with which you can both use and develop complete asynchronous networked applications and protocols. It is *not* part of the Python Standard Library as of this writing and must be downloaded and installed separately (you can use the link at the end of the chapter). It provides a significant amount of support for you to build complete systems, including network protocols, threading, security and authentication, chat/IM, DBM and RDBMS database integration, Web/Internet, e-mail, command-line arguments, GUI toolkit integration, etc.

Using Twisted to implement our tiny simplistic example is like using a sledgehammer to pound a thumbtack, but you have to get started somehow, and our application is the equivalent to the "hello world" of networked applications.

Like SocketServer, most of the functionality of Twisted lies in its classes. In particular for our examples, we will be using the classes found in the reactor and protocol subpackages of Twisted's Internet component.

2.6.1   Creating a Twisted Reactor TCP Server

You will find the code in Example 2-10 similar to that of the SocketServer example. Instead of a handler class, however, we create a protocol class and override several methods in the same manner as installing callbacks. Also, this example is asynchronous. Let's take a look at the server now.

Example 2-10   Twisted Reactor Timestamp TCP Server (tsTservTW.py)

This is a timestamp TCP server that uses Twisted Internet classes.

```
1   #!/usr/bin/env python
2
3   from twisted.internet import protocol, reactor
4   from time import ctime
5
6   PORT = 21567
7
8   class TSServProtocol(protocol.Protocol):
9       def connectionMade(self):
10          clnt = self.clnt = self.transport.getPeer().host
11          print '...connected from:', clnt
12      def dataReceived(self, data):
13          self.transport.write('[%s] %s' % (
14                  ctime(), data))
15
16  factory = protocol.Factory()
17  factory.protocol = TSServProtocol
18  print 'waiting for connection...'
19  reactor.listenTCP(PORT, factory)
20  reactor.run()
```

Line-by-Line Explanation

Lines 1–6

The setup lines of code include the usual module imports, most notably the `protocol` and `reactor` subpackages of `twisted.internet` and our constant port number.

Lines 8–14

We derive the `Protocol` class and call ours `TSServProtocol` for our timestamp server. We then override `connectionMade()`, a method that is executed when a client connects to us, and `dataReceived()`, called when a client sends a piece of data across the network. The reactor passes in the data as an argument to this method so that we can get access to it right away without having to extract it ourselves.

   The transport instance object is how we can communicate with the client. You can see how we use it in `connectionMade()` to get the host information about who is connecting to us as well as in `dataReceived()` to return data back to the client.

Lines 16–20

In the final part of our server, we create a protocol `Factory`. It is called a factory because an instance of our protocol is "manufactured" every time we get an incoming connection. We then install a TCP listener in our reactor to check for service requests; when it receives a request, it creates a `TSServProtocol` instance to take care of that client.

2.6.2   Creating a Twisted Reactor TCP Client

Unlike the `SocketServer` TCP client, Example 2-11 will not look like all the other clients—this one is distinctly Twisted.

Example 2-11   Twisted Reactor Timestamp TCP Client (`tsTclntTW.py`)

Our familiar timestamp TCP client, written from a Twisted point of view.

```
1   #!/usr/bin/env python
2
3   from twisted.internet import protocol, reactor
4
```

(Continued)

Example 2-11   Twisted Reactor Timestamp TCP Client (`tsTclntTW.py`)
               (Continued)

```
5   HOST = 'localhost'
6   PORT = 21567
7
8   class TSClntProtocol(protocol.Protocol):
9       def sendData(self):
10          data = raw_input('> ')
11          if data:
12              print '...sending %s...' % data
13              self.transport.write(data)
14          else:
15              self.transport.loseConnection()
16
17      def connectionMade(self):
18          self.sendData()
19
20      def dataReceived(self, data):
21          print data
22          self.sendData()
23
24  class TSClntFactory(protocol.ClientFactory):
25      protocol = TSClntProtocol
26      clientConnectionLost = clientConnectionFailed = \
27          lambda self, connector, reason: reactor.stop()
28
29  reactor.connectTCP(HOST, PORT, TSClntFactory())
30  reactor.run()
```

Line-by-Line Explanation

Lines 1–6

Again, nothing really new here apart from the import of Twisted components. It is very similar to all of our other clients.

Lines 8–22

Like the server, we extend `Protocol` by overriding the `connectionMade()` and `dataReceived()` methods. Both execute for the same reason as the server. We also add our own method for when data needs to be sent and call it `sendData()`.

Because this time we are the client, we are the ones initiating a conversation with the server. Once that connection has been established, we take the first step and send a message. The server replies, and we handle it by displaying it to the screen and sending another message to the server.

This continues in a loop until we terminate the connection by giving no input when prompted. Instead of calling the `write()` method of the transport object to send another message to the server, `loseConnection()` is executed, closing the socket. When this occurs, the factory's `clientConnectionLost()` method will be called and our reactor is stopped, completing execution of our script. We also stop the reactor if a `clientConnectionFailed()` for some other reason.

The final part of the script is where we create a client factory and make a connection to the server and run the reactor. Note that we instantiate the client factory here instead of passing it in to the reactor, as we did in the server. This is because we are not the server waiting for clients to talk to us, and its factory makes a new protocol object for each connection. *We* are one client, so we make a single protocol object that connects to the server, whose factory makes one to talk to ours.

2.6.3   Executing Our TCP Server and Client(s)

The Twisted client displays output similar to all of our other clients:

```
$ tsTclntTW.py
> Where is hope
...sending Where is hope...
[Tue Apr 18 23:53:09 2006] Where is hope
> When words fail
...sending When words fail...
[Tue Apr 18 23:53:14 2006] When words fail
>
$
```

The server is back to a single connection. Twisted maintains the connection and does not close the transport after every message:

```
$ tsTservTW.py
waiting for connection...
...connected from: 127.0.0.1
```

The "connection from" output does not have the other information because we only asked for the host/address from the `getPeer()` method of the server's transport object.

Keep in mind that most applications based on Twisted are much more complex than the examples built in this subsection. It is a feature-rich library, but it does come with a level of complexity for which you need to be prepared.

2.7   Related Modules

Table 2-4 lists some of the other Python modules that are related to network and socket programming. The `select` module is usually used in conjunction with the `socket` module when developing lower-level socket applications. It provides the `select()` function, which manages sets of socket objects. One of the most useful things it does is to take a set of sockets and listen for active connections on them. The `select()` function will block until at least one socket is ready for communication, and when that happens, it provides you with a set of those that are ready for reading. (It can also determine which sockets are ready for writing, although that is not as common as the former operation.)

Table 2-4   Network/Socket Programming Related Modules

Module	Description
socket	Lower-level networking interface, as discussed in this chapter
asyncore/ asynchat	Provide infrastructure to create networked applications that process clients asynchronously
select	Manages multiple socket connections in a single-threaded network server application
SocketServer	High-level module that provides server classes for networked applications, complete with forking or threading varieties

The `async*` and `SocketServer` modules both provide higher-level functionality as far as creating servers is concerned. Written on top of the `socket` and/or `select` modules, they enable more rapid development of client/server systems because all the lower-level code is handled for you. All you have to do is to create or subclass the appropriate base classes, and you are on your way. As we mentioned earlier, `SocketServer` even provides the capability of integrating threading or new processes into the server, which affords a more parallel-like processing of client requests.

Although `async*` provides the only asynchronous development support in the standard library, in the previous section, you were introduced to Twisted, a third-party package that is more powerful than those older modules. Although the example code we have seen in this chapter is slightly longer than the barebones scripts, Twisted provides a much more powerful and flexible framework and has implemented many protocols for you already. You can find out more about Twisted at its Web site:

http://twistedmatrix.com

A more modern networking framework is Concurrence, which is the engine behind the Dutch social network, Hyves. Concurrence is a high-performance I/O system paired with *libevent*, the lower-level event callback dispatching system. Concurrence follows an asynchronous model, using lightweight threads (executing callbacks) in an event-driven way to do the work and message-passing for interthread communication. You can find out more info about Concurrence at:

http://opensource.hyves.org/concurrence

Modern networking frameworks follow one of many asynchronous models (greenlets, generators, etc.) to provide high-performance asynchronous servers. One of the goals of these frameworks is to push the complexity of asynchronous programming so as to allow users to code in a more familiar, synchronous manner.

The topics we have covered in this chapter deal with network programming with sockets in Python and how to create custom applications using lower-level protocol suites such as TCP/IP and UDP/IP. If you want to develop higher-level Web and Internet applications, we strongly encourage you to move ahead to Chapter 3, "Internet Client Programming," or perhaps skip to Part II of the book.

2.8   Exercises

2-1. *Sockets*. What is the difference between connection-oriented and connectionless sockets?

2-2. *Client/Server Architecture*. Describe in your own words what this term means and give several examples.

2-3. *Sockets*. Between TCP and UDP, which type of servers accept connections and hands them off to separate sockets for client communication?

2-4. *Clients.* Update the TCP (`tsTclnt.py`) and UDP (`tsUclnt.py`) clients so that the server name is not hardcoded into the application. Allow the user to specify a hostname and port number, and only use the default values if either or both parameters are missing.

2-5. *Internetworking and Sockets.* Implement the sample TCP client/server programs found in the Python Library Reference documentation on the `socket` module and get them to work. Set up the server and then the client. An online version of the source is also available here:

http://docs.python.org/library/socket#example

You decide the server is too boring. Update the server so that it can do much more, recognizing the following commands:

date   Server will return its current date/timestamp, that is, `time.ctime()`.

os   Get OS information (`os.name`).

ls   Give a listing of the current directory. (Hints: `os.listdir()` lists a directory, `os.curdir` is the current directory.) Extra Credit: Accept `ls dir` and return `dir`'s file listing.

You do not need a network to do this assignment—your computer can communicate with itself. Be aware that after the server exits, the binding must be cleared before you can run it again. You might experience "port already bound" errors. The operating system usually clears the binding within 5 minutes, so be patient.

2-6. *Daytime Service.* Use the `socket.getservbyname()` to determine the port number for the "daytime" service under the UDP protocol. Check the documentation for `getservbyname()` to get the exact usage syntax (i.e., `socket.getservbyname.__doc__`). Now write an application that sends a dummy message over and wait for the reply. Once you have received a reply from the server, display it to the screen.

2-7. *Half-Duplex Chat.* Create a simple, *half-duplex* chat program. By half-duplex, we mean that when a connection is made and the service starts, only one person can type. The other participant must wait to get a message before being prompted to enter a message. Once a message is sent, the sender must wait for a reply before being allowed to send another message. One participant will be on the server side; the other will be on the client side.

2-8. *Full-Duplex Chat.* Update your solution to the previous exercise so that your chat service is now *full-duplex*, meaning that both parties can send and receive, independent of each other.

2-9. *Multi-User Full Duplex Chat.* Further update your solution so that your chat service is multi-user.

2-10. *Multi-User, Multiroom, Full Duplex Chat.* Now make your chat service multi-user *and* multiroom.

2-11. *Web Client.* Write a TCP client that connects to port 80 of your favorite Web site (remove the "http://" and any trailing information; use only the hostname). Once a connection has been established, send the HTTP command string GET /\n and write all the data that the server returns to a file. (The GET command retrieves a Web page, the / file indicates the file to get, and the \n sends the command to the server.) Examine the contents of the retrieved file. What is it? How can you check to make sure the data you received is correct? (Note: You might have to insert one or two NEWLINEs after the command string. One usually works.)

2-12. *Sleep Server.* Create a *sleep* server. A client will request to be "put to sleep" for a number of seconds. The server will issue the command on behalf of the client then return a message to the client indicating success. The client should have slept or should have been idle for the exact time requested. This is a simple implementation of a remote procedure call, where a client's request invokes commands on another computer across the network.

2-13. *Name Server.* Design and implement a name server. Such a server is responsible for maintaining a database of host-name-port number pairs, perhaps along with the string description of the service that the corresponding servers provide. Take one or more existing servers and have them register their service with your name server. (Note that these servers are, in this case, clients of the name server.)

Every client that starts up has no idea where the server is that it is looking for. Also as clients of the name server, these clients should send a request to the name server indicating what type of service they are seeking. The name server, in reply, returns a hostname-port number pair to this client, which then connects to the appropriate server to process its request.

Extra Credit:

1) Add caching to your name server for popular requests.

2) Add logging capability to your name server, keeping track of which servers have registered and which services clients are requesting.

3) Your name server should periodically ping the registered hosts at their respective port numbers to ensure that the service is indeed up. Repeated failures will cause a server to be delisted from the list of services.

You can implement real services for the servers that register for your name service, or just use dummy servers (which merely acknowledge a request).

2-14. *Error Checking and Graceful Shutdown.* All of the sample client/server code presented in this chapter is poor in terms of error-checking. We do not handle scenarios such as when users press Ctrl+C to exit out of a server or Ctrl+D to terminate client input, nor do we check other improper input to raw_input() or handle network errors. Because of this weakness, quite often we terminate an application without closing our sockets, potentially losing data. Choose a client/server pair of one of our examples, and add enough error-checking so that each application properly shuts down, that is, closes network connections.

2-15. *Asynchronicity and SocketServer/socketserver.* Take the example TCP server and use either mix-in class to support an asynchronous server. To test your server, create and run multiple clients simultaneously and show output that your server is serving requests from both, interleaved.

2-16. *Extending SocketServer Classes.* In the SocketServer TCP
server code, we had to change our client from the original
base TCP client because the SocketServer class does not
maintain the connection between requests.

    a) Subclass the TCPServer and StreamRequestHandler
       classes and re-design the server so that it maintains
       and uses a single connection for each client (not one per
       request).

    b) Integrate your solution for the previous exercise with
       your solution to part (a), such that multiple clients are
       being serviced in parallel.

2-17. *Asynchronous Systems.* Research at least five different
Python-based asynchronous systems—choose from Twisted,
Greenlets, Tornado, Diesel, Concurrence, Eventlet, Gevent,
etc. Describe what they are, categorize them, find similarities
and differences, and then create some demonstration code
samples.

3

Internet Client Programming

*You can't take something off the Internet, that's like trying to take
pee out of a swimming pool. Once it's in there, it's in there.*
—Joe Garrelli, March 1996
(verbally via "Joe Rogan," a character from
NewsRadio [television program]),

In this chapter...

- What Are Internet Clients?
- Transferring Files
- Network News
- E-Mail
- Related Modules

In Chapter 2, "Network Programming," we took a look at low-level networking communication protocols using sockets. This type of networking is at the heart of most of the client/server protocols that exist on the Internet today. These protocols include those for transferring files (FTP, etc.), reading Usenet newsgroups (Network News Transfer Protocol), sending e-mail (SMTP), and downloading e-mail from a server (POP3, IMAP), etc. These protocols work in a way much like the client/server examples in Chapter 2. The only difference is that now we have taken lower-level protocols such as TCP/IP and created newer, more specific protocols on top of them to implement these higher-level services.

3.1 What Are Internet Clients?

Before we take a look at these protocols, we first must ask, "What is an Internet client?" To answer this question, we simplify the Internet to a place where data is exchanged, and this interchange is made up of someone offering a service and a user of such services. You will hear the term *producer-consumer* in some circles (although this phrase is generally reserved for conversations on operating systems). Servers are the producers, providing the services, and clients consume the offered services. For any one particular service, there is usually only one server (process, host, etc.) and more than one consumer. We previously examined the client/server model, and although we do not need to create Internet clients with the low-level socket operations seen earlier, the model is an accurate match.

In this chapter, we'll explore a variety of these Internet protocols and create clients for each. When finished, you should be able to recognize how similar the application programming interfaces (APIs) of all of these protocols are—this is done by design, as keeping interfaces consistent is a worthy cause—and most importantly, the ability to create real clients of these and other Internet protocols. And even though we are only highlighting these three specific protocols, at the end of this chapter, you should feel confident enough to write clients for just about *any* Internet protocol.

3.2   Transferring Files

3.2.1   File Transfer Internet Protocols

One of the most popular Internet activities is file exchange. It happens *all the time*. There have been many protocols to transfer files over the Internet, with some of the most popular including the File Transfer Protocol, the Unix-to-Unix Copy Protocol (UUCP), and of course, the Web's Hypertext Transfer Protocol (HTTP). We should also include the remote (Unix) file copy command, `rcp` (and now its more secure and flexible cousins, `scp` and `rsync`).

HTTP, FTP, and `scp/rsync` are still quite popular today. HTTP is primarily used for Web-based file download and accessing Web services. It generally doesn't require clients to have a login and/or password on the server host to obtain documents or service. The majority of all HTTP file transfer requests are for Web page retrieval (file downloads).

On the other hand, `scp` and `rsync` require a user login on the server host. Clients must be authenticated before file transfers can occur, and files can be sent (upload) or retrieved (download). Finally, we have FTP. Like `scp/rsync`, FTP can be used for file upload or download; and like `scp/rsync`, it employs the Unix multi-user concepts of usernames and passwords. FTP clients must use the login/password of existing users; however, FTP also allows anonymous logins. Let's now take a closer look at FTP.

3.2.2   File Transfer Protocol

The File Transfer Protocol (FTP) was developed by the late Jon Postel and Joyce Reynolds in the Internet Request for Comment (RFC) 959 document and published in October 1985. It is primarily used to download publicly accessible files in an anonymous fashion. It can also be used to transfer files between two computers, especially when you're using a Unix-based system for file storage or archiving and a desktop or laptop PC for work. Before the Web became popular, FTP was one of the primary methods of transferring files on the Internet, and one of the only ways to download software and/or source code.

As mentioned previously, you must have a login/password to access the remote host running the FTP server. The exception is anonymous logins, which are designed for guest downloads. These permit clients who do not have accounts to download files. The server's administrator must set up an

FTP server with anonymous logins to enable this. In these cases, the login of an unregistered user is called *anonymous*, and the password is generally the e-mail address of the client. This is akin to a public login and access to directories that were designed for general consumption as opposed to logging in and transferring files as a particular user. The list of available commands via the FTP protocol is also generally more restrictive than that for real users.

The protocol is diagrammed in Figure 3-1 and works as follows:

1. Client contacts the FTP server on the remote host
2. Client logs in with username and password (or anonymous and e-mail address)
3. Client performs various file transfers or information requests
4. Client completes the transaction by logging out of the remote host and FTP server

Of course, this is generally how it works. Sometimes there are circumstances whereby the entire transaction is terminated before it's completed. These include being disconnected from the network if one of the two hosts crash or because of some other network connectivity issue. For inactive clients, FTP connections will generally time out after 15 minutes (900 seconds) of inactivity.

Under the hood, it is good to know that FTP uses only TCP (see Chapter 2) —it does not use UDP in any way. Also, FTP can be seen as a more unusual example of client/server programming because both the clients and the servers use a pair of sockets for communication: one is the control or command port (port 21), and the other is the data port (sometimes port 20).

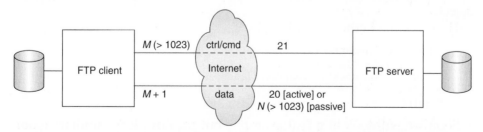

Figure 3-1 FTP Clients and Servers on the Internet. The client and server communicate using the FTP protocol on the command or control port data; is transferred using the data port.

We say sometimes because there are two FTP modes: Active and Passive, and the server's data port is only 20 for Active mode. After the server sets up 20 as its data port, it "actively" initiates the connection to the client's data port. For Passive mode, the server is only responsible for letting the client know where its random data port is; the client must initiate the data connection. As you can see in this mode, the FTP server is taking a more passive role in setting up the data connection. Finally, there is now support for a new Extended Passive Mode to support version 6 Internet Protocol (IPv6) addresses—see RFC 2428.

Python supports most Internet protocols, including FTP. Other supported client libraries can be found at http://docs.python.org/library/internet. Now let's take a look at just how easy it is to create an Internet client with Python.

3.2.3   Python and FTP

So, how do we write an FTP client by using Python? What we just described in the previous section covers it pretty well. The only additional work required is to import the appropriate Python module and make the appropriate calls in Python. So let's review the protocol briefly:

1. Connect to server
2. Log in
3. Make service request(s) (and hopefully get response[s])
4. Quit

When using Python's FTP support, all you do is import the ftplib module and instantiate the ftplib.FTP class. All FTP activity—logging in, transferring files, and logging out—will be accomplished using your object.

Here is some Python pseudocode:

```
from ftplib import FTP
f = FTP('some.ftp.server')
f.login('anonymous', 'your@email.address')
    :
f.quit()
```

Soon we will look at a real example, but for now, let's familiarize ourselves with methods from the ftplib.FTP class, which you will likely use in your code.

3.2.4 `ftplib.FTP` Class Methods

We outline the most popular methods in Table 3-1. The list is not comprehensive—see the source code for the class itself for all methods—but the ones presented here are those that make up the API for FTP client programming in Python. In other words, you don't really need to use the others because they are either utility or administrative functions or are used by the API methods later.

Table 3-1 Methods for FTP Objects

Method	Description
`login(user='anonymous', passwd='', acct='')`	Log in to FTP server; all arguments are optional
`pwd()`	Current working directory
`cwd(path)`	Change current working directory to *path*
`dir([path[,...[,cb]]])`	Displays directory listing of *path*; optional callback *cb* passed to `retrlines()`
`nlst([path[,...])`	Like `dir()` but returns a list of filenames instead of displaying
`retrlines(cmd[, cb])`	Download text file given FTP *cmd*, for example, RETR `filename`; optional callback *cb* for processing each line of file
`retrbinary(cmd, cb[, bs=8192[, ra]])`	Similar to `retrlines()` except for binary file; callback cb for processing each block (size *bs* defaults to 8K) downloaded *required*
`storlines(cmd, f)`	Upload text file given FTP *cmd*, for example, STOR `filename`; open file object f required
`storbinary(cmd, f[, bs=8192])`	Similar to `storlines()` but for binary file; open file object f required, upload blocksize *bs* defaults to 8K
`rename(old, new)`	Rename remote file from *old* to *new*
`delete(path)`	Delete remote `file` located at *path*
`mkd(directory)`	Create remote *directory*
`rmd(directory)`	Remove remote *directory*
`quit()`	Close connection and quit

The methods you will most likely use in a normal FTP transaction include login(), cwd(), dir(), pwd(), stor*(), retr*(), and quit(). There are more FTP object methods not listed in the table that you might find useful. For more detailed information about FTP objects, read the Python documentation available at http://docs.python.org/library/ftplib#ftp-objects.

3.2.5   An Interactive FTP Example

An example of using FTP with Python is so simple to use that you do not even have to write a script. You can just do it all from the interactive interpreter and see the action and output in real time. Here is a sample session from a few years ago when there was still an FTP server running at python.org, but it will not work today, so this is just an example of what you might experience with a running FTP server:

```
>>> from ftplib import FTP
>>> f = FTP('ftp.python.org')
>>> f.login('anonymous', 'guido@python.org')
'230 Guest login ok, access restrictions apply.'
>>> f.dir()
total 38
drwxrwxr-x   10 1075      4127         512 May 17  2000 .
drwxrwxr-x   10 1075      4127         512 May 17  2000 ..
drwxr-xr-x    3 root      wheel        512 May 19  1998 bin
drwxr-sr-x    3 root      1400         512 Jun  9  1997 dev
drwxr-xr-x    3 root      wheel        512 May 19  1998 etc
lrwxrwxrwx    1 root      bin            7 Jun 29  1999 lib -> usr/lib
-r--r--r--    1 guido     4127          52 Mar 24  2000 motd
drwxrwsr-x    8 1122      4127         512 May 17  2000 pub
drwxr-xr-x    5 root      wheel        512 May 19  1998 usr
>>> f.retrlines('RETR motd')
Sun Microsystems Inc.   SunOS 5.6        Generic August 1997
'226 Transfer complete.
>>> f.quit()
'221 Goodbye.'
```

3.2.6   A Client Program FTP Example

We mentioned previously that an example script is not even necessary because you can run one interactively and not get lost in any code. We will try anyway. For example, suppose that you want a piece of code that goes to download the latest copy of Bugzilla from the Mozilla Web site. Example 3-1 is what we came up with. We are attempting an application here, but even so, you can probably run this one interactively, too. Our application uses the FTP library to download the file and includes some error-checking.

Example 3-1   FTP Download Example (`getLatestFTP.py`)

This program is used to download the latest version of a file from a Web site. You can tweak it to download your favorite application.

```python
1    #!/usr/bin/env python
2
3    import ftplib
4    import os
5    import socket
6
7    HOST = 'ftp.mozilla.org'
8    DIRN = 'pub/mozilla.org/webtools'
9    FILE = 'bugzilla-LATEST.tar.gz'
10
11   def main():
12       try:
13           f = ftplib.FTP(HOST)
14       except (socket.error, socket.gaierror) as e:
15           print 'ERROR: cannot reach "%s"' % HOST
16           return
17       print '*** Connected to host "%s"' % HOST
18
19       try:
20           f.login()
21       except ftplib.error_perm:
22           print 'ERROR: cannot login anonymously'
23           f.quit()
24           return
25       print '*** Logged in as "anonymous"'
26
27       try:
28           f.cwd(DIRN)
29       except ftplib.error_perm:
30           print 'ERROR: cannot CD to "%s"' % DIRN
31           f.quit()
32           return
33       print '*** Changed to "%s" folder' % DIRN
34
35       try:
36           f.retrbinary('RETR %s' % FILE,
37                   open(FILE, 'wb').write)
38       except ftplib.error_perm:
39           print 'ERROR: cannot read file "%s"' % FILE
40           os.unlink(FILE)
41       else:
42           print '*** Downloaded "%s" to CWD' % FILE
43       f.quit()
44
45   if __name__ == '__main__':
46       main()
```

Be aware that this script is not automated, so it is up to you to run it whenever you want to perform the download, or if you are on a Unix-based system, you can set up a `cron` job to automate it for you. Another issue is that it will break if either the file or directory names change.

If no errors occur when we run our script, we get the following output:

```
$ getLatestFTP.py
*** Connected to host "ftp.mozilla.org"
*** Logged in as "anonymous"
*** Changed to "pub/mozilla.org/webtools" folder
*** Downloaded "bugzilla-LATEST.tar.gz" to CWD
$
```

Line-by-Line Explanation

Lines 1–9

The initial lines of code import the necessary modules (mainly to grab exception objects) and set a few constants.

Lines 11–44

The `main()` function consists of various steps of operation: create an FTP object and attempt to connect to the FTPs server (lines 12–17) and (return and) quit on any failure. We attempt to login as *anonymous* and abort if unsuccessful (lines 19–25). The next step is to change to the distribution directory (lines 27–33), and finally, we try to download the file (lines 35–44).

For line 14 and all other exception handlers in this book where you're saving the exception instance—in this case *e*—if you're using Python 2.5 and older, you need to change the **as** to a comma, because this new syntax was introduced (but not required) in version 2.6 to help with 3.x migration. Python 3 only understands the new syntax shown in line 14.

2.6

On lines 35–36, we pass a callback to `retrbinary()` that should be executed for every block of binary data downloaded. This is the `write()` method of a file object we create to write out the local version of the file. We are depending on the Python interpreter to adequately close our file after the transfer is done and to not lose any of our data. Although more convenient, I usually try to avoid using this style, because the programmer should be responsible for freeing resources directly allocated rather than depending on other code. In this case, we should save the open file object to a variable, say `loc`, and then pass `loc.write` in the call to `ftp.retrbinary()`.

After the transfer has completed, we would call `loc.close()`. If for some reason we are not able to save the file, we remove the empty file to avoid cluttering up the file system (line 40). We should put some error-checking around that call to `os.unlink(FILE)` in case the file does not exist. Finally, to avoid another pair of lines (lines 43–44) that close the FTP connection and return, we use an **else** clause (lines 35–42).

Lines 46–47

This is the usual idiom for running a stand-alone script.

3.2.7   Miscellaneous FTP

Python supports both Active and Passive modes. Note, however, that in Python 2.0 and older releases, Passive mode was *off* by default; in Python 2.1 and all successive releases, it is *on* by default.

2.1

Here is a list of typical FTP clients:

- **Command-line client program:** This is where you execute FTP transfers by running an FTP client program such as /bin/ftp, or NcFTP, which allows users to interactively participate in an FTP transaction via the command line.

- **GUI client program:** Similar to a command-line client program, except that it is a GUI application like WS_FTP, Filezilla, CuteFTP, Fetch, or SmartFTP.

- **Web browser:** In addition to using HTTP, most Web browsers (also referred to as a client) can also speak FTP. The first directive in a URL/URI is the protocol, that is, "http://blahblah." This tells the browser to use HTTP as a means of transferring data from the given Web site. By changing the protocol, one can make a request using FTP, as in "ftp://blahblah." It looks pretty much exactly the same as a URL, which uses HTTP. (Of course, the "blahblah" can expand to the expected "host/path?attributes" after the protocol directive "ftp://".) Because of the login requirement, users can add their logins and passwords (in clear text) into their URL, for example, "ftp://user:passwd@host/path?attr1=val1&attr2=val2...".

- **Custom application:** A program you write that uses FTP to transfer files. It generally does not allow the user to interact with the server as the application was created for specific purposes.

All four types of clients can be created by using Python. We used ftplib above to create our custom application, but you can just as well create an interactive command-line application. On top of that, you can even bring a GUI toolkit such as Tk, wxWidgets, GTK+, Qt, MFC, and even Swing into the mix (by importing their respective Python [or Jython] interface modules) and build a full GUI application on top of your command-line client code. Finally, you can use Python's urllib module to parse and perform FTP transfers using FTP URLs. At its heart, urllib imports and uses ftplib making urllib *another* client of ftplib.

FTP is not only useful for downloading client applications to build and/ or use, but it can also be helpful in your everyday job for moving files between systems. For example, suppose that you are an engineer or a system administrator needing to transfer files. It is an obvious choice to use the `scp` or `rsync` commands when crossing the Internet boundary or pushing files to an externally visible server. However, there is a penalty when moving extremely large logs or database files between internal computers on a secure network in that manner: security, encryption, compression/decompression, etc. If what you want to do is just build a simple FTP application that moves files for you quickly during the after-hours, using Python is a great way to do it!

You can read more about FTP in the FTP Protocol Definition/Specification (RFC 959) at http://tools.ietf.org/html/rfc959 as well as on the www. network sorcery.com/enp/protocol/ftp.htm Web page. Other related RFCs include 2228, 2389, 2428, 2577, 2640, and 4217. To find out more about Python's FTP support, you can start at http://docs.python.org/library/ftplib.

3.3   Network News

3.3.1   Usenet and Newsgroups

The *Usenet News System* is a global archival bulletin board. There are newsgroups for just about any topic, from poems to politics, linguistics to computer languages, software to hardware, planting to cooking, finding or announcing employment opportunities, music and magic, breaking up or finding love. Newsgroups can be general and worldwide or targeted toward a specific geographic region.

The entire system is a large global network of computers that participate in sharing Usenet postings. Once a user uploads a message to his local Usenet computer, it will then be propagated to other adjoining Usenet computers, and then to the neighbors of *those* systems, until it's gone around the world and everyone has received the posting. Postings will live on Usenet for a finite period of time, either dictated by a Usenet system administrator or the posting itself via an expiration date/time.

Each system has a list of newsgroups that it *subscribes* to and only accepts postings of interest—not all newsgroups may be archived on a server. Usenet news service is dependent on which provider you use. Many are open to the public; others only allow access to specific users, such as paying subscribers, or students of a particular university, etc. A login and password are optional, configurable by the Usenet system administrator. The ability to post only download is another parameter configurable by the administrator.

Usenet has lost its place as the global bulletin board, superseded in large part by online forums. Still it's worthwhile looking at Usenet here specifically for its network protocol.

While older incarnations of the Usenet used UUCP as its network transport mechanism, another protocol arose in the mid-1980s when most network traffic began to migrate to TCP/IP. We'll look at this new protocol next.

3.3.2   Network News Transfer Protocol

The method by which users can download newsgroup postings or *articles* or perhaps post new articles, is called the Network News Transfer Protocol (NNTP). It was authored by Brian Kantor (University of California, San Diego) and Phil Lapsley (University of California, Berkeley) in RFC 977, published in February 1986. The protocol has since been updated in RFC 2980, published in October 2000.

As another example of client/server architecture, NNTP operates in a fashion similar to FTP; however, it is much simpler. Rather than having a whole set of different port numbers for logging in, data, and control, NNTP uses only one standard port for communication, 119. You give the server a request, and it responds appropriately, as shown in Figure 3-2.

3.3.3   Python and NNTP

Based on your experience with Python and FTP in the previous section, you can probably guess that there is an `nntplib` and an `nntplib.NNTP` class that you need to instantiate, and you would be right. As with FTP, all we need to do is to import that Python module and make the appropriate calls in Python. So let's review the protocol briefly:

1. Connect to server
2. Log in (if applicable)
3. Make service request(s)
4. Quit

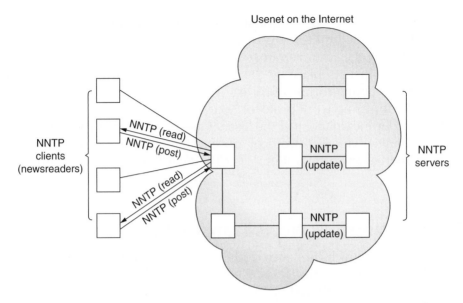

Figure 3-2 NNTP Clients and Servers on the Internet. Clients mostly read news but can also post. Articles are then distributed as servers update each other.

Look somewhat familiar? It should, because it's practically a carbon copy of using the FTP protocol. The only change is that the login step is optional, depending on how an NNTP server is configured.

Here is some Python pseudocode to get started:

```
from nntplib import NNTP
n = NNTP('your.nntp.server')
r,c,f,l,g = n.group('comp.lang.python')
...
n.quit()
```

Typically, once you log in, you will choose a newsgroup of interest and call the group() method. It returns the server reply, a count of the number of articles, the ID of the first and last articles, and superfluously, the group name again. Once you have this information, you will then perform some sort of action, such as scroll through and browse articles, download entire postings (headers and body of article), or perhaps post an article.

Before we take a look at a real example, let's introduce some of the more popular methods of the nntplib.NNTP class.

3.3.4   `nntplib.NNTP` Class Methods

As in the previous section outlining the `ftplib.FTP` class methods, we will not show you all methods of `nntplib.NNTP`, just the ones you need in order to create an NNTP client application.

As with the FTP objects in Table 3-1, there are more NNTP object methods than are described in Table 3-2. To avoid clutter, we list only the ones we think you would most likely use. For the rest, we again refer you to the Python Library Reference.

Table 3-2   Methods for NNTP Objects

Method	Description
group(*name*)	Select newsgroup name and return a tuple (rsp, ct, fst, lst, group): server response, number of articles, first and last article numbers and group name, all of which are strings (name == group)
xhdr(*hdr*, *artrg*[, *ofile*])	Returns list of *hdr* headers for article range *artrg* ("first-last" format) or outputs data to file *ofile*
body(*id*[, *ofile*])	Get article body given its *id*, which is either a message ID (enclosed in <...>) or an article number (as a string); returns tuple (*rsp, anum, mid, data*): server response, article number (as a string), message ID (enclosed in <...>), and list of article lines or outputs *data* to file *ofile*
head(*id*)	Similar to body(); same tuple returned except lines only contain article headers
article(*id*)	Also similar to body(); same tuple returned except lines contain both headers and article body
stat(*id*)	Set article "pointer" to id (message ID or article number as above); returns tuple similar to body (rsp, anum, mid) but contains no data from article
next()	Used with stat(), moves article pointer to next article and returns similar tuple
last()	Also used with stat(), moves article pointer to last article and returns similar tuple
post(*ufile*)	Upload data from ufile file object (using ufile.readline()) and post to current newsgroup
quit()	Close connection and quit

3.3.5   An Interactive NNTP Example

Here is an interactive example of how to use Python's NNTP library. It should look similar to the interactive FTP example. (The e-mail addresses have been changed for privacy reasons.)

When connecting to a group, you get a 5-tuple back from the group() method, as described in Table 3-2.

```
>>> from nntplib import NNTP
>>> n = NNTP('your.nntp.server')
>>> rsp, ct, fst, lst, grp = n.group('comp.lang.python')
>>> rsp, anum, mid, data = n.article('110457')
>>> for eachLine in data:
...     print eachLine
From: "Alex Martelli" <alex@...>
Subject: Re: Rounding Question
Date: Wed, 21 Feb 2001 17:05:36 +0100
"Remco Gerlich" <remco@...> wrote:
> Jacob Kaplan-Moss <jacob@...> wrote in comp.lang.python:
>> So I've got a number between 40 and 130 that I want to round up to
>> the nearest 10.  That is:
>>
>>    40 --> 40, 41 --> 50, ..., 49 --> 50, 50 --> 50, 51 --> 60
> Rounding like this is the same as adding 5 to the number and then
> rounding down. Rounding down is substracting the remainder if you were
> to divide by 10, for which we use the % operator in Python.
This will work if you use +9 in each case rather than +5 (note that he
doesn't really want rounding -- he wants 41 to 'round' to 50, for ex).
Alex
>>> n.quit()
'205 closing connection - goodbye!'
>>>
```

3.3.6   Client Program NNTP Example

For our NNTP client in Example 3-2, we are going to try to be more adventurous. It will be similar to the FTP client example in that we are going to download the latest of something—this time it will be the latest article available in the Python language newsgroup, comp.lang.python.

Once we have it, we will display (up to) the first 20 lines in the article, and on top of that, (up to) the first 20 *meaningful* lines of the article. By that, we mean lines of real data, not quoted text (which begin with ">" or "|") or even quoted text introductions like "In article <...>, soAndSo@some.domain wrote:".

Finally, we are going to process blank lines intelligently. We will display one blank line when we see one in the article, but if there are more than one consecutive blank lines, we only show the first blank line of the set. Only lines with real data are counted toward the first 20 lines, so it is possible to display a maximum of 39 lines of output, 20 real lines of data interleaved with 19 blank lines.

Example 3-2   NNTP Download Example (`getFirstNNTP.py`)

This script downloads and displays the first meaningful (up to 20) lines of the most recently available article in `comp.lang.python`, the Python newsgroup.

```
1    #!/usr/bin/env python
2
3    import nntplib
4    import socket
5
6    HOST = 'your.nntp.server'
7    GRNM = 'comp.lang.python'
8    USER = 'wesley'
9    PASS = 'youllNeverGuess'
10
11   def main():
12
13       try:
14           n = nntplib.NNTP(HOST)
15           #, user=USER, password=PASS)
16       except socket.gaierror as e:
17           print 'ERROR: cannot reach host "%s"' % HOST
18           print '    ("%s")' % eval(str(e))[1]
19           return
20       except nntplib.NNTPPermanentError as e:
21           print 'ERROR: access denied on "%s"' % HOST
22           print '    ("%s")' % str(e)
23           return
24       print '*** Connected to host "%s"' % HOST
25
26       try:
27           rsp, ct, fst, lst, grp = n.group(GRNM)
28       except nntplib.NNTPTemporaryError as ee:
29           print 'ERROR: cannot load group "%s"' % GRNM
30           print '    ("%s")' % str(e)
31           print '    Server may require authentication'
32           print '    Uncomment/edit login line above'
33           n.quit()
34           return
```

(Continued)

Example 3-2   NNTP Download Example (`getFirstNNTP.py`) *(Continued)*

```
35      except nntplib.NNTPTemporaryError as ee:
36        print 'ERROR: group "%s" unavailable' % GRNM
37        print '        ("%s")' % str(e)
38        n.quit()
39        return
40      print '*** Found newsgroup "%s"' % GRNM
41
42      rng = '%s-%s' % (lst, lst)
43      rsp, frm = n.xhdr('from', rng)
44      rsp, sub = n.xhdr('subject', rng)
45      rsp, dat = n.xhdr('date', rng)
46      print '''*** Found last article (#%s):
47
48      From: %s
49      Subject: %s
50      Date: %s
51  '''% (lst, frm[0][1], sub[0][1], dat[0][1])
52
53      rsp, anum, mid, data = n.body(lst)
54      displayFirst20(data)
55      n.quit()
56
57  def displayFirst20(data):
58      print '*** First (<= 20) meaningful lines:\n'
59      count = 0
60      lines = (line.rstrip() for line in data)
61      lastBlank = True
62      for line in lines:
63          if line:
64              lower = line.lower()
65              if (lower.startswith('>') and not \
66                  lower.startswith('>>>')) or \
67                  lower.startswith('|') or \
68                  lower.startswith('in article') or \
69                  lower.endswith('writes:') or \
70                  lower.endswith('wrote:'):
71                      continue
72          if not lastBlank or (lastBlank and line):
73              print '    %s' % line
74              if line:
75                  count += 1
76                  lastBlank = False
77              else:
78                  lastBlank = True
79          if count == 20:
80              break
81
82  if __name__ == '__main__':
83      main()
```

If no errors occur when we run our script, we might see something like
this:

```
$ getLatestNNTP.py
*** Connected to host "your.nntp.server"
*** Found newsgroup "comp.lang.python"
*** Found last article (#471526):
    From: "Gerard Flanagan" <grflanagan@...>
    Subject: Re: Generate a sequence of random numbers that sum up to 1?
    Date: Sat Apr 22 10:48:20 CEST 2006
*** First (<= 20) meaningful lines:
    def partition(N=5):
        vals = sorted( random.random() for _ in range(2*N) )
        vals = [0] + vals + [1]
        for j in range(2*N+1):
            yield vals[j:j+2]
    deltas = [ x[1]-x[0] for x in partition() ]
    print deltas
    print sum(deltas)
    [0.10271966686994982, 0.13826576491042208, 0.064146913555132801,
    0.11906452454467387, 0.10501198456091299, 0.011732423830768779,
    0.11785369256442912, 0.065927165520102249, 0.098351305878176198,
    0.077786747076205365, 0.099139810689226726]
    1.0
$
```

This output is given the original newsgroup posting, which looks like this:

```
From: "Gerard Flanagan" <grflanagan@...>
Subject: Re: Generate a sequence of random numbers that sum up to 1?
Date: Sat Apr 22 10:48:20 CEST 2006
Groups: comp.lang.python
Gerard Flanagan wrote:
> Anthony Liu wrote:
> > I am at my wit's end.
> > I want to generate a certain number of random numbers.
> >  This is easy, I can repeatedly do uniform(0, 1) for
> > example.
> > But, I want the random numbers just generated sum up
> > to 1 .
> > I am not sure how to do this.  Any idea?  Thanks.
> ---------------------------------------------------------------
> import random
> def partition(start=0,stop=1,eps=5):
>     d = stop - start
>     vals = [ start + d * random.random() for _ in range(2*eps) ]
>     vals = [start] + vals + [stop]
>     vals.sort()
>     return vals
> P = partition()
> intervals = [ P[i:i+2] for i in range(len(P)-1) ]
> deltas = [ x[1] - x[0] for x in intervals ]
> print deltas
```

```
> print sum(deltas)
> -------------------------------------------------------------
def partition(N=5):
      vals = sorted( random.random() for _ in range(2*N) )
      vals = [0] + vals + [1]
      for j in range(2*N+1):
          yield vals[j:j+2]
deltas = [ x[1]-x[0] for x in partition() ]
print deltas
print sum(deltas)
[0.10271966686994982, 0.13826576491042208, 0.064146913555132801,
0.11906452454467387, 0.10501198456091299, 0.011732423830768779,
0.11785369256442912, 0.065927165520102249, 0.098351305878176198,
0.077786747076205365, 0.099139810689226726]
1.0
```

Of course, the output will always be different, because articles are always being posted. No two executions will result in the same output unless your news server has not been updated with another article since you last ran the script.

Line-by-Line Explanation

Lines 1–9

This application starts with a few **import** statements and some constants, much like the FTP client example.

Lines 11–40

In the first section, we attempt to connect to the NNTP host server and abort if unsuccessful (lines 13–24). Line 15 is commented out deliberately in case your server requires authentication (with login and password)—if so, uncomment this line and edit it in line 14. This is followed by trying to load up the specific newsgroup. Again, it will quit if that newsgroup does not exist, is not archived by this server, or if authentication is required (lines 26–40).

Lines 42–55

In the next part, we get some headers to display (lines 42–51). The ones that have the most meaning are the author, subject, and date. This data is retrieved and displayed to the user. Each call to the xhdr() method requires us to give the range of articles from which to extract the headers. We are only interested in a single message, so the range is "X-X," where X is the last message number.

xhdr() returns a 2-tuple consisting of a server response (rsp) and a list of the headers in the range we specify. Because we are only requesting this information for one message (the last one), we just take the first element of the list (*hdr*[0]). *That* data item is a 2-tuple consisting of the article number and the data string. Because we already know the article number (we give it in our range request), we are only interested in the second item, the data string (*hdr*[0][1]).

The last part is to download the body of the article itself (lines 53–55). It consists of a call to the body() method, a display of the first 20 or fewer meaningful lines (as defined at the beginning of this section), a logout of the server, and complete execution.

Lines 57–80

The core piece of processing is done by the displayFirst20() function (lines 57–80). It takes the set of lines that make up the article body and does some preprocessing, such as setting our counter to 0, creating a generator expression that lazily iterates through our (possibly large) set of lines making up the body, and "pretends" that we have just seen and displayed a blank line (more on this later; lines 59–61). "Genexps" were added in Python 2.4, so if you're still using version 2.0–2.3, change this to a list comprehension, instead. (Really, you shouldn't be using anything older than version 2.4.) When we strip the line of data, we only remove the trailing whitespace (rstrip()) because leading spaces might be intended lines of Python code.

One criterion we have is that we should not show any quoted text or quoted text introductions. That is what the big **if** statement is for on lines 65–71 (also include line 64). We do this checking if the line is not blank (line 63). We lowercase the line so that our comparisons are case-insensitive (line 64).

If a line begins with ">" or "|," it means it is usually a quote. We make an exception for lines that start with ">>>" because it might be an interactive interpreter line, although this does introduce a flaw that a triply-old message (one quoted three times for the fourth responder) is displayed. (One of the exercises at the end of the chapter is to remove this flaw.) Lines that begin with "in article. . .", and/or end with "writes:" or "wrote:", both with trailing colons (:), are also quoted text introductions. We skip all these with the **continue** statement.

Now to address the blank lines. We want our application to be smart. It should show blank lines as seen in the article, but it should be smart about it. If there is more than one blank line consecutively, only show the first

2.4

one so that the user does not see unneccessary lines, scrolling useful information off the screen. We should also not count any blank lines in our set of 20 meaningful lines. All of these requirements are taken care of in lines 72–78.

The `if` statement on line 72 only displays the line if the last line was not blank, *or* if the last line was blank but now we have a non-blank line. In other words, if we fall through and we print the current line, it is because it is either a line with data or a blank line, as long as the previous line was not blank. Now the other tricky part: if we have a non-blank line, count it and set the `lastBlank` flag to `False` because this line was not empty (lines 74–76). Otherwise, we have just seen a blank line, so set the flag to `True`.

Now back to the business on line 61. We set the `lastBlank` flag to `True`, because if the first real (non-introductory or quoted) line of the body is a blank, we do not want to display it; we want to show the first real *data* line!

Finally, if we have seen 20 non-blank lines, then we quit and discard the remaining lines (lines 79–80). Otherwise, we would have exhausted all the lines and the `for` loop terminates normally.

3.3.7   Miscellaneous NNTP

You can read more about NNTP in the NNTP Protocol Definition/ Specification (RFC 977) at http://tools.ietf.org/html/rfc977 as well as on the http://www.networksorcery.com/enp/protocol/nntp.htm Web page. Other related RFCs include 1036 and 2980. To find out more about Python's NNTP support, you can start at http://docs.python.org/library/nntplib.

3.4   E-Mail

E-mail, is both archaic and modern at the same time. For those of us who have been using the Internet since the early days, e-mail seems so "old," especially compared to newer and more immediate communication mechanisms, such as Web-based online chat, instant messaging (IM), and digital telephony such as Voice over Internet Protocol (VoIP) applications. The next section gives a high-level overview of how e-mail works. If you are already familiar with this and just want to move on to developing e-mail-related clients in Python, skip to the succeeding sections.

Before we take a look at the e-mail infrastructure, have you ever asked yourself what is the exact definition of an e-mail message? Well, according to RFC 2822, "[a] message consists of header fields (collectively called 'the header of the message') followed, optionally, by a body." When we think of e-mail as users, we immediately think of its contents, whether it be a real message or an unsolicited commercial advertisement (a.k.a. *spam*). However, the RFC states that the body itself is optional and that only the headers are required. Imagine that!

3.4.1   E-Mail System Components and Protocols

Despite what you might think, e-mail actually existed before the modern Internet came around. It actually started as a simple message exchange between mainframe users; there wasn't even any networking involved as senders and receivers all used the same computer. Then when networking became a reality, it was possible for users on different hosts to exchange messages. This, of course, was a complicated concept because people used different computers, which more than likely also used different networking protocols. It was not until the early 1980s that message exchange settled on a single *de facto* standard for moving e-mail around the Internet.

Before we get into the details, let's first ask ourselves, how *does* e-mail work? How does a message get from sender to recipient across the vastness of all the computers accessible on the Internet? To put it simply, there is the originating computer (the sender's message departs from here) and the destination computer (recipient's mail server). The optimal solution is if the sending computer knows exactly how to reach the receiving host, because then it can make a direct connection to deliver the message. However, this is usually not the case.

The sending computer queries to find another intermediate host that can pass the message along its way to the final recipient host. Then *that* host searches for the next host who is another step closer to the destination. So in between the originating and final destination hosts are any number of computers. These are called *hops*. If you look carefully at the full e-mail headers of any message you receive, you will see a "passport" stamped with all the places your message bounced to before it finally reached you.

To get a clearer picture, let's take a look at the components of the e-mail system. The foremost component is the *message transport agent* (MTA). This is a server process running on a mail exchange host that is responsible for the routing, queuing, and sending of e-mail. These represent all the hosts that an e-mail message bounces from, beginning at the source host all the way to the final destination host and all hops in between. Thus, they are "agents" of "message transport."

For all this to work, MTAs need to know two things: 1) how determine the next MTA to forward a message to, and 2) how to talk to another MTA. The first is solved by using a *domain name service* (DNS) lookup to find the MX (Mail eXchange) of the destination domain. This is not necessarily the final recipient; it might simply be the next recipient who can eventually get the message to its final destination. Next, how do MTAs forward messages to other MTAs?

3.4.2   Sending E-Mail

To send e-mail, your mail client must connect to an MTA, and the only language they understand is a communication protocol. The way MTAs communicate with one another is by using a *message transport system* (MTS). This protocol must be recognized by a pair of MTAs before they can communicate with one another. As we described at the beginning of this section, such communication was dicey and unpredictable in the early days because there were so many different types of computer systems, each running different networking software. In addition, computers were using both networked transmission as well as dial-up modem, so delivery times were unpredictable. In fact, this author remembers a message not showing up for almost nine months after the message was originally sent! How is *that* for Internet speed? Out of this complexity rose the *Simple Mail Transfer Protocol* (SMTP), one of the foundations of modern e-mail.

SMTP, ESMTP, LMTP

SMTP was originally authored by the late Jonathan Postel (ISI) in RFC 821, published in August 1982 and has gone through a few revisions since then. In November 1995, via RFC 1869, SMTP received a set of service extensions (ESMTP), and both SMTP and ESMTP were rolled into the current RFC 5321, published in October 2008. We'll just use the term "SMTP" to refer to both SMTP and ESMTP. For general applications, you really only need to be able to log in to a server, send a message, and quit. Everything else is supplemental.

There is also one other alternative known as LMTP (Local Mail Transfer Protocol) based on SMTP and ESMTP, defined in October 1996 as RFC 2033. One requirement for SMTP is having mail queues, but this requires additional storage and management, so LMTP provides for a more light-weight system that avoids the necessity of mail queues but does require messages to be delivered immediately (and not queued). LMTP servers aren't exposed externally and work directly with a mail gateway that *is* Internet-facing to indicate whether messages are accepted or rejected. The gateway serves as the queue for LMTP.

MTAs

Some well-known MTAs that have implemented SMTP include:

Open Source MTAs

- Sendmail
- Postfix
- Exim
- qmail

Commercial MTAs

- Microsoft Exchange
- Lotus Notes Domino Mail Server

Note that although they have all implemented the minimum SMTP protocol requirements, most of them, especially the commercial MTAs, have added even more features to their servers, going above and beyond the protocol definition.

SMTP is the MTS that is used by most of the MTAs on the Internet for message exchange. It is the protocol used by MTAs to transfer e-mail from (MTA) host to (MTA) host. When you send e-mail, you must connect to an outgoing SMTP server, with which your mail application acts as an SMTP client. Your SMTP server, therefore, is the first hop for your message.

3.4.3   Python and SMTP

Yes, there is an `smtplib` and an `smtplib.SMTP` class to instantiate. Let's review this familiar story:

1. Connect to server
2. Log in (if applicable)
3. Make service request(s)
4. Quit

As with NNTP, the login step is optional and only required if the server has SMTP authentication (SMTP-AUTH) enabled. SMTP-AUTH is defined in RFC 2554. Also similar to NNTP, speaking SMTP only requires communicating with one port on the server; this time, it's port 25.

Here is some Python pseudocode to get started:

```
from smtplib import SMTP
n = SMTP('smtp.yourdomain.com')
...
n.quit()
```

Before we take a look at a real example, let's introduce some of the more popular methods of the `smtplib.SMTP` class.

3.4.4   `smtplib.SMTP` Class Methods

2.6   In addition to the `smtplib.SMTP` class, Python 2.6 introduced another pair: `SMTP_SSL` and `LMTP`. The latter implements LMTP, as described earlier in Section 3.4.2, whereas the former works just like SMTP, except that it communicates over an encrypted socket and is an alternative to SMTP using TLS. If omitted, the default port for SMTP_SSL is 465.

As in the previous sections, we won't show you all methods which belong to the class, just the ones you need in order to create an SMTP client application. For most e-mail sending applications, only two are required: `sendmail()` and `quit()`.

All arguments to `sendmail()` should conform to RFC 2822; that is, e-mail addresses must be properly formatted, and the message body should have appropriate leading headers and contain lines that must be delimited by carriage-return and NEWLINE pairs (\r\n).

Note that an actual message body is not required. According to RFC 2822, "[the] only required header fields are the origination date field and the originator address field(s)," for example, "Date:" and "From:" (MAIL FROM, RCPT TO, DATA).

Table 3-3 presents some common SMTP object methods. There are a few more methods not described here, but they are not normally required to send an e-mail message. For more information about all the SMTP object methods, refer to the Python documentation.

Table 3-3 Common Methods for SMTP Objects

Method	Description
sendmail(*from*, *to*, *msg*[, *mopts*, *ropts*])	Sends *msg* from *from* to *to* (list/tuple) with optional ESMTP mail (*mopts*) and recipient (*ropts*) options.
ehlo() or helo()	Initiates a session with an SMTP or ESMTP server using EHLO or HELO, respectively. Should be optional because sendmail() will call these as necessary.
starttls(*keyfile*=None, *certfile*=None)	Directs server to begin Transport Layer Security (TLS) mode. If either keyfile or certfile are given, they are used in the creation of the secure socket.
set_debuglevel(*level*)	Sets the debug level for server communication.
quit()	Closes connection and quits.
login(*user*, *passwd*)[a]	Log in to SMTP server with *user* name and *passwd*.

a. SMTP-AUTH only.

3.4.5   Interactive SMTP Example

Once again, we present an interactive example:

```
>>> from smtplib import SMTP as smtp
>>> s = smtp('smtp.python.is.cool')
>>> s.set_debuglevel(1)
>>> s.sendmail('wesley@python.is.cool', ('wesley@python.is.cool',
'chun@python.is.cool'), ''' From: wesley@python.is.cool\r\nTo:
wesley@python.is.cool, chun@python.is.cool\r\nSubject: test
msg\r\n\r\nxxx\r\n.''')
send: 'ehlo myMac.local\r\n'
reply: '250-python.is.cool\r\n'
reply: '250-7BIT\r\n'
reply: '250-8BITMIME\r\n'
```

```
reply: '250-AUTH CRAM-MD5 LOGIN PLAIN\r\n'
reply: '250-DSN\r\n'
reply: '250-EXPN\r\n'
reply: '250-HELP\r\n'
reply: '250-NOOP\r\n'
reply: '250-PIPELINING\r\n'
reply: '250-SIZE 15728640\r\n'
reply: '250-STARTTLS\r\n'
reply: '250-VERS V05.00c++\r\n'
reply: '250 XMVP 2\r\n'
reply: retcode (250); Msg: python.is.cool
7BIT
8BITMIME
AUTH CRAM-MD5 LOGIN PLAIN
DSN
EXPN
HELP
NOOP
PIPELINING
SIZE 15728640
STARTTLS
VERS V05.00c++
XMVP 2
send: 'mail FROM:<wesley@python.is.cool> size=108\r\n'
reply: '250 ok\r\n'
reply: retcode (250); Msg: ok
send: 'rcpt TO:<wesley@python.is.cool>\r\n'
reply: '250 ok\r\n'
reply: retcode (250); Msg: ok
send: 'data\r\n'
reply: '354 ok\r\n'
reply: retcode (354); Msg: ok
data: (354, 'ok')
send: 'From: wesley@python.is.cool\r\nTo:
wesley@python.is.cool\r\nSubject: test msg\r\n\r\nxxx\r\n..\r\n.\r\n'
reply: '250 ok ; id=20051226235837013000r7hhe\r\n'
reply: retcode (250); Msg: ok ; id=20051226235837013000r7hhe
data: (250, 'ok ; id=20051226235837013000r7hhe')
{}
>>> s.quit()
send: 'quit\r\n'
reply: '221 python.is.cool\r\n'
reply: retcode (221); Msg: python.is.cool
```

3.4.6   Miscellaneous SMTP

You can read more about SMTP in the SMTP Protocol Definition/Specification, RFC 5321, at http://tools.ietf.org/html/rfc2821. To find out more about Python's SMTP support, go to http://docs.python.org/library/smtplib.

One of the more important aspects of e-mail which we have not discussed yet is how to properly format Internet addresses as well as e-mail messages themselves. This information is detailed in the latest Internet Message Format specification, RFC 5322, which is accessible at http://tools.ietf.org/html/rfc5322.

3.4.7   Receiving E-Mail

Back in the day, communicating by e-mail on the Internet was relegated to university students, researchers, and employees of private industry and commercial corporations. Desktop computers were predominantly still Unix-based workstations. Home users focused mainly on dial-up Web access on PCs and really didn't use e-mail. When the Internet began to explode in the mid-1990s, e-mail came home to everyone.

Because it was not feasible for home users to have workstations in their dens running SMTP, a new type of system had to be devised to leave e-mail on an incoming mail host while periodically downloading mail for offline reading. Such a system had to consist of both a new application and a new protocol to communicate with the mail server.

The application, which runs on a home computer, is called a *mail user agent* (MUA). An MUA will download mail from a server, perhaps automatically deleting it from the server in the process (or leaving the mail on the server to be deleted manually by the user). However, an MUA must also be able to send mail; in other words, it should also be able to speak SMTP to communicate directly to an MTA when sending mail. We have already seen this type of client in the previous section when we looked at SMTP. How about downloading mail then?

3.4.8   POP and IMAP

The first protocol developed for downloading was the *Post Office Protocol*. As stated in the original RFC document, RFC 918 published in October 1984, "The intent of the Post Office Protocol (POP) is to allow a user's workstation to access mail from a mailbox server. It is expected that mail will be posted from the workstation to the mailbox server via the Simple Mail Transfer Protocol (SMTP)." The most recent version of POP is version 3, otherwise known as POP3. POP3, defined in RFC 1939, is still widely used today.

A competing protocol came a few years after POP, known as the *Internet Message Access Protocol*, or IMAP. (IMAP has also been known by various other names: "Internet Mail Access Protocol," "Interactive Mail Access Protocol," and "Interim Mail Access Protocol.") The first version was experimental, and it was not until version 2 that its RFC was published (RFC 1064 in July 1988). It is stated in RFC 1064 that IMAP2 was inspired by the second version of POP, POP2.

The intent of IMAP is to provide a more complete solution than POP; however, it is more complex than POP. For example, IMAP is extremely suitable for today's needs due to users interacting with their e-mail messages from more than a single device, such as desktop/laptop/tablet computers, mobile phones, video game systems, etc. POP does not work well with multiple mail clients, and although still widely used, is mostly obsolete. Note that many ISPs currently only provide POP for receiving (and SMTP for sending) e-mail. We anticipate more adoption of IMAP as we move forward.

The current version of IMAP in use today is IMAP4rev1, and it, too, is widely used. In fact, Microsoft Exchange, one of the predominant mail servers in the world today, uses IMAP as its download mechanism. At the time of this writing, the latest draft of the IMAP4rev1 protocol definition is spelled out in RFC 3501, published in March 2003. We use the term "IMAP4" to refer to both the IMAP4 and IMAP4rev1 protocols, collectively.

For further reading, we suggest that you take a look at the aforementioned RFC documents. The diagram in Figure 3-3 illustrates this complex system we know simply as e-mail.

Now let's take a closer look at POP3 and IMAP4 support in Python.

3.4.9   Python and POP3

No surprises here: import `poplib` and instantiate the `poplib.POP3` class; the standard conversation is as expected:

1. Connect to server
2. Log in
3. Make service request(s)
4. Quit

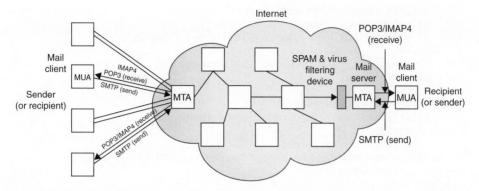

Figure 3-3 E-Mail Senders and Recipients on the Internet. Clients download and send mail via their MUAs, which talk to their corresponding MTAs. E-mail "hops" from MTA to MTA until it reaches the correct destination.

And the expected Python pseudocode:

```
from poplib import POP3
p = POP3('pop.python.is.cool')
p.user(...)
p.pass_(...)
...
p.quit()
```

Before we take a look at a real example, we should mention that there is also a `poplib.POP3_SSL` class (added in version 2.4) which performs mail transfer over an encrypted connection, provided the appropriate credentials are supplied. Let's take a look at an interactive example as well as introduce the basic methods of the `poplib.POP3` class.

2.4

3.4.10 An Interactive POP3 Example

Below is an interactive example that uses Python's `poplib`. The exception you see comes from deliberately entering an incorrect password just to demonstrate what you'll get back from the server in practice. Here is the interactive output:

```
>>> from poplib import POP3
>>> p = POP3('pop.python.is.cool')
>>> p.user('wesley')
'+OK'
>>> p.pass_("you'llNeverGuess")
```

```
Traceback (most recent call last):
  File "<stdin>", line 1, in ?
  File "/usr/local/lib/python2.4/poplib.py", line 202,
in pass_
    return self._shortcmd('PASS %s' % pswd)
  File "/usr/local/lib/python2.4/poplib.py", line 165,
in _shortcmd
    return self._getresp()
  File "/usr/local/lib/python2.4/poplib.py", line 141,
in _getresp
    raise error_proto(resp)
poplib.error_proto: -ERR directory status: BAD PASSWORD
>>> p.user('wesley')
'+OK'
>>> p.pass_('youllNeverGuess')
'+OK ready'
>>> p.stat()
(102, 2023455)
>>> rsp, msg, siz = p.retr(102)
>>> rsp, siz
('+OK', 480)
>>> for eachLine in msg:
...    print eachLine
...
Date: Mon, 26 Dec 2005 23:58:38 +0000 (GMT)
Received: from c-42-32-25-43.smtp.python.is.cool
          by python.is.cool (scmrch31) with ESMTP
          id <20051226235837013000r7hhe>; Mon, 26 Dec 2005 23:58:37
+0000
From: wesley@python.is.cool
To: wesley@python.is.cool
Subject: test msg

xxx
.
>>> p.quit()
'+OK python.is.cool'
```

3.4.11   poplib.POP3 Class Methods

The POP3 class provides numerous methods to help you download and manage your inbox offline. Those most widely used are included in Table 3-4.

Table 3-4   Common Methods for POP3 Objects

Method	Description
user(*login*)	Sends the login name to the server; awaits reply indicating the server is waiting for user's password
pass_(*passwd*)	Sends *passwd* (after user logs in with user()); an exception occurs on login/passwd failure
stat()	Returns mailbox status, a 2-tuple (*msg_ct*, *mbox_siz*): the total message count and total message size, a.k.a. octets
list([*msgnum*])	Superset of stat(); returns entire message list from server as a 3-tuple (*rsp*, *msg_list*, *rsp_siz*): server response, message list, response message size; if *msgnum* given, return data for that message only
retr(*msgnum*)	Retrieves message *msgnum* from server and sets its "seen" flag; returns a 3-tuple (*rsp*, *msglines*, *msgsiz*): server response, all lines of message *msgnum*, and message size in bytes/octets
dele(*msgnum*)	Tag message number *msgnum* for deletion; most servers process deletes upon *quit()*
quit()	Logs out, commits changes (e.g., process "seen," "delete" flags, etc.), unlocks mailbox, terminates connection, and then quits

When logging in, the user() method not only sends the login name to the server, but it also awaits the reply that indicates the server is waiting for the user's password. If pass_() fails due to authentication issues, the exception raised is poplib.error_proto. If it is successful, it gets back a positive reply, for example, "+OK ready," and the mailbox on the server is locked until quit() is called.

For the list() method, the *msg_list* is of the form ['*msgnum msgsiz*',...] where *msgnum* and *msgsiz* are the message number and message sizes, respectively, of each message.

There are a few other methods that are not listed here. For the full details, check out the documentation for poplib in the Python Library Reference.

3.4.12   SMTP and POP3 Example

Example 3-3 shows how to use both SMTP and POP3 to create a client that both receives and downloads e-mail as well as one that uploads and sends it. What we are going to do is send an e-mail message to ourselves (or some test account) via SMTP, wait for a bit—we arbitrarily chose ten seconds—and then use POP3 to download our message and assert that the messages are identical. Our operation will be a success if the program completes silently, meaning that there should be no output or any errors.

Example 3-3   SMTP and POP3 Example (myMail.py)

This script sends a test e-mail message to the destination address (via the outgoing/ SMTP mail server) and retrieves it immediately from the (incoming mail/POP) server. You must change the server names and e-mail addresses to make it work properly.

```
1    #!/usr/bin/env python
2
3    from smtplib import SMTP
4    from poplib import POP3
5    from time import sleep
6
7    SMTPSVR = 'smtp.python.is.cool'
8    POP3SVR = 'pop.python.is.cool'
9
10   who = 'wesley@python.is.cool'
11   body = '''\
12   From: %(who)s
13   To: %(who)s
14   Subject: test msg
15
16   Hello World!
17   ''' % {'who': who}
18
19   sendSvr = SMTP(SMTPSVR)
20   errs = sendSvr.sendmail(who, [who], origMsg)
21   sendSvr.quit()
22   assert len(errs) == 0, errs
23   sleep(10)      # wait for mail to be delivered
24
25   recvSvr = POP3(POP3SVR)
26   recvSvr.user('wesley')
27   recvSvr.pass_('youllNeverGuess')
28   rsp, msg, siz = recvSvr.retr(recvSvr.stat()[0])
29   # strip headers and compare to orig msg
30   sep = msg.index('')
31   recvBody = msg[sep+1:]
32   assert origBody == recvBody # assert identical
```

Line-by-Line Explanation

Lines 1–8

This application starts with a few **import** statements and some constants, much like the other examples in this chapter. The constants here are the outgoing (SMTP) and incoming (POP3) mail servers.

Lines 10–17

These lines represent the preparation of the message contents. For this test message, the sender and the recipient will be the same user. Don't forget the RFC 2822-required line delimiters with a blank line separating the two sections.

Lines 19–23

We connect to the outgoing (SMTP) server and send our message. There is another pair of From and To addresses here. These are the "real" e-mail addresses, or the envelope sender and recipient(s). The recipient field should be an iterable. If a string is passed in, it will be transformed into a list of one element. For unsolicited spam e-mail, there is usually a discrepancy between the message headers and the envelope headers.

The third argument to sendmail() is the e-mail message itself. Once it has returned, we log out of the SMTP server and check that no errors have occurred. Then we give the servers some time to send and receive the message.

Lines 25–32

The final part of our application downloads the just-sent message and asserts that both it and the received messages are identical. A connection is made to the POP3 server with a username and password. After successfully logging in, a stat() call is made to get a list of available messages. The first message is chosen ([0]), and retr() is instructed to download it.

We look for the blank line separating the headers and message, discard the headers, and compare the original message body with the incoming message body. If they are identical, nothing is displayed and the program ends successfully. Otherwise, an assertion is made.

Note that due to the numerous errors, we left out all the error-checking for this script to make it a bit more easy on the eyes. (One of the exercises at the end of the chapter is to add the error-checking.)

Now you have a very good idea of how sending and receiving e-mail works in today's environment. If you wish to continue exploring this realm of programming expertise, see the next section for other e-mail-related Python modules, which will prove valuable in application development.

3.4.13   Python and IMAP4

Python supports IMAP4 via the `imaplib` module. Its use is quite similar to that of other Internet protocols described in this chapter. To begin, import `imaplib` and instantiate one of the `imaplib.IMAP4*` classes; the standard conversation is as expected:

1. Connect to server
2. Log in
3. Make service request(s)
4. Quit

The Python pseudocode is also similar to what we've seen before:

```
from imaplib import IMAP4
s= IMAP4('imap.python.is.cool')
s.login(...)
...
s.close()
s.logout()
```

This module defines three classes, `IMAP4`, `IMAP4_SSL`, and `IMAP4_stream` with which you can use to connect to an IMAP4-compatible server. Like `POP3_SSL` for POP, `IMAP4_SSL` lets you connect to an IMAP4 server by using an SSL-encrypted socket. Another subclass of IMAP is `IMAP4_stream` which gives you a file-like object interface to an IMAP4 server. The latter pair of classes was added in Python 2.3.

2.3

Now let's take a look at an interactive example as well as introduce the basic methods of the `imaplib.IMAP4` class.

3.4.14   An Interactive IMAP4 Example

Here is an interactive example that uses Python's `imaplib`:

```
>>> s = IMAP4('imap.python.is.cool') # default port: 143
>>> s.login('wesley', 'youllneverguess')
('OK', ['LOGIN completed'])
>>> rsp, msgs = s.select('INBOX', True)
>>> rsp
'OK'
```

```
>>> msgs
['98']
>>> rsp, data = s.fetch(msgs[0], '(RFC822)')
>>> rsp
'OK'
>>> for line in data[0][1].splitlines()[:5]:
...     print line
...
Received: from mail.google.com
    by mx.python.is.cool (Internet Inbound) with ESMTP id
316ED380000ED
    for <wesley@python.is.cool>; Fri, 11 Mar 2011 10:49:06 -0500 (EST)
Received: by gyb11 with SMTP id 11so125539gyb.10
        for <wesley@python.is.cool>; Fri, 11 Mar 2011 07:49:03 -0800
(PST)
>>> s.close()
('OK', ['CLOSE completed'])
>>> s.logout()
('BYE', ['IMAP4rev1 Server logging out'])
```

3.4.15   Common `imaplib.IMAP4` Class Methods

As we mentioned earlier, the IMAP protocol is more complex than POP, so there are many more methods that we're not documenting here. Table 3-5 lists just the basic ones you are most likely to use for a simple e-mail application.

Table 3-5   Common Methods for IMAP4 Objects

Method	Description
close()	Closes the current mailbox. If access is not set to read-only, any deleted messages will be discarded.
fetch(*message_set*, *message_parts*)	Retrieve e-mail messages (or requested parts via *message_parts*) stated by *message_set*.
login(*user*, *password*)	Logs in *user* by using given *password*.
logout()	Logs out from the server.

(Continued)

Table 3-5   Common Methods for IMAP4 Objects *(Continued)*

Method	Description
noop()	Ping the server but take no action ("no operation").
search(*charset*, **criteria*)	Searches mailbox for messages matching at least one piece of *criteria*. If *charset* is False, it defaults to US-ASCII.
select(*mailbox*= '*INBOX*', *read-only=False*)	Selects a *mailbox* (default is INBOX); user not allowed to modify contents if *readonly* is set.

Below are some examples of using some of these methods.

- NOP, NOOP, or "no operation." This is meant as a keepalive to the server:

```
>>> s.noop()
('OK', ['NOOP completed'])
```

- Get information about a specific message:

```
>>> rsp, data = s.fetch('98', '(BODY)')
>>> data[0]
'98 (BODY ("TEXT" "PLAIN" ("CHARSET" "ISO-8859-1" "FORMAT" "flowed"
"DELSP" "yes") NIL NIL "7BIT" 1267 33))'
```

- Get just the headers of a message:

```
>>> rsp, data = s.fetch('98', '(BODY[HEADER])')
>>> data[0][1][:45]
'Received: from mail-gy.google.com (mail-gy.go'
```

- Get the IDs of the messages that have been viewed (try also using 'ALL', 'NEW', etc.):

```
>>> s.search(None, 'SEEN')
('OK', ['1 2 3 4 5 6 7 8 9 10 11 12 13 14 15 16 17 18 19 20 21 22 23
24 25 26 27 28 29 30 31 32 33 34 35 36 37 38 39 40 41 42 59 60 61 62
63 64 97'])
```

- Get more than one message (use a colon (:) as the delimiter; note ')' is used to delimit results):

```
>>> rsp, data = s.fetch('98:100', '(BODY[TEXT])')
>>> data[0][1][:45]
'Welcome to Google Accounts.  To activate your'
```

```
>>> data[2][1][:45]
'\r\n-b1_aeb1ac91493d87ea4f2aa7209f56f909\r\nCont'
>>> data[4][1][:45]
'This is a multi-part message in MIME format.'
>>> data[1], data[3], data[5]
(')', ')', ')')
```

3.5   In Practice

3.5.1   E-Mail Composition

So far, we've taken a pretty in-depth look at the various ways Python helps you download e-mail messages. We've even discussed how to create simple text e-mail messages and then connect to SMTP servers to *send* them. However, what has been missing is guidance on how to construct slightly more complex messages in Python. As you can guess, I'm speaking about e-mail messages that are more than plain text, with attachments, alternative formats, etc. Now is the right time to briefly visit this topic.

These longer messages are comprised normally of multiple parts, say a plain text portion for the message, optionally an HTML equivalent for those with Web browsers as their mail clients, and one or more attachments. The global standard for identifying and differentiating each of these parts is known as *Mail Interchange Message Extension* format, or MIME for short.

Python's email package is perfectly suited to handle and manage MIME parts of entire e-mail messages, and we'll be using it for this entire subsection along with smtplib, of course. The email package has separate components that parse as well as construct e-mail. We will start with the latter then conclude with a quick look at parsing and message walkthrough.

In Example 3-4, you'll see two examples of creating e-mail messages, make_mpa_msg() and make_img_msg(), both of which make a single e-mail message with one attachment. The former creates a single multipart alternative message and sends it, and the latter creates an e-mail message containing one image and sends *that*. Following the example is the line-by-line explanation.

Example 3-4   Composing E-Mail (`email-examples.py`)

This Python 2 script creates and sends two different e-mail message types.

```python
1   #!/usr/bin/env python
2   'email-examples.py - demo creation of email messages'
3
4   from email.mime.image import MIMEImage
5   from email.mime.multipart import MIMEMultipart
6   from email.mime.text import MIMEText
7   from smtplib import SMTP
8
9   # multipart alternative: text and html
10  def make_mpa_msg():
11      email = MIMEMultipart('alternative')
12      text = MIMEText('Hello World!\r\n', 'plain')
13      email.attach(text)
14      html = MIMEText(
15          '<html><body><h4>Hello World!</h4>'
16          '</body></html>', 'html')
17      email.attach(html)
18      return email
19
20  # multipart: images
21  def make_img_msg(fn):
22      f = open(fn, 'r')
23      data = f.read()
24      f.close()
25      email = MIMEImage(data, name=fn)
26      email.add_header('Content-Disposition',
27          'attachment; filename="%s"' % fn)
28      return email
29
30  def sendMsg(fr, to, msg):
31      s = SMTP('localhost')
32      errs = s.sendmail(fr, to, msg)
33      s.quit()
34
35  if __name__ == '__main__':
36      print 'Sending multipart alternative msg...'
37      msg = make_mpa_msg()
38      msg['From'] = SENDER
39      msg['To'] = ', '.join(RECIPS)
40      msg['Subject'] = 'multipart alternative test'
41      sendMsg(SENDER, RECIPS, msg.as_string())
42
43      print 'Sending image msg...'
44      msg = make_img_msg(SOME_IMG_FILE)
45      msg['From'] = SENDER
46      msg['To'] = ', '.join(RECIPS)
47      msg['Subject'] = 'image file test'
48      sendMsg(SENDER, RECIPS, msg.as_string())
```

Line-by-Line Explanation

Lines 1–7

In addition to the standard startup line and docstring, we see the import of `MIMEImage`, `MIMEMultipart`, `MIMEText`, and `SMTP` classes.

Lines 9–18

Multipart alternative messages usually consist of the following two parts: the body of an e-mail message in plain text and its equivalent on the HTML side. It was up to the mail client to determine which gets shown. For example, a Web-based e-mail system would generally show the HTML version, whereas a command-line mail reader would only show the plain text version.

To create this type of message, you need to use the `email.mime.multiple.MIMEMultipart` class and instantiate it by passing in `'alternative'` as its only argument. If you don't pass this value in, each of the two parts will be a separate attachment; thus, some e-mail systems might show both parts.

The `email.mime.text.MIMEText` class was used for both parts (because they really are both bodies of plain text). Each part is then attached to the entire e-mail message because they are created before the return message is returned.

Lines 20–28

The `make_img_msg()` function takes a single parameter, a filename. Its data is absorbed then fed directly to a new instance of `email.mime.image.MIMEImage`. A `Content-Disposition` header is added and then a message is returned to the user.

Lines 30–33

The sole purpose of `sendMsg()` is to take the basic e-mail-sending criteria (sender, recipient[s], message body), transmit the message, and then return to the caller.

Looking for more verbose output? Try this extension: `s.set_debuglevel(True)`, where "s" is the `smtplib.SMTP` server. Finally, we'll repeat what we said earlier that many SMTP servers require logins, so you'd do that here (just after logging in but before sending an e-mail message).

Lines 35–48

The "main" part of this script just tests each of these two functions. The functions create the message, add the From, To, and Sender fields, and then transmit the message to those recipients. Naturally, you need to fill in all of the following for your application to work: SENDER, RECIPS, and SOME_IMG_FILE.

3.5.2   E-Mail Parsing

Parsing is somewhat easier than constructing a message from scratch. You would typically use several tools from the email package: the email.message_from_string() function as well as the message.walk() and message.get_payload() methods. Here is the typical pattern:

```
def processMsg(entire_msg):
    body = ''
    msg = email.message_from_string(entire_msg)
    if msg.is_multipart():
        for part in msg.walk():
            if part.get_content_type() == 'text/plain':
                body = part.get_payload()
                break
        else:
            body = msg.get_payload(decode=True)
    else:
        body = msg.get_payload(decode=True)
    return body
```

This snippet should be fairly simple to figure out. Here are the major players:

- email.message_from_string(), used to parse the message.

- msg.walk(): Let's "walk down" the attachment hierarchy of a mall stand/shop.

- part.get_content_type(): Guess the correct MIME type.

- msg.get_payload(): Pull out the specific part from the message body. Typically the decode flag is set to True so as to decode the body part as per the Content-Transfer-Encoding header.

3.5.3   Web-Based Cloud E-Mail Services

The use of the protocols that we've covered so far in this chapter, for the most part, have been ideal: there hasn't been much of a focus on security or the messiness that comes with it. Of course, we did mention that some servers require logins.

However, when coding in real life, we need to come back down to earth and recognize that servers that are actively maintained really don't want to be the focus or target of hackers who want a free spam and/or phishing e-mail relay or other nefarious activity. Such systems, predominantly e-mail systems, are locked down appropriately. The e-mail examples given earlier in the chapter are for generic e-mail services that come with your ISP. Because you're paying a monthly fee for your Internet service, you generally get e-mail uploading/sending and downloading/receiving for "free."

Let's take a look at some public Web-based e-mail services such as Yahoo! Mail and Google's Gmail service. Because such software as a service (SaaS) cloud services don't require you to pay a monthly fee up front, it seems completely free to you. However, users generally "pay" by being exposed to advertising. The better the ad relevance, the more likely the service provider is able to recoup some of the costs of offering such services free of charge.

Gmail features algorithms that scan e-mail messages to get a sense of its context and hopefully, with good machine learning algorithms, presents ads that are more likely to be clicked by users than generic ad inventory. The ads are generally in plain text and along the right side of the e-mail message panel. Because of the efficacy of their algorithms, Google not only offers Web access to their Gmail service for free, they even allow outbound transfer of messages through a client service via POP3 and IMAP4 as well as the ability to send e-mail using SMTP.

Yahoo!, on the other hand, shows more general ads in image format embedded in parts of their Web application. Because their ads don't target as well, they likely don't derive as much revenue, which might be a contributing factor for why they require a paid subscription service (called Yahoo! Mail Plus) in order to download your e-mail. Another reason could be that they don't want users to easily be able to move their mail elsewhere. Yahoo! currently does not charge for sending e-mail via SMTP at the time of this writing. We will look at some code examples of both in the remainder of this subsection.

3.5.4   Best Practices: Security, Refactoring

We need to take a moment to also discuss best practices, including security and refactoring. Sometimes, the best laid plans are thwarted because of the reality that different releases of a programming language will have improvements and bugfixes that aren't found in older releases, so in practice, you might have to do a little bit more work than you had originally planned.

Before we look at the two e-mail services from Google and Yahoo!, let's look at some boilerplate code that we'll use for each set of examples:

```python
from imaplib import IMAP4_SSL
from poplib import POP3_SSL
from smtplib import SMTP_SSL

from secret import * # where MAILBOX, PASSWD come from

who = . . . # xxx@yahoo/gmail.com where MAILBOX = xxx
from_ = who
to = [who]

headers = [
    'From: %s' % from_,
    'To: %s' % ', '.join(to),
    'Subject: test SMTP send via 465/SSL',
]

body = [
    'Hello',
    'World!',
]

msg = '\r\n\r\n'.join(('\r\n'.join(headers), '\r\n'.join(body)))
```

The first thing you'll notice is that we're no longer in utopia; the realities of living and working, nay even *existing*, on the Web requires that we use secure connections, so we're using the SSL-equivalents of all three protocols; hence, the "_SSL" appended to the end of each of the original class names.

Secondly, we can't use our mailboxes (login names) and passwords in plain text as we did in the codes examples in previous sections. In practice, putting account names and passwords in plain text and embedding them in source code is... well, horrific to say the least. In practice, they should be fetched from either a secure database, imported from a bytecode-compiled .pyc or .pyo file, or retrieved from some live server or broker found somewhere on your company's intranet. For our example, we'll assume they're in a secret.pyc file that contains MAILBOX and PASSWD attributes associated with the equivalent privileged information.

The last set of variables just represent the actual e-mail message plus sender and receiver (both the same people to make it easy). The way we've structured the e-mail message itself is slightly more complex than we did in the earlier example, in which the body was a single string that required us to fill in the necessary field data:

```
body = '''\
From: %(who)s
To: %(who)s
Subject: test msg

Hello World!
''' % {'who': who}
```

However, we chose to use lists instead, because in practice, the body of the e-mail message is more likely to be generated or somehow controlled by the application instead of being a hardcoded string. The same may be true of the e-mail headers. By making them lists, you can easily add (or even remove) lines to (from) an e-mail message. Then when ready for transmission, the process only requires a couple of str.join() calls with \r\n pairs. (Recall from an earlier subsection in this chapter that this is the official delimiter accepted by RFC5322-compliant SMTP servers—some servers won't accept only NEWLINEs.)

We've also made another minor tweak to the message body data: there might be more than one receiver, so the to variable has also been changed to a list. We then have to str.join() them together when creating the final set of e-mail headers. Finally, let's look at a specific utility function we're going to use for our upcoming Yahoo! Mail and Gmail examples; it's a short snippet that just goes and grabs the Subject line from inbound e-mail messages.

```
def getSubject(msg, default='(no Subject line)'):
    '''\
    getSubject(msg) - 'msg' is an iterable, not a
    delimited single string; this function iterates
    over 'msg' look for Subject: line and returns
    if found, else the default is returned if one isn't
    found in the headers
    '''
    for line in msg:
        if line.startswith('Subject:'):
            return line.rstrip()
        if not line:
            return default
```

The getSubject() function is fairly simplistic; it looks for the Subject line only within the headers. As soon as one is found, the function returns immediately. The headers have completed when a blank line is reached, so if one hasn't been found at this point, return a default, which is a local variable with a default argument allowing the user to pass in a custom default string as desired. Yeah, I know some of you performance buffs will want to use `line[:8]` `==` `'Subject:'` to avoid the `str.startswith()` method call, but guess what? Don't forget that `line[:8]` results in a `str.__getslice__()` call; although to be honest, for this case it *is* about 40 percent faster than `str.startswith()`, as shown in a few `timeit` tests:

```
>>> t = timeit.Timer('s[:8] == "Subject:"', 's="Subject: xxx"')
>>> t.timeit()
0.14157199859619141
>>> t.timeit()
0.1387479305267334
>>> t.timeit()
0.13623881340026855
>>>
>>> t = timeit.Timer('s.startswith("Subject:")', 's="Subject: xxx"')
>>> t.timeit()
0.23016810417175293
>>> t.timeit()
0.23104190826416016
>>> t.timeit()
0.24139499664306641
```

Using `timeit` is another best practice and we've just gone over one of its most common use cases: you have a pair of snippets that do the same thing, so you're in a situation in which you need to know which one is more efficient. Now let's see how we can apply some of this knowledge on some real code.

3.5.5   Yahoo! Mail

Assuming that all of the preceding boilerplate code has been executed, we'll start with Yahoo! Mail. The code we're going to look at is an extension of Example 3-3. We'll also send e-mail via SMTP but will retrieve messages via both POP then IMAP. Here's the prototype script:

```
s = SMTP_SSL('smtp.mail.yahoo.com', 465)
s.login(MAILBOX, PASSWD)
s.sendmail(from_, to, msg)
s.quit()
print 'SSL: mail sent!'

s = POP3_SSL('pop.mail.yahoo.com', 995)
s.user(MAILBOX)
s.pass_(PASSWD)
rv, msg, sz = s.retr(s.stat()[0])
s.quit()
```

```
line = getSubject(msg)
print 'POP:', line

s = IMAP4_SSL('imap.n.mail.yahoo.com', 993)
s.login(MAILBOX, PASSWD)
rsp, msgs = s.select('INBOX', True)
rsp, data = s.fetch(msgs[0], '(RFC822)')
line = getSubject(StringIO(data[0][1]))
s.close()
s.logout()
print 'IMAP:', line
```

Assuming we stick all of this into a `ymail.py` file, our execution might look something like this:

```
$ python ymail.py
SSL mail sent!
POP: Subject:Meet singles for dating, romance and more.
IMAP: Subject: test SMTP send via 465/SSL
```

In our case, we had a Yahoo! Mail Plus account, which allows us to download e-mail. (The sending is free regardless of whether you're a paying or non-paying subscriber.) However, note a couple of things that didn't work out quite right. The first is that the message obtained via POP was *not* that of our sent message, whereas IMAP was able to find it. In general, you'll find IMAP more reliable. Also in the preceding example, we're assuming that you're a paying customer and using a current version of Python (version 2.6.3+); reality sets in rather quickly if you're not.

If you're not paying for Yahoo! Mail Plus, you're not allowed to download e-mail. Here's a sample traceback that you'll get if you attempt it:

```
Traceback (most recent call last):
  File "ymail.py", line 101, in <module>
    s.pass_(PASSWD)
  File "/Library/Frameworks/Python.framework/Versions/2.7/lib/
python2.7/poplib.py", line 189, in pass_
    return self._shortcmd('PASS %s' % pswd)
  File "/Library/Frameworks/Python.framework/Versions/2.7/lib/
python2.7/poplib.py", line 152, in _shortcmd
    return self._getresp()
  File "/Library/Frameworks/Python.framework/Versions/2.7/lib/
python2.7/poplib.py", line 128, in _getresp
    raise error_proto(resp)
poplib.error_proto: -ERR [SYS/PERM] pop not allowed for user.
```

Furthermore, the SMTP_SSL class was only added in version 2.6, and on top of that, it was buggy until version 2.6.3, so that's the minimum version you need in order to be able to write code that uses SMTP over SSL. If you

2.6

using a release older than version 2.6, you won't even get that class, and if you're using version 2.6(.0)–2.6.2, you'll get an error that looks like this:

```
Traceback (most recent call last):
  File "ymail.py", line 61, in <module>
    s.login(MAILBOX, PASSWD)
  File "/System/Library/Frameworks/Python.framework/Versions/2.6/lib/
python2.6/smtplib.py", line 549, in login
    self.ehlo_or_helo_if_needed()
  File "/System/Library/Frameworks/Python.framework/Versions/2.6/lib/
python2.6/smtplib.py", line 509, in ehlo_or_helo_if_needed
    if not (200 <= self.ehlo()[0] <= 299):
  File "/System/Library/Frameworks/Python.framework/Versions/2.6/lib/
python2.6/smtplib.py", line 382, in ehlo
    self.putcmd(self.ehlo_msg, name or self.local_hostname)
  File "/System/Library/Frameworks/Python.framework/Versions/2.6/lib/
python2.6/smtplib.py", line 318, in putcmd
    self.send(str)
  File "/System/Library/Frameworks/Python.framework/Versions/2.6/lib/
python2.6/smtplib.py", line 310, in send
    raise SMTPServerDisconnected('please run connect() first')
smtplib.SMTPServerDisconnected: please run connect() first
```

These are just some of the issues you'll discover in practice; it's never as perfect as what you'd find in a textbook. There are always weird, unanticipated gotchas that end up biting you. By simulating it here, hopefully it will be less shocking for you.

Let's clean up the output a bit. But more importantly, let's add all these (version) checks that you'd have to do in real life, just to get used to it. Our final version of ymail.py can be found in Example 3-5.

Example 3-5   Yahoo! Mail SMTP, POP, IMAP Example (ymail.py)

This script exercises SMTP, POP, and IMAP for the Yahoo! Mail service.

```
1   #!/usr/bin/env python
2   'ymail.py - demo Yahoo!Mail SMTP/SSL, POP, IMAP'
3
4   from cStringIO import StringIO
5   from imaplib import IMAP4_SSL
6   from platform import python_version
7   from poplib import POP3_SSL, error_proto
8   from socket import error
9
10  # SMTP_SSL added in 2.6, fixed in 2.6.3
11  release = python_version()
12  if release > '2.6.2':
13      from smtplib import SMTP_SSL, SMTPServerDisconnected
```

```
14  else:
15      SMTP_SSL = None
16
17  from secret import *    # you provide MAILBOX, PASSWD
18
19  who = '%s@yahoo.com' % MAILBOX
20  from_ = who
21  to = [who]
22
23  headers = [
24      'From: %s' % from_,
25      'To: %s' % ', '.join(to),
26      'Subject: test SMTP send via 465/SSL',
27  ]
28  body = [
29      'Hello',
30      'World!',
31  ]
32  msg = '\r\n\r\n'.join(('\r\n'.join(headers), '\r\n'.join(body)))
33
34  def getSubject(msg, default='(no Subject line)'):
35      '''\
36      getSubject(msg) - iterate over 'msg' looking for
37      Subject line; return if found otherwise 'default'
38      '''
39      for line in msg:
40          if line.startswith('Subject:'):
41              return line.rstrip()
42          if not line:
43              return default
44
45  # SMTP/SSL
46  print '*** Doing SMTP send via SSL...'
47  if SMTP_SSL:
48      try:
49          s = SMTP_SSL('smtp.mail.yahoo.com', 465)
50          s.login(MAILBOX, PASSWD)
51          s.sendmail(from_, to, msg)
52          s.quit()
53          print '    SSL mail sent!'
54      except SMTPServerDisconnected:
55          print '    error: server unexpectedly disconnected... try
    again'
56  else:
57      print '    error: SMTP_SSL requires 2.6.3+'
58
59  # POP
60  print '*** Doing POP recv...'
```

(Continued)

Example 3-5   Yahoo! Mail SMTP, POP, IMAP Example (`ymail.py`)
                  (Continued)

```
61  try:
62      s = POP3_SSL('pop.mail.yahoo.com', 995)
63      s.user(MAILBOX)
64      s.pass_(PASSWD)
65      rv, msg, sz = s.retr(s.stat()[0])
66      s.quit()
67      line = getSubject(msg)
68      print '    Received msg via POP: %r' % line
69  except error_proto:
70      print '    error: POP for Yahoo!Mail Plus subscribers only'
71
72  # IMAP
73  print '*** Doing IMAP recv...'
74  try:
75      s = IMAP4_SSL('imap.n.mail.yahoo.com', 993)
76      s.login(MAILBOX, PASSWD)
77      rsp, msgs = s.select('INBOX', True)
78      rsp, data = s.fetch(msgs[0], '(RFC822)')
79      line = getSubject(StringIO(data[0][1]))
80      s.close()
81      s.logout()
82      print '    Received msg via IMAP: %r' % line
83  except error:
84      print '    error: IMAP for Yahoo!Mail Plus subscribers only
```

Line-by-Line Explanation

Lines 1–8

These are the normal header and import lines.

Lines 10–15

Here we ask for the Python release number as a string which comes from `platform.python_version()`. We only perform the import `smtplib` attributes if we're using version 2.6.3 and newer; otherwise, set `SMTP_SSL` to None.

Lines 17–21

As mentioned earlier, instead of hardcoding privileged information such as login and password, we put them in somewhere else, such as a byte-code-compiled secret.pyc file, where the average user cannot reverse engineer the `MAILBOX` and `PASSWD` data. As this is just a test application, after obtaining that information (line 17), we set the envelope sender and recipient variables as the same person (lines 19–21). Why is the sender variable named `from_` instead of `from`?

Lines 23–32

These next set of lines constitute the body of the e-mail message. Lines 23–27 represent the headers (which you can have easily generated by some code), lines 28–31 are for the actual body of the message (which can also be generated or in an iterable). At the end (line 32), we have the line of code that merges all of the previous information (headers + body) and creates the entire e-mail message body with the correct delimiter(s).

Lines 34–43

We have already discussed the `getSubject()` function, whose sole purpose is to seek the Subject line within an inbound message's e-mail headers, taking a default string if no Subject line is found. It's optional as we've implemented a default value for `default`.

Lines 45–57

This is the SMTP code. Earlier in lines 10–15, we decided whether to use `SMTP_SSL` or assign `None` to that value. Here, if we *did* get the class (line 7), try to connect to the server, login, execute the e-mail send, and then quit (lines 48–53). Otherwise, alert the user that version 2.6.3 or newer is required (lines 56–57). Occasionally you might get disconnected from the server due to a variety of reasons such as poor connectivity, etc. In such cases, usually a retry does the trick, so we inform the user about the retry attempt (lines 54–55).

Lines 59–70

This is the POP3 code that we already covered earlier for the most part (lines 62–68). The only difference is that we've added a check in case you're not paying for the POP access but are trying to download your mail anyway, which is why we need to catch the `poplib.error_proto` exception (lines 69–70), seen earlier.

Lines 72–84

The same is true for the IMAP4 code. We wrap the basic functionality in a **try** block (lines 74–82) and catch `socket.error` (lines 83–84). Did you also notice that this is where we subtly use the `cStringIO.StringIO` object (line 79)? The reason for this is because IMAP returns the e-mail message as a single large string. Because `getSubject()` iterates over multiple lines, we need to provide it something similar that it can work with, so that's what we get from `StringIO`—it takes a long string and gives it a file-like interface.

So that, in practice, is how you would actually deal with Yahoo! Mail. Gmail is very similar, except that all the access is "free." In addition, Gmail also allows standard SMTP (using TLS).

3.5.6   Gmail

Example 3-6 looks at Google's Gmail service. In addition to SMTP over SSL, Gmail also offers SMTP using *Transport Layer Security* (TLS), so we'll see one additional import of the `smtplib.SMTP` class with its own section of code. As far as everything else (SMTP over SSL, POP, and IMAP), they'll look quite similar to their equivalents for Yahoo! Mail. Because e-mail download is completely free, we do not need the exception handler to process access errors due to not being a subscriber.

Example 3-6   Gmail SMTPx2, POP, IMAP Example (`gmail.py`)

This script exercises SMTP, POP, and IMAP of the Google Gmail service.

```
1    #!/usr/bin/env python
2    'gmail.py - demo Gmail SMTP/TLS, SMTP/SSL, POP, IMAP'
3
4    from cStringIO import StringIO
5    from imaplib import IMAP4_SSL
6    from platform import python_version
7    from poplib import POP3_SSL
8    from smtplib import SMTP
9
10   # SMTP_SSL added in 2.6
11   release = python_version()
12   if release > '2.6.2':
13       from smtplib import SMTP_SSL  # fixed in 2.6.3
14   else:
15       SMTP_SSL = None
16
17   from secret import *   # you provide MAILBOX, PASSWD
18
19   who = '%s@gmail.com' % MAILBOX
20   from_ = who
21   to = [who]
22
23   headers = [
24       'From: %s' % from_,
25       'To: %s' % ', '.join(to),
26       'Subject: test SMTP send via 587/TLS',
27   ]
28   body = [
29       'Hello',
30       'World!',
31   ]
32   msg = '\r\n\r\n'.join(('\r\n'.join(headers), '\r\n'.join(body)))
33
```

```
34  def getSubject(msg, default='(no Subject line)'):
35      '''\
36      getSubject(msg) - iterate over 'msg' looking for
37      Subject line; return if found otherwise 'default'
38      '''
39      for line in msg:
40          if line.startswith('Subject:'):
41              return line.rstrip()
42          if not line:
43              return default
44
45  # SMTP/TLS
46  print '*** Doing SMTP send via TLS...'
47  s = SMTP('smtp.gmail.com', 587)
48  if release < '2.6':
49      s.ehlo()     # required in older releases
50  s.starttls()
51  if release < '2.5':
52      s.ehlo()     # required in older releases
53  s.login(MAILBOX, PASSWD)
54  s.sendmail(from_, to, msg)
55  s.quit()
56  print '    TLS mail sent!'
57
58  # POP
59  print '*** Doing POP recv...'
60  s = POP3_SSL('pop.gmail.com', 995)
61  s.user(MAILBOX)
62  s.pass_(PASSWD)
63  rv, msg, sz = s.retr(s.stat()[0])
64  s.quit()
65  line = getSubject(msg)
66  print '    Received msg via POP: %r' % line
67
68  body = body.replace('587/TLS', '465/SSL')
69
70  # SMTP/SSL
71  if SMTP_SSL:
72      print '*** Doing SMTP send via SSL...'
73      s = SMTP_SSL('smtp.gmail.com', 465)
74      s.login(MAILBOX, PASSWD)
75      s.sendmail(from_, to, msg)
76      s.quit()
77      print '    SSL mail sent!'
78
79  # IMAP
80  print '*** Doing IMAP recv...'
81  s = IMAP4_SSL('imap.gmail.com', 993)
82  s.login(MAILBOX, PASSWD)
83  rsp, msgs = s.select('INBOX', True)
84  rsp, data = s.fetch(msgs[0], '(RFC822)')
85  line = getSubject(StringIO(data[0][1]))
86  s.close()
87  s.logout()
88  print '    Received msg via IMAP: %r' % line
```

Line-by-Line Explanation

Lines 1–8

These are the usual header and import lines with one addition: the import of `smtplib.SMTP`. We will use this class with TLS to send an e-mail message.

Lines 10–43

These are pretty much the same as the equivalent lines in `ymail.py`. One difference is that our `who` variable will have an `@gmail.com` e-mail address, of course (line 19). The other change is that we'll start with SMTP/TLS, so the Subject line reflects this. We also don't import the `smtplib.SMTPServer-Disconnected` exception, because this exception wasn't observed throughout our testing.

Lines 45–56

This is the SMTP code that connects to the server by using TLS. As you can see, successive releases of Python (lines 48–52) have resulted in less boilerplate necessary to communicate with the server. It also has a different port number than SMTP/SSL (line 47).

Lines 58–88

The rest of the script is nearly identical to the equivalent in Yahoo! Mail. As we mentioned earlier, there are fewer error checks because those issues either don't exist for Gmail or have not been observed when using Gmail. One final minor difference is that as a result of sending both SMTP/TLS and SMTP/SSL messages, the Subject line needed to be tweaked (line 68).

What we're hoping that readers get out of these final pair of applications includes being able to take the concepts learned earlier in the chapter and apply some realism to every day application development; how in practice, security is a necessity; and yes, sometimes there are minor differences between Python releases. As much as we'd prefer solutions that are more pure, we know this isn't reality, and such issues are just examples of things that you have to take into consideration on any development project.

3.6   Related Modules

One of Python's greatest assets is the strength of its networking support in the standard library, particularly those oriented toward Internet protocols and client development. The subsections that follow present related modules, first focusing on e-mail, followed by Internet protocols in general.

3.6.1   E-Mail

Python features numerous e-mail modules and packages to help you with building an application. Some of them are listed in Table 3-6.

Table 3-6 E-Mail-Related Modules

Module/Package	Description
email	Package for processing e-mail (also supports MIME)
smtpd	SMTP server
base64	Base-16, 32, and 64 data encodings (RFC 3548)
mhlib	Classes for handling MH folders and messages
mailbox	Classes to support parsing mailbox file formats
mailcap	Support for handling "mailcap" files
mimetools	(deprecated) MIME message parsing tools (use email)
mimetypes	Converts between filenames/URLs and associated MIME types
MimeWriter	(deprecated) MIME message processing (use email)
mimify	(deprecated) Tools to MIME-process messages with (use email)
quopri	Encode/decode MIME quoted-printable data
binascii	Binary and ASCII conversion
binhex	Binhex4 encoding and decoding support

3.6.2   Other Internet "Client" Protocols

Table 3-7 presents other Internet "Client" Protocol-Related Modules.

Table 3-7   Internet "Client" Protocol-Related Modules

Module	Description
ftplib	FTP protocol client
xmlrpclib	XML-RPC protocol client
httplib	HTTP and HTTPS protocol client
imaplib	IMAP4 protocol client
nntplib	NNTP protocol client
poplib	POP3 protocol client
smtplib	SMTP protocol client

3.7   Exercises

FTP

3-1. *Simple FTP Client.* Given the FTP examples from this chapter, write a small FTP client program that goes to your favorite Web sites and downloads the latest versions of the applications you use. This can be a script that you run every few months to ensure that you're using the "latest and greatest." You should probably keep some sort of table with FTP location, login, and password information for your convenience.

3-2. *Simple FTP Client and Pattern-Matching.* Use your solution to Exercise 3-1 as a starting point for creating another simple FTP client that either pushes or pulls a set of files from a remote host by using patterns. For example, if you want to move a set of Python or PDF files from one host to another, allow users to enter *.py or doc*.pdf and only transfer those files whose names match.

3-3. *Smart FTP Command-Line Client.* Create a command-line FTP application similar to the vanilla Unix /bin/ftp program; however, make it a "better FTP client," meaning it should have additional useful features. You can take a look at the ncFTP application as motivation. It can be found at http://ncftp.com. For example, it has the following features: history, bookmarks (saving FTP locations with log in and password), download progress, etc. You might need to implement read-line functionality for history and curses for screen control.

3-4. *FTP and Multithreading.* Create an FTP client that uses Python threads to download files. You can either upgrade your existing Smart FTP client, as in Exercise 3-3, or just write a more simple client to download files. This can be either a command-line program in which you enter multiple files as arguments to the program, or a GUI in which you let the user select 1+ file(s) to transfer. Extra Credit: Allow patterns, that is, *.exe. Use individual threads to download each file.

3-5. *FTP and GUI.* Take the smart FTP client that you developed earlier and add a GUI layer on top of it to form a complete FTP application. You can choose from any of the modern Python GUI toolkits.

3-6. *Subclassing.* Derive ftplib.FTP and make a new class FTP2 where you do not need to give STOR filename and RETR filename commands with all four (4) retr*() and stor*() methods; you only need to pass in the filename. You can choose to either override the existing methods or create new ones with a 2 suffix, for example, retrlines2().

The file Tools/scripts/ftpmirror.py in the Python source distribution is a script that can mirror FTP sites, or portions thereof, using the ftplib module. It can be used as an extended example that applies to this module. The next five exercises feature the creation of solutions that revolve around code such as ftpmirror.py. You can use code in ftpmirror.py or implement your own solution with its code as your motivation.

3-7. *Recursion.* The ftpmirror.py script copies a remote directory recursively. Create a simpler FTP client in the spirit of ftpmirror.py but one that does *not* recurse by default. Create an -r option that instructs the application to recursively copy subdirectories to the local filesystem.

3-8. *Pattern-Matching.* The ftpmirror.py script has an -s option that lets users skip files that match the given pattern, such as .exe. Create your own simpler FTP client or update your solution to Exercise 3-7 so that it lets the user supply a pattern and only copy those files matching that pattern. Use your solution to an earlier exercise as a starting point.

3-9. *Recursion and Pattern-Matching.* Create an FTP client that integrates both Exercises 3-7 and 3-8.

3-10. *Recursion and ZIP files.* This exercise is similar to Exercise 3-7; however, instead of copying the remote files to the local filesystem, either update your existing FTP client or create a new one to download remote files and compress them into a ZIP (or TGZ or BZ2) file. This -z option allows your users to back up an FTP site in an automated manner.

3-11. *Kitchen Sink.* Implement a single, final, all-encompassing FTP application that has all the solutions to Exercises 3-7, 3-8, 3-9, and 3-10, that is, -r, -s, and -z options.

NNTP

3-12. *Introduction to NNTP.* Change Example 3-2 (getLatestNNTP.py) so that instead of the most recent article, it displays the first available article, meaningfully.

3-13. *Improving Code.* Fix the flaw in getLatestNNTP.py where triple-quoted lines show up in the output. This is because we want to display Python interactive interpreter lines but not triple-quoted text. Solve this problem by checking whether the stuff that comes after the ">>>" is real Python code. If so, display it as a line of data; if not, do not display this quoted text. Extra Credit: Use your solution to solve another minor problem—leading whitespace is not stripped from the body because it might represent indented Python code. If it really is code, display it; otherwise, it is text, so lstrip() that before displaying.

3-14. *Finding Articles.* Create an NNTP client application that lets the user log in and choose a newsgroup of interest. Once that has been accomplished, prompt the user for keywords to search article Subject lines. Bring up the list of articles that match the requirement and display them to the user. The user should then be allowed to choose an article to read from that list—display them and provide simple navigation like pagination, etc. If no search field is entered, bring up all current articles.

3-15. *Searching Bodies.* Upgrade your solution to Exercise 3-14 by searching both Subject lines and article bodies. Allow for AND or OR searching of keywords. Also allow for AND or OR searching of Subject lines and article bodies; that is, keyword(s) must be in Subject lines only, article bodies only, either, or both.

3-16.   *Threaded Newsreader.* This doesn't mean write a multi-threaded newsreader—it means organize related postings into "article threads." In other words, group related articles together, independent of when the individual articles were posted. All the articles belonging to individual threads should be listed chronologically though. Allow the user to do the following:

a) Select individual articles (bodies) to view, then have the option to go back to the list view or to previous or next article, either sequentially or related to the current thread.

b) Allow replies to threads, option to copy and quote previous article, and reply to the entire newsgroup via another post. Extra Credit: Allow personal reply to individual via e-mail.

c) Permanently delete threads—no future related articles should show up in the article list. For this, you will have to temporarily keep a persistent list of deleted threads so that they don't show up again. You can assume a thread is dead if no one posts an article with the same Subject line after several months.

3-17.   *GUI Newsreader.* Similar to an FTP exercise above, choose a Python GUI toolkit to implement a complete standalone GUI newsreader application.

3-18.   *Refactoring.* Like `ftpmirror.py` for FTP, there is a demo script for NNTP: `Demo/scripts/newslist.py`. Run it. This script was written a long time ago and can use a facelift. For this exercise, you are to refactor this program using features of the latest versions of Python as well as your developing skills in Python to perform the same task but run and complete in less time. This can include using list comprehensions or generator expressions, using smarter string concatenation, not calling unnecessary functions, etc.

3-19.   *Caching.* Another problem with `newslist.py` is that, according to its author, "I should really keep a list of ignored empty groups and re-check them for articles on every run, but I haven't got around to it yet." Make this improvement a reality. You can use the default version as-is or your newly improved one from Exercise 3-18.

E-Mail

3-20. *Identifiers*. The POP3 method `pass_()` is used to send the password to the server after giving it the login name by using `login()`. Can you give any reasons why you believe this method was named with a trailing underscore (`pass_()`), instead of just plain, old `pass()`?

3-21. *POP and IMAP*. Write an application using one of the `poplib` classes (`POP3` or `POP3_SSL`) to download e-mail, then do the same thing using `imaplib`. You can borrow some of the code seen earlier in this chapter. Why would you want to leave your login and password information out of the source code?

The next set of exercises deal with the `myMail.py` application presented in Example 3-3.

3-22. *E-Mail Headers*. In `myMail.py`, the last few lines compared the originally sent body with the body in the received e-mail. Create similar code to assert the original headers. Hint: Ignore newly added headers.

3-23. *Error Checking*. Add SMTP and POP error-checking.

3-24. *SMTP and IMAP*. Add support for IMAP. Extra Credit: Support both mail download protocols, giving the user the ability to choose which to use.

3-25. *E-Mail Composition*. Further develop your solution to Exercise 3-24 by giving the users of your application the ability to compose and send e-mail.

3-26. *E-Mail Application*. Further develop your e-mail application, turning it into something more useful by adding in mailbox management. Your application should be able to read in the current set of e-mail messages in a user's imbeds and display their Subject lines. Users should be able to select messages to view. Extra Credit: Add support to view attachments via external applications.

3-27. *GUI*. Add a GUI layer on top of your solution to the previous problem to make it practically a full e-mail application.

3-28. *Elements of SPAM*. Unsolicited junk e-mail, or spam, is a very real and significant problem today. There are many good solutions out there, validating this market. We do not want you to (necessarily) reinvent the wheel, but we would like you to get a taste of some of the elements of spam processing.

a) *"mbox" format.* Before we can get started, we should convert any e-mail messages you want to work on to a common format, such as the *mbox* format. (There are others that you can use if you prefer. Once you have several (or all) work messages in mbox format, merge them all into a single file. Hint: See the `mailbox` module and `email` package.

b) *Headers.* Most of the clues of spam lie in the e-mail headers. (You might want to use the e-mail package or parse them manually yourself.) Write code that answers questions such as:

   – What e-mail client appears to have originated this message? (Check out the `X-Mailer` header.)

   – Is the message ID (`Message-ID` header) format valid?

   – Are there domain name mismatches between the `From`, `Received`, and perhaps `Return-Path` headers? What about domain name and IP address mismatches? Is there an `X-Authentication-Warning` header? If so, what does it report?

c) *Information Servers.* Based on an IP address or domain, servers such as WHOIS, SenderBase.org, etc., might be able to help you identify the location where a piece of bulk e-mail originated. Find one or more of these services and build code to the find the country of origin, and optionally the city, network owner name, contact information, etc.

d) *Keywords.* Certain words keep popping up in spam. You have no doubt seen them before, and in all of their variations, including using a number resembling a letter, capitalizing random letters, etc. Build a list of frequent words that you have seen definitely tied to spam and quarantine them. Extra Credit: Develop an algorithm or add keyword variations to spot such trickery in messages.

e) *Phishing.* These spam messages attempt to disguise themselves as valid e-mail from major banking institutions or well-known Internet Web sites. They contain links that lure readers to Web sites in an attempt to harvest private and extremely sensitive information such as login names, passwords, and credit card numbers. These fakers do a pretty good job of giving their fraudulent messages an accurate look-and-feel. However, they cannot hide the fact that the actual link that they direct users to does not belong to the company they are masquerading as. Many of them are obvious giveaways; for example, horrible-looking domain names, raw IP addresses, and even IP addresses in 32-bit integer format rather than in octets. Develop code that can determine whether e-mail that looks like official communication is real or bogus.

E-Mail Composition

The following set of exercises deal with composing e-mail messages by using the e-mail package and specifically refers to the code we looked at in `email-examples.py`.

3-29. *Multipart Alternative*. What does multipart alternative mean, anyway? We took a quick look at it earlier in the `make_mpa_msg()` function, but what does it really signify? How would the behavior of `make_mpa_msg()` change if we removed `'alternative'` when we instantiated the `MIMEMultipart` class, that is, `email = MIMEMultipart()`?

3-30. *Python 3*. Port the `email-examples.py` script to Python 3 (or create a hybrid that runs without modification under both versions 2.x and 3.x).

3-31. *Multiple attachments*. In the section on composing e-mail, we looked at the `make_img_msg()` function, which created a single e-mail message made up of a single image. While that's a great start, it isn't as useful in the real world. Create a more generalized function called `attachImgs()`, `attach_images()`, or whatever you want to call it, with which users can pass in more than one image file. Take those files and make them individual attachments of the entire e-mail message body and return a single multipart message object.

3-32. *Robustness*. Improve the solution for Exercise 3-31 for `attachImgs()` by making sure that users are passing in only image files (and throwing exceptions if not). In other words, check the filename to ensure that the extension matches .png, .jpg, .gif, .tif, etc. Extra Credit: Support file introspection to take files with *any*, *incorrect*, or *no* extension and determine what type they really are. To help you get started, check out the Wikipedia page at http://en.wikipedia.org/wiki/File_format.

3-33. *Robustness, Networking*. Further enhance the `attachImgs()` function so that in addition to local files, users can pass in a URL to an online picture such as http://docs.python.org/_static/py.png.

3-34. *Spreadsheets*. Create a function called `attachSheets()` that attaches one or more spreadsheet files to a multipart e-mail message. Support the most common formats such as `.csv`, `.xls`, `.xlsx`, `.ods`, `.uof/.uos`, etc.). You can use `attachImgs()` as a model; however, instead of using `email.mime.image.MIMEImage`, you'll be using `email.mime.base.MIMEBase` as well as need to specify an appropriate MIME type (for example, `'application/vnd.ms-excel'`). Also don't forget the `Content-Disposition` header.

3-35. *Documents*. Similar to Exercise 3-34, create a function called `attachDocs()` that attaches document files to a multipart e-mail message. Support common formats, such as `.doc`, `.docx`, `.odt`, `.rtf`, `.pdf`, `.txt`, `.uof/.uot`, etc.

3-36. *Multiple Attachment Types*. Let's broaden the scope defined by your solutions to Exercise 3-35. Create a new, more generalized function called `attachFiles()`, which takes *any* type of attachment. You are welcome to merge any of the code from the solutions for any of these exercises.

Miscellaneous

A list of various Internet protocols, including the three highlighted in this chapter, can be found at http://networksorcery.com/enp/topic/ipsuite.htm. A list of specific Internet protocols supported by Python can be found at http://docs. python.org/library/internet.

3-37. *Developing Alternate Internet Clients*. Now that you have seen four examples of how Python can help you to develop Internet clients, choose another protocol with client support in a Python Standard Library module and write a client application for it.

3-38. **Developing New Internet Clients*. Much more difficult: find an uncommon or upcoming protocol *without* Python support and implement it. Be serious enough that you will consider writing and submitting a PEP to have your module included in the standard library distribution of a future Python release.

CHAPTER 4

Multithreaded Programming

> *With Python you can start a thread, but you can't stop it.*
> *Sorry. You'll have to wait until it reaches the end of execution.*
> *So, just the same as [comp.lang.python], then?*
> —Cliff Wells, Steve Holden
> (and Timothy Delaney), February 2002

In this chapter...

- Introduction/Motivation
- Threads and Processes
- Threads and Python
- The thread Module
- The threading Module
- Comparing Single vs. Multithreaded Execution
- Multithreading in Practice
- Producer-Consumer Problem and the Queue/queue Module
- Alternative Considerations to Threads
- Related Modules

I n this section, we will explore the different ways by which you can achieve more parallelism in your code. We will begin by differentiating between processes and threads in the first few of sections of this chapter. We will then introduce the notion of multithreaded programming and present some multithreaded programming features found in Python. (Those of you already familiar with multithreaded programming can skip directly to Section 4.3.5.) The final sections of this chapter present some examples of how to use the threading and Queue modules to accomplish multithreaded programming with Python.

4.1   Introduction/Motivation

Before the advent of *multithreaded* (MT) programming, the execution of computer programs consisted of a single sequence of steps that were executed in synchronous order by the host's CPU. This style of execution was the norm whether the task itself required the sequential ordering of steps or if the entire program was actually an aggregation of multiple subtasks. What if these subtasks were independent, having no *causal* relationship (meaning that results of subtasks do not affect other subtask outcomes)? Is it not logical, then, to want to run these independent tasks all at the same time? Such parallel processing could significantly improve the performance of the overall task. This is what MT programming is all about.

MT programming is ideal for programming tasks that are asynchronous in nature, require multiple concurrent activities, and where the processing of each activity might be *nondeterministic*, that is, random and unpredictable. Such programming tasks can be organized or partitioned into multiple streams of execution wherein each has a specific task to accomplish. Depending on the application, these subtasks might calculate intermediate results that could be merged into a final piece of output.

While CPU-bound tasks might be fairly straightforward to divide into subtasks and executed sequentially or in a multithreaded manner, the task of managing a single-threaded process with multiple external sources of input is not as trivial. To achieve such a programming task without multithreading, a sequential program must use one or more timers and implement a multiplexing scheme.

A sequential program will need to sample each I/O terminal channel to check for user input; however, it is important that the program does not block when reading the I/O terminal channel, because the arrival of user input is nondeterministic, and blocking would prevent processing of other I/O channels. The sequential program must use non-blocked I/O or blocked I/O with a timer (so that blocking is only temporary).

Because the sequential program is a single thread of execution, it must juggle the multiple tasks that it needs to perform, making sure that it does not spend too much time on any one task, and it must ensure that user response time is appropriately distributed. The use of a sequential program for this type of task often results in a complicated flow of control that is difficult to understand and maintain.

Using an MT program with a shared data structure such as a `Queue` (a multithreaded queue data structure, discussed later in this chapter), this programming task can be organized with a few threads that have specific functions to perform:

- `UserRequestThread`: Responsible for reading client input, perhaps from an I/O channel. A number of threads would be created by the program, one for each current client, with requests being entered into the queue.

- `RequestProcessor`: A thread that is responsible for retrieving requests from the queue and processing them, providing output for yet a third thread.

- `ReplyThread`: Responsible for taking output destined for the user and either sending it back (if in a networked application) or writing data to the local file system or database.

Organizing this programming task with multiple threads reduces the complexity of the program and enables an implementation that is clean, efficient, and well organized. The logic in each thread is typically less complex because it has a specific job to do. For example, the `UserRequestThread` simply reads input from a user and places the data into a queue for further processing by another thread, etc. Each thread has its own job to do; you merely have to design each type of thread to do one thing and do it well. Use of threads for specific tasks is not unlike Henry Ford's assembly line model for manufacturing automobiles.

4.2   Threads and Processes

4.2.1   What Are Processes?

Computer *programs* are merely executables, binary (or otherwise), which reside on disk. They do not take on a life of their own until loaded into memory and invoked by the operating system. A *process* (sometimes called a *heavyweight process*) is a program in execution. Each process has its own address space, memory, a data stack, and other auxiliary data to keep track of execution. The operating system manages the execution of all processes on the system, dividing the time fairly between all processes. Processes can also *fork* or *spawn* new processes to perform other tasks, but each new process has its own memory, data stack, etc., and cannot generally share information unless *interprocess communication* (IPC) is employed.

4.2.2   What Are Threads?

Threads (sometimes called *lightweight processes*) are similar to processes except that they all execute within the same process, and thus all share the same context. They can be thought of as "mini-processes" running in parallel within a main process or "main thread."

A thread has a beginning, an execution sequence, and a conclusion. It has an instruction pointer that keeps track of where within its context it is currently running. It can be preempted (interrupted) and temporarily put on hold (also known as *sleeping*) while other threads are running—this is called *yielding*.

Multiple threads within a process share the same data space with the main thread and can therefore share information or communicate with one another more easily than if they were separate processes. Threads are generally executed in a concurrent fashion, and it is this parallelism and data sharing that enable the coordination of multiple tasks. Naturally, it is impossible to run truly in a concurrent manner in a single CPU system, so threads are scheduled in such a way that they run for a little bit, then yield to other threads (going to the proverbial back of the line to await more CPU time again). Throughout the execution of the entire process, each thread performs its own, separate tasks, and communicates the results with other threads as necessary.

Of course, such sharing is not without its dangers. If two or more threads access the same piece of data, inconsistent results can arise because of the ordering of data access. This is commonly known as a *race condition*. Fortunately, most thread libraries come with some sort of synchronization primitives that allow the thread manager to control execution and access.

Another caveat is that threads cannot be given equal and fair execution time. This is because some functions block until they have completed. If not written specifically to take threads into account, this skews the amount of CPU time in favor of such greedy functions.

4.3   Threads and Python

In this section, we discuss how to use threads in Python. This includes the limitations of threads due to the global interpreter lock and a quick demo script.

4.3.1   Global Interpreter Lock

Execution of Python code is controlled by the *Python Virtual Machine* (a.k.a. the *interpreter main loop*). Python was designed in such a way that only one thread of control may be executing in this main loop, similar to how multiple processes in a system share a single CPU. Many programs can be in memory, but only *one* is live on the CPU at any given moment. Likewise, although multiple threads can run within the Python interpreter, only one thread is being executed by the interpreter at any given time.

Access to the Python Virtual Machine is controlled by the *global interpreter lock* (GIL). This lock is what ensures that exactly one thread is running. The Python Virtual Machine executes in the following manner in an MT environment:

1. Set the GIL
2. Switch in a thread to run
3. Execute either of the following:
   a. For a specified number of bytecode instructions, or
   b. If the thread voluntarily yields control (can be accomplished `time.sleep(0)`)
4. Put the thread back to sleep (switch out thread)
5. Unlock the GIL
6. Do it all over again (lather, rinse, repeat)

When a call is made to external code—that is, any C/C++ extension built-in function—the GIL will be locked until it has completed (because there are no Python bytecodes to count as the interval). Extension programmers do have the ability to unlock the GIL, however, so as the Python developer, you shouldn't have to worry about your Python code locking up in those situations.

As an example, for any Python I/O-oriented routines (which invoke built-in operating system C code), the GIL is released before the I/O call is made, allowing other threads to run while the I/O is being performed. Code that *doesn't* have much I/O will tend to keep the processor (and GIL) for the full interval a thread is allowed before it yields. In other words, I/O-bound Python programs stand a much better chance of being able to take advantage of a multithreaded environment than CPU-bound code.

Those of you who are interested in the source code, the interpreter main loop, and the GIL can take a look at the `Python/ceval.c` file.

4.3.2   Exiting Threads

When a thread completes execution of the function it was created for, it exits. Threads can also quit by calling an exit function such as `thread.exit()`, or any of the standard ways of exiting a Python process such as `sys.exit()` or raising the `SystemExit` exception. You cannot, however, go and "kill" a thread.

We will discuss in detail the two Python modules related to threads in the next section, but of the two, the `thread` module is the one we do *not* recommend. There are many reasons for this, but an obvious one is that when the main thread exits, all other threads die without cleanup. The other module, `threading`, ensures that the whole process stays alive until all "important" child threads have exited. (For a clarification of what important means, read the upcoming Core Tip, "Avoid using the thread module.")

Main threads should always be good managers, though, and perform the task of knowing what needs to be executed by individual threads, what data or arguments each of the spawned threads requires, when they complete execution, and what results they provide. In so doing, those main threads can collate the individual results into a final, meaningful conclusion.

4.3.3   Accessing Threads from Python

Python supports multithreaded programming, depending on the operating system on which it's running. It is supported on most Unix-based platforms, such as Linux, Solaris, Mac OS X, *BSD, as well as Windows-based PCs. Python uses POSIX-compliant threads, or *pthreads*, as they are commonly known.

By default, threads are enabled when building Python from source (since Python 2.0) or the Win32 installed binary. To determine whether threads are available for your interpreter, simply attempt to import the `thread` module from the interactive interpreter, as shown here (no errors occur when threads are available):

```
>>> import thread
>>>
```

If your Python interpreter was *not* compiled with threads enabled, the module import fails:

```
>>> import thread
Traceback (innermost last):
  File "<stdin>", line 1, in ?
ImportError: No module named thread
```

In such cases, you might need to recompile your Python interpreter to get access to threads. This usually involves invoking the `configure` script with the `--with-thread` option. Check the `README` file for your distribution to obtain specific instructions on how to compile Python with threads for your system.

4.3.4   Life Without Threads

For our first set of examples, we are going to use the `time.sleep()` function to show how threads work. `time.sleep()` takes a floating point argument and "sleeps" for the given number of seconds, meaning that execution is temporarily halted for the amount of time specified.

Let's create two time loops: one that sleeps for 4 seconds (`loop0()`), and one that sleeps for 2 seconds (`loop1()`), respectively. (We use the names "loop0" and "loop1" as a hint that we will eventually have a sequence of loops.) If we were to execute `loop0()` and `loop1()` sequentially in a one-process or single-threaded program, as `onethr.py` does in Example 4-1, the total execution time would be at least 6 seconds. There might or might not be a 1-second gap between the starting of `loop0()` and `loop1()` as well as other execution overhead which can cause the overall time to be bumped to 7 seconds.

Example 4-1   Loops Executed by a Single Thread (onethr.py)

This script executes two loops consecutively in a single-threaded program. One loop must complete before the other can begin. The total elapsed time is the sum of times taken by each loop.

```
1    #!/usr/bin/env python
2
3    from time import sleep, ctime
4
5    def loop0():
6        print 'start loop 0 at:', ctime()
7        sleep(4)
```

```
8          print 'loop 0 done at:', ctime()
9
10  def loop1():
11          print 'start loop 1 at:', ctime()
12          sleep(2)
13          print 'loop 1 done at:', ctime()
14
15  def main():
16          print 'starting at:', ctime()
17          loop0()
18          loop1()
19          print 'all DONE at:', ctime()
20
21  if __name__ == '__main__':
22          main()
```

We can verify this by executing onethr.py, which renders the following output:

```
$ onethr.py
starting at: Sun Aug 13 05:03:34 2006
start loop 0 at: Sun Aug 13 05:03:34 2006
loop 0 done at: Sun Aug 13 05:03:38 2006
start loop 1 at: Sun Aug 13 05:03:38 2006
loop 1 done at: Sun Aug 13 05:03:40 2006
all DONE at: Sun Aug 13 05:03:40 2006
```

Now, assume that rather than sleeping, loop0() and loop1() were separate functions that performed individual and independent computations, all working to arrive at a common solution. Wouldn't it be useful to have them run in parallel to cut down on the overall running time? That is the premise behind MT programming that we now introduce.

4.3.5   Python Threading Modules

Python provides several modules to support MT programming, including the thread, threading, and Queue modules. Programmers can us the thread and threading modules to create and manage threads. The thread module provides basic thread and locking support; threading provides higher-level, fully-featured thread management. With the Queue module, users can create a queue data structure that can be shared across multiple threads. We will take a look at these modules individually and present examples and intermediate-sized applications.

CORE TIP: Avoid using the `thread` module

We recommend using the high-level `threading` module instead of the `thread` module for many reasons. `threading` is more contemporary, has better thread support, and some attributes in the `thread` module can conflict with those in the `threading` module. Another reason is that the lower-level `thread` module has few synchronization primitives (actually only one) while `threading` has many.

However, in the interest of learning Python and threading in general, we do present some code that uses the `thread` module. We present these for learning purposes only; hopefully they give you a much better insight as to why you would want to avoid using `thread`. We will also show you how to use more appropriate tools such as those available in the `threading` and `Queue` modules.

Another reason to avoid using `thread` is because there is no control of when your process exits. When the main thread finishes, any other threads will also die, without warning or proper cleanup. As mentioned earlier, at least `threading` allows the important child threads to finish first before exiting.

3.x   Use of the `thread` module is recommended only for experts desiring lower-level thread access. To emphasize this, it is renamed to `_thread` in Python 3. Any multithreaded application you create should utilize `threading` and perhaps other higher-level modules.

4.4   The `thread` Module

Let's take a look at what the `thread` module has to offer. In addition to being able to spawn threads, the `thread` module also provides a basic synchronization data structure called a *lock object* (a.k.a. *primitive lock, simple lock, mutual exclusion lock, mutex,* and *binary semaphore*). As we mentioned earlier, such synchronization primitives go hand in hand with thread management.

Table 4-1 lists the more commonly used thread functions and `LockType` lock object methods.

Table 4-1   thread Module and Lock Objects

Function/Method	Description
thread *Module Functions*	
start_new_thread(*function*, *args*, *kwargs*=None)	Spawns a new thread and executes function with the given args and optional *kwargs*
allocate_lock()	Allocates LockType lock object
exit()	Instructs a thread to exit
LockType Lock *Object Methods*	
acquire(*wait*=None)	Attempts to acquire lock object
locked()	Returns True if lock acquired, False otherwise
release()	Releases lock

The key function of the thread module is start_new_thread(). It takes a function (object) plus arguments and optionally, keyword arguments. A new thread is spawned specifically to invoke the function.

Let's take our onethr.py example and integrate threading into it. By slightly changing the call to the loop*() functions, we now present mtsleepA.py in Example 4-2:

Example 4-2   Using the thread Module (mtsleepA.py)

The same loops from onethr.py are executed, but this time using the simple multithreaded mechanism provided by the thread module. The two loops are executed concurrently (with the shorter one finishing first, obviously), and the total elapsed time is only as long as the slowest thread rather than the total time for each separately.

```
1   #!/usr/bin/env python
2
3   import thread
4   from time import sleep, ctime
5
6   def loop0():
7       print 'start loop 0 at:', ctime()
```

(Continued)

Example 4-2   Using the thread Module (mtsleepA.py) *(Continued)*

```
8       sleep(4)
9       print 'loop 0 done at:', ctime()
10
11  def loop1():
12      print 'start loop 1 at:', ctime()
13      sleep(2)
14      print 'loop 1 done at:', ctime()
15
16  def main():
17      print 'starting at:', ctime()
18      thread.start_new_thread(loop0, ())
19      thread.start_new_thread(loop1, ())
20      sleep(6)
21      print 'all DONE at:', ctime()
22
23  if __name__ == '__main__':
24      main()
```

---

start_new_thread() requires the first two arguments, so that is the reason for passing in an empty tuple even if the executing function requires no arguments.

Upon execution of this program, our output changes drastically. Rather than taking a full 6 or 7 seconds, our script now runs in 4 seconds, the length of time of our longest loop, plus any overhead.

```
$ mtsleepA.py
starting at: Sun Aug 13 05:04:50 2006
start loop 0 at: Sun Aug 13 05:04:50 2006
start loop 1 at: Sun Aug 13 05:04:50 2006
loop 1 done at: Sun Aug 13 05:04:52 2006
loop 0 done at: Sun Aug 13 05:04:54 2006
all DONE at: Sun Aug 13 05:04:56 2006
```

The pieces of code that sleep for 4 and 2 seconds now occur concurrently, contributing to the lower overall runtime. You can even see how loop 1 finishes before loop 0.

The only other major change to our application is the addition of the sleep(6) call. Why is this necessary? The reason is that if we did not stop the main thread from continuing, it would proceed to the next statement, displaying "all done" and exit, killing both threads running loop0() and loop1().

We did not have any code that directed the main thread to wait for the child threads to complete before continuing. This is what we mean by threads requiring some sort of synchronization. In our case, we used another sleep() call as our synchronization mechanism. We used a value of 6 seconds because we know that both threads (which take 4 and 2 seconds) should have completed by the time the main thread has counted to 6.

You are probably thinking that there should be a better way of managing threads than creating that extra delay of 6 seconds in the main thread. Because of this delay, the overall runtime is no better than in our single-threaded version. Using sleep() for thread synchronization as we did is not reliable. What if our loops had independent and varying execution times? We could be exiting the main thread too early or too late. This is where locks come in.

Making yet another update to our code to include locks as well as getting rid of separate loop functions, we get mtsleepB.py, which is presented in Example 4-3. Running it, we see that the output is similar to mtsleepA.py. The only difference is that we did not have to wait the extra time for mtsleepA.py to conclude. By using locks, we were able to exit as soon as both threads had completed execution. This renders the following output:

```
$ mtsleepB.py
starting at: Sun Aug 13 16:34:41 2006
start loop 0 at: Sun Aug 13 16:34:41 2006
start loop 1 at: Sun Aug 13 16:34:41 2006
loop 1 done at: Sun Aug 13 16:34:43 2006
loop 0 done at: Sun Aug 13 16:34:45 2006
all DONE at: Sun Aug 13 16:34:45 2006
```

Example 4-3   Using thread and Locks (mtsleepB.py)

Rather than using a call to sleep() to hold up the main thread as in mtsleepA.py, the use of locks makes more sense.

```
1    #!/usr/bin/env python
2
3    import thread
4    from time import sleep, ctime
5
6    loops = [4,2]
7
8    def loop(nloop, nsec, lock):
9        print 'start loop', nloop, 'at:', ctime()
10       sleep(nsec)
11       print 'loop', nloop, 'done at:', ctime()
12       lock.release()
13
```

(Continued)

Example 4-3   Using `thread` and Locks (`mtsleepB.py`) *(Continued)*

```
14    def main():
15        print 'starting at:', ctime()
16        locks = []
17        nloops = range(len(loops))
18
19      for i in nloops:
20          lock = thread.allocate_lock()
21          lock.acquire()
22          locks.append(lock)
23
24    for i in nloops:
25        thread.start_new_thread(loop,
26            (i, loops[i], locks[i]))
27
28        for i in nloops:
29            while locks[i].locked(): pass
30
31        print 'all DONE at:', ctime()
32
33  if __name__ == '__main__':
34      main()
```

So how did we accomplish our task with locks? Let's take a look at the source code.

Line-by-Line Explanation

Lines 1–6

After the Unix startup line, we import the `thread` module and a few familiar attributes of the `time` module. Rather than hardcoding separate functions to count to 4 and 2 seconds, we use a single `loop()` function and place these constants in a list, `loops`.

Lines 8–12

The `loop()` function acts as a proxy for the deleted `loop*()` functions from our earlier examples. We had to make some cosmetic changes to `loop()` so that it can now perform its duties using locks. The obvious changes are that we need to be told which loop number we are as well as the sleep duration. The last piece of new information is the lock itself. Each thread will be allocated an acquired lock. When the `sleep()` time has concluded, we release the corresponding lock, indicating to the main thread that this thread has completed.

Lines 14–34

The bulk of the work is done here in main(), using three separate **for** loops. We first create a list of locks, which we obtain by using the thread.allocate_lock() function and acquire (each lock) with the acquire() method. Acquiring a lock has the effect of "locking the lock." Once it is locked, we add the lock to the lock list, locks. The next loop actually spawns the threads, invoking the loop() function per thread, and for each thread, provides it with the loop number, the sleep duration, and the acquired lock for that thread. So why didn't we start the threads in the lock acquisition loop? There are two reasons. First, we wanted to synchronize the threads, so that all the horses started out the gate around the same time, and second, locks take a little bit of time to be acquired. If your thread executes too fast, it is possible that it completes before the lock has a chance to be acquired.

It is up to each thread to unlock its lock object when it has completed execution. The final loop just sits and spins (pausing the main thread) until both locks have been released before continuing execution. Because we are checking each lock sequentially, we might be at the mercy of all the slower loops if they are more toward the beginning of the set of loops. In such cases, the majority of the wait time may be for the first loop(s). When that lock is released, remaining locks may have already been unlocked (meaning that corresponding threads have completed execution). The result is that the main thread will fly through those lock checks without pause. Finally, you should be well aware that the final pair of lines will execute main() only if we are invoking this script directly.

As hinted in the earlier Core Note, we presented the thread module only to introduce the reader to threaded programming. Your MT application should use higher-level modules such as the threading module, which we discuss in the next section.

4.5   The threading Module

We will now introduce the higher-level threading module, which gives you not only a Thread class but also a wide variety of synchronization mechanisms to use to your heart's content. Table 4-2 presents a list of all the objects available in the threading module.

Table 4-2   `threading` Module Objects

Object	Description
Thread	Object that represents a single thread of execution
Lock	Primitive lock object (same lock as in `thread` module)
RLock	Re-entrant lock object provides ability for a single thread to (re)acquire an already-held lock (recursive locking)
Condition	Condition variable object causes one thread to wait until a certain "condition" has been satisfied by another thread, such as changing of state or of some data value
Event	General version of condition variables, whereby any number of threads are waiting for some event to occur and all will awaken when the event happens
Semaphore	Provides a "counter" of finite resources shared between threads; block when none are available
BoundedSemaphore	Similar to a `Semaphore` but ensures that it never exceeds its initial value
Timer	Similar to `Thread`, except that it waits for an allotted period of time before running
Barrier[a]	Creates a "barrier," at which a specified number of threads must all arrive before they're all allowed to continue

3.2

a.   New in Python 3.2.

In this section, we will examine how to use the `Thread` class to implement threading. Because we have already covered the basics of locking, we will not cover the locking primitives here. The `Thread()` class also contains a form of synchronization, so explicit use of locking primitives is not necessary.

CORE TIP: Daemon threads

Another reason to avoid using the `thread` module is that it does not support the concept of daemon (or daemonic) threads. When the main thread exits, all child threads will be killed, regardless of whether they are doing work. The concept of daemon threads comes into play here if you do not desire this behavior.

Support for daemon threads is available in the `threading` module, and here is how they work: a *daemon* is typically a server that waits for client requests to service. If there is no client work to be done, the daemon sits idle. If you set the daemon flag for a thread, you are basically saying that it is non-critical, and it is okay for the process to exit without waiting for it to finish. As you have seen in Chapter 2, "Network Programming," server threads run in an infinite loop and do not exit in normal situations.

If your main thread is ready to exit and you do not care to wait for the child threads to finish, then set their daemon flags. A value of true denotes a thread is not important or more likely, not doing anything but waiting for a client.

To set a thread as daemonic, make this assignment: `thread.daemon = True` before you start the thread. (The old-style way of calling `thread.setDaemon(True)` is deprecated.) The same is true for checking on a thread's daemonic status; just check that value (versus calling `thread.isDaemon()`). A new child thread inherits its daemonic flag from its parent. The entire Python program (read as: the main thread) will stay alive until all non-daemonic threads have exited—in other words, when no active non-daemonic threads are left.

4.5.1   The Thread Class

The `Thread` class of the `threading` module is your primary executive object. It has a variety of functions not available to the `thread` module. Table 4-3 presents a list of attributes and methods.

Table 4-3   Thread Object Attributes and Methods

Attribute	Description
Thread object data attributes	
`name`	The name of a thread.
`ident`	The identifier of a thread.
`daemon`	Boolean flag indicating whether a thread is daemonic.
Thread object methods	
`__init__(`*group*`=None,` *target*`=None,` *name*`=None,` *args*`=(),` *kwargs*`={},` *verbose*`=None,` *daemon*`=None)`[c]	Instantiate a Thread object, taking target `callable` and any *args* or *kwargs*. A *name* or *group* can also be passed but the latter is unimplemented. A *verbose* flag is also accepted. Any *daemon* value sets the `thread.daemon` attribute/flag.
`start()`	Begin thread execution.
`run()`	Method defining thread functionality (usually overridden by application writer in a subclass).
`join(`*timeout*`=None)`	Suspend until the started thread terminates; blocks unless *timeout* (in seconds) is given.
`getName()`[a]	Return name of thread.
`setName(`*name*`)`[a]	Set name of thread.
`isAlive/is_alive()`[b]	Boolean flag indicating whether thread is still running.
`isDaemon()`[c]	Return `True` if thread daemonic, `False` otherwise.
`setDaemon(`*daemonic*`)`[c]	Set the daemon flag to the given Boolean *daemonic* value (must be called before thread `start()`.

a. Deprecated by setting (or getting) `thread.name` attribute or passed in during instantiation.
b. CamelCase names deprecated and replaced starting in Python 2.6.
c. `is/setDaemon()` deprecated by setting `thread.daemon` attribute; `thread.daemon` can also be set during instantiation via the optional daemon value—new in Python 3.3.

There are a variety of ways by which you can create threads using the Thread class. We cover three of them here, all quite similar. Pick the one you feel most comfortable with, not to mention the most appropriate for your application and future scalability (we like the final choice the best):

- Create Thread instance, passing in function
- Create Thread instance, passing in callable class instance
- Subclass Thread and create subclass instance

You'll discover that you will pick either the first or third option. The latter is chosen when a more object-oriented interface is desired and the former, otherwise. The second, honestly, is a bit more awkward and slightly harder to read, as you'll discover.

Create Thread Instance, Passing in Function

In our first example, we will just instantiate Thread, passing in our function (and its arguments) in a manner similar to our previous examples. This function is what will be executed when we direct the thread to begin execution. Taking our mtsleepB.py script from Example 4-3 and tweaking it by adding the use of Thread objects, we have mtsleepC.py, as shown in Example 4-4.

Example 4-4   Using the threading Module (mtsleepC.py)

The Thread class from the threading module has a join() method that lets the main thread wait for thread completion.

```
1    #!/usr/bin/env python
2
3    import threading
4    from time import sleep, ctime
5
6    loops = [4,2]
7
8    def loop(nloop, nsec):
9        print 'start loop', nloop, 'at:', ctime()
10       sleep(nsec)
11       print 'loop', nloop, 'done at:', ctime()
12
13   def main():
14       print 'starting at:', ctime()
15       threads = []
```

(Continued)

Example 4-4   Using the threading Module (mtsleepC.py) *(Continued)*

```
16      nloops = range(len(loops))
17
18      for i in nloops:
19          t = threading.Thread(target=loop,
20              args=(i, loops[i]))
21          threads.append(t)
22
23      for i in nloops:          # start threads
24          threads[i].start()
25
26      for i in nloops:          # wait for all
27          threads[i].join()     # threads to finish
28
29      print 'all DONE at:', ctime()
30
31  if __name__ == '__main__':
32      main()
```

When we run the script in Example 4-4, we see output similar to that of its predecessors:

```
$ mtsleepC.py
starting at: Sun Aug 13 18:16:38 2006
start loop 0 at: Sun Aug 13 18:16:38 2006
start loop 1 at: Sun Aug 13 18:16:38 2006
loop 1 done at: Sun Aug 13 18:16:40 2006
loop 0 done at: Sun Aug 13 18:16:42 2006
all DONE at: Sun Aug 13 18:16:42 2006
```

So what *did* change? Gone are the locks that we had to implement when using the thread module. Instead, we create a set of Thread objects. When each Thread is instantiated, we dutifully pass in the function (target) and arguments (args) and receive a Thread instance in return. The biggest difference between instantiating Thread (calling Thread()) and invoking thread.start_new_thread() is that the new thread does not begin execution right away. This is a useful synchronization feature, especially when you don't want the threads to start immediately.

Once all the threads have been allocated, we let them go off to the races by invoking each thread's start() method, but not a moment before that. And rather than having to manage a set of locks (allocating, acquiring, releasing, checking lock state, etc.), we simply call the join() method for each thread. join() will wait until a thread terminates, or, if provided, a timeout occurs. Use of join() appears much cleaner than an infinite loop that waits for locks to be released (which is why these locks are sometimes known as *spin locks*).

One other important aspect of join() is that it does not need to be called at all. Once threads are started, they will execute until their given function completes, at which point, they will exit. If your main thread has things to do other than wait for threads to complete (such as other processing or waiting for new client requests), it should do so. join() is useful only when you *want* to wait for thread completion.

Create Thread Instance, Passing in Callable Class Instance

A similar offshoot to passing in a function when creating a thread is having a callable class and passing in an instance for execution—this is the more object-oriented approach to MT programming. Such a callable class embodies an execution environment that is much more flexible than a function or choosing from a set of functions. You now have the power of a class object behind you, as opposed to a single function or a list/tuple of functions.

Adding our new class ThreadFunc to the code and making other slight modifications to mtsleepC.py, we get mtsleepD.py, shown in Example 4-5.

Example 4-5   Using Callable Classes (mtsleepD.py)

In this example, we pass in a callable class (instance) as opposed to just a function. It presents more of an object-oriented approach than mtsleepC.py.

```
1   #!/usr/bin/env python
2
3   import threading
4   from time import sleep, ctime
5
6   loops = [4,2]
7
8   class ThreadFunc(object):
9
10      def __init__(self, func, args, name=''):
11          self.name = name
12          self.func = func
13          self.args = args
14
15      def __call__(self):
16          self.func(*self.args)
17
```

(Continued)

Example 4-5   Using Callable classes (`mtsleepD.py`) *(Continued)*

```
18   def loop(nloop, nsec):
19       print 'start loop', nloop, 'at:', ctime()
20       sleep(nsec)
21       print 'loop', nloop, 'done at:', ctime()
22
23   def main():
24       print 'starting at:', ctime()
25       threads = []
26       nloops = range(len(loops))
27
28       for i in nloops:  # create all threads
29           t = threading.Thread(
30               target=ThreadFunc(loop, (i, loops[i]),
31               loop.__name__))
32           threads.append(t)
33
34       for i in nloops:  # start all threads
35           threads[i].start()
36
37       for i in nloops:  # wait for completion
38           threads[i].join()
39
40       print 'all DONE at:', ctime()
41
42   if __name__ == '__main__':
43       main()
```

When we run `mtsleepD.py`, we get the expected output:

```
$ mtsleepD.py
starting at: Sun Aug 13 18:49:17 2006
start loop 0 at: Sun Aug 13 18:49:17 2006
start loop 1 at: Sun Aug 13 18:49:17 2006
loop 1 done at: Sun Aug 13 18:49:19 2006
loop 0 done at: Sun Aug 13 18:49:21 2006
all DONE at: Sun Aug 13 18:49:21 2006
```

So what are the changes this time? The addition of the `ThreadFunc` class and a minor change to instantiate the `Thread` object, which also instantiates `ThreadFunc`, our callable class. In effect, we have a double instantiation going on here. Let's take a closer look at our `ThreadFunc` class.

We want to make this class general enough to use with functions other than our `loop()` function, so we added some new infrastructure, such as having this class hold the arguments for the function, the function itself, and also a function name string. The constructor `__init__()` just sets all the values.

When the `Thread` code calls our `ThreadFunc` object because a new thread is created, it will invoke the `__call__()` special method. Because we already have our set of arguments, we do not need to pass it to the `Thread()` constructor and can call the function directly.

Subclass Thread and Create Subclass Instance

The final introductory example involves subclassing Thread(), which turns out to be extremely similar to creating a callable class as in the previous example. Subclassing is a bit easier to read when you are creating your threads (lines 29–30). We will present the code for mtsleepE.py in Example 4-6 as well as the output obtained from its execution, and leave it as an exercise for you to compare mtsleepE.py to mtsleepD.py.

Example 4-6   Subclassing Thread (mtsleepE.py)

Rather than instantiating the Thread class, we subclass it. This gives us more flexibility in customizing our threading objects and simplifies the thread creation call.

```
1   #!/usr/bin/env python
2
3   import threading
4   from time import sleep, ctime
5
6   loops = (4, 2)
7
8   class MyThread(threading.Thread):
9       def __init__(self, func, args, name=''):
10          threading.Thread.__init__(self)
11          self.name = name
12          self.func = func
13          self.args = args
14
15      def run(self):
16          self.func(*self.args)
17
18  def loop(nloop, nsec):
19      print 'start loop', nloop, 'at:', ctime()
20      sleep(nsec)
21      print 'loop', nloop, 'done at:', ctime()
22
23  def main():
24      print 'starting at:', ctime()
25      threads = []
26      nloops = range(len(loops))
27
28      for i in nloops:
29          t = MyThread(loop, (i, loops[i]),
30              loop.__name__)
31          threads.append(t)
32
```

(Continued)

Example 4-6   Subclassing Thread (mtsleepE.py) *(Continued)*

```
33        for i in nloops:
34            threads[i].start()
35
36        for i in nloops:
37            threads[i].join()
38
39        print 'all DONE at:', ctime()'
40
41    if __name__ == '__main__':
42        main()
```

Here is the output for mtsleepE.py. Again, it's just as we expected:

```
$ mtsleepE.py
starting at: Sun Aug 13 19:14:26 2006
start loop 0 at: Sun Aug 13 19:14:26 2006
start loop 1 at: Sun Aug 13 19:14:26 2006
loop 1 done at: Sun Aug 13 19:14:28 2006
loop 0 done at: Sun Aug 13 19:14:30 2006
all DONE at: Sun Aug 13 19:14:30 2006
```

While you compare the source between the mtsleep4 and mtsleep5 modules, we want to point out the most significant changes: 1) our MyThread subclass constructor must first invoke the base class constructor (line 9), and 2) the former special method __call__() must be called run() in the subclass.

We now modify our MyThread class with some diagnostic output and store it in a separate module called myThread (look ahead to Example 4-7) and import this class for the upcoming examples. Rather than simply calling our functions, we also save the result to instance attribute self.res, and create a new method to retrieve that value, getResult().

Example 4-7   MyThread Subclass of Thread (myThread.py)

To generalize our subclass of Thread from mtsleepE.py, we move the subclass to a separate module and add a getResult() method for callables that produce return values.

```
1    #!/usr/bin/env python
2
3    import threading
4    from time import ctime
5
```

```
6    class MyThread(threading.Thread):
7      def __init__(self, func, args, name=''):
8          threading.Thread.__init__(self)
9          self.name = name
10         self.func = func
11         self.args = args
12
13     def getResult(self):
14         return self.res
15
16     def run(self):
17         print 'starting', self.name, 'at:', \
18             ctime()
19         self.res = self.func(*self.args)
20         print self.name, 'finished at:', \
21             ctime()
```

4.5.2   Other Threading Module Functions

In addition to the various synchronization and threading objects, the Threading module also has some supporting functions, as detailed in Table 4-4.

Table 4-4   threading Module Functions

Function	Description
activeCount/ active_count()[a]	Number of currently active Thread objects
currentThread()/ current_thread[a]	Returns the current Thread object
enumerate()	Returns list of all currently active Threads
settrace(*func*)[b]	Sets a trace *function* for all threads
setprofile(*func*)[b]	Sets a profile *function* for all threads
stack_size(*size*=0)[c]	Returns stack size of newly created threads; optional *size* can be set for subsequently created threads

a. CamelCase names deprecated and replaced starting in Python 2.6.
b. New in Python 2.3.
c. An alias to thread.stack_size(); (both) new in Python 2.5.

4.6   Comparing Single vs. Multithreaded Execution

The `mtfacfib.py` script, presented in Example 4-8 compares execution of the recursive Fibonacci, factorial, and summation functions. This script runs all three functions in a single-threaded manner. It then performs the same task by using threads to illustrate one of the advantages of having a threading environment.

Example 4-8   Fibonacci, Factorial, Summation (`mtfacfib.py`)

In this MT application, we execute three separate recursive functions—first in a single-threaded fashion, followed by the alternative with multiple threads.

```
1   #!/usr/bin/env python
2
3   from myThread import MyThread
4   from time import ctime, sleep
5
6   def fib(x):
7       sleep(0.005)
8       if x < 2: return 1
9       return (fib(x-2) + fib(x-1))
10
11  def fac(x):
12      sleep(0.1)
13      if x < 2: return 1
14      return (x * fac(x-1))
15
16  def sum(x):
17      sleep(0.1)
18      if x < 2: return 1
19      return (x + sum(x-1))
20
21  funcs = [fib, fac, sum]
22  n = 12
23
24  def main():
25      nfuncs = range(len(funcs))
26
27      print '*** SINGLE THREAD'
28      for i in nfuncs:
29          print 'starting', funcs[i].__name__, 'at:', \
30              ctime()
31          print funcs[i](n)
32          print funcs[i].__name__, 'finished at:', \
33              ctime()
34
35      print '\n*** MULTIPLE THREADS'
36      threads = []
```

```
37        for i in nfuncs:
38            t = MyThread(funcs[i], (n,),
39                funcs[i].__name__)
40            threads.append(t)
41
42        for i in nfuncs:
43            threads[i].start()
44
45        for i in nfuncs:
46            threads[i].join()
47            print threads[i].getResult()
48
49        print 'all DONE'
50
51    if __name__ == '__main__':
52        main()
```

Running in single-threaded mode simply involves calling the functions one at a time and displaying the corresponding results right after the function call.

When running in multithreaded mode, we do not display the result right away. Because we want to keep our MyThread class as general as possible (being able to execute callables that do and do not produce output), we wait until the end to call the getResult() method to finally show you the return values of each function call.

Because these functions execute so quickly (well, maybe except for the Fibonacci function), you will notice that we had to add calls to sleep() to each function to slow things down so that we can see how threading can improve performance, if indeed the actual work had varying execution times—you certainly wouldn't pad your work with calls to sleep(). Anyway, here is the output:

```
$ mtfacfib.py
*** SINGLE THREAD
starting fib at: Wed Nov 16 18:52:20 2011
233
fib finished at: Wed Nov 16 18:52:24 2011
starting fac at: Wed Nov 16 18:52:24 2011
479001600
fac finished at: Wed Nov 16 18:52:26 2011
starting sum at: Wed Nov 16 18:52:26 2011
78
sum finished at: Wed Nov 16 18:52:27 2011

*** MULTIPLE THREADS
starting fib at: Wed Nov 16 18:52:27 2011
starting fac at: Wed Nov 16 18:52:27 2011
starting sum at: Wed Nov 16 18:52:27 2011
```

```
fac finished at: Wed Nov 16 18:52:28 2011
sum finished at: Wed Nov 16 18:52:28 2011
fib finished at: Wed Nov 16 18:52:31 2011
233
479001600
78
all DONE
```

4.7   Multithreading in Practice

So far, none of the simplistic sample snippets we've seen so far represent code that you'd write in practice. They don't really do anything useful beyond demonstrating threads and the different ways that you can create them—the way we've started them up and wait for them to finish are all identical, and they all just sleep, too.

We also mentioned earlier in Section 4.3.1 that due to the fact that the Python Virtual Machine is single-threaded (the GIL), greater concurrency in Python is only possible when threading is applied to an I/O-bound application (versus CPU-bound applications, which only do round-robin), so let's look at an example of this, and for a further exercise, try to port it to Python 3 to give you a sense of what that process entails.

4.7.1   Book Rankings Example

The bookrank.py script shown in Example 4-9 is very staightforward. It goes to the one of my favorite online retailers, Amazon, and asks for the current rankings of books written by yours truly. In our sample code, you'll see a function, getRanking(), that uses a regular expression to pull out and return the current ranking plus showRanking(), which displays the result to the user.

Note that, according to their *Conditions of Use* guidelines, "*Amazon grants you a limited license to access and make personal use of this site and not to download (other than page caching) or modify it, or any portion of it, except with express written consent of Amazon.*" For our application, all we're doing is looking at the current book rankings for a specific book and then throwing everything away; we're not even caching the page.

Example 4-9 is our first (but nearly-final) attempt at bookrank.py, which is a non-threaded version.

Example 4-9   Book Rankings "Screenscraper" (bookrank.py)

This script makes calls to download book ranking information via separate threads.

```python
1   #!/usr/bin/env python
2
3   from atexit import register
4   from re import compile
5   from threading import Thread
6   from time import ctime
7   from urllib2 import urlopen as uopen
8
9   REGEX = compile('#([\d,]+) in Books ')
10  AMZN = 'http://amazon.com/dp/'
11  ISBNs = {
12      '0132269937': 'Core Python Programming',
13      '0132356139': 'Python Web Development with Django',
14      '0137143419': 'Python Fundamentals',
15  }
16
17  def getRanking(isbn):
18      page = uopen('%s%s' % (AMZN, isbn)) # or str.format()
19      data = page.read()
20      page.close()
21      return REGEX.findall(data)[0]
22
23  def _showRanking(isbn):
24      print '- %r ranked %s' % (
25          ISBNs[isbn], getRanking(isbn))
26
27  def _main():
28      print 'At', ctime(), 'on Amazon...'
29      for isbn in ISBNs:
30          _showRanking(isbn)
31
32  @register
33  def _atexit():
34      print 'all DONE at:', ctime()
35
36  if __name__ == '__main__':
37      main()
```

Line-by-Line Explanation

Lines 1–7

These are the startup and import lines. We'll use the `atexit.register()` function to tell us when the script is over (you'll see why later). We'll also use the regular expression `re.compile()` function for the pattern that matches a book's ranking on Amazon's product pages. Then, we save the `threading.Thread` import for future improvement (coming up a bit later), `time.ctime()` for the current timestamp string, and `urllib2.urlopen()` for accessing each link.

Lines 9–15

We use three constants in this script: `REGEX`, the regular expression object (compiled from the regex pattern that matches a book's ranking); `AMZN`, the base Amazon product link—all we need to complete each link is a book's International Standard Book Number (ISBN), which serves as a book's ID, differentiating one written work from all others. There are two standards: the ISBN-10 ten-character value and its successor, the ISBN-13 thirteen-character ISBN. Currently, Amazon's systems understand both ISBN types, so we'll just use ISBN-10 because they're shorter. These are stored in the `ISBNs` dictionary along with the corresponding book titles.

Lines 17–21

The purpose of `getRanking()` is to take an ISBN, create the final URL with which to communicate to Amazon's servers, and then call `urllib2.urlopen()` on it. We used the string format operator to put together the URL (on line 18) but if you're using version 2.6 and newer, you can also try the `str.format()` method, for example, `'{0}{1}'.format(AMZN,isbn)`.

Once you have the full URL, call `urllib2.urlopen()`—we shortened it to `uopen()`—and expect the file-like object back once the Web server has been contacted. Then the `read()` call is issued to download the entire Web page, and "file" is closed. If the regex is as precise as we have planned, there should only be exactly one match, so we grab it from the generated list (any additional would be dropped) and return it back to the caller.

Lines 23–25

The `_showRanking()` function is just a short snippet of code that takes an ISBN, looks up the title of the book it represents, calls `getRanking()` to get its current ranking on Amazon's Web site, and then outputs both of these values to the user. The leading single-underscore notation indicates that this is a special function only to be used by code within this module and should not be imported by any other application using this as a library or utility module.

Lines 27–30

_main() is also a special function, only executed if this module is run directly from the command-line (and not imported for use by another module). It shows the start and end times (to let users know how long it took to run the entire script) and calls _showRanking() for each ISBN to lookup and display each book's current ranking on Amazon.

Lines 32–37

These lines present something completely different. What is atexit.register()? It's a function (used in a decorator role here) that registers an *exit function* with the Python interpreter, meaning it's requesting a special function be called just before the script quits. (Instead of the decorator, you could have also done register (_atexit()).

Why are we using it here? Well, right now, it's definitely not needed. The print statement could very well go at the end of _main() in lines 27–31, but that's not a really great place for it. Plus this is functionality that you might really want to use in a real production application at some point. We assume that you know what lines 36–37 are about, so onto the output:

```
$ python bookrank.py
At Wed Mar 30 22:11:19 2011 PDT on Amazon...
- 'Core Python Programming' ranked 87,118
- 'Python Fundamentals' ranked 851,816
- 'Python Web Development with Django' ranked 184,735
all DONE at: Wed Mar 30 22:11:25 2011
```

If you're wondering, we've separated the process of retrieving (getRanking()) and displaying (_showRanking() and _main()) the data in case you wish to do something *other* than dumping the results out to the user via the terminal. In practice, you might need to send this data back via a Web template, store it in a database, text it to a mobile phone, etc. If you put all of this code into a single function, it makes it harder to reuse and/or repurpose.

Also, if Amazon changes the layout of their product pages, you might need to modify the regular expression "screenscraper" to continue to be able to extract the data from the product page. By the way, using a regex (or even plain old string processing) for this simple example is fine, but you might need a more powerful markup parser, such as HTMLParser from the standard library or third-party tools like BeautifulSoup, html5lib, or lxml. (We demonstrate a few of these in Chapter 9, "Web Clients and Servers.")

Add threading

Okay, you don't have to tell me that this is still a silly single-threaded program. We're going to change our application to use threads instead. It is an I/O-bound application, so this is a good candidate to do so. To simplify things, we won't use any of the classes and object-oriented programming; instead, we'll use threading.Thread directly, so you can think of this more as a derivative of mtsleepC.py than any of the succeeding examples. We'll just spawn the threads and start them up immediately.

Take your application and modify the _showRanking(isbn) call to the following:

```
Thread(target=_showRanking, args=(isbn,)).start().
```

That's it! Now you have your final version of bookrank.py and can see that the application (typically) runs faster because of the added concurrency. But, your still only as fast as the slowest response.

```
$ python bookrank.py
At Thu Mar 31 10:11:32 2011 on Amazon...
 - 'Python Fundamentals' ranked 869,010
 - 'Core Python Programming' ranked 36,481
 - 'Python Web Development with Django' ranked 219,228
all DONE at: Thu Mar 31 10:11:35 2011
```

As you can see from the output, instead of taking six seconds as our single-threaded version, our threaded version only takes three. Also note that the output is in "by completion" order, which is variable, versus the single-threaded display. With the non-threaded version, the order is always by key, but now the queries all happen in parallel with the output coming as each thread completes its work.

In the earlier mtsleepX.py examples, we used Thread.join() on all the threads to block execution until each thread exits. This effectively prevents the main thread from continuing until all threads are done, so the print statement of "all DONE at" is called at the correct time.

In those examples, it's not necessary to join() all the threads because none of them are daemon threads. The main thread is not going to exit the script until all the spawned threads have completed anyway. Because of this reasoning, we've dropped all the join()s in mtsleepF.py. However, realize that if we displayed "all done" from the same spot, it would be incorrect.

The main thread would have displayed "all done" before the threads have completed, so we can't have that print call above in _main(). There are only 2 places we can put this print: after line 37 when _main() returns (the very final line executed of our script), or use atexit.register() to register an exit function. Because the latter is something we haven't discussed before *and* might be something useful to you later on, we thought this would be a good place to introduce it to you. This is also one interface that remains constant between Python 2 and 3, our upcoming challenge.

Porting to Python 3

The next thing we want is a working Python 3 version of this script. As projects and applications continue down the migration path, this is something with which you need to become familiar, anyway. Fortunately, there are few tools to help you, one of them being the 2to3 tool. There are generally two ways of using it:

3.x

```
$ 2to3 foo.py     # only output diff
$ 2to3 -w foo.py  # overwrites w/3.x code
```

In the first command, the 2to3 tool just displays the differences between the version 2.x original script and its generated 3.x equivalent. The -w flag instructs 2to3 to overwrite the original script with the newly minted 3.x version while renaming the 2.x version to foo.py.bak.

Let's run 2to3 on bookrank.py, writing over the existing file. It not only spits out the differences, it also saves the new version, as we just described:

```
$ 2to3 -w bookrank.py
RefactoringTool: Skipping implicit fixer: buffer
RefactoringTool: Skipping implicit fixer: idioms
RefactoringTool: Skipping implicit fixer: set_literal
RefactoringTool: Skipping implicit fixer: ws_comma
--- bookrank.py (original)
+++ bookrank.py (refactored)
@@ -4,7 +4,7 @@
 from re import compile
 from threading import Thread
 from time import ctime
-from urllib2 import urlopen as uopen
+from urllib.request import urlopen as uopen

 REGEX = compile('#([\d,]+) in Books ')
 AMZN = 'http://amazon.com/dp/'
@@ -21,17 +21,17 @@
     return REGEX.findall(data)[0]

 def _showRanking(isbn):
-    print '- %r ranked %s' % (
-        ISBNs[isbn], getRanking(isbn))
+    print('- %r ranked %s' % (
+        ISBNs[isbn], getRanking(isbn)))
```

```
    def _main():
-       print 'At', ctime(), 'on Amazon...'
+       print('At', ctime(), 'on Amazon...')
        for isbn in ISBNs:
            Thread(target=_showRanking,
args=(isbn,)).start()#_showRanking(isbn)

    @register
    def _atexit():
-       print 'all DONE at:', ctime()
+       print('all DONE at:', ctime())

    if __name__ == '__main__':
        _main()
RefactoringTool: Files that were modified:
RefactoringTool: bookrank.py
```

The following step is optional for readers, but we renamed our files to
bookrank.py and bookrank3.py by using these POSIX commands (Windows-
based PC users should use the ren command):

```
$ mv bookrank.py bookrank3.py
$ mv bookrank.py.bak bookrank.py
```

If you try to run our new next-generation script, it's probably wishful
thinking that it's a perfect translation and that you're done with your
work. Something bad happened, and you'll get the following exception in
each thread (this output is for just one thread as they're all the same):

```
$ python3 bookrank3.py
Exception in thread Thread-1:
Traceback (most recent call last):
  File "/Library/Frameworks/Python.framework/Versions/
      3.2/lib/python3.2/threading.py", line 736, in
      _bootstrap_inner
    self.run()
  File "/Library/Frameworks/Python.framework/Versions/
      3.2/lib/python3.2/threading.py", line 689, in run
    self._target(*self._args, **self._kwargs)
  File "bookrank3.py", line 25, in _showRanking
    ISBNs[isbn], getRanking(isbn)))
  File "bookrank3.py", line 21, in getRanking
    return REGEX.findall(data)[0]
TypeError: can't use a string pattern on a bytes-like object
        :
```

Darn it! Apparently the problem is that the regular expression is a (Unicode) string, whereas the data that comes back from urlopen() file-like
object's read() method is an ASCII/bytes string. The fix here is to compile
a bytes object instead of a text string. Therefore, change line 9 so that
re.compile() is compiling a bytes string (by adding the bytes string. To

do this, add the `bytes` string designation b just before the opening quote, as shown here:

```
REGEX = compile(b'#([\d,]+) in Books ')
```

Now let's try it again:

```
$ python3 bookrank3.py
At Sun Apr  3 00:45:46 2011 on Amazon...
- 'Core Python Programming' ranked b'108,796'
- 'Python Web Development with Django' ranked b'268,660'
- 'Python Fundamentals' ranked b'969,149'
all DONE at: Sun Apr  3 00:45:49 2011
```

Aargh! What's wrong now? Well, it's a *little* bit better (no errors), but the output looks weird. The ranking values grabbed by the regular expressions, when passed to `str()` show the b and quotes. Your first instinct might be to try ugly string slicing:

```
>>> x = b'xxx'
>>> repr(x)
"b'xxx'"
>>> str(x)
"b'xxx'"
>>> str(x)[2:-1]
'xxx'
```

However, it's just more appropriate to convert it to a real (Unicode string, perhaps using UTF-8:

```
>>> str(x, 'utf-8')
'xxx'
```

To do that in our script, make a similar change to line 53 so that it now reads as:

```
 return str(REGEX.findall(data)[0], 'utf-8')
```

Now, the output of our Python 3 script matches that of our Python 2 script:

```
$ python3 bookrank3.py
At Sun Apr  3 00:47:31 2011 on Amazon...
- 'Python Fundamentals' ranked 969,149
- 'Python Web Development with Django' ranked 268,660
- 'Core Python Programming' ranked 108,796
all DONE at: Sun Apr  3 00:47:34 2011
```

In general, you'll find that porting from version 2.x to version 3.x follows a similar pattern: you ensure that all your unit and integration tests pass, knock down all the basics using 2to3 (and other tools), and then clean up the aftermath by getting the code to run and pass the same tests. We'll try this exercise again with our next example which demonstrates the use of synchronization with threads.

4.7.2   Synchronization Primitives

In the main part of this chapter, we looked at basic threading concepts and how to utilize threading in Python applications. However, we neglected to mention one very important aspect of threaded programming: synchronization. Often times in threaded code, you will have certain functions or blocks in which you don't (or shouldn't) want more than one thread executing. Usually these involve modifying a database, updating a file, or anything similar that might cause a race condition, which, if you recall from earlier in the chapter, is when different code paths or behaviors are exhibited or inconsistent data was rendered if one thread ran before another one and vice versa. (You can read more about race conditions on the Wikipedia page at http://en.wikipedia.org/wiki/Race_condition.)

Such cases require synchronization. Synchronization is used when any number of threads can come up to one of these critical sections of code (http://en.wikipedia.org/wiki/Critical_section), but only one is allowed through at any given time. The programmer makes these determinations and chooses the appropriate synchronization primitives, or thread control mechanisms to perform the synchronization. There are different types of process synchronization (see http://en.wikipedia.org/wiki/Synchronization_ (computer_ science)) and Python supports several types, giving you enough choices to select the best one to get the job done.

We introduced them all to you earlier at the beginning of this section, so here we'd like to demonstrate a couple of sample scripts that use two types of synchronization primitives: locks/mutexes, and semaphores. A lock is the simplest and lowest-level of all these mechanisms; while semaphores are for situations in which multiple threads are contending for a finite resource. Locks are easier to explain, so we'll start there, and then discuss semaphores.

4.7.3   Locking Example

Locks have two states: locked and unlocked (surprise, surprise). They support only two functions: acquire and release. These actions mean exactly what you think.

As multiple threads vie for a lock, the first thread to acquire one is permitted to go in and execute code in the critical section. All other threads coming along are blocked until the first thread wraps up, exits the critical section, and releases the lock. At this moment, any of the other waiting threads can acquire the lock and enter the critical section. Note that there is no ordering (first come, first served) for the blocked threads; the selection of the "winning" thread is not deterministic and can vary between different implementations of Python.

Let's see why locks are necessary. `mtsleepF.py` is an application that spawns a random number of threads, each of which outputs when it has completed. Take a look at the core chunk of (Python 2) source here:

```python
from atexit import register
from random import randrange
from threading import Thread, currentThread
from time import sleep, ctime

class CleanOutputSet(set):
    def __str__(self):
        return ', '.join(x for x in self)

loops = (randrange(2,5) for x in xrange(randrange(3,7)))
remaining = CleanOutputSet()

def loop(nsec):
    myname = currentThread().name
    remaining.add(myname)
    print '[%s] Started %s' % (ctime(), myname)
    sleep(nsec)
    remaining.remove(myname)
    print '[%s] Completed %s (%d secs)' % (
        ctime(), myname, nsec)
    print '    (remaining: %s)' % (remaining or 'NONE')

def _main():
    for pause in loops:
        Thread(target=loop, args=(pause,)).start()

@register
def _atexit():
    print 'all DONE at:', ctime()
```

We'll have a longer line-by-line explanation once we've finalized our code with locking, but basically what `mtsleepF.py` does is expand on our earlier examples. Like `bookrank.py`, we simplify the code a bit by skipping object-oriented programming, drop the list of thread objects and thread `join()`s, and (re)use `atexit.register()` (for all the same reasons as `bookrank.py`).

Also as a minor change to the earlier `mtsleepX.py` examples, instead of hardcoding a pair of loops/threads sleeping for 4 and 2 seconds, respectively, we wanted to mix it up a little by randomly creating between 3 and 6 threads, each of which can sleep anywhere between 2 and 4 seconds.

One of the new features that stands out is the use of a set to hold the names of the remaining threads still running. The reason why we're sub-classing the set object instead of using it directly is because we just want to demonstrate another use case, altering the default printable string representation of a set.

When you display a set, you get output such as set([X, Y, Z, ...]). The issue is that the users of our application don't (and shouldn't) need to know anything about sets or that we're using them. We just want to display something like X, Y, Z, ..., instead; thus the reason why we derived from set and implemented its __str__() method.

With this change, and if you're lucky, the output will be all nice and lined up properly:

```
$ python mtsleepF.py
[Sat Apr  2 11:37:26 2011] Started Thread-1
[Sat Apr  2 11:37:26 2011] Started Thread-2
[Sat Apr  2 11:37:26 2011] Started Thread-3
[Sat Apr  2 11:37:29 2011] Completed Thread-2 (3 secs)
    (remaining: Thread-3, Thread-1)
[Sat Apr  2 11:37:30 2011] Completed Thread-1 (4 secs)
    (remaining: Thread-3)
[Sat Apr  2 11:37:30 2011] Completed Thread-3 (4 secs)
    (remaining: NONE)
all DONE at: Sat Apr  2 11:37:30 2011
```

However, if you're *un*lucky, you might get strange output such as this pair of example executions:

```
$ python mtsleepF.py
[Sat Apr  2 11:37:09 2011] Started Thread-1
 [Sat Apr  2 11:37:09 2011] Started Thread-2
[Sat Apr  2 11:37:09 2011] Started Thread-3
[Sat Apr  2 11:37:12 2011] Completed Thread-1 (3 secs)
 [Sat Apr  2 11:37:12 2011] Completed Thread-2 (3 secs)
    (remaining: Thread-3)
    (remaining: Thread-3)
[Sat Apr  2 11:37:12 2011] Completed Thread-3 (3 secs)
    (remaining: NONE)
all DONE at: Sat Apr  2 11:37:12 2011

$ python mtsleepF.py
[Sat Apr  2 11:37:56 2011] Started Thread-1
[Sat Apr  2 11:37:56 2011] Started Thread-2
 [Sat Apr  2 11:37:56 2011] Started Thread-3
[Sat Apr  2 11:37:56 2011] Started Thread-4

[Sat Apr  2 11:37:58 2011] Completed Thread-2 (2 secs)
 [Sat Apr  2 11:37:58 2011] Completed Thread-4 (2 secs)
    (remaining: Thread-3, Thread-1)
    (remaining: Thread-3, Thread-1)
```

```
[Sat Apr  2 11:38:00 2011] Completed Thread-1 (4 secs)
    (remaining: Thread-3)
[Sat Apr  2 11:38:00 2011] Completed Thread-3 (4 secs)
    (remaining: NONE)
all DONE at: Sat Apr  2 11:38:00 2011
```

What's wrong? Well, for one thing, the output might appear partially garbled (because multiple threads might be executing I/O in parallel). You can see some examples of preceding code in which the output is interleaved, too. Another problem identified is when you have two threads modifying the same variable (the set containing the names of the remaining threads).

Both the I/O and access to the same data structure are part of critical sections; therefore, we need locks to prevent more than one thread from entering them at the same time. To add locking, you need to add a line of code to import the Lock (or RLock) object and create a lock object, so add/modify your code to contain these lines in the right places:

```
from threading import Thread, Lock, currentThread
lock = Lock()
```

Now you mut *use* your lock. The following code highlights the acquire() and release() calls that we should insert into our loop() function:

```
def loop(nsec):
    myname = currentThread().name
    lock.acquire()
    remaining.add(myname)
    print '[%s] Started %s' % (ctime(), myname)
    lock.release()
    sleep(nsec)
    lock.acquire()
    remaining.remove(myname)
    print '[%s] Completed %s (%d secs)' % (
        ctime(), myname, nsec)
    print '    (remaining: %s)' % (remaining or 'NONE')
    lock.release()
```

Once the changes are made, you should no longer get strange output:

```
$ python mtsleepF.py
[Sun Apr  3 23:16:59 2011] Started Thread-1
[Sun Apr  3 23:16:59 2011] Started Thread-2
[Sun Apr  3 23:16:59 2011] Started Thread-3
[Sun Apr  3 23:16:59 2011] Started Thread-4
[Sun Apr  3 23:17:01 2011] Completed Thread-3 (2 secs)
    (remaining: Thread-4, Thread-2, Thread-1)
[Sun Apr  3 23:17:01 2011] Completed Thread-4 (2 secs)
    (remaining: Thread-2, Thread-1)
```

```
[Sun Apr  3 23:17:02 2011] Completed Thread-1 (3 secs)
    (remaining: Thread-2)
[Sun Apr  3 23:17:03 2011] Completed Thread-2 (4 secs)
    (remaining: NONE)
all DONE at: Sun Apr  3 23:17:03 2011
```

The modified (and final) version of `mtsleepF.py` is shown in Example 4-10.

Example 4-10   Locks and More Randomness (`mtsleepF.py`)

In this example, we demonstrate the use of locks and other threading tools.

```
1    #!/usr/bin/env python
2
3    from atexit import register
4    from random import randrange
5    from threading import Thread, Lock, currentThread
6    from time import sleep, ctime
7
8    class CleanOutputSet(set):
9        def __str__(self):
10           return ', '.join(x for x in self)
11
12   lock = Lock()
13   loops = (randrange(2,5) for x in xrange(randrange(3,7)))
14   remaining = CleanOutputSet()
15
16   def loop(nsec):
17       myname = currentThread().name
18       lock.acquire()
19       remaining.add(myname)
20       print '[%s] Started %s' % (ctime(), myname)
21       lock.release()
22       sleep(nsec)
23       lock.acquire()
24       remaining.remove(myname)
25       print '[%s] Completed %s (%d secs)' % (
26           ctime(), myname, nsec)
27       print '    (remaining: %s)' % (remaining or 'NONE')
28       lock.release()
29
30   def _main():
31       for pause in loops:
32           Thread(target=loop, args=(pause,)).start()
33
34   @register
35   def _atexit():
36       print 'all DONE at:', ctime()
37
38   if __name__ == '__main__':
39       _main()
```

Line-by-Line Explanation

Lines 1–6

These are the usual startup and import lines. Be aware that `threading.currentThread()` is renamed to `threading.current_thread()` starting in version 2.6 but with the older name remaining intact for backward compatibility.

2.6

Lines 8–10

This is the set subclass we described earlier. It contains an implementation of `__str__()` to change the output from the default to a comma-delimited string of its elements.

Lines 12–14

Our global variables consist of the lock, an instance of our modified set from above, and a random number of threads (between three and six), each of which will pause or sleep for between two and four seconds.

Lines 16–28

The `loop()` function saves the name of the current thread executing it, then acquires a lock so that the addition of that name to the `remaining` set and an output indicating the thread has started is atomic (where no other thread can enter this critical section). After releasing the lock, this thread sleeps for the predetermined random number of seconds, then re-acquires the lock in order to do its final output before releasing it.

Lines 30–39

The `_main()` function is only executed if this script was not imported for use elsewhere. Its job is to spawn and execute each of the threads. As mentioned before, we use `atexit.register()` to register the `_atexit()` function that the interpreter can execute before exiting.

As an alternative to maintaining your own set of currently running threads, you might consider using `threading.enumerate()`, which returns a list of all threads that are still running (including daemon threads, but not those which haven't started yet). We didn't use it for our example here because it gives us two extra threads that we need to remove to keep our output short: the current thread (because it hasn't completed yet) as well as the main thread (not necessary to show this either).

Also don't forget that you can also use the `str.format()` method instead of the string format operator if you're using Python 2.6 or newer (including version 3.x). In other words, this `print` statement

```
print '[%s] Started %s' % (ctime(), myname)
```

2.6-2.7   can be replaced by this one in 2.6+

```
print '[{0}] Started {1}'.format(ctime(), myname)
```

3.x   or this call to the `print()` function in version 3.x:

```
print('[{0}] Started {1}'.format(ctime(), myname))
```

If you just want a count of currently running threads, you can use `threading.activeCount()` (renamed to `active_count()` starting in version 2.6), instead.

Using Context Management

2.5   Another option for those of you using Python 2.5 and newer is to have neither the lock `acquire()` nor `release()` calls at all, simplifying your code. When using the `with` statement, the context manager for each object is responsible for calling `acquire()` before entering the suite and `release()` when the block has completed execution.

The `threading` module objects `Lock`, `RLock`, `Condition`, `Semaphore`, and `BoundedSemaphore`, all have context managers, meaning they can be used with the **with** statement. By using **with**, you can further simplify `loop()` to:

```
from __future__ import with_statement # 2.5 only
def loop(nsec):
    myname = currentThread().name
    with lock:
        remaining.add(myname)
        print '[%s] Started %s' % (ctime(), myname)
    sleep(nsec)
    with lock:
        remaining.remove(myname)
        print '[%s] Completed %s (%d secs)' % (
            ctime(), myname, nsec)
        print '    (remaining: %s)' % (
            remaining or 'NONE',)
```

Porting to Python 3

3.x   Now let's do a seemingly easy port to Python 3.x by running the 2to3 tool on the preceding script (this output is truncated because we saw a full `diff` dump earlier):

```
$ 2to3 -w mtsleepF.py
RefactoringTool: Skipping implicit fixer: buffer
RefactoringTool: Skipping implicit fixer: idioms
RefactoringTool: Skipping implicit fixer: set_literal
RefactoringTool: Skipping implicit fixer: ws_comma
     :
RefactoringTool: Files that were modified:
RefactoringTool: mtsleepF.py
```

After renaming `mtsleepF.py` to `mtsleepF3.py` and `mtsleep.py.bak` to `mtsleepF.py`, we discover, much to our pleasant surprise, that this is one script that ported perfectly, with no issues:

```
$ python3 mtsleepF3.py
[Sun Apr  3 23:29:39 2011] Started Thread-1
[Sun Apr  3 23:29:39 2011] Started Thread-2
[Sun Apr  3 23:29:39 2011] Started Thread-3
[Sun Apr  3 23:29:41 2011] Completed Thread-3 (2 secs)
    (remaining: Thread-2, Thread-1)
[Sun Apr  3 23:29:42 2011] Completed Thread-2 (3 secs)
    (remaining: Thread-1)
[Sun Apr  3 23:29:43 2011] Completed Thread-1 (4 secs)
    (remaining: NONE)
all DONE at: Sun Apr  3 23:29:43 2011
```

Now let's take our knowledge of locks, introduce semaphores, and look at an example that uses both.

4.7.4   Semaphore Example

As stated earlier, locks are pretty simple to understand and implement. It's also fairly easy to decide when you should need them. However, if the situation is more complex, you might need a more powerful synchronization primitive, instead. For applications with finite resources, using semaphores might be a better bet.

Semaphores are some of the oldest synchronization primitives out there. They're basically counters that decrement when a resource is being consumed (and increment again when the resource is released). You can think of semaphores representing their resources as either available or unavailable. The action of consuming a resource and decrementing the counter is traditionally called P() (from the Dutch word probeer/proberen) but is also known as *wait, try, acquire, pend,* or *procure.* Conversely, when a thread is done with a resource, it needs to return it back to the pool. To do this, the action used is named "V()" (from the Dutch word verhogen/verhoog) but also known as *signal, increment, release, post, vacate.* Python simplifies all the naming and uses the same function/method names as locks: acquire and release. Semaphores are more flexible than locks because you can have multiple threads, each using one of the instances of the finite resource.

For our example, we're going to simulate an oversimplified candy vending machine as an example. This particular machine has only five slots available to hold inventory (candy bars). If all slots are taken, no more candy can be added to the machine, and similarly, if there are no more of one particular type of candy bar, consumers wishing to purchase that product are out-of-luck. We can track these finite resources (candy slots) by using a semaphore.

Example 4-11 shows the source code (candy.py).

Example 4-11   Candy Vending Machine and Semaphores (candy.py)

This script uses locks and semaphores to simulate a candy vending machine.

```
1    #!/usr/bin/env python
2
3    from atexit import register
4    from random import randrange
5    from threading import BoundedSemaphore, Lock, Thread
6    from time import sleep, ctime
7
8    lock = Lock()
9    MAX = 5
10   candytray = BoundedSemaphore(MAX)
11
12   def refill():
13       lock.acquire()
14       print 'Refilling candy...',
15       try:
16           candytray.release()
17       except ValueError:
18           print 'full, skipping'
19       else:
20           print 'OK'
21       lock.release()
22
23   def buy():
24       lock.acquire()
25       print 'Buying candy...',
26       if candytray.acquire(False):
27           print 'OK'
28       else:
29           print 'empty, skipping'
30       lock.release()
31
```

```
32   def producer(loops):
33       for i in xrange(loops):
34           refill()
35           sleep(randrange(3))
36
37   def consumer(loops):
38       for i in xrange(loops):
39           buy()
40           sleep(randrange(3))
41
42   def _main():
43       print 'starting at:', ctime()
44       nloops = randrange(2, 6)
45       print 'THE CANDY MACHINE (full with %d bars)!' % MAX
46       Thread(target=consumer, args=(randrange(
47           nloops, nloops+MAX+2),)).start() # buyer
48       Thread(target=producer, args=(nloops,)).start() #vndr
49
50   @register
51   def _atexit():
52       print 'all DONE at:', ctime()
53
54   if __name__ == '__main__':
55       _main()
```

Line-by-Line Explanation

Lines 1–6

The startup and import lines are quite similar to examples earlier in this chapter. The only thing new is the semaphore. The threading module comes with two semaphore classes, Semaphore and BoundedSemaphore. As you know, semaphores are really just counters; they start off with some fixed number of a finite resource.

This counter decrements when one unit of this is allocated, and when that unit is returned to the pool, the counter increments. The additional feature you get with a BoundedSemaphore is that the counter can never increment beyond its initial value; in other words, it prevents the aberrant use case where a semaphore is released more times than it's acquired.

Lines 8–10

The global variables in this script are the lock, a constant representing the maximum number of items that can be inventoried, and the tray of candy.

Lines 12–21

The refill() function is performed when the owner of the fictitious vending machines comes to add one more item to inventory. The entire routine represents a critical section; this is why acquiring the lock is the only way to execute all lines. The code outputs its action to the user as well as warns when someone has exceeded the maximum inventory (lines 17–18).

Lines 23–30

buy() is the converse of refill(); it allows a consumer to acquire one unit of inventory. The conditional (line 26) detects when all finite resources have been consumed already. The counter can never go below zero, so this call would normally block until the counter is incremented again. By passing the nonblocking flag as False, this instructs the call to not block but to return a False if it *would've* blocked, indicating no more resources.

Lines 32–40

The producer() and consumer() functions merely loop and make corresponding calls to refill() and buy(), pausing momentarily between calls.

Lines 42–55

The remainder of the code contains the call to _main() if the script was executed from the command-line, the registration of the exit function, and finally, _main(), which seeds the newly created pair of threads representing the producer and consumer of the candy inventory.

The additional math in the creation of the consumer/buyer is to randomly suggest positive bias where a customer might actually consume more candy bars than the vendor/producer puts in the machine (otherwise, the code would never enter the situation in which the consumer attempts to buy a candy bar from an empty machine).

Running the script results in output similar to the following:

```
$ python candy.py
starting at: Mon Apr  4 00:56:02 2011
THE CANDY MACHINE (full with 5 bars)!
Buying candy... OK
Refilling candy... OK
Refilling candy... full, skipping
Buying candy... OK
Buying candy... OK
Refilling candy... OK
Buying candy... OK
Buying candy... OK
Buying candy... OK
all DONE at: Mon Apr  4 00:56:08 2011
```

CORE TIP: Debugging might involve intervention

At some point, you might need to debug a script that uses semaphores, but to do this, you might need to know exactly what value is in the semaphore's counter at any given time. In one of the exercises at the end of the chapter, you will implement such a solution to `candy.py`, perhaps calling it `candydebug.py`, and give it the ability to display the counter's value. To do this, you'll need to look at the source code for `threading.py` (and probably in both the Python 2 and Python 3 versions).

You'll discover that the `threading` module's synchronization primitives are not class names even though they use CamelCase capitalization to look like a class. In fact, they're really just one-line functions that instantiate the objects you're expecting. There are two problems to consider: the first one is that you can't subclass them (because they're functions); the second problem is that the variable name changed between version 2.x and 3.x.

3.x

The entire issue could be avoided if the object gives you clean/easy access to a counter, which it doesn't. You can directly access the counter's value because it's just an attribute of the class, as we just mentioned, the variable name changed from `self.__value`, meaning `self._Semaphore__value`, in Python 2 to `self._value` in Python 3.

For developers, the cleanest application programming interface (API) (at least in our opinion) is to derive from `threading._BoundedSemaphore` class and implement an `__len__()` method but use the correct counter value we just discussed if you plan to support this on both version 2.x and version 3.x.

Porting to Python 3

Similar to `mtsleepF.py`, `candy.py` is another example of how the `2to3` tool is sufficient to generate a working Python 3 version, which we have renamed to `candy3.py`. We'll leave this as an exercise for the reader to confirm.

Summary

We've demonstrated only a couple of the synchronization primitives that come with the `threading` module. There are plenty more for you to explore. However, keep in mind that that's still only what they are: "primitives." There's nothing wrong with using them to build your own classes and data structures that are thread-safe. The Python Standard Library comes with one, the `Queue` object.

4.8   Producer-Consumer Problem and the Queue/queue Module

The final example illustrates the producer-consumer scenario in which a producer of goods or services creates goods and places it in a data structure such as a queue. The amount of time between producing goods is nondeterministic, as is the consumer consuming the goods produced by the producer.

3.x

We use the Queue module (Python 2.x; renamed to queue in version 3.x) to provide an interthread communication mechanism that allows threads to share data with each other. In particular, we create a queue into which the producer (thread) places new goods and the consumer (thread) consumes them. Table 4-5 itemizes the various attributes that can be found in this module.

Table 4-5   Common Queue/queue Module Attributes

Attribute	Description
Queue/queue *Module Classes*	
Queue(*maxsize*=0)	Creates a FIFO queue of given *maxsize* where inserts block until there is more room, or (if omitted), unbounded
LifoQueue(*maxsize*=0)	Creates a LIFO queue of given *maxsize* where inserts block until there is more room, or (if omitted), unbounded
PriorityQueue(*maxsize*=0)	Creates a priority queue of given *maxsize* where inserts block until there is more room, or (if omitted), unbounded
Queue/queue *Exceptions*	
Empty	Raised when a get*() method called for an empty queue
Full	Raised when a put*() method called for a full queue

Attribute	Description
Queue/queue *Object Methods*	
qsize()	Returns queue size (approximate, whereas queue may be getting updated by other threads)
empty()	Returns True if queue empty, False otherwise
full()	Returns True if queue full, False otherwise
put(*item*, *block*=True, *timeout*=None)	Puts *item* in queue; if *block* True (the default) and *timeout* is None, blocks until room is available; if *timeout* is positive, blocks at most timeout seconds or if *block* False, raises the Empty exception
put_nowait(*item*)	Same as put(item, False)
get(*block*=True, *timeout*=None)	Gets *item* from queue, if *block* given (not 0), block until an item is available
get_nowait()	Same as get(False)
task_done()	Used to indicate work on an enqueued item completed, used with join() below
join()	Blocks until all items in queue have been processed and signaled by a call to task_done() above

We'll use Example 4-12 (prodcons.py), to demonstrate producer-consumer Queue/queue. The following is the output from one execution of this script:

```
$ prodcons.py
starting writer at: Sun Jun 18 20:27:07 2006
producing object for Q... size now 1
starting reader at: Sun Jun 18 20:27:07 2006
consumed object from Q... size now 0
producing object for Q... size now 1
consumed object from Q... size now 0
producing object for Q... size now 1
producing object for Q... size now 2
producing object for Q... size now 3
consumed object from Q... size now 2
consumed object from Q... size now 1
writer finished at: Sun Jun 18 20:27:17 2006
consumed object from Q... size now 0
reader finished at: Sun Jun 18 20:27:25 2006
all DONE
```

Example 4-12   Producer-Consumer Problem (`prodcons.py`)

This implementation of the Producer–Consumer problem uses `Queue` objects and a random number of goods produced (and consumed). The producer and consumer are individually—and concurrently—executing threads.

```python
1   #!/usr/bin/env python
2
3   from random import randint
4   from time import sleep
5   from Queue import Queue
6   from myThread import MyThread
7
8   def writeQ(queue):
9       print 'producing object for Q...',
10      queue.put('xxx', 1)
11      print "size now", queue.qsize()
12
13  def readQ(queue):
14      val = queue.get(1)
15      print 'consumed object from Q... size now', \
16              queue.qsize()
17
18  def writer(queue, loops):
19      for i in range(loops):
20          writeQ(queue)
21          sleep(randint(1, 3))
22
23  def reader(queue, loops):
24      for i in range(loops):
25          readQ(queue)
26          sleep(randint(2, 5))
27
28  funcs = [writer, reader]
29  nfuncs = range(len(funcs))
30
31  def main():
32      nloops = randint(2, 5)
33      q = Queue(32)
34
35      threads = []
36      for i in nfuncs:
37          t = MyThread(funcs[i], (q, nloops),
38              funcs[i].__name__)
39          threads.append(t)
40
41      for i in nfuncs:
42          threads[i].start()
43
44      for i in nfuncs:
45          threads[i].join()
46
47      print 'all DONE'
48
49  if __name__ == '__main__':
50      main()
```

As you can see, the producer and consumer do not necessarily alternate in execution. (Thank goodness for random numbers!) Seriously, though, real life is generally random and non-deterministic.

Line-by-Line Explanation

Lines 1–6

In this module, we use the `Queue.Queue` object as well as our thread class `myThread.MyThread`, seen earlier. We use `random.randint()` to make production and consumption somewhat varied. (Note that `random.randint()` works just like `random.randrange()` but is *inclusive* of the upper/end value).

Lines 8–16

The `writeQ()` and `readQ()` functions each have a specific purpose: to place an object in the queue—we are using the string `'xxx'`, for example—and to consume a queued object, respectively. Notice that we are producing one object and reading one object each time.

Lines 18–26

The `writer()` is going to run as a single thread whose sole purpose is to produce an item for the queue, wait for a bit, and then do it again, up to the specified number of times, chosen randomly per script execution. The `reader()` will do likewise, with the exception of consuming an item, of course.

You will notice that the random number of seconds that the writer sleeps is in general shorter than the amount of time the reader sleeps. This is to discourage the reader from trying to take items from an empty queue. By giving the writer a shorter time period of waiting, it is more likely that there will already be an object for the reader to consume by the time their turn rolls around again.

Lines 28–29

These are just setup lines to set the total number of threads that are to be spawned and executed.

Lines 31–47

Finally, we have our `main()` function, which should look quite similar to the `main()` in all of the other scripts in this chapter. We create the appropriate threads and send them on their way, finishing up when both threads have concluded execution.

We infer from this example that a program that has multiple tasks to perform can be organized to use separate threads for each of the tasks. This can result in a much cleaner program design than a single-threaded program that attempts to do all of the tasks.

In this chapter, we illustrated how a single-threaded process can limit an application's performance. In particular, programs with independent, non-deterministic, and non-causal tasks that execute sequentially can be improved by division into separate tasks executed by individual threads. Not all applications will benefit from multithreading due to overhead and the fact that the Python interpreter is a single-threaded application, but now you are more cognizant of Python's threading capabilities and can use this tool to your advantage when appropriate.

4.9   Alternative Considerations to Threads

Before you rush off and do some threading, let's do a quick recap: threading in general is a good thing. However, because of the restrictions of the GIL in Python, threading is more appropriate for I/O-bound applications (I/O releases the GIL, allowing for more concurrency) than for CPU-bound applications. In the latter case, to achieve greater parallelism, you'll need processes that can be executed by other cores or CPUs.

Without going into too much detail here (some of these topics have already been covered in the "Execution Environment" chapter of *Core Python Programming* or *Core Python Language Fundamentals*), when looking at multiple threads or processes, the primary alternatives to the `threading` module include:

4.9.1   The subprocess Module

This is the primary alternative when desiring to spawn processes, whether to purely execute stuff or to communicate with another process via the standard files (`stdin`, `stdout`, `stderr`). It was introduced to Python in version 2.4.

2.4

4.9.2 The `multiprocessing` Module

This module, added in Python 2.6, lets you spawn processes for multiple cores or CPUs but with an interface very similar to that of the threading module; it also contains various mechanisms to pass data between processes that are cooperating on shared work.

2.6

4.9.3 The `concurrent.futures` Module

This is a new high-level library that operates only at a "job" level, which means that you no longer have to fuss with synchronization, or managing threads or processes. you just *specify* a thread or process pool with a certain number of "workers," submit jobs, and collate the results. It's new in Python 3.2, but a port for Python 2.6+ is available at http://code.google.com/p/pythonfutures.

3.2

What would `bookrank3.py` look like with this change? Assuming everything else stays the same, here's the new import and modified _main() function:

```
from concurrent.futures import ThreadPoolExecutor
    . . .
def _main():
    print('At', ctime(), 'on Amazon...')
    with ThreadPoolExecutor(3) as executor:
        for isbn in ISBNs:
            executor.submit(_showRanking, isbn)
    print('all DONE at:', ctime())
```

The argument given to `concurrent.futures.ThreadPoolExecutor` is the thread pool size, and our application is looking for the rankings of three books. Of course, this is an I/O-bound application for which threads are more useful. For a CPU-bound application, we would use `concurrent.futures.ProcessPoolExecutor`, instead.

Once we have an executor (whether threads or processes), which is responsible for dispatching the jobs and collating the results, we can call its `submit()` method to execute what we would have had to spawn a thread to run previously.

If we do a "full" port to Python 3 by replacing the string format operator with the `str.format()` method, making liberal use of the **with** statement, and using the executor's `map()` method, we can actually delete _showRanking() and roll its functionality into _main(). In Example 4-13, you'll find our final `bookrank3CF.py` script.

Example 4-13   Higher-Level Job Management (bookrank3CF.py)

Our friend, the book rank screenscraper, but this time using
concurrent.futures.

```
 1   #!/usr/bin/env python
 2
 3   from concurrent.futures import ThreadPoolExecutor
 4   from re import compile
 5   from time import ctime
 6   from urllib.request import urlopen as uopen
 7
 8   REGEX = compile(b'#([\d,]+) in Books ')
 9   AMZN = 'http://amazon.com/dp/'
10   ISBNs = {
11       '0132269937': 'Core Python Programming',
12       '0132356139': 'Python Web Development with Django',
13       '0137143419': 'Python Fundamentals',
14   }
15
16   def getRanking(isbn):
17       with uopen('{0}{1}'.format(AMZN, isbn)) as page:
18           return str(REGEX.findall(page.read())[0], 'utf-8')
19
20   def _main():
21       print('At', ctime(), 'on Amazon...')
22       with ThreadPoolExecutor(3) as executor:
23           for isbn, ranking in zip(
24                   ISBNs, executor.map(getRanking, ISBNs)):
25               print('- %r ranked %s' % (ISBNs[isbn], ranking)
26       print('all DONE at:', ctime())
27
28   if __name__ == '__main__':
29       main()
```

Line-by-Line Explanation

Lines 1–14

Outside of the new **import** statement, everything in the first half of this
script is identical to the bookrank3.py file we looked at earlier in this chapter.

Lines 16–18

The new getRanking() uses the **with** statement and str.format(). You can
make the same change to bookrank.py because both features are available
in version 2.6+ (they are not unique to version 3.x).

Lines 20–26

In the previous code example, we used executor.submit() to spawn the
jobs. Here, we tweak this slightly by using executor.map() because it

allows us to absorb the functionality from _showRanking(), letting us remove it entirely from our code.

The output is nearly identical to what we've seen earlier:

```
$ python3 bookrank3CF.py
At Wed Apr  6 00:21:50 2011 on Amazon...
- 'Core Python Programming' ranked 43,992
- 'Python Fundamentals' ranked 1,018,454
- 'Python Web Development with Django' ranked 502,566
all DONE at: Wed Apr  6 00:21:55 2011
```

You can read more about the concurrent.futures module origins at the link below.

- http://docs.python.org/dev/py3k/library/concurrent.futures.html

- http://code.google.com/p/pythonfutures/

- http://www.python.org/dev/peps/pep-3148/

A summary of these options and other threading-related modules and packages can be found in the next section.

4.10 Related Modules

Table 4-6 lists some of the modules that you can use when programming multithreaded applications.

Table 4-6 Threading-Related Standard Library Modules

Module	Description
thread[a]	Basic, lower-level thread module
threading	Higher-level threading and synchronization objects
multiprocessing[b]	Spawn/use subprocesses with a "threading" interface
subprocess[c]	Skip threads altogether and execute processes instead
Queue	Synchronized FIFO queue for multiple threads
mutex[d]	Mutual exclusion objects

(Continued)

Table 4-6   Threading-Related Standard Library Modules *(Continued)*

Module	Description
`concurrent.futures`[e]	High-level library for asynchronous execution
`SocketServer`	Create/manage threaded TCP or UDP servers

a. Renamed to _thread in Python 3.0.
b. New in Python 2.6.
c. New in Python 2.4.
d. Deprecated in Python 2.6 and removed in version 3.0.
e. New in Python 3.2 (but available outside the standard library for version 2.6+).

4.11   Exercises

4-1. *Processes versus Threads.* What are the differences between processes and threads?

4-2. *Python Threads.* Which type of multithreaded application will tend to fare better in Python, I/O-bound or CPU-bound?

4-3. *Threads.* Do you think anything significant happens if you have multiple threads on a multiple CPU system? How do you think multiple threads run on these systems?

4-4. *Threads and Files.*

a) Create a function that obtains a byte value and a filename (as parameters or user input) and displays the number of times that byte appears in the file.

b) Suppose now that the input file is extremely large. Multiple readers in a file is acceptable, so modify your solution to create multiple threads that count in different parts of the file such that each thread is responsible for a certain part of the file. Collate the data from each thread and provide the correct total. Use the `timeit` module to time both the single- threaded new multithreaded solutions and say something about the difference in performance, if any.

4-5. *Threads, Files, and Regular Expressions.* You have a very large mailbox file—if you don't have one, put all of your e-mail messages together into a single text file. Your job is to take the regular expressions you designed earlier in this book that recognize e-mail addresses and Web site URLs and use them to convert all e-mail addresses and URLs in this large file into live links so that when the new file is saved as an `.html` (or `.htm`) file, it will show up in a Web browser as live and clickable. Use threads to segregate the conversion process across the large text file and collate the results into a single new `.html` file. Test the results on your Web browser to ensure the links are indeed working.

4-6. *Threads and Networking*. Your solution to the chat service application in the previous chapter required you to use heavyweight threads or processes as part of your solution. Convert your solution to be multithreaded.

4-7. **Threads and Web Programming*. The `Crawler` application in Chapter 10, "Web Programming: CGI and WSGI," is a single-threaded application that downloads Web pages. It would benefit from MT programming. Update `crawl.py` (you could call it `mtcrawl.py`) such that independent threads are used to download pages. Be sure to use some kind of locking mechanism to prevent conflicting access to the links queue.

4-8. *Thread Pools*. Instead of a producer thread and a consumer thread, change the code for `prodcons.py`, in Example 4-12 so that you have any number of consumer threads (a *thread pool*) which can process or consume more than one item from the `Queue` at any given moment.

4-9. *Files*. Create a set of threads to count how many lines there are in a set of (presumably large) text files. You can choose the number of threads to use. Compare the performance against a single-threaded version of this code. Hint: Review the exercises at the end of the Chapter 9, in *Core Python Programming* or *Core Python Language Fundamentals*.

4-10. *Concurrent Processing*. Take your solution to Exercise 4-9 and adopt it to a task of your selection, for example, processing a set of e-mail messages, downloading Web pages, processing RSS or Atom feeds, enhancing message processing as part of a chat server, solving a puzzle, etc.

4-11. *Synchronization Primitives*. Investigate each of the synchronization primitives in the threading module. Describe what they do, what they might be useful for, and create working code examples for each.

The next couple of exercises deal with the candy.py script featured in Example 4-11.

4-12. *Porting to Python 3*. Take the candy.py script and run the 2to3 tool on it to create a Python 3 version called candy3.py.

4-13. *The* threading *module*. Add debugging to the script. Specifically, for applications that use semaphores (whose initial value is going to be greater than 1), you might need to know exactly the counter's value at any given time. Create a variation of candy.py, perhaps calling it candydebug.py, and give it the ability to display the counter's value. You will need to look at the threading.py source code, as alluded to earlier in the CORE TIP sidebar. Once you're done with the modifications, you can alter its output to look something like the following:

```
$ python candydebug.py
starting at: Mon Apr  4 00:24:28 2011
THE CANDY MACHINE (full with 5 bars)!
Buying candy... inventory: 4
Refilling candy... inventory: 5
Refilling candy... full, skipping
Buying candy... inventory: 4
Buying candy... inventory: 3
Refilling candy... inventory: 4
Buying candy... inventory: 3
Buying candy... inventory: 2
Buying candy... inventory: 1
Buying candy... inventory: 0
Buying candy... empty, skipping
all DONE at: Mon Apr  4 00:24:36 2011
```

CHAPTER 5

GUI Programming

GUI stuff is supposed *to be hard. It builds character.*
— Jim Ahlstrom, May 1995
(verbally at Python Workshop)

In this chapter...

- Introduction
- Tkinter and Python Programming
- Tkinter Examples
- A Brief Tour of Other GUIs
- Related Modules and Other GUIs

I n this chapter, we will give you a brief introduction to the subject of graphical user interface (GUI) programming. If you are somewhat new to this area or want to learn more about it, or if you want to see how it is done in Python, then this chapter is for you. We cannot show you everything about GUI application development in this one chapter, but we will give you a very solid introduction to it. The primary GUI toolkit we will be using is Tk, Python's default GUI. We'll access Tk from its Python interface called Tkinter (short for "Tk interface").

Tk is not the latest and greatest, nor does it have the most robust set of GUI building blocks, but it is fairly simple to use, and with it, you can build GUIs that run on most platforms. We will present several simple and intermediate examples using Tkinter, followed by a few examples using other toolkits. Once you have completed this chapter, you will have the skills to build more complex applications and/or move to a more modern toolkit. Python has *bindings* or *adapters* to most of the current major toolkits, including commercial systems.

5.1   Introduction

Before getting started with GUI programming, we first discuss Tkinter as Python's default UI toolkit. We begin by looking at installation because Tkinter is not always on by default (especially when building Python yourself). This is followed by a quick review of client/server architecture, which is covered in Chapter 2, "Network Programming," but has relevance here.

5.1.1   What Are Tcl, Tk, and Tkinter?

Tkinter is Python's default GUI library. It is based on the Tk toolkit, originally designed for the *Tool Command Language* (Tcl). Due to Tk's popularity, it has been ported to a variety of other scripting languages, including Perl (Perl/Tk), Ruby (Ruby/Tk), and Python (Tkinter). The combination of Tk's GUI development portability and flexibility along with the simplicity of a scripting language integrated with the power of systems language gives you the tools to rapidly design and implement a wide variety of commercial-quality GUI applications.

If you are new to GUI programming, you will be pleasantly surprised at how easy it is. You will also find that Python, along with Tkinter, provides a fast and exciting way to build applications that are fun (and perhaps useful) and that would have taken much longer if you had to program directly in C/C++ with the native windowing system's libraries. Once you have designed the application and the look and feel that goes along with your program, you will use basic building blocks known as *widgets* to piece together the desired components, and finally, to attach functionality to "make it real."

If you are an old hand at using Tk, either with Tcl or Perl, you will find Python a refreshing way to program GUIs. On top of that, it provides an even faster rapid prototyping system for building them. Remember that you also have Python's system accessibility, networking functionality, XML, numerical and visual processing, database access, and all the other standard library and third-party extension modules.

Once you get Tkinter up on your system, it will take less than 15 minutes to get your first GUI application running.

5.1.2 Getting Tkinter Installed and Working

Tkinter is not necessarily turned on by default on your system. You can determine whether Tkinter is available for your Python interpreter by attempting to import the `Tkinter` module (in Python 1 and 2; renamed to `tkinter` in Python 3). If Tkinter is available, then no errors occur, as demonstrated in the following:

```
>>> import Tkinter
>>>
```

If your Python interpreter was *not* compiled with Tkinter enabled, the module import fails:

```
>>> import Tkinter
Traceback (innermost last):
  File "<stdin>", line 1, in ?
  File "/usr/lib/pythonX.Y/lib-tk/Tkinter.py", line 8, in ?
    import _tkinter # If this fails your Python may not
be configured for Tk
ImportError: No module named _tkinter
```

You might need to recompile your Python interpreter to gain access to Tkinter. This usually involves editing the `Modules/Setup` file and then enabling all the correct settings to compile your Python interpreter with hooks to Tkinter, or choosing to have Tk installed on your system. Check the `README` file for your Python distribution for specific instructions for compiling Tkinter on your system. After compiling the interpreter, be sure that you start the *new* Python interpreter otherwise, it will act just like your old one without Tkinter (and in fact, it *is* your old one).

5.1.3   Client/Server Architecture—Take Two

In Chapter 2, we introduced the concept of client/server computing. A windowing system is another example of a software server. These run on a computer with an attached display, such as a monitor. There are clients, too—programs that require a windowing environment in which to execute, also known as GUI applications. Such applications cannot run without a windows system.

The architecture becomes even more interesting when networking comes into play. Usually when a GUI application is executed, it displays to the computer that it started on (via the windowing server), but it is possible in some networked windowing environments, such as the X Window system on Unix, to choose another computer's window server to which the application displays. Thus, you can be running a GUI program on one computer, but display it on another.

5.2   Tkinter and Python Programming

In this section, we'll introduce GUI programming in general then focus on how to use Tkinter and its components to build GUIs in Python.

5.2.1   The Tkinter Module: Adding Tk to your Applications

So what do you need to do to have Tkinter as part of your application? First, it is not necessary to have an application already. You can create a pure GUI if you want, but it probably isn't too useful without some underlying software that does something interesting.

There are basically five main steps that are required to get your GUI up and running:

1. Import the Tkinter module (or **from** Tkinter **import** *).
2. Create a top-level windowing object that contains your entire GUI application.
3. Build all your GUI components (and functionality) on top (or within) of your top-level windowing object.
4. Connect these GUI components to the underlying application code.
5. Enter the main event loop.

The first step is trivial: all GUIs that use Tkinter must import the Tkinter module. Getting access to Tkinter is the first step (see Section 5.1.2).

5.2.2   Introduction to GUI Programming

Before going to the examples, we will give you a brief introduction to GUI application development. This will provide you with some of the general background you need to move forward.

Setting up a GUI application is similar to how an artist produces a painting. Conventionally, there is a single canvas onto which the artist must put all the work. Here's how it works: you start with a clean slate, a "top-level" windowing object on which you build the rest of your components. Think of it as a foundation to a house or the easel for an artist. In other words, you have to pour the concrete or set up your easel before putting together the actual structure or canvas on top of it. In Tkinter, this foundation is known as the *top-level window object*.

Windows and Widgets

In GUI programming, a top-level root windowing object contains all of the little windowing objects that will be part of your complete GUI application. These can be text labels, buttons, list boxes, etc. These individual little GUI components are known as *widgets*. So when we say create a top-level window, we just mean that you need a place where you put all your widgets. In Python, this would typically look like this line:

```
top = Tkinter.Tk() # or just Tk() with "from Tkinter import *"
```

The object returned by `Tkinter.Tk()` is usually referred to as the *root window*; hence, the reason why some applications use root rather than top to indicate as such. Top-level windows are those that show up stand-alone as part of your application. You can have more than one top-level window for your GUI, but only one of them should be your root window. You can choose to completely design all your widgets first, and then add the real functionality, or do a little of this and a little of that along the way. (This means mixing and matching steps 3 and 4 from our list.)

Widgets can be stand-alone or be containers. If a widget contains other widgets, it is considered the *parent* of those widgets. Accordingly, if a widget is contained in another widget, it's considered a *child* of the parent, the parent being the next immediate enclosing container widget.

Usually, widgets have some associated behaviors, such as when a button is pressed, or text is filled into a text field. These types of user behaviors are called *events*, and the GUI's response to such events are known as *callbacks*.

Event-Driven Processing

Events can include the actual button press (and release), mouse movement, hitting the Return or Enter key, etc. The entire system of events that occurs from the beginning until the end of a GUI application is what drives it. This is known as *event-driven processing*.

One example of an event with a callback is a simple mouse move. Suppose that the mouse pointer is sitting somewhere on top of your GUI application. If you move the mouse to another part of your application, something has to cause the movement of the mouse to be replicated by the cursor on your screen so that it *looks* as if it is moving according to the motion of your hand. These are mouse move events that the system must process portray your cursor moving across the window. When you release the mouse, there are no more events to process, so everything just remains idle on the screen again.

The event-driven processing nature of GUIs fits right in with client/ server architecture. When you start a GUI application, it must perform some setup procedures to prepare for the core execution, just as how a network server must allocate a socket and bind it to a local address. The GUI application must establish all the GUI components, then draw (a.k.a. render or paint) them to the screen. This is the responsibility of the *geometry manager* (more about this in a moment). When the geometry manager has completed arranging all of the widgets, including the top-level window, GUI applications enter their server-like infinite loop. This loop runs forever waiting for GUI events, processing them, and then going to wait for more events to process.

Geometry Managers

Tk has three geometry managers that help with positioning your widgetset. The original one was called the *Placer*. It was very straightforward: you provide the size of the widgets and locations to *place* them; the manager then places them for you. The problem is that you have to do this with all the widgets, burdening the developer with coding that should otherwise take place automatically.

The second geometry manager, and the main one that you will use, is the *Packer*, named appropriately because it packs widgets into the correct places (namely the containing parent widgets, based on your instruction), and for every succeeding widget, it looks for any remaining "real estate" into which to pack the next one. The process is similar to how you would pack elements into a suitcase when traveling.

A third geometry manager is the *Grid*. You use the Grid to specify GUI widget placement, based on grid coordinates. The Grid will render each object in the GUI in their grid position. For this chapter, we will stick with the Packer.

Once the Packer has determined the sizes and alignments of all your widgets, it will then place them on the screen for you.

When all the widgets are in place, we instruct the application to enter the aforementioned infinite main loop. In Tkinter, the code that does this is:

```
Tkinter.mainloop()
```

This is normally the last piece of sequential code your program runs. When the main loop is entered, the GUI takes over execution from there. All other actions are handled via callbacks, even exiting your application. When you select the File menu and then click the Exit menu option or close the window directly, a callback must be invoked to end your GUI application.

5.2.3   Top-Level Window: `Tkinter.Tk()`

We mentioned earlier that all main widgets are built on the top-level window object. This object is created by the `Tk` class in Tkinter and is instantiated as follows:

```
>>> import Tkinter
>>> top = Tkinter.Tk()
```

Within this window, you place individual widgets or multiple-component pieces together to form your GUI. So what kinds of widgets are there? We will now introduce the Tk widgets.

5.2.4   Tk Widgets

At the time of this writing, there were 18 types of widgets in Tk. We describe these widgets in Table 5-1. The newest of the widgets are `LabelFrame`, `PanedWindow,` and `Spinbox`, all three of which were added in Python 2.3 (via Tk 8.4).

2.3

Table 5-1   Tk Widgets

Widget	Description
Button	Similar to a Label but provides additional functionality for mouse-overs, presses, and releases, as well as keyboard activity/events
Canvas	Provides ability to draw shapes (lines, ovals, polygons, rectangles); can contain images or bitmaps
Checkbutton	Set of boxes, of which any number can be "checked" (similar to HTML checkbox input)
Entry	Single-line text field with which to collect keyboard input (similar to HTML text input)
Frame	Pure container for other widgets
Label	Used to contain text or images
LabelFrame	Combo of a label and a frame but with extra label attributes
Listbox	Presents the user with a list of choices from which to choose
Menu	Actual list of choices "hanging" from a Menubutton from which the user can choose
Menubutton	Provides infrastructure to contain menus (pulldown, cascading, etc.)
Message	Similar to a Label, but displays multiline text
PanedWindow	A container widget with which you can control other widgets placed within it
Radiobutton	Set of buttons, of which only one can be "pressed" (similar to HTML radio input)
Scale	Linear "slider" widget providing an exact value at current setting; with defined starting and ending values
Scrollbar	Provides scrolling functionality to supporting widgets, for example, Text, Canvas, Listbox, and Entry
Spinbox	Combination of an entry with a button letting you adjust its value

Widget	Description
Text	Multiline text field with which to collect (or display) text from user (similar to HTML `textarea`)
Toplevel	Similar to a `Frame`, but provides a separate window container

We won't go over the Tk widgets in detail as there is plenty of good documentation available for you to read, either from the Tkinter topics page at the main Python Web site or the abundant number of Tcl/Tk printed and online resources (some of which are available in Appendix B, "Reference Tables"). However, we will present several simple examples to help you get started.

 CORE NOTE: Default arguments are your friend

GUI development really takes advantage of default arguments in Python because there are numerous default actions in Tkinter widgets. Unless you know every single option available to you for every single widget that you are using, it's best to start out by setting only the parameters that you are aware of and letting the system handle the rest. These defaults were chosen carefully. If you do not provide these values, do not worry about your applications appearing odd on the screen. They were created with an optimized set of default arguments as a general rule, and only when you know how to exactly customize your widgets should you use values other than the default.

5.3   Tkinter Examples

Now we'll look at our first GUI scripts, each introducing another widget and perhaps showing a different way of using a widget that we've looked at before. Very basic examples lead to more intermediate ones, which have more relevance to coding GUIs in practice.

5.3.1   Label Widget

In Example 5-1, we present `tkhello1.py`, which is the Tkinter version of "Hello World!" In particular, it shows you how a Tkinter application is set up and highlights the `Label` widget.

Example 5-1   Label Widget Demo (`tkhelloA.py`)

Our first Tkinter example is—well, what else could it be but "Hello World!"? In particular, we introduce our first widget: the `Label`.

```
1   #!/usr/bin/env python
2
3   import Tkinter
4
5   top = Tkinter.Tk()
6   label = Tkinter.Label(top, text='Hello World!')
7   label.pack()
8   Tkinter.mainloop()
```

In the first line, we create our top-level window. That is followed by our `Label` widget, which contains the all-too-famous string. We instruct the Packer to manage and display our widget, and then finally call `mainloop()` to run our GUI application. Figure 5-1 shows what you will see when you run this GUI application.

Unix (twm)   Windows

Figure 5-1 The Tkinter `Label` widget.

5.3.2   The Button Widget

The next example (`tkhelloB.py`) is pretty much the same as the first. However, instead of a simple text label, we will create a button. Example 5-2 presents the source code.

Example 5-2   Button Widget Demo (`tkhelloB.py`)

This example is exactly the same as `tkhello1.py`, except that rather than using a `Label` widget, we create a `Button` widget.

```
1   #!/usr/bin/env python
2
3   import Tkinter
4
5   top = Tkinter.Tk()
6   quit = Tkinter.Button(top, text='Hello World!',
7       command=top.quit)
8   quit.pack()
9   Tkinter.mainloop()
```

The first few lines are identical. Things differ only when we create the `Button` widget. Our button has one additional parameter, the `Tkinter.quit()` method. This installs a callback to our button so that if it is pressed (and released), the entire application will exit. The final two lines are the usual `pack()` and invocation of the `mainloop()`. This simple button application is shown in Figure 5-2.

Unix   Windows

Figure 5-2 The Tkinter `Label` widget.

5.3.3   The `Label` and `Button` Widgets

In Example 5-3, we combine `tkhelloA.py` and `tkhelloB.py` into `tkhelloC.py`, a script that has both a label and a button. In addition, we are providing more parameters now than before when we were comfortable using all of the default arguments that are automatically set for us.

Example 5-3   Label and Button Widget Demo (`tkhelloC.py`)

This example features both a `Label` and a `Button` widget. Rather than primarily using default arguments when creating the widget, we are able to specify additional parameters now that we know more about `Button` widgets and how to configure them.

```
1   #!/usr/bin/env python
2
3   import Tkinter
4   top = Tkinter.Tk()
5
6   hello = Tkinter.Label(top, text='Hello World!')
7   hello.pack()
8
9   quit = Tkinter.Button(top, text='QUIT',
10      command=top.quit, bg='red', fg='white')
11  quit.pack(fill=Tkinter.X, expand=1)
12
13  Tkinter.mainloop()
```

Besides additional parameters for the widgets, we also see some arguments for the Packer. The `fill` parameter tells it to let the QUIT button take up the rest of the horizontal real estate, and the `expand` parameter directs it to visually fill out the entire horizontal landscape, stretching the button to the left and right sides of the window.

As you can see in Figure 5-3, without any other instructions to the Packer, the widgets are placed vertically (on top of each other). Horizontal placement requires creating a new `Frame` object with which to add the buttons. That frame will take the place of the parent object as a single child object (see the buttons in the `listdir.py` module, [Example 5-6] in Section 5.3.6).

Unix   Windows

Figure 5-3 Tkinter `Label` widget, together.

5.3.4   Label, Button, and Scale Widgets

Our final trivial example, `tkhelloD.py`, involves the addition of a `Scale` widget. In particular, the `Scale` is used to interact with the `Label` widget. The `Scale` slider is a tool that controls the size of the text font in the `Label` widget. The greater the slider position, the larger the font, and vice versa. The code for `tkhelloD.py` is presented in Example 5-4.

Example 5-4   Label, Button, and Scale Demonstration (`tkhelloD.py`)

Our final introductory widget example introduces the `Scale` widget and highlights how widgets can "communicate" with each other by using callbacks (such as `resize()`). The text in the `Label` widget is affected by actions taken on the `Scale` widget.

```
1    #!/usr/bin/env python
2
3    from Tkinter import *
4
```

```
5    def resize(ev=None):
6        label.config(font='Helvetica -%d bold' % \
7            scale.get())
8
9    top = Tk()
10   top.geometry('250x150')
11
12   label = Label(top, text='Hello World!',
13       font='Helvetica -12 bold')
14   label.pack(fill=Y, expand=1)
15
16   scale = Scale(top, from_=10, to=40,
17       orient=HORIZONTAL, command=resize)
18   scale.set(12)
19   scale.pack(fill=X, expand=1)
20
21   quit = Button(top, text='QUIT',
22       command=top.quit, activeforeground='white',
23       activebackground='red')
24   quit.pack()
25
26   mainloop()
```

New features of this script include a resize() callback function (lines 5–7), which is attached to the Scale. This is the code that is activated when the slider on the Scale is moved, resizing the size of the text in the Label.

We also define the size (250 × 150) of the top-level window (line 10). The final difference between this script and the first three is that we import the attributes from the Tkinter module into our namespace by using **from** Tkinter **import** *. Although this is not recommended because it "pollutes" your namespace, we do it here mainly because this application involves a great number of references to Tkinter attributes. This would require the use of their fully qualified names for each and every attribute access. By using the undesired shortcut, we are able to access attributes with less typing and have code that is easier to read, at some cost.

As you can see in Figure 5-4, both the slider mechanism as well as the current set value show up in the main part of the window. The figure also shows the state of the GUI after the user moves the scale/slider to a value of 36. Notice in the code that the initial setting for the scale when the application starts is 12 (line 18).

Unix

Windows

Figure 5-4 Tkinter `Label`, `Button`, and `Scale` widgets.

5.3.5   Partial Function Application Example

Before looking at a longer GUI application, we want to review the Partial Function Application (PFA), as introduced in *Core Python Programming* or *Core Python Language Fundamentals*.

2.5   PFAs were added to Python in version 2.5 and are one piece in a series of significant improvements in functional programming. Using PFAs, you can cache function parameters by effectively "freezing" those predetermined arguments, and then at runtime, when you have the remaining arguments you need, you can thaw them out, send in the final arguments, and have that function called with all parameters.

Best of all, PFAs are not limited to just functions. They will work with any "callable," which is any object that has a functional interface, just by using parentheses, including, classes, methods, or callable instances. The use of PFAs fits perfectly into a situation for which there are many callables and many of the calls feature the same arguments over and over again.

GUI programming makes a great use case, because there is good probability that you want some consistency in GUI widget look-and-feel, and this consistency comes about when the same parameters are used to create similar objects. We are now going to present an application in which multiple buttons will have the same foreground and background colors. It would be a waste of typing to give the same arguments to the same instantiators every time we wanted a slightly different button: the foreground and background colors are the same, but the text is slightly different.

We are going to use traffic road signs as our example, with our application attempting to create textual versions of road signs by dividing them up into various categories of sign types, such as critical, warning, or informational (just like logging levels). The sign type determines the color scheme when they are created. For example, critical signs have the text in bright red with a white background; warning signs are in black text on a goldenrod background; and informational or regulatory signs feature black text on a white background. We have the "Do Not Enter" and "Wrong Way" signs, which are both critical, plus "Merging Traffic" and "Railroad Crossing," both of which are warnings. Finally, we have the regulatory "Speed Limit" and "One Way" signs.

The application in Example 5-5 creates the signs, which are just buttons. When users press the buttons, they display the corresponding Tk dialog in a pop-up window, critical/error, warning, or informational. It is not too exciting, but how the buttons are built is.

Example 5-5   Road Signs PFA GUI Application (`pfaGUI.py`)

Create road signs with the appropriate foreground and background colors, based on sign type. Use PFAs to help "templatize" common GUI parameters.

```
1   #!/usr/bin/env python
2
3   from functools import partial as pto
4   from Tkinter import Tk, Button, X
5   from tkMessageBox import showinfo, showwarning, showerror
6
7   WARN = 'warn'
8   CRIT = 'crit'
9   REGU = 'regu'
10
11  SIGNS = {
12    'do not enter': CRIT,
```

(Continued)

Example 5-5   Road Signs PFA GUI Application (pfaGUI.py) *(Continued)*

```
13      'railroad crossing': WARN,
14      '55\nspeed limit': REGU,
15      'wrong way': CRIT,
16      'merging traffic': WARN,
17      'one way': REGU,
18    }
19
20    critCB = lambda: showerror('Error', 'Error Button Pressed!')
21    warnCB = lambda: showwarning('Warning',
22      'Warning Button Pressed!')
23    infoCB = lambda: showinfo('Info', 'Info Button Pressed!')
24
25    top = Tk()
26    top.title('Road Signs')
27    Button(top, text='QUIT', command=top.quit,
28      bg='red', fg='white').pack()
29
30    MyButton = pto(Button, top)
31    CritButton = pto(MyButton, command=critCB, bg='white', fg='red')
32    WarnButton = pto(MyButton, command=warnCB, bg='goldenrod1')
33    ReguButton = pto(MyButton, command=infoCB, bg='white')
34
35    for eachSign in SIGNS:
36      signType = SIGNS[eachSign]
37      cmd = '%sButton(text=%r%s).pack(fill=X, expand=True)' % (
38          signType.title(), eachSign,
39          '.upper()' if signType == CRIT else '.title()')
40      eval(cmd)
41
42    top.mainloop()
```

When you execute this application, you will see a GUI that will look
something like Figure 5-5.

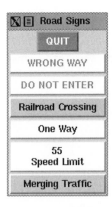

Figure 5-5 The Road signs PFA GUI application on XDarwin in Mac OS X.

Line-by-Line Explanation

Lines 1–18

We begin our application by importing `functools.partial()`, a few `Tkinter` attributes, and the Tk dialogs (lines 1–5). Next, we define some signs along with their categories (lines 7–18).

Lines 20–28

The Tk dialogs are assigned as button callbacks, which we will use for each button created (lines 20–23). We then launch Tk, set the title, and create a QUIT button (lines 25–28).

Lines 30–33

These lines represent our PFA magic. We use two levels of PFA. The first templatizes the `Button` class and the root window `top`. This means that every time we call `MyButton`, it will call `Button` (`Tkinter.Button()` creates a button.) with `top` as its first argument. We have frozen this into `MyButton`.

The second level of PFA is where we use our first one, `MyButton`, and templatize *that*. We create separate button types for each of our sign categories. When users create a critical button `CritButton` (by calling it, for example, `CritButton()`), it will then call `MyButton` along with the appropriate button callback and background and foreground colors, which means calling `Button` with `top`, callback, and colors. You can see how it unwinds and goes down the layers until at the very bottom, it has the call that you would have originally had to make if this feature did not exist yet. We repeat with `WarnButton` and `ReguButton`.

Lines 35–42

With the setup completed, we look at our list of signs and create them. We put together a string that Python can evaluate, consisting of the correct button name, pass in the button label as the text argument, and `pack()` it. If it is a critical sign, then we capitalize the button text; otherwise, we titlecase it. This last bit is done in line 39, demonstrating another feature introduced in Python 2.5, the ternary/conditional operator. Each button is instantiated with `eval()`, resulting in what is shown in Figure 5-5. Finally, we start the GUI by entering the main event loop.

2.5

You can easily replace the use of the ternary operator with the old "and/ or" syntax if running with version 2.4 or older, but `functools.partial()` is a more difficult feature to replicate, so we recommend you use version 2.5 or newer with this example application.

5.3.6   Intermediate Tkinter Example

We conclude this section with a larger script, listdir.py, which is presented in Example 5-6. This application is a directory tree traversal tool. It starts in the current directory and provides a file listing. Double-clicking any other directory in the list causes the tool to change to the new directory as well as replace the original file listing with the files from the new directory.

Example 5-6   File System Traversal GUI (listdir.py)

This slightly more advanced GUI expands on the use of widgets, adding listboxes, text entry fields, and scrollbars to our repertoire. There are also a good number of callbacks such as mouse clicks, key presses, and scrollbar action.

```
1    #!/usr/bin/env python
2
3    import os
4    from time import sleep
5    from Tkinter import *
6
7    class DirList(object):
8
9        def __init__(self, initdir=None):
10           self.top = Tk()
11           self.label = Label(self.top,
12               text='Directory Lister v1.1')
13           self.label.pack()
14
15           self.cwd = StringVar(self.top)
16
17           self.dirl = Label(self.top, fg='blue',
18               font=('Helvetica', 12, 'bold'))
19           self.dirl.pack()
20
21           self.dirfm = Frame(self.top)
22           self.dirsb = Scrollbar(self.dirfm)
23           self.dirsb.pack(side=RIGHT, fill=Y)
24           self.dirs = Listbox(self.dirfm, height=15,
25               width=50, yscrollcommand=self.dirsb.set)
26           self.dirs.bind('<Double-1>', self.setDirAndGo)
27           self.dirsb.config(command=self.dirs.yview)
28           self.dirs.pack(side=LEFT, fill=BOTH)
29           self.dirfm.pack()
30
31           self.dirn = Entry(self.top, width=50,
32               textvariable=self.cwd)
33           self.dirn.bind('<Return>', self.doLS)
34           self.dirn.pack()
35
36           self.bfm = Frame(self.top)
37           self.clr = Button(self.bfm, text='Clear',
38               command=self.clrDir,
39               activeforeground='white',
40               activebackground='blue')
```

```
41              self.ls = Button(self.bfm,
42                  text='List Directory',
43                  command=self.doLS,
44                  activeforeground='white',
45                  activebackground='green')
46              self.quit = Button(self.bfm, text='Quit',
47                  command=self.top.quit,
48                  activeforeground='white',
49                  activebackground='red')
50              self.clr.pack(side=LEFT)
51              self.ls.pack(side=LEFT)
52              self.quit.pack(side=LEFT)
53              self.bfm.pack()
54
55              if initdir:
56                  self.cwd.set(os.curdir)
57                  self.doLS()
58
59          def clrDir(self, ev=None):
60              self.cwd.set('')
61
62          def setDirAndGo(self, ev=None):
63              self.last = self.cwd.get()
64              self.dirs.config(selectbackground='red')
65              check = self.dirs.get(self.dirs.curselection())
66              if not check:
67                  check = os.curdir
68              self.cwd.set(check)
69              self.doLS()
70
71          def doLS(self, ev=None):
72              error = ''
73              tdir = self.cwd.get()
74              if not tdir: tdir = os.curdir
75
76              if not os.path.exists(tdir):
77                  error = tdir + ': no such file'
78              elif not os.path.isdir(tdir):
79                  error = tdir + ': not a directory'
80
81              if error:
82                  self.cwd.set(error)
83                  self.top.update()
84                  sleep(2)
85                  if not (hasattr(self, 'last') \
86                      and self.last):
87                      self.last = os.curdir
88                  self.cwd.set(self.last)
89                  self.dirs.config(\
90                      selectbackground='LightSkyBlue')
91                  self.top.update()
92                  return
93
```

(Continued)

Example 5-6   File System Traversal GUI (`listdir.py`) *(Continued)*

```
94              self.cwd.set(\
95                  'FETCHING DIRECTORY CONTENTS...')
96              self.top.update()
97              dirlist = os.listdir(tdir)
98              dirlist.sort()
99              os.chdir(tdir)
100             self.dirl.config(text=os.getcwd())
101             self.dirs.delete(0, END)
102             self.dirs.insert(END, os.curdir)
103             self.dirs.insert(END, os.pardir)
104             for eachFile in dirlist:
105                 self.dirs.insert(END, eachFile)
106             self.cwd.set(os.curdir)
107             self.dirs.config(\
108                 selectbackground='LightSkyBlue')
109
110 def main():
111     d = DirList(os.curdir)
112     mainloop()
113
114 if __name__ == '__main__':
115     main()
```

In Figure 5-6, we present what this GUI looks like on a Windows-based PC. The POSIX UI screenshot of this application is shown in Figure 5-7.

Line-by-Line Explanation

Lines 1–5

These first few lines contain the usual Unix startup line and importation of the os module, the `time.sleep()` function, and all attributes of the Tkinter module.

Lines 9–13

These lines define the constructor for the `DirList` class, an object that represents our application. The first `Label` we create contains the main title of the application and the version number.

Lines 15–19

We declare a Tk variable named cwd to hold the name of the directory we are on—we will see where this comes in handy later. Another `Label` is created to display the name of the current directory.

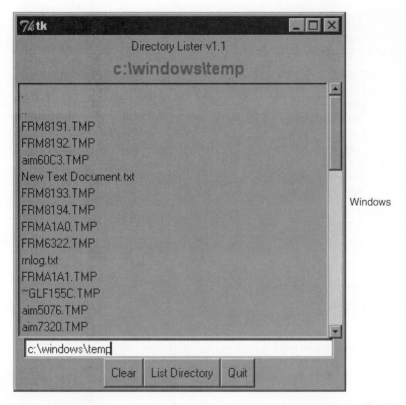

Windows

Figure 5-6   Our List directory GUI application as it appears in Windows.

Lines 21–29

This section defines the core part of our GUI, the Listbox dirs, which contain the list of files of the directory that is being listed. A Scrollbar is employed to allow the user to move through a listing if the number of files exceeds the size of the Listbox. Both of these widgets are contained in a Frame widget. Listbox entries have a callback (setDirAndGo) tied to them by using the Listbox bind() method.

Binding means to tie a keystroke, mouse action, or some other event to a callback to be executed when such an event is generated by the user. setDirAndGo() will be called if any item in the Listbox is double-clicked. The Scrollbar is tied to the Listbox by calling the Scrollbar.config() method.

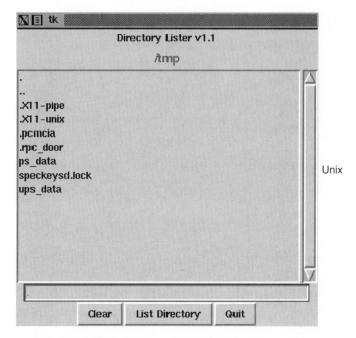

Figure 5-7 The List directory GUI application as it appears in Unix.

Lines 31–34

We then create a text Entry field for the user to enter the name of the directory he wants to traverse and see its files listed in the Listbox. We add a Return or Enter key binding to this text entry field so that the user can press Return as an alternative to clicking a button. The same applies for the mouse binding we saw earlier in the Listbox. When the user double-clicks a Listbox item, it has the same effect as entering the directory name manually into the text Entry field and then clicking the Go button.

Lines 36–53

We then define a Button frame (bfm) to hold our three buttons: a "clear" button (clr), a "go" button (ls), and a "quit" button (quit). Each button has its own configuration and callbacks, if pressed.

Lines 55–57

The final part of the constructor initializes the GUI program, starting with the current working directory.

Lines 59–60

The clrDir() method clears the cwd Tk string variable, which contains the current active directory. This variable is used to keep track of what directory we are in and, more important, helps keep track of the previous directory in case errors arise. You will notice the ev variables in the callback functions with a default value of None. Any such values would be passed in by the windowing system. They might or might not be used in your callback.

Lines 62–69

The setDirAndGo() method sets the directory to which to traverse and issues the call to the method that makes it all happen, doLS().

Lines 71–108

doLS() is, by far, the key to this entire GUI application. It performs all the safety checks (e.g., is the destination a directory and does it exist?). If there is an error, the last directory is reset to be the current directory. If all goes well, it calls os.listdir() to get the actual set of files and replaces the listing in the Listbox. While the background work is going on to pull in the information from the new directory, the highlighted blue bar becomes bright red. When the new directory has been installed, it reverts to blue.

Lines 110–115

The last pieces of code in listdir.py represent the main part of the code. main() is executed only if this script is invoked directly; when main() runs, it creates the GUI application, and then calls mainloop() to start the GUI, which is passed control of the application.

We leave all other aspects of the application as an exercise for you to undertake, recommending that it is easier to view the entire application as a combination of a set of widgets and functionality. If you see the individual pieces clearly, then the entire script will not appear as daunting.

We hope that we have given you a good introduction to GUI programming with Python and Tkinter. Remember that the best way to become familiar with Tkinter programming is by practicing and stealing a few examples! The Python distribution comes with a large number of demonstration applications that you can study.

If you download the source code, you will find Tkinter demonstration code in Lib/lib-tk, Lib/idlelib, and Demo/tkinter. If you have installed the Win32 version of Python and C:\Python2x, then you can get access to the demonstration code in Lib\lib-tk and Lib\idlelib. The latter

directory contains the most significant sample Tkinter application: the
IDLE IDE itself. For further reference, there are several books on Tk programming, one specifically on Tkinter.

5.4   A Brief Tour of Other GUIs

We hope to eventually develop an independent chapter on general GUI
development that makes use of the abundant number of graphical toolkits
that exist under Python, but alas, that is for the future. As a proxy, we
would like to present a single, simple GUI application written by using
four of the more popular toolkits: Tix (Tk Interface eXtensions), Pmw
(Python MegaWidgets Tkinter extension), wxPython (Python binding to
wxWidgets), and PyGTK (Python binding to GTK+). The final example
demonstrates how to use Tile/Ttk—in both Python 2 and 3. You can find
links to more information and/or download these toolkits in the reference
section at the end of this chapter.

The Tix module is already available in the Python Standard Library.
You must download the others, which are third party. Since Pmw is just an
extension to Tkinter, it is the easiest to install (just extract it into your site packages). wxPython and PyGTK involve the download of more than one file and
building (unless you opt for the Win32 versions for which binaries are usually available). Once the toolkits are installed and verified, we can begin.
Rather than just sticking with the widgets we've already seen in this chapter, we'd like to introduce a few more complex widgets for these examples.

In addition to the Label and Button widgets, we would like to introduce
the Control or SpinButton and ComboBox. The Control widget is a combination of a text widget that contains a value which is "controlled" or "spun
up or down" by a set of arrow buttons close by. The ComboBox is usually a
text widget and a pulldown menu of options where the currently active or
selected item in the list is displayed in the text widget.

Our application is fairly basic: pairs of animals are being moved
around, and the number of total animals can range from a pair to a maximum of a dozen. The Control is used to keep track of the total number,
while the ComboBox is a menu containing the various types of animals that can
be selected. In Figure 5-8, each image shows the state of the GUI application
immediately after launching. Note that the default number of animals is
two, and no animal type has been selected yet.

Things are different once we start to play around with the application,
as evidenced in Figure 5-9, which shows some of the elements after we
have modified them in the Tix application.

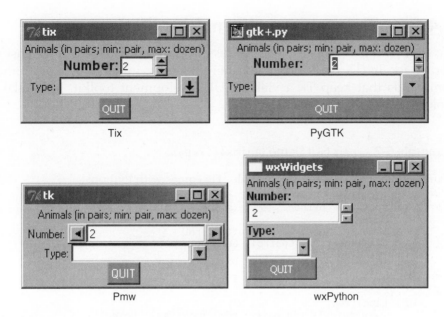

Figure 5-8 Application using various GUIs under Win32.

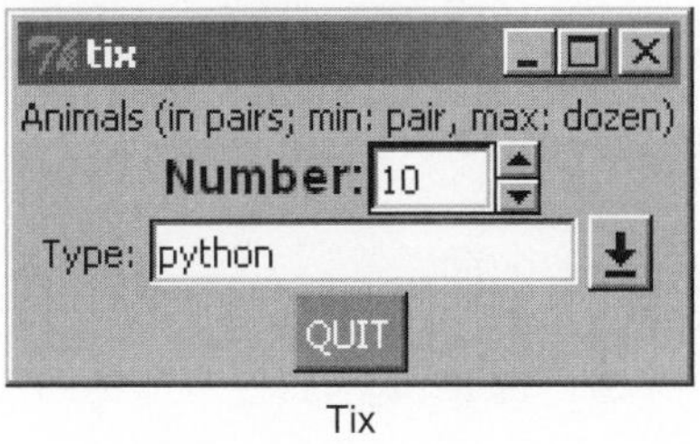

Figure 5-9 The Tix GUI modified version of our application.

You can view the code for all four versions of our GUI in Examples 5-7 through 5-10. Example 5-11, which uses Tile/Ttk (the code is supported in Python 2 and 3) supersedes these first four examples. You will note that although relatively similar, each one differs in its own special way. Also, we use the .*pyw* extension to suppress DOS command or terminal window pop-ups.

5.4.1   Tk Interface eXtensions (Tix)

We start with Example 5-7, which uses the `Tix` module. Tix is an extension library for Tcl/Tk that adds many new widgets, image types, and other commands that keep Tk a viable GUI development toolkit. Let's take a look at how to use Tix with Python.

Example 5-7   Tix GUI Demo (`animalTix.pyw`)

Our first example uses the `Tix` module. Tix comes with Python!

```
1   #!/usr/bin/env python
2
3   from Tkinter import Label, Button, END
4   from Tix import Tk, Control, ComboBox
5
6   top = Tk()
7   top.tk.eval('package require Tix')
8
9   lb = Label(top,
10      text='Animals (in pairs; min: pair, max: dozen)')
11  lb.pack()
12
13  ct = Control(top, label='Number:',
14      integer=True, max=12, min=2, value=2, step=2)
15  ct.label.config(font='Helvetica -14 bold')
16  ct.pack()
17
18  cb = ComboBox(top, label='Type:', editable=True)
19  for animal in ('dog', 'cat', 'hamster', 'python'):
20      cb.insert(END, animal)
21  cb.pack()
22
23  qb = Button(top, text='QUIT',
24      command=top.quit, bg='red', fg='white')
25  qb.pack()
26
27  top.mainloop()
```

Line-by-Line Explanation

Lines 1–7

This is all the setup code, module imports, and basic GUI infrastructure. Line 7 asserts that the `Tix` module is available to the application.

Lines 8–27

These lines create all the widgets: `Label` (lines 9–11), `Control` (lines 13–16), `ComboBox` (lines 18–21), and quit `Button` (lines 23–25). The constructors and arguments for the widgets are fairly self-explanatory and do not require elaboration. Finally, we enter the main GUI event loop in line 27.

5.4.2   Python MegaWidgets (PMW)

Next we take a look at Python MegaWidgets (shown in Example 5-8). This module was created to address the aging Tkinter. It basically helps to extend its longevity by adding more modern widgets to the GUI palette.

Example 5-8   Pmw GUI Demo (`animalPmw.pyw`)

Our second example uses the Python MegaWidgets package.

```
1   #!/usr/bin/env python
2
3   from Tkinter import Button, END, Label, W
4   from Pmw import initialise, ComboBox, Counter
5
6   top = initialise()
7
8   lb = Label(top,
9       text='Animals (in pairs; min: pair, max: dozen)')
10  lb.pack()
11
12  ct = Counter(top, labelpos=W, label_text='Number:',
13      datatype='integer', entryfield_value=2,
14      increment=2, entryfield_validate={'validator':
15      'integer', 'min': 2, 'max': 12})
16  ct.pack()
17
18  cb = ComboBox(top, labelpos=W, label_text='Type:')
19  for animal in ('dog', 'cat', 'hamster', 'python'):
20      cb.insert(end, animal)
21  cb.pack()
22
23  qb = Button(top, text='QUIT',
24      command=top.quit, bg='red', fg='white')
25  qb.pack()
26
27  top.mainloop()
```

The Pmw example is so similar to our Tix example that we leave line-by-line analysis to the reader. The line of code that differs the most is the constructor for the control widget, the Pmw Counter. It provides for entry validation. Instead of specifying the smallest and largest possible values as keyword arguments to the widget constructor, Pmw uses a "validator" to ensure that the values do not fall outside our accepted range.

Tix and Pmw are extensions to Tk and Tkinter, respectively, but now we are going to leave the Tk world behind and change gears to look at completely different toolkits: wxWidgets and GTK+. You will notice that the number of lines of code starts to increase as we start programming in a more object-oriented way with these more modern and robust GUI toolkits.

5.4.3   wxWidgets and wxPython

wxWidgets (formerly known as wxWindows) is a cross-platform toolkit that you can use to build graphical user applications. It is implemented by using C++ and is available on a wide range of platforms to which wxWidgets defines a consistent and common applications programming interface (API). The best part of all is that wxWidgets uses the native GUI on each platform, so your program will have the same look-and-feel as all the other applications on your desktop. Another feature is that you are not restricted to developing wxWidgets applications in C++; there are interfaces to both Python and Perl. Example 5-9 shows our animal application using wxPython.

Example 5-9   wxPython GUI Demo (`animalWx.pyw`)

Our third example uses wxPython (and wxWidgets). Note that we have placed all of our widgets inside a "sizer" for organization. Also, take note of the more object-oriented nature of this application.

```
1    #!/usr/bin/env python
2
3    import wx
4
5    class MyFrame(wx.Frame):
6        def __init__(self, parent=None, id=-1, title=''):
7            wx.Frame.__init__(self, parent, id, title,
8                size=(200, 140))
9            top = wx.Panel(self)
10           sizer = wx.BoxSizer(wx.VERTICAL)
11           font = wx.Font(9, wx.SWISS, wx.NORMAL, wx.BOLD)
12           lb = wx.StaticText(top, -1,
13             'Animals (in pairs; min: pair, max: dozen)')
14           sizer.Add(lb)
15
16           c1 = wx.StaticText(top, -1, 'Number:')
17           c1.SetFont(font)
18           ct = wx.SpinCtrl(top, -1, '2', min=2, max=12)
```

```
19          sizer.Add(c1)
20          sizer.Add(ct)
21
22          c2 = wx.StaticText(top, -1, 'Type:')
23          c2.SetFont(font)
24          cb = wx.ComboBox(top, -1, '',
25            choices=('dog', 'cat', 'hamster','python'))
26          sizer.Add(c2)
27          sizer.Add(cb)
28
29          qb = wx.Button(top, -1, "QUIT")
30          qb.SetBackgroundColour('red')
31          qb.SetForegroundColour('white')
32          self.Bind(wx.EVT_BUTTON,
33              lambda e: self.Close(True), qb)
34          sizer.Add(qb)
35
36          top.SetSizer(sizer)
37          self.Layout()
38
39  class MyApp(wx.App):
40      def OnInit(self):
41          frame = MyFrame(title="wxWidgets")
42          frame.Show(True)
43          self.SetTopWindow(frame)
44          return True
45
46  def main():
47      pp = MyApp()
48      app.MainLoop()
49
50  if __name__ == '__main__':
51      main()
```

Line-by-Line Explanation

Lines 5–37

Here we instantiate a `Frame` class (lines 5–8), of which the sole member is the constructor. This method's only purpose in life is to create our widgets. Inside the frame, we have a `Panel`. Inside the panel we use a `BoxSizer` to contain and layout all of our widgets (lines 10, 36), which consist of a `Label` (lines 12–14), `SpinCtrl` (lines 16–20), `ComboBox` (lines 22–27), and quit `Button` (lines 29–34).

We have to manually add `Label`s to the `SpinCtrl` and `ComboBox` widgets because they apparently do not come with them. Once we have them all, we add them to the sizer, set the sizer to our panel, and lay everything out. On line 10, you will note that the sizer is vertically oriented, meaning that our widgets will be placed top to bottom.

One weakness of the `SpinCtrl` widget is that it does not support "step" functionality. With the other three examples, we are able to click an arrow selector which increments or decrements by units of two, but that is not possible with this widget.

Lines 39–51

Our application class instantiates the `Frame` object we just designed, renders it to the screen, and sets it as the top-most window of our application. Finally, the setup lines just instantiate our GUI application and start it running.

5.4.4   GTK+ and PyGTK

Finally, we have the PyGTK version, which is quite similar to the wxPython GUI (See Example 5-10). The biggest difference is that we use only one class, and it seems more tedious to set the foreground and background colors of objects, buttons in particular.

Example 5-10   PyGTK GUI Demo (`animalGtk.pyw`)

Our final example uses PyGTK (and GTK+). Like the wxPython example, this one also uses a class for our application. It is interesting to note how similar yet different all of our GUI applications are. This is not surprising and allows programmers to switch between toolkits with relative ease.

```
1    #!/usr/bin/env python
2
3    import pygtk
4    pygtk.require('2.0')
5    import gtk
6    import pango
7
8    class GTKapp(object):
9      def __init__(self):
10       top = gtk.Window(gtk.WINDOW_TOPLEVEL)
11       top.connect("delete_event", gtk.main_quit)
12       top.connect("destroy", gtk.main_quit)
13       box = gtk.VBox(False, 0)
14       lb = gtk.Label(
15         'Animals (in pairs; min: pair, max: dozen)')
16       box.pack_start(lb)
17
18       sb = gtk.HBox(False, 0)
19       adj = gtk.Adjustment(2, 2, 12, 2, 4, 0)
```

```
20        sl = gtk.Label('Number:')
21        sl.modify_font(
22            pango.FontDescription("Arial Bold 10"))
23        sb.pack_start(sl)
24        ct = gtk.SpinButton(adj, 0, 0)
25        sb.pack_start(ct)
26        box.pack_start(sb)
27
28        cb = gtk.HBox(False, 0)
29        c2 = gtk.Label('Type:')
30        cb.pack_start(c2)
31        ce = gtk.combo_box_entry_new_text()
32        for animal in ('dog', 'cat','hamster', 'python'):
33            ce.append_text(animal)
34        cb.pack_start(ce)
35        box.pack_start(cb)
36
37        qb = gtk.Button("")
38        red = gtk.gdk.color_parse('red')
39        sty = qb.get_style()
40        for st in (gtk.STATE_NORMAL,
41            gtk.STATE_PRELIGHT, gtk.STATE_ACTIVE):
42            sty.bg[st] = red
43        qb.set_style(sty)
44        ql = qb.child
45        ql.set_markup('<span color="white">QUIT</span>')
46        qb.connect_object("clicked",
47            gtk.Widget.destroy, top)
48        box.pack_start(qb)
49        top.add(box)
50        top.show_all()
51
52  if __name__ == '__main__':
53      animal = GTKapp()
54      gtk.main()
```

Line-by-Line Explanation

Lines 1–6

We import three different modules and packages, PyGTK, GTK, and Pango, a library for layout and rendering of text, specifically for I18N purposes. We need it here because it represents the core of text and font handling for GTK+ (version 2.x).

Lines 8–50

The GTKapp class represents all the widgets of our application. The topmost window is created (with handlers for closing it via the window manager), and a vertically oriented sizer (VBox) is created to hold our primary widgets. This is exactly what we did in the wxPython GUI.

However, wanting the static labels for the `SpinButton` and `ComboBoxEntry` to be next to them (unlike above them for the wxPython example), we create little horizontally-oriented boxes to contain the label-widget pairs (lines 18–35) and placed those `HBox`es into the all-encompassing `VBox`.

After creating the quit `Button` and adding the `VBox` to our topmost window, we render everything on screen. You will notice that we create the button with an empty label at first. We do this so that a `Label` (child) object will be created as part of the button. Then on lines 44–45, we get access to the label and set the text with white font color.

The reason we do this is because if you set the style foreground, for instance, in the loop and auxiliary code on lines 40–43, the foreground only affects the button's foreground and not the label—for example, if you set the foreground style to white and highlight the button (by pressing the Tab key until it is "selected") you will see that the inside dotted box identifying the selected widget *is* white, but the label text would still be black if you did not alter it such as we did with the markup on line 45.

Lines 52–54

Here, we create our application and enter the main event loop.

5.4.5   Tile/Ttk

Since its inception, the Tk library has established a solid reputation as a flexible and simple library and toolkit with which to build GUI tools. However, after its first decade, a perception grew among the current user base as well as new developers that without new features, major changes, and upgrades, it became perceived as being dated and not keeping up with more current toolkits such as wxWidgets and GTK+.

Tix attempts to address this by providing new widgets, image types, and new commands to extend Tk. Some of its core widgets even used native UI code, giving them a more similar look and feel to other applications on the same windowing system. However, this effort merely *extended* Tk's capabilities.

In the mid-2000s, a more radical approach was proposed: the Tile widget set, which is a reimplementation of most of Tk's core widgets while adding several new ones. Not only is native code more prevalent, but Tile comes with a *themeing engine*.

Themed widget sets and the ability to easily create, import, and export themes give developers (and users) much more control over the visual appearance of applications and lends to a more seamless integration with the operating system and the windowing system that runs on it. This aspect of Tile was compelling enough to cause it to be integrated with the Tk core in version 8.5 as Ttk. Rather than being a replacement, the Ttk widget set is provided as an adjunct to the original core Tk widget set.

Tile/Ttk made its debut in Python 2.7 and 3.1. To use Ttk, the Python **2.7** version you're using needs to have access to either Tk 8.5 as a minimum; recent but older versions will also work, as long as Tile is installed. In Python 2.7+, Tile/Ttk is made available via the `ttk` module; while in 3.1+, it **3.1** has been absorbed under the `tkinter` umbrella, so you would import `tkinter.ttk`.

In Examples 5-11 and 5-12, you'll find Python 2 and 3 versions of our `animalTtk.pyw` and `animalTtk3.pyw` applications. Whether using Python 2 or 3, a UI application screen similar to that found in Figure 5-10 will be what you'll get upon execution.

Example 5-11   Tile/Ttk GUI Demo (`animalTtk.pyw`)

A demonstration application using the Tile toolkit (named Ttk when integrated into Tk 8.5).

```
1   #!/usr/bin/env python
2
3   from Tkinter import Tk, Spinbox
4   from ttk import Style, Label, Button, Combobox
5
6   top = Tk()
7   Style().configure("TButton",
8       foreground='white', background='red')
9
10  Label(top,
11      text='Animals (in pairs; min: pair, '
12      'max: dozen)').pack()
13  Label(top, text='Number:').pack()
14
15  Spinbox(top, from_=2, to=12,
16      increment=2, font='Helvetica -14 bold').pack()
17
18  Label(top, text='Type:').pack()
19
20  Combobox(top, values=('dog',
21      'cat', 'hamster', 'python')).pack()
22
23  Button(top, text='QUIT',
24      command=top.quit, style="TButton").pack()
25
26  top.mainloop()
```

Example 5-12   Tile/Ttk Python 3 GUI Demo (`animalTtk3.pyw`)

A Python 3 demonstration using the Tile toolkit (named Ttk when integrated into Tk 8.5).

```python
1   #!/usr/bin/env python3
2
3   from tkinter import Tk, Spinbox
4   from tkinter.ttk import Style, Label, Button, Combobox
5
6   top = Tk()
7   Style().configure("TButton",
8       foreground='white', background='red')
9
10  Label(top,
11      text='Animals (in pairs; min: pair, '
12      'max: dozen)').pack()
13  Label(top, text='Number:').pack()
14
15  Spinbox(top, from_=2, to=12,
16      increment=2, font='Helvetica -14 bold').pack()
17
18  Label(top, text='Type:').pack()
19
20  Combobox(top, values=('dog',
21      'cat', 'hamster', 'python')).pack()
22
23  Button(top, text='QUIT',
24      command=top.quit, style="TButton").pack()
25
26  top.mainloop()
```

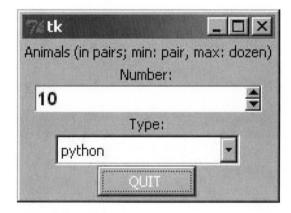

Figure 5-10 The animal UI in Tile/Ttk.

Line-by-Line Explanation

Lines 1–4

The Tk core widgets received three new widgets in Tk 8.4. One of them was the `Spinbox`, which we'll be using in this application. (The other two are `LabelFrame` and `PanedWindow`.) All others used here are Tile/Ttk widgets: `Label`, `Button`, and `Combobox`, plus the `Style` class, which helps with the widget themeing.

Lines 6–8

These lines just initiate the root window as well as a `Style` object, which contains the themed elements for widgets that choose to use it. It helps define a common look and feel to your widgets. Although it seems like a waste to use it just for our quit button, you cannot specify individual foreground and background colors directly for buttons. This forces you to program in a more disciplined way. The minor inconvenience in this trivial example will prove a more useful habit in practice.

Lines 10–26

The majority of the rest of the code defines (and packs) the entire widgetset, which matches pretty much what you've seen in this application using the other UIs introduced in this chapter: a Label defining the application, a `Label` and `Spinbox` combo that controls the numeric range of possible values (and increment), a `Label` and `Combobox` pair letting users select an animal, and a quit `Button`. We end by entering the GUI mainloop.

This line-by-line explanation is identical to that of its Python 3 sibling shown in Example 5-12, with the only changes being in imports: `Tkinter` is renamed to `tkinter` in Python 3, and the `ttk` module becomes a submodule of `tkinter`.

5.5   Related Modules and Other GUIs

There are other GUI development systems that can be used with Python. We present the appropriate modules along with their corresponding window systems in Table 5-2.

Table 5-2   GUI Systems Available for Python

GUI Library	Description
Tk-Related Modules	
Tkinter/tkinter[a]	TK INTERface: Python's default GUI toolkit http://wiki.python.org/moin/TkInter
Pmw	Python MegaWidgets (Tkinter extension) http://pmw.sf.net
Tix	Tk Interface eXtension (Tk extension) http://tix.sf.net
Tile/Ttk	Tile/Ttk themed widget set http://tktable.sf.net
TkZinc (Zinc)	Extended Tk canvas type (Tk extension) http://www.tkzinc.org
EasyGUI (easygui)	Very simple, non-event-driven GUIs (Tkinter extension) http://ferg.org/easygui
TIDE + (IDE Studio)	Tix Integrated Development Environment (including IDE Studio, a Tix-enhanced version of the standard IDLE IDE) http://starship.python.net/crew/mike
wxWidgets-Related Modules	
wxPython	Python binding to wxWidgets, a cross-platform GUI framework (formerly known as wxWindows) http://wxpython.org
Boa Constructor	Python IDE and wxPython GUI builder http://boa-constructor.sf.net
PythonCard	wxPython-based desktop application GUI construction kit (inspired by HyperCard) http://pythoncard.sf.net
wxGlade	another wxPython GUI designer (inspired by Glade, the GTK+/GNOME GUI builder) http://wxglade.sf.net
GTK+/GNOME-Related Modules	
PyGTK	Python wrapper for the GIMP Toolkit (GTK+) library http://pygtk.org

GUI Library	Description
GTK+/GNOME-Related Modules	
GNOME-Python	Python binding to GNOME desktop and development libraries http://gnome.org/start/unstable/bindings http://download.gnome.org/sources/gnome-python
Glade	A GUI builder for GTK+ and GNOME http://glade.gnome.org
PyGUI (GUI)	Cross-platform "Pythonic" GUI API (built on Cocoa [Mac OS X] and GTK+ [POSIX/X11 and Win32]) http://www.cosc.canterbury.ac.nz/~greg/python_gui
Qt/KDE-Related Modules	
PyQt	Python binding for the Qt GUI/XML/SQL C++ toolkit from Trolltech (partially open source [dual-license]) http://riverbankcomputing.co.uk/pyqt
PyKDE	Python binding for the KDE desktop environment http://riverbankcomputing.co.uk/pykde
eric	Python IDE written in PyQt using QScintilla editor widget http://die-offenbachs.de/detlev/eric3 http://ericide.python-hosting.com/
PyQtGPL	Qt (Win32 Cygwin port), Sip, QScintilla, PyQt bundle http://pythonqt.vanrietpaap.nl
Other Open-Source GUI Toolkits	
FXPy	Python binding to FOX toolkit (http://fox-toolkit.org) http://fxpy.sf.net
pyFLTK (fltk)	Python binding to FLTK toolkit (http://fltk.org) http://pyfltk.sf.net
PyOpenGL (OpenGL)	Python binding to OpenGL (http://opengl.org) http://pyopengl.sf.net
Commercial	
win32ui	Microsoft MFC (via Python for Windows Extensions) http://starship.python.net/crew/mhammond/win32
swing	Sun Microsystems Java/Swing (via Jython) http://jython.org

a. Tkinter for Python 2 and tkinter for Python 3.

You can find out more about all GUIs related to Python from the general GUI Programming page on the Python wiki at http://wiki.python.org/moin/GuiProgramming.

5.6   Exercises

5-1. *Client/Server Architecture.* Describe the roles of a windows (or windowing) server and a windows client.

5-2. *Object-Oriented Programming.* Describe the relationship between child and parent widgets.

5-3. *Label Widgets.* Update the tkhello1.py script to display your own message instead of "Hello World!"

5-4. *Label and Button Widgets.* Update the tkhello3.py script so that there are three new buttons in addition to the QUIT button. Pressing any of the three buttons will result in changing the text label so that it will then contain the text of the Button (widget) that was pressed. Hint: You will need three separate handlers or customize one handler with arguments preset (still three function objects).

5-5. *Label, Button, and Radiobutton Widgets.* Modify your solution to Exercise 5-4 so that there are three Radiobuttons presenting the choices of text for the Label. There are two buttons: the QUIT button and an Update button. When the Update button is pressed, the text label will then be changed to contain the text of the selected Radiobutton. If no Radiobutton has been checked, the Label will remain unchanged.

5-6. *Label, Button, and Entry Widgets.* Modify your solution to Exercise 5-5 so that the three Radiobuttons are replaced by a single Entry text field widget with a default value of "Hello World!" (to reflect the initial string in the Label). The Entry field can be edited by the user with a new text string for the Label, which will be updated if the Update button is pressed.

5-7. *Label and Entry Widgets and Python I/O.* Create a GUI application that provides an Entry field in which the user can provide the name of a text file. Open the file and read it, displaying its contents in a Label.

Extra Credit (Menus): Replace the Entry widget with a menu that has a File Open option that pops up a window to allow the user to specify the file to read. Also add an Exit or Quit option to the menu to augment the QUIT button.

5-8. *Simple Text Editor.* Use your solution to the previous problem to create a simple text editor. A file can be created from scratch or read and displayed into a Text widget that can be edited by the user. When the user quits the application (either by using the QUIT button or the Quit/Exit menu option), the user is prompted whether to save the changes or quit without saving.

Extra Credit: Interface your script to a spellchecker and add a button or menu option to spellcheck the file. The words that are misspelled should be highlighted by using a different foreground or background color in the Text widget.

5-9. *Multithreaded Chat Applications.* The chat programs from the earlier chapters need completion. Create a fully-functional, multithreaded chat server. A GUI is not really necessary for the server unless you want to create one as a front-end to its configuration, for example, port number, name, connection to a name server, etc. Create a multithreaded chat client that has separate threads to monitor user input (and sends the message to the server for broadcast) and another thread to accept incoming messages to display to the user. The client front-end GUI should have two portions of the chat window: a larger section with multiple lines to hold all the dialog, and a smaller text entry field to accept input from the user.

5-10. *Using Other GUIs.* The example GUI applications using the various toolkits are very similar; however, they are not the same. Although it is impossible to make them all look *exactly* alike, tweak them so that they are more consistent than they are now.

5-11. *Using GUI Builders.* GUI builders help you to create GUI applications faster by auto-generating the boilerplate code for you so that all you have to do is "the hard stuff." Download a GUI builder tool and implement the animal GUI by just dragging the widgets from the corresponding palette. Hook it up with callbacks so that they behave just like the sample applications we looked at in this chapter.

What GUI builders are out there? For wxWidgets, see Python-Card, wxGlade, XRCed, wxFormBuilder, or even Boa Constructor (no longer maintained), and for GTK+, there's Glade (plus its friend GtkBuilder). For more tools like these, check out the "GUI Design Tools and IDEs" section of the GUI tools wiki page at http://wiki.python.org/moin/GuiProgramming.

CHAPTER 6

Database Programming

Did you really name your son Robert');
DROP TABLE Students;-- ?
—Randall Munroe, XKCD, October 2007

In this chapter...

- Introduction
- The Python DB-API
- ORMs
- Non-Relational Databases
- Related References

In this chapter, we discuss how to communicate with databases by using Python. Files or simplistic persistent storage can meet the needs of smaller applications, but larger server or high-data-volume applications might require a full-fledged database system, instead. Thus, we cover both relational and non-relational databases as well as Object-Relational Mappers (ORMs).

6.1   Introduction

This opening section will discuss the need for databases, present the Structured Query Language (SQL), and introduce readers to Python's database application programming interface (API).

6.1.1   Persistent Storage

In any application, there is a need for persistent storage. Generally, there are three basic storage mechanisms: files, a database system, or some sort of hybrid, such as an API that sits on top of one of those existing systems, an ORM, file manager, spreadsheet, configuration file, etc.

In the Files chapter of *Core Python Language Fundamentals* or *Core Python Programming*, we discussed persistent storage using both plain file access as well as a Python and database manager (DBM), which is an old Unix persistent storage mechanism, overlay on top of files, that is, *dbm, dbhash/ bsddb files, shelve (combination of pickle and DBM), and using their dictionary-like object interface.

This chapter will focus on using databases for the times when files or creating your own data storage system does not suffice for larger projects. In such cases, you will have many decisions to make. Thus, the goal of this chapter is to introduce you to the basics and show you as many of your options as possible (and how to work with them from within Python) so that you can make the right decision. We start off with SQL and relational databases first, because they are still the prevailing form of persistent storage.

6.1.2   Basic Database Operations and SQL

Before we dig into databases and how to use them with Python, we want to present a quick introduction (or review if you have some experience) to some elementary database concepts and SQL.

Underlying Storage

Databases usually have a fundamental persistent storage that uses the file system, that is, normal operating system files, special operating system files, and even raw disk partitions.

User Interface

Most database systems provide a command-line tool with which to issue SQL commands or queries. There are also some GUI tools that use the command-line clients or the database client library, affording users a much more comfortable interface.

Databases

A relational database management system (RDBMS) can usually manage multiple databases, such as sales, marketing, customer support, etc., all on the same server (if the RDBMS is server-based; simpler systems are usually not). In the examples we will look at in this chapter, MySQL demonstrates a server-based RDBMS because there is a server process running continuously, waiting for commands; neither SQLite nor Gadfly have running servers.

Components

The *table* is the storage abstraction for databases. Each *row* of data will have fields that correspond to database *columns*. The set of table definitions of columns and data types per table all put together define the database *schema*.

Databases are *created* and *dropped*. The same is true for tables. Adding new rows to a database is called *inserting*; changing existing rows in a table is called *updating*; and removing existing rows in a table is called *deleting*. These actions are usually referred to as database *commands* or *operations*. Requesting rows from a database with optional criteria is called *querying*.

When you query a database, you can *fetch* all of the results (rows) at once, or just iterate slowly over each resulting row. Some databases use the concept of a *cursor* for issuing SQL commands, queries, and grabbing results, either all at once or one row at a time.

SQL

Database commands and queries are given to a database via SQL. Not all databases use SQL, but the majority of relational databases do. Following are some examples of SQL commands. Note that most databases are configured to be case-insensitive, especially database commands. The accepted style is to use CAPS for database keywords. Most command-line programs require a trailing semicolon (;) to terminate a SQL statement.

Creating a Database

```
CREATE DATABASE test;
GRANT ALL ON test.* to user(s);
```

The first line creates a database named "test," and assuming that you are a database administrator, the second line can be used to grant permissions to specific users (or all of them) so that they can perform the database operations that follow.

Using a Database

```
USE test;
```

If you logged into a database system without choosing which database you want to use, this simple statement allows you to specify one with which to perform database operations.

Dropping a Database

```
DROP DATABASE test;
```

This simple statement removes all the tables and data from the database and deletes it from the system.

Creating a Table

```
CREATE TABLE users (login VARCHAR(8), userid INT, projid INT);
```

This statement creates a new table with a string column login and a pair of integer fields, userid and projid.

Dropping a Table

```
DROP TABLE users;
```

This simple statement drops a database table, along with all its data.

Inserting a Row

```
INSERT INTO users VALUES('leanna', 2111, 1);
```

You can insert a new row in a database by using the INSERT statement. You specify the table and the values that go into each field. For our example, the string 'leanna' goes into the login field, and 2111 and 1 to userid and projid, respectively.

Updating a Row

```
UPDATE users SET projid=4 WHERE projid=2;
UPDATE users SET projid=1 WHERE userid=311;
```

To change existing table rows, you use the UPDATE statement. Use SET for the columns that are changing and provide any criteria for determining which rows should change. In the first example, all users with a "project ID" (or projid) of 2 will be moved to project #4. In the second example, we take one user (with a UID of 311) and move him to project #1.

Deleting a Row

```
DELETE FROM users WHERE projid=%d;
DELETE FROM users;
```

To delete a table row, use the DELETE FROM command, specify the table from which you want to delete rows, and any optional criteria. Without it, as in the second example, all rows will be deleted.

Now that you are up to speed on basic database concepts, it should make following the rest of the chapter and its examples much easier. If you need additional help, there are plenty of database tutorial books available that can do the trick.

6.1.3   Databases and Python

We are going to cover the Python database API and look at how to access relational databases from Python—either directly through a database interface, or via an ORM—and how you can accomplish the same task but without necessarily having to give explicit commands in SQL.

Topics such as database principles, concurrency, schema, atomicity, integrity, recovery, proper complex left JOINs, triggers, query optimization, transactions, stored procedures, etc., are all beyond the scope of this text, and we will not be discussing them in this chapter other than direct use from a Python application. Rather, we will present how to store and retrieve data to and from RDBMSs while playing within a Python framework. You can then decide which is best for your current project or application and be able to study sample code that can get you started instantly. The goal is to get you on top of things as quickly as possible if you need to integrate your Python application with some sort of database system.

We are also breaking out of our mode of covering only the "batteries included" features of the Python Standard Library. While our original goal was to play only in that arena, it has become clear that being able to work with databases is really a core component of everyday application development in the Python world.

As a software engineer, you can probably only make it so far in your career without having to learn something about databases: how to use one (command-line and/or GUI interfaces), how to extract data by using the SQL, perhaps how to add or update information in a database, etc. If Python is your programming tool, then a lot of the hard work has already been done for you as you add database access to your Python universe. We first describe what the Python database API, or *DB-API* is, then give examples of database interfaces that conform to this standard.

We will show some examples using popular open-source RDBMSs. However, we will not include discussions of open-source versus commercial products. Adapting to those other RDBMS systems should be fairly straightforward. A special mention will be given to Aaron Watters's Gadfly database, a simple RDBMS written completely in Python.

The way to access a database from Python is via an *adapter*. An adapter is a Python module with which you can interface to a relational database's client library, usually in C. It is recommended that all Python adapters conform to the API of the Python database special interest group (DB-SIG). This is the first major topic of this chapter.

Figure 6-1 illustrates the layers involved in writing a Python database application, with and without an ORM. The figure demonstrates that the DB-API is your interface to the C libraries of the database client.

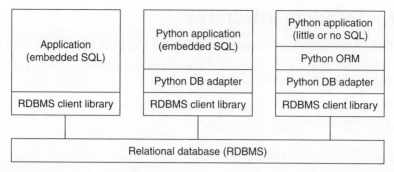

Figure 6-1 Multitiered communication between application and database. The first box is generally a C/C++ program, whereas DB-API-compliant adapters let you program applications in Python. ORMs can simplify an application by handling all of the database-specific details.

6.2   The Python DB-API

Where can one find the interfaces necessary to talk to a database? Simple. Just go to the database topics section at the main Python Web site. There you will find links to the full and current DB-API (version 2.0), existing database modules, documentation, the special interest group, etc. Since its inception, the DB-API has been moved into PEP 249. (This PEP supersedes the old DB-API 1.0 specification, which is PEP 248.) What is the DB-API?

The API is a specification that states a set of required objects and database access mechanisms to provide consistent access across the various database adapters and underlying database systems. Like most community-based efforts, the API was driven by strong need.

In the "old days," we had a scenario of many databases and many people implementing their own database adapters. It was a wheel that was being reinvented over and over again. These databases and adapters were implemented at different times by different people without any consistency of functionality. Unfortunately, this meant that application code using such interfaces also had to be customized to which database module they chose to use, and any changes to that interface also meant updates were needed in the application code.

SIG for Python database connectivity was formed, and eventually, an API was born: the DB-API version 1.0. The API provides for a consistent interface to a variety of relational databases, and porting code between different databases is much simpler, usually only requiring tweaking several lines of code. You will see an example of this later on in this chapter.

6.2.1   Module Attributes

The DB-API specification mandates that the features and attributes listed below must be supplied. A DB-API-compliant module must define the global attributes as shown in Table 6-1.

Table 6-1   DB-API Module Attributes

Attribute	Description
apilevel	The version of the DB-API with which an adapter is compliant
threadsafety	Level of thread safety of this module
paramstyle	SQL statement parameter style of this module
connect()	Connect() function
(Various exceptions)	*(See Table 6-4)*

Data Attributes

apilevel

This string (not float) indicates the highest version of the DB-API with which the module is compliant, for example, 1.0, 2.0, etc. If absent, 1.0 should be assumed as the default value.

threadsafety

This an integer that can take the following possible values:

- 0: Not threadsafe, so threads should not share the module at all
- 1: Minimally threadsafe: threads can share the module but not connections
- 2: Moderately threadsafe: threads can share the module and connections but not cursors
- 3: Fully threadsafe: threads can share the module, connections, and cursors

If a resource is shared, a synchronization primitive such as a spin lock or semaphore is required for atomic-locking purposes. Disk files and global variables are not reliable for this purpose and can interfere with standard mutex operation. See the `threading` module or go back to Chapter 4, "Multithreaded Programming," for more information on how to use a lock.

paramstyle

The API supports a variety of ways to indicate how parameters should be integrated into an SQL statement that is eventually sent to the server for execution. This argument is just a string that specifies the form of string substitution you will use when building rows for a query or command (see Table 6-2).

Table 6-2   `paramstyle` Database Parameter Styles

Parameter Style	Description	Example
`numeric`	Numeric positional style	`WHERE name=:1`
`named`	Named style	`WHERE name=:name`
`pyformat`	Python dictionary `printf()` format conversion	`WHERE name=%(name)s`
`qmark`	Question mark style	`WHERE name=?`
`format`	ANSI C `printf()` format conversion	`WHERE name=%s`

Function Attribute(s)

`connect()` Function access to the database is made available through `Connection` objects. A compliant module must implement a `connect()` function, which creates and returns a `Connection` object. Table 6-3 shows the arguments to `connect()`.

Table 6-3   connect() Function Attributes

Parameter	Description
user	Username
password	Password
host	Hostname
database	Database name
dsn	Data source name

You can pass in database connection information as a string with multiple parameters (DSN) or individual parameters passed as positional arguments (if you know the exact order), or more likely, keyword arguments. Here is an example of using connect() from PEP 249:

```
connect(dsn='myhost:MYDB',user='guido',password='234$')
```

The use of DSN versus individual parameters is based primarily on the system to which you are connecting. For example, if you are using an API like Open Database Connectivity (ODBC) or Java DataBase Connectivity (JDBC), you would likely be using a DSN, whereas if you are working directly with a database, then you are more likely to issue separate login parameters. Another reason for this is that most database adapters have not implemented support for DSN. The following are some examples of non-DSN connect() calls. Note that not all adapters have implemented the specification exactly, e.g., MySQLdb uses db instead of database.

- `MySQLdb.connect(host='dbserv', db='inv', user='smith')`
- `PgSQL.connect(database='sales')`
- `psycopg.connect(database='template1', user='pgsql')`
- `gadfly.dbapi20.connect('csrDB', '/usr/local/database')`
- `sqlite3.connect('marketing/test')`

Exceptions

Exceptions that should also be included in the compliant module as globals are shown in Table 6-4.

Table 6-4 DB-API Exception Classes

Exception	Description
`Warning`	Root warning exception class
`Error`	Root error exception class
`InterfaceError`	Database interface (not database) error
`DatabaseError`	Database error
`DataError`	Problems with the processed data
`OperationalError`	Error during database operation execution
`IntegrityError`	Database relational integrity error
`InternalError`	Error that occurs within the database
`ProgrammingError`	SQL command failed
`NotSupportedError`	Unsupported operation occurred

6.2.2   Connection Objects

Connections are how your application communicates with the database. They represent the fundamental mechanism by which commands are sent to the server and results returned. Once a connection has been established (or a pool of connections), you create cursors to send requests to and receive replies from the database.

Connection Object Methods

Connection objects are not required to have any data attributes but should define the methods shown in Table 6-5.

Table 6-5   `Connection` Object Methods

Method Name	Description
`close()`	Close database connection
`commit()`	Commit current transaction
`rollback()`	Cancel current transaction
`cursor()`	Create (and return) a cursor or cursor-like object using this connection
`errorhandler(`*cxn, cur,* *errcls, errval*`)`	Serves as a handler for given connection cursor

When `close()` is used, the same connection cannot be used again without running into an exception.

The `commit()` method is irrelevant if the database does not support transactions or if it has an auto-commit feature that has been enabled. You can implement separate methods to turn auto-commit off or on if you wish. Since this method is required as part of the API, databases that do not support transactions should just implement "pass" for this method.

Like `commit()`, `rollback()` only makes sense if transactions are supported in the database. After execution, `rollback()` should leave the database in the same state as it was when the transaction began. According to PEP 249, "*Closing a connection without committing the changes first will cause an implicit rollback to be performed.*"

If the RDBMS does not support cursors, `cursor()` should still return an object that faithfully emulates or imitates a real cursor object. These are just the minimum requirements. Each individual adapter developer can always add special attributes specifically for their interface or database.

It is also recommended but not required for adapter writers to make all database module exceptions (see earlier) available via a connection. If not, then it is assumed that `Connection` objects will throw the corresponding module-level exception. Once you have completed using your connection and cursors are closed, you should `commit()` any operations and `close()` your connection.

6.2.3   Cursor Objects

Once you have a connection, you can begin communicating with the database. As we mentioned earlier in the introductory section, a cursor lets a user issue database commands and retrieve rows resulting from queries. A Python DB-API cursor object functions as a cursor for you, even if cursors are not supported in the database. In this case, if you are creating a database adapter, you must implement cursor objects so that they act like cursors. This keeps your Python code consistent when you switch between database systems that support or do not support cursors.

Once you have created a cursor, you can execute a query or command (or multiple queries and commands) and retrieve one or more rows from the results set. Table 6-6 presents Cursor object data attributes and methods.

Table 6-6 Cursor Object Attributes

Object Attribute	Description
arraysize	Number of rows to fetch at a time with fetchmany(); default is 1
connection	Connection that created this cursor (optional)
description	Returns cursor activity (7-item tuples): (name, type_code, display_size, internal_ size, precision, scale, null_ok); only *name* and type_code are required
lastrowid	Row ID of last modified row (optional; if row IDs not supported, default to None)
rowcount	Number of rows that the last execute*() produced or affected
callproc(*func*[, *args*])	Call a stored procedure
close()	Close cursor
execute(*op*[, *args*])	Execute a database query or command
executemany(*op*, *args*)	Like execute() and map() combined; prepare and execute a database query or command over given arguments

(Continued)

Table 6-6   Cursor Object Attributes *(Continued)*

Object Attribute	Description
`fetchone()`	Fetch next row of query result
`fetchmany ([size= cursor.arraysize])`	Fetch next size rows of query result
`fetchall()`	Fetch all (remaining) rows of a query result
`__iter__()`	Create iterator object from this cursor (optional; also see `next()`)
`messages`	List of messages (set of tuples) received from the database for cursor execution (optional)
`next()`	Used by iterator to fetch next row of query result (optional; like `fetchone()`, also see `__iter__()`)
`nextset()`	Move to next results set (if supported)
`rownumber`	Index of cursor (by row, 0-based) in current result set (optional)
`setinputsizes(sizes)`	Set maximum input size allowed (required but implementation optional)
`setoutputsize(size[,col])`	Set maximum buffer size for large column fetches (required but implementation optional)

The most critical attributes of cursor objects are the `execute*()` and the `fetch*()` methods; all service requests to the database are performed by these. The `arraysize` data attribute is useful in setting a default size for `fetchmany()`. Of course, closing the cursor is a good thing, and if your database supports stored procedures, then you will be using `callproc()`.

6.2.4   Type Objects and Constructors

Oftentimes, the interface between two different systems are the most fragile. This is seen when converting Python objects to C types and vice versa. Similarly, there is also a fine line between Python objects and native database objects. As a programmer writing to Python's DB-API, the parameters you send to a database are given as strings, but the database might need to convert it to a variety of different, supported data types that are correct for any particular query.

For example, should the Python string be converted to a VARCHAR, a TEXT, a BLOB, or a raw BINARY object, or perhaps a DATE or TIME object if that is what the string is supposed to be? Care must be taken to provide database input in the expected format; therefore, another requirement of the DB-API is to create constructors that build special objects that can easily be converted to the appropriate database objects. Table 6-7 describes classes that can be used for this purpose. SQL NULL values are mapped to and from Python's NULL object, None.

Table 6-7   Type Objects and Constructors

Type Object	Description
Date(*yr,mo,dy*)	Object for a date value
Time(*hr,min,sec*)	Object for a time value
Timestamp (*yr,mo,dy,hr,min,sec*)	Object for a timestamp value
DateFromTicks(*ticks*)	Date object, given in number of seconds since the epoch
TimeFromTicks(*ticks*)	Time object, given in number of seconds since the epoch
TimestampFromTicks(*ticks*)	Timestamp object, given in number of seconds since the epoch
Binary(*string*)	Object for a binary (long) string value
STRING	Object describing string-based columns, for example, VARCHAR
BINARY	Object describing (long) binary columns, for example, RAW, BLOB
NUMBER	Object describing numeric columns
DATETIME	Object describing date/time columns
ROWID	Object describing "row ID" columns

Changes to API Between Versions

Several important changes were made when the DB-API was revised from version 1.0 (1996) to 2.0 (1999):

- The required `dbi` module was removed from the API.

- Type objects were updated.

- New attributes were added to provide better database bindings.

- `callproc()` semantics and the return value of `execute()` were redefined.

- Conversion to class-based exceptions.

Since version 2.0 was published, some of the additional, optional DB-API extensions that you just read about were added in 2002. There have been no other significant changes to the API since it was published. Continuing discussions of the API occur on the DB-SIG mailing list. Among the topics brought up over the last five years include the possibilities for the next version of the DB-API, tentatively named DB-API 3.0. These include the following:

- Better return value for `nextset()` when there is a new result set.

- Switch from `float` to `Decimal`.

- Improved flexibility and support for parameter styles.

- Prepared statements or statement caching.

- Refine the transaction model.

- State the role of API with respect to portability.

- Add unit testing.

If you have strong feelings about the API or its future, feel free to participate and join in the discussion. Here are some references that you might find handy.

- http://python.org/topics/database

- http://linuxjournal.com/article/2605 (outdated but historical)

- http://wiki.python.org/moin/DbApi3

6.2.5   Relational Databases

So, you are now ready to go, but you probably have one burning question: "which interfaces to database systems are available to me in Python?" That inquiry is similar to, "which platforms is Python available for?" The answer is, "Pretty much all of them." Following is a broad (but not exhaustive) list of interfaces:

Commercial RDBMSs

- IBM Informix
- Sybase
- Oracle
- Microsoft SQL Server
- IBM DB2
- SAP
- Embarcadero Interbase
- Ingres

Open-Source RDBMSs

- MySQL
- PostgreSQL
- SQLite
- Gadfly

Database APIs

- JDBC
- ODBC

Non-Relational Databases

- MongoDB
- Redis
- Cassandra
- SimpleDB

- Tokyo Cabinet

- CouchDB

- Bigtable (via Google App Engine Datastore API)

To find an updated (but not necessarily the most recent) list of what databases are supported, go to the following Web site:

http://wiki.python.org/moin/DatabaseInterfaces

6.2.6   Databases and Python: Adapters

For each of the databases supported, there exists one or more adapters that let you connect to the target database system from Python. Some databases, such as Sybase, SAP, Oracle, and SQLServer, have more than one adapter available. The best thing to do is to determine which ones best fit your needs. Your questions for each candidate might include: how good is its performance, how useful is its documentation and/or Web site, whether it has an active community or not, what is the overall quality and stability of the driver, etc. You have to keep in mind that most adapters provide just the basic necessities to get you connected to the database. It is the extras that you might be looking for. Keep in mind that you are responsible for higher-level code like threading and thread management as well as management of database connection pools, etc.

If you are squeamish and want less hands-on interaction—for example, if you prefer to do as little SQL or database administration as possible—then you might want to consider ORMs, which are covered later in this chapter.

Let's now look at some examples of how to use an adapter module to communicate with a relational database. The real secret is in setting up the connection. Once you have this and use the DB-API objects, attributes, and object methods, your core code should be pretty much the same, regardless of which adapter and RDBMS you use.

6.2.7   Examples of Using Database Adapters

First, let's look at a some sample code, from creating a database to creating a table and using it. We present examples that use MySQL, PostgreSQL, and SQLite.

MySQL

We will use MySQL as the example here, along with the most well-known MySQL Python adapter: MySQLdb, a.k.a. MySQL-python—we'll discuss the other MySQL adapter, MySQL Connector/Python, when our conversation turns to Python 3. In the various bits of code that follow, we'll also expose you (deliberately) to examples of error situations so that you have an idea of what to expect, and for which you might want to create handlers.

We first log in as an administrator to create a database and grant permissions, then log back in as a normal client, as shown here:

```
>>> import MySQLdb
>>> cxn = MySQLdb.connect(user='root')
>>> cxn.query('DROP DATABASE test')
Traceback (most recent call last):
  File "<stdin>", line 1, in ?
_mysql_exceptions.OperationalError: (1008, "Can't drop, database
'test'; database doesn't exist")
>>> cxn.query('CREATE DATABASE test')
>>> cxn.query("GRANT ALL ON test.* to ''@'localhost'")
>>> cxn.commit()
>>> cxn.close()
```

In the preceding code, we did not use a cursor. Some adapters have Connection objects, which can execute SQL queries with the query() method, but not all. We recommend you either not use it or check your adapter to ensure that it is available.

The commit() was optional for us because auto-commit is turned on by default in MySQL. We then connect back to the new database as a regular user, create a table, and then perform the usual queries and commands by using SQL to get our job done via Python. This time we use cursors and their execute() method.

The next set of interactions shows us creating a table. An attempt to create it again (without first dropping it) results in an error:

```
>>> cxn = MySQLdb.connect(db='test')
>>> cur = cxn.cursor()
>>> cur.execute('CREATE TABLE users(login VARCHAR(8), userid INT)')
0L
```

Now we will insert a few rows into the database and query them out:

```
>>> cur.execute("INSERT INTO users VALUES('john', 7000)")
1L
>>> cur.execute("INSERT INTO users VALUES('jane', 7001)")
1L
>>> cur.execute("INSERT INTO users VALUES('bob', 7200)")
1L
```

```
>>> cur.execute("SELECT * FROM users WHERE login LIKE 'j%'")
2L
>>> for data in cur.fetchall():
...   print '%s\t%s' % data
...
john    7000
jane    7001
```

The last bit features updating the table, either by updating or deleting rows:

```
>>> cur.execute("UPDATE users SET userid=7100 WHERE userid=7001")
1L
>>> cur.execute("SELECT * FROM users")
3L
>>> for data in cur.fetchall():
...   print '%s\t%s' % data
...
john    7000
jane    7100
bob     7200
>>> cur.execute('DELETE FROM users WHERE login="bob"')
1L
>>> cur.execute('DROP TABLE users')
0L
>>> cur.close()
>>> cxn.commit()
>>> cxn.close()
```

MySQL is one of the most popular open-source databases in the world, and it is no surprise that a Python adapter is available for it.

PostgreSQL

Another popular open-source database is PostgreSQL. Unlike MySQL, there are no less than three Python adapters available for Postgres: psycopg, PyPgSQL, and PyGreSQL. A fourth, PoPy, is now defunct, having contributed its project to combine with that of PyGreSQL in 2003. Each of the three remaining adapters has its own characteristics, strengths, and weaknesses, so it would be a good idea to practice due diligence to determine which is right for you.

Note that while we demonstrate the use of each of these, PyPgSQL has not been actively developed since 2006, whereas PyGreSQL released its most recent version (4.0) in 2009. This inactivity clearly leaves psycopg as the sole leader of the PostgreSQL adapters, and this will be the final version of this book featuring examples of those adapters. psycopg is on its second version, meaning that even though our examples use the version 1 psycopg module, when you download it today, you'll be using psycopg2, instead.

The good news is that the interfaces are similar enough that you can create an application that, for example, measures the performance between all three (if that is a metric that is important to you). The following presents the setup code to get a Connection object for each adapter.

psycopg

```
>>> import psycopg
>>> cxn = psycopg.connect(user='pgsql')
```

PyPgSQL

```
>>> from pyPgSQL import PgSQL
>>> cxn = PgSQL.connect(user='pgsql')
```

PyGreSQL

```
>>> import pgdb
>>> cxn = pgdb.connect(user='pgsql')
```

Here is some generic code that will work for all three adapters:

```
>>> cur = cxn.cursor()
>>> cur.execute('SELECT * FROM pg_database')
>>> rows = cur.fetchall()
>>> for i in rows:
...    print i
>>> cur.close()
>>> cxn.commit()
>>> cxn.close()
```

Finally, you can see how the output from each adapter is slightly different from one another.

PyPgSQL

```
sales
template1
template0
```

psycopg

```
('sales', 1, 0, 0, 1, 17140, '140626', '3221366099', '', None, None)
('template1', 1, 0, 1, 1, 17140, '462', '462', '', None, '{pgsql=C*T*/
pgsql}')
('template0', 1, 0, 1, 0, 17140, '462', '462', '', None, '{pgsql=C*T*/
pgsql}')
```

PyGreSQL

```
['sales', 1, 0, False, True, 17140L, '140626', '3221366099', '', None,
None]
```

```
['template1', 1, 0, True, True, 17140L, '462', '462', '', None,
'{pgsql=C*T*/pgsql}']
['template0', 1, 0, True, False, 17140L, '462', '462', '', None,
'{pgsql=C*T*/pgsql}']
```

SQLite

For extremely simple applications, using files for persistent storage usually suffices, but the most complex and data-driven applications demand a full relational database. SQLite targets the intermediate systems, and indeed is a hybrid of the two. It is extremely lightweight and fast, plus it is serverless and requires little or no administration.

SQLite has experienced a rapid growth in popularity, and it is available on many platforms. With the introduction of the pysqlite database adapter in Python 2.5 as the `sqlite3` module, this marks the first time that the Python Standard Library has featured a database adapter in any release.

It was bundled with Python not because it was favored over other databases and adapters, but because it is simple, uses files (or memory) as its back-end store like the DBM modules do, does not require a server, and does not have licensing issues. It is simply an alternative to other similar persistent storage solutions included with Python but which happens to have a SQL interface.

Having a module like this in the standard library allows you to develop rapidly in Python by using SQLite, and then migrate to a more powerful RDBMS such as MySQL, PostgreSQL, Oracle, or SQL Server for production purposes, if this is your intention. If you don't need all that horsepower, `sqlite3` is a great solution.

Although the database adapter is now provided in the standard library, you still have to download the actual database software yourself. However, once you have installed it, all you need to do is start up Python (and import the adapter) to gain immediate access:

```
>>> import sqlite3
>>> cxn = sqlite3.connect('sqlite_test/test')
>>> cur = cxn.cursor()
>>> cur.execute('CREATE TABLE users(login VARCHAR(8),
        userid INTEGER)')
>>> cur.execute('INSERT INTO users VALUES("john", 100)')
>>> cur.execute('INSERT INTO users VALUES("jane", 110)')
>>> cur.execute('SELECT * FROM users')
>>> for eachUser in cur.fetchall():
...     print eachUser
...
(u'john', 100)
(u'jane', 110)
```

```
>>> cur.execute('DROP TABLE users')
<sqlite3.Cursor object at 0x3d4320>
>>> cur.close()
>>> cxn.commit()
>>> cxn.close()
```

Okay, enough of the small examples. Next, we look at an application similar to our earlier example with MySQL, but which does a few more things:

- Creates a database (if necessary)

- Creates a table

- Inserts rows into the table

- Updates rows in the table

- Deletes rows from the table

- Drops the table

For this example, we will use two other open-source databases. SQLite has become quite popular of late. It is very small, lightweight, and extremely fast for all of the most common database functions. Another database involved in this example is Gadfly, a mostly SQL-compliant RDBMS written entirely in Python. (Some of the key data structures have a C module available, but Gadfly can run without it [slower, of course].)

Some notes before we get to the code. Both SQLite and Gadfly require that you specify the location to store database files (MySQL has a default area and does not require this information). The most current incarnation of Gadfly is not yet fully DB-API 2.0 compliant, and as a result, it is missing some functionality, most notably the cursor attribute, rowcount, in our example.

6.2.8 A Database Adapter Example Application

In the example that follows, we demonstrate how to use Python to access a database. For the sake of variety and exposing you to as much code as possible, we added support for three different database systems: Gadfly, SQLite, and MySQL. To mix things up even further, we're first going to dump out the entire Python 2.x source, without a line-by-line explanation.

The application works in exactly the same ways as described via the bullet points in the previous subsection. You should be able to understand its functionality without a full explanation—just start with the main() function at the bottom. (To keep things simple, for a full system such as

MySQL that has a server, we will just login as the root user, although it's discouraged to do this for a production application.) Here's the source code for this application, which is called ushuffle_db.py:

```python
#!/usr/bin/env python

import os
from random import randrange as rand

COLSIZ = 10
FIELDS = ('login', 'userid', 'projid')
RDBMSs = {'s': 'sqlite', 'm': 'mysql', 'g': 'gadfly'}
DBNAME = 'test'
DBUSER = 'root'
DB_EXC = None
NAMELEN = 16

tformat = lambda s: str(s).title().ljust(COLSIZ)
cformat = lambda s: s.upper().ljust(COLSIZ)

def setup():
    return RDBMSs[raw_input('''
Choose a database system:

(M)ySQL
(G)adfly
(S)QLite

Enter choice: ''').strip().lower()[0]]

def connect(db):
    global DB_EXC
    dbDir = '%s_%s' % (db, DBNAME)

    if db == 'sqlite':
        try:
            import sqlite3
        except ImportError:
            try:
                from pysqlite2 import dbapi2 as sqlite3
            except ImportError:
                return None

        DB_EXC = sqlite3
        if not os.path.isdir(dbDir):
            os.mkdir(dbDir)
        cxn = sqlite3.connect(os.path.join(dbDir, DBNAME))

    elif db == 'mysql':
        try:
            import MySQLdb
            import _mysql_exceptions as DB_EXC
```

```python
        except ImportError:
            return None

        try:
            cxn = MySQLdb.connect(db=DBNAME)
        except DB_EXC.OperationalError:
            try:
                cxn = MySQLdb.connect(user=DBUSER)
                cxn.query('CREATE DATABASE %s' % DBNAME)
                cxn.commit()
                cxn.close()
                cxn = MySQLdb.connect(db=DBNAME)
            except DB_EXC.OperationalError:
                return None

    elif db == 'gadfly':
        try:
            from gadfly import gadfly
            DB_EXC = gadfly
        except ImportError:
            return None

        try:
            cxn = gadfly(DBNAME, dbDir)
        except IOError:
            cxn = gadfly()
            if not os.path.isdir(dbDir):
                os.mkdir(dbDir)
            cxn.startup(DBNAME, dbDir)
    else:
        return None
    return cxn

def create(cur):
    try:
        cur.execute('''
            CREATE TABLE users (
                login   VARCHAR(%d),
                userid INTEGER,
                projid INTEGER)
        ''' % NAMELEN)
    except DB_EXC.OperationalError:
        drop(cur)
        create(cur)

drop = lambda cur: cur.execute('DROP TABLE users')

NAMES = (
    ('aaron', 8312), ('angela', 7603), ('dave', 7306),
    ('davina',7902), ('elliot', 7911), ('ernie', 7410),
    ('jess', 7912), ('jim', 7512), ('larry', 7311),
    ('leslie', 7808), ('melissa', 8602), ('pat', 7711),
```

```
        ('serena', 7003), ('stan', 7607), ('faye', 6812),
        ('amy', 7209), ('mona', 7404), ('jennifer', 7608),
)

def randName():
    pick = set(NAMES)
    while pick:
        yield pick.pop()

def insert(cur, db):
    if db == 'sqlite':
        cur.executemany("INSERT INTO users VALUES(?, ?, ?)",
            [(who, uid, rand(1,5)) for who, uid in randName()])
    elif db == 'gadfly':
        for who, uid in randName():
            cur.execute("INSERT INTO users VALUES(?, ?, ?)",
                (who, uid, rand(1,5)))
    elif db == 'mysql':
        cur.executemany("INSERT INTO users VALUES(%s, %s, %s)",
            [(who, uid, rand(1,5)) for who, uid in randName()])

getRC = lambda cur: cur.rowcount if hasattr(cur, 'rowcount') else -1

def update(cur):
    fr = rand(1,5)
    to = rand(1,5)
    cur.execute(
        "UPDATE users SET projid=%d WHERE projid=%d" % (to, fr))
    return fr, to, getRC(cur)

def delete(cur):
    rm = rand(1,5)
    cur.execute('DELETE FROM users WHERE projid=%d' % rm)
    return rm, getRC(cur)

def dbDump(cur):
    cur.execute('SELECT * FROM users')
    print '\n%s' % ''.join(map(cformat, FIELDS))
    for data in cur.fetchall():
        print ''.join(map(tformat, data))

def main():
    db = setup()
    print '*** Connect to %r database' % db
    cxn = connect(db)
    if not cxn:
        print 'ERROR: %r not supported or unreachable, exiting' % db
        return
    cur = cxn.cursor()

    print '\n*** Create users table (drop old one if appl.)'
    create(cur)
```

```
        print '\n*** Insert names into table'
        insert(cur, db)
        dbDump(cur)

        print '\n*** Move users to a random group'
        fr, to, num = update(cur)
        print '\t(%d users moved) from (%d) to (%d)' % (num, fr, to)
        dbDump(cur)

        print '\n*** Randomly delete group'
        rm, num = delete(cur)
        print '\t(group #%d; %d users removed)' % (rm, num)
        dbDump(cur)

        print '\n*** Drop users table'
        drop(cur)
        print '\n*** Close cxns'
        cur.close()
        cxn.commit()
        cxn.close()

    if __name__ == '__main__':
        main()
```

Trust me, this application runs. It's available for download from this book's Web site if you really want to try it out. However, before we execute it here in the book, there's one more matter to take care of. No, we're not going to give you the line-by-line explanation yet.

Don't worry, the line-by-line is coming up, but we wanted to use this example for another purpose: to demonstrate another example of porting to Python 3 and how it's possible to build scripts that will run under both Python 2 and 3 with a single source .py file and without the need for conversion using tools like 2to3 or 3to2. After the port, we'll officially make it Example 6-1. Furthermore, we'll use and reuse the attributes from this example in the examples for the remainder of the chapter, porting it to use ORMs as well as non-relational databases.

3.x

Porting to Python 3

A handful of porting recommendations are provided in the best practices chapter of *Core Python Language Fundamentals*, but we wanted to share some specific tips here and implement them by using ushuffle_db.py.

One of the big porting differences between Python 2 and 3 is **print**, which is a statement in Python 2 but a built-in function (BIF) in Python 3. Instead of using either, you can proxy for both by using the distutils.log.warn() function—at least you could at the time of this writing. It's identical in

Python 2 and 3; thus, it doesn't require any changes. To keep the code from getting confusing, we rename this function to `printf()` in our application, in homage to the **print**/`print()`-equivalent in C/C++. Also see the related exercise at the end of this chapter.

The second tip is for the Python 2 BIF `raw_input()`. It changes its name to `input()` in Python 3. This is further complicated by the fact that there is also an `input()` function in Python 2 that is a security hazard and removed from the language. In other words, `raw_input()` replaces and is renamed to `input()` in Python 3. To continue honoring C/C++, we call this function `scanf()` in our application.

The next tip is to remind you of the changes in the syntax for handling exceptions. This subject is covered in detail in the Errors and Exceptions chapter of *Core Python Language Fundamentals* and *Core Python Programming*. You can read more about the update there, but for now, the fundamental change that you need to know about is this:

Old: **except** *Exception, instance*

New: **except** *Exception* **as** *instance*

However, this only matters if you save the instance because you're interested in the cause of the exception. If it doesn't matter or you're not intending to use it, just leave it out. There's nothing wrong with just: **except** *Exception*.

That syntax does not change between Python 2 and 3. In earlier editions of this book, we used **except** *Exception*, e. For this edition, we've removed the ", e" altogether rather than changing it to "**as** e" to make porting easier.

Finally, the last change we're going to do is tied specifically to our example, whereas those other changes are general porting suggestions. At the time of this writing, the main C-based MySQL-Python adapter, better known by its package name, `MySQLdb`, has not yet been ported to Python 3. However, there is another MySQL adapter, and it's called MySQL Connector/Python and has a package name of `mysql.connector`.

MySQL Connector/Python implements the MySQL client protocol in pure Python, so neither MySQL libraries nor compilation are necessary, and best of all, there is a port to Python 3. Why is this a big deal? It gives Python 3 users access to MySQL databases, that's all!

Making all of these changes and additions to ushuffle_db.py, we arrive at what I'd like to refer to as the "universal" version of the application, ushuffle_dbU.py, which you can see in Example 6-1.

Example 6-1   Database Adapter Example (ushuffle_dbU.py)

This script performs some basic operations by using a variety of databases (MySQL, SQLite, Gadfly). It runs under Python 2 and 3 without any code changes, and components will be (re)used in future sections of this chapter.

```python
1    #!/usr/bin/env python
2
3    from distutils.log import warn as printf
4    import os
5    from random import randrange as rand
6
7    if isinstance(__builtins__, dict) and 'raw_input' in __builtins__:
8        scanf = raw_input
9    elif hasattr(__builtins__, 'raw_input'):
10        scanf = raw_input
11    else:
12        scanf = input
13
14    COLSIZ = 10
15    FIELDS = ('login', 'userid', 'projid')
16    RDBMSs = {'s': 'sqlite', 'm': 'mysql', 'g': 'gadfly'}
17    DBNAME = 'test'
18    DBUSER = 'root'
19    DB_EXC = None
20    NAMELEN = 16
21
22    tformat = lambda s: str(s).title().ljust(COLSIZ)
23    cformat = lambda s: s.upper().ljust(COLSIZ)
24
25    def setup():
26        return RDBMSs[raw_input('''
27    Choose a database system:
28
29    (M)ySQL
30    (G)adfly
31    (S)QLite
32
33    Enter choice: ''').strip().lower()[0]]
34
35    def connect(db, DBNAME):
36        global DB_EXC
37        dbDir = '%s_%s' % (db, DBNAME)
38
```

(Continued)

Example 6-1   Database Adapter Example (ushuffle_dbU.py) *(Continued)*

```
39      if db == 'sqlite':
40          try:
41                  import sqlite3
42          except ImportError:
43              try:
44                      from pysqlite2 import dbapi2 as sqlite3
45              except ImportError:
46                  return None
47
48          DB_EXC = sqlite3
49          if not os.path.isdir(dbDir):
50              os.mkdir(dbDir)
51          cxn = sqlite.connect(os.path.join(dbDir, DBNAME))
52
53      elif db == 'mysql':
54          try:
55                  import MySQLdb
56                  import _mysql_exceptions as DB_EXC
57
58              try:
59                  cxn = MySQLdb.connect(db=DBNAME)
60              except DB_EXC.OperationalError:
61                  try:
62                      cxn = MySQLdb.connect(user=DBUSER)
63                      cxn.query('CREATE DATABASE %s' % DBNAME)
64                      cxn.commit()
65                      cxn.close()
66                      cxn = MySQLdb.connect(db=DBNAME)
67                  except DB_EXC.OperationalError:
68                      return None
69          except ImportError:
70              try:
71                  import mysql.connector
72                  import mysql.connector.errors as DB_EXC
73                  try:
74                      cxn = mysql.connector.Connect(**{
75                          'database': DBNAME,
76                          'user': DBUSER,
77                      })
78                  except DB_EXC.InterfaceError:
79                      return None
80              except ImportError:
81                      return None
82
83      elif db == 'gadfly':
84          try:
85                  from gadfly import gadfly
86                  DB_EXC = gadfly
87          except ImportError:
88                  return None
89
```

```
90          try:
91              cxn = gadfly(DBNAME, dbDir)
92          except IOError:
93              cxn = gadfly()
94              if not os.path.isdir(dbDir):
95                  os.mkdir(dbDir)
96              cxn.startup(DBNAME, dbDir)
97      else:
98          return None
99      return cxn
100
101 def create(cur):
102     try:
103         cur.execute('''
104           CREATE TABLE users (
105             login  VARCHAR(%d),
106             userid INTEGER,
107             projid INTEGER)
108         ''' % NAMELEN)
109     except DB_EXC.OperationalError, e:
110         drop(cur)
111         create(cur)
112
113 drop = lambda cur: cur.execute('DROP TABLE users')
114
115 NAMES = (
116     ('aaron', 8312), ('angela', 7603), ('dave', 7306),
117     ('davina',7902), ('elliot', 7911), ('ernie', 7410),
118     ('jess', 7912), ('jim', 7512), ('larry', 7311),
119     ('leslie', 7808), ('melissa', 8602), ('pat', 7711),
120     ('serena', 7003), ('stan', 7607), ('faye', 6812),
121     ('amy', 7209), ('mona', 7404), ('jennifer', 7608),
122 )
123
124 def randName():
125     pick = set(NAMES)
126     while pick:
127         yield pick.pop()
128
129 def insert(cur, db):
130     if db == 'sqlite':
131         cur.executemany("INSERT INTO users VALUES(?, ?, ?)",
132             [(who, uid, rand(1,5)) for who, uid in randName()])
133     elif db == 'gadfly':
134         for who, uid in randName():
135             cur.execute("INSERT INTO users VALUES(?, ?, ?)",
136                 (who, uid, rand(1,5)))
137     elif db == 'mysql':
138         cur.executemany("INSERT INTO users VALUES(%s, %s, %s)",
139             [(who, uid, rand(1,5)) for who, uid in randName()])
140
141 getRC = lambda cur: cur.rowcount if hasattr(cur,
  'rowcount') else -1
142
```

(Continued)

Example 6-1   Database Adapter Example (ushuffle_dbU.py) *(Continued)*

```
143  def update(cur):
144      fr = rand(1,5)
145      to = rand(1,5)
146      cur.execute(
147        "UPDATE users SET projid=%d WHERE projid=%d" % (to, fr))
148      return fr, to, getRC(cur)
149
150  def delete(cur):
151      rm = rand(1,5)
152      cur.execute('DELETE FROM users WHERE projid=%d' % rm)
153      return rm, getRC(cur)
154
155  def dbDump(cur):
156      cur.execute('SELECT * FROM users')
157      printf('\n%s' % ''.join(map(cformat, FIELDS)))
158      for data in cur.fetchall():
159          printf(''.join(map(tformat, data)))
160
161  def main():
162      db = setup()
163      printf('*** Connect to %r database' % db)
164      cxn = connect(db)
165      if not cxn:
166        printf('ERROR: %r not supported or unreachable, exit' % db)
167          return
168      cur = cxn.cursor()
169
170      printf('\n*** Creating users table')
171      create(cur)
172
173      printf('\n*** Inserting names into table')
174      insert(cur, db)
175      dbDump(cur)
176
177      printf('\n*** Randomly moving folks')
178      fr, to, num = update(cur)
179      printf('\t(%d users moved) from (%d) to (%d)' % (num, fr, to))
180      dbDump(cur)
181
182      printf('\n*** Randomly choosing group')
183      rm, num = delete(cur)
184      printf('\t(group #%d; %d users removed)' % (rm, num))
185      dbDump(cur)
186
187      printf('\n*** Dropping users table')
188      drop(cur)
189      printf('\n*** Close cxns')
190      cur.close()
191      cxn.commit()
192      cxn.close()
193
194  if __name__ == '__main__':
195      main()
```

Line-by-Line Explanation

Lines 1–32

The first part of this script imports the necessary modules, creates some global constants (the column size for display and the set of databases we are supporting), and features the `tformat()`, `cformat()`, and `setup()` functions.

After the **import** statements, you'll find some curious code (lines 7–12) that finds the right function to which to alias from `scanf()`, our designated command-line user input function. The **elif** and **else** are simpler to explain: we're checking to see if `raw_input()` exists as a BIF. If it does, we're in Python (1 or) 2 and should use that. Otherwise, we're in Python 3 and should use its new name, `input()`.

The other bit of complexity is the **if** statement. `__builtins__` is only a module in your application. In an imported module, `__builtins__` is a dict. The conditional basically says that if we were imported, check if 'raw_input' is a name in this dictionary; otherwise, it's a module, so drop down to the **elif** and **else**. Hope that makes sense!

With regard to the `tformat()` and `cformat()` functions, the former is the format string for showing the titles; for instance, "tformat" means "title-case formatter." It's just a cheap way to take names from the database, which can be all lowercase (such as what we have), first letter capped correctly, all CAPS, etc., and make all the names uniform. The latter function's name stands for "CAPS formatter." All it does is take each column name and turn it into a header by calling the `str.upper()` method.

Both formatters left-justify their output and limit it to ten characters in width because it's not expected the data will exceed that—our sample data certainly doesn't, so if you want to use your own, change `COLSIZ` to whatever works for your data. It was simpler to write these as **lambda**s rather than traditional functions although you can certainly do that, as well.

One can argue that this is probably a lot of effort to do this when all `scanf()` will do is prompt the user in `setup()` to select the RDBMS to use for any particular execution of this script (or derivatives in the remainder of the chapter). However, the point is to show you some code that you might be able to use elsewhere. We haven't claimed that this is a script you'd use in production have we?

We already have the user output function—as mentioned earlier, we're using `distutils.log.warn()` in place of **print** for Python 2 and `print()` for Python 3. In our application, we import it (line 3) as `printf()`.

Most of the constants are fairly self-explanatory. One exception is `DB_EXC`, which stands for DataBase EXCeption. This variable will eventually be assigned the database exception module for the specific database system with which users choose to use to run this application. In other words, for users who choose MySQL, DB_EXC will be _mysql_exceptions, etc. If we built this application in a more object-oriented way, we would have a class in which this would simply be an instance attribute, such as self.db_exc_module.

Lines 35–99

The guts of consistent database access happen here in the connect() function. At the beginning of each section ("section" here refers to each database's **if** clause), we attempt to load the corresponding database modules. If a suitable one is not found, **None** is returned to indicate that the database system is not supported.

Once a connection is made, all of other code is database and adapter independent and should work across all connections. (The only exception in our script is insert().) In all three subsections of this set of code, you will notice that a valid connection should be passed back as cxn.

If SQLite is chosen, we attempt to load a database adapter. We first try to load the standard library's sqlite3 module (Python 2.5+). If that fails, we look for the third-party pysqlite2 package. This is to support version 2.4.x and older systems with the pysqlite adapter installed. If either is found, we then check to ensure that the directory exists, because the database is file based. (You can also choose to create an in-memory database by substituting :memory: as the filename.) When the connect() call is made to SQLite, it will either use one that already exists or make a new one using that path if one does not exist.

MySQL uses a default area for its database files and does not require this to come from the user. The most popular MySQL adapter is the MySQLdb package, so we try to import this first. Like SQLite, there is a "plan B," the mysql.connector package—a good choice because it's compatible with both Python 2 and 3. If neither is found, MySQL isn't supported and **None** is returned.

The last database supported by our application is Gadfly. (At the time of this writing, this database is mostly, but not fully, DB-API-compliant, and you will see this in this application.) It uses a startup mechanism similar to that of SQLite: it starts up with the directory where the database files should be. If it is there, fine, but if not, you have to take a roundabout way to start up a new database. (Why this is, we are not sure. We believe that the startup() functionality should be merged into that of the constructor gadfly.gadfly().)

Lines 101–113

The create() function creates a new users table in our database. If there is an error, it is almost always because the table already exists. If this is the case, drop the table and re-create it by recursively calling this function again. This code is dangerous in that if the re-creation of the table still fails, you will have infinite recursion until your application runs out of memory. You will fix this problem in one of the exercises at the end of the chapter.

The table is dropped from the database with the one-liner drop(), written as a lambda.

Lines 115–127

The next blocks of code feature a constant set of NAMES and user IDs, followed by the generator randName(). NAMES is a tuple that must be converted to a set for use in randName() because we alter it in the generator, removing one name at a time until the names are exhausted. Because this is destructive behavior and is used often in the application, it's best to set NAMES as the canonical source and just copy its contents to another data structure to be destroyed each time the generator is used.

Lines 129–139

The insert() function is the only other place where database-dependent code lives. This is because each database is slightly different in one way or another. For example, both the adapters for SQLite and MySQL are DB-API-compliant, so both of their cursor objects have an executemany() function, whereas Gadfly does not, so rows must be inserted one at a time.

Another quirk is that both SQLite and Gadfly use the qmark parameter style, whereas MySQL uses format. Because of this, the format strings are different. If you look carefully, however, you will see that the arguments themselves are created in a very similar fashion.

What the code does is this: for each name-userID pair, it assigns that individual to a project group (given by its project ID or projid). The project ID is chosen randomly out of four different groups (randrange(1,5)).

Line 141

This single line represents a conditional expression (read as: Python ternary operator) that returns the rowcount of the last operation (in terms of rows altered), or if the cursor object does not support this attribute (meaning it is not DB-API–compliant), it returns –1.

2.5   Conditional expressions were added in Python 2.5, so if you are using version 2.4.x or older, you will need to convert it back to the "old-style" way of doing it:

```
getRC = lambda cur: (hasattr(cur, 'rowcount') \
    and [cur.rowcount] or [-1])[0]
```

If you are confused by this line of code, don't worry about it. Check the FAQ to see why this is, and get a taste of why conditional expressions were finally added to Python in version 2.5. If you *are* able to figure it out, then you have developed a solid understanding of Python objects and their Boolean values.

Lines 143–153

The update() and delete() functions randomly choose folks from one group. If the operation is update, move them from their current group to another (also randomly chosen); if it is delete, remove them altogether.

Lines 155–159

The dbDump() function pulls all rows from the database, formats them for printing, and displays them to the user. The displayed output requires the assistance of the cformat() (to display the column headers) and tformat() (to format each user row).

First, you should see that the data was extracted after the SELECT by the fetchall() method. So as we iterate each user, take the three columns (login, userid, projid) and pass them to tformat() via map() to convert them to strings (if they are not already), format them as titlecase, and then format the complete string to be COLSIZ columns, left-justified (right-hand space padding).

Lines 161–195

The director of this movie is main(). It makes individual calls to each function described above that defines how this script works (assuming that it does not exit due to either not finding a database adapter or not being able to obtain a connection [lines 164–166]). The bulk of it should be fairly self-explanatory, given the proximity of the output statements. The last bits wrap up the cursor and connection.

6.3   ORMs

As seen in the previous section, a variety of different database systems are available today, and most of them have Python interfaces with which you can harness their power. The only drawback to those systems is the need to know SQL. If you are a programmer who feels more comfortable with manipulating Python objects instead of SQL queries, yet still want to use a relational database as your data back-end, then you would probably prefer to use ORMs.

6.3.1   Think Objects, Not SQL

Creators of these systems have abstracted away much of the pure SQL layer and implemented objects in Python that you can manipulate to accomplish the same tasks without having to generate the required lines of SQL. Some systems allow for more flexibility if you do have to slip in a few lines of SQL, but for the most part, you can avoid almost all the general SQL required.

Database tables are magically converted to Python classes with columns and features as attributes, and methods responsible for database operations. Setting up your application to an ORM is somewhat similar to that of a standard database adapter. Because of the amount of work that ORMs perform on your behalf, some things are actually more complex or require more lines of code than using an adapter directly. Hopefully, the gains you achieve in productivity make up for a little bit of extra work.

6.3.2   Python and ORMs

The most well-known Python ORMs today are SQLAlchemy (http://sqlalchemy.org) and SQLObject (http://sqlobject.org). We will give you examples of both because the systems are somewhat disparate due to different philosophies, but once you figure these out, moving on to other ORMs is much simpler.

Some other Python ORMs include Storm, PyDO/PyDO2, PDO, Dejavu, PDO, Durus, QLime, and ForgetSQL. Larger Web-based systems can also have their own ORM component such as WebWare MiddleKit and

Django's Database API. Be advised that "well-known" does not mean best for your application. Although these others were not included in our discussion, that does not mean that they would not be right for your application.

Setup and Installation

Because neither SQLAlchemy nor SQLObject are in the standard library, you'll need to download and install them on your own. (Usually this is easily taken care of with the `easy_install` or `pip` tools.)

At the time of this writing, all of the software packages described in this chapter are available in Python 2; only SQLAlchemy, SQLite, and the MySQL Connector/Python adapter are available in Python 3. The `sqlite3` package is part of the standard library for Python 2.5+ and 3.x, so you don't need to do anything unless you're using version 2.4 and older.

2.5, 3.x

If you're starting on a computer with only Python 3 installed, you'll need to get Distribute (which includes `easy_install`) first. You'll need a Web browser (or the `curl` command if you have it) and to download the installation file (available at http://python-distribute.org/distribute_setup.py), and then get SQLAlchemy with `easy_install`. Here is what this entire process might look like on a Windows-based PC:

```
C:\WINDOWS\Temp>C:\Python32\python distribute_setup.py
Extracting in c:\docume~1\wesley\locals~1\temp\tmp8mcddr
Now working in c:\docume~1\wesley\locals~1\temp\tmp8mcddr\distribute-
0.6.21
Installing Distribute
warning: no files found matching 'Makefile' under directory 'docs'
warning: no files found matching 'indexsidebar.html' under directory
'docs'
creating build
creating build\src
        :
Installing easy_install-3.2.exe script to C:\python32\Scripts

Installed c:\python32\lib\site-packages\distribute-0.6.21-py3.2.egg
Processing dependencies for distribute==0.6.21
Finished processing dependencies for distribute==0.6.21
After install bootstrap.
Creating C:\python32\Lib\site-packages\setuptools-0.6c11-py3.2.egg-info
Creating C:\python32\Lib\site-packages\setuptools.pth
```

```
C:\WINDOWS\Temp>
C:\WINDOWS\Temp>C:\Python32\Scripts\easy_install sqlalchemy
Searching for sqlalchemy
Reading http://pypi.python.org/simple/sqlalchemy/
Reading http://www.sqlalchemy.org
Best match: SQLAlchemy 0.7.2
Downloading http://pypi.python.org/packages/source/S/SQLAlchemy/
SQLAlchemy-0.7.2.tar.gz#md5=b84a26ae2e5de6f518d7069b29bf8f72
      :
Adding sqlalchemy 0.7.2 to easy-install.pth file
Installed c:\python32\lib\site-packages\sqlalchemy-0.7.2-py3.2.egg
Processing dependencies for sqlalchemy
Finished processing dependencies for sqlalchemy
```

6.3.3   Employee Role Database Example

We will port our user shuffle application ushuffle_db.py to both SQLAl-chemy and SQLObject. MySQL will be the back-end database server for both. You will note that we implement these as classes because there is more of an object feel to using ORMs, as opposed to using raw SQL in a database adapter. Both examples import the set of NAMES and the random name chooser from ushuffle_db.py. This is to avoid copying and pasting the same code everywhere as code reuse is a good thing.

6.3.4   SQLAlchemy

We start with SQLAlchemy because its interface is somewhat closer to SQL than SQLObject's. SQLObject is simpler, more Pythonic, and faster, whereas SQLAlchemy abstracts really well to the object world and also gives you more flexibility in issuing raw SQL, if you have to.

Examples 6-2 and 6-3 illustrate that the ports of our user shuffle exam-ples using both these ORMs are very similar in terms of setup, access, and overall number of lines of code. Both also borrow the same set of func-tions and constants from ushuffle_db{,U}.py.

Example 6-2   SQLAlchemy ORM Example (`ushuffle_sad.py`)

This user shuffle Python 2.x and 3.x-compatible application features the
SQLAlchemy ORM paired up with MySQL or SQLite databases as back-ends.

```
1    #!/usr/bin/env python
2
3    from distutils.log import warn as printf
4    from os.path import dirname
5    from random import randrange as rand
6    from sqlalchemy import Column, Integer, String, create_engine, exc, orm
7    from sqlalchemy.ext.declarative import declarative_base
8    from ushuffle_dbU import DBNAME, NAMELEN, randName,
   FIELDS, tformat, cformat, setup
9
10   DSNs = {
11       'mysql': 'mysql://root@localhost/%s' % DBNAME,
12       'sqlite': 'sqlite:///:memory:',
13   }
14
15   Base = declarative_base()
16   class Users(Base):
17       __tablename__ = 'users'
18       login = Column(String(NAMELEN))
19       userid  = Column(Integer, primary_key=True)
20       projid  = Column(Integer)
21       def __str__(self):
22           return ''.join(map(tformat,
23               (self.login, self.userid, self.projid)))
24
25   class SQLAlchemyTest(object):
26       def __init__(self, dsn):
27           try:
28               eng = create_engine(dsn)
29           except ImportError:
30               raise RuntimeError()
31
32           try:
33               eng.connect()
34           except exc.OperationalError:
35               eng = create_engine(dirname(dsn))
36               eng.execute('CREATE DATABASE %s' % DBNAME).close()
37               eng = create_engine(dsn)
38
39           Session = orm.sessionmaker(bind=eng)
40           self.ses = Session()
41           self.users = Users.__table__
42           self.eng = self.users.metadata.bind = eng
43
```

```
44        def insert(self):
45            self.ses.add_all(
46                Users(login=who, userid=userid, projid=rand(1,5)) \
47                    for who, userid in randName()
48            )
49            self.ses.commit()
50
51        def update(self):
52            fr = rand(1,5)
53            to = rand(1,5)
54            i = -1
55            users = self.ses.query(
56                Users).filter_by(projid=fr).all()
57            for i, user in enumerate(users):
58                user.projid = to
59            self.ses.commit()
60            return fr, to, i+1
61
62        def delete(self):
63            rm = rand(1,5)
64            i = -1
65            users = self.ses.query(
66                Users).filter_by(projid=rm).all()
67            for i, user in enumerate(users):
68                self.ses.delete(user)
69            self.ses.commit()
70            return rm, i+1
71
72        def dbDump(self):
73            printf('\n%s' % ''.join(map(cformat, FIELDS)))
74            users = self.ses.query(Users).all()
75            for user in users:
76                printf(user)
77            self.ses.commit()
78
79        def __getattr__(self, attr):    # use for drop/create
80            return getattr(self.users, attr)
81
82        def finish(self):
83            self.ses.connection().close()
84
85    def main():
86        printf('*** Connect to %r database' % DBNAME)
87        db = setup()
88        if db not in DSNs:
89            printf('\nERROR: %r not supported, exit' % db)
90            return
91
92        try:
93            orm = SQLAlchemyTest(DSNs[db])
94        except RuntimeError:
95            printf('\nERROR: %r not supported, exit' % db)
96            return
97
```

(Continued)

Example 6-2   SQLAlchemy ORM Example (`ushuffle_sad.py`) *(Continued)*

```
 98        printf('\n*** Create users table (drop old one if appl.)')
 99        orm.drop(checkfirst=True)
100        orm.create()
101
102        printf('\n*** Insert names into table')
103        orm.insert()
104        orm.dbDump()
105
106        printf('\n*** Move users to a random group')
107        fr, to, num = orm.update()
108        printf('\t(%d users moved) from (%d) to (%d)' % (num, fr, to))
109        orm.dbDump()
110
111        printf('\n*** Randomly delete group')
112        rm, num = orm.delete()
113        printf('\t(group #%d; %d users removed)' % (rm, num))
114        orm.dbDump()
115
116        printf('\n*** Drop users table')
117        orm.drop()
118        printf('\n*** Close cxns')
119        orm.finish()
120
121    if __name__ == '__main__':
122        main()
```

Line-by-Line Explanation

Lines 1–13

As expected, we begin with module imports and constants. We follow the suggested style guideline of importing Python Standard Library modules first (`distutils`, `os.path`, `random`), followed by third-party or external modules (`sqlalchemy`), and finally, local modules to our application (`ushuffle_dbU`), which in our case is providing the majority of the constants and utility functions.

The other constant contains the Database Source Names (DSNs), which you can think of as database connection URIs. In previous editions of this book, this application only supported MySQL, so we're happy to be able to add SQLite to the mix. In the `ushuffle_dbU.py` application seen earlier, we used the file system with SQLite. Here we'll use the in-memory version (line 12).

CORE NOTE: Active Record pattern

Active Record is a software design pattern (http://en.wikipedia.org/wiki/Active_record_pattern) that ties manipulation of objects to equivalent actions on a database. ORM objects essentially represent database rows such that when an object is created, a row representing its data is written to the database automatically. When an object is updated, so is the corresponding row. Similarly, when an object is removed, its row in the database is deleted.

In the beginning, SQLAlchemy didn't have an Active Record flavored declarative layer to make working with the ORM less complex. Instead, it followed the "Data Mapper" pattern in which objects do not have the ability to modify the database itself; rather, they come with actions that the user can call upon to make those changes happen. Yes, an ORM can substitute for having to issue raw SQL, but developers are still responsible for explicitly making the equivalent database operations to persist additions, updates, and deletions.

A desire for an Active Record-like interface spawned the creation of projects like ActiveMapper and TurboEntity. Eventually, both were replaced by Elixir (http://elixir.ematia.de), which became the most popular declarative layer for SQLAlchemy. Some developers find it Rails-like in nature, whereas others find it overly simplistic, abstracting away too much functionality.

However, SQLAlchemy eventually came up with its own declarative layer which also adheres to the Active Record pattern. It's fairly lightweight, simple, and gets the job done, so we'll use it in our example because it's is more beginner-friendly. However, if you do find it too lightweight, you can still use the `__table__` object for more traditional access.

Lines 15–23

The next code block represents the use of SQLAlchemy's declarative layer. Its use defines objects that, as manipulated, will result in the equivalent database operation. As mentioned in the preceding Core Note, it might not be as feature-rich as the third-party tools, but it suffices for our simple example here.

To use it, you must import `sqlalchemy.ext.declarative_base` (line 7) and use it to make a `Base` class (line 15) from which you derive your data subclasses (line 16).

The next part of the class definition contains the __tablename__ attribute, which is the database table name to which it is mapped. Alternatively, you can define a lower-level sqlalchemy.Table object explicitly, in which case you would alias to __table__, instead. In this application, we're taking a hybrid approach, mostly using the objects for row access, but we've saved off the table (line 41) for table-level actions (create and drop).

After that are the "column" attributes; check the docs for all allowed data types. Finally, we have an __str__() method definition which returns a human-readable string representation of a row of data. Because this output is customized (with the help of the tformat() function), we don't recommend this in practice. If you wanted to reuse this code in another application, that's made more difficult because you might wish the output to be formatted differently. More likely, you'll subclass this one and modify the child class __str__() method, instead. SQLAlchemy does support table inheritance.

Lines 25–42

The class initializer, like ushuffle_dbU.connect(), does everything it can to ensure that there is a database available, and then saves a connection to it. First, it attempts to use the DSN to create an engine to the database. An engine is the main database manager. For debugging purposes, you might wish to see the ORM-generated SQL. To do that, just set the echo parameter, e.g., create_engine('sqlite:///:memory:', echo=True).

Engine creation failure (lines 29–30) means that SQLAlchemy isn't able to support the chosen database, usually an ImportError, because it cannot find an installed adapter. In this case, we fail back to the setup() function to inform the user.

Assuming that an engine was successfully created, the next step is to try a database connection. A failure usually means that the database itself (or its server) is reachable, but in this case, the database you want to use to store your data does not exist, so we attempt to create it here and retry the connection (lines 34–37). Notice that we were sneaky in using os.path.dirname() to strip off the database name and leave the rest of the DSN intact so that the connection works (line 35).

This is the only place you will see raw SQL (line 36) because this type of activity is typically an operational task, not application-oriented. All other database operations happen under the table (pun not originally intended) via object manipulation or by calling a database table method via delegation (more on this a bit later in lines 44–70).

The last section of code (lines 39–42) creates a session object to manage individual transaction-flavored objects involving one or more database operations that all must be committed for the data to be written. We then save the session object plus the user's table and engine as instance attributes. The additional binding of the engine to the table's metadata (line 42) means to bind all operations on this table to the given engine. (You can bind to other engines or connections.)

Lines 44–70

These next three methods represent the core database functionality of row insertion (lines 44–49), update (lines 51–60), and deletion (lines 62–70). Insertion employs a `session.add_all()` method, which takes an iterable and builds up a set of insert operations. At the end, you can decide whether to issue a commit as we did (line 49) or a rollback.

Both `update()` and `delete()` feature a session query and use the `query.filter_by()` method for lookup. Updating randomly chooses members from one product group (`fr`) and moves them to another project by changing those IDs to another value (`to`). The counter (`i`) tracks the row-count of how many users were affected. Deleting involves randomly choosing a theoretical company project by ID (`rm`) that was cancelled, and because of which, employees laid-off. Both commit via the session object once the operations are carried out.

Note that there are equivalent query object `update()` and `delete()` methods that we aren't using in our application. They reduce the amount of code necessary as they operate in bulk and return the rowcount. Porting `ushuffle_sad.py` to using these methods is an exercise at the end of the chapter.

Here are some of the more commonly-used query methods:

- `filter_by()`   Extract values with specific column values as keyword parameters.

- `filter()`   Similar to `filter_by()` but more flexible as you provide an expression, instead. For example:
  query.`filter_by(userid=1)` is the same as
  query.`filter(Users.userid==1)`.

- `order_by()`   Analogous to the SQL ORDER BY directive. The default is ascending. You'll need to import `sqlalchemy.desc()` for descending sort.

- `limit()`   Analogous to the SQL LIMIT directive.

- `offset()`   Analogous to the SQL `OFFSET` directive.

- `all()`   Return all objects that match the query.

- `one()`   Return only one (the next) object that matches the query.

- `first()`   Return the first object that matches the query.

- `join()`   Create a SQL `JOIN` given the desired JOIN criteria.

- `update()`   Bulk update rows.

- `delete()`   Bulk delete rows.

Most of these methods result in another `Query` object and can thus be chained together, for example, *query*`.order_by(desc(Users.userid))`. `limit(5).offset(5)`.

If you wish to use `LIMIT` and `OFFSET`, the more Pythonic way is to take your query object and apply a slice to it, for example, *query*`.order_by (User.userid)` `[10:20]` for the second group of ten users with the oldest user IDs.

To see `Query` methods, read the documentation at http://www. sqlalchemy. org/docs/orm/query.html#sqlalchemy.orm.query.Query. JOINs are a large topic on their own, so there is additional and more specific information at http://www.sqlalchemy.org/docs/orm/tutorial.html#ormtutorial-joins.   You'll get a chance to play with some of these methods in the chapter exercises.

So far, we've only discussed querying, thus row-level operations. What about table create and drop actions? Shouldn't there be functions that look like the following?

```
def drop(self):
    self.users.drop()
```

Here we made a decision to use delegation again (as introduced in the object-oriented programming chapter in *Core Python Language Fundamentals* or *Core Python Programming*). Delegation is where missing attributes in an instance are required from another object in our instance (`self.users`) which has it; for example, wherever you see `__getattr__()`, `self.users.` `create()`, `self.users.drop()`, etc. (lines 79–80, 98–99, 116), think delegation.

Lines 72–77

The responsibility of displaying proper output to the screen belongs to the `dbDump()` method. It extracts the rows from the database and pretty-prints the data just like its equivalent in `ushuffle_dbU.py`. In fact, they are nearly identical.

Lines 79–83

We just discussed delegation, and using __getattr__() lets us deliberately avoid creating drop() and create() methods because it would just respectively call the table's drop() or create() methods, anyway. There is no added functionality, so why create yet another function to have to maintain? We would like to remind you that __getattr__() is only called whenever an attribute lookup fails. (This is as opposed to __getattribute__(), which is called, regardless.)

If we call orm.drop() and find no such method, getattr(orm, 'drop') is invoked. When that happens, __getattr__() is called and delegates the attribute name to self.users. The interpreter will find that self.users has a drop attribute and pass that method call to it: self. users.drop().

The last method is finish(), which does the final cleanup of closing the connection. Yes, we could have written this as a lambda but chose not to in case cleaning up of cursors and connections, etc. requires more than a single statement.

Lines 85–122

The main() function drives our application. It creates a SQLAlchemyTest object and uses that for all database operations. The script is the same as that of our original application, ushuffle_dbU.py. You will notice that the database parameter db is optional and does not serve any purpose here in ushuffle_sad.py or the upcoming SQLObject version, ushuffle_so.py. This is a placeholder for you to add support for other RDBMSs in these applications (see the exercises at the end of the chapter).

Upon running this script, you might get output that looks like this on a Windows-based PC:

```
C:\>python ushuffle_sad.py
*** Connect to 'test' database

Choose a database system:

(M)ySQL
(G)adfly
(S)QLite

Enter choice: s

*** Create users table (drop old one if appl.)
```

```
*** Insert names into table

LOGIN      USERID   PROJID
Faye       6812     2
Serena     7003     4
Amy        7209     2
Dave       7306     3
Larry      7311     2
Mona       7404     2
Ernie      7410     1
Jim        7512     2
Angela     7603     1
Stan       7607     2
Jennifer   7608     4
Pat        7711     2
Leslie     7808     3
Davina     7902     3
Elliot     7911     4
Jess       7912     2
Aaron      8312     3
Melissa    8602     1

*** Move users to a random group
        (3 users moved) from (1) to (3)

LOGIN      USERID   PROJID
Faye       6812     2
Serena     7003     4
Amy        7209     2
Dave       7306     3
Larry      7311     2
Mona       7404     2
Ernie      7410     3
Jim        7512     2
Angela     7603     3
Stan       7607     2
Jennifer   7608     4
Pat        7711     2
Leslie     7808     3
Davina     7902     3
Elliot     7911     4
Jess       7912     2
Aaron      8312     3
Melissa    8602     3

*** Randomly delete group
        (group #3; 7 users removed)

LOGIN      USERID   PROJID
Faye       6812     2
Serena     7003     4
Amy        7209     2
```

```
Larry      7311    2
Mona       7404    2
Jim        7512    2
Stan       7607    2
Jennifer   7608    4
Pat        7711    2
Elliot     7911    4
Jess       7912    2

*** Drop users table

*** Close cxns
C:\>
```

Explicit/"Classical" ORM Access

We mentioned early on that we chose to use the declarative layer in SQL-Alchemy for our example. However, we feel it's also educational to look at the more "explicit" form of `ushuffle_sad.py` (User shuffle SQLAlchemy declarative), which we'll name as `ushuffle_sae.py` (User shuffle SQLAlchemy explicit). You'll notice that they look extremely similar to each other.

A line-by-line explanation isn't provided due to its similarity with `ushuffle_sad.py`, but it can be downloaded from http://corepython.com. The point is to both preserve this from previous editions as well as to let you compare explicit versus declarative. SQLAlchemy has matured since the book's previous edition, so we wanted to bring it up-to-date, as well. Here is `ushuffle_sae.py`:

```python
#!/usr/bin/env python

from distutils.log import warn as printf
from os.path import dirname
from random import randrange as rand
from sqlalchemy import Column, Integer, String, create_engine, \
    exc, orm, MetaData, Table
from sqlalchemy.ext.declarative import declarative_base
from ushuffle_dbU import DBNAME, NAMELEN, randName, FIELDS, \
    tformat, cformat, setup

DSNs = {
    'mysql': 'mysql://root@localhost/%s' % DBNAME,
    'sqlite': 'sqlite:///:memory:',
}

class SQLAlchemyTest(object):
    def __init__(self, dsn):
        try:
            eng = create_engine(dsn)
```

```
        except ImportError, e:
            raise RuntimeError()

        try:
            cxn = eng.connect()
        except exc.OperationalError:
            try:
                eng = create_engine(dirname(dsn))
                eng.execute('CREATE DATABASE %s' % DBNAME).close()
                eng = create_engine(dsn)
                cxn = eng.connect()
            except exc.OperationalError:
                raise RuntimeError()

        metadata = MetaData()
        self.eng = metadata.bind = eng
        try:
            users = Table('users', metadata, autoload=True)
        except exc.NoSuchTableError:
            users = Table('users', metadata,
                Column('login',  String(NAMELEN)),
                Column('userid', Integer),
                Column('projid', Integer),
            )

        self.cxn = cxn
        self.users = users

    def insert(self):
        d = [dict(zip(FIELDS, [who, uid, rand(1,5)])) \
            for who, uid in randName()]
        return self.users.insert().execute(*d).rowcount

    def update(self):
        users = self.users
        fr = rand(1,5)
        to = rand(1,5)
        return (fr, to,
            users.update(users.c.projid==fr).execute(
            projid=to).rowcount)

    def delete(self):
        users = self.users
        rm = rand(1,5)
        return (rm,
            users.delete(users.c.projid==rm).execute().rowcount)

    def dbDump(self):
        printf('\n%s' % ''.join(map(cformat, FIELDS)))
        users = self.users.select().execute()
```

```python
        for user in users.fetchall():
            printf(''.join(map(tformat, (user.login,
                user.userid, user.projid))))

    def __getattr__(self, attr):
        return getattr(self.users, attr)

    def finish(self):
        self.cxn.close()

def main():
    printf('*** Connect to %r database' % DBNAME)
    db = setup()
    if db not in DSNs:
        printf('\nERROR: %r not supported, exit' % db)
        return

    try:
        orm = SQLAlchemyTest(DSNs[db])
    except RuntimeError:
        printf('\nERROR: %r not supported, exit' % db)
        return

    printf('\n*** Create users table (drop old one if appl.)')
    orm.drop(checkfirst=True)
    orm.create()

    printf('\n*** Insert names into table')
    orm.insert()
    orm.dbDump()

    printf('\n*** Move users to a random group')
    fr, to, num = orm.update()
    printf('\t(%d users moved) from (%d) to (%d)' % (num, fr, to))
    orm.dbDump()

    printf('\n*** Randomly delete group')
    rm, num = orm.delete()
    printf('\t(group #%d; %d users removed)' % (rm, num))
    orm.dbDump()

    printf('\n*** Drop users table')
    orm.drop()
    printf('\n*** Close cxns')
    orm.finish()

if __name__ == '__main__':
    main()
```

The noticeable major differences between `ushuffle_sad.py` and `ushuffle_sae.py` are:

- Creates a `Table` object instead of declarative `Base` object
- Our election not to use `Sessions`; instead performing individual units of work, auto-commit, non-transactional, etc.
- Uses the `Table` object for all database interaction rather than `Session Querys`

To show sessions and explicit operations are not tied together, you'll get an exercise to roll `Sessions` into `ushuffle_sae.py`. Now that you've learned SQLAlchemy, let's move onto SQLObject and see a similar tool.

SQLObject

SQLObject was Python's first major ORM. In fact, it's a decade old! Ian Bicking, its creator, released the first alpha version to the world in October 2002. (SQLAlchemy didn't come along until February 2006.) At the time of this writing, SQLObject is only available for Python 2.

As we mentioned earlier, SQLObject is more object-flavored (some feel more Pythonic) and implemented the Active Record pattern for implicit object-to-database access early on but doesn't give you as much freedom to use raw SQL for more ad hoc or customized queries. Many users claim that it is easy to learn SQLAlchemy, but we'll let you be the judge. Take a look at `ushuffle_so.py` in Example 6-3, which is our port of `ushuffle_dbU.py` and `ushuffle_sad.py` to SQLObject.

Example 6-3   SQLObject ORM Example (`ushuffle_so.py`)

This user shuffle Python 2.x and 3.x-compatible application features the SQLObject ORM paired up with MySQL or SQLite databases as back-ends.

```
1    #!/usr/bin/env python
2
3    from distutils.log import warn as printf
4    from os.path import dirname
5    from random import randrange as rand
6    from sqlobject import *
7    from ushuffle_dbU import DBNAME, NAMELEN, randName, FIELDS,
     tformat, cformat, setup
8
```

```
9   DSNs = {
10      'mysql': 'mysql://root@localhost/%s' % DBNAME,
11      'sqlite': 'sqlite:///:memory:',
12  }
13
14  class Users(SQLObject):
15      login  = StringCol(length=NAMELEN)
16      userid = IntCol()
17      projid = IntCol()
18      def __str__(self):
19          return ''.join(map(tformat,
20              (self.login, self.userid, self.projid)))
21
22  class SQLObjectTest(object):
23      def __init__(self, dsn):
24          try:
25              cxn = connectionForURI(dsn)
26          except ImportError:
27              raise RuntimeError()
28          try:
29              cxn.releaseConnection(cxn.getConnection())
30          except dberrors.OperationalError:
31              cxn = connectionForURI(dirname(dsn))
32              cxn.query("CREATE DATABASE %s" % dbName)
33              cxn = connectionForURI(dsn)
34          self.cxn = sqlhub.processConnection = cxn
35
36      def insert(self):
37          for who, userid in randName():
38              Users(login=who, userid=userid, projid=rand(1,5))
39
40      def update(self):
41          fr = rand(1,5)
42          to = rand(1,5)
43          i = -1
44          users = Users.selectBy(projid=fr)
45          for i, user in enumerate(users):
46              user.projid = to
47          return fr, to, i+1
48
49      def delete(self):
50          rm = rand(1,5)
51          users = Users.selectBy(projid=rm)
52          i = -1
53          for i, user in enumerate(users):
54              user.destroySelf()
55          return rm, i+1
56
57      def dbDump(self):
58          printf('\n%s' % ''.join(map(cformat, FIELDS)))
59          for user in Users.select():
60              printf(user)
61
62      def finish(self):
63          self.cxn.close()
64
```

(Continued)

Example 6-3   SQLObject ORM Example (ushuffle_so.py) *(Continued)*

```
65  def main():
66      printf('*** Connect to %r database' % DBNAME)
67      db = setup()
68      if db not in DSNs:
69          printf('\nERROR: %r not supported, exit' % db)
70          return
71
72      try:
73          orm = SQLObjectTest(DSNs[db])
74      except RuntimeError:
75          printf('\nERROR: %r not supported, exit' % db)
76          return
77
78      printf('\n*** Create users table (drop old one if appl.)')
79      Users.dropTable(True)
80      Users.createTable()
81
82      printf('\n*** Insert names into table')
83      orm.insert()
84      orm.dbDump()
85
86      printf('\n*** Move users to a random group')
87      fr, to, num = orm.update()
88      printf('\t(%d users moved) from (%d) to (%d)' % (num, fr, to))
89      orm.dbDump()
90
91      printf('\n*** Randomly delete group')
92      rm, num = orm.delete()
93      printf('\t(group #%d; %d users removed)' % (rm, num))
94      orm.dbDump()
95
96      printf('\n*** Drop users table')
97      Users.dropTable()
98      printf('\n*** Close cxns')
99      orm.finish()
100
101  if __name__ == '__main__':
102      main()
```

Line-by-Line Explanation

Lines 1–12

The imports and constant declarations for this module are practically identical to those of ushuffle_sad.py, except that we are using SQLObject instead of SQLAlchemy.

Lines 14–20

The Users table extends the SQLObject.SQLObject class. We define the same columns as before and also provide an __str__() for display output.

Lines 22–34

The constructor for our class does everything it can to ensure that there is a database available and returns a connection to it, just like our SQLAlchemy example. Similarly, this is the only place you will see real SQL. The code works as described in the following, which bails on all errors:

- Try to establish a connection to an existing table (line 29); if it works, we are done. It has to dodge exceptions like an RDBMS adapter being available and the server online, and then beyond that, the existence of the database.

- Otherwise, create the table; if so, we are done (lines 31–33).

- Once successful, we save the connection object in self.cxn.

Lines 36–55

The database operations happen in these lines. We have Insert (lines 36–38), Update (lines 40–47), and Delete (lines 49–55). These are analogous to the SQLAlchemy equivalents.

 CORE TIP (HACKER'S CORNER): Reducing insert() **down to one (long) line of Python**

We can reduce the code from the insert() method into a more obfuscated "one-liner:"

```
[Users(**dict(zip(FIELDS, (who, userid, rand(1,5))))) \
    for who, userid in randName()]
```

We're not in the business to encourage code that damages readability or executes code explicitly by using a list comprehension; however, the existing solution does have one flaw: it requires you to create new objects by explicitly naming the columns as keyword arguments. By using FIELDS, you don't need to know the column names and wouldn't need to fix as much code if those column names changed, especially if FIELDS was in some configuration (not application) module.

Lines 57–63

This block starts with the same (and expected) dbDump() method, which pulls the rows from the database and displays things nicely to the screen. The finish() method (lines 62–63) closes the connection. We could not use delegation for table drop as we did for the SQLAlchemy example because the would-be delegated method for it is called dropTable(), not drop().

Lines 65–102

This is the `main()` function again. It works just like the one in `ushuffle_sad.py`. Also, the `db` argument and DSNs constant are building blocks for you to add support for other RDBMSs in these applications (see the exercises at the end of the chapter).

Here is what your output might look like if you run `ushuffle_so.py` (which is going to be nearly identical to the output from the `ushuffle_dbU.py` and `ushuffle_sa?.py` scripts):

```
$ python ushuffle_so.py
*** Connect to 'test' database

Choose a database system:

(M)ySQL
(G)adfly
(S)QLite

Enter choice: s

*** Create users table (drop old one if appl.)

*** Insert names into table

LOGIN      USERID    PROJID
Jess       7912      2
Ernie      7410      1
Melissa    8602      1
Serena     7003      1
Angela     7603      1
Aaron      8312      4
Elliot     7911      3
Jennifer   7608      1
Leslie     7808      4
Mona       7404      4
Larry      7311      1
Davina     7902      3
Stan       7607      4
Jim        7512      2
Pat        7711      1
Amy        7209      2
Faye       6812      1
Dave       7306      4

*** Move users to a random group
        (5 users moved) from (4) to (2)

LOGIN      USERID    PROJID
Jess       7912      2
Ernie      7410      1
```

```
Melissa    8602     1
Serena     7003     1
Angela     7603     1
Aaron      8312     2
Elliot     7911     3
Jennifer   7608     1
Leslie     7808     2
Mona       7404     2
Larry      7311     1
Davina     7902     3
Stan       7607     2
Jim        7512     2
Pat        7711     1
Amy        7209     2
Faye       6812     1
Dave       7306     2

*** Randomly delete group
      (group #3; 2 users removed)

LOGIN      USERID   PROJID
Jess       7912     2
Ernie      7410     1
Melissa    8602     1
Serena     7003     1
Angela     7603     1
Aaron      8312     2
Jennifer   7608     1
Leslie     7808     2
Mona       7404     2
Larry      7311     1
Stan       7607     2
Jim        7512     2
Pat        7711     1
Amy        7209     2
Faye       6812     1
Dave       7306     2

*** Drop users table

*** Close cxns
$
```

6.4   Non-Relational Databases

At the beginning of this chapter, we introduced you to SQL and looked at relational databases. We then showed you how to get data to and from those types of systems and presented a short lesson in porting to Python 3, as well. Those sections were followed by sections on ORMs and how they let users avoid SQL by taking on more of an "object" approach, instead. However, under the hood, both SQLAlchemy and SQLObject generate SQL on your behalf. In the final section of this chapter, we'll stay on objects but move away from relational databases.

6.4.1   Introduction to NoSQL

Recent trends in Web and social services have led to the generation of data in amounts and/or rates greater than relational databases can handle. Think Facebook or Twitter scale data generation. Developers of Facebook games or applications that handle Twitter stream data, for example, might have applications that need to write to persistent storage at a rate of millions of rows or objects per hour. This scalability issue has led to the creation, explosive growth, and deployment of *non-relational* or *NoSQL* databases.

There are plenty of options available here, but they're not all the same. In the non-relational (or *non-rel* for short) category alone, there are object databases, key-value stores, document stores (or datastores), graph databases, tabular databases, columnar/extensible record/wide-column databases, multivalue databases, etc. At the end of the chapter, we'll provide some links to help you with your NoSQL research. At the time of this writing, one of the more popular document store non-rel databases is MongoDB.

6.4.2   MongoDB

MongoDB has experienced a recent boost in popularity. Besides users, documentation, community, and professional support, it has its own regular set of conferences—another sign of adoption. The main Web site claims a variety of marquee users, including Craigslist, Shutterfly, foursquare, bit.ly, SourceForge, etc. See http://www.mongodb.org/display/DOCS/ Production+Deployments for these and more. Regardless of its user base, we feel that MongoDB is a good choice to introduce readers to NoSQL and document datastores. For those who are curious, MongoDB's document storage system is written in C++.

If you were to compare document stores (MongoDB, CouchDB, Riak, Amazon SimpleDB) in general to other non-rel databases, they fit somewhere between simple key-value stores, such as Redis, Voldemort, Amazon Dynamo, etc., and column-stores, such as Cassandra, Google Bigtable, and HBase. They're somewhat like schemaless derivatives of relational databases, simpler and less constrained than columnar-based storage but more flexible than plain key-value stores. They generally store their data as JavaScript Object Notation (JSON) objects, which allows for data types, such as strings, numbers, lists, as well as for nesting.

Some of the MongoDB (and NoSQL) terminology is also different from those of relational database systems. For example, instead of thinking about rows and columns, you might have to consider documents and collections, instead. To better wrap your head around the change in terms, you can take a quick look at the SQL-to-Mongo Mapping Chart at http://www.mongodb.org/display/DOCS/SQL+to+Mongo+Mapping+Chart

MongoDB in particular stores its JSON payloads (documents)—think a single Python dictionary—in a binary-encoded serialization, commonly known as BSON format. However, regardless of its storage mechanism, the main idea is that to developers, it looks like JSON, which in turn looks like Python dictionaries, which brings us to where we want to be. MongoDB is popular enough to have adapters available for most platforms, including Python.

6.4.3   PyMongo: MongoDB and Python

Although there are a variety of MongoDB drivers for Python, the most formal of them is PyMongo. The others are either more lightweight adapters or are special-purpose. You can perform a search on *mongo* at the Cheeseshop (http://pypi.python.org) to see all MongoDB-related Python packages. You can try any of them, as you prefer, but our example in this chapter uses PyMongo.

Another benefit of the pymongo package is that it has been ported to Python 3. Given the techniques already used earlier in this chapter, we will only present one Python application that runs on both Python 2 and 3, and depending on which interpreter you use to execute the script, it in turn will utilize the appropriately-installed version of pymongo.

We won't spend much time on installation as that is primarily beyond the scope of this book; however, we can point you to mongodb.org to download MongoDB and let you know that you can use easy_install or pip to install PyMongo and/or PyMongo3. (Note: I didn't have any problems getting pymongo3 on my Mac, but the install process choked in Windows.) Whichever one you install (or both), it'll look the same from your code: **import** pymongo.

To confirm that you have MongoDB installed and working correctly, check out the QuickStart guide at http://www.mongodb.org/display/ DOCS/Quickstart and similarly, to confirm the same for PyMongo, ensure that you can import the pymongo package. To get a feel for using MongoDB with Python, run through the PyMongo tutorial at http://api.mongodb. org/python/current/tutorial.html.

What we're going to do here is port our existing user shuffle (ushuffle_*.py) application that we've been looking at throughout this chapter to use MongoDB as its persistent storage. You'll notice that the flavor of the application is similar to that of SQLAlchemy and SQLObject, but it is even less substantial in that there isn't as much overhead with MongoDB as there is a typical relational database system such as MySQL. Example 6-4 presents the Python 2 and 3-compatible ushuffle_mongo.py, followed by the line-by-line explanation.

Example 6-4   MongoDB Example (ushuffle_mongo.py)

Our user shuffle Python 2.x and 3.x-compatible MongoDB and PyMongo application.

```
1   #!/usr/bin/env python
2
3   from distutils.log import warn as printf
4   from random import randrange as rand
5   from pymongo import Connection, errors
6   from ushuffle_dbU import DBNAME, randName, FIELDS, tformat, cformat
7
8   COLLECTION = 'users'
9
10  class MongoTest(object):
11      def __init__(self):
12          try:
13              cxn = Connection()
14          except errors.AutoReconnect:
15              raise RuntimeError()
16          self.db = cxn[DBNAME]
17          self.users = self.db[COLLECTION]
18
19      def insert(self):
20          self.users.insert(
21              dict(login=who, userid=uid, projid=rand(1,5)) \
22              for who, uid in randName())
23
24      def update(self):
25          fr = rand(1,5)
26          to = rand(1,5)
27          i = -1
28          for i, user in enumerate(self.users.find({'projid': fr})):
```

```
29                 self.users.update(user,
30                     {'$set': {'projid': to}})
31             return fr, to, i+1
32
33     def delete(self):
34         rm = rand(1,5)
35         i = -1
36         for i, user in enumerate(self.users.find({'projid': rm})):
37             self.users.remove(user)
38         return rm, i+1
39
40     def dbDump(self):
41         printf('\n%s' % ''.join(map(cformat, FIELDS)))
42         for user in self.users.find():
43             printf(''.join(map(tformat,
44                 (user[k] for k in FIELDS))))
45
46     def finish(self):
47         self.db.connection.disconnect()
48
49 def main():
50     printf('*** Connect to %r database' % DBNAME)
51     try:
52         mongo = MongoTest()
53     except RuntimeError:
54         printf('\nERROR: MongoDB server unreachable, exit')
55         return
56
57     printf('\n*** Insert names into table')
58     mongo.insert()
59     mongo.dbDump()
60
61     printf('\n*** Move users to a random group')
62     fr, to, num = mongo.update()
63     printf('\t(%d users moved) from (%d) to (%d)' % (num, fr, to))
64     mongo.dbDump()
65
66     printf('\n*** Randomly delete group')
67     rm, num = mongo.delete()
68     printf('\t(group #%d; %d users removed)' % (rm, num))
69     mongo.dbDump()
70
71     printf('\n*** Drop users table')
72     mongo.db.drop_collection(COLLECTION)
73     printf('\n*** Close cxns')
74     mongo.finish()
75
76 if __name__ == '__main__':
77     main()
```

Line-by-Line Explanation

Lines 1–8

The main import line is to bring in PyMongo's `Connection` object and the package's exceptions (`errors`). Everything else you've seen earlier in this chapter. Like the ORM examples, we yet again borrow most constants and common functions from our earlier `ushuffle_dbU.py` application. The last statement sets our collection ("table") name.

Lines 10–17

The first part of the initializer for our `MongoTest` class creates a connection, raising an exception if the server cannot be reached (lines 12–15). The next two lines are very easy to skip over because they look like mere assignments, but under the hood, these create a database or reuse an existing one (line 16) and create or reuse an existing "users" collection, which you can sort of consider as analogous to a database table.

Tables have defined columns then rows for each record, whereas collections don't have any schema requirements; they have individual documents for each record. You will notice the conspicuous absence of a "data model" class definition in this part of the code. Each record defines itself, so to speak—whatever record you save is what goes into the collection.

Lines 19–22

The `insert()` method adds values to a MongoDB collection. A collection is made up of documents. You can think of a document as a single record in the form of a Python dictionary. We create one by using the `dict()` factory function of those for each record, and all are streamed to the collection's `insert()` method via a generator expression.

Lines 24–31

The `update()` method works in the same manner as earlier in the chapter. The difference is the collection's `update()` method which, gives developers more options than a typical database system. Here, (lines 29–30) we use the MongoDB `$set` directive, which updates an existing value explicitly.

Each MongoDB directive represents a modifier operation that is both highly-efficient, useful, and convenient to the developer when updating existing values. In addition to `$set`, there are also operations for incrementing a field by a value, removing a field (key-value pair), appending and removing values to/from an array, etc.

Working backward somewhat, before the update, however, we first need to query for all the users in the system (line 28) to find those with a project ID (`projid`) that matches the group we want to update. To do this, you use the collection `find()` method and pass in the criteria. This takes the place of a SQL `SELECT` statement.

It's also possible to use the `Collection.update()` method to modify multiple documents; you would just need to set the multi flag to True. The only bad news with this is that it currently doesn't return the total number of documents modified.

For more complex queries than just the single criteria for our simple script, check the corresponding page in the official documentation at http://www.mongodb.org/display/DOCS/Advanced+Queries.

Lines 33–38

The `delete()` method reuses the same query as for `update()`. Once we have all the users that match the query, we `remove()` them one at a time (lines 36–37) and return the results. If you don't care about the total number of documents removed, then you can simply make a single call to `self.users.remove()`, which deletes all documents from a collection.

Lines 40–44

The query performed in `dbDump()` has no criteria (line 42), so all users in the collection are returned, followed by the data, string-formatted and displayed to the user (lines 43–44).

Lines 46–47

The final method defined and called during application execution disconnects from the MongoDB server.

Lines 49–77

The `main()` driver function is self-documenting and following the exact same script as the previous applications seen in this chapter: connect to database server and do preparation work; insert users into the collection ("table") and dump database contents; move users from one project to another (and dump contents); remove an entire group (and dump contents); drop the entire collection; and then finally, disconnect.

While this closes our look at non-relational databases for Python, it should only be the beginning for you. As mentioned at the beginning of this section, there are plenty of NoSQL options to look at, and you'll need to investigate and perhaps prototype each to determine which among them might be the right tool for the job. In the next section, we give various additional references for you to read further.

6.4.4 Summary

We hope that we have provided you with a good introduction to using relational databases with Python. When your application's needs go beyond those offered by plain files, or specialized files, such as DBM, pickled, etc., you have many options. There are a good number of RDBMSs out there, not to mention one completely implemented in Python, freeing you from having to install, maintain, or administer a real database system.

In the following section, you will find information on many of the Python adapters plus database and ORM systems. Furthermore, the community has been augmented with non-relational databases now to help out in those situations when relational databases don't scale to the level that your application needs.

We also suggest checking out the DB-SIG pages as well as the Web pages and mailing lists of all systems of interest. Like all other areas of software development, Python makes things easy to learn and simple to experiment with.

6.5 Related References

Table 6-8 lists most of the common databases available, along with working Python modules and packages that serve as adapters to those database systems. Note that not all adapters are DB-API-compliant.

Table 6-8 Database-Related Modules/Packages and Web sites

Name	Online Reference
Relational Databases	
Gadfly	gadfly.sf.net
MySQL	mysql.com or mysql.org
MySQLdb a.k.a. MySQL-python	sf.net/projects/mysql-python
MySQL Connector/Python	launchpad.net/myconnpy

Name	Online Reference
Relational Databases	
PostgreSQL	postgresql.org
psycopg	initd.org/psycopg
PyPgSQL	pypgsql.sf.net
PyGreSQL	pygresql.org
SQLite	sqlite.org
pysqlite	trac.edgewall.org/wiki/PySqlite
sqlite3[a]	docs.python.org/library/sqlite3
APSW	code.google.com/p/apsw
MaxDB (SAP)	maxdb.sap.com
sdb.dbapi	maxdb.sap.com/doc/7_7/46/ 702811f2042d87e10000000a1553f6/content.htm
sdb.sql	maxdb.sap.com/doc/7_7/46/ 71b2a816ae0284e10000000a1553f6/content.htm
sapdb	sapdb.org/sapdbPython.html
Firebird (InterBase)	firebirdsql.org
KInterbasDB	firebirdsql.org/en/python-driver
SQL Server	microsoft.com/sql
pymssql	code.google.com/p/pymssql (requires FreeTDS [freetds.org])
adodbapi	adodbapi.sf.net
Sybase	sybase.com
sybase	www.object-craft.com.au/projects/sybase
Oracle	oracle.com

2.5

(Continued)

Table 6-8   Database-Related Modules/Packages and Web sites *(Continued)*

Name	Online Reference
cx_Oracle	cx-oracle.sf.net
DCOracle2	zope.org/Members/matt/dco2 (older, for Oracle8 only)
Ingres	ingres.com
Ingres DBI	community.actian.com/wiki/ Ingres_Python_Development_Center
ingmod	www.informatik.uni-rostock.de/~hme/software/
NoSQL Document Datastores	
MongoDB	mongodb.org
PyMongo	pypi.python.org/pypi/pymongo Docs at api.mongodb.org/python/current
PyMongo3	pypi.python.org/pypi/pymongo3
Other adapters	api.mongodb.org/python/current/tools.html
CouchDB	couchdb.apache.org
couchdb-python	code.google.com/p/couchdb-python Docs at packages.python.org/CouchDB
ORMs	
SQLObject	sqlobject.org
SQLObject2	sqlobject.org/2
SQLAlchemy	sqlalchemy.org
Storm	storm.canonical.com
PyDO/PyDO2	skunkweb.sf.net/pydo.html

a. `pysqlite` added to Python 2.5 as `sqlite3` module.

In addition to the database-related modules/packages, the following are yet more online references that you can consider:

Python and Databases

- wiki.python.org/moin/DatabaseProgramming

- wiki.python.org/moin/DatabaseInterfaces

Database Formats, Structures, and Development Patterns

- en.wikipedia.org/wiki/DSN

- www.martinfowler.com/eaaCatalog/dataMapper.html

- en.wikipedia.org/wiki/Active_record_pattern

- blog.mongodb.org/post/114440717/bson

Non-relational Databases

- en.wikipedia.org/wiki/Nosql

- nosql-database.org/

- www.mongodb.org/display/DOCS/MongoDB,+CouchDB,
  +MySQL+Compare+Grid

6.6   Exercises

Databases

6-1.   *Database API.* What is the Python DB-API? Is it a good thing? Why (or why not)?

6-2.   *Database API.* Describe the differences between the database module parameter styles (see the `paramstyle` module attribute).

6-3.   *Cursor Objects.* What are the differences between the cursor `execute*()` methods?

6-4.   *Cursor Objects.* What are the differences between the cursor `fetch*()` methods?

6-5.   *Database Adapters.* Research your RDBMS and its Python module. Is it DB-API compliant? What additional features are available for that module that are extras not required by the API?

6-6.   *Type Objects.* Study using `Type` objects for your database and DB-API adapter, and then write a small script that uses at least one of those objects.

6-7. *Refactoring.* In the `ushuffle_dbU.create()` function, a table that already exists is dropped and re-created by recursively calling `create()` again. This is dangerous, because if re-creation of the table fails (again), you will then have infinite recursion. Fix this problem by creating a more practical solution that does not involve copying the create query (`cur.execute()`) again in the exception handler. Extra Credit: Try to recreate the table a maximum of three times before returning failure back to the caller.

6-8. *Database and HTML.* Take any existing database table, and use your Web programming knowledge to create a handler that outputs the contents of that table as HTML for browsers.

6-9. *Web Programming and Databases.* Take our user shuffle example (`ushuffle_db.py`) and create a Web interface for it.

6-10. *GUI Programming and Databases.* Take our user shuffle example (`ushuffle_db.py`) and throw a GUI for it.

6-11. *Stock Portfolio Class.* Create an application that manages the stock portfolios for multiple users. Use a relational database as the back-end and provide a Web-based user interface. You can use the stock database class from the object-oriented programming chapter of *Core Python Language Fundamentals* or *Core Python Programming*.

6-12. *Debugging & Refactoring.* The `update()` and `remove()` functions each have a minor flaw: `update()` might move users from one group into the same group. Change the random destination group to be different from the group from which the user is moving. Similarly, `remove()` might try to remove people from a group that has no members (because they don't exist or were moved up with `update()`).

ORMs

6-13. *Stock Portfolio Class.* Create an alternative solution to the Stock Portfolio (Exercise 6-11) by using an ORM instead of direct to an RDBMS.

6-14. *Debugging and Refactoring.* Port your solutions to Exercise 6-13 to both the SQLAlchemy and SQLObject examples.

6-15. *Supporting Different RDBMSs.* Take either the SQLAlchemy (`ushuffle_sad.py`) or SQLObject (`ushuffle_so.py`) application, which currently support MySQL and SQLite, and add yet another relational database of your choice.

For the next four exercises, focus on the `ushuffle_dbU.py` script, which features some code near the top (lines 7–12) that determines which function should be used to get user input from the command-line.

6-16. *Importing and Python.* Review that code again. Why do we need to check if `__builtins__` is a `dict` versus a module?

6-17. *Porting to Python 3.* Using `distutils.log.warn()` is not a perfect substitute for **print**/`print()`. Prove it. Provide code snippets to show where `warn()` is not compatible with `print()`.

6-18. *Porting to Python 3.* Some users believe that they can use `print()` in Python 2 just like in Python 3. Prove them wrong. Hint: From Guido himself: `print(x, y)`

6-19. *Python Language.* Assume that you want to use `print()` in Python 3 but `distutils.log.warn()` in Python 2, and you want to use the `printf()` name. What's wrong with the code below?

```
from distutils.log import warn
if hasattr(__builtins__, 'print'):
    printf = print
else:
    printf = warn
```

6-20. *Exceptions.* When establishing our connection to the server using our designated database name in `ushuffle_sad.py`, a failure (`exc.OperationalError`) indicated that our table did not exist, so we had to back up and create the database first before retrying the database connection. However, this is not the only source of errors: if using MySQL and the server itself is down, the same exception is also thrown. In this situation, execution of `CREATE DATABASE` will fail, as well. Add another handler to take care of this situation, raising `RuntimeError` back to the code attempting to create an instance.

6-21. *SQLAlchemy.* Augment the `ushuffle_sad.dbDump()` function by adding a new default parameter named `newest5` which defaults to `False`. If `True` is passed in, rather than displaying all users, reverse sort the list by order of `Users.userid` and show only the top five representing the newest employees. Make this special call in `main()` right after the call to `orm.insert()` and `orm.dbDump()`.

   a) Use the `Query` `limit()` and `offset()` methods.

   b) Use the Python slicing syntax, instead.

The updated output would look something like this:

```
. . .
Jess       7912      4
Aaron      8312      3
Melissa    8602      2

*** Top 5 newest employees

LOGIN      USERID    PROJID
Melissa    8602      2
Aaron      8312      3
Jess       7912      4
Elliot     7911      3
Davina     7902      3

*** Move users to a random group
        (4 users moved) from (3) to (1)

LOGIN      USERID    PROJID
Faye       6812      4
Serena     7003      2
Amy        7209      1
. . .
```

6-22. *SQLAlchemy.* Change ushuffle_sad.update() to use the Query update() method, dropping down to 5 lines of code. Use the timeit module to show whether it's faster than the original.

6-23. *SQLAlchemy.* Same as Exercise 6-22 but for ushuffle_sad.delete(), use the Query delete() method.

6-24. *SQLAlchemy.* In the explicitly non-declarative version of ushuffle_sad.py, ushuffle_sae.py, we removed the use of the declarative layer as well as sessions. While using an Active Record model is more optional, the concept of Sessions isn't a bad idea at all. Change all of the code that performs database operations in ushuffle_sae.py so that they all use/share a Session object, as in the declarative ushuffle_sad.py.

6-25. *Django Data Models.* Take the Users data model class, as implemented in our SQLAlchemy or SQLObject examples, and create the equivalent by using the Django ORM. You might want to read ahead to Chapter 11, "Web Frameworks: Django."

6-26. *Storm ORM.* Port the ushuffle_s*.py application to the Storm ORM.

Non-Relational (NoSQL) Databases

6-27. *NoSQL.* What are some of reasons why non-relational databases have become popular? What do they offer over traditional relational databases?

6-28. *NoSQL.* There are at least four different types of non-relational databases. Categorize each of the major types and name the most well-known projects in each category. Note the specific ones that have at least one Python adapter.

6-29. *CouchDB.* CouchDB is another document datastore that's often compared to MongoDB. Review some of the online comparisons in the final section of this chapter, and then download and install CouchDB. Morph `ushuffle_mongo.py` into a CouchDB-compatible `ushuffle_couch.py`.

*Programming
Microsoft Office

Whatever you have to do, there is always a limiting factor *that determines how quickly and well you get it done. Your job is to study the task and identify the limiting factor or constraint within it. You must then focus all of your energies on alleviating that single choke point.*
—Brian Tracy, March 2001
(from *Eat That Frog*, 2001, Berrett-Koehler)

In this chapter...

- Introduction
- COM Client Programming with Python
- Introductory Examples
- Intermediate Examples
- Related Modules/Packages

> Note that the examples in this chapter require a Windows operating system; they will not work on Apple computers running Microsoft Office for Mac.

T his chapter represents a departure from most other sections of this book, meaning that instead of focusing on developing networked, GUI, Web, or command-line-based applications, we'll be using Python for something completely different: controlling proprietary software, specifically Microsoft Office applications, via Component Object Model (COM) client programming.

7.1   Introduction

Like it or not, we developers live in a world in which we will interact with Windows-based PCs. It might be intermittent or something you have to deal with on a daily basis, but regardless of how much exposure you face, the power of Python can be used to make our lives easier.

In this chapter, we will explore COM client programming by using Python to control and communicate with Microsoft Office applications such as Word, Excel, PowerPoint, and Outlook. COM is a service through which PC applications can interact with each other. Specifically, well-known applications such as those in the Office suite provide COM services, and COM client programs can be written to drive these applications.

Traditionally, COM clients are written in Microsoft Visual Basic (VB)/ Visual Basic for Applications (VBA) or (Visual) C++, two very powerful but very different tools. For COM programming, Python is often viewed as a viable substitute because it is more powerful than VB, and it is more expressive and less time-consuming than developing in C++.

IronPython, .NET, and VSTO (Visual Studio Tools for Office) are all newer tools that help you to write applications that communicate with Office tools, as well, but if you look under the hood, you'll find COM, so the material in this chapter still applies, even if you're using some of these more advanced tools.

This chapter is designed for both COM developers who want to learn how they can apply Python in their world, and also for Python programmers who need to learn how to create COM clients to automate tasks such as generating Excel spreadsheets, creating form letters as Word documents, building slide presentations by using PowerPoint, sending e-mail via Outlook, etc. We will not be discussing the principles or concepts of COM, waxing philosophically on such thoughts as "Why COM?" Nor will we be learning about COM+, ATL, IDL, MFC, DCOM, ADO, .NET, IronPython, VSTO, etc.

Instead, we will immerse you in COM client programming by learning how to use Python to communicate with Office applications.

7.2   COM Client Programming with Python

One of the most useful things that you can do in an everyday business environment is to integrate support for Windows applications. Being able to read data from and write data to such applications can often be very handy. Your department might not be running in a Windows environment, but chances are, your management and other project teams are. Mark Hammond's Windows Extensions for Python allows programmers to interact with Windows applications in their native environment.

The Windows programming universe is expansive; most of it available from the Windows Extensions for Python package. This bundle includes the Windows applications programming interface (API), spawning processes, Microsoft Foundation Classes (MFC) Graphical User Interface (GUI) development, Windows multithreaded programming, services, remote access, pipes, server-side COM programming, and events. For the remainder of the chapter, we are going to focus on one part of the Windows universe: COM client programming.

7.2.1   Client-Side COM Programming

We can use COM (or its marketing name, ActiveX), to communicate with tools such as Outlook and Excel. For programmers, the pleasure comes with being able to "control" a native Office application directly from their Python code.

Specifically, when discussing the use of a COM object, for example, launching of an application and allowing code to access methods and data of that application, this is referred to as COM *client-side* programming. *Server-side* COM programming is the implementation of a COM object for clients to access.

 CORE NOTE: Python and Microsoft COM (client-side) programming

Python on the Windows 32-bit platform contains connectivity to COM, a Microsoft interfacing technology that allows objects to talk to one another, thus facilitating higher-level applications to talk to one another, without any language or format dependence. We will see in this section how the combination of Python and COM (client programming) presents a unique opportunity to create scripts that can communicate directly with Microsoft Office applications such as Word, Excel, PowerPoint, and Outlook.

7.2.2   Getting Started

The prerequisites to this section include using a PC (or other system containing a virtual machine) that is running a 32-bit or 64-bit version of Windows. You also must have .NET 2.0 (at least) installed as well as both Python and the Python Extensions for Windows. (You can get the extensions from http://pywin32.sf.net.) Finally, you must have one or more Microsoft applications available with which to try the examples. You can develop from the command-line or with the PythonWin IDE that comes with the Extensions distribution.

I must confess that I'm neither a COM expert or a Microsoft software developer, however I am skilled enough to show you how to use Python to control Office applications. Naturally our examples can be vastly improved. We solicit you to drop us a line and send us any comments, suggestions, or improvements that you would consider for the general audience.

The rest of the chapter is made up of demonstration applications to get you started in programming each of the major Office applications; it then concludes with several intermediate examples. Before we show you examples, we want to point out that client-side COM applications all follow similar steps in execution. The typical way in which you would interact with these applications is something like this:

1. Launch application
2. Add appropriate document to work on (or load an existing one)
3. Make application visible (if desired)
4. Perform all desired work on document
5. Save or discard document
6. Quit

Enough talking; let's take a look at some code. In the following section are a series of scripts that each control a different Microsoft application. All import the `win32com.client` module as well as a couple of Tk modules to control the launch (and completion) of each application. Also, as we did in Chapter 5, "GUI Programming," we used the `.pyw` file extension to suppress the unneeded DOS command window.

7.3   Introductory Examples

In this section, we will take a look at basic examples that will get you started developing with four major Office applications: Excel, Word, PowerPoint, and Outlook.

7.3.1   Excel

Our first example is a demonstration using Excel. Of the entire Office suite, we find Excel to be the most programmable. It is quite useful to pass data to Excel so that you can both take advantage of the spreadsheet's features as well as view data in a nice, printable format. It is also useful to be able to read data from a spreadsheet and process it with the power of a real programming language such as Python. We will present a more complex example at the end of this section, but we have to start somewhere, so let's start with Example 7-1.

Example 7-1   Excel Example (`excel.pyw`)

This script launches Excel and writes data to spreadsheet cells.

```
1   #!/usr/bin/env python
2
3   from Tkinter import Tk
4   from time import sleep
5   from tkMessageBox import showwarning
6   import win32com.client as win32
7
8   warn = lambda app: showwarning(app, 'Exit?')
9   RANGE = range(3, 8)
10
11  def excel():
12      app = 'Excel'
13      xl = win32.gencache.EnsureDispatch('%s.Application' % app)
14      ss = xl.Workbooks.Add()
15      sh = ss.ActiveSheet
16      xl.Visible = True
17      sleep(1)
18
19      sh.Cells(1,1).Value = 'Python-to-%s Demo' % app
20      sleep(1)
21      for i in RANGE:
22          sh.Cells(i,1).Value = 'Line %d' % i
23          sleep(1)
24      sh.Cells(i+2,1).Value = "Th-th-th-that's all folks!"
25
```

```
26      warn(app)
27      ss.Close(False)
28      xl.Application.Quit()
29
30   if __name__=='__main__':
31      Tk().withdraw()
32      excel()
```

Line-by-Line Explanation

Lines 1–6, 31

We import `Tkinter` and `tkMessageBox` only to use the `showwarning` message box upon termination of the demonstration. We `withdraw()` the Tk top-level window to suppress it (line 31) before bringing up the dialog box (line 26). If you do not initialize the top level beforehand, one will automatically be created for you; it won't be withdrawn and will be an annoyance on screen.

Lines 11–17

After the code starts (or "dispatches") Excel, we add a *workbook* (a spreadsheet that contains *sheets* to which the data is written; these sheets are organized as tabs in the workbook), and then grab a handle to the *active sheet* (the sheet that is displayed). Do not get all worked up about the terminology, which can be confusing mostly because a *spreadsheet contains sheets*.

 CORE NOTE: Static and dynamic dispatch

On line 13, we use what is known as static dispatch. Before starting up the script, we ran the **Makepy** utility from PythonWin. (Start the IDE, select `Tools`, `COM Makepy utility`, and then choose the appropriate application object library.) This utility creates and caches the objects that are needed for the application. Without this preparatory work, the objects and attributes will need to be built during runtime; this is known as *dynamic dispatch*. If you want to run dynamically, then use the regular `Dispatch()` function:

```
xl = win32com.client.Dispatch('%s.Application' % app)
```

The Visible flag must be set to True to make the application visible on your desktop; pause so that you can see each step in the demonstration (line 16).

Lines 19–24

In the application portion of the script, we write out the title of our demonstration to the first (upper-left) cell, (A1) or (1, 1). We then skip a row and write "Line *N*" where *N* is numbered from 3 to 7, pausing 1 second in between each row so that you can see our updates happening live. (The cell updates would occur too quickly without the delay. This is the reason for all the sleep() calls throughout the script.)

Lines 26–32

A warning dialog box appears after the demonstration, stating that you can quit once you have observed the output. The spreadsheet is closed without saving, ss.Close([SaveChanges=]False), and the application exits. Finally, the "main" part of the script initializes Tk and runs the core part of the application.

Running this script results in an Excel application window, which should look similar to Figure 7-1.

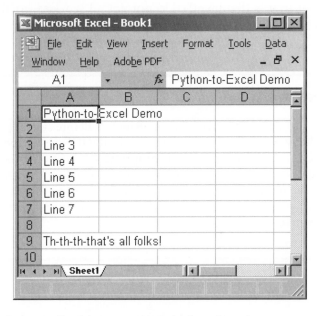

Figure 7-1 The Python-to-Excel demonstration script (excel.pyw).

7.3.2   Word

The next demonstration involves Word. Using Word for documents is not as applicable to the programming world because there is not much data involved. However, you could consider using Word for generating form letters. In Example 7-2, we create a document by writing one line of text after another.

Example 7-2   Word Example (word.pyw)

This script launches Word and writes data to the document.

```
1    #!/usr/bin/env python
2
3    from Tkinter import Tk
4    from time import sleep
5    from tkMessageBox import showwarning
6    import win32com.client as win32
7
8    warn = lambda app: showwarning(app, 'Exit?')
9    RANGE = range(3, 8)
10
11   def word():
12       app = 'Word'
13       word = win32.gencache.EnsureDispatch('%s.Application' % app)
14       doc = word.Documents.Add()
15       word.Visible = True
16       sleep(1)
17
18       rng = doc.Range(0,0)
19       rng.InsertAfter('Python-to-%s Test\r\n\r\n' % app)
20       sleep(1)
21       for i in RANGE:
22           rng.InsertAfter('Line %d\r\n' % i)
23           sleep(1)
24       rng.InsertAfter("\r\nTh-th-th-that's all folks!\r\n")
25
26       warn(app)
27       doc.Close(False)
28       word.Application.Quit()
29
30   if __name__=='__main__':
31       Tk().withdraw()
32       word()
```

The Word example follows pretty much the same script as the Excel example. The only difference is that instead of writing in cells, we insert the strings into the text "range" of our document and move the cursor forward after each write. We also must manually provide the line termination characters, carriage RETURN followed by NEWLINE (\r\n).

When you run this script, the resulting screen might look like Figure 7-2.

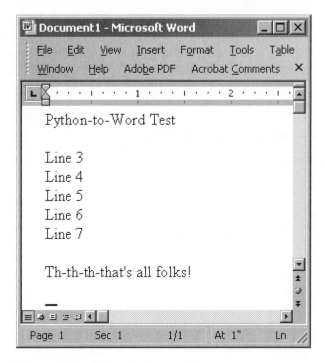

Figure 7-2 The Python-to-Word demonstration script (word.pyw).

7.3.3   PowerPoint

Applying PowerPoint in an application might not seem commonplace, but you could consider using it when you are rushed to make a presentation. You can create your bullet points in a text file on the plane, and then upon arrival at the hotel that evening, use a script that parses the file and auto-generates a set of slides. You can further enhance those slides by adding in a background, animation, etc., all of which are possible through the COM interface. Another use case would be if you had to auto-generate or modify new or existing presentations. You can create a COM script controlled via a shell script to create and tweak each presentation. Okay, enough speculation; let's take a look at Example 7-3 to see our PowerPoint example in action.

Example 7-3   PowerPoint Example (ppoint.pyw)

This script launches PowerPoint and writes data to the "shapes" on a slide.

```
 1   #!/usr/bin/env python
 2
 3   from Tkinter import Tk
 4   from time import sleep
 5   from tkMessageBox import showwarning
 6   import win32com.client as win32
 7
 8   warn = lambda app: showwarning(app, 'Exit?')
 9   RANGE = range(3, 8)
10
11   def ppoint():
12       app = 'PowerPoint'
13       ppoint = win32.gencache.EnsureDispatch('%s.Application' % app)
14       pres = ppoint.Presentations.Add()
15       ppoint.Visible = True
16
17       s1 = pres.Slides.Add(1, win32.constants.ppLayoutText)
18       sleep(1)
19       s1a = s1.Shapes[0].TextFrame.TextRange
20       s1a.Text = 'Python-to-%s Demo' % app
21       sleep(1)
22       s1b = s1.Shapes[1].TextFrame.TextRange
23       for i in RANGE:
24           s1b.InsertAfter("Line %d\r\n" % i)
25           sleep(1)
26       s1b.InsertAfter("\r\nTh-th-th-that's all folks!")
27
28       warn(app)
29       pres.Close()
30       ppoint.Quit()
31
32   if __name__=='__main__':
33       Tk().withdraw()
34       ppoint()
```

Again, you will notice similarities to both the preceding Excel and Word demonstrations. Where PowerPoint differs is in the objects to which you write data. Instead of a single active sheet or document, PowerPoint is somewhat trickier because with a presentation, you have multiple slides, and each slide can have a different layout. (Recent versions of PowerPoint have 30 different layouts!) The actions you can perform on a slide depend on which layout you have chosen.

In our example, we just use a title and text layout (line 17) and fill in the main title (lines 19–20), Shape[0] or Shape(1)—Python sequences begin at index 0 while Microsoft software starts at 1—and the text portion (lines 22–26), Shape[1] or Shape(2). To figure out which constant to use, you will need a list of all those that are available to you. For example, ppLayoutText is defined as a constant with a value of 2 (integer), ppLayoutTitle is 1, etc. You can find the constants in most Microsoft VB/Office programming books or online by just searching on the names. Alternatively, you can just use the integer constants without having to name them via win32.constants.

The PowerPoint screenshot is shown in Figure 7-3.

Figure 7-3 The Python-to-PowerPoint demonstration script (ppoint.pyw).

7.3.4   Outlook

Finally, we present an Outlook demonstration, which uses even more constants than PowerPoint. As a fairly common and versatile tool, use of Outlook in an application makes sense, like it does for Excel. There are always e-mail addresses, messages, and other data that can be easily manipulated in a Python program. Example 7-4 is an Outlook example that does a little bit more than our previous examples.

Example 7-4   Outlook Example (olook.pyw)

This script launches Outlook, creates a new message, sends it, and lets you view it by opening and displaying both the Outbox and the message itself.

```
1   #!/usr/bin/env python
2
3   from Tkinter import Tk
4   from tkMessageBox import showwarning
5   import win32com.client as win32
6
7   warn = lambda app: showwarning(app, 'Exit?')
8   RANGE = range(3, 8)
9
10  def outlook():
11      app = 'Outlook'
12      olook = win32.gencache.EnsureDispatch('%s.Application' % app)
13
14      mail = olook.CreateItem(win32.constants.olMailItem)
15      recip = mail.Recipients.Add('you@127.0.0.1')
16      subj = mail.Subject = 'Python-to-%s Demo' % app
17      body = ["Line %d" % i for i in RANGE]
18      body.insert(0, '%s\r\n' % subj)
19      body.append("\r\nTh-th-th-that's all folks!")
20      mail.Body = '\r\n'.join(body)
21      mail.Send()
22
23      ns = olook.GetNamespace("MAPI")
24      obox = ns.GetDefaultFolder(win32.constants.olFolderOutbox)
25      obox.Display()
26      obox.Items.Item(1).Display()
27
28      warn(app)
29      olook.Quit()
30
31  if __name__=='__main__':
32      Tk().withdraw()
33      outlook()
```

In this example, we use Outlook to send an e-mail to ourselves. To make the demonstration work, you need to turn off your network access so that you do not really send the message, and thus are able to view it in your Outbox folder (and delete it after viewing, if you like). After launching Outlook, we create a new mail message and fill out the various fields such as recipient, subject, and body (lines 15–21). We then call the send() method (line 22) to spool the message to the Outbox where it will be moved to "Sent Mail" once the message has actually been transmitted to the mail server.

Like PowerPoint, there are many constants available; `olMailItem` (with a constant value of 0) is the one used for e-mail messages. Other popular Outlook items include `olAppointmentItem` (1), `olContactItem` (2), and `olTaskItem` (3). Of course, there are more, so you will need to find a VB/Office programming book or search for the constants and their values online.

In the next section (lines 24–27), we use another constant, `olFolder-Outbox` (4), to open the Outbox folder and bring it up for display. We find the most recent item (hopefully the one we just created) and display it, as well. Other popular folders include: `olFolderInbox` (6), `olFolderCalendar` (9), `olFolderContacts` (10), `olFolderDrafts` (16), `olFolderSentMail` (5), and `olFolderTasks` (13). If you use dynamic dispatch, you will likely have to use the numeric values instead of the constants' names (see the previous Core Note).

Figure 7-4 shows a screen capture of just the message window.

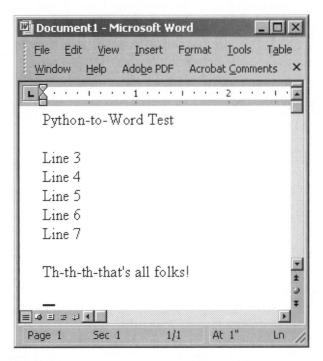

Figure 7-4 The Python-to-Outlook demonstration script (`olook.pyw`).

Before we get this far, however, from its history we know that Outlook has been vulnerable to all kinds of attacks, so Microsoft has built in some protection that restricts access to your address book and the ability to send mail on your behalf. When attempting to access your Outlook data, the screen shown in Figure 7-5 pops up, in which you must explicitly give permission to an outside program.

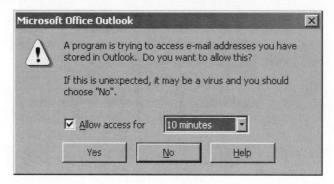

Figure 7-5 Outlook address book access warning.

Then, when you are trying to send a message from an external program, a warning dialog appears, as shown in Figure 7-6; you must wait until the timer expires before you are allowed to select Yes.

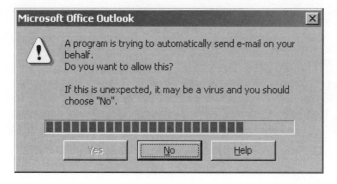

Figure 7-6 Outlook e-mail transmission warning.

Once you pass all the security checks, everything else should work smoothly. There is software available to help get you around these checks but they have to be downloaded and installed separately.

On this book's Web site at http://corepython.com, you will find an alternative script that combines these four smaller ones into a single application that lets users choose which of these demonstrations to run.

7.4   Intermediate Examples

The examples we've looked at so far in this chapter are to get you started with using Python to control Microsoft Office products. Now let's look at several real-world useful applications, some of which I've used regularly for work.

7.4.1   Excel

In this example, we're going to combine the material from this chapter with that of Chapter 13, "Web Services." In this chapter, we feature a script `stock.py` as Example 13-1, that uses the Yahoo! Finance service and asks for stock quote data. Example 7-5 shows how we can merge the stock quote example with our Excel demonstration script; we will end up with an application that can download stock quotes from the Net and insert them directly into Excel, without having to create or use CSV files as a medium.

Example 7-5   Stock Quote and Excel Example (`estock.pyw`)

This script downloads stock quotes from Yahoo! and writes the data to Excel.

```
1   #!/usr/bin/env python
2
3   from Tkinter import Tk
4   from time import sleep, ctime
5   from tkMessageBox import showwarning
6   from urllib import urlopen
7   import win32com.client as win32
8
9   warn = lambda app: showwarning(app, 'Exit?')
10  RANGE = range(3, 8)
11  TICKS = ('YHOO', 'GOOG', 'EBAY', 'AMZN')
12  COLS = ('TICKER', 'PRICE', 'CHG', '%AGE')
13  URL = 'http://quote.yahoo.com/d/quotes.csv?s=%s&f=sl1c1p2'
14
15  def excel():
16      app = 'Excel'
17      xl = win32.gencache.EnsureDispatch('%s.Application' % app)
18      ss = xl.Workbooks.Add()
19      sh = ss.ActiveSheet
20      xl.Visible = True
21      sleep(1)
22
23      sh.Cells(1, 1).Value = 'Python-to-%s Stock Quote Demo' % app
24      sleep(1)
25      sh.Cells(3, 1).Value = 'Prices quoted as of: %s' % ctime()
26      sleep(1)
27      for i in range(4):
28          sh.Cells(5, i+1).Value = COLS[i]
```

```
29          sleep(1)
30          sh.Range(sh.Cells(5, 1), sh.Cells(5, 4)).Font.Bold = True
31          sleep(1)
32          row = 6
33
34          u = urlopen(URL % ','.join(TICKS))
35          for data in u:
36              tick, price, chg, per = data.split(',')
37              sh.Cells(row, 1).Value = eval(tick)
38              sh.Cells(row, 2).Value = ('%.2f' % round(float(price), 2))
39              sh.Cells(row, 3).Value = chg
40              sh.Cells(row, 4).Value = eval(per.rstrip())
41              row += 1
42              sleep(1)
43          u.close()
44
45          warn(app)
46          ss.Close(False)
47          xl.Application.Quit()
48
49   if __name__=='__main__':
50          Tk().withdraw()
51          excel()
```

Line-by-Line Explanation

Lines 1–13

Looking ahead in Chapter 13, we will explore a simple script that fetches stock quotes from the Yahoo! Finance service. In this chapter, we take the core component from that script and integrate it into an example that takes the data and imports it into an Excel spreadsheet.

Lines 15–32

The first part of the core function launches Excel (lines 17–21), as seen earlier. The title and timestamp are then written to cells (lines 23–29), along with the column headings, which are then styled as bold (line 30). The remaining cells are dedicated to writing the actual stock quote data, starting in row 6 (line 32).

Lines 34–43

We open the URL as before (line 34), but instead of just writing the data to standard output, we fill in the spreadsheet cells, one column of data at a time, and one company per row (lines 35–42).

Lines 45–51

The remaining lines of our script mirror code that we have seen before.

Figure 7-7 shows a window with real data after executing our script.

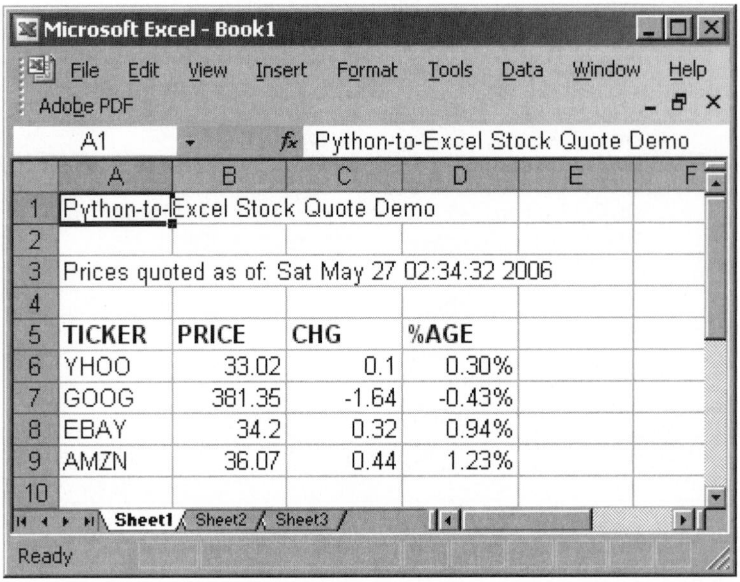

Figure 7-7 The Python-to-Excel stock quote demonstration script (estock.pyw).

Note that the data columns lose the original formatting of the numeric strings because Excel stores them as numbers, using the default cell format. We lose the formatting of the numbers to two places after the decimal point; for example, "34.2" is displayed, even though Python passed in "34.20." For the "change from previous close column," we lose not only the decimal places but also the plus sign (+) that indicates a positive change in value. (Compare the output in Excel to the output from the original text version, which you can see in Example 13-1 [stock.py], in Chapter 13. These problems will be addressed by an exercise at the end of this chapter.)

7.4.2   Outlook

At first, we wanted to give readers examples of Outlook scripts that manipulate your address book or that send and receive e-mail. However, given all the security issues with Outlook, we decided to avoid those categories, yet still give you a very useful example.

Those of us who work daily on the command-line building applications are used to certain text editors to help us do our work. Without getting into any religious wars, these tools include Emacs, vi (or its modern replacement vim or gVim), and others. For users of these tools, editing an e-mail reply in an Outlook dialog window may not exactly be their cup of tea. In comes Python to the rescue.

This script, inspired by John Klassa's original 2001 creation, is very simple: when you reply to an e-mail message in Outlook, it launches your editor of choice, brings in the content of the e-mail reply that is currently in the crude-editing dialog window, lets you edit the rest of the message to your heart's desire in your favorite editor, and then when exiting, replaces the dialog window content with the text you just edited. You only need to click the Send button.

You can run the tool from the command-line. We've named it outlook_edit.pyw. The .pyw extension is used to indicate the suppression of the terminal, meaning the intention is to run a GUI application for which user interaction isn't necessary. Before we look at the code, let's describe how it works. When it's started, you'll see its simple user interface, as shown in Figure 7-8.

Figure 7-8 The Outlook e-mail editor GUI control panel (outlook_edit.pyw).

As your going through your e-mail, there might be one to which you want to respond, so you click the Reply button to bring up a pop-up window similar to that (except for the contents, of course) in Figure 7-9.

Now, rather than editing in this poor dialog window, you prefer to do so in a different editor (your editor of choice) rather than taking what's given to you. Once you've set up one to use with outlook_edit.py, click the GUI's Edit button. We hardcoded it to be gVim 7.3 in this example, but there's no reason why you can't use an environment variable or let the user specify this on the command-line (see the related exercise at the end of the chapter).

For the figures in this section, we're using Outlook 2003. When this version of Outlook detects an outside script that is requesting access to it, it displays the same warning dialog as that shown in Figure 7-5. Once you

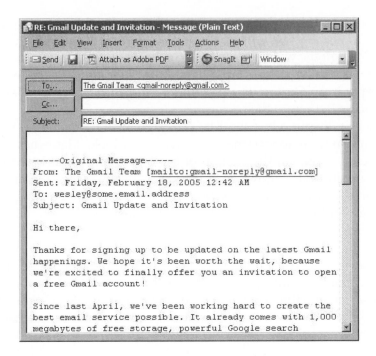

Figure 7-9 Standard Outlook reply dialog window.

"opt-in," a new gVim window pops open, including the contents of the Outlook reply dialog box. An example of ours is shown in Figure 7-10.

At this point, you can add your reply, editing any other part of the message as desired. We'll just do a quick and friendly reply (Figure 7-11). Saving the file and quitting the editor results in that window closing and the contents of your reply pushed back into the Outlook reply dialog box (see Figure 7-12) that you didn't want to deal with to begin with. The only thing you need to do here is to click the Send button, and you're done!

Now let's take a look at the script itself, shown in Example 7-6. You will see from the line-by-line description of the code that this script is broken up into four main parts: hook into Outlook and grab the current item being worked on; clean the text in the Outlook dialog and transfer it to a temporary file; spawn the editor opened against the temporary text file; and reading the contents of the edited text file and pushing it back into that dialog window.

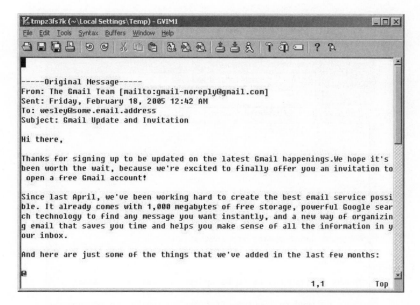

Figure 7-10 Outlook dialog contents in a spawned gVim editor window.

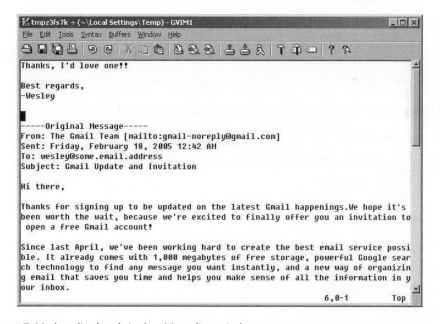

Figure 7-11 An edited reply in the gVim editor window.

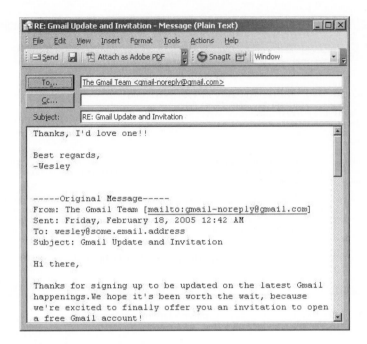

Figure 7-12 Back to the Outlook dialog with our modified contents.

Example 7-6   Outlook Editor Example (outlook_edit.pyw)

Why edit your Outlook new or reply messages in a dialog window?

```
1   #!/usr/bin/env python
2
3   from Tkinter import Tk, Frame, Label, Button, BOTH
4   import os
5   import tempfile
6   import win32com.client as win32
7
8   def edit():
9       olook = win32.Dispatch('Outlook.Application')
10      insp = olook.ActiveInspector()
11      if insp is None:
12          return
13      item = insp.CurrentItem
14      if item is None:
15          return
16
17      body = item.Body
18      tmpfd, tmpfn = tempfile.mkstemp()
19      f = os.fdopen(tmpfd, 'a')
```

```
20       f.write(body.encode(
21            'ascii', 'ignore').replace('\r\n', '\n'))
22       f.close()
23
24       #ed = r"d:\emacs-23.2\bin\emacsclientw.exe"
25       ed = r"c:\progra~1\vim\vim73\gvim.exe"
26       os.spawnv(os.P_WAIT, ed, [ed, tmpfn])
27
28       f = open(tmpfn, 'r')
29       body = f.read().replace('\n', '\r\n')
30       f.close()
31       os.unlink(tmpfn)
32       item.Body = body
33
34   if __name__=='__main__':
35       tk = Tk()
36       f = Frame(tk, borderwidth=2)
37       f.pack(fill=BOTH)
38       Label(f,
39            text="Outlook Edit Launcher v0.3").pack()
40       Button(f, text="Edit",
41            fg='blue', command=edit).pack(fill=BOTH)
42       Button(f, text="Quit",
43            fg='red', command=tk.quit).pack(fill=BOTH)
44       tk.mainloop()
```

Line-by-Line Explanation

Lines 1–6

Although Tk does not play a huge role in any of the examples in this chapter, it provides an *execution shell* with which to control the interface between the user and the target Office application. Accordingly, we need a bunch of Tk constants and widgets for this application. There are a bunch of operating system items that we need, so we import the os module (well, nt actually). tempfile is a Python module that we haven't really discussed, but it provides a variety of utilities and classes that developers can use to create temporary files, filenames, and directories. Finally, we need our PC connectivity to Office applications and their COM servers.

Lines 8–15

The only real PC COM client lines of code are here, obtaining a handle to the running instance of Outlook, looking for the active dialog (should be a olMailItem) that is being worked on. If it cannot do this inspection or find the current item, the application quits quietly. You will know if this is the case because control of the Edit button comes back immediately rather than being grayed-out (if all went well and the editor window pops up).

Note that we're choosing to use dynamic dispatch here instead of static (`win32.Dispatch()` vs. `win32.gencache.EnsureDispatch()`) because dynamic usually has quicker startup, and we're not using any of the cached constant values in this script.

Lines 16–22

Once the current dialog (compose new or reply) window is identified, the first thing we do in this section is to grab the text and write it to a temporary file. Admittedly, the handling of Unicode text and diacritic characters is not good here; we're filtering all non-ASCII characters out of the dialog box. (One of the exercises at the end of the this chapter is to right this wrong and tweak the script so it works correctly with Unicode.)

Originally, Unix-flavored editors did not like to deal with the carriage RETURN-NEWLINE pair used as line termination characters in files created on PCs, so another piece of processing that's done pre- and post-editing is to convert these to pure NEWLINEs before sending the file to the editor and then add them back after editing is complete. Modern text-based editors handle \r\n more cleanly, so this isn't as much of an issue as it was in the past.

Lines 24–26

Here's where a bit of magic happens: after setting our editor (on line 25, where we specify the location of the vim binary on our system; Emacs users will do something like line 24 which is commented out), we launch the editor with the temporary filename as the argument (assuming that the editor takes the target filename on the command-line as the first argument after the program name). This is done via the call to `os.spawnv()` on line 26.

The `P_WAIT` flag is used to "pause" the main (parent) process until the spawned (child) process has completed. In other words, we do want to keep the Edit button grayed-out so that the user does not try to edit more than one reply at a time. It sounds like a limitation, but it helps the user focus and not have partially-edited replies all over the desktop.

To further expand on what else you can do with `spawnv()`, this flag works on both POSIX and Windows systems just like `P_NOWAIT` (which does the opposite—do *not* wait for the child to finish, running both processes in parallel). The last two possible flags, `P_OVERLAY` and `P_DETACH`, are only valid on Windows. `P_OVERLAY` causes the child to replace the parent like the POSIX `exec()` call, and `P_DETACH`, like `P_NOWAIT`, starts the child running in parallel with the parent, except it does so in the background, "detached" from a keyboard or console.

One of the exercises at the end of this chapter is to make this part of the code more flexible. As we hinted a bit earlier, you should be able to specify your editor of choice here via the command-line or through the use of an environment variable.

Lines 28–32

The next block of code opens the updated temporary file after the editor has closed, takes its contents, deletes the temporary file, and replaces the text in the dialog window. Note that we are merely sending this data back to Outlook—it does *not* prevent Outlook from mucking with your message; that is, there can be a variety of side effects, some of which include adding your signature (again), removing NEWLINEs, etc.

Lines 34–44

The application is built around `main()` which uses Tk(inter) to draw up a simple user interface with a single frame containing a Label with the application description, plus a pair of buttons: Edit spawns an editor on the active Outlook dialog window, and Quit terminates this application.

7.4.3   PowerPoint

Our final example of a more realistic application is one that Python users have requested of me for many years now, and I'm happy to say that I'm finally able to present it to the community. If you have ever seen me deliver a presentation at a conference, you will likely have seen my ploy of showing the audience a plain text version of my talk, perhaps to the shock and horror of some of the attendees who have yet to hear me speak.

I then launch this script on that plain text file and let the power of Python autogenerate a PowerPoint presentation, complete with style template, and then start the slide show, much to the amazement of the audience. However, once you realize it's only a small, easily-written Python script, you might be less impressed but satisfied that you can do the same thing too!

The way it works is this: the GUI comes up (see Figure 7-13a) prompting the user to enter the location of the text file. If the user types in a valid location for the file, things progress, but if the file is not found or "DEMO" is entered, a demonstration will start. If a filename is given but somehow can't be opened by the application, the DEMO string is installed into the text entry along with the error stating that the file can't be opened (Figure 7-13b).

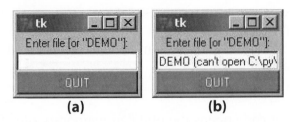

Figure 7-13 Text-to-PowerPoint GUI control panel (`txt2ppt.pyw`).
(a) Filename entry field clear on start-up (b) DEMO if demo request or error otherwise.

As shown in Figure 7-14, the next step is to connect to the existing PowerPoint application that is running (or launch one if it isn't and then get a handle to it), create a title slide (based on the ALL CAPS slide title), and then create any other slides based on contents of the plain text file formatted in a pseudo-Python syntax.

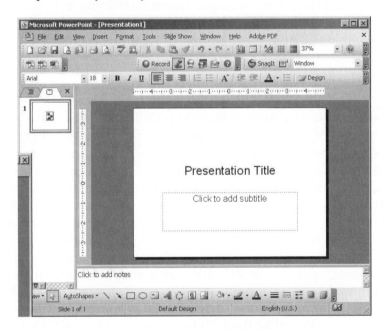

Figure 7-14 PowerPoint creating the title slide of the demo presentation.

Figure 7-15 shows the script in mid-flight, creating the final slide of the demonstration. When this screen was captured, the final line had not been added to the slide yet (so it's not a bug in the code).

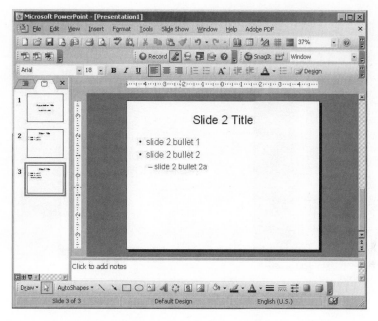

Figure 7-15 Creating the final slide of the demo presentation.

Finally, the code adds one more auxiliary slide to tell the user the slide-show is set to go (Figure 7-16) and gives a cute little countdown from three to zero. (The screenshot was taken as the count had already started and progressed down to two.) The slideshow is then started without any additional processing. Figure 7-17 depicts the plain look (black text on a white background).

To show it works, now we apply a presentation template (Figure 7-18) to give it the desired look and feel, and then you can drive it from here on out.

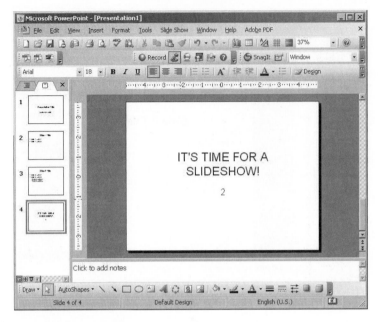

Figure 7-16 Counting down to start the slideshow.

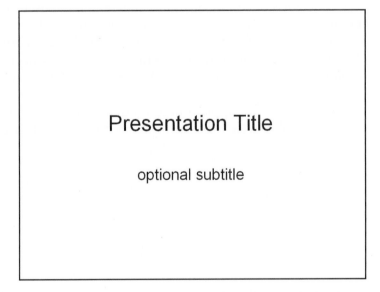

Figure 7-17 The slideshow has started, but no template has been applied (yet).

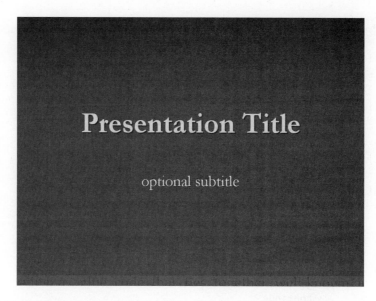

Figure 7-18 The finished PowerPoint slideshow after the template is applied.

Example 7-7 presents the `txt2ppt.pyw` script, followed by the corresponding code walkthrough.

Example 7-7   Text-to-PowerPoint converter (`txt2ppt.pyw`)

This script generates a PowerPoint presentation from a plain text file formatted like Python code.

```
 1   #!/usr/bin/env python
 2
 3   from Tkinter import Tk, Label, Entry, Button
 4   from time import sleep
 5   import win32com.client as win32
 6
 7   INDENT = '    '
 8   DEMO = '''
 9   PRESENTATION TITLE
10       optional subtitle
11
```

(Continued)

Example 7-7   Text-to-PowerPoint converter (txt2ppt.pyw) *(Continued)*

```
12   slide 1 title
13       slide 1 bullet 1
14       slide 1 bullet 2
15
16   slide 2 title
17       slide 2 bullet 1
18       slide 2 bullet 2
19           slide 2 bullet 2a
20           slide 2 bullet 2b
21   '''
22
23   def txt2ppt(lines):
24       ppoint = win32.gencache.EnsureDispatch(
25           'PowerPoint.Application')
26       pres = ppoint.Presentations.Add()
27       ppoint.Visible = True
28       sleep(2)
29       nslide = 1
30       for line in lines:
31           if not line:
32               continue
33           linedata = line.split(INDENT)
34           if len(linedata) == 1:
35               title = (line == line.upper())
36               if title:
37                   stype = win32.constants.ppLayoutTitle
38               else:
39                   stype = win32.constants.ppLayoutText
40
41               s = pres.Slides.Add(nslide, stype)
42               ppoint.ActiveWindow.View.GotoSlide(nslide)
43               s.Shapes[0].TextFrame.TextRange.Text = line.title()
44               body = s.Shapes[1].TextFrame.TextRange
45               nline = 1
46               nslide += 1
47               sleep((nslide<4) and 0.5 or 0.01)
48           else:
49               line = '%s\r\n' % line.lstrip()
50               body.InsertAfter(line)
51               para = body.Paragraphs(nline)
52               para.IndentLevel = len(linedata) - 1
53               nline += 1
54               sleep((nslide<4) and 0.25 or 0.01)
55
56       s = pres.Slides.Add(nslide,win32.constants.ppLayoutTitle)
57       ppoint.ActiveWindow.View.GotoSlide(nslide)
58       s.Shapes[0].TextFrame.TextRange.Text = "It's time for a slide-
     show!".upper()
59       sleep(1.)
60       for i in range(3, 0, -1):
61           s.Shapes[1].TextFrame.TextRange.Text = str(i)
62           sleep(1.)
63
```

```
64        pres.SlideShowSettings.ShowType = win32.constants.ppShowType-
   Speaker
65        ss = pres.SlideShowSettings.Run()
66        pres.ApplyTemplate(r'c:\Program Files\Microsoft
   Office\Templates\Presentation Designs\Stream.pot')
67        s.Shapes[0].TextFrame.TextRange.Text = 'FINIS'
68        s.Shapes[1].TextFrame.TextRange.Text = ''
69
70  def _start(ev=None):
71        fn = en.get().strip()
72        try:
73            f = open(fn, 'U')
74        except IOError, e:
75            from cStringIO import StringIO
76            f = StringIO(DEMO)
77            en.delete(0, 'end')
78            if fn.lower() == 'demo':
79                en.insert(0, fn)
80            else:
81                import os
82                en.insert(0,
83                    r"DEMO (can't open %s: %s)" % (
84                    os.path.join(os.getcwd(), fn), str(e)))
85            en.update_idletasks()
86        txt2ppt(line.rstrip() for line in f)
87        f.close()
88
89  if __name__=='__main__':
90        tk = Tk()
91        lb = Label(tk, text='Enter file [or "DEMO"]:')
92        lb.pack()
93        en = Entry(tk)
94        en.bind('<Return>', _start)
95        en.pack()
96        en.focus_set()
97        quit = Button(tk, text='QUIT',
98            command=tk.quit, fg='white', bg='red')
99        quit.pack(fill='x', expand=True)
100       tk.mainloop()
```

Line-by-Line Explanation

Lines 1–5

Surprisingly, there aren't that many things to import. Python has almost everything we need to solve this problem. Like the Outlook dialog editor, we need to bring in some basic Tk functionality for a shell GUI application to capture user input. Naturally, you can choose to do it via a command-line interface, as well, but you have enough knowledge to do that on your own. Sometimes it's more convenient to have the tool sitting on your desktop waiting for you to use.

The use of the `time.sleep()` function is purely academic. We're only using it to slow down our application. You can choose to leave out all those calls if you prefer. The reason why we're using it here as well as our Excel stock demonstration earlier is to slow things down a bit because the code generally executes so quickly, people are skeptical that it even did anything or that it was staged.

The last bit of course, is the lynchpin: the PC library.

Lines 7–21

These are a pair of general global variables that represent two values. The first is the default indentation level of four spaces, much like the recommended indentation for Python code per the PEP 8 style guide, only this time, we're defining the presentation bullet level. The other one is a demonstration slide presentation in case you prefer to see a demonstration of how the script works or as a backup in case the desired source text file cannot be found by the script. This static string also serves as an example of how you should structure your source text file. Once you've created a presentation, you won't need to look at this again.

Lines 23–29

These first few lines of the main function, `txt2ppt()`, launch PowerPoint, create a new presentation, make the PowerPoint application show up on the desktop, pause for a few seconds, and then reset the slide count to one.

Lines 30–54

The `txt2ppt()` function takes one argument: all the lines of the source text file that comprise the presentation. You can pretty much feed this function any iterable with one or more lines, and a slide presentation will be created for you. For the demonstration bullet points, we use `cStringIO.StringIO` object to iterate through the text, and for a real file, we use a generator expression for each line. Naturally, if you're using Python 2.3 or older, you'll need to change the "genexp" to a list comprehension. True, it's not as great for memory, especially large source files, but what are you going do?

Back to the processor loop; we skip blank lines, then do a little bit of magic by string splitting on the indentation. A look at this code snippet will show you exactly what we're doing:

```
>>> 'slide title'.split('    ')
['slide title']
>>> '    1st level bullet'.split('    ')
```

```
['', '1st level bullet']
>>> '        2nd level bullet'.split('    ')
['', '', '2nd level bullet']
```

When there is no indentation, meaning that splitting on the indentation only leaves a single string, this means we're starting a new slide and the text is the slide title. If the length of this list is greater than one, this means that we have at least one level of indentation and that this is continuing material of a previous slide (and not the beginning of a new one). For the former, this affirmative part of the `if` clause makes up lines 35 to 47. We'll focus on this block first, followed by the rest.

The next five lines (35–39) determine whether this is a title slide or a standard text slide. This is where the ALL CAPS for a title slide comes in. We just compare the contents to an all-capitalized version of it. If they match, meaning the text is in CAPS, this means that this slide should use the title layout, designated by the PC constant `ppLayoutTitle`. Otherwise, this is a standard slide with a title and text body (`ppLayoutText`).

After we've determined the slide layout, the new slide is created on line 41, PowerPoint is directed (in line 42) to that slide (by making it the active slide), and the title or main shape text is set to the content, using title case (line 43). Note that Python starts counting at zero (`Shape[0]`), whereas Microsoft likes to start counting at one (`Shape(1)`)—either syntax is acceptable.

The remaining content to come will be part of `Shape[1]` (or `Shape(2)`), and we call that the body (line 44); for a title slide it will be the subtitle, and for a standard slide it's going to be bulleted lines of text.

On the remaining lines in this clause (45–47), we mark that we've written the first line on this slide, increment the counter tracking the total number of slides in the presentation, and then pause so that the user can see how the Python script was able to control PowerPoint's execution.

Jumping over the wall to the `else`-clause, we move to the code that's executed for the remaining list on the same slide, filling in the second shape or body of the slide. Because we have already used the indentation to indicate where we are and the indentation level, we don't need those leading spaces any more, so we strip (`str.lstrip()`) them out, and then insert the text into the body (lines 49–50).

The rest of the block indents the text to the correct bullet level (or no indentation at all if it's a title slide—setting an indentation level of zero has no effect on the text), increments the linecount, and adds the minor pause at the end to slow things down (lines 51–54).

Lines 56–62

After all the main slides have been created, we add one more title slide at the end, announcing that it's time for a slideshow by changing the text dynamically, counting down by seconds from three to zero.

Lines 64–68

The primary purpose of these lines is to start the slideshow. Actually only the first two lines (64 and 65) do this. Line 66 applies the template. We do this after the slideshow has started so that you can see it—it's more impressive that way. The last pair of lines in this block of code (67–68) reset the "it's time for a slideshow" slide and countdown used earlier.

Lines 70–100

The _start() function is only useful if we ran this script from the command-line. We leave txt2ppt() as importable to be used elsewhere, but _start() requires the GUI. Jumping down momentarily to lines 90–100, you can see that we create a Tk GUI with a text entry field (with a label prompting the user to enter a filename or "DEMO" to see the demonstration) and a Quit button.

So _start() begins (on line 71) by extracting the contents of this entry field and attempts to open this file (line 73; see the related exercise at the end of the chapter). If the file is opened successfully, it skips the except clause and calls txt2ppt() to process the file then closes it when complete (lines 86–87).

If an exception is encountered, the handler checks to see if the demo was selected (lines 77–79). If so, it reads the demonstration string into a cStringIO.StringIO object (line 76) and passes *that* to txt2ppt(); otherwise, it runs the demonstration anyway but inserts an error message in the text field to inform the user why the failure occurred (lines 81–84).

7.4.4   Summary

Hopefully, by studying this chapter, you will have received a strong introduction to COM client programming with Python. Although the COM servers on the Microsoft Office applications are the most robust and full-featured, the material you learned here will apply to other applications with COM servers, or even OpenOffice, the open-source version of Star-Office, another alternative to Microsoft Office.

Since the acquisition by Oracle of Sun Microsystems, the original corporate sponsor of StarOffice and OpenOffice, the successor to StarOffice has been announced as Oracle Open Office, and those in the open-source community who feel that the status of OpenOffice has become jeopardized have forked it as LibreOffice. Since they both come from the same codebase, they share the same COM-style interface known as Universal Network Objects (UNO). You can use the PyUNO module to drive OpenOffice or LibreOffice applications to process documents, such as, writing PDF files, converting from Microsoft Word to the OpenDocument text (ODT) format, HTML, etc.

7.5   Related Modules/Packages

Python Extensions for Windows

>   http://pywin32.sf.net

xlrd, xlwt (Python 3 versions available)

>   http://www.lexicon.net/sjmachin/xlrd.htm
>
>   http://pypi.python.org/pypi/xlwt
>
>   http://pypi.python.org/pypi/xlrd

pyExcelerator

>   http://sourceforge.net/projects/pyexcelerator/

PyUNO

>   http://udk.openoffice.org/python/python-bridge.html

7.6   Exercises

7-1. *Web Services.* Take the Yahoo! stock quote example (stock.py) and change the application to save the quote data to a file instead of displaying it to the screen. Optional: You can change the script so that users can choose to display the quote data or save it to a file.

7-2. *Excel and Web Pages.* Create an application that will read data from an Excel spreadsheet and map all of it to an equivalent HTML table. (You can use the third-party HTMLgen module if desired.)

7-3. *Office Applications and Web Services.* Interface to any existing Web service, whether REST or URL-based, and write data to an Excel spreadsheet, or format the data nicely into a Word document. Format them properly for printing. Extra Credit: Support both Excel *and* Word.

7-4. *Outlook and Web Services.* Similar to Exercise 7-3, do the same thing, but put the data into a new e-mail message that you send by using Outlook. Extra Credit: Do the same thing but send the e-mail by using regular SMTP instead. (You might want to refer to Chapter 3, "Internet Client Programming.")

7-5. *Slideshow Generation.* In Exercises 7-15 through 7-24, you'll build new features into the slideshow generator we introduced earlier in this chapter, txt2ppt.pyw. This exercise prompts you to think about just the basics but with a non-proprietary format. Implement a script with similar functionality to txt2ppt.pyw, except instead of interfacing with PowerPoint, your output should use an open-source standard such as HTML5. Take a look at projects such as Land-Slide, DZSlides, and HTML5Wow for inspiration. You can find others at http://en.wikipedia.org/wiki/Web-based_slideshow. Create a plain-text specification format for your users, document it, and let your users use this tool to produce something that they can use on stage.

7-6. *Outlook, Databases, and Your Address Book.* Write a program that will extract the contents of an Outlook address book and store the desired fields into a database. The database can be a text file, DBM file, or even an RDBMS. (You might want to refer to Chapter 6, "Database Programming.") Extra Credit: Do the reverse; read in contact information from a database (or allow for direct user input) and create or update records in Outlook.

7-7. *Microsoft Outlook and E-mail.* Develop a program that backs up your e-mail by taking the contents of your Inbox and/or other important folders and saves it in (as close to) regular "mbox" format to disk.

7-8. *Outlook Calendar.* Write a simple script that creates new Outlook appointments. Take at least the following as user input: start date and time, appointment name or subject, and duration of appointment.

7-9. *Outlook Calendar.* Build an application that dumps the contents of your appointments to a destination of your choice, for example, to the screen, to a database, to Excel, etc. Extra Credit: Do the same thing to your set of Outlook tasks.

7-10. *Multithreading.* Update the Excel version of the stock quote download script (`estock.pyw`) so that the downloads of data happen concurrently using multiple Python threads. Optional: You might also try this exercise with Visual C++ threads using `win32process.beginthreadex()`.

7-11. *Excel Cell Formatting.* In the spreadsheet version of the stock quote download script (`estock.pyw`), we saw in Figure 7-7 how the stock price does not default to two places after the decimal point, even if we pass in a string with the trailing zero(s). When Excel converts it to a number, it uses the default setting for the number format.

   a) Change the numeric format to correctly go out to two decimal places by changing the cell's `NumberFormat` attribute to `0.00`.

   b) We also saw that the "change from previous close" column loses the "+" character in addition to the decimal point formatting. However, we discovered that making the correction in part (a) to both columns only solves the decimal place problem; the plus sign is automatically dropped for any number. The solution here is to change this column to be text instead of a number. You can do this by changing the cell's `NumberFormat` attribute to `@`.

   c) By changing the cell's numeric format to text, however, we lose the right alignment that comes automatically with numbers. In addition to your solution to part (b), you must also now set the cell's `HorizontalAlignment` attribute to the PC Excel constant `xlRight`. After you come up with the solutions to all three parts, your output will now look more acceptable, as shown in Figure 7-19.

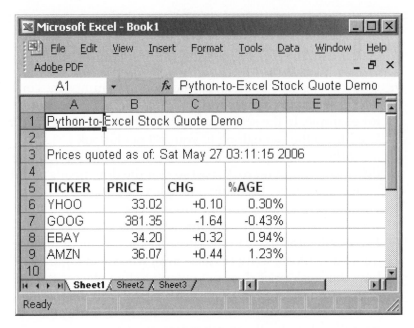

Figure 7-19 Improving the Python-to-Excel stock quote script (estock.pyw).

7-12. *Python 3.* Example 7-8 shows the Python 3 version of our first Excel example (excel3.pyw) along with the changes (in italics). Given this solution, port all the other scripts in this chapter to Python 3.

Example 7-8   Python 3 version of Excel Example (excel3.pyw)

Porting the original excel.pyw script is as simple as running the 2to3 tool.

```
1    #!/usr/bin/env python3
2
3    from time import sleep
4    from tkinter import Tk
5    from tkinter.messagebox import showwarning
6    import win32com.client as win32
7
```

```
 8    warn = lambda app: showwarning(app, 'Exit?')
 9    RANGE = list(range(3, 8))
10
11    def excel():
12        app = 'Excel'
13        xl = win32.gencache.EnsureDispatch('%s.Application' % app)
14        ss = xl.Workbooks.Add()
15        sh = ss.ActiveSheet
16        xl.Visible = True
17        sleep(1)
18
19        sh.Cells(1,1).Value = 'Python-to-%s Demo' % app
20        sleep(1)
21        for i in RANGE:
22            sh.Cells(i,1).Value = 'Line %d' % i
23            sleep(1)
24        sh.Cells(i+2,1).Value = "Th-th-th-that's all folks!"
25
26        warn(app)
27        ss.Close(False)
28        xl.Application.Quit()
29
30    if __name__=='__main__':
31        Tk().withdraw()
32        excel()
```

The next pair of exercises pertain to Example 7-6 (outlook_edit.pyw).

7-13. *Unicode Support.* Fix the outlook_edit.pyw script so that it works flawlessly with Unicode and diacritic characters. In other words, do not strip these out. Instead, preserve them, pass them to the editor, and accept them in messages after editing so that they can be sent in e-mail messages.

7-14. *Robustness.* Make the script more flexible by allowing the user to specify the editor she prefers to use from the command-line. If one is not provided, the application should fall back to an environment variable setting, or finally, bring up one of the editors hardcoded as a last resort.

The next set of exercises pertain to Example 7-7 (txt2ppt.pyw).

7-15. *Skip Comments.* Modify your script to support comments: if a line in the text file begins with an hash mark ('#', a.k.a. pound sign, octothorpe, etc.), assume this line doesn't exist and move to the next one.

7-16. *Improving Title Slide Designation.* Come up with a better way to signify a title slide. Using all capital letters is nice except for certain situations in which title casing is not desired. For example, if the user created a talk entitled, "Intro to TCP/IP", it will contain errors due to the capitalization of "to" and the lowercase "cp" and "p" in "Tcp/Ip":

```
>>> 'Intro to TCP/IP'.title()
'Intro To Tcp/Ip'
```

7-17. *Side Effects.* What happens in `_start()` if there is a text file named "demo" in the current folder? Is this a bug or a feature? Can we improve this situation in any way? If so, code it. If not, indicate why not.

7-18. *Template Specification.* Currently in the script, all presentations will apply the design template `C:\Program Files\Microsoft Office\Templates\Presentation Designs\Stream.pot`. That's boring.

(a) Allow the user to choose from any of the other templates in that folder or wherever your installation is.

(b) Allow the user to specify their own template (and its location) from a new entry field in the GUI, the command-line, or from an environment variable (your choice). Extra Credit: Support all options here in the order of precedence given, or give the user a pulldown in the user interface for the default template options from part (a).

7-19. *Hyperlinking.* A talk might feature links in the plain text file. Make those links active from PowerPoint. Hint: You will need to set the `Hyperlink.Address` as the URL to spawn a browser to visit if a viewer clicks the link in the slide (see the `ActionSettings` for a `ppMouseClick`). Extra Credit: Support hyperlinks only on the URL text when the link isn't the only text on the same line; that is, set the active part of the link to be just the URL and not any other text on that line.

7-20. *Text Formatting.* Add the ability to have bold, italics, and monospaced (for example, Courier) text to presentation contents by supporting some sort of lightweight markup formatting in source text files. We strongly recommend reST (reStructuredText), Markdown, or similar, like Wiki-style formatting, such as, 'monospaced', *bold*, _italic_, etc. For more examples, see http://en.wikipedia.org/wiki/Lightweight_markup_language.

7-21. *Text Formatting.* Add support for other formatting services, such as underlining, shadowing, other fonts, text color, justification change (left, right, centered, etc.), font sizing, headers and footers, or anything else that PowerPoint supports.

7-22. *Images.* One important feature we need to add to our application is the ability to have slides with images. Let's make the problem easier by requiring you to only support slides with a title and a single image (resized and centered on a presentation slide). You'll need to specify a customized syntax for your users to embed image filenames with, for example, `:IMG:C:/py/talk/images/cover.png`. Hints: So far, we've only used the `ppLayoutTitle` or `ppLayoutText` slide layouts; for this exercise, we recommend `ppLayoutTitleOnly`. Insert images using `Shapes.AddPicture()` and resize them using `ScaleHeight()` and `ScaleWidth()` along with data points provided by `PageSetup.SlideHeight` and `PageSetup.SlideWidth` plus the image's `Height` and `Width` attributes.

7-23. *Different Layouts.* Further extend your solution to Exercise 7-22 so that your script supports slides with multiple images or slides with images and bulleted text. Mainly, this means playing around with other layout styles.

7-24. *Embedded Videos.* Another advanced feature you can add is the ability to embed YouTube video clips (or other Adobe Flash applications) in presentations. Similar to Exercise 7-23, you'll need to define your own syntax to support this, for example, `:VID:http://youtube.com/v/Tj5UmH5TdfI`. Hints: We recommend the `ppLayoutTitleOnly` layout again here. In addition, you'll need to use `Shapes.AddOLEDObject()` with a type of `'ShockwaveFlash.ShockwaveFlash.10'` or whatever version your Flash player is.

8

Extending Python

C is very efficient. Unfortunately, C gets that efficiency by
requiring you to do a lot of low-level management of resources.
With today's machines as powerful as they are, this is usually a bad
tradeoff—it's smarter to use a language that uses the machine's
time less efficiently, but your time much more *efficiently.*
Thus, Python.
—Eric Raymond, October 1996

In this chapter...

- Introduction/Motivation
- Extending Python by Writing Extensions
- Related Topics

In this chapter, we will discuss how to take code written externally and integrate that functionality into the Python programming environment. We will first present the motivation for why you do it, and then take you through the step-by-step process of how to do it. We should point out, though, that because extensions are primarily done in the C language, all of the example code you will see in this section is pure C, as a lowest common denominator. You can also use C++ if you want because it's a superset of C; if you're building extensions on PCs by using Microsoft Visual Studio, you *will* be using (Visual) C++.

8.1   Introduction/Motivation

In this opening section of the chapter, we'll define what Python extensions are, and then try to justify why you would (or wouldn't) consider creating one.

8.1.1   What Are Extensions?

In general, any code that you write that can be integrated or imported into another Python script can be considered an extension. This new code can be written in pure Python or in a compiled language such as C and C++, (or Java for Jython and C# or VisualBasic.NET for IronPython).

One great feature of Python is that its extensions interact with the interpreter in exactly the same way as the regular Python modules. Python was designed so that the abstraction of module import hides the underlying implementation details from the code that uses such extensions. Unless the client programmer searches the file system, he simply wouldn't be able to tell whether a module is written in Python or in a compiled language.

 CORE NOTE: Creating extensions on different platforms

We will note here that extensions are generally available in a development environment in which you compile your own Python interpreter. There is a subtle relationship between manual compilation versus obtaining the binaries. Although compilation can be a bit trickier than just downloading and installing binaries, you have the most flexibility in customizing the version of Python that you are using. If you intend to create extensions, you should perform this task in a similar environment.

The examples in this chapter are built on a Unix-based system (which usually comes with a compiler), but assuming you do have access to a C/C++ (or Java) compiler and a Python development environment in C/C++ (or Java), the only differences are in your compilation method. The actual code to make your extensions usable in the Python world is the same on any platform.

If you are developing for Windows-based PCs, you'll need Visual C++ "Developer Studio." The Python distribution comes with project files for version 7.1, but you can use older versions of VC++.

For more information on building extensions in general:

- C++ on PCs–http://docs.python.org/extending/windows
- Java/Jython–http://wiki.python.org/jython
- IronPython–http://ironpython.codeplex.com

Caution: Although moving binaries between different hosts of the same architecture is generally a non-issue, sometimes slight differences in the compiler or CPU will cause code not to work consistently.

8.1.2   Why You Want to Extend Python

Throughout the brief history of software engineering, programming languages have always been taken at face value. What you see is what you get; it was impossible to add new functionality to an existing language. In today's programming environment, however, the ability to customize one's programming environment is now a desired feature; it also promotes code reuse. Languages such as Tcl and Python are among the first languages to provide the ability to extend the base language. So why would you want to extend a language like Python, which is already feature-rich? There are several good reasons:

- **Added/extra (non-Python) functionality**   One reason for extending Python is the need to have new functionality that is not provided by the core part of the language. This can be accomplished in either pure Python or as a compiled extension, but there are certain things such as creating new data types or embedding Python in an existing application that must be compiled.

- **Bottleneck performance improvement**   It is well known that interpreted languages do not perform as fast as compiled languages because that translation must happen on the fly, and during runtime. In general, moving a body of code into an extension will improve overall performance. The problem is that it is sometimes not advantageous if the cost is high in terms of resources.

  From the perspective of percentage, it is a wiser bet to do some simple profiling of the code to identify what the bottlenecks are, and move *those* pieces of code out to an extension. The gain can be seen more quickly and without expending as much in terms of resources.

- **Keep proprietary source code private**   Another important reason to create extensions is due to one side effect of having a scripting language. For all the ease-of-use such languages bring to the table, there really is no privacy as far as source code is concerned because the executable is the source code.

  Code that is moved out of Python and into a compiled language helps keep proprietary code private because you ship a binary object. Because these objects are compiled, they are not as easily reverse-engineered; thus, the source remains more private. This is key when it involves special algorithms, encryption or software security, etc.

  Another alternative to keeping code private is to ship pre-compiled `.pyc` files only. It serves as a good middle ground between releasing the actual source (`.py` files) and having to migrate that code to extensions.

8.1.3   Why You Don't Want to Extend Python

Before we get into how to write extensions, we want to warn you that you might not want to do this, after all. You can consider this section a caveat so that you don't think there's any false advertising going on here. Yes, there are definitely benefits to writing extensions such as those just outlined, however there are some drawbacks too:

- You have to write C/C++ code.

- You'll need to understand how to pass data between Python and C/C++.

- You need to manage references on your own.

- There are tools that accomplish the same thing—that is, they generate and take advantage of the performance of C/C++ code without you writing any C/C++ at all. You'll find some of these tools at the end of this chapter.

Don't say we didn't warn you! Now you may proceed...

8.2   Extending Python by Writing Extensions

Creating extensions for Python involves three main steps:

1. Creating application code
2. Wrapping code with boilerplates
3. Compilation and testing

In this section, we will break out and expose all three stages.

8.2.1   Creating Your Application Code

First, before any code becomes an extension, you need to create a stand-alone "library." In other words, create your code keeping in mind that it is going to turn into a Python module. Design your functions and objects with the vision that Python code will be communicating and sharing data with your C code, and vice versa.

Next, create test code to bulletproof your software. You can even use the Pythonic development method of designating your main() function in C as the testing application so that if your code is compiled, linked, and loaded into an executable (as opposed to just a shared object), the invocation of such an executable will result in a regression test of your software library. For our extension example that follows, this is exactly what we do.

The test case involves two C functions that we want to bring to the world of Python programming. The first is the recursive factorial function, fac(). The second, reverse(), is a simple string reverse algorithm, whose main purpose is to reverse a string "in place," that is, to return a string whose characters are all reversed from their original positions, all without allocating a separate string to copy in reverse order. Because this involves the use of pointers, we need to carefully design and debug our code before bringing Python into the picture.

Our first version, `Extest1.c`, is presented in Example 8-1.

Example 8-1   Pure C Version of Library (`Extest1.c`)

This code represents our library of C functions, which we want to wrap so that we can use it from within the Python interpreter. `main()` is our tester function.

```c
1   #include <stdio.h>
2   #include <stdlib.h>
3   #include <string.h>
4
5   int fac(int n)
6   {
7       if (n < 2) return(1); /* 0! == 1! == 1 */
8       return (n)*fac(n-1); /* n! == n*(n-1)! */
9   }
10
11  char *reverse(char *s)
12  {
13      register char t,                    /* tmp */
14              *p = s,                     /* fwd */
15              *q = (s + (strlen(s)-1));   /* bwd */
16
17      while (p < q)            /* if p < q */
18      {                        /* swap & mv ptrs */
19          t = *p;
20          *p++ = *q;
21          *q-- = t;
22      }
23      return s;
24  }
25
26  int main()
27  {
28      char s[BUFSIZ];
29      printf("4! == %d\n", fac(4));
30      printf("8! == %d\n", fac(8));
31      printf("12! == %d\n", fac(12));
32      strcpy(s, "abcdef");
33      printf("reversing 'abcdef', we get '%s'\n", \
34          reverse(s));
35      strcpy(s, "madam");
36      printf("reversing 'madam', we get '%s'\n", \
37          reverse(s));
38      return 0;
39  }
```

This code consists of a pair of functions, fac() and reverse(), which are implementations of the functionality we just described. fac() takes a single integer argument and recursively calculates the result, which is eventually returned to the caller once it exits the outermost call.

The last piece of code is the required main() function. We use it to be our tester, sending various arguments to fac() and reverse(). With this function, we can determine whether our code actually works.

Now we should compile the code. For many versions of Unix with the gcc compiler, we can use the following command:

```
$ gcc Extest1.c -o Extest
$
```

To run our program, we issue the following command and get the output:

```
$ Extest
4! == 24
8! == 40320
12! == 479001600
reversing 'abcdef', we get 'fedcba'
reversing 'madam', we get 'madam'
$
```

We stress again that you should try to complete your code as much as possible, because you do not want to mix debugging of your library with potential bugs when integrating with Python. In other words, keep the debugging of your core code separate from the debugging of the integration. The closer you write your code to Python interfaces, the sooner your code will be integrated and work correctly.

Each of our functions takes a single value and returns a single value. It's pretty cut and dried, so there shouldn't be a problem integrating with Python. Note that, so far, we have not seen any connection or relationship with Python. We are simply creating a standard C or C++ application.

8.2.2   Wrapping Your Code in Boilerplate

The entire implementation of an extension primarily revolves around the "wrapping" concept that should seem familiar to you: composite classes, decorator functions, class delegation, etc. You should design your code in such a way that there is a smooth transition between the world of Python and your implementing language. This interfacing code is commonly called *boilerplate* code because it is a necessity if your code is to talk to the Python interpreter.

There are four main pieces to the boilerplate software:

1. Include a Python header file
2. Add `PyObject* Module_func()` Python wrappers for each module function
3. Add a `PyMethodDef Module`Methods`[]` array/table for each module function
4. Add a `void init`Module`()` module initializer function

Including the Python Header File

The first thing you should do is to find your Python include files and ensure that your compiler has access to that directory. On most Unix-based systems, this would be either `/usr/local/include/python2.x` or `/usr/include/python2.x`, where `2.x` is your version of Python. If you compiled and installed your Python interpreter, you should not have a problem, because the system generally knows where your files are installed.

Add the inclusion of the `Python.h` header file to your source. The line will look something like:

```
#include "Python.h"
```

That is the easy part. Now you have to add the rest of the boilerplate software.

Add `PyObject* Module_func()` Python Wrappers for Each Function

This part is the trickiest. For each function that you want accessible to the Python environment, you will create a **static** PyObject* function with the module name along with an underscore (_) prepended to it.

For example, we want `fac()` to be one of the functions available for import from Python and we will use Extest as the name of our final module, so we create a *wrapper* called `Extest_fac()`. In the client Python script, there will be an **import** Extest and an `Extest.fac()` call somewhere (or just `fac()` for **from** Extest **import** fac).

The job of the wrapper is to take Python values, convert them to C, and then make a call to the appropriate function with what we want. When our function has completed, and it is time to return to the world of Python; it is also the job of this wrapper to take whatever return values we designate, convert them to Python, and then perform the return, passing back any values as necessary.

In the case of `fac()`, when the client program invokes `Extest.fac()`, our wrapper will be called. We will accept a Python integer, convert it to a C integer, call our C function `fac()`, and then obtain another integer result. We then have to take that return value, convert it back to a Python integer, and then return from the call. (keep in mind that you are writing the code that will proxy for a **def** fac(n) declaration. When you are returning, it is as if that imaginary Python `fac()` function is completing.)

So, you're asking, how does this conversion take place? The answer is with the `PyArg_Parse*()` functions when going from Python to C, and `Py_BuildValue()` when returning from C to Python.

The `PyArg_Parse*()` functions are similar to the C `sscanf()` function. It takes a stream of bytes, and then, according to some format string, parcels them off to corresponding container variables, which, as expected, take pointer addresses. They both return 1 on successful parsing, and 0 otherwise.

`Py_BuildValue()` works like `sprintf()`, taking a format string and converting all arguments to a single returned object containing those values in the formats that you requested.

You will find a summary of these functions in Table 8-1.

Table 8-1 Converting Data Between Python and C/C++

Function	Description
Python to C	
`int` `PyArg_ParseTuple()`	Converts (a tuple of) arguments passed from Python to C
`int` `PyArg_ParseTupleAndKeywords()`	Same as `PyArg_ParseTuple()` but also parses keyword arguments
C to Python	
`PyObject*` `Py_BuildValue()`	Converts C data values into a Python return object, either a single object or a single tuple of objects

A set of conversion codes is used to convert data objects between C and Python; they are given in Table 8-2.

Table 8-2 Python[a] and C/C++ Conversion "Format Units"

Format Unit	Python Type	C/C++ Type
s, s#	str/unicode, len()	char*(, int)
z, z#	str/unicode/None, len()	char*/NULL(, int)
u, u#	unicode, len()	(Py_UNICODE*, int)
i	int	int
b	int	char
h	int	short
l	int	long
k	int or long	unsigned long
I	int or long	unsigned int
B	int	unsigned char
H	int	unsigned short
L	long	long long
K	long	unsigned long long
c	str	char
d	float	double
f	float	float
D	complex	Py_Complex*
O	(any)	PyObject*
S	str	PyStringObject
N[b]	(any)	PyObject*
O&	(any)	(any)

a. These format codes are for Python 2 but have near equivalents in Python 3.
b. Like "O" except it does not increment object's reference count.

These conversion codes are the ones given in the respective format strings that dictate how the values should be converted when moving between both languages. Note that the conversion types are different for Java because all data types are classes. Consult the Jython documentation to obtain the corresponding Java types for Python objects. The same applies for C# and VB.NET.

Here, we show you our completed `Extest_fac()` wrapper function:

```
static PyObject *
Extest_fac(PyObject *self, PyObject *args) {

    int res;                // parse result
    int num;                // arg for fac()
    PyObject* retval;       // return value

    res = PyArg_ParseTuple(args, "i", &num);
    if (!res) {             // TypeError
        return NULL;
    }
    res = fac(num);
    retval = (PyObject*)Py_BuildValue("i", res);
    return retval;
}
```

The first step is to parse the data received from Python. It should be a regular integer, so we use the "i" conversion code to indicate as such. If the value was indeed an integer, then it is stored in the `num` variable. Otherwise, `PyArg_ParseTuple()` will return a NULL, in which case we also return one. In our case, it will generate a `TypeError` exception that informs the client user that we are expecting an integer.

We then call `fac()` with the value stored in `num` and put the result in `res`, reusing that variable. Now we build our return object, a Python integer, again using a conversion code of "i." `Py_BuildValue()` creates an integer Python object, which we then return. That's all there is to it!

In fact, once you have created wrapper after wrapper, you tend to shorten your code somewhat to avoid the extraneous use of variables. Try to keep your code legible, though. We take our `Extest_fac()` function and reduce it to its smaller version given here, using only one variable, `num`:

```
static PyObject *
Extest_fac(PyObject *self, PyObject *args) {
    int num;
    if (!PyArg_ParseTuple(args, "i", &num))
        return NULL;
    return (PyObject*)Py_BuildValue("i", fac(num));
}
```

What about `reverse()`? Well, given you already know how to return a single value, we are going to change our `reverse()` example somewhat, returning two values instead of one. We will return a pair of strings as a tuple; the first element being the string as passed in to us, and the second being the newly reversed string.

To show you that there is some flexibility, we will call this function `Extest.doppel()` to indicate that its behavior differs from `reverse()`. Wrapping our code into an `Extest_doppel()` function, we get:

```
static PyObject *
Extest_doppel(PyObject *self, PyObject *args) {
    char *orig_str;
    if (!PyArg_ParseTuple(args, "s", &orig_str)) return NULL;
    return (PyObject*)Py_BuildValue("ss", orig_str, \
        reverse(strdup(orig_str)));
}
```

As in `Extest_fac()`, we take a single input value, this time a string, and store it into `orig_str`. Notice that we use the "s" conversion code now. We then call `strdup()` to create a copy of the string. (Because we want to return the original one, as well, we need a string to reverse, so the best candidate is just a copy of the string.) `strdup()` creates and returns a copy, which we immediately dispatch to `reverse()`. We get back a reversed string.

As you can see, `Py_BuildValue()` puts together both strings using a conversion string of `ss`. This creates a tuple of two strings: the original string and the reversed one. End of story, right? Unfortunately, no.

We got caught by one of the perils of C programming: the memory leak (when memory is allocated but not freed). Memory leaks are analogous to borrowing books from the library but not returning them. You should always release resources that you have acquired when you no longer require them. How did we commit such a crime with our code (which looks innocent enough)?

When `Py_BuildValue()` puts together the Python object to return, it makes copies of the data that has been passed to it. In our case here, that would be a pair of strings. The problem is that we allocated the memory for the second string, but we did not release that memory when we finished, leaking it. What we really want to do is to build the return object, and then free the memory that we allocated in our wrapper. We have no choice but to lengthen our code to:

```
static PyObject *
Extest_doppel(PyObject *self, PyObject *args) {
    char *orig_str;              // original string
    char *dupe_str;              // reversed string
    PyObject* retval;
```

```
if (!PyArg_ParseTuple(args, "s", &orig_str)) return NULL;
retval = (PyObject*)Py_BuildValue("ss", orig_str, \
    dupe_str=reverse(strdup(orig_str)));
free(dupe_str);
return retval;
}
```

We introduce the `dupe_str` variable to point to the newly allocated string and build the return object. Then we `free()` the memory allocated and finally return back to the caller. *Now* we are done.

Adding PyMethodDef *Module*Methods[] Array/Table for Each Module Function

Now that both of our wrappers are complete, we want to list them somewhere so that the Python interpreter knows how to import and access them. This is the job of the *Module*Methods[] array.

It is made up of an array of arrays, with each individual array containing information about each function, terminated by a NULL array that marks the end of the list. For our `Extest` module, we create the following ExtestMethods[] array:

```
static PyMethodDef
ExtestMethods[] = {
    { "fac", Extest_fac, METH_VARARGS },
    { "doppel", Extest_doppel, METH_VARARGS },
    { NULL, NULL },
};
```

The Python-accessible names are given, followed by the corresponding wrapping functions. The constant METH_VARARGS is given, indicating a set of arguments in the form of a tuple. If we are using PyArg_ParseTuple AndKeywords() with keyworded arguments, we would logically OR this flag with the METH_KEYWORDS constant. Finally, a pair of NULLs properly terminates our list of two functions.

Adding a void init*Module*() Module Initializer Function

The final piece to our puzzle is the module initializer function. This code is called when our module is imported for use by the interpreter. In this code, we make one call to Py_Init*Module*() along with the module name and the name of the *Module*Methods[] array so that the interpreter can access our module functions. For our Extest module, our **initExtest()** procedure looks like this:

```
void initExtest() {
        Py_InitModule("Extest", ExtestMethods);
}
```

We are now done with all our wrapping. We add all this code to our original code from Extest1.c and merge the results into a new file called Extest2.c, concluding the development phase of our example.

Another approach to creating an extension would be to make your wrapping code first, using *stubs* or test or dummy functions which will, during the course of development, be replaced by the fully-functional pieces of implemented code. This way, you can ensure that your interface between Python and C is correct, and then use Python to test your C code.

8.2.3   Compilation

Now we are on to the compilation phase. To get your new wrapper Python extension to build, you need to get it to compile with the Python library. This task has been standardized (since version 2.0) across platforms to make life a lot easier for extension writers. The distutils package is used to build, install, and distribute modules, extensions, and packages. It came about back in Python 2.0 and replaced the old version 1.x way of building extensions that used "makefiles." Using distutils, we can follow this easy recipe:

1. Create setup.py
2. Compile and link your code by running setup.py
3. Import your module from Python
4. Test the function

Creating setup.py

The next step is to create a setup.py file. The bulk of the work will be done by the setup() function. All the lines of code that come before that call are preparatory steps. For building extension modules, you need to create an Extension instance per extension. Since we only have one, we only need one Extension instance:

```
Extension('Extest', sources=['Extest2.c'])
```

The first argument is the (full) extension name, including any high-level packages, if necessary. The name should be in full dotted-attribute notation. Ours is stand-alone, hence the name "Extest." sources is a list of all the source files. Again, we only have the one, Extest2.c.

Now we are ready to call `setup()`. It takes a name argument for what it is building and a list of the items to build. Because we are creating an extension, we set it a list of extension modules to build as `ext_modules`. The syntax will be like this:

```
setup('Extest', ext_modules=[...])
```

Because we only have one module, we combine the instantiation of our extension module into our call to `setup()`, setting the module name as "constant" `MOD` on the preceding line:

```
MOD = 'Extest'
setup(name=MOD, ext_modules=[
    Extension(MOD, sources=['Extest2.c'])])
```

There are many more options to `setup()`; in fact, they are too numerous to list here. You can find out more about creating `setup.py` and calling `setup()` in the official Python documentation that we refer to at the end of this chapter. Example 8-2 shows the complete script that we are using for our example.

Example 8-2   The Build Script (`setup.py`)

This script compiles our extension into the `build/lib.*` subdirectory.

```
1   #!/usr/bin/env python
2
3   from distutils.core import setup, Extension
4
5   MOD = 'Extest'
6   setup(name=MOD, ext_modules=[
7       Extension(MOD, sources=['Extest2.c'])])
```

Compile and Link Your Code by Running `setup.py`

Now that we have our `setup.py` file, we can build our extension by running it with the `build` directive, as we have done here on our Mac (your output will differ based on the version of the operating system you are running as well as the version of Python you are using):

```
$ python setup.py build
running build
running build_ext
building 'Extest' extension
creating build
creating build/temp.macosx-10.x-fat-2.x
gcc -fno-strict-aliasing -Wno-long-double -no-cpp-
precomp -mno-fused-madd -fno-common -dynamic -DNDEBUG -g
```

```
-I/usr/include -I/usr/local/include -I/sw/include -I/
usr/local/include/python2.x -c Extest2.c -o build/temp.macosx-10.x-
fat-2.x/Extest2.o
creating build/lib.macosx-10.x-fat-2.x
gcc -g -bundle -undefined dynamic_lookup -L/usr/lib -L/
usr/local/lib -L/sw/lib -I/usr/include -I/usr/local/
include -I/sw/include build/temp.macosx-10.x-fat-2.x/Extest2.o -o
build/lib.macosx-10.x-fat-2.x/Extest.so
```

8.2.4   Importing and Testing

The final step is to go back into Python and use our new extension as if it
were written in pure Python.

Importing Your Module from Python

Your extension module will be created in the `build/lib.*` directory from
where you ran your `setup.py` script. You can either change to that directory to test your module or install it into your Python distribution with:

```
$ python setup.py install
```

If you do install it, you will get the following output:

```
running install
running build
running build_ext
running install_lib
copying build/lib.macosx-10.x-fat-2.x/Extest.so ->
/usr/local/lib/python2.x/site-packages
```

Now we can test our module from the interpreter:

```
>>> import Extest
>>> Extest.fac(5)
120
>>> Extest.fac(9)
362880
>>> Extest.doppel('abcdefgh')
('abcdefgh', 'hgfedcba')
>>> Extest.doppel("Madam, I'm Adam.")
("Madam, I'm Adam.", ".madA m'I ,madaM")
```

Adding a Test Function

The one last thing we want to do is to add a test function. In fact, we
already have one, in the form of the `main()` function. Be aware that it is
potentially dangerous to have a `main()` function in our code because
there should only be one `main()` in the system. We remove this danger by

changing the name of our `main()` to `test()` and wrapping it, adding `Extest_test()` and updating the `ExtestMethods` array so that they both look like this:

```
static PyObject *
Extest_test(PyObject *self, PyObject *args) {
    test();
    return (PyObject*)Py_BuildValue("");
}
static PyMethodDef
ExtestMethods[] = {
    { "fac", Extest_fac, METH_VARARGS },
    { "doppel", Extest_doppel, METH_VARARGS },
    { "test", Extest_test, METH_VARARGS },
    { NULL, NULL },
};
```

The `Extest_test()` module function just runs `test()` and returns an empty string, resulting in a Python value of `None` being returned to the caller.

Now we can run the same test from Python:

```
>>> Extest.test()
4! == 24
8! == 40320
12! == 479001600
reversing 'abcdef', we get 'fedcba'
reversing 'madam', we get 'madam'
>>>
```

In Example 8-3, we present the final version of `Extest2.c` that was used to generate the output we just saw.

Example 8-3   Python-Wrapped Version of C Library (`Extest2.c`)

```
1   #include <stdio.h>
2   #include <stdlib.h>
3   #include <string.h>
4
5   int fac(int n)
6   {
7       if (n < 2) return(1);
8       return (n)*fac(n-1);
9   }
10
11  char *reverse(char *s)
12  {
13      register char t,
14                  *p = s,
15                  *q = (s + (strlen(s) - 1));
16
```

```
17      while (s && (p < q))
18      {
19          t = *p;
20          *p++ = *q;
21          *q-- = t;
22      }
23      return s;
24  }
25
26  int test()
27  {
28      char s[BUFSIZ];
29      printf("4! == %d\n", fac(4));
30      printf("8! == %d\n", fac(8));
31      printf("12! == %d\n", fac(12));
32      strcpy(s, "abcdef");
33      printf("reversing 'abcdef', we get '%s'\n", \
34          reverse(s));
35      strcpy(s, "madam");
36      printf("reversing 'madam', we get '%s'\n", \
37          reverse(s));
38      return 0;
39  }
40
41  #include "Python.h"
42
43  static PyObject *
44  Extest_fac(PyObject *self, PyObject *args)
45  {
46      int num;
47      if (!PyArg_ParseTuple(args, "i", &num))
48          return NULL;
49      return (PyObject*)Py_BuildValue("i", fac(num));}
50  }
51
52  static PyObject *
53  Extest_doppel(PyObject *self, PyObject *args)
54  {
55      char *orig_str;
56      char *dupe_str;
57      PyObject* retval;
58
59      if (!PyArg_ParseTuple(args, "s", &orig_str))
60          return NULL;
61      retval = (PyObject*)Py_BuildValue("ss", orig_str, \
62          dupe_str=reverse(strdup(orig_str)));
63      free(dupe_str);
64      return retval;
65  }
66
```

(Continued)

Example 8-3   Python-Wrapped Version of C Library (`Extest2.c`)
                    (Continued)

```
67  static PyObject *
68  Extest_test(PyObject *self, PyObject *args)
69  {
70      test();
71      return (PyObject*)Py_BuildValue("");
72  }
73
74  static PyMethodDef
75  ExtestMethods[] =
76  {
77      { "fac", Extest_fac, METH_VARARGS },
78      { "doppel", Extest_doppel, METH_VARARGS },
79      { "test", Extest_test, METH_VARARGS },
80      { NULL, NULL },
81  };
82
83  void initExtest()
84  {
85      Py_InitModule("Extest", ExtestMethods);
86  }
```

In this example, we chose to segregate our C code from our Python code. It just kept things easier to read and is no problem with our short example. In practice, these source files tend to get large, and some choose to implement their wrappers completely in a different source file such as `ExtestWrappers.c` or something of that nature.

8.2.5   Reference Counting

You might recall that Python uses reference counting as a means of keeping track of objects and de-allocating objects no longer referenced, as part of the garbage collection mechanism. When creating extensions, you must pay extra special attention to how you manipulate Python objects, because you must be mindful of whether you need to change the reference count for such objects.

There are two types of references that you can have to an object, one of which is an *owned reference*, meaning that the reference count to the object is incremented by one to indicate your ownership. One situation for which you would definitely have an owned reference is when you create a Python object from scratch.

When you are done with a Python object, you must dispose of your ownership, either by decrementing the reference count, transferring your ownership by passing it on, or storing the object. Failure to dispose of an owned reference creates a memory leak.

You can also have a *borrowed reference* to an object. Somewhat lower on the responsibility ladder, this is when you are passed the reference of an object, but otherwise do not manipulate the data in any way. Nor do you have to worry about its reference count, as long as you do not hold on to this reference after its reference count has decreased to zero. You might convert your borrowed reference to an owned reference simply by incrementing an object's reference count.

Python provides a pair of C macros which are used to change the reference count to a Python object. They are given in Table 8-3.

Table 8-3   Macros for Performing Python Object Reference Counting

Function	Description
Py_INCREF(*obj*)	Increment the reference count to *obj*
Py_DECREF(*obj*)	Decrement the reference count to *obj*

In our above `Extest_test()` function, we return `None` by building a `PyObject` with an empty string; however, this can also be accomplished by becoming an owner of the `None` object, `PyNone`, incrementing your reference count to it, and returning it explicitly, as in the following alternative piece of code:

```
static PyObject *
Extest_test(PyObject *self, PyObject *args) {
        test();
        Py_INCREF(Py_None);
        return PyNone;
}
```

`Py_INCREF()` and `Py_DECREF()` also have versions that check for NULL objects. They are `Py_XINCREF()` and `Py_XDECREF()`, respectively.

We strongly urge that you consult the Python documentation regarding extending and embedding Python for all the details with regard to reference counting (see the documentation reference in Appendix C, "Python 3: The Evolution of a Programming Language").

8.2.6   Threading and the GIL

Extension writers must be aware that their code might be executed in a multi-threaded Python environment. In Chapter 4, "Multithreaded Programming," in Section 4.3.1, we introduced the Python Virtual Machine (PVM) and the Global Interpreter Lock (GIL), describing how only one thread of execution can be running at any given time in the PVM and that the GIL is responsible for keeping other threads from running. Furthermore, we indicated that code calling external functions, such as in extension code, would keep the GIL locked until the call returns.

We also hinted that there was a remedy, a way for the extension programmer to release the GIL, for example, before performing a system call. This is accomplished by "blocking" your code off to where threads may (and may not) run safely using another pair of C macros, `Py_BEGIN_ALLOW_THREADS` and `Py_END_ALLOW_THREADS`. A block of code bounded by these macros will permit other threads to run.

As with the reference counting macros, we urge that you consult the documentation regarding extending and embedding Python as well as the Python/C API reference manual.

8.3   Related Topics

In this final section of this chapter, we'll look at various tools representing alternatives to writing extensions (in any supported language). We'll introduce you to SWIG, Pyrex, Cython, psyco, and PyPy. We end the chapter with a brief discussion about a related topic, Embedding Python.

8.3.1   The Simplified Wrapper and Interface Generator

There is an external tool available called Simplified Wrapper and Interface Generator (SWIG). It was written by David Beazley, who is also the author of *Python Essential Reference* (Addison-Wesley, 2009). It is a software tool that can take annotated C/C++ header files and generate wrapped code, ready to compile for Python, Tcl, and Perl. Using SWIG frees you from having to write the boilerplate code we've seen in this chapter. You only need to worry about coding the solution part of your project in C/C++. All you have to do is create your files in the SWIG format, and it will do the background work on your behalf. You can find out more information about SWIG from its main Web site:

http://swig.org

http://en.wikipedia.org/wiki/SWIG

8.3.2   Pyrex

One obvious weakness of creating C/C++ extensions (raw or with SWIG) is that you have to write C/C++ (surprise, surprise), with all of its strengths, and, more importantly, its pitfalls. Pyrex gives you practically all of the gains of writing extensions but none of the headache. Pyrex is a new language created specifically for writing Python extensions. It is a hybrid of C and Python, leaning much more toward Python; in fact, the Pyrex Web site goes as far as saying that *"Pyrex is Python with C data types."* You only need to write code in the Pyrex syntax and run the Pyrex compiler on the source. Pyrex creates C files, which can then be compiled and used as you would a normal extension. Some have sworn off C programming forever upon discovering Pyrex. You can get Pyrex at its home page:

http://cosc.canterbury.ac.nz/~greg/python/Pyrex

http://en.wikipedia.org/wiki/Pyrex_(programming_language)

8.3.3   Cython

Cython is a fork of Pyrex from 2007—the first release of Cython was 0.9.6, which came out around the same time as Pyrex 0.9.6. The Cython developers have a more agile and aggressive approach to Cython's development over the Pyrex team in that the latter takes a more cautious approach. The result is that more patches, improvements, and extensions make it into Cython faster/sooner than into Pyrex, but both are considered active projects. You can read more about Cython and its distinctions from Pyrex via the links below.

http://cython.org

http://wiki.cython.org/DifferencesFromPyrex

http://wiki.cython.org/FAQ

8.3.4   Psyco

Pyrex and Cython offer the benefit of no longer having to write pure C code. However, do you need to learn some new syntax (sigh... yet another language to have to deal with.) In the end, your Pyrex/Cython code turns into C anyway. Developers write extensions or use tools like SWIG or Pyrex/Cython for that performance boost. However, what if you can obtain such performance gains *without* having to write code in a language other than pure Python?

Psyco's concept is quite different from those other approaches. Rather than writing C code, why not just make your existing Python code run faster? Psyco serves as a just-in-time (JIT) compiler, so you do not have to change to your source other than importing the Psyco module and telling it to start optimizing your code (during runtime).

Psyco can also profile your code to establish where it can make the most significant improvements. You can even enable logging to see what Psyco does while optimizing your code. The only restriction is that it solely supports 32-bit Intel 386 architectures (Linux, Max OS X, Windows, BSD) running **2.2-2.6** Python 2.2.2-2.6.x but not version 3.x. Version 2.7 support is not complete (at the time of this writing). For more information, go to the following links:

> http://psyco.sf.net
>
> http://en.wikipedia.org/wiki/Psyco

8.3.5   PyPy

PyPy is the successor project to Psyco. It has a much more ambitious goal of creating a generalized environment for developing interpreted languages, independent of platform or target execution environment. It all started innocently, to create a Python interpreter written in Python—in fact, this is what most people still think PyPy is, while in fact, this specific interpreter is just part of the entire PyPy ecosystem.

However, this toolset comprises the "real goods," the power to allow language designers to only be concerned with the parsing and semantic analysis of their interpreter language *du jour*. All of the difficult stuff in translating to a native architecture, such as memory management, byte-code translation, garbage collection, internal representation of numeric types, primitive data structures, native architecture, etc., are taken care of for you.

The way it works is that you take your language and implement it with a restricted, statically-typed version of Python, called RPython. As mentioned above, Python was the first target language, so an interpreter for it was written in RPython—this is as close to the term "PyPy" as you're going to get. However, you can implement any language you want with RPython, not just Python.

This toolchain will translate your RPython code into something lower-level, like C, Java bytecode, or Common Intermediate Language (CIL), which is the bytecode for languages written against the Common Language Infrastructure (CLI) standard. In other words, interpreted language developers only need to worry about language design and much less about implementation and target architecture. For more information, go to:

http://pypy.org

http://codespeak.net/pypy

http://en.wikipedia.org/wiki/PyPy

8.3.6   Embedding

Embedding is another feature available in Python. It is the inverse of an extension. Rather than taking C code and wrapping it into Python, you take a C application and wrap a Python interpreter inside it. This has the effect of giving a potentially large, monolithic, and perhaps rigid, proprietary, and/or mission-critical application the power of having an embedded Python interpreter. Once you have Python, well, it's like a whole new ball game.

For extension writer, there is a set of official documents that you should refer to for additional information.

Here are links to some of the Python documentation related to this chapter's topics: http://docs.python.org/extending/embedding.

Extending and Embedding

http://docs.python.org/ext

Python/C API

http://docs.python.org/c-api

Distributing Python Modules

http://docs.python.org/distutils

8.4   Exercises

8-1.   *Extending Python*. What are some of the advantages of Python extensions?

8-2.   *Extending Python*. Can you see any disadvantages or dangers of using extensions?

8-3.   *Writing Extensions*. Obtain a C/C++ compiler and (re)familiarize yourself with C/C++ programming. Create a simple utility function that you can make available and configure as an extension. Demonstrate that your utility executes in both C/C++ and Python.

8-4.   *Porting from Python to C*. Take several of the exercises you did in earlier chapters and port them to C/C++ as extension modules.

8-5.   *Wrapping C Code*. Find a piece of C/C++ code, which you might have done a long time ago but want to port to Python. Instead of porting, make it an extension module.

8-6.   *Writing Extensions*. In one of the exercises in the object-oriented programming chapter of *Core Python Programming* or *Core Python Language Fundamentals*, you created a `dollarize()` function as part of a class to format a floating-point value into a financial numeric string. Create an extension featuring a wrapped `dollarize()` function and integrate a regression testing function, for example, `test()`, into the module. Extra Credit: In addition to creating a C extension, also rewrite `dollarize()` in Pyrex or Cython.

8-7.   *Extending vs. Embedding*. What is the difference between extending and embedding?

8-8.   *Not Writing Extensions*. Take the C/C++ code you used in Exercise 8-3, 8-4, or 8-5 and redo it in pseudo-Python via Pyrex or Cython. Describe your experiences using Pyrex/Cython versus integrating that code all as part of a C extension.

PART

II

Web Development

9

Web Clients and Servers

If you have a browser from CERN's WWW project
(World Wide Web, a distributed hypertext system) you can
browse a WWW hypertext version of the manual.
—Guido van Rossum, November 1992
(first mention of the Web on the Python mailing list)

In this chapter...

- Introduction
- Python Web Client Tools
- Web Clients
- Web (HTTP) Servers
- Related Modules

9.1   Introduction

Because the universe of Web applications is so expansive, we've (re)organized this book in a way that allows readers to focus specifically on multiple aspects of Web development via a set of chapters that cover individual topics.

Before getting into the nitty-gritty, this introductory chapter on Web programming will start you off by again focusing on client/server architecture, but this time the perspective of the Web. It provides a solid foundation for the material in the remaining chapters of the book.

9.1.1   Web Surfing: Client/Server Computing

Web surfing falls under the same client/server architecture umbrella that we have seen repeatedly. This time, however, *Web clients* are browsers, which, of course, are applications that allow users to view documents on the World Wide Web. On the other side are *Web servers*, which are processes that run on an information provider's host computers. These servers wait for clients and their document requests, process them, and then return the requested data. As with most servers in a client/server system, Web servers are designed to run indefinitely. The Web surfing experience is best illustrated by Figure 9-1. Here, a user runs a Web client program, such as a browser, and makes a connection to a Web server elsewhere on the Internet to obtain information.

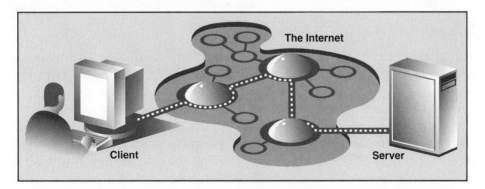

Figure 9-1 A Web client and Web server on the Internet. A client sends a request out over the Internet to the server, which then responds by sending the requested data back to the client.

Clients can issue a variety of requests to Web servers. Such requests might include obtaining a Web page for viewing or submitting a form with data for processing. The request is then serviced by the Web server (and possibly other systems), and the reply comes back to the client in a special format for display purposes.

The language that is spoken by Web clients and servers, the standard protocol used for Web communication, is called HyperText Transfer Protocol (HTTP). HTTP is written on top of the TCP and IP protocol suite, meaning that it relies on TCP and IP to carry out its lower-level communication needs. Its responsibility is not to route or deliver messages—TCP and IP handle that—but to respond to client requests (by sending and receiving HTTP messages).

HTTP is known as a *stateless* protocol because it does not keep track of information from one client request to the next, similar to the client/server architecture we have seen so far. The server stays running, but client interactions are singular events structured in such a way that once a client request is serviced, it quits. New requests can always be sent, but they are considered separate service requests. Because of the lack of context per request, you might notice that some URLs have a long set of variables and values chained as part of the request to provide some sort of state information. Another alternative is the use of *cookies*—static data stored on the client side that generally contain state information, as well. In later parts of this chapter, we will look at how to use both long URLs and cookies to maintain state information.

9.1.2   The Internet

The Internet is a moving and fluctuating "cloud" or "pond" of interconnected clients and servers scattered around the globe. Metaphorically speaking, communication from client to server consists of a series of connections from one lily pad on the pond to another, with the last step connecting to the server. As a client user, all this detail is kept hidden from your view. The abstraction is to have a direct connection between you (the client) and the server you are visiting, but the underlying HTTP, TCP, and IP protocols are hidden underneath, doing all of the dirty work. Information regarding the intermediate *nodes* is of no concern or consequence to the general user, anyway, so it's good that the implementation is hidden. Figure 9-2 shows an expanded view of the Internet.

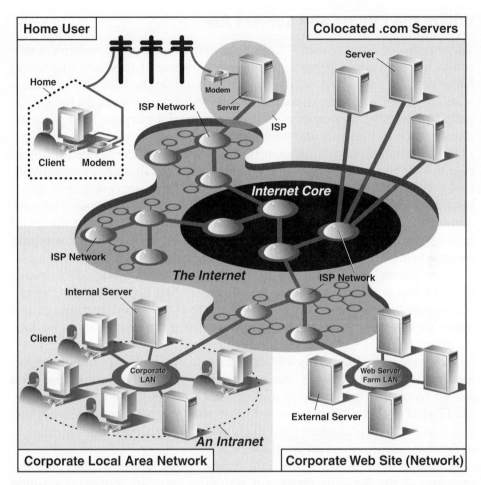

Figure 9-2 A grand view of the Internet. The left side illustrates where you would find Web clients; the right side hints as to where Web servers are typically located.

It's worth mentioning that with all of the data moving around the Internet, there might be some that is more sensitive. There is no encryption service available by default, so standard protocols just transmit the data as they're sent from applications. An additional level of security has been added to ordinary sockets, called the *secure socket layer* (SSL), to encrypt all transmission going across a socket created with this additional level. Now developers can determine whether they want this additional security or not.

Where the Clients and Servers Are

As you can see from Figure 9-2, the Internet is made up of multiple, inter-connected networks, all working with some sense of (perhaps disjointed) harmony. The left half of the diagram is focused on the Web clients—users who are either at home, connected via their ISP, or at work on their com-pany's LAN. Missing from the diagram are special-purpose (and popular) devices such as firewalls and proxy servers.

Firewalls help fight against unauthorized access to a corporate (or home) network by blocking known entry points, configurable on a per-network basis. Without one of these, computers that have servers might allow intruders to enter an unprotected port and gain system access. Network administrators reduce the chances of hacking by locking everything out and only opening up ports for well-known services like Web servers and secure shell (SSH) access, the latter based on the aforementioned SSL.

Proxy servers are another useful tool that can work alongside firewalls (or not). Network administrators might prefer that only a certain number of computers have Internet access, perhaps to better monitor traffic in and out of their networks. Another useful feature is if the proxy can cache data. As an example, if Linda accesses a Web page which is proxy-cached, when her co-worker Heather visits the same page later, she'll experience a faster loading time. Her browser did not need to go all the way to the Web server; instead, it got everything it needed from the proxy. Furthermore, the IT staff at their company now knows that at least two employees vis-ited that Web site and when (and likely who). Such servers are also known as *forward proxies*, based on what they do.

A similar type of computer is a *reverse proxy*. These do (sort-of) the opposite of the forward proxy. (In actuality, you can configure a single computer to perform as both a forward and reverse proxy.) A reverse proxy acts like a server with which clients can connect. They will likely access hit a *back-end server* to obtain the information for which the clients are requesting. Reverse proxies can also cache such server data and return it directly back to the client as if they were one of the back-ends.

As you can surmise, instead of caching on their behalf, "living closer to," and serving clients, reverse proxies live closer to (back-end) servers. They act on the behalf of servers, possibly caching for them, load balancing, etc. You can also use reverse proxies as firewalls or to encrypt data (SSL, HTTPS, Secure FTP (SFTP), etc.). They're very useful, and it's highly likely that you'll come across more than one reverse proxy during daily Web surf-ing. Now let's talk about where some of those back-end Web servers are.

The right side of Figure 9-2 concentrates more on Web servers and where they can be found. Corporations with larger Web sites will typically have an entire *Web server farm* located at their ISPs. Such physical placement is called *co-location*, meaning that a company's servers reside at an ISP along with computers from other corporate customers. These servers are either all providing different data to clients or are part of a redundant system with duplicated information designed for heavy demand (high number of clients). Smaller corporate Web sites might not require as much hardware and networking gear, and hence, might only have one or several co-located servers at their ISP.

In either case, most co-located servers are stored with a larger ISP sitting on a network *backbone*, meaning that they have a "fatter" (read wider) and presumably faster connection to the Internet—closer to the core of the Internet, if you will. This permits clients to access the servers quickly—being on a backbone means clients do not have to hop across as many networks to access a server, thus allowing more clients to be serviced within a given time period.

Internet Protocols

You should also keep in mind that although Web surfing is the most common Internet application, it is not the only one and is certainly not the oldest. The Internet predates the Web by almost three decades. Before the Web, the Internet was mainly used for educational and research purposes, and many of the original Internet protocols, such as FTP, SMTP, and NNTP are still around today.

Since Python was initially known for Internet programming, you will find support for all of the protocols discussed above in addition to many others. We differentiate between "Internet programming" and "Web programming" by stating that the latter pertains only to applications developed specifically for the Web, such as Web clients and servers, which are the focus for this chapter.

Internet programming covers a wider range of applications, including applications that use some of the Internet protocols we previously mentioned, plus network and socket programming in general, all of which are covered in previous chapters in this book.

9.2   Python Web Client Tools

One thing to keep in mind is that a browser is only one type of Web client. Any application that makes a request for data from a Web server is considered a client. Yes, it is possible to create other clients that retrieve documents or data from the Internet. One important reason to do this is that a browser provides only limited capacity; it is used primarily for viewing and interacting with Web sites. A client program, on the other hand, has the ability to do more—not only can it download data, but it can also store it, manipulate it, or perhaps even transmit it to another location or application.

Applications that use the `urllib` module to download or access information on the Web (using either `urllib.urlopen()` or `urllib.urlretrieve()`) can be considered a simple Web client. All you need to do is provide a valid Web address.

9.2.1   Uniform Resource Locators

Simple Web surfing involves using Web addresses called *Uniform Resource Locators* (URLs). Such addresses are used to locate a document on the Web or to call a CGI program to generate a document for your client. URLs are part of a larger set of identifiers known as *Uniform Resource Identifiers* (URIs). This superset was created in anticipation of other naming conventions that have yet to be developed. A URL is simply a URI that uses an existing protocol or scheme (i.e., http, ftp, etc.) as part of its addressing. To complete this picture, we'll add that non-URL URIs are sometimes known as *Uniform Resource Names* (URNs), but because URLs are the only URIs in use today, you really don't hear much about URIs or URNs, save for perhaps XML identifiers.

Like street addresses, Web addresses have some structure. An American street address usually is of the form "number/street designation," for example, 123 Main Street. It can differ from other countries, which might have their own rules. A URL uses the format:

```
prot_sch://net_loc/path;params?query#frag
```

Table 9-1 describes each of the components.

Table 9-1 Web Address Components

URL Component	Description
prot_sch	Network protocol or download scheme
net_loc	Location of server (and perhaps user information)
path	Slash (/) delimited path to file or CGI application
params	Optional parameters
query	Ampersand (&) delimited set of "key=value" pairs
frag	Fragment to a specific anchor within document

net_loc can be broken down into several more components, some required, others optional. The *net_loc* string looks like this:

```
user:passwd@host:port
```

These individual components are described in Table 9-2.

Table 9-2 Network Location Components

Component	Description
user	User name or login
passwd	User password
host	Name or address of the computer running the Web server (required)
port	Port number (if not 80, which is the default)

Of the four, the host name is the most important. The port number is necessary only if the Web server is running on a different port number from the default. (If you aren't sure what a port number is, read Chapter 2, "Network Programming.")

User names and perhaps passwords are used only when making FTP connections, and even then they usually aren't necessary because the majority of such connections are anonymous.

Python supplies two different modules, each dealing with URLs in completely different functionality and capacities. One is `urlparse`, and the other is `urllib`. We will briefly introduce some of their functions here.

9.2.2   The `urlparse` Module

The `urlparse` module provides basic functionality with which to manipulate URL strings. These functions include `urlparse()`, `urlunparse()`, and `urljoin()`.

`urlparse.urlparse()`

`urlparse()` breaks up a URL string into some of the major components described earlier. It has the following syntax:

```
urlparse(urlstr, defProtSch=None, allowFrag=None)
```

`urlparse()` parses *urlstr* into a 6-tuple (`prot_sch`, `net_loc`, `path`, `params`, `query`, `frag`). Each of these components has been described earlier. *defProtSch* specifies a default network protocol or download scheme in case one is not provided in `urlstr`. *allowFrag* is a flag that signals whether a fragment part of a URL is allowed. Here is what `urlparse()` outputs when given a URL:

```
>>> urlparse.urlparse('http://www.python.org/doc/FAQ.html')
('http', 'www.python.org', '/doc/FAQ.html', '', '', '')
```

`urlparse.urlunparse()`

`urlunparse()` does the exact opposite of `urlparse()`—it merges a 6-tuple (`prot_sch`, `net_loc`, `path`, `params`, `query`, `frag`)—*urltup*, which could be the output of `urlparse()`, into a single URL string and returns it. Accordingly, we state the following equivalence:

```
urlunparse(urlparse(urlstr)) ≡ urlstr
```

You might have already surmised that the syntax of `urlunparse()` is as follows:

```
urlunparse(urltup)
```

urlparse.urljoin()

The urljoin() function is useful in cases for which many related URLs are needed, for example, the URLs for a set of pages to be generated for a Web site. The syntax for urljoin() is:

```
urljoin(baseurl, newurl, allowFrag=None)
```

urljoin() takes *baseurl* and joins its base path (*net_loc* plus the full path up to, but not including, a file at the end) with *newurl*. For example:

```
>>> urlparse.urljoin('http://www.python.org/doc/FAQ.html',
... 'current/lib/lib.htm')
'http://www.python.org/doc/current/lib/lib.html'
```

A summary of the functions in urlparse can be found in Table 9-3.

Table 9-3   Core urlparse Module Functions

urlparse Functions	Description
urlparse(*urlstr*, *defProtSch*=None, *allowFrag*=None)	Parses *urlstr* into separate components, using *defProtSch* if the protocol or scheme is not given in *urlstr*; *allowFrag* determines whether a URL fragment is allowed
urlunparse(*urltup*)	Unparses a tuple of URL data (*urltup*) into a single URL string
urljoin(*baseurl*, *newurl*, *allowFrag*=None)	Merges the base part of the *baseurl* URL with *newurl* to form a complete URL; *allowFrag* is the same as for urlparse()

9.2.3   urllib Module/Package

 CORE MODULE: urllib in Python 2 and Python 3

Unless you are planning on writing a more lower-level network client, the urllib module provides all the functionality you need. urllib provides a high-level Web communication library, supporting the basic Web protocols, HTTP, FTP, and Gopher, as well as providing access to local files. Specifically, the functions of the urllib module are designed to download data (from the Internet, local network, or local host) using the aforementioned protocols. Use of this module generally obviates the need for using the `httplib`, `ftplib`, and `gopherlib` modules unless you desire their lower-level functionality. In those cases, such modules can be considered as alternatives. (Note: most modules named *lib are generally for developing clients of the corresponding protocols. This is not always the case, however, as perhaps `urllib` should then be renamed "internetlib" or something similar!)

3.x

With *urllib, urlparse, urllib2,* and others in Python 2, a step was taken in Python 3 to streamline all of these related modules under a single package named *urllib*, so you'll find pieces of *urllib* and *urllib2* unified into the *urllib.request* module and *urlparse* turned into *urllib.parse*. The *urllib* package in Python 3 also includes the *response, error,* and *robotparser* submodules. Keep these changes in mind as you read this chapter and try the examples or exercises.

The `urllib` module provides functions to download data from given URLs as well as encoding and decoding strings to make them suitable for including as part of valid URL strings. The functions we will be looking at in the upcoming section include `urlopen()`, `urlretrieve()`, `quote()`, `unquote()`, `quote_plus()`, `unquote_plus()`, and `urlencode()`. We will also look at some of the methods available to the file-like object returned by `urlopen()`.

urllib.urlopen()

`urlopen()` opens a Web connection to the given URL string and returns a file-like object. It has the following syntax:

```
urlopen(urlstr, postQueryData=None)
```

`urlopen()` opens the URL pointed to by *urlstr*. If no protocol or download scheme is given, or if a "file" scheme is passed in, `urlopen()` will open a local file.

For all HTTP requests, the normal request type is GET. In these cases, the query string provided to the Web server (key-value pairs encoded or quoted, such as the string output of the `urlencode()` function), should be given as part of *urlstr*.

If the POST request method is desired, then the query string (again encoded) should be placed in the *postQueryData* variable. (We'll discuss GET and POST some more later in the chapter, but such HTTP commands are general to Web programming and HTTP itself, not tied specifically to Python.)

When a successful connection is made, `urlopen()` returns a file-like object, as if the destination was a file opened in read mode. If our file object is f, for example, then our "handle" would support the expected read methods such as f.read(), f.readline(), f.readlines(), f.close(), and f.fileno().

In addition, a f.info() method is available which returns the Multipurpose Internet Mail Extension (MIME) headers. Such headers give the browser information regarding which application can view returned file types. For example, the browser itself can view HTML, plain text files, and render *PNG* (Portable Network Graphics) and *JPEG* (Joint Photographic Experts Group) or the old *GIF* (Graphics Interchange Format) graphics files. Other files, such as multimedia or specific document types, require external applications in order to view.

Finally, a geturl() method exists to obtain the true URL of the final opened destination, taking into consideration any redirection that might have occurred. A summary of these file-like object methods is given in Table 9-4.

Table 9-4 urllib.urlopen() File-like Object Methods

urlopen() Object Methods	Description
f.read([*bytes*])	Reads all or bytes bytes from f
f.readline()	Reads a single line from f
f.readlines()	Reads a all lines from f into a list
f.close()	Closes URL connection for f
f.fileno()	Returns file number of f
f.info()	Gets MIME headers of f
f.geturl()	Returns true URL opened for f

If you expect to be accessing more complex URLs or want to be able to handle more complex situations, such as basic and digest authentication, redirections, cookies, etc., then we suggest using the urllib2 module. It too, has a urlopen() function, but it also provides other functions and classes for opening a variety of URLs.

If you're staying with version 2.x for now, we strongly recommend that you use urllib2.urlopen(), instead, because it deprecates the original one in urllib starting in version 2.6; the old one is removed in version 3.0. As **2.6, 3.0** you read in the Core Module sidebar earlier, the functionality for both modules are merged into `urllib.request` in Python 3. This is just another way of saying that the version 3.x `urllib.request.urlopen()` function is ported directly from version 2.x `urllib2.urlopen()` (and not `urllib.urlopen()`).

urllib.urlretrieve()

Rather than opening a URL and letting you access it like a file, `urlretrieve()` just downloads the entire HTML and saves it as a file. Here is the syntax for `urlretrieve()`:

urlretrieve(*url*, *filename*=None, *reporthook*=None, *data*=None)

Rather than reading from the URL like `urlopen()` does, `urlretrieve()` simply downloads the entire HTML file located at *urlstr* to your local disk. It stores the downloaded data into *localfile*, if given, or a temporary file if not. If the file has already been copied from the Internet or if the file is local, no subsequent downloading will occur.

The *downloadStatusHook*, if provided, is a function that is called after each block of data has been downloaded and delivered. It is called with the following three arguments: number of blocks read so far, the block size in bytes, and the total (byte) size of the file. This is very useful if you are implementing download status information to the user in a text-based or graphical display.

`urlretrieve()` returns a 2-tuple (*filename*, *mime_hdrs*). *filename* is the name of the local file containing the downloaded data. *mime_hdrs* is the set of MIME headers returned by the responding Web server. For more information, see the `Message` class of the `mimetools` module. *mime_hdrs* is None for local files.

urllib.quote() and urllib.quote_plus()

The `quote*()` functions take URL data and encode it so that it is fit for inclusion as part of a URL string. In particular, certain special characters that are unprintable or cannot be part of valid URLs to a Web server must be converted. This is what the `quote*()` functions do for you. Both `quote*()` functions have the following syntax:

quote(*urldata*, *safe*='/')

Characters that are never converted include commas, underscores, periods, and dashes, as well as alphanumerics. All others are subject to conversion. In particular, the disallowed characters are changed to their hexadecimal ordinal equivalents, prepended with a percent sign (%), for example, %xx, where xx is the hexadecimal representation of a character's ASCII value. When calling quote*(), the *urldata* string is converted to an equivalent string that can be part of a URL string. The *safe* string should contain a set of characters that should also *not* be converted. The default is the slash (/).

quote_plus() is similar to quote(), except that it also encodes spaces to plus signs (+). Here is an example using quote() versus quote_plus():

```
>>> name = 'joe mama'
>>> number = 6
>>> base = 'http://www/~foo/cgi-bin/s.py'
>>> final = '%s?name=%s&num=%d' % (base, name, number)
>>> final
'http://www/~foo/cgi-bin/s.py?name=joe mama&num=6'
>>>
>>> urllib.quote(final)
'http:%3a//www/%7efoo/cgi-bin/s.py%3fname%3djoe%20mama%26num%3d6'
>>>
>>> urllib.quote_plus(final)
'http%3a//www/%7efoo/cgi-bin/s.py%3fname%3djoe+mama%26num%3d6'
```

urllib.unquote() and urllib.unquote_plus()

As you have probably guessed, the unquote*() functions do the exact opposite of the quote*() functions—they convert all characters encoded in the %xx fashion to their ASCII equivalents. The syntax of unquote*() is as follows:

```
unquote*(urldata)
```

Calling unquote() will decode all URL-encoded characters in urldata and return the resulting string. unquote_plus() will also convert plus signs back to space characters.

urllib.urlencode()

urlencode() takes a dictionary of key-value pairs and encodes them to be included as part of a query in a CGI request URL string. The pairs are in key=value format and are delimited by ampersands (&). Furthermore, the keys and their values are sent to quote_plus() for proper encoding. Here is an example output from urlencode():

```
>>> aDict = { 'name': 'Georgina Garcia', 'hmdir': '~ggarcia' }
>>> urllib.urlencode(aDict)
'name=Georgina+Garcia&hmdir=%7eggarcia'
```

There are other functions in urllib and urlparse that we don't have the opportunity to cover here. Refer to the documentation for more information.

A summary of the urllib functions discussed in this section can be found in Table 9-5.

Table 9-5 Core urllib Module Functions

urllib Functions	Description
urlopen(*urlstr*, *postQueryData*=None)	Opens the URL *urlstr*, sending the query data in *postQueryData* if a POST request
urlretrieve(*urlstr*, *localfile*=None, *downloadStatusHook*=None)	Downloads the file located at the *urlstr* URL to *localfile* or a temporary file if *localfile* not given; if present, *downloaStatusHook* is a function that can receive download statistics
quote(*urldata*, *safe*='/')	Encodes invalid URL characters of *urldata*; characters in *safe* string are *not* encoded
quote_plus(*urldata*, *safe*='/')	Same as quote() except encodes spaces as plus (+) signs (rather than as %20)
unquote(*urldata*)	Decodes encoded characters of *urldata*
unquote_plus(*urldata*)	Same as unquote() but converts plus signs to spaces
urlencode(*dict*)	Encodes the key-value pairs of *dict* into a valid string for CGI queries and encodes the key and value strings with quote_plus()

SSL Support

Before wrapping up our discussion on urllib and looking at some examples, we want to mention that it supports opening HTTP connections using the SSL. (The core change to add SSL is implemented in the socket module.) The httplib module supports URLs using the "https" connection scheme. In addition to those two modules, other protocol client modules with SSL support include: imaplib, poplib, and smtplib.

9.2.4   An Example of `urllib2` HTTP Authentication

As mentioned in the previous subsection, `urllib2` can handle more complex URL opening. One example is for Web sites with basic authentication (login and password) requirements. The most straightforward solution to getting past security is to use the extended `net_loc` URL component, as described earlier in this chapter, for example, http://*username:passwd@* www.python.org. The problem with this solution is that it is not programmatic. Using `urllib2`, however, we can tackle this problem in two different ways.

We can create a basic authentication handler (`urllib2.HTTPBasicAuth Handler`) and register a login password given the base URL and *realm*, meaning a string defining the secure area of the Web site. Once you have a handler, you build an opener with it and install a URL-opener with it so that all URLs opened will use our handler.

The realm comes from the defined `.htaccess` file for the secure part of the Web site. One example of such a file appears here:

```
AuthType        basic
AuthName        "Secure Archive"
AuthUserFile    /www/htdocs/.htpasswd
require         valid-user
```

For this part of the Web site, the string listed for `AuthName` is the realm. The username and (encrypted) password are created by using the `htpasswd` command (and installed in the `.htpasswd` file). For more on realms and Web authentication, see RFC 2617 (HTTP Authentication: Basic and Digest Access Authentication) as well as the WikiPedia page at http://en.wikipedia.org/ wiki/Basic_access_authentication.

The alternative to creating an opener with a authentication handler is to simulate a user typing the username and password when prompted by a browser; that is, to send an HTTP client request with the appropriate authorization headers. In Example 9-1, we demonstrate these two methods.

Example 9-1   Basic HTTP Authentication (`urlopen_auth.py`)

This script uses both techniques described earlier for basic HTTP authentication. You must use `urllib2` because this functionality isn't in `urllib`.

```
1   #!/usr/bin/env python
2
3   import urllib2
4
```

(Continued)

Example 9-1   Basic HTTP Authentication (`urlopen_auth.py`) *(Continued)*

```
5   LOGIN = 'wesley'
6   PASSWD = "you'llNeverGuess"
7   URL = 'http://localhost'
8   REALM = 'Secure Archive'
9
10  def handler_version(url):
11      from urlparse import urlparse
12      hdlr = urllib2.HTTPBasicAuthHandler()
13      hdlr.add_password(REALM,
14              urlparse(url)[1], LOGIN, PASSWD)
15      opener = urllib2.build_opener(hdlr)
16      urllib2.install_opener(opener)
17      return url
18
19  def request_version(url):
20      from base64 import encodestring
21      req = urllib2.Request(url)
22      b64str = encodestring('%s:%s' % (LOGIN, PASSWD))[:-1]
23      req.add_header("Authorization", "Basic %s" % b64str)
24      return req
25
26  for funcType in ('handler', 'request'):
27      print '*** Using %s:' % funcType.upper()
28      url = eval('%s_version' % funcType)(URL)
29      f = urllib2.urlopen(url)
30      print f.readline()
31      f.close()
```

Line-by-Line Explanation

Lines 1–8

This is the usual, expected setup plus some constants for the rest of the script to use. We don't need to remind you that sensitive information should come from a secure database, or at least from environment variables or pre-compiled .pyc files rather than being hardcoded in plain text in a source file.

Lines 10–17

The "handler" version of the code allocates a basic handler class as described earlier, and then adds the authentication information. The handler is then used to create a URL-opener that is subsequently installed so that all URLs opened will use the given authentication. This code was adapted from the official Python documentation for the urllib2 module.

Lines 19–24

The "request" version of our code just builds a Request object and adds the simple base64-encoded authentication header into our HTTP request. This request is then used to substitute the URL string when calling `urlopen()` upon returning back to "main." Note that the original URL was "baked into" the `urllib2.Request` object, hence the reason why it was not a problem to replace it in the subsequent call to `urllib2.urlopen()`. This code was inspired by Michael Foord's and Lee Harr's recipes in the *Python Cookbook*, which you can obtain at:

http://aspn.activestate.com/ASPN/Cookbook/Python/
Recipe/305288

http://aspn.activestate.com/ASPN/Cookbook/Python/
Recipe/267197

It would have been great to have been able to use Harr's `HTTPRealm Finder` class so that we do not need to hard-code it in our example.

Lines 26–31
The rest of this script just opens the given URL by using both techniques and displays the first line (dumping the others) of the resulting HTML page returned by the server once authentication has been validated. Note that an HTTP error (and no HTML) would be returned if the authentication information is invalid.

The output should look something like this:

```
$ python urlopen_auth.py
*** Using HANDLER:
<html>

*** Using REQUEST:
<html>
```

In addition to the official Python documentation for `urllib2`, you may find this companion piece useful:

http://www.voidspace.org.uk/python/articles/urllib2.shtml.

9.2.5   Porting the HTTP Authentication Example to Python 3

At the time of this writing, porting this application requires a bit more work than just using the `2to3` tool. Of course, it does the heavy lifting, but it does require a softer (or is that "software"?) touch afterwards. Let's take our `urlauth_open.py` script and run the tool on it:

3.x

```
$ 2to3 -w urlopen_auth.py
. . .
```

You would use a similar command on PCs, but as you might have already seen from earlier chapters, the output shows the differences that were changed between the Python 2 and Python 3 versions of the script, and the original file is overridden with the Python 3 version, whereas the Python 2 version was backed up automatically.

Rename the new file from urlopen_auth.py to urlopen_auth3.py and the backup from urlopen_auth.py.bak to urlopen_auth.py. On a POSIX system, execute these file rename commands (and on PCs, you would do it from Windows or use the ren DOS command):

```
$ mv urlopen_auth.py urlopen_auth3.py
$ mv urlopen_auth.py.bak urlopen_auth.py
```

This keeps with our naming strategy to help recognize our code that's in Python 2 versus those ported to Python 3. Anyway, running the tool is just the beginning. If we're optimistic that it will run the first time, our hopes are dashed quickly:

```
$ python3 urlopen_auth3.py
*** Using HANDLER:
b'<HTML>\n'
*** Using REQUEST:
Traceback (most recent call last):
  File "urlopen_auth3.py", line 28, in <module>
    url = eval('%s_version' % funcType)(URL)
  File "urlopen_auth3.py", line 22, in request_version
    b64str = encodestring('%s:%s' % (LOGIN, PASSWD))[:-1]
  File "/Library/Frameworks/Python.framework/Versions/3.2/lib/
python3.2/base64.py", line 353, in encodestring
    return encodebytes(s)
  File "/Library/Frameworks/Python.framework/Versions/3.2/lib/
python3.2/base64.py", line 341, in encodebytes
    raise TypeError("expected bytes, not %s" % s.__class__.__name__)
TypeError: expected bytes, not str
```

Going with our gut instinct, change the string in line 22 to a bytes string by adding a leading "b" before the opening quote, as in b'%s:%s' % (LOGIN, PASSWD). Now if we run it again, we get another error—welcome to the Python 3 porting club!

```
$ python3 urlopen_auth3.py
*** Using HANDLER:
b'<HTML>\n'
*** Using REQUEST:
Traceback (most recent call last):
  File "urlopen_auth3.py", line 28, in <module>
    url = eval('%s_version' % funcType)(URL)
  File "urlopen_auth3.py", line 22, in request_version
    b64str = encodestring(b'%s:%s' % (LOGIN, PASSWD))[:-1]
TypeError: unsupported operand type(s) for %: 'bytes' and 'tuple'
```

Apparently, `bytes` objects do not support the string format operator because, technically, you're not supposed to use them as strings. Instead, we need to format the string as (Unicode) text, and then convert the whole thing into a `bytes` object: `bytes('%s:%s' % (LOGIN, PASSWD), 'utf-8')`. The output after this change is much closer to what we want:

```
$ python3 urlopen_auth3.py

*** Using HANDLER:
b'<HTML>\n'
*** Using REQUEST:
b'<HTML>\n'
```

It's still slightly off because we're seeing the designation of the bytes objects (leading "b", quotes, etc.) instead of just the text in which we're interested. Change the `print()` call to this: `print(str(f.readline(), 'utf-8'))`. Now the output of the Python 3 version is identical to that of the Python 2 script:

```
$ python3 urlopen_auth3.py
*** Using HANDLER:
<html>

*** Using REQUEST:
<html>
```

As you can see, porting requires a bit of handholding, but it's not impossible. Again, as we noted earlier, `urllib`, `urllib2`, and `urlparse` are all merged together under the `urllib` package umbrella in Python 3. Because of how the 2to3 tool works, an import of `urllib.parse` already exists at the top. It is thus is superfluous in the definition of `handler_version()` and removed. You'll find that change along with the others in Example 9-2.

Example 9-2   Python 3 HTTP Authentication Script (`urlopen_auth3.py`)

This represents the Python 3 version to our `urlopen_auth.py` script.

```
1   #!/usr/bin/env python3
2
3   import urllib.request, urllib.error, urllib.parse
4
5   LOGIN = 'wesley'
6   PASSWD = "you'llNeverGuess"
7   URL = 'http://localhost'
8   REALM = 'Secure Archive'
9
```

(Continued)

```
10  def handler_version(url):
11      hdlr = urllib.request.HTTPBasicAuthHandler()
12      hdlr.add_password(REALM,
13          urllib.parse.urlparse(url)[1], LOGIN, PASSWD)
14      opener = urllib.request.build_opener(hdlr)
15      urllib.request.install_opener(opener)
16      return url
17
18  def request_version(url):
19      from base64 import encodestring
20      req = urllib.request.Request(url)
21      b64str = encodestring(
22          bytes('%s:%s' % (LOGIN, PASSWD), 'utf-8'))[:-1]
23      req.add_header("Authorization", "Basic %s" % b64str)
24      return req
25
26  for funcType in ('handler', 'request'):
27      print('*** Using %s:' % funcType.upper())
28      url = eval('%s_version' % funcType)(URL)
29      f = urllib.request.urlopen(url)
30      print(str(f.readline(), 'utf-8')
31      f.close()
```

Let's now turn our attention to slightly more advanced Web clients.

9.3   Web Clients

Web browsers are basic Web clients. They are used primarily for searching and downloading documents from the Web. You can also create Web clients that do more than that, though. We'll take a look at several in this section.

9.3.1   A Simple Web Crawler/Spider/Bot

One example of a slightly more complex Web client is a *crawler* (a.k.a. *spider*, *[ro]bot*). These are programs that explore and download pages from the Internet for a variety of reasons, some of which include:

- Indexing into a large search engine such as Google or Yahoo!

- Offline browsing—downloading documents onto a local hard disk and rearranging hyperlinks to create almost a mirror image for local browsing

- Downloading and storing for historical or archival purposes, or

- Web page caching to save superfluous downloading time on Web site revisits.

The crawler in Example 9-3, `crawl.py`, takes a starting Web address (URL), downloads that page and all other pages whose links appear in succeeding pages, but only those that are in the same domain as the starting page. Without such limitations, you will run out of disk space.

Example 9-3   Web Crawler (`crawl.py`)

The crawler consists of two classes: one to manage the entire crawling process (`Crawler`), and one to retrieve and parse each downloaded Web page (`Retriever`). (Refactored from earlier editions of this book.)

```python
1    #!/usr/bin/env python
2
3    import cStringIO
4    import formatter
5    from htmllib import HTMLParser
6    import httplib
7    import os
8    import sys
9    import urllib
10   import urlparse
11
12   class Retriever(object):
13       __slots__ = ('url', 'file')
14       def __init__(self, url):
15           self.url, self.file = self.get_file(url)
16
17       def get_file(self, url, default='index.html'):
18           'Create usable local filename from URL'
19           parsed = urlparse.urlparse(url)
20           host = parsed.netloc.split('@')[-1].split(':')[0]
21           filepath = '%s%s' % (host, parsed.path)
22           if not os.path.splitext(parsed.path)[1]:
23               filepath = os.path.join(filepath, default)
24           linkdir = os.path.dirname(filepath)
25           if not os.path.isdir(linkdir):
26               if os.path.exists(linkdir):
27                   os.unlink(linkdir)
28               os.makedirs(linkdir)
29           return url, filepath
30
```

(Continued)

Example 9-3   Web Crawler (`crawl.py`) *(Continued)*

```
31        def download(self):
32            'Download URL to specific named file'
33            try:
34                retval = urllib.urlretrieve(self.url, self.file)
35            except (IOError, httplib.InvalidURL) as e:
36                retval = (('*** ERROR: bad URL "%s": %s' % (
37                    self.url, e)),)
38            return retval
39
40        def parse_links(self):
41            'Parse out the links found in downloaded HTML file'
42            f = open(self.file, 'r')
43            data = f.read()
44            f.close()
45            parser = HTMLParser(formatter.AbstractFormatter(
46                formatter.DumbWriter(cStringIO.StringIO())))
47            parser.feed(data)
48            parser.close()
49            return parser.anchorlist
50
51    class Crawler(object):
52        count = 0
53
54        def __init__(self, url):
55            self.q = [url]
56            self.seen = set()
57            parsed = urlparse.urlparse(url)
58            host = parsed.netloc.split('@')[-1].split(':')[0]
59            self.dom = '.'.join(host.split('.')[-2:])
60
61        def get_page(self, url, media=False):
62            'Download page & parse links, add to queue if nec'
63            r = Retriever(url)
64            fname = r.download()[0]
65            if fname[0] == '*':
66                print fname, '... skipping parse'
67                return
68            Crawler.count += 1
69            print '\n(', Crawler.count, ')'
70            print 'URL:', url
71            print 'FILE:', fname
72            self.seen.add(url)
73            ftype = os.path.splitext(fname)[1]
74            if ftype not in ('.htm', '.html'):
75                return
76
77            for link in r.parse_links():
78                if link.startswith('mailto:'):
79                    print '... discarded, mailto link'
80                    continue
```

```
81                  if not media:
82                      ftype = os.path.splitext(link)[1]
83                      if ftype in ('.mp3', '.mp4', '.m4v', '.wav'):
84                          print '... discarded, media file'
85                          continue
86                  if not link.startswith('http://'):
87                      link = urlparse.urljoin(url, link)
88              print '*', link,
89              if link not in self.seen:
90                  if self.dom not in link:
91                      print '... discarded, not in domain'
92                  else:
93                      if link not in self.q:
94                          self.q.append(link)
95                          print '... new, added to Q'
96                      else:
97                          print '... discarded, already in Q'
98              else:
99                  print '... discarded, already processed'
100
101     def go(self, media=False):
102         'Process next page in queue (if any)'
103         while self.q:
104             url = self.q.pop()
105             self.get_page(url, media)
106
107 def main():
108     if len(sys.argv) > 1:
109         url = sys.argv[1]
110     else:
111         try:
112             url = raw_input('Enter starting URL: ')
113         except (KeyboardInterrupt, EOFError):
114             url = ''
115     if not url:
116         return
117     if not url.startswith('http://') and \
118         not url.startswith('ftp://'):
119         url = 'http://%s/' % url
120     robot = Crawler(url)
121     robot.go()
122
123 if __name__ == '__main__':
124     main()
```

Line-by-Line (Class-by-Class) Explanation

Lines 1–10

The top part of the script consists of the standard Python Unix startup line and the import of the modules/packages to be used. Here are some brief explanations:

- cStringIO, formatter, htmllib   We use various classes in these modules for parsing HTML.

- `httplib`   We only need an exception from this module.

- `os`   This provides various file system functions.

- `sys`   We are just using `argv` for command-line arguments.

- `urllib`   We only need the `urlretrieve()` function for downloading Web pages.

- `urlparse`   We use the `urlparse()` and `urljoin()` functions for URL manipulation.

Lines 12–29

The `Retriever` class has the responsibility of downloading pages from the Web and parsing the links located within each document, adding them to the "to-do" queue, if necessary. A `Retriever` instance object is created for each page that is downloaded from the Internet. `Retriever` consists of several methods to aid in its functionality: a constructor (`__init__()`), `get_file()`, `download()`, and `parse_links()`.

Skipping ahead momentarily, the `get_file()` method takes the given URL and comes up with a safe and sane corresponding filename to store the file locally—we are downloading this file from the Web. Basically, it works by removing the `http://` prefix from the URL, getting rid of any extras such as username, password, and port number in order to arrive at the hostname (line 20).

URLs without trailing file extensions will be given the default filename `index.html` and can be overridden by the caller. You can see how this works as well as the final `filepath` created on lines 21–23.

We then pull out the final destination directory (line 24) and check if it is already a directory—if so, we leave it alone and return the URL-filepath pair. If we enter this `if` clause, this means the directory either doesn't exist or is a plain file. In the case it is the latter, so it will be erased. Finally, the target directory and any parents are created by using `os.makedirs()` in line 28.

Now let's go back up to the initializer `__init__()`. A `Retriever` object is created and stores both the URL (`str`) and the corresponding filename returned by `get_file()` as (instance) attributes. In our current design, instances are created for every file downloaded. In the case of a Web site with many, many files, a small instance like this can cause additional memory usage. To help minimize consumed resources, we create a `__slots__` variable, indicating that the only attributes that instances can have are `self.url` and `self.file`.

Lines 31–49

We'll see the crawler momentarily, but this is a heads-up that it creates `Retriever` objects for each downloaded file. The `download()` method, as you can imagine, actually goes out to the Internet to download the page with the given link (line 34). It calls `urllib.urlretrieve()` with the URL and saves it to the filename (the one returned by `get_file()`).

If the download was successful, the filename is returned (line 34), but if there's an error, an error string prefixed with ******* is returned instead (lines 35–36). The crawler checks this return value and calls `parse_links()` to parse links out of the just-downloaded page only if all went well.

The more serious method in this part of our application is the `parse_links()` method. Yes, the job of a crawler is to download Web pages, but a *recursive* crawler (like ours) looks for additional links in each downloaded page and processes them, too. It first opens up the down-loaded Web page and extracts the entire HTML content as a single string (lines 42–44).

The magic you see in lines 45–49 is a well-known recipe that uses the `htmllib.HTMLParser` class. We would like to say something to the effect that this is a recipe that's been passed down by Python programmers from generation to generation, but we would just be lying to you. Anyway, we digress.

The main point of how it works is that the parser class doesn't do I/O, so it takes a `formatter` object to handle that. Formatter objects—Python only has one real formatter: `formatter.AbstractFormatter`—parse the data and use a writer object to dispatch its output. Similarly, Python only has one useful writer object: `formatter.DumbWriter`. It optionally takes a file object to which to write the output. If you omit it, it writes to standard output, which is probably undesirable. To that effect, we instantiate a `cStringIO`. `StringIO` object to absorb this output (think /dev/null, if you know what that is.) You can search online for any of the class names and find similar code snippets in many places along with additional commentary.

Because `htmllib.HTMLParser` is fairly long in the tooth and deprecated starting in version 2.6, a smaller example demonstrating some of the more contemporary tools comes in the next subsection. We leave it in this exam-ple because it is/was such a common recipe and still can be the right tool for this job.

Anyway, all the complexity in creating the parser is entirely contained in a single call (lines 45–46). The rest of this block consists of passing in the HTML, closing the parser, and then returning a list of parsed links/anchors.

Lines 51–59

The `Crawler` class is the star of the show, managing the entire crawling process for one Web site. If we added threading to our application, we would create separate instances for each site crawled. The `Crawler` consists of three items stored by the constructor during the instantiation phase, the first of which is `self.q`, a queue of links to download. Such a list will fluctuate during execution, shrinking as each page is processed and expanding as new links are discovered within each downloaded page.

The other two data values for the `Crawler` include `self.seen`, a set containing all the links that we have seen (downloaded) already. And finally, we store the domain name for the main link, `self.dom`, and use that value to determine whether any succeeding links are part of the same domain. All three values are created in the initializer method `__init__()` in lines 54–59.

Note that we parse the domain by using `urlparse.urlparse()` (line 58) in the same way that we grab the hostname out of the URL in the `Retriever`. The domain name comes by just taking the final two parts of the hostname. Note that because we don't use the host for anything else, you can make your code harder to read by combining lines 58 and 59 like this:

```
self.dom = '.'.join(urlparse.urlparse(
    url).netloc.split('@')[-1].split(':')[0].split('.')[-2:])
```

Right above `__init__()`, the `Crawler` also has a static data item named `count`. The purpose of this counter is just to keep track of the number of objects we have downloaded from the Internet. It is incremented for every successfully downloaded page.

Lines 61-105

`Crawler` has a pair of other methods in addition to its constructor: `get_page()` and `go()`. `go()` is simply the method that is used to start the `Crawler`. It is called from the main body of code. `go()` consists of a loop that will continue to execute as long as there are new links in the queue that need to be downloaded. The workhorse of this class, though, is the `get_page()` method.

`get_page()` instantiates a `Retriever` object with the first link and lets it go off to the races. If the page was downloaded successfully, the counter is incremented (otherwise, links that error-out are skipped [lines 65–67]) and the link added to the "already seen" set (line 72). We use a set because order doesn't matter and its lookup is much faster than using a list.

`get_page()` looks at all the links featured inside each downloaded page (skipping all non-Web pages [lines 73–75]) and determines whether any more links should be added to the queue (lines 77–99). The main loop in go() will continue to process links until the queue is empty, at which time victory is declared (lines 103–105).

Links that are a part of another domain (lines 90–91), or have already been downloaded (lines 98–99), are already in the queue waiting to be processed (lines 96–97), or are mailto: links are ignored and not added to the queue (lines 78–80). The same applies for media files (lines 81–85).

Lines 107–124

main() needs a URL to begin processing. If one is entered on the command line (for example, when this script is invoked directly; lines 108–109), it will just go with the one given. Otherwise, the script enters interactive mode, prompting the user for a starting URL (line 112). With a starting link in hand, the Crawler is instantiated, and away we go (lines 120–121).

One sample invocation of crawl.py might look like this:

```
$ crawl.py
Enter starting URL: http://www.null.com/home/index.html

( 1 )
URL: http://www.null.com/home/index.html
FILE: www.null.com/home/index.html
* http://www.null.com/home/overview.html ... new, added to Q
* http://www.null.com/home/synopsis.html ... new, added to Q
* http://www.null.com/home/order.html ... new, added to Q
* mailto:postmaster@null.com ... discarded, mailto link
* http://www.null.com/home/overview.html ... discarded, already in Q
* http://www.null.com/home/synopsis.html ... discarded, already in Q
* http://www.null.com/home/order.html ... discarded, already in Q
* mailto:postmaster@null.com ... discarded, mailto link
* http://bogus.com/index.html ... discarded, not in domain

( 2 )
URL: http://www.null.com/home/order.html
FILE: www.null.com/home/order.html
* mailto:postmaster@null.com ... discarded, mailto link
* http://www.null.com/home/index.html ... discarded, already processed
* http://www.null.com/home/synopsis.html ... discarded, already in Q
* http://www.null.com/home/overview.html ... discarded, already in Q

( 3 )
URL: http://www.null.com/home/synopsis.html
FILE: www.null.com/home/synopsis.html
* http://www.null.com/home/index.html ... discarded, already processed
* http://www.null.com/home/order.html ... discarded, already processed
* http://www.null.com/home/overview.html ... discarded, already in Q
```

```
( 4 )
URL: http://www.null.com/home/overview.html
FILE: www.null.com/home/overview.html
* http://www.null.com/home/synopsis.html ... discarded, already
processed
* http://www.null.com/home/index.html ... discarded, already processed
* http://www.null.com/home/synopsis.html ... discarded, already
processed
* http://www.null.com/home/order.html ... discarded, already processed
```

After execution, a `www.null.com` directory would be created in the local file system, with a `home` subdirectory. You will find all the processed files within `home`.

If after reviewing the code you're still wondering where writing a crawler in Python can get you, you might be surprised to learn that the original Google Web crawlers were written in Python. For more information, see http://infolab.stanford.edu/~backrub/google.html.

9.3.2   Parsing Web Content

In the previous subsection, we took a look at a crawler Web client. Part of the spidering process involved parsing of links, or *anchors* as they're officially called. For a long while, the well-known recipe `htmllib.HTMLParser` was employed for parsing Web pages; however, newer and improved modules and packages have come along. We'll be demonstrating some of these in this subsection.

In Example 9-4, we explore one standard library tool, the `HTMLParser` class in the `HTMLParser` module (added in version 2.2). `HTMLParser.HTMLParser` was supposed to replace `htmllib.HTMLParser` because it was simpler, provided a lower-level view of the content, and handled XHTML, whereas the latter was older and more complex because it was based on the `sgmllib` module (meaning it had to understand the intricacies of Standard Generalized Markup Language [SGML]). The official documentation is fairly sparse when describing how to use `HTMLParser.HTMLParser`, so hopefully we'll give a more useful example here.

We'll also demonstrate the use of two of the other three most popular Web parsers, `BeautifulSoup` and `html5lib`, which are available as separate downloads outside of the standard library. You can access them both at the Cheeseshop, or from http://pypi.python.org. For a less stressful installation, you can also use the `easy_install` or `pip` tools to get either one.

The one we skipped was lxml; we'll leave that as an exercise for you to undertake. You'll find more exercises at the end of the chapter that will help you learn these more thoroughly by substituting them for htmllib. HTMLParser in the crawler.

The parse_links.py script in Example 9-4 only consists of parsing anchors out of any input data. Given a URL, it will extract all links, attempt to make any necessary adjustments to make them full URLs, sort, and display them to the user. It runs each URL through all three parsers. For BeautifulSoup in particular, we provide two different solutions: the first one is simpler, parsing all tags then looking for all the anchor tags; the second requires the use of the SoupStrainer class, which specifically targets anchor tags and only parses those.

Example 9-4   Link Parser (parse_links.py)

This script uses three different parsers to extract links from HTML anchor tags. It features the HTMLParser standard library module as well as the third-party BeautifulSoup and html5lib packages.

```
1   #!/usr/bin/env python
2
3   from HTMLParser import HTMLParser
4   from cStringIO import StringIO
5   from urllib2 import urlopen
6   from urlparse import urljoin
7
8   from BeautifulSoup import BeautifulSoup, SoupStrainer
9   from html5lib import parse, treebuilders
10
11  URLs = (
12      'http://python.org',
13      'http://google.com',
14  )
15
16  def output(x):
17      print '\n'.join(sorted(set(x)))
18
19  def simpleBS(url, f):
20      'simpleBS() - use BeautifulSoup to parse all tags to get anchors'
21      output(urljoin(url, x['href']) for x in BeautifulSoup(
22          f).findAll('a'))
23
```

(Continued)

Example 9-4   Link Parser (parse_links.py) *(Continued)*

```
24  def fasterBS(url, f):
25      'fasterBS() - use BeautifulSoup to parse only anchor tags'
26      output(urljoin(url, x['href']) for x in BeautifulSoup(
27          f, parseOnlyThese=SoupStrainer('a')))
28
29  def htmlparser(url, f):
30      'htmlparser() - use HTMLParser to parse anchor tags'
31      class AnchorParser(HTMLParser):
32          def handle_starttag(self, tag, attrs):
33              if tag != 'a':
34                  return
35              if not hasattr(self, 'data'):
36                  self.data = []
37              for attr in attrs:
38                  if attr[0] == 'href':
39                      self.data.append(attr[1])
40      parser = AnchorParser()
41      parser.feed(f.read())
42      output(urljoin(url, x) for x in parser.data)
43
44  def html5libparse(url, f):
45      'html5libparse() - use html5lib to parse anchor tags'
46      output(urljoin(url, x.attributes['href']) \
47          for x in parse(f) if isinstance(x,
48          treebuilders.simpletree.Element) and \
49          x.name == 'a')
50
51  def process(url, data):
52      print '\n*** simple BS'
53      simpleBS(url, data)
54      data.seek(0)
55      print '\n*** faster BS'
56      fasterBS(url, data)
57      data.seek(0)
58      print '\n*** HTMLParser'
59      htmlparser(url, data)
60      data.seek(0)
61      print '\n*** HTML5lib'
62      html5libparse(url, data)
63
64  def main():
65      for url in URLs:
66          f = urlopen(url)
67          data = StringIO(f.read())
68          f.close()
69          process(url, data)
70
71  if __name__ == '__main__':
72      main()
```

Line-by-Line Explanation

Lines 1–9

In this script, we use four modules from the standard library. HTMLParser is one of the parsers; the other three are for general use throughout. The second group of imports are of third-party (non-standard library) modules/packages. This ordering is the generally accepted standard for imports: standard library modules/packages first, followed by third-party installations, and finally, any modules/packages local to the application.

Lines 11–17

The URLs variable contains the Web pages to parse; feel free to add, change, or remove URLs here. The output() function takes an iterable of links, removes duplicates by putting them all into a set, sorts them in lexicographic order, and then merges them into a NEWLINE-delimited string that is displayed to the user.

Lines 19–27

We highlight the use of BeautifulSoup in the simpleBS() and fasterBS() functions. In simpleBS(), the parsing happens when you instantiate BeautifulSoup with the file handle. In the following short snippet, we do exactly that, using an already downloaded page from the PyCon Web site as pycon.html.

```
>>> from BeautifulSoup import BeautifulSoup as BS
>>> f = open('pycon.html')
>>> bs = BS(f)
```

When you get the instance and call its findAll() method requesting anchor ('a') tags, it returns a list of tags, as shown here:

```
>>> type(bs)
<class 'BeautifulSoup.BeautifulSoup'>
>>> tags = bs.findAll('a')
>>> type(tags)
<type 'list'>
>>> len(tags)
19
>>> tag = tags[0]
>>> tag
<a href="/2011/">PyCon 2011 Atlanta</a>
>>> type(tag)
<class 'BeautifulSoup.Tag'>
>>> tag['href']
u'/2011/'
```

Because the `Tag` object is an anchor, it should have an `'href'` tag, so we ask for it. We then call `urlparse.urljoin()` and pass along the head URL along with the link to get the full URL. Here's our continuing example (assuming the PyCon URL):

```
>>> from urlparse import urljoin
>>> url = 'http://us.pycon.org'
>>> urljoin(url, tag['href'])
u'http://us.pycon.org/2011/'
```

The generator expression iterates over all the final links created by `urlparse.urljoin()` from all of the anchor tags and sends them to `output()`, which processes them as just described. If the code is slightly more difficult to understand because of the use of the generator expression, we can expand out the code to the equivalent:

```
def simpleBS(url, f):
    parsed = BeautifulSoup(f)
    tags = parsed.findAll('a')
    links = [urljoin(url, tag['href']) for tag in tags]
    output(links)
```

For readability purposes, this wins over our single line version, and we would recommend that when developing open-source, work, or group collaborative projects, you always consider this over a more cryptic one-liner.

Although the `simpleBS()` function is fairly easy to understand, one of its drawbacks is that the way we're processing it isn't as efficient as it can be. We use `BeautifulSoup` to parse all the tags in this document and *then* look for the anchors. It would be quicker if we could just filter only the anchor tags (and ignore the rest).

This is what `fasterBS()` does, accomplishing what we just described by using the `SoupStrainer` helper class (and passing that request to filter only anchor tags as the `parseOnlyThese` parameter). By using `SoupStrainer`, you can tell `BeautifulSoup` to skip all the elements it isn't interested in when building the parse tree, so it saves time as well as memory. Also, once parsing has completed, only the anchors make up the parse tree, so there's no need to use the `findAll()` method before iterating.

Lines 29–42

In `htmlparser()`, we use the standard library class `HTMLParser.HTMLParser` to do the parsing. You can see why `BeautifulSoup` is a popular parser; code is shorter and less complex than using `HTMLParser`. Our use of `HTMLParser` is also slower here because you have to manually build a list, that is, create an empty list and repeatedly call its `append()` method.

You can also tell that HTMLParser is lower level than BeautifulSoup. You subclass it and have to create a method called handle_starttag() that's called every time a new tag is encountered in the file stream (lines 31–39). We skip all non-anchor tags (lines 33–34), and then add all anchor links to self.data (lines 37–39), initializing self.data when necessary (lines 35–36).

To use your new parser, you instantiate and feed it (lines 40–41). The results, as you know, are placed into parser.data, and we create the full URLs and display them (line 42) as in our previous BeautifulSoup example.

Lines 44–49

The final example uses html5lib, a parser for HTML documents that follow the HTML5 specification. The simplest way of using html5lib is to call its parse() function with the payload (line 47). It builds and outputs a tree in its custom simpletree format.

You can also choose to use any of a variety of popular tree formats, including minidom, ElementTree, lxml, or BeautifulSoup. To choose an alternative tree format, just pass the name of the desired format in to parse() as the treebuilder argument:

```python
import html5lib
f = open("pycon.html")
tree = html5lib.parse(f, treebuilder="lxml")
f.close()
```

Unless you need a specific tree, usually simpletree is good enough. If you were to perform a trial run and parse a generic document, you'd see output looking something like this:

```python
>>> import html5lib
>>> f = open("pycon.html")
>>> tree = html5lib.parse(f)
>>> f.close()
>>> for x in data:
...   print x, type(x)
...
<html> <class 'html5lib.treebuilders.simpletree.DocumentType'>
<html> <class 'html5lib.treebuilders.simpletree.Element'>
<head> <class 'html5lib.treebuilders.simpletree.Element'>
<None> <class 'html5lib.treebuilders.simpletree.TextNode'>
<meta> <class 'html5lib.treebuilders.simpletree.Element'>
<None> <class 'html5lib.treebuilders.simpletree.TextNode'>
<title> <class 'html5lib.treebuilders.simpletree.Element'>
<None> <class 'html5lib.treebuilders.simpletree.TextNode'>
<None> <class 'html5lib.treebuilders.simpletree.CommentNode'>
        . . .
<img> <class 'html5lib.treebuilders.simpletree.Element'>
<None> <class 'html5lib.treebuilders.simpletree.TextNode'>
<h1> <class 'html5lib.treebuilders.simpletree.Element'>
```

```
<a> <class 'html5lib.treebuilders.simpletree.Element'>
<None> <class 'html5lib.treebuilders.simpletree.TextNode'>
<h2> <class 'html5lib.treebuilders.simpletree.Element'>
<None> <class 'html5lib.treebuilders.simpletree.TextNode'>
        . . .
```

Most of the traversed items are either `Element` or `TextNode` objects. We don't really care about `TextNode` objects in our example here; we're only concerned with one specific type of `Element` object, the anchor. To filter these out, we have two checks in the **if** clause of the generator expression: only look at `Elements`, and of those, only anchors (lines 47–49). For those that meet this criteria, we pull out their `'href'` attribute, merge into a complete URL, and output that as before (line 46).

Lines 51–72

The drivers of this application are the `main()` function, which process each of links found on lines 11–14. It makes one call to download the Web page and immediately sticks the data into a `StringIO` object (lines 65–68) so that we can iterate over them using each of the parsers (line 69) via a call to `process()`.

The `process()` function (lines 51–62) takes the target URL and the `StringIO` object, and then calls on each parser to perform its duty and output its result. With every successive parse (after the first), `process()` must also reset the `StringIO` object back to the beginning (lines 54, 57, and 60) for the next parser.

Once you're satisfied with the code and have it working, you can run it and see how each parser outputs all links (sorted in alphabetical order) found in anchor tags within the Web page's URL. Note that at the time of this writing, there is a preliminary port of `BeautifulSoup` to Python 3 but not `html5lib`.

9.3.3   Programmatic Web Browsing

In this final section on Web clients, we'll present a slightly different example that uses a third-party tool, Mechanize (based on a similarly-named tool written for Perl), which is designed to simulate a browser. It also spawned off a Ruby version.

In the previous example (`parse_links.py`), `BeautifulSoup` was one of the parsers we used to decipher Web page content. We'll use that again here.

If you wish to play along, you'll need to have both Mechanize and `BeautifulSoup` installed on your system. Again, you can obtain and install them separately, or you can use a tool like `easy_install` or `pip`.

Example 9-5 presents the mech.py script, which is very much of a *script* or batch-style application. There are no classes or functions. The whole thing is just one large main() broken up into seven parts, each of which explores one page of the Web site we're examining today: the PyCon conference Web site from 2011. We chose this because the site is not likely to change over time (more recent conferences will get their own customized application).

If it *does* change, however, there are many Web sites to which you can adapt this example, such as logging in to any Web-based e-mail service you subscribe to or some tech news or blog site you frequent. By going over mech.py and what it does, you should have a good enough understanding of how it works to easily port the sample code to work elsewhere.

Example 9-5   Programmatic Web Browsing (mech.py)

In a very batch-like, straightforward script, we employ the Mechanize third-party tool to explore the PyCon 2011 Web site, parsing it with another non-standard tool, BeautifulSoup.

```
1   #!/usr/bin/env python
2
3   from BeautifulSoup import BeautifulSoup, SoupStrainer
4   from mechanize import Browser
5
6   br = Browser()
7
8   # home page
9   rsp = br.open('http://us.pycon.org/2011/home/')
10  print '\n***', rsp.geturl()
11  print "Confirm home page has 'Log in' link; click it"
12  page = rsp.read()
13  assert 'Log in' in page, 'Log in not in page'
14  rsp = br.follow_link(text_regex='Log in')
15
16  # login page
17  print '\n***', rsp.geturl()
18  print 'Confirm at least a login form; submit invalid creds'
19  assert len(list(br.forms())) > 1, 'no forms on this page'
20  br.select_form(nr=0)
```

(Continued)

Example 9-5   Programmatic Web Browsing (`mech.py`) *(Continued)*

```
21  br.form['username'] = 'xxx'  # wrong login
22  br.form['password'] = 'xxx'  # wrong passwd
23  rsp = br.submit()
24
25  # login page, with error
26  print '\n***', rsp.geturl()
27  print 'Error due to invalid creds; resubmit w/valid creds'
28  assert rsp.geturl() == 'http://us.pycon.org/2011/account/login/',
    rsp.geturl()
29  page = rsp.read()
30  err = str(BS(page).find("div",
31      {"id": "errorMsg"}).find('ul').find('li').string)
32  assert err == 'The username and/or password you specified are not cor-
    rect.', err
33  br.select_form(nr=0)
34  br.form['username'] = YOUR_LOGIN
35  br.form['password'] = YOUR_PASSWD
36  rsp = br.submit()
37
38  # login successful, home page redirect
39  print '\n***', rsp.geturl()
40  print 'Logged in properly on home page; click Account link'
41  assert rsp.geturl() == 'http://us.pycon.org/2011/home/', rsp.geturl()
42  page = rsp.read()
43  assert 'Logout' in page, 'Logout not in page'
44  rsp = br.follow_link(text_regex='Account')
45
46  # account page
47  print '\n***', rsp.geturl()
48  print 'Email address parseable on Account page; go back'
49  assert rsp.geturl() == 'http://us.pycon.org/2011/account/email/',
    rsp.geturl()
50  page = rsp.read()
51  assert 'Email Addresses' in page, 'Missing email addresses'
52  print '    Primary e-mail: %r' % str(
53      BS(page).find('table').find('tr').find('td').find('b').string)
54  rsp = br.back()
55
56  # back to home page
57  print '\n***', rsp.geturl()
58  print 'Back works, on home page again; click Logout link'
59  assert rsp.geturl() == 'http://us.pycon.org/2011/home/', rsp.geturl()
60  rsp = br.follow_link(url_regex='logout')
61
62  # logout page
63  print '\n***', rsp.geturl()
64  print 'Confirm on Logout page and Log in link at the top'
65  assert rsp.geturl() == 'http://us.pycon.org/2011/account/logout/',
    rsp.geturl()
66  page = rsp.read()
67  assert 'Log in' in page, 'Log in not in page'
68  print '\n*** DONE'
```

Line-by-Line Explanation

Lines 1–6

This script is fairly simplistic. In fact, we don't use any standard library packages/modules, so all you see here are the imports of the `Mechanize.Browser` and `BeautifulSoup.BeautifulSoup` classes.

Lines 8–14

The first place we visit on the PyCon 2011 Web site is the home page. We display the URL to the user as a confirmation (line 10). Note that this is the final URL that is visited because the original link might have redirected the user elsewhere. The last part of this section (lines 12–14) confirms that the user is not logged in by looking for the `'Log in'` link and following it.

Lines 16–23

Once we've confirmed that we're on a login page (that has at least one form on it), we select the first (and only) form, fill in the authentication fields with erroneous data (unless, unfortunately, your login and password are both `'xxx'`), and submit it.

Lines 25–36

Upon confirmation of a login error on the login page (lines 28–32), we fill in the fields with the correct credentials (which the reader must supply [YOUR_LOGIN, YOUR_PASSWD]) and resubmit.

Lines 38–44

Once authentication has been validated, you are directed back to the home page. This is confirmed (on lines 41–43) by checking for a "Logout" link (which wouldn't be there if you had not successfully logged in). We then click the Account link.

Lines 46–54

You must register by using an e-mail address. You can have more than one, but there must be a single primary address. Your e-mail addresses are the first tab that you arrive at when visiting this page for your Account information. We use `BeautifulSoup` to parse and display the e-mail address table and peek into the first cell of the first row of the table (lines 52–53). The next step is to click the "click on the back button" to return to the home page.

Lines 56–60

This is the shortest of all the sections; we really don't do much here except confirm that we're back on the home page (lines 59), then follow the "Logout" link.

Lines 62–68

The last section confirms we're on the logout page and that you're not logged in. This is accomplished by checking to see if there's a "Log in" link on this page (lines 66–67).

This application demonstrates that, using `Mechanize.Browser` is fairly straightforward. You just need to mentally map user activity in a browser to the right method calls. Ultimately, the primary concern is whether the underlying Web page or application will be altered by its developers, potentially rendering our script out-of-date. Note that at the time of this writing, there is no Python 3 port of Mechanize yet.

Summary

This concludes our look at various types of Web clients. We can now turn our attention to Web servers.

9.4   Web (HTTP) Servers

Until now, we have been discussing the use of Python in creating Web clients and performing tasks to aid Web servers in request processing. We know (and saw earlier in this chapter) that Python can be used to create both simple and complex Web clients.

However, we have yet to explore the creation of Web servers, and that is the focus of this section. If Google Chrome, Mozilla Firefox, Microsoft Internet Explorer, and Opera are among the most popular Web clients, then what are the most common Web servers? They are Apache, ligHTTPD, Microsoft IIS, LiteSpeed Technologies LiteSpeed, and ACME Laboratories thttpd. For situations in which these servers might be overkill for your desired application, Python can be used to create simple yet useful Web servers.

Note that although these servers are simplistic and not meant for production, they can be very useful in providing development servers for your users. Both the Django and Google App Engine development servers are based on the `BaseHTTPServer` module described in the next section.

9.4.1   Simple Web Servers in Python

The base code needed is already available in the Python standard library—you just need to customize it for your needs. To create a Web server, a base server and a *handler* are required.

The base Web server is a boilerplate item—a must-have. Its role is to perform the necessary HTTP communication between client and server. The base server class is (appropriately) named `HTTPServer` and is found in the `BaseHTTPServer` module.

The handler is the piece of software that does the majority of the Web serving. It processes the client request and returns the appropriate file, whether static or dynamically generated. The complexity of the handler determines the complexity of your Web server. The Python Standard Library provides three different handlers.

The most basic, plain, vanilla handler, `BaseHTTPRequestHandler`, is found in the `BaseHTTPServer` module, along with the base Web server. Other than taking a client request, no other handling is implemented at all, so you have to do it all yourself, such as in our `myhttpd.py` server coming up.

The `SimpleHTTPRequestHandler`, available in the `SimpleHTTP-Server` module, builds on `BaseHTTPRequestHandler` by implementing the standard GET and HEAD requests in a fairly straightforward manner. Still nothing sexy, but it gets the simple jobs done.

Finally, we have the `CGIHTTPRequestHandler`, available in the `CGIHTTPServer` module, which takes the `SimpleHTTPRequestHandler` and adds support for POST requests. It has the ability to call common gateway interface (CGI) scripts to perform the requested processing and can send the generated HTML back to the client. In this chapter, we're only going to explore a CGI-processing server; the next chapter will describe to you why CGI is no longer the way the world of the Web works, but you still need to know the concepts.

To simplify the user experience, consistency, and code maintenance, these modules (actually their classes) have been combined into a single module named `server.py` and installed as part of the `http` package in Python 3. (Similarly, the Python 2 `httplib` [HTTP client] module has been renamed to `http.client` in Python 3.) The three modules, their classes, and the Python 3 `http.server` umbrella package are summarized in Table 9-6.

3.x

Table 9-6   Web Server Modules and Classes

Module	Description
BaseHTTPServer[a]	Provides the base Web server and base handler classes, HTTPServer and BaseHTTPRequestHandler, respectively
SimpleHTTPServer[a]	Contains the SimpleHTTPRequestHandler class to perform GET and HEAD requests
CGIHTTPServer[a]	Contains the CGIHTTPRequestHandler class to process POST requests and perform CGI execution
http.server[b]	All three Python 2 modules and classes above combined into a single Python 3 package.

a. Removed in Python 3.0.
b. New in Python 3.0.

Implementing a Simple Base Web server

To be able to understand how the more advanced handlers found in the SimpleHTTPServer and CGIHTTPServer modules work, we will implement simple GET processing for a BaseHTTPRequestHandler. In Example 9-6, we present the code for a fully working Web server, myhttpd.py.

Example 9-6   Simple Web Server (myhttpd.py)

This simple Web server can read GET requests, fetch a Web page (.html file), and return it to the calling client. It uses the BaseHTTPRequestHandler found in BaseHTTPServer and implements the do_GET() method to enable processing of GET requests.

```
1    #!/usr/bin/env python
2
3    from BaseHTTPServer import \
4        BaseHTTPRequestHandler, HTTPServer
5
6    class MyHandler(BaseHTTPRequestHandler):
7        def do_GET(self):
8            try:
9                f = open(self.path[1:], 'r')
10               self.send_response(200)
11               self.send_header('Content-type', 'text/html')
```

```
12                    self.end_headers()
13                    self.wfile.write(f.read())
14                    f.close()
15           except IOError:
16               self.send_error(404,
17                   'File Not Found: %s' % self.path)
18
19   def main():
20       try:
21           server = HTTPServer(('', 80), MyHandler)
22           print 'Welcome to the machine...',
23           print 'Press ^C once or twice to quit.'
24           server.serve_forever()
25       except KeyboardInterrupt:
26           print '^C received, shutting down server'
27           server.socket.close()
28
29   if __name__ == '__main__':
30       main()
```

This server derives from `BaseHTTPRequestHandler` and consists of a single do_GET() method (lines 6–7), which is called when the base server receives a GET request. We attempt to open the path (removing the leading '/') passed in by the client (line 9), and if all goes well, return an "OK" status (200) and forward the downloaded Web page to the user (line 13) via the `wfile` pipe. If the file was not found, it returns a 404 status (lines 15–17).

The main() function simply instantiates our Web server class and invokes it to run our familiar infinite server loop, shutting it down if interrupted by Ctrl+C or similar keystroke. If you have appropriate access and can run this server, you will notice that it displays loggable output, which will look something like this:

```
# myhttpd.py
Welcome to the machine... Press ^C once or twice to quit
localhost - - [26/Aug/2000 03:01:35] "GET /index.html HTTP/1.0" 200 -
localhost - - [26/Aug/2000 03:01:29] code 404, message File Not Found:
x.html
localhost - - [26/Aug/2000 03:01:29] "GET /dummy.html HTTP/1.0" 404 -
localhost - - [26/Aug/2000 03:02:03] "GET /hotlist.htm HTTP/1.0" 200 -
```

Of course, our simple little Web server is so simple, it cannot even process plain text files. We leave that as an exercise for you to undertake (see Exercise 9-10 at the end of this chapter).

More Power, Less Code: A Simple CGI Web Server

The previous example is also weak in that it cannot process CGI requests. BaseHTTPServer is as basic as it gets. One step higher, we have the SimpleHTTPServer. It provides the do_HEAD() and do_GET() methods on your behalf, so you don't have to create either, such as we did with the BaseHTTPServer.

The highest-level (take that with a grain of salt) server provided in the standard library is CGIHTTPServer. In addition to do_HEAD() and do_GET(), it defines do_POST(), with which you can process form data. Because of these amenities, a CGI-capable development server can be created with just two real lines of code (so short we're not even bothering making it a code example in this chapter, because you can just recreate it by typing it up on your computer now):

```
#!/usr/bin/env python
import CGIHTTPServer
CGIHTTPServer.test()
```

Note that we left off the check to quit the server by using Ctrl+C and other fancy output, taking whatever the CGIHTTPServer.test() function gives us, which is a lot. You start the server by just invoking it from your shell. Below is an example of running this code on a PC—it's quite similar to what you'll experience on a POSIX machine:

```
C:\py>python cgihttpd.py
Serving HTTP on 0.0.0.0 port 8000 ...
```

It starts a server by default on port 8000 (but you can change that at run-time by providing a port number as a command-line argument:

```
C:\py\>python cgihttpd.py 8080
Serving HTTP on 0.0.0.0 port 8080 ...
```

To test it out, just make sure that a cgi-bin folder exists (with some CGI Python scripts) at the same level as the script. There's no point in setting up Apache, setting CGI handler prefixes, and all that extra stuff when you just want to test a simple script. We'll show you how to write CGI scripts in Chapter 10, "Web Programming: CGI and WSGI," as well as tell you why you should avoid doing so.

As you can see, it doesn't take much to have a Web server up and running in pure Python. Again, you shouldn't be writing servers all the time. Generally you're creating Web applications that run on Web servers. These server modules are meant only to create servers that are useful during development, regardless of whether you develop applications or Web frameworks.

In production, your live service will instead be using servers that are production-worthy such as Apache, ligHTTPD, or any of the others listed at the beginning of this section. However, we hope this section will have enlightened you such that you realize doing complex tasks can be simplified with the power that Python gives you.

9.5 Related Modules

In Table 9-7, we present a list of modules, some of which are covered in this chapter (and others not), that you might find useful for Web development.

Table 9-7 Web Programming Related Modules

Module/Package	Description
Web Applications	
cgi	Retrieves CGI form data
cgitb[c]	Handles CGI tracebacks
htmllib	Older HTML parser for simple HTML files; HTML- Parser class extends from sgmllib.SGMLParser
HTMLparser[c]	Newer, non-SGML-based parser for HTML and XHTML
htmlentitydefs	HTML general entity definitions
Cookie	Server-side cookies for HTTP state management
cookielib[e]	Cookie-handling classes for HTTP clients
webbrowser[b]	Controller: launches Web documents in a browser
sgmllib	Parses simple SGML files
robotparser[a]	Parses robots.txt files for URL "fetchability" analysis
httplib[a]	Used to create HTTP clients

(Continued)

Table 9-7   Web Programming Related Modules *(Continued)*

Module/Package	Description
Web Applications	
`urllib`	Access servers via URL, other URL-related utilities; `urllib.urlopen()` replaced by `urllib2.urlopen()` in Python 3 as `urllib.request.urlopen()`
`urllib2`; `urllib.request`[g], `urllib.error`[g]	Classes and functions to open (real-world) URLs; broken up into the second two subpackages in Python 3
`urlparse`, `urllib.parse`[g]	Utilities for parsing URL strings; renamed as `urllib.parse` in Python 3.
XML Processing	
`xmllib`	Original simple XML parser (outdated/deprecated)
`xml`[b]	XML package featuring various parsers (some following)
`Xml.sax`[b]	Simple API for XML (SAX) SAX2-compliant XML parser
`xml.dom`[b]	Document Object Model [DOM] XML parser
`xml.etree`[f]	Tree-oriented XML parser based on the Element flexible container object
`xml.parsers.expat`[b]	Interface to the non-validating Expat XML parser
`xmlrpclib`[c]	Client support for XML Remote Procedure Call (RPC) via HTTP
`SimpleXMLRPCServer`[c]	Basic framework for Python XML-RPC servers
`DocXMLRPCServer`[d]	Framework for self-documenting XML-RPC servers

Module/Package	Description
Web Servers	
BaseHTTPServer	Abstract class with which to develop Web servers
SimpleHTTPServer	Serve the simplest HTTP requests (HEAD and GET)
CGIHTTPServer	In addition to serving Web files such as SimpleHTTPServers, can also process CGI (HTTP POST) requests
http.server[g]	New name for the combined package merging together BaseHTTPServer, SimpleHTTPServer, and CGIHTTPServer modules in Python 3
wsgiref[f]	Package defining a standard interface between Web servers and Web applications
Third-Party Packages (not in standard library)	
HTMLgen	CGI helper converts Python objects into valid HTML http://starship.python.net/crew/friedrich/ HTMLgen/html/main.html
BeautifulSoup	HTML and XML parser and screen-scraper http://crummy.com/software/BeautifulSoup
Mechanize	Web-browsing package based on WWW: Mechanize http://wwwsearch.sourceforge.net/mechanize/

a. New in Python 1.6.
b. New in Python 2.0.
c. New in Python 2.2.
d. New in Python 2.3.
e. New in Python 2.4.
f. New in Python 2.5.
g. New in Python 3.0.

9.6   Exercises

9-1. *urllib Module.* Write a program that takes a user-input URL (either a Web page or an FTP file such as http://python.org or ftp://ftp.python.org/pub/python/README), and downloads it to your computer with the same filename (or modified name similar to the original if it is invalid on your system). Web pages (HTTP) should be saved as .htm or .html files, and FTP'd files should retain their extension.

9-2. *urllib Module.* Rewrite the grabWeb.py script of Example 11-4 of *Core Python Programming* or *Core Python Language Fundamentals*, which downloads a Web page and displays the first and last non-blank lines of the resulting HTML file so that you use urlopen() instead of urlretrieve() to process the data directly (as opposed to downloading the entire file first before processing it).

9-3. *URLs and Regular Expressions.* Your browser can save your favorite Web site URLs as a bookmarks HTML file (Mozilla-flavored browsers do this) or as a set of .url files in a "favorites" directory (Internet Explorer does this). Find your browser's method of recording your "hot links" and the location of where and how they are stored. Without altering any of the files, strip the URLs and names of the corresponding Web sites (if given) and produce a two-column list of names and links as output, and then store this data into a disk file. Truncate site names or URLs to keep each line of output within 80 characters in length.

9-4. *URLs, urllib Module, Exceptions, and Regular Expressions.* As a follow-up problem to Exercise 9-3, add code to your script to test each of your favorite links. Report back a list of dead links (and their names) such as Web sites that are no longer active or a Web page that has been removed. Only output and save to disk the still-valid links.

Exercises 9-5 to 9-8 below pertain to *Web server access log files and regular expressions.* Web servers (and their administrators) generally have to maintain an access log file (usually logs/access_log from the main Web, server directory) which tracks requests. Over a period of time, such files become large and either need to be stored or truncated. Why not save only the pertinent information and delete the files to conserve disk space? The exercises below are designed to give you some exercise with regular expressions and how they can be used to help archive and analyze Web server data.

9-5. Count how many of each type of request (GET versus POST) exist in the log file.

9-6. Count the successful page/data downloads. Display all links that resulted in a return code of 200 (OK [no error]) and how many times each link was accessed.

9-7. Count the errors: Show all links that resulted in errors (return codes in the 400s or 500s) and how many times each link was accessed.

9-8. Track IP addresses: for each IP address, output a list of each page/data downloaded and how many times that link was accessed.

9-9. *Web Browser Cookies and Web Site Registration.* The user login registration database you worked on in various chapters (7, 9, 13) of *Core Python Programming* or *Core Python Language Fundamentals* had you creating a pure text-based, menu-driven script. Port it to the Web so that your user-password information should now be site authentication system.

Extra Credit: Familiarize yourself with setting Web browser cookies and maintain a login session for four hours from the last successful login.

9-10. *Creating Web Servers.* Our code for myhttpd.py (Example 9-6) is only able to read HTML files and return them to the calling client. Add support for plain text files with the .txt ending. Be sure that you return the correct MIME type of "text/plain."

Extra Credit: Add support for JPEG files ending with either .jpg or .jpeg and having a MIME type of "image/jpeg."

Exercises 9-11 through 9-14 require you to update Example 9-3, crawl.py, the Web crawler.

9-11. *Web Clients.* Port crawl.py so that it uses either HTMLParser, BeautifulSoup, html5lib, or lxml parsing systems.

9-12. *Web Clients.* URLs given as input to crawl.py must have the leading "http://" protocol indicator and top-level URLs must contain a trailing slash, for example, http://www.prenhall-professional.com/. Make crawl.py more robust by allowing the user to input just the hostname (without the protocol part [make it assume HTTP]) and also make the trailing slash optional. For example, www.prenhallprofessional.com should now be acceptable input.

9-13. *Web Clients.* Update the `crawl.py` script to also download links that use the `ftp:` scheme. All `mailto:` links are ignored by `crawl.py`. Add support to ensure that it also ignores `telnet:`, `news:`, `gopher:`, and `about:` links.

9-14. *Web Clients.* The `crawl.py` script only downloads `.html` files via links found in Web pages at the same site and does not handle/save images that are also valid "files" for those pages. It also does not handle servers that are susceptible to URLs that are missing the trailing slash (/). Add a pair of classes to `crawl.py` to deal with these problems.

A `My404UrlOpener` class should subclass `urllib.Fancy URLOpener` and consist of a single method, `http_error_404()` which determines if a 404 error was reached because of a URL without a trailing slash. If so, it adds the slash and retries the request again (and only once). If it still fails, return a real 404 error. You must set `urllib._urlopener` with an instance of this class so that `urllib` uses it.

Create another class called `LinkImageParser`, which derives from `htmllib.HTMLParser`. This class should contain a constructor to call the base class constructor as well as initialize a list for the image files parsed from Web pages. The `handle_image()` method should be overridden to add image filenames to the image list (instead of discarding them like the current base class method does).

The final set of exercises pertain to the `parse_links.py` file, shown earlier in this chapter as Example 9-4.

9-15. *Command-line Arguments.* Add command-line arguments to let the user see output from one or more parsers (instead of just all of them [which could be the default]).

9-16. *lxml Parser.* Download and install `lxml`, and then add support for `lxml` to `parse_links.py`.

9-17. *Markup Parsers.* Subsitute each parser into the crawler replacing `htmllib.HTMLParser`.

a) `HTMLParser.HTMLParser`

b) `html5lib`

c) `BeaufifulSoup`

d) `lxml`

9-18. *Refactoring.* Change the `output()` function to be able to support other forms of output.

   a) Writing to a file

   b) Sending to another process (i.e., writing to a socket)

9-19. *Pythonic Coding.* In the Line-by-Line Explanation of `parse_links.py`, we expanded `simpleBS()` from a less-readable one-liner to a block of properly formatted Python code. Do the same thing with `fasterBS()` and `html5libparse()`.

9-20. *Performance and Profiling.* Earlier, we described how `fasterBS()` performs better than `simpleBS()`. Use `timeit` to show it runs faster, and then find a Python memory tool online to show it saves memory. Describe what the memory profiler tool is and where you found it. Do any of the three standard library profilers (`profile`, `hotshot`, `cProfile`) show memory usage information?

9-21. *Best Practices.* In `htmlparser()`, suppose that we didn't like the thought of having to create a blank list and having to call its `append()` method repeatedly to build the list; instead, you wanted to use a list comprehension to replace lines 35–39 with the following single line of code:

```
self.data = [v for k, v in attrs if k == 'href']
```

Is this a valid substitution? In other words, could we make this change and still have it all execute correctly? Why (or why not)?

9-22. *Data Manipulation.* In `parse_links.py`, we sort the URLs alphabetically (actually lexicographically). However, this might not be the best way to organize links:

http://python.org/psf/

http://python.org/search

http://roundup.sourceforge.net/

http://sourceforge.net/projects/mysql-python

http://twistedmatrix.com/trac/

http://wiki.python.org/moin/

http://wiki.python.org/moin/CgiScripts

http://www.python.org/

Instead, a sort by domain name might make more sense:

http://python.org/psf/

http://python.org/search

http://wiki.python.org/moin/

http://wiki.python.org/moin/CgiScripts

http://www.python.org/

http://roundup.sourceforge.net/

http://sourceforge.net/projects/mysql-python

http://twistedmatrix.com/trac/

Give your script the ability to sort by domain in addition to the alpha/ lexicographic sort.

10

Web Programming: CGI and WSGI

[The] benefits of WSGI are primarily for Web framework authors and Web server authors, not Web application authors. This is not an application API, it's a framework-to-server glue API.
—Phillip J. Eby, August 2004

In this chapter...

- Introduction
- Helping Web Servers Process Client Data
- Building CGI Applications
- Using Unicode with CGI
- Advanced CGI
- Introduction to WSGI
- Real-World Web Development
- Related Modules

10.1   Introduction

This introductory chapter on Web programming will give you a quick and broad overview of the kinds of things you can do with Python on the Internet, from Web surfing to creating user feedback forms, from recognizing URLs to generating dynamic Web page output. We'll first explore the *common gateway interface* (CGI) then discuss the *web server gateway interface* (WSGI).

10.2   Helping Web Servers Process Client Data

In this section, we'll introduce you to CGI, what it means, why it exists, and how it works in relation to Web servers. We'll then show you how to use Python to create CGI applications.

10.2.1   Introduction to CGI

The Web was initially developed to be a global online repository or archive of documents (mostly educational and research-oriented). Such pieces of information generally come in the form of static text and usually in HTML.

HTML is not as much a language as it is a text formatter, indicating changes in font types, sizes, and styles. The main feature of HTML is in its hypertext capability. This refers to the ability to designate certain text (usually highlighted in some fashion) or even graphic elements as *links* that point to other "documents" or locations on the Internet and Web that are related in context to the original. Such a document can be accessed by a simple mouse click or other user selection mechanism. These (static) HTML documents live on the Web server and are sent to clients when requested.

As the Internet and Web services evolved, there grew a need to process user input. Online retailers needed to be able to take individual orders, and online banks and search engine portals needed to create accounts for individual users. Thus fill-out forms were invented; they were the only way a Web site could get specific information from users (until Java applets came along). This, in turn, required that the HTML be generated on the fly, for each client submitting user-specific data.

But, Web servers are only really good at one thing: getting a user request for a file and returning that file (i.e., an HTML file) to the client. They do not have the "brains" to be able to deal with user-specific data such as those which come from fields. Given this is not their responsibility, Web servers farm out such requests to external applications which create the dynamically generated HTML that is returned to the client.

The entire process begins when the Web server receives a client request (i.e., GET or POST) and calls the appropriate application. It then waits for the resulting HTML—meanwhile, the client also waits. Once the application has completed, it passes the dynamically generated HTML back to the server, which then (finally) forwards it back to the user. This process of the server receiving a form, contacting an external application, and receiving and returning the HTML takes place through the CGI. An overview of how CGI works is presented in Figure 10-1, which shows you the execution and data flow, step-by-step, from when a user submits a form until the resulting Web page is returned.

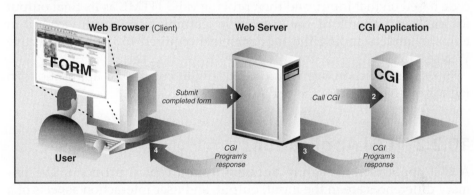

Figure 10-1 Overview of how CGI works. CGI represents the interaction between a Web server and the application that is required to process a user's form and generate the dynamic HTML that is eventually returned.

Forms input on the client and sent to a Web server can include processing and perhaps some form of storage in a back-end database. Just keep in mind that any time a Web page contains items that require user input (text fields, radio buttons, etc.) and/or a Submit button or image, it most likely involves some sort of CGI activity.

CGI applications that create the HTML are usually written in one of many higher-level programming languages that have the ability to accept user data, process it, and then return HTML back to the server. Before we take a look at CGI, we have to issue the caveat that the typical production Web application is no longer being implemented in CGI.

Because of its significant limitations and limited ability to allow Web servers to process an abundant number of simultaneous clients, CGI is a dinosaur. Mission-critical Web services rely on compiled languages like C/C++ to scale. A modern-day Web server is typically composed of Apache and integrated components for database access (MySQL or PostgreSQL), Java (Tomcat), PHP, and various modules for dynamic languages such as Python or Ruby, and secure sockets layer (SSL)/security. However, if you are working on small personal Web sites or those of small organizations and do not need the power and complexity required by mission critical Web services, CGI is a quick way to get started. It can also be used for testing.

Furthermore, there are a good number of Web application development frameworks out there as well as content management systems, all of which make building CGI a relic of past. However, beneath all the fluff and abstraction, they must still, in the end, follow the same model that CGI originally provided, and that is being able to take user input, execute code based on that input, and then provide valid HTML as its final output for the client. Therefore, the exercise in learning CGI is well worth it in terms of understanding the fundamentals required to develop effective Web services.

In this next section, we will look at how to create CGI applications in Python, with the help of the cgi module.

10.2.2   CGI Applications

A CGI application is slightly different from a typical program. The primary differences are in the input, output, and user interaction aspects of a computer program. When a CGI script starts, it needs to retrieve the user-supplied form data, but it has to obtain this data from the Web client, not a user on the server computer or a disk file. This is usually known as *the request*.

The output differs in that any data sent to standard output will be sent back to the connected Web client rather than to the screen, GUI window, or disk file. This is known as *the response*. The data sent back must be a set of valid headers followed by HTML-tagged data. If it is not and the Web client is a browser, an error (specifically, an Internal Server Error) will occur because Web clients understand only valid HTTP data (i.e., MIME headers and HTML).

Finally, as you can probably guess, there is no user interaction with the script. All communication occurs among the Web client (on behalf of a user), the Web server, and the CGI application.

10.2.3   The cgi Module

There is one primary class in the cgi module that does all the work: the FieldStorage class. This class reads in all the pertinent user information from the Web client (via the Web server); thus, it should be instantiated when a Python CGI script begins. Once it has been instantiated, it will consist of a dictionary-like object that contains a set of key-value pairs. The keys are the names of the input items that were passed in via the form. The values contain the corresponding data.

Values can be one of three objects. The first are FieldStorage objects (instances). The second are instances of a similar class called MiniField Storage, which is used in cases for which no file uploads or multiple-part form data is involved. MiniFieldStorage instances contain only the key-value pair of the name and the data. Lastly, they can be a list of such objects. This occurs when a form contains more than one input item with the same field name.

For simple Web forms, you will usually find all MiniFieldStorage instances. All of our examples that follow pertain only to this general case.

10.2.4   The cgitb Module

As we mentioned earlier, a valid response back to the Web server (which would then forward it to the user/browser) must contain valid HTTP headers and HTML-tagged data. Have you thought about the returned data if your CGI application crashes? What happens when you run a Python script that results in an error? That's right: a traceback occurs. Would the text of a traceback be considered as valid HTTP headers or HTML? No.

A Web server receiving a response it doesn't understand will just throw up its hands and give up, returning a "500 error." The 500 is an HTTP response code that means an internal Web server error has occurred, most likely from the application that is being executed. The output on the browser doesn't aid the developer either, as the screen is either blank or shows "Internal Server Error," or something similar.

When our Python programs were running on the command-line or in an *integrated development environment* (IDE), errors resulted in a traceback, upon which we could take action. Not so in the browser. What we really want is to see the Web application's traceback on the browser screen, not "Internal Server Error." This is where the cgitb module comes in.

To enable a dump of tracebacks, all we need to do is to insert the following import and call in our CGI applications:

```
import cgitb
cgitb.enable()
```

You'll have plenty of opportunity as we explore CGI for the first half of this chapter. For now, just leave these two lines out as we undertake some simple examples. First, I want you to see the "Internal Server Error" messages and debug them the hard way. Once you realize how the server's not throwing you a bone, you'll add these two lines religiously, on your own.

10.3   Building CGI Applications

In this section of the chapter, we go hands-on, showing you how to set up a Web server, followed by a step-by-step breakdown of how to create a CGI application in Python. We start with a simple script, then build on it incrementally. The practices you learn here can be used for developing applications using any Web framework.

10.3.1   Setting Up a Web Server

To experiment with CGI development in Python, you need to first install a Web server, configure it for handling Python CGI requests, and then give the Web server access to your CGI scripts. Some of these tasks might require assistance from your system administrator.

Production Servers

If you want a real Web server, you will likely download and install Apache, ligHTTPD, or thttpd. For Apache, there are various plug-ins or modules for handling Python CGI, but they are not required for our examples. You might want to install those if you are planning on "going live" to the world with your service. But even this might be overkill.

Developer Servers

For learning purposes or for simple Web sites, it might suffice to use the Web servers that come with Python. In Chapter 9, "Web Clients and Servers," you were exposed to creating and configuring simple Python-based Web servers. Our examples in this chapter are simpler, use only Python's CGI Web server.

If you want to start up this most basic Web server, execute it directly in Python 2.x, as follows:

2.x

```
$ python -m CGIHTTPServer [port]
```

This won't work as easily in Python 3 because all three Web servers and their handlers have been merged into a single module (`http.server`), with one base server and three request handler classes (`BaseHTTPRequestHandler`, `SimpleHTTPRequestHandler`, and `CGIHTTPRequestHandler`).

3.x

If you don't provide the optional port number for the server, it starts at port 8000 by default. Also, the -m option is new in version 2.4. If you are using an older version of Python or want to see alternative ways of running it, here are your options:

2.4

- Executing the module from a command shell

    This method is somewhat troublesome because you need to know where the `CGIHTTPServer.py` file is physically located. On Windows-based PCs, this is easier because the typical installation folder is C:\Python2X:

    ```
    C:\>python C:\Python27\Lib\CGIHTTPServer.py
    Serving HTTP on 0.0.0.0 port 8000 ...
    ```

    On POSIX systems, you need to do a bit more sleuthing:

    ```
    >>> import sys, CGIHTTPServer
    >>> sys.modules['CGIHTTPServer']
    <module 'CGIHTTPServer' from '/usr/local/lib/python2.7/
        CGIHTTPServer.py'>
    >>>^D
    $ python /usr/local/lib/python2.7/CGIHTTPServer.py
    Serving HTTP on 0.0.0.0 port 8000 ...
    ```

- Use the -c option

    Using the -c option you can run a string consisting of Python statements. Therefore, import `CGIHTTPServer` and execute the `test()` function, use the following:

    ```
    $ python -c "import CGIHTTPServer; CGIHTTPServer.test()"
    Serving HTTP on 0.0.0.0 port 8000 ...
    ```

    Because `CGIHTTPServer` is merged into `http.server` in version 3.x, you can issue the equivalent call (by using, for example, Python 3.2) as the following:

    3.x

    ```
    $ python3.2 -c "from http.server import
    CGIHTTPRequestHandler,test;test(CGIHTTPRequestHandler)"
    ```

- Create a quick script

  Take the `import` and `test()` call from the previous option and insert it into an arbitrary file, say `cgihttpd.py` file (Python 2 or 3). For Python 3, because there is no `CGIHTTPServer.py` module to execute, the only way to get your server to start from the command-line on a port other than 8000 is to use this script:

```
$ python3.2 cgihttpd.py 8080
Serving HTTP on 0.0.0.0 port 8080 ...
```

Any of these four techniques will start a Web server on port 8000 (or whatever you chose) on your current computer from the current directory. Then you can just create a `cgi-bin` directory right under the directory from which you started the server and put your Python CGI scripts there. Put some HTML files in that directory and perhaps some .py CGI scripts in `cgi-bin`, and you are ready to "surf" directly to this Web site with addresses looking something like these:

http://localhost:8000/friends.htm

http://localhost:8080/cgi-bin/friendsB.py

Be sure to start up your server where there is a `cgi-bin` directory and ensure that your .py files are there; otherwise, the development server will return your Python files as static text rather than executing them.

10.3.2   Creating the Form Page

In Example 10-1, we present the code for a simple Web form, `friends.htm`. As you can see in the HTML, the form contains two input variables: `person` and `howmany`. The values of these two fields will be passed to our CGI script, `friendsA.py`.

You will notice in our example that we install our CGI script into the default `cgi-bin` directory (see the `ACTION` link) on the local host. (If this information does not correspond with your development environment, update the form action before attempting to test the Web page and CGI script.) Also, because a METHOD subtag is missing from the form action, all requests will be of the default type, GET. We choose the GET method because we do not have very many form fields, and also, we want our query string to show up in the Location (a.k.a. "Address," "Go To") bar so that you can see what URL is sent to the server.

Example 10-1   Static Form Web Page (`friends.htm`)

This HTML file presents a form to the user with an empty field for the user's name and a set of radio buttons from which the user can choose.

```
1    <HTML><HEAD><TITLE>
2    Friends CGI Demo (static screen)
3    </TITLE></HEAD>
4    <BODY><H3>Friends list for: <I>NEW USER</I></H3>
5    <FORM ACTION="/cgi-bin/friendsA.py">
6    <B>Enter your Name:</B>
7    <INPUT TYPE=text NAME=person VALUE="NEW USER" SIZE=15>
8    <P><B>How many friends do you have?</B>
9    <INPUT TYPE=radio NAME=howmany VALUE="0" CHECKED> 0
10   <INPUT TYPE=radio NAME=howmany VALUE="10"> 10
11   <INPUT TYPE=radio NAME=howmany VALUE="25"> 25
12   <INPUT TYPE=radio NAME=howmany VALUE="50"> 50
13   <INPUT TYPE=radio NAME=howmany VALUE="100"> 100
14   <P><INPUT TYPE=submit></FORM></BODY></HTML>
```

Figure 10-2 and 10-3 show the screen that is rendered by `friends.htm` in clients running on both Mac and Windows.

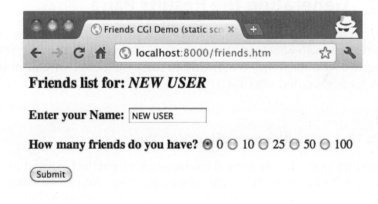

Figure 10-2 The Friends form page in Chrome "incognito mode," on Mac OS X.

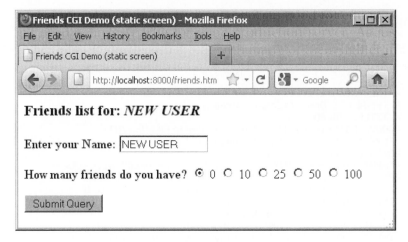

Figure 10-3 The Friends form page in Firefox 6 on Windows.

10.3.3   Generating the Results Page

The input is entered by the user when the Submit button is clicked. (Alternatively, the user can also press the Return or Enter key within the text field to invoke the same action.) When this occurs, the script in Example 10-2, friendsA.py, is executed via CGI.

Example 10-2   Results Screen CGI code (friendsA.py)

This CGI script grabs the person and howmany fields from the form and uses that data to create the dynamically generated results screen. Add parentheses to the **print** statement on line 17 for the Python 3 version, friendsA3.py (not displayed here). Both are available at corepython.com.

```
1    #!/usr/bin/env python
2
3    import cgi
4
5    reshtml = '''Content-Type: text/html\n
6    <HTML><HEAD><TITLE>
7    Friends CGI Demo (dynamic screen)
8    </TITLE></HEAD>
9    <BODY><H3>Friends list for: <I>%s</I></H3>
10   Your name is: <B>%s</B><P>
```

```
11    You have <B>%s</B> friends.
12    </BODY></HTML>'''
13
14    form = cgi.FieldStorage()
15    who = form['person'].value
16    howmany = form['howmany'].value
17    print reshtml % (who, who, howmany)
```

This script contains all the programming power to read the form input and process it as well as return the resulting HTML page back to the user. All the "real" work in this script takes place in only four lines of Python code (lines 14–17).

The form variable is our FieldStorage instance, containing the values of the person and howmany fields. We read these into the Python who and howmany variables, respectively. The reshtml variable contains the general body of HTML text to return, with a few fields filled in dynamically, using the data just read in from the form.

 CORE TIP: HTTP headers separate from HTML

Here's something that always catches beginners: when sending results back via a CGI script, the CGI script must return the appropriate HTTP headers *first* before any HTML. Furthermore, to distinguish between these headers and the resulting HTML, there must be one blank line (a pair of NEWLINE characters) inserted between both sets of data, as in line 5 of our friendsA.py example (one explicit \n plus the implicit one at the end of line 5). You'll notice this in the other examples, too.

One possible resulting screen appears in Figure 10-4, (assuming the user typed in "Annalee Lenday" as the name and clicked the "25 friends" radio button).

If you are a Web site producer, you might be thinking, "Gee, wouldn't it be nice if I could automatically capitalize this person's name, especially if she forgot?" With Python CGI, you can accomplish this easily. (And we shall do so soon!)

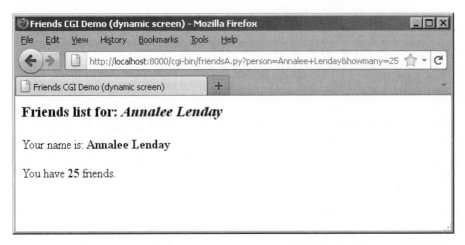

Figure 10-4 The Friends results page after the name and number of friends has been submitted.

Notice how on a GET request that our form variables and their values are added to the form action URL in the Address bar. Also, did you observe that the title for the `friends.htm` page has the word "static" in it, whereas the output screen from `friends.py` has the word "dynamic" in its title? We did that for a reason: to indicate that the `friends.htm` file is a static text file while the results page is dynamically generated. In other words, the HTML for the results page did not exist on disk as a text file; rather, it was generated by our CGI script, which returned it as if it *were* a local file.

In our next example, we bypass static files altogether by updating our CGI script to be somewhat more multifaceted.

10.3.4   Generating Form and Results Pages

We obsolete `friends.html` and merge it into `friendsB.py`. The script will now generate both the form page as well as the results page. But how can we tell which page to generate? Well, if there is form data being sent to us, that means that we should be creating a results page. If we do not get any information at all, that tells us that we should generate a form page for the user to enter his data. Our new `friendsB.py` script is presented in Example 10-3.

Example 10-3   Generating Form and Results Pages (friendsB.py)

Both friends.htm and friendsA.py are merged into friendsB.py. The
resulting script can now output both form and results pages as dynamically
generated HTML and has the smarts to know which page to output. To port this
to the Python 3 version, friendsB3.py, you need to add parentheses to both
print statements and change the form action to friendsB3.py.

```
1   #!/usr/bin/env python
2
3   import cgi
4
5   header = 'Content-Type: text/html\n\n'
6
7   formhtml = '''<HTML><HEAD><TITLE>
8   Friends CGI Demo</TITLE></HEAD>
9   <BODY><H3>Friends list for: <I>NEW USER</I></H3>
10  <FORM ACTION="/cgi-bin/friendsB.py">
11  <B>Enter your Name:</B>
12  <INPUT TYPE=hidden NAME=action VALUE=edit>
13  <INPUT TYPE=text NAME=person VALUE="NEW USER" SIZE=15>
14  <P><B>How many friends do you have?</B>
15  %s
16  <P><INPUT TYPE=submit></FORM></BODY></HTML>'''
17
18  fradio = '<INPUT TYPE=radio NAME=howmany VALUE="%s" %s> %s\n'
19
20  def showForm():
21      friends = []
22      for i in (0, 10, 25, 50, 100):
23          checked = ''
24          if i == 0:
25              checked = 'CHECKED'
26          friends.append(fradio % (str(i), checked, str(i)))
27
28      print '%s%s' % (header, formhtml % ''.join(friends))
29
30  reshtml = '''<HTML><HEAD><TITLE>
31  Friends CGI Demo</TITLE></HEAD>
32  <BODY><H3>Friends list for: <I>%s</I></H3>
33  Your name is: <B>%s</B><P>
34  You have <B>%s</B> friends.
35  </BODY></HTML>'''
36
37  def doResults(who, howmany):
38      print header + reshtml % (who, who, howmany)
39
40  def process():
41      form = cgi.FieldStorage()
```

(Continued)

Example 10-3   Generating Form and Results Pages (`friendsB.py`)
                    (Continued)

```
42       if 'person' in form:
43           who = form['person'].value
44       else:
45           who = 'NEW USER'
46
47       if 'howmany' in form:
48           howmany = form['howmany'].value
49       else:
50           howmany = 0
51
52       if 'action' in form:
53           doResults(who, howmany)
54       else:
55           showForm()
56
57   if __name__ == '__main__':
58       process()
```

Line-by-Line Explanation

Lines 1–5

In addition to the usual startup and module import lines, we separate the HTTP MIME header from the rest of the HTML body because we will use it for both types of pages (form page and results page) returned and we don't want to duplicate the text. We will add this header string to the corresponding HTML body when it's time for output to occur.

Lines 7–28

All of this code is related to the now-integrated `friends.htm` form page in our CGI script. We have a variable for the form page text, `formhtml`, and we also have a string to build the list of radio buttons, `fradio`. We could have duplicated this radio button HTML text as it is in `friends.htm`, but we wanted to show how we could use Python to generate more dynamic output—see the **for** loop in lines 22–26.

The `showForm()` function has the responsibility of generating a form for user input. It builds a set of text for the radio buttons, merges those lines of HTML into the main body of `formhtml`, prepends the header to the form, and then returns the entire collection of data back to the client by sending the entire string to standard output.

There are a couple of interesting things to note about this code. The first is the "hidden" variable in the form called `action`, containing the value edit on line 12. This field is the only way we can tell which screen to display (i.e., the form page or the results page). We will see this field come into play in lines 53–56.

Also, observe that we set the 0 radio button as the default by "checking" it within the loop that generates all the buttons. This will also allow us to update the layout of the radio buttons and/or their values on a single line of code (line 18) rather than over multiple lines of text. It will also offer some more flexibility in letting the logic determine which radio button is checked—see the next update to our script, friendsC.py, coming up.

Now you might be thinking, "Why do we need an action variable when I could just as well be checking for the presence of person or howmany?" That is a valid question, because yes, you could have just used person or howmany in this situation.

However, the action variable is a more conspicuous presence, insofar as its name as well as what it does—the code is easier to understand. The person and howmany variables are used for their values, whereas the action variable is used as a flag.

The other reason for creating action is that we will be using it again to help us determine which page to generate. In particular, we will need to display a form *with* the presence of a person variable (rather than a results page). This will break your code if you are solely relying on there being a person variable.

Lines 30–38

The code to display the results page is practically identical to that of friendsA.py.

Lines 40–55

Because there are different pages that can result from this one script, we created an overall process() function to get the form data and decide which action to take. The main portion of process() will also look familiar to the main body of code in friendsA.py. There are two major differences, however.

Because the script might or might not be getting the expected fields (invoking the script the first time to generate a form page, for example, will not pass any fields to the server), we need to "bracket" our retrieval of the form fields with **if** statements to check if they are even there. Also, we mentioned the action field above, which helps us decide which page to bring up. The code that performs this determination is in lines 52–55.

Figure 10-5 illustrates that the auto-generated form looks identical to the static form presented in Figure 10-2; however, instead of a link ending in .html, it ends in .py. If we enter "Cynthia Gilbert" for the name and select 50 friends, clicking the **Submit** button results in what is shown in Figure 10-6.

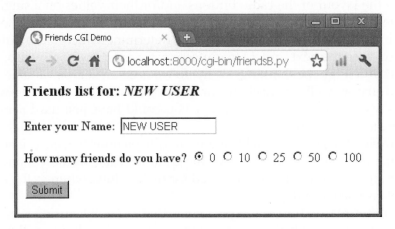

Figure 10-5 The autogenerated Friends form page in Chrome on Windows.

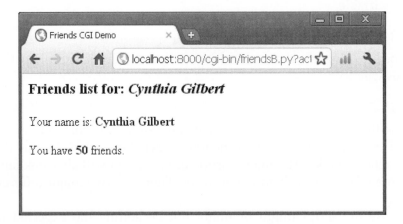

Figure 10-6 The Friends results page after submitting the name and friend count.

Note that a static friends.htm does not show up in the URL because friendsB.py is responsible for both the form and results pages.

10.3.5 Fully Interactive Web Sites

Our final example will complete the circle. As in the past, a user enters her information from the form page. We then process the data and output a results page. This time, however, we will add a link to the results page that will allow the user to go *back* to the form page, but rather than presenting a blank form, we will fill in the data that the user has already provided. We will also add some error processing to give you an example of how it can be accomplished. The new `friendsC.py` is shown in Example 10-4.

Example 10-4   Full User Interaction and Error Processing (`friendsC.py`)

By adding a link to return to the form page with information already provided, we have come full circle, giving the user a fully interactive Web surfing experience. Our application also now performs simple error checking, which notifies the user if no radio button was selected.

```
1    #!/usr/bin/env python
2
3    import cgi
4    from urllib import quote_plus
5
6    header = 'Content-Type: text/html\n\n'
7    url = '/cgi-bin/friendsC.py'
8
9    errhtml = '''<HTML><HEAD><TITLE>
10   Friends CGI Demo</TITLE></HEAD>
11   <BODY><H3>ERROR</H3>
12   <B>%s</B><P>
13   <FORM><INPUT TYPE=button VALUE=Back
14   ONCLICK="window.history.back()"></FORM>
15   </BODY></HTML>'''
16
17   def showError(error_str):
18     print header + errhtml % error_str
19
20   formhtml = '''<HTML><HEAD><TITLE>
21   Friends CGI Demo</TITLE></HEAD>
22   <BODY><H3>Friends list for: <I>%s</I></H3>
23   <FORM ACTION="%s">
24   <B>Enter your Name:</B>
25   <INPUT TYPE=hidden NAME=action VALUE=edit>
26   <INPUT TYPE=text NAME=person VALUE="%s" SIZE=15>
27   <P><B>How many friends do you have?</B>
28   %s
29   <P><INPUT TYPE=submit></FORM></BODY></HTML>'''
30
```

(Continued)

Example 10-4   Full User Interaction and Error Processing (`friendsC.py`)
(*Continued*)

```
31  fradio = '<INPUT TYPE=radio NAME=howmany VALUE="%s" %s> %s\n'
32
33  def showForm(who, howmany):
34      friends = []
35      for i in (0, 10, 25, 50, 100):
36          checked = ''
37          if str(i) == howmany:
38              checked = 'CHECKED'
39          friends.append(fradio % (str(i), checked, str(i)))
40      print '%s%s' % (header, formhtml % (
41          who, url, who, ''.join(friends)))
42
43  reshtml = '''<HTML><HEAD><TITLE>
44  Friends CGI Demo</TITLE></HEAD>
45  <BODY><H3>Friends list for: <I>%s</I></H3>
46  Your name is: <B>%s</B><P>
47  You have <B>%s</B> friends.
48  <P>Click <A HREF="%s">here</A> to edit your data again.
49  </BODY></HTML>'''
50
51  def doResults(who, howmany):
52      newurl = url + '?action=reedit&person=%s&howmany=%s'%\
53          (quote_plus(who), howmany)
54      print header + reshtml % (who, who, howmany, newurl)
55
56  def process():
57      error = ''
58      form = cgi.FieldStorage()
59
60      if 'person' in form:
61          who = form['person'].value.title()
62      else:
63          who = 'NEW USER'
64
65      if 'howmany' in form:
66          howmany = form['howmany'].value
67      else:
68          if 'action' in form and \
69                  form['action'].value == 'edit':
70              error = 'Please select number of friends.'
71          else:
72              howmany = 0
73
74      if not error:
75          if 'action' in form and \
76                  form['action'].value != 'reedit':
77              doResults(who, howmany)
78          else:
79              showForm(who, howmany)
80      else:
81              showError(error)
82
83  if __name__ == '__main__':
84      process()
```

`friendsC.py` is not too unlike `friendsB.py`. We invite you to compare the differences; we present a brief summary of the major changes for you here.

Abridged Line-by-Line Explanation

Line 7

We take the URL out of the form because we now need it in two places, the results page being the new customer in addition to the user input form.

Lines 9–18, 68–70, 74–81

All of these lines deal with the new feature of having an error screen. If the user does not select a radio button indicating the number of friends, the `howmany` field is not passed to the server. In such a case, the `showError()` function returns the error page to the user.

The error page also features a JavaScript "Back" button. Because buttons are input types, we need a form, but no action is needed because we are just going back one page in the browsing history. Although our script currently supports (a.k.a. tests for) only one type of error, we still use a generic `error` variable in case we want to continue development of this script to add more error detection in the future.

Lines 26–28, 37–40, 47, and 51–54

One goal for this script is to create a meaningful link back to the form page from the results page. This is implemented as a link to give the user the ability to return to a form page to update or edit the data he entered. The new form page makes sense only if it contains information pertaining to the data that has already been entered by the user. (It is frustrating for users to re-enter their information from scratch!)

To accomplish this, we need to embed the current values into the updated form. In line 26, we add a value for the name. This value will be inserted into the name field, if given. Obviously, it will be blank on the initial form page. In Lines 37–38, we set the radio box corresponding to the number of friends currently chosen. Finally, on lines 48 and the updated `doResults()` function on lines 52–54, we create the link with all the existing information, which returns the user to our modified form page.

Line 61

Finally, we added a simple feature that we thought would be a nice aesthetic touch. In the screens for `friendsA.py` and `friendsB.py`, the text entered by the user as her name is taken verbatim. If you look at the equivalent line in friendsA.py and friendsB.py, you'll notice that we leave the names alone from form to display. This means that if users enter names in all lowercase, they will show up in all lowercase, etc. So, we added a call to `str.title()` to automatically capitalize a user's name. The `title()` string method titlecases the passed-in string. This might or might not be a desired feature, but we thought that we would share it with you so that you know that such functionality exists.

Figures 10-7 through 10-10 show the progression of user interaction with this CGI form and script.

In Figure 10-7, we invoke `friendsC.py` to bring up the form page. We enter a name "foo bar," but deliberately avoid checking any of the radio buttons. The resulting error after submitting the form can be seen in Figure 10-8.

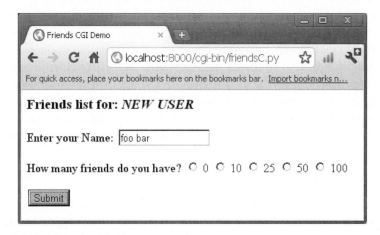

Figure 10-7 The Friends initial form page without friends selection.

Figure 10-8 An error page appears due to invalid user input.

We click the Back button, click the 50 radio button, and then resubmit our form. The results page, shown in Figure 10-9, is also familiar, but now has an extra link at the bottom, which will take us back to the form page. The only difference between the new form page and our original is that all the data filled in by the user is now set as the default settings, meaning that the values are already available in the form. (Hopefully you'll notice the automatic name capitalization too.) We can see this in Figure 10-10.

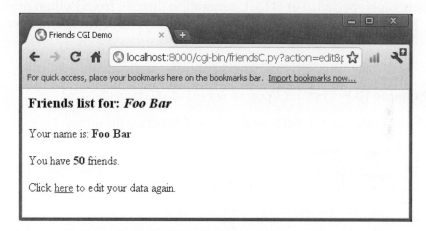

Figure 10-9 The Friends results page with valid input.

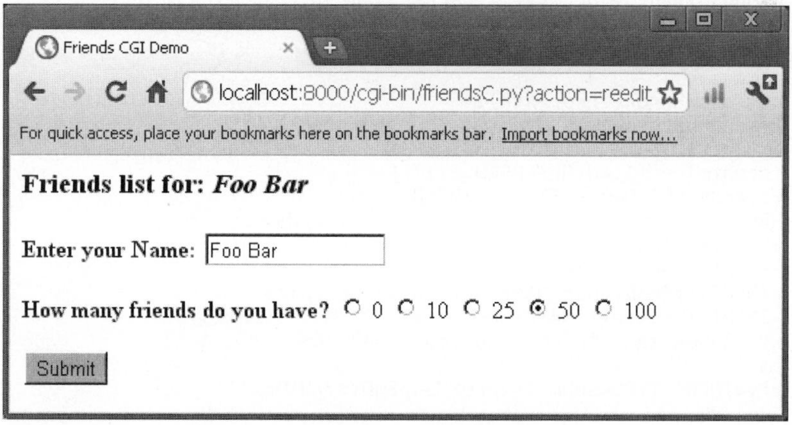

Figure 10-10 The Friends form page redux.

Now the user is able to make changes to either of the fields and resubmit her form.

As the developer, however, you will no doubt begin to notice that as our forms and data become more complicated, so does the generated HTML, especially for complex results pages. If you ever get to a point where generating the HTML text is interfering with your application, you might consider trying Python packages, such as HTMLgen, xist, or HSC. These third-party tools specialize in HTML generation directly from Python objects.

Finally, in Example 10-5, we want to show you the Python 3 equivalent, friendsC3.py.

Example 10-5   Python 3 port of friendsC.py (friendsC3.py)

The equivalent of friendsC.py in Python 3. What are the differences?

```
1    #!/usr/bin/env python
2
3    import cgi
4    from urllib.parse import quote_plus
5
6    header = 'Content-Type: text/html\n\n'
7    url = '/cgi-bin/friendsC3.py'
8
9    errhtml = '''<HTML><HEAD><TITLE>
10   Friends CGI Demo</TITLE></HEAD>
11   <BODY><H3>ERROR</H3>
12   <B>%s</B><P>
13   <FORM><INPUT TYPE=button VALUE=Back
14   ONCLICK="window.history.back()"></FORM>
15   </BODY></HTML>'''
16
17   def showError(error_str):
18       print(header + errhtml % (error_str))
19
20   formhtml = '''<HTML><HEAD><TITLE>
21   Friends CGI Demo</TITLE></HEAD>
22   <BODY><H3>Friends list for: <I>%s</I></H3>
23   <FORM ACTION="%s">
24   <B>Enter your Name:</B>
25   <INPUT TYPE=hidden NAME=action VALUE=edit>
26   <INPUT TYPE=text NAME=person VALUE="%s" SIZE=15>
27   <P><B>How many friends do you have?</B>
28   %s
29   <P><INPUT TYPE=submit></FORM></BODY></HTML>'''
30
```

```
31   fradio = '<INPUT TYPE=radio NAME=howmany VALUE="%s" %s> %s\n'
32
33   def showForm(who, howmany):
34       friends = []
35       for i in (0, 10, 25, 50, 100):
36           checked = ''
37           if str(i) == howmany:
38               checked = 'CHECKED'
39           friends.append(fradio % (str(i), checked, str(i)))
40       print('%s%s' % (header, formhtml % (
41           who, url, who, ''.join(friends))))
42
43   reshtml = '''<HTML><HEAD><TITLE>
44   Friends CGI Demo</TITLE></HEAD>
45   <BODY><H3>Friends list for: <I>%s</I></H3>
46   Your name is: <B>%s</B><P>
47   You have <B>%s</B> friends.
48   <P>Click <A HREF="%s">here</A> to edit your data again.
49   </BODY></HTML>'''
50
51   def doResults(who, howmany):
52       newurl = url + '?action=reedit&person=%s&howmany=%s' % (
53           quote_plus(who), howmany)
54       print(header + reshtml % (who, who, howmany, newurl))
55
56   def process():
57       error = ''
58       form = cgi.FieldStorage()
59
60       if 'person' in form:
61           who = form['person'].value.title()
62       else:
63           who = 'NEW USER'
64
65       if 'howmany' in form:
66           howmany = form['howmany'].value
67       else:
68           if 'action' in form and \
69                   form['action'].value == 'edit':
70               error = 'Please select number of friends.'
71           else:
72               howmany = 0
73
74       if not error:
75           if 'action' in form and \
76                   form['action'].value != 'reedit':
77               doResults(who, howmany)
78           else:
79               showForm(who, howmany)
80       else:
81           showError(error)
82
83   if __name__ == '__main__':
84       process()
```

10.4   Using Unicode with CGI

In the "Sequences" chapter of *Core Python Programming* or *Core Python Language Fundamentals*, we introduced the use of Unicode strings. In one particular section, we gave a simple example of a script that takes a Unicode string, writes it out to a file, and then reads it back in. Here, we'll demonstrate a similar CGI script that produces Unicode output. We'll show you how to give your browser enough clues to be able to render the characters properly. The one requirement is that you must have East Asian fonts installed on your computer so that the browser can display them.

To see Unicode in action, we will build a CGI script to generate a multilingual Web page. First, we define the message in a Unicode string. We assume that your text editor can only enter ASCII. Therefore, the non-ASCII characters are input by using the \u escape. In practice, the message can also be read from a file or database.

```
# Greeting in English, Spanish,
# Chinese and Japanese.
UNICODE_HELLO = u"""
Hello!
\u00A1Hola!
\u4F60\u597D!
\u3053\u3093\u306B\u3061\u306F!
"""
```

The first output generated by the CGI is the content-type HTTP header. It is very important to declare here that the content is transmitted in the UTF-8 encoding so that the browser can correctly interpret it.

```
print 'Content-type: text/html; charset=UTF-8\r'
print '\r'
```

Then, output the actual message. Use the string's encode() method to translate the string into UTF-8 sequences first.

```
print UNICODE_HELLO.encode('UTF-8')
```

You can look through the code in Example 10-6, whose output will look like the browser window shown in Figure 10-11.

Example 10-6   Simple Unicode CGI Example (uniCGI.py)

This script outputs Unicode strings to your Web browser.

```
 1  #!/usr/bin/env python
 2
 3  CODEC = 'UTF-8'
 4  UNICODE_HELLO = u'''
 5  Hello!
 6  \u00A1Hola!
 7  \u4F60\u597D!
 8  \u3053\u3093\u306B\u3061\u306F!
 9  '''
10
11  print 'Content-Type: text/html; charset=%s\r' % CODEC
12  print '\r'
13  print '<HTML><HEAD><TITLE>Unicode CGI Demo</TITLE></HEAD>'
14  print '<BODY>'
15  print UNICODE_HELLO.encode(CODEC)
16  print '</BODY></HTML>'
```

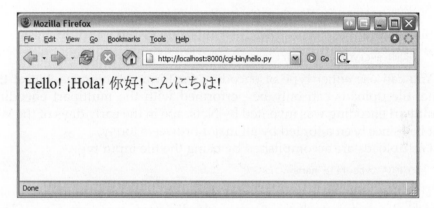

Figure 10-11 A simple Simple Unicode CGI demonstration output in Firefox.

10.5   Advanced CGI

We will now take a look at some of the more advanced aspects of CGI programming. These include the use of *cookies* (cached data saved on the client side), multiple values for the same CGI field, and file upload using multipart form submissions. To save space, we show you all three of these features with a single application. Let's take a look at multipart submissions first.

10.5.1   Multipart Form Submission and File Uploading

Currently, the CGI specifications only allow two types of form encodings: "application/x-www-form-urlencoded" and "multipart/form-data." Because the former is the default, there is never a need to state the encoding in the FORM tag like this:

```
<FORM enctype="application/x-www-form-urlencoded" ...>
```

But for multipart forms, you must explicitly give the encoding as:

```
<FORM enctype="multipart/form-data" ...>
```

You can use either type of encoding for form submissions, but at this time, file uploads can only be performed with the multipart encoding. Multipart encoding was invented by Netscape in the early days of the Web but has since been adopted by all major browsers today.

File uploads are accomplished by using the file input type:

```
<INPUT type=file name=...>
```

This directive presents an empty text field with a button on the side which allows you to browse your file directory structure for a file to upload. When using multipart, your Web client's form submission to the server will look amazingly like (multipart) e-mail messages with attachments. A separate encoding was needed because it would not be wise to "urlencode" a file, especially a binary file. The information still gets to the server, but it is just packaged in a different way.

Regardless of whether you use the default encoding or the multipart, the cgi module will process them in the same manner, providing keys and corresponding values in the form submission. You will simply access the data through your FieldStorage instance, as before.

10.5.2   Multivalued Fields

In addition to file uploads, we are going to show you how to process fields with multiple values. The most common case is when you provide checkboxes for a user to select from various choices. Each of the checkboxes is labeled with the same field name, but to differentiate them, each will have a different value associated with a particular checkbox.

As you know, the data from the user is sent to the server in key-value pairs during form submission. When more than one checkbox is submitted, you will have multiple values associated with the same key. In these cases, rather than being given a single `MiniFieldStorage` instance for your data, the `cgi` module will create a list of such instances that you will iterate over to obtain the different values. Not too painful at all.

10.5.3   Cookies

Finally, we will use cookies in our example. If you are not familiar with cookies, they are just bits of data information which a server at a Web site will request to be saved on the client side (the browser).

Because HTTP is a stateless protocol, information that has to be carried from one page to another can be accomplished by using key-value pairs in the request, as you have seen in the GET requests and screens earlier in this chapter. Another way of doing it, as we have also seen before, is by using hidden form fields such as the action variable in some of the later `friends*.py` scripts. These variables and their values are managed by the server because the pages they return to the client must embed these in generated pages.

One alternative to maintaining persistency in state across multiple page views is to save the data on the client side, instead. This is where cookies come in. Rather than embedding data to be saved in the returned Web pages, a server will make a request to the client to save a cookie. The cookie is linked to the domain of the originating server (so a server cannot set or override cookies from other Web sites) and has an expiration date (so your browser doesn't become cluttered with cookies).

These two characteristics are tied to a cookie along with the key-value pair representing the data item of interest. There are other attributes of cookies such as a domain subpath or a request that a cookie should only be delivered in a secure environment.

By using cookies, we no longer have to pass the data from page to page to track a user. Although they have been subject to a good amount of controversy with regard to privacy, most Web sites use cookies responsibly. To prepare you for the code, a Web server requests that a client store a cookie by sending the "Set-Cookie" header immediately before the requested file.

Once cookies are set on the client side, requests to the server will automatically have those cookies sent to the server using the HTTP_COOKIE environment variable. The cookies are delimited by semicolons (;), and each key-value pair is separated by equal signs (=). All your application needs to do to access the data values is to split the string several times (i.e., using str.split() or manual parsing).

Like multipart encoding, cookies originated from Netscape, which wrote up the first specification that is still mostly valid today. You can access this document at the following Web site:

http://www.netscape.com/newsref/std/cookie_spec.html

Once cookies are standardized and this document finally made obsolete, you will be able to get more current information from Request for Comment documents (RFCs). The first published on cookies was RFC 2109 in 1997. It was then replaced by RFC 2965 a few years later in 2000. The most recent one (which supersedes the other two) at the time of this writing is RFC 6265, published in April 2011.

10.5.4   Cookies and File Upload

We now present our CGI application, advcgi.py, which has code and functionality not too unlike the friendsC.py script earlier in this chapter. The default first page is a user fill-out form consisting of four main parts: user-set cookie string, name field, checkbox list of programming languages, and file submission box. Figure 10-12 presents an image of this screen along with some sample input.

All of the data is submitted to the server using multipart encoding, and retrieved in the same manner on the server side using the FieldStorage instance. The only tricky part is in retrieving the uploaded file. In our application, we choose to iterate over the file, reading it line by line. It is also possible to read in the entire contents of the file if you are not wary of its size.

Because this is the first occasion data is received by the server, it is at this time, when returning the results page back to the client, that we use the "Set-Cookie:" header to cache our data in browser cookies.

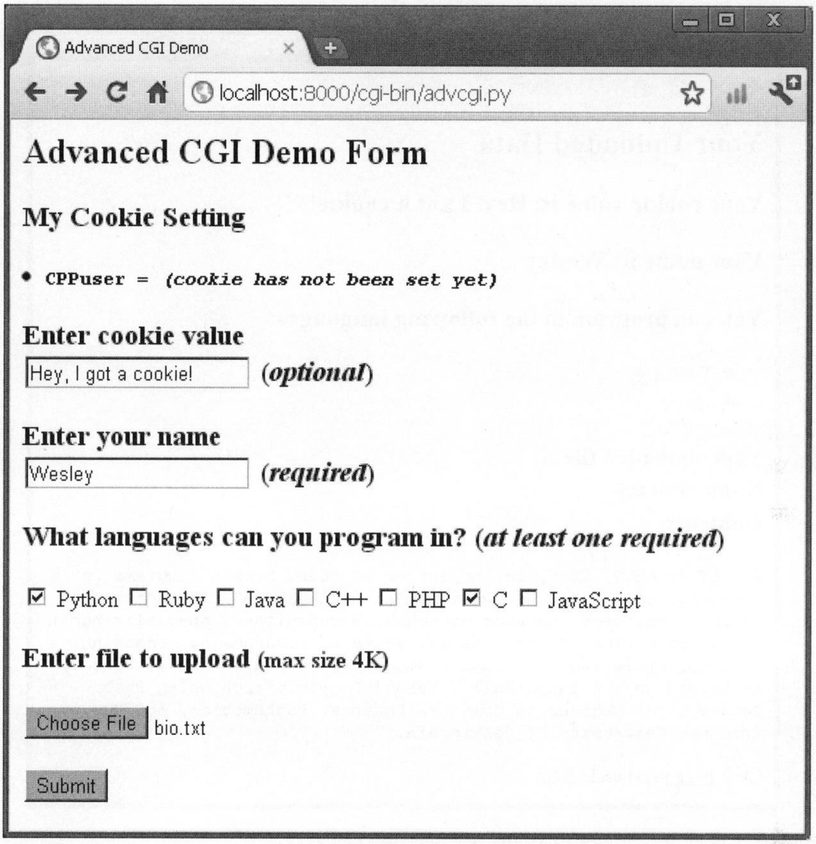

Figure 10-12 An advanced CGI cookie, upload, and multivalue form page.

In Figure 10-13, you will see the results after submitting our form data. All the fields the user entered are shown on the page. The given file in the final dialog box was uploaded to the server and displayed, as well.

You will also notice the link at the bottom of the results page, which returns us to the form page, again using the same CGI script.

If we click that link at the bottom, no form data is submitted to our script, causing a form page to be displayed. Yet, as you can see from Figure 10-14, what shows up is anything but an empty form; information previously entered by the user is already present. How did we accomplish this with no form data (either hidden or as query arguments in the URL)? The secret is that the data is stored on the client side in cookies—two of them, in fact.

Figure 10-13 Our advanced CGI application results page.

The user cookie holds the string of data typed in by the user in the "Enter cookie value" form field, and the user's name, languages he is familiar with, and uploaded files are stored in the information cookie.

When the script detects no form data, it shows the form page, but before the form page has been created, it grabs the cookies from the client (which are automatically transmitted by the client when the user clicks the link) and fills out the form accordingly. So when the form is finally displayed, all the previously entered information appears to the user like magic.

We are certain you are eager to take a look at this application, so take a look at it in Example 10-7.

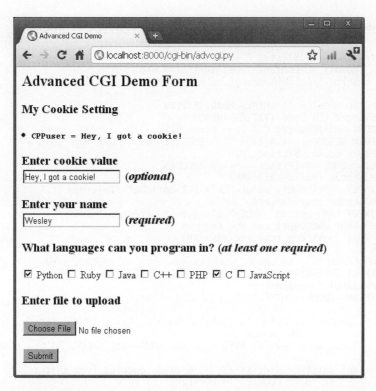

Figure 10-14 The new form page with data loaded from cookies, except the uploaded file.

Example 10-7   Advanced CGI Application (`advcgi.py`)

This script has one main class that does a bit more, `AdvCGI.py`. It has methods to show either form, error, or results pages, as well as those that read or write cookies from/to the client (a Web browser).

```
1    #!/usr/bin/env python
2
3    from cgi import FieldStorage
4    from os import environ
5    from cStringIO import StringIO
6    from urllib import quote, unquote
7
```

(Continued)

Example 10-7   Advanced CGI Application (advcgi.py) *(Continued)*

```
8    class AdvCGI(object):
9        header = 'Content-Type: text/html\n\n'
10       url = '/cgi-bin/advcgi.py'
11
12       formhtml = '''<HTML><HEAD><TITLE>
13   Advanced CGI Demo</TITLE></HEAD>
14   <BODY><H2>Advanced CGI Demo Form</H2>
15   <FORM METHOD=post ACTION="%s" ENCTYPE="multipart/form-data">
16   <H3>My Cookie Setting</H3>
17   <LI> <CODE><B>CPPuser = %s</B></CODE>
18   <H3>Enter cookie value<BR>
19   <INPUT NAME=cookie value="%s"> (<I>optional</I>)</H3>
20   <H3>Enter your name<BR>
21   <INPUT NAME=person VALUE="%s"> (<I>required</I>)</H3>
22   <H3>What languages can you program in?
23   (<I>at least one required</I>)</H3>
24   %s
25   <H3>Enter file to upload <SMALL>(max size 4K)</SMALL></H3>
26   <INPUT TYPE=file NAME=upfile VALUE="%s" SIZE=45>
27   <P><INPUT TYPE=submit>
28   </FORM></BODY></HTML>'''
29
30       langSet = ('Python', 'Ruby', 'Java', 'C++', 'PHP', 'C',
                    'JavaScript')
31       langItem = '<INPUT TYPE=checkbox NAME=lang VALUE="%s"%s> %s\n'
32
33       def getCPPCookies(self):    # reads cookies from client
34           if 'HTTP_COOKIE' in environ:
35               cookies = [x.strip() for x in environ['HTTP_
                     COOKIE'].split(';')]
36               for eachCookie in cookies:
37                   if len(eachCookie)>6 and eachCookie[:3]=='CPP':
38                       tag = eachCookie[3:7]
39                       try:
40                           self.cookies[tag] = eval(unquote(
                                 eachCookie[8:]))
41                       except (NameError, SyntaxError):
42                           self.cookies[tag] = unquote(
                                 eachCookie[8:])
43               if 'info' not in self.cookies:
44                   self.cookies['info'] = ''
45               if 'user' not in self.cookies:
46                   self.cookies['user'] = ''
47           else:
48               self.cookies['info'] = self.cookies['user'] = ''
49
```

```
50          if self.cookies['info'] != '':
51              self.who, langStr, self.fn = self.cookies['info'].split(':')
52              self.langs = langStr.split(',')
53          else:
54              self.who = self.fn = ' '
55              self.langs = ['Python']
56
57      def showForm(self):
58          self.getCPPCookies()
59
60          # put together language checkboxes
61          langStr = []
62          for eachLang in AdvCGI.langSet:
63              langStr.append(AdvCGI.langItem % (eachLang,
64                  ' CHECKED' if eachLang in self.langs else '',
65                  eachLang))
66
67          # see if user cookie set up yet
68          if not ('user' in self.cookies and self.cookies['user']):
69              cookStatus = '<I>(cookie has not been set yet)</I>'
70              userCook = ''
71          else:
72              userCook = cookStatus = self.cookies['user']
73
74          print '%s%s' % (AdvCGI.header, AdvCGI.formhtml % (
75              AdvCGI.url, cookStatus, userCook, self.who,
76              ''.join(langStr), self.fn))
77
78      errhtml = '''<HTML><HEAD><TITLE>
79 Advanced CGI Demo</TITLE></HEAD>
80 <BODY><H3>ERROR</H3>
81 <B>%s</B><P>
82 <FORM><INPUT TYPE=button VALUE=Back
83 ONCLICK="window.history.back()"></FORM>
84 </BODY></HTML>'''
85
86      def showError(self):
87          print AdvCGI.header + AdvCGI.errhtml % (self.error)
88
89      reshtml = '''<HTML><HEAD><TITLE>
90 Advanced CGI Demo</TITLE></HEAD>
91 <BODY><H2>Your Uploaded Data</H2>
92 <H3>Your cookie value is: <B>%s</B></H3>
93 <H3>Your name is: <B>%s</B></H3>
94 <H3>You can program in the following languages:</H3>
95 <UL>%s</UL>
96 <H3>Your uploaded file...<BR>
97 Name: <I>%s</I><BR>
```

(Continued)

Example 10-7   Advanced CGI Application (advcgi.py) *(Continued)*

```
98   Contents:</H3>
99   <PRE>%s</PRE>
100  Click <A HREF="%s"><B>here</B></A> to return to form.
101  </BODY></HTML>'''
102
103      def setCPPCookies(self):# tell client to store cookies
104          for eachCookie in self.cookies.keys():
105              print 'Set-Cookie: CPP%s=%s; path=/' % \
106                  (eachCookie, quote(self.cookies[eachCookie]))
107
108      def doResults(self):# display results page
109          MAXBYTES = 4096
110          langList = ''.join(
111              '<LI>%s<BR>' % eachLang for eachLang in self.langs)
112          filedata = self.fp.read(MAXBYTES)
113          if len(filedata) == MAXBYTES and f.read():
114              filedata = '%s%s' % (filedata,
115                  '... <B><I>(file truncated due to size)</I></B>')
116          self.fp.close()
117          if filedata == '':
118              filedata = <B><I>(file not given or upload error)</I></B>'
119          filename = self.fn
120
121          # see if user cookie set up yet
122          if not ('user' in self.cookies and self.cookies['user']):
123              cookStatus = '<I>(cookie has not been set yet)</I>'
124              userCook = ''
125          else:
126              userCook = cookStatus = self.cookies['user']
127
128          # set cookies
129          self.cookies['info'] = ':'.join(
130              (self.who, ','.join(self.langs, ','), filename))
131          self.setCPPCookies()
132
133          print '%s%s' % (AdvCGI.header, AdvCGI.reshtml % (
134                  cookStatus, self.who, langList,
135                  filename, filedata, AdvCGI.url)
136
137      def go(self):          # determine which page to return
138          self.cookies = {}
139          self.error = ''
140          form = FieldStorage()
141          if not form.keys():
142              self.showForm()
143              return
144
145          if 'person' in form:
146              self.who = form['person'].value.strip().title()
147              if self.who == '':
148                  self.error = 'Your name is required. (blank)'
```

```
149            else:
150                self.error = 'Your name is required. (missing)'
151
152            self.cookies['user'] = unquote(form['cookie'].value.strip()) if
      'cookie' in form else ''
153            if 'lang' in form:
154                langData = form['lang']
155                if isinstance(langData, list):
156                    self.langs = [eachLang.value for eachLang in langData]
157                else:
158                    self.langs = [langData.value]
159            else:
160                self.error = 'At least one language required.'
161
162            if 'upfile' in form:
163                upfile = form['upfile']
164                self.fn = upfile.filename or ''
165                if upfile.file:
166                    self.fp = upfile.file
167                else:
168                    self.fp = StringIO('(no data)')
169            else:
170                self.fp = StringIO('(no file)')
171                self.fn = ''
172
173            if not self.error:
174                self.doResults()
175            else:
176                self.showError()
177
178 if __name__ == '__main__':
179     page = AdvCGI()
180     page.go()
```

advcgi.py looks strikingly similar to our friendsC.py CGI scripts seen earlier in this chapter. It has a form, results, and error pages to return. In addition to all of the advanced CGI features that are part of our new script, we are also infusing more of an object-oriented feel to our script by using a class with methods instead of just a set of functions. The HTML text for our pages is now static data for our class, meaning that they will remain constant across all instances—even though there is actually only one instance in our case.

Line-by-Line Explanation

Lines 1–6

The usual startup and import lines appear here. If you're not familiar with the StringIO class, it's is a file-like data structure whose core element is a string—think in-memory text stream.

For Python 2, this class is found in either the `StringIO` module or its C-equivalent, `cStringIO`. In Python 3, it has been moved into the `io` package. Similarly, the Python 2 `urllib.quote()` and `urllib.unquote()` functions have been moved into the `urllib.parse` package for Python 3.

Lines 8–28

After the `AdvCGI` class is declared, the `header` and `url` (static class) variables are created for use by the methods displaying all the different pages. The static text form HTML comes next, followed by the programming language set and HTML element for each language.

Lines 33–55

This example uses cookies. Somewhere further down in this application is the `setCPPCookies()` method, which our application calls to send cookies (from the Web server) back to the browser and store them there.

The `getCPPCookies()` method does the opposite. When a browser makes subsequent calls to the application, it sends those same cookies back to the server via HTTP headers. By the time our application executes, those values are available to us (the application) via the `HTTP_COOKIE` environment variable.

This method parses the cookies, specifically seeking those that start with the `CPP` string (line 37). In our application, we're only looking for cookies named "CPPuser" and "CPPinfo." The keys `'user'` and `'info'` are extracted as the tag on line 38, the equal sign at index 7 skipped, and the value starting at index 8 unquoted and evaluated into a Python object occurs on lines 39–42. The exception handler looks for cookie payloads that are not valid Python objects and just saves the string value. If either of the cookies are missing, they are assigned to the empty string (lines 43–48). The `getCPPCookies()` method is only called from `showForm()`.

We parse the cookies ourselves in this simple example, but if things get more complex, you will likely use the `Cookie` module (renamed to `http.cookies` in Python 3) to perform this task.

Similarly, if you're writing Web clients and need to manage all the cookies stored in the browser (a *cookie jar*) and communication to Web servers, you'll likely use the `cookielib` module (renamed to `http.cookiejar` in Python 3).

Lines 57–76

The `checkUserCookie()` method is used by both `showForm()` and `doResults()` to check whether the user-supplied cookie value has been set. Both the form and results HTML templates display this value.

The showForm() method's only purpose is to display the form to the user. It relies on getCPPCookies() to retrieve cookies from previous requests (if any) and format the form as appropriate.

Lines 78–87

This block of code is responsible for the error page.

Lines 89–101

This is just the HTML template for the results page. It is used in doResults(), which fills in all the required data.

Lines 102–135

The results page is created by using these blocks of code. The setCPPCookies() method requests that a client store the cookies for our application, and the doResults() method puts together all the data and sends the output back to the client.

The latter, called from the go() method, does all the heavy lifting to put together the output. In the first block of this method (lines 109–119), we process the user input: the set of programming languages chosen (at least one required—see the go() method), any uploaded file and the user-supplied cookie value, both of which are optional.

The final steps of doResults() (lines 128–135) cram all this data into a single "CPPinfo" cookie for use later, and then renders the results template with all the data.

Lines 137–180

The script begins by instantiating an AdvCGI page object and then calling its go() method to start the ball rolling. The go() method contains the logic that reads all incoming data and decides which page to show.

The error page will be displayed if no name was given or if no languages were checked. The showForm() method is called to output the form if no input data was received; otherwise, the doResults() method is invoked to display the results page. Error situations are created by setting the self.error variable, which serves two purposes. It lets you set an error reason as a string and also serves as a flag to indicate that an error has occurred. If this value is not blank, the user will be forwarded to the error page.

Handling the person field (lines 145–150) is the same as we have seen in the past: a single key-value pair. However, collecting the language information (lines 153–160) is a bit trickier because we must check for either a

(Mini)FieldStorage instance or a list of such instances. We will employ the familiar isinstance() built-in function for this purpose. In the end, we will have a list of a single language name or many, depending on the user's selections.

The use of cookies to contain data illustrates how they can be used to avoid using any kind of CGI field pass-through. In our previous examples in this chapter, we passed such values as CGI variables. Now we are only using cookies. You will notice in the code that obtains such data that no CGI processing is invoked, meaning that the data does not come from the FieldStorage object. The data is passed to us by the Web client with each request and the values (user's chosen data as well as information to fill in a succeeding form with pre-existing information) are obtained from cookies.

Because the showResults() method receives the new input from the user, it has the responsibility of setting the cookies, for example, by calling setCPPCookies(). However, showForm(), must read in the cookies' values in order to display a form page with the current user selections. This is done by its invocation of the getCPPCookies() method.

Finally, we get to the file upload processing (lines 162–171). Regardless of whether a file was actually uploaded, FieldStorage is given a file handle in the file attribute. On line 171, if there was no filename given, then we just set it to a blank string. As a better alternative, you can access the file pointer—the file attribute—and perhaps read only one line at a time or other kind of slower processing.

In our case, file uploads are only part of user submissions, so we simply pass on the file pointer to the doResults() function to extract the data from the file. doResults() will display only the first 4KB (as set on line 112) of the file for space reasons and to show you that it is not necessary (or necessarily productive or useful) to display a 4GB binary file.

Existing *Core Python* readers will notice that we have refactored this code significantly from previous editions of this book. The original was over a decade old and did not reflect contemporary Python practices. It is likely this incarnation of advcgi.py will not run in Python older than version 2.5. However, you can still access the code from earlier editions of this script from the book's Web site as well as the equivalent Python 3 version.

2.5

10.6   Introduction to WSGI

This section of the chapter introduces you to everything you need to know about WSGI, starting with the motivation and background. The second half of this section covers how to write Web applications without having to worry about how they will be executed.

10.6.1   Motivation (CGI Alternatives)

Okay, now you have a good understanding of what CGI does and why something like it is needed: servers cannot create dynamic content; they don't have knowledge of user-specific application information data, such as authentication, bank accounts, online purchases, etc. Web servers must communicate with an outside process to do this custom work.

In the first two-thirds of this chapter, we discussed how CGI solves this problem and taught you how it works. We also mentioned that it is woefully inadequate because it does not scale; CGI processes (like Python interpreters) are created per-request then thrown away. If your application receives thousands of requests, spawning of a like-number of language interpreters will quickly bring your servers to a halt. Two widely-used methods to combat this performance issue are: server integration and external processes. Let's briefly discuss each of these.

10.6.2   Server Integration

Server integration is also known as a *server API*. These include proprietary solutions like the Netscape Server Application Programming Interface (NSAPI) and Microsoft's Internet Server Application Programming Interface (ISAPI). The most widely-user server solution today (since the mid-1990s) is the Apache HTTP Web server, an open-source solution. *Apache* as it is commonly called, has a server API, as well, and uses the term *module* to describe compiled plug-in components that extend its functionality and capability.

All three of these and similar solutions address the CGI performance problem by integrating the gateway into the server. In other words, instead of the server forking off a separate language interpreter to handle a request, it merely makes a function call, running any application code and coming up with the response in-process. These servers may process their work via a set of pre-created processes or threads, depending on its API. Most can be adjusted to suit the requirements of the supported applications. General features that servers also provide include compression, security, proxying, and virtual hosting, to name a few.

Of course, no solution is without its downsides, and for server APIs, this includes a variety of issues such as buggy code affecting server performance, language implementations that are not-fully compatible, requiring the API developer to have to code in the same programming language as the Web server implementation, integration into a proprietary solution (if not using an open-source server API), requiring that applications must be thread-safe, etc.

10.6.3   External Processes

Another solution is an external process. These are CGI applications that permanently run outside of the server. When a request comes in, the server passes it off to such a process. They scale better than pure CGI because these processes are long-lived as opposed to being spawned for individual requests then terminated. The most well-known external process solution is *FastCGI*. With external processes, you get the benefits of server APIs but not as many of the drawbacks because, for instance, you get to run outside the server, they can be implemented in your language of choice, application defects might not affect the Web server, you're not forced to code against a proprietary source, etc.

Naturally, there is a Python implementation of FastCGI, as well as a variety of Python modules for Apache (`PyApache`, `mod_snake`, `mod_python`, etc.), some of which are no longer being maintained. All these plus the original pure CGI solution make up the gamut of Web server API gateway solutions to calling Python Web applications.

Because of these different invocation mechanisms, an additional burden has been placed on the developer. You not only need to build your application, but you must also decide on integration with these Web servers. In fact, when you write your application, you need to know exactly in which one of these mechanisms it will execute and code it that way.

This problem is more acute for Web framework developers, because you want to give your users the most flexibility. If you don't want to force them to create multiple versions of their applications, you'll need to provide interfaces to all server solutions in order to promote adoption of your framework. This dilemma certainly doesn't sound like it lends itself to being Pythonic, thus it has led to the creation of the Web Server Gateway Interface (WSGI) standard.

10.6.4   Introducing WSGI

It's not a server, an API you program against, or an actual piece of code, but it does define an interface. The WSGI specification was created as PEP 333 in 2003 to address the wide proliferation of disparate Web frameworks, Web servers, and various invocation styles just discussed (pure CGI, server API, external process).

The goal was to reduce this type of interoperability and fragmentation with a standard that targets a common API between the Web server and Web framework layers. Since its creation, WSGI adoption has become commonplace. Nearly all of the Python-based Web servers are WSGI-compliant. Having WSGI as a standard is advantageous to application developers, framework creators, and the community as a whole.

A WSGI application is defined as a callable which (always) takes the following parameters: a dictionary containing the server environment variables, and another callable that initializes the response with an HTTP status code and HTTP headers to return back to the client. This callable must return an iterable which makes up the payload.

In the sample "Hello World" WSGI application that follows, these variables are named `environ` and `start_response()`, respectively:

```
def simple_wsgi_app(environ, start_response):
    status = '200 OK'
    headers = [('Content-type', 'text/plain')]
    start_response(status, headers)
    return ['Hello world!']
```

The `environ` variable contains familiar environment variables, such as `HTTP_HOST`, `HTTP_USER_AGENT`, `SERVER_PROTOCOL`, etc. The `start_response()` callable that must be executed within the application to prepare the response that will eventually be sent back to the client. The response must include an HTTP return code (200, 300, etc.) as well as HTTP response headers.

In this first version of the WSGI standard, `start_response()` should also return a `write()` function in order to support legacy servers that stream results back. It is recommended against using it and returning just an iterable to let the Web server manage returning the data back to the client (instead of having the application do so as that is *not* in its realm of expertise). Because of this, most applications just drop the return value from `start_response()` or don't use or save it otherwise.

In the previous example, you can see that a 200 status code is set as well as the `Content-Type` header. Both are passed into `start_response()` to formally begin the response. Everything else that comes after should be some iterable, such as, list, generator, etc. that make up the actual response payload. In this example, we're only returning a list containing a single string, but you can certainly imagine a lot more data going back. It can also be any iterable not just a list; a generator or callable instance are great alternatives.

The last thing we wanted to say about `start_response()` is the third and optional exception information parameter, usually known by its abbreviation, `exc_info`. If an application has set the headers to say "200 OK" (but has not actually *sent* them) and encounters problems during execution, it's possible to change the headers to something else, like "403 Forbidden" or "500 Internal Server Error," if desired.

To make this happen, we can assume that the application called `start_response()` with the regular pair of parameters at the beginning of execution. When errors occur, `start_response()` can be called again, but with exc_info passed in along with the new status and headers that will replace the existing ones.

It is an error to call `start_response()` a second time without exc_info. Again, this must all happen before any HTTP headers are sent. If the headers have already been sent, an exception must be raised, such as, `raise exc_info[0]`, `exc_info[1]`, or `exc_info[2]`.

For more information on the `start_response()` callable, refer to PEP 333 at http://www.python.org/dev/peps/pep-0333/#the-start-response-callable.

10.6.5   WSGI servers

On the server side, we need to call the application (as we discussed previously), pass in the environment and `start_response()` callable, and then wait for the application to complete. When it does, we should get an iterable as the return value and return this data back to the client. In the following script, we present a simplistic and limited example of what a WSGI Web server would look like:

```python
import StringIO
import sys

def run_wsgi_app(app, environ):
    body = StringIO.StringIO()

    def start_response(status, headers):
        body.write('Status: %s\r\n' % status)
        for header in headers:
            body.write('%s: %s\r\n' % header)
        return body.write

    iterable = app(environ, start_response)
    try:
      if not body.getvalue():
            raise RuntimeError("start_response() not called by app!")
      body.write('\r\n%s\r\n' % '\r\n'.join(line for line in iterable))
    finally:
        if hasattr(iterable, 'close') and callable(iterable.close):
            iterable.close()

    sys.stdout.write(body.getvalue())
    sys.stdout.flush()
```

The underlying server/gateway will take the application as provided by the developer and put it together the with environ dictionary with the contents of `os.environ()` plus the WSGI-specified `wsgi.*` environment variables (see the PEP, but expect elements, such as `wsgi.input`, `wsgi.errors`, `wsgi.version`, etc.) as well as any framework or middleware environment variables. (More on middleware coming soon.) With both of these items, it will then call `run_wsgi_app()`, which returns the response back to the client.

In reality as an application developer, you wouldn't be interested in minutia such as this. Creating servers is for those wanting to provide, with WSGI specifications, a consistent execution framework for applications. You can see from the preceding example that WSGI provides a clean break between the application side and the server side. Any application can be passed to the server described above (or any other WSGI server). Similarly, in any application, you don't care what kind of server is calling you; all you care about is the environment you're given and the `start_response()` callable that you need to execute before returning data to the client.

10.6.6   Reference Server

As we just mentioned, application developers shouldn't be forced to write servers too, so rather than having to create and manage code like `run_wsgi_app()`, you should be able to choose any WSGI server you want, and if none are handy, Python provides a simple reference server in the standard library: `wsgiref.simple_server.WSGIServer`.

You can build one using the class directly; however, the `wsgiref` package itself features a convenience function called `make_server()` that you can employ for simple access to the reference server. Let's do so with our sample application, `simple_wsgi_app()`:

```python
#!/usr/bin/env python

from wsgiref.simple_server import make_server

httpd = make_server('', 8000, simple_wsgi_app)
print "Started app serving on port 8000..."
httpd.serve_forever()
```

This takes the application we created earlier, `simple_wsgi_app()`, wraps it in a server running on port 8000, and starts the server loop. If you visit http://localhost:8000 in a browser (or whatever [host, port] pair you're using), you should see the plain text output of "Hello World!"

For the truly lazy, you don't have to write the application or the server. The `wsgiref` module also has a demonstration application, `wsgiref.simple_server.demo_app()`. The `demo_app()` is nearly identical to `simple_wsgi_app()`, except that in addition, it displays the environment variables. Here's the code for running the demonstration application with the reference server:

```
#!/usr/bin/env python

from wsgiref.simple_server import make_server, demo_app

httpd = make_server('', 8000, demo_app)
print "Started app serving on port 8000..."
httpd.serve_forever()
```

Start up a CGI server, and then browse to the application; you should see the "Hello World!" output along with the environment variable dump.

This is just the reference model for a WSGI-compliant server. It is not full-featured or intended to serve in production use. However, server creators can take a page from this to design their own products and make them WSGI-compliant. The same is true for `demo_app()` as a reference WSGI-compliant application for application developers.

10.6.7 Sample WSGI Applications

As mentioned earlier, WSGI is now the standard, and nearly all Python Web frameworks support it, even if it doesn't look like it. For example, an Google App Engine handler class, given the usual imports, might contain code that looks something like this:

```
class MainHandler(webapp.RequestHandler):
    def get(self):
        self.response.out.write('Hello world!')

application = webapp.WSGIApplication([
    ('/', MainHandler)], debug=True)
run_wsgi_app(application)
```

Not all frameworks will have an exact match as far as code goes, but you can clearly see the WSGI reference. For a much closer comparison, you can go one level lower and take a look at the `run_bare_wsgi_app()` function found in the `util.py` module of the `webapp` subpackage of the App Engine Python SDK. You'll find this code looks much more like a derivative of `simple_wsgi_app()`.

10.6.8   Middleware and Wrapping WSGI Applications

There might be situations in which you want to let the application run as-is, but you want to inject pre or post-processing before (the request) or after the application executes (the response). This is commonly known as *middleware*, which is additional functionality that sits between the Web server and the Web application. You're either massaging the data coming from the user before passing it to the application, or you need to do some final tweaks to the results from the application before returning the payload back to the user. This is commonly referred to as a *middleware onion*, indicating the application is at the heart, with additional layers in between.

Preprocessing can include activities, such as intercepting the request parameters; modifying them; adding or removing them; altering the environment (including any user-submitted form [CGI] variables); using the URL path to dispatch application functionality; forwarding or redirecting requests; load-balancing based on network traffic via the inbound client IP address; delegating to altered functionality (e.g., using the User-Agent header to send mobile users to a simplified UI/app); etc.

Examples of post-processing primarily involves manipulating the output from the application. The following script is an example, similar to the timestamp server that we created in Chapter 2, "Network Programming": for each line from the application's results, we're going to prepend it with a timestamp. In practice of course, this is much more complicated, but this is an example similar to others you can find online that capitalize or lower-case application output. Here, we'll wrap our call to simple_wsgi_app() with ts_simple_wsgi_app() and install the latter as the application that the server registers:

```python
#!/usr/bin/env python

from time import ctime
from wsgiref.simple_server import make_server

def ts_simple_wsgi_app(environ, start_response):
    return ('[%s] %s' % (ctime(), x) for x in \
        simple_wsgi_app(environ, start_response))

httpd = make_server('', 8000, ts_simple_wsgi_app)
print "Started app serving on port 8000..."
httpd.serve_forever()
```

For those of you with more of an object bent, you can use a class wrapper instead of a function wrapper. On top of this, we can reduce environ and start_response() into a single variable argument tuple (see stuff in the example that follows) to shorten the code a bit because we added some with the inclusion of a class and definition of a pair of methods:

```
class Ts_ci_wrapp(object):
    def __init__(self, app):
        self.orig_app = app

    def __call__(self, *stuff):
        return ('[%s] %s' % (ctime(), x) for x in
            self.orig_app(*stuff))

httpd = make_server('', 8000, Ts_ci_wrapp(simple_wsgi_app))
print "Started app serving on port 8000..."
httpd.serve_forever()
```

We've named the class Ts_ci_wrapp, which is short for "timestamp callable instance wrapped application" that is instantiated when we create the server. The initializer takes the original application and caches it for use later. When the server executes the application, it still passes in the environ dict and start_response() callable, as before. With this change, the instance itself will be called (hence the __call__() method definition). Both environ and start_response() are passed to the original application via stuff.

Although we used a callable instance here and a function earlier, keep in mind that any callable will work. Also note that none of these last few examples modify simple_wsgi_app() in any way. The main point is that WSGI provides a clean break between the Web application and the Web server. This helps compartmentalize development, allow teams to more easily divide the work, and gives a consistent and flexible way to allow Web application's to run with any type of WSGI-compliant back-end. It also frees the Web server creator from having to incorporate any custom or specific hooks for users who choose to run applications by using their (Web) server software.

10.6.9   Updates to WSGI in Python 3

3.x

PEP 333 defined the WSGI standard for Python 2. PEP 3333 offers enhances to PEP 333 to bring the standard to Python 3. Specifically, it calls out that the network traffic is all done in bytes. While such strings are native to Python 2, native Python 3 strings are Unicode to emphasize that they represent text data while the original ASCII strings were renamed to the bytes type.

Specifically, PEP 3333 clarifies that "native" strings—the data type named `str`, regardless of whether you're using Python 2 or 3—are those used for all HTTP headers and corresponding metadata. It also states that "byte" strings are those which are used for the HTTP payloads (requests/responses, GET/POST/PUT input data, HTML output, etc.). For more information on PEP 333, take a look at its definition, which you can find at www.python.org/dev/peps/pep-3333/.

Independent of PEP 3333, there are other related proposals that will make for good reading. One is PEP 444, which is a first attempt to define a "WSGI 2," if such a thing takes on that name. The community generally regards PEP 3333 as a "WSGI 1.0.1," an enhancement to the original PEP 333 specification, whereas PEP 444 is a consideration for WSGI's next generation.

10.7   Real-World Web Development

CGI was the way things used to work, and the concepts it brought still apply in Web programming today; hence, the reason why we spent so much time looking at it. The introduction to WSGI brought you one step closer to reality.

Today, new Python Web programmers have a wealth of choices, and while the big names in the Web framework space are still Django, Pyramid, and Google App Engine, there are plenty more options for users to choose from—perhaps a mind-numbing selection, actually. Frameworks aren't even necessary: you could go straight down to a WSGI-compliant Web server without any of the extra "fluff" or framework features. However, the chances are more likely that you will go with a framework because of the convenience of having the rest of the Web stack available to you.

A modern Web execution environment will likely consist of either a multithreaded or multiprocess server model, signed/secure cookies, basic user authentication, and session management. Many of these things regular application developers already know; authentication represents user registration with a login name and password, and cookies are ways of maintaining user information, sometimes session information, as well. We also know that in order to scale, Web servers need to be able to handle requests from multiple users; hence, the use of threads or processes. However, one thing that hasn't been covered is the need for sessions.

If you look at all the application code in this entire chapter that runs on Web servers, it might take a while for you to know that aside from the obvious differences from scripts that run from beginning to end or server loops which just run forever, Web applications (or *servlets* in Java parlance) are executed for every request. There's no state saved within the code, and we already mentioned that HTTP is stateless, as well. In other words, don't expect data to be saved in variables, global or otherwise. Think of a request like a single transaction. It comes in, does its business, and finishes, leaving nothing behind in the codebase.

This is why *session management*—saving of a user's state across one or more requests within a well-defined duration of time—is needed. Generally, this is accomplished by using some sort of persistent storage, such as memcache, flat (or not-so-flat) files, and even databases. Developers can certainly roll their own, especially when writing lower-level code, as we've seen in this chapter. But without question this wheel has already been (re)invented several times, which is why many of the larger, more well-known Web frameworks, including Django, come with their own session management software. (This leads directly into our next chapter.)

10.8   Related Modules

In Table 10-1, we present a list of modules that you might find useful for Web development. You might also take a look at Chapter 3, "Internet Client Programming," and Chapter 13, "Web Services," for other useful Web application modules.

Table 10-1 Web Programming Related Modules

Module/Package	Description
Web Applications	
`cgi`	Retrieves CGI form data
`cgitb`[c]	Handles CGI tracebacks
`htmllib`	Older HTML parser for simple HTML files; `HTML-Parser` class extends from `sgmllib.SGMLParser`
`HTMLparser`[c]	Newer, non-SGML-based parser for HTML and XHTML
`htmlentitydefs`	HTML general entity definitions
`Cookie`	Server-side cookies for HTTP state management
`cookielib`[e]	Cookie-handling classes for HTTP clients

Module/Package	Description
Web Applications	
webbrowser[b]	Controller: launches Web documents in a browser
sgmllib	Parses simple SGML files
robotparser[a]	Parses robots.txt files for URL "fetchability" analysis
httplib[a]	Used to create HTTP clients
Web Servers	
BaseHTTPServer	Abstract class with which to develop Web servers
SimpleHTTPServer	Serve the simplest HTTP requests (HEAD and GET)
CGIHTTPServer	In addition to serving Web files like SimpleHTTPServers, can also process CGI (HTTP POST) requests
http.server[g]	New name for the combined package merging together BaseHTTPServer, SimpleHTTPServer, and CGIHTTPServer modules in Python 3
wsgiref[f]	WSGI reference module
3rd party packages (not in standard library)	
BeautifulSoup	Regex-based HTML and XML parser http://crummy.com/software/BeautifulSoup
html5lib	HTML5 parser http://code.google.com/p/html5lib
lxml	Comprehensive HTML and XML parser (supports both of the above parsers) http://lxml.de

a. New in Python 1.6.
b. New in Python 2.0.
c. New in Python 2.2.
d. New in Python 2.3.
e. New in Python 2.4.
f. New in Python 2.5.
g. New in Python 3.0.

10.9   Exercises

CGI and Web Applications

10-1.   *urllib Module and Files*. Update the `friendsC.py` script so that it stores names and corresponding number of friends into a two-column text file on disk and continues to add names each time the script is run.

Extra Credit: Add code to dump the contents of such a file to the Web browser (in HTML format). Additional Extra Credit: Create a link that clears all the names in this file.

10-2.   *Error Checking*. The `friendsC.py` script reports an error if no radio button was selected to indicate the number of friends. Update the CGI script to also report an error if no name (e.g., blank or whitespace) is entered.

Extra Credit: We have so far explored only server-side error checking. Explore JavaScript programming and implement client-side error checking by creating JavaScript code to check for both error situations so that these errors are stopped before they reach the server.

10-3.   *Simple CGI*. Create a "Comments" or "Feedback" page for a Web site. Take user feedback via a form, process the data in your script, and then return a "thank you" screen.

10-4.   *Simple CGI*. Create a Web guestbook. Accept a name, an e-mail address, and a journal entry from a user, and then log it to a file (format of your choice). Like Exercise 10-3, return a "thanks for filling out a guestbook entry" page. Also provide a link so that users can view guestbooks.

10-5.   *Web Browser Cookies and Web Site Registration*. Create a user authentication service for a Web site. Manager user names and passwords in an encrypted way. You may have done a plain text version of this exercise in either *Core Python Programming* or *Core Python Language Fundamentals* and can use parts of that solution if you wish.

Extra Credit: Familiarize yourself with setting Web browser cookies and maintain a login session for four hours from the last successful login.

Extra Credit: Allow for *federated authentication* via OpenID, allowing users to log in via Google, Yahoo!, AOL, Word-Press, or even proprietary authentication systems such as "Facebook Connect" or "sign in with Twitter." You can also use the Google Identity Toolkit that you can download from http://code. google.com/apis/identitytoolkit.

10-6. *Errors*. What happens when a CGI script crashes? How can the `cgitb` module be helpful?

10-7. *CGI, File Updates, and Zip Files*. Create a CGI application that not only saves files to the server's disk, but also intelligently unpacks Zip files (or other archive) into a subdirectory named after the archive file.

10-8. *Web Database Application*. Think of a database schema that you want to provide as part of a Web database application. For this multi-user application, you want to grant everyone read access to the entire contents of the database, but perhaps only write access to each individual. One example might be an address book for your family and relatives. Each family member, once successfully logged in, is presented with a Web page with several options, add an entry, view my entry, update my entry, remove or delete my entry, and view all entries (entire database).

Design a `UserEntry` class and create a database entry for each instance of this class. You can use any solution created for any previous problem to implement the registration framework. Finally, you can use any type of storage mechanism for your database, either a relational database such as MySQL or some of the simpler Python persistent storage modules such as `anydbm` or `shelve`.

10-9. *Electronic Commerce Engine*. Create an e-commerce/online shopping Web service that is generic and can be "reskinned" for multiple clients. Add your own authentication system as well as classes for users and shopping carts (If you have *Core Python Programming* or *Core Python Language Fundamentals*, you can use the classes created for your solutions to Exercises 4 and 11 in the Object-Oriented Programming chapter.) Don't forget that you will also need code to manage your products, whether they are hard goods or services. You might want to connect to a payment system such as those offered by PayPal or Google. After reading the next few chapters, port this temporary CGI solution to Django, Pyramid, or Google App Engine.

10-10.   *Python 3*. Examine the differences between `friendsC.py` and `friendsC3.py`. Describe each change.

10-11.   *Python 3, Unicode/Text vs. Data/Bytes*. Port the Unicode example, `uniCGI.py`, to Python 3.

WSGI

10-12.   *Background*. What is WSGI and what were some of the reasons behind its creation?

10-13.   *Background*. What are/were some of the techniques used to get around the scalability issue of CGI?

10-14.   *Background*. Name some well-known frameworks that are WSGI-compliant, and do some research to find some that are not.

10-15.   *Background*. What is the difference between WSGI and CGI?

10-16.   *WSGI Applications*. WSGI applications can be what kind(s) of Python object(s)?

10-17.   *WSGI Applications*. What are the two required arguments for a WSGI application? Go into more detail about the second one.

10-18.   *WSGI Applications*. What is (are) the possible return type(s) of a WSGI application?

10-19.   *WSGI Applications*. Solutions to Exercises 10-1 through 10-11 only work if/when your server processes form data in the same manner as CGI. Choose one of them to port to WSGI, where it will work regardless of which WSGI-compliant server you choose, with perhaps only slight modifications.

10-20.   *WSGI Servers*. The WSGI servers presented in Section 10.6.5 featured a sample `run_wsgi_app()` server function which executes a WSGI application.

   a) The `run_wsgi_app()` function currently does not feature the optional third parameter `exc_info`. Study PEPs 333 and 3333 and add support for `exc_info`.

   b) Create a Python 3 port of this function.

10-21.   *Case Study*. Compare and contrast the WSGI implementations of the following Python Web frameworks: Werkzeug, WebOb, Django, Google App Engine's webapp.

10-22.   *Standards*. While PEP 3333 includes clarifications and enhancements to PEP 333 for Python 3, PEP 444 is something else. Describe what PEP 444 is all about and how it relates to the existing PEPs.

CHAPTER 11

Web Frameworks: Django

Python: the only language with more Web frameworks than keywords.
—Harald Armin Massa, December 2005

In this chapter...

- Introduction
- Web Frameworks
- Introduction to Django
- Projects and Apps
- Your "Hello World" Application (A Blog)
- Creating a Model to Add Database Service
- The Python Application Shell
- The Django Administration App

- Creating the Blog's User Interface
- Improving the Output
- Working with User Input
- Forms and Model Forms
- More About Views
- *Look-and-Feel Improvements
- *Unit Testing
- *An Intermediate Django App: The TweetApprover
- Resources

11.1   Introduction

In this chapter, we'll go outside the Python Standard Library and explore one popular Web framework for Python: Django. We'll first go over Web frameworks in general, and then expose you to developing applications by using Django. This discussion starts with the basics and a "Hello World" application then takes you beyond that with other areas that you'll likely come across when developing a real application. This roadmap essentially defines the structure of this chapter: a solid introduction followed by an intermediate application involving Twitter, e-mail, and OAuth, which is an open protocol for *authorization* to gain access to data via application programming interfaces (APIs).

The goal is to introduce you to a real tool that Python developers use every day to get their jobs done. We'll give you the skills and provide enough knowledge for you to build more complex applications via Django. You can also take these skills and jump to any of the other Python Web frameworks. To get started, let's define the topic.

11.2   Web Frameworks

We hope that you gained a greater understanding of Web development from the material presented in Chapter 10, "Web Programming: CGI and WSGI." Rather than doing everything by hand, you can take advantage of the significant body of work done by others to make your life easier. These Web development environments are generically called *Web frameworks*, and their goal is to help you to perform your job by pushing common tasks "under the hood" and/or providing resources for you to create, update, execute, and scale applications with a minimal amount of work.

Also, we explained earlier, using CGI is no longer an option, due to scalability limitations. So, people in the Python community look to more powerful Web server solutions such as Apache, ligHTTPD (pronounced as "lighty"), or nginx. Some servers, such as Pylons and CherryPy, have their own framework ecosystem around them. However, serving content is only one aspect of creating Web applications. You still need to worry about ancillary tools such as a JavaScript framework, an object-relational mapper (ORM) or lower-level database adapter, a web templating system, and orthogonal but necessary for any type of development: a unit-testing and/ or continuous integration framework. Python Web frameworks are either individual (or multiple) subcomponents or complete *full-stack* systems.

The term full-stack means that you can develop code for all phases and levels of a Web application. Frameworks that are considered as such will provide all related services, such as a Web server, database ORM, templating, and all necessary middleware hooks. Some even provide a JavaScript library. Django is arguably one of the most well-known Web frameworks on the market today; many consider it as Python's answer to Ruby on Rails. It includes all of the services mentioned above as a single, all-in-one solution (except for a built-in JavaScript library, because you can use whichever one you like). We'll see in Chapter 12, "Cloud Computing: Google App Engine," that Google App Engine also provides many of these components but is geared more specifically for scalability and fast request/response Web *and* non-Web applications hosted by the Internet giant.

Although Django was created as a single entity by one engineering team, not all frameworks follow in this philosophy. TurboGears, for example, is a best-of-breed full-stack system, built by a scattered team of developers, serving as glue code that ties together well-known individual components in the stack, such as ToscaWidgets (high-level Web widgets that can utilize a variety of JavaScript frameworks, such as Ex1tJS, jQuery, etc.), SQLAlchemy (ORM), Pylons (Web server), and Genshi (templating). Frameworks that follow this architectural style provide greater flexibility in that users can choose from a variety of templating systems, JS libraries, tools to generate raw SQL, and multiple Web servers. You only need to sacrifice a bit of consistency and any peace of mind that comes with using only one tool. However, that might not be that different from what you're used to.

Pyramid is also very popular and is the successor to both `repoze.bfg` (or "BFG" for short) and the Pylons Web frameworks. Its approach is even simpler: it only provides with you the basics, such as URL dispatch, templating, security, and resources. If you need anything else, you must add those capabilities yourself. Its minimalistic approach along with its strong sense of testing and documentation, plus its inheritance of users from both the Pylons and BFG communities, make it a strong contender in today's set of Web frameworks available for Python.

If you're new to Python, you might be coming from Rails or perhaps PHP, which has significantly expanded from its original intention as an HTML-embedded scripting language to its own large monolithic universe. One benefit you gain from Python is that you're not locked to a "single language, single framework" type of scenario. There are many frameworks out there from which to choose; hence, the quote at the beginning of this chapter. Web framework popularity was accelerated by the creation of the web server gateway interface (WSGI) standard, defined by PEP 333 at http://python.org/dev/peps/pep-0333.

If you don't already know about WSGI, it's not really code or an API as much as it is an interface definition that frees the Web framework developer from having to create a custom Web server for the framework, which in turn frees application developers from having to *use* that server when perhaps they would prefer something else. With WSGI, it's easy for application developers to swap between WSGI-compliant servers (or develop new ones) without worrying about being forced to change application code. For more on WSGI, take a look back at Chapter 10.

I don't know if it's a good thing to say this (especially in print), but when passionate Python developers become dissatisfied with the choices out there, they'll just come up with a new framework. After all, there are more Web frameworks than keywords in Python, right? Other frameworks you'll undoubtedly hear about at some point will include web2py, web.py, Tornado, Diesel, and Zope. One good resource is the wiki page on the Python Web site at http://wiki.python.org/moin/WebFrameworks.

Okay, enough idle chatter, let's engage our Web development knowledge and take a look at Django.

11.3   Introduction to Django

Django bills itself as *"the Web framework for perfectionists with deadlines."* It originated in the early 2000s, created by Web developers at the online presence of the *Lawrence Journal-World* newspaper, which introduced it to the world in 2005 as a way of *"developing code with journalism deadlines."* We'll put ourselves on a deadline and see how fast we can produce a very simple blog by using Django, and later do the same with Google App Engine. (You'll have to work on your perfectionist side on your own.) Although we're going to blast through this example, we'll still give you enough in the way of explanation so that you know what's going on. However, if you would like to explore a full treatment of this exact example, you'll find it in Chapter 2 of *Python Web Development with Django* (Addison-Wesley, 2009), written by my esteemed colleagues, Jeff Forcier (lead developer of Fabric) and Paul Bissex (creator of dpaste), plus yours truly.

CORE TIP: Python 3 availability forthcoming

At the time of this writing, Django is not available for Python 3, so all of the examples in this chapter are Python 2.x only. However, because the Python 3 port currently passes all tests (at the time of this writing), a release will be forthcoming once the documentation is ready. When this occurs, look for Python 3 versions of the code from this chapter on the book's Web site. I strongly believe that Python 3 adoption will definitely experience a significant uptick once large frameworks like Django, along with other infrastructure libraries such as database adapters, become available on that next generation platform.

3.x

11.3.1 Installation

Before jumping into Django development, we first need to install the necessary components, which include installation of the prerequisites followed by Django itself.

Prerequisites

Before you install Django, Python must already be installed. Because you're more than knee-deep in a Python book, we're going to assume that's already been taken care of. Also, most POSIX-compliant (Mac OS X, Linux, *BSD) operating systems already come with Python installed. Microsoft Windows users are typically the only ones that need to download and install Python.

Apache is the king of Web servers, so this is what most deployments use. The Django team recommends the mod_wsgi Apache module and provides simple instructions at http://docs.djangoproject.com/en/dev/topics/install/#install-apache-and-mod-wsgi as well as a more comprehensive document at http://docs.djangoproject.com/en/dev/howto/deployment/modwsgi/. Another great document for more complex installations—those that host multiple Django Web sites (projects) using only one instance of Apache—can be found at http://forum.webfaction.com/viewtopic.php?id=3646. If you're wondering about mod_python, it's mostly found in older installations or part of operating system distributions before mod_wsgi became the standard. Support for mod_python is now officially deprecated (and in fact removed in Django 1.5).

As we close our discussion of Web servers,[1] it's good to remind you that you don't need to use Apache for your production server. As just mentioned there are other options, as well, with many of them lighter in memory footprint and faster; perhaps one of those might be a better fit for your application. You can find out more about some of the possible Web server arrangements at http://code.djangoproject.com/wiki/ServerArrangements.

Django does require a database. The standard version of Django (currently) only runs on SQL-based relational database management systems (RDBMSs). The four main databases employed by users are PostgreSQL, MySQL, Oracle, and SQLite. By far, the easiest to set up is SQLite. Furthermore, SQLite is the only one of the four that does not require running a database server, so it's also the simplest. Of course, that doesn't make it a toy; it performs admirably against its more well-known brethren.

Why is it easy to set up? The SQLite database adapter comes bundled in all versions of Python, starting with version 2.5. Be aware that we're only talking about the adapter here. Some distributions come bundled with SQLite, others link to the system-installed SQLite, and everyone else will need to download and install it manually.

SQLite is just one RDBMS supported by Django, so don't feel you're stuck with that, especially if your company is already using one of the server-based databases. You can read more about Django and database installation at http://docs.djangoproject.com/en/dev/topics/install/#database-installation.

We have also seen a recent rapid proliferation of non-relational (NoSQL) databases. Presumably this is due to the additional scalability offered by such systems in the face of an ever-increasing amount of data. If you're talking about the volume of data on the scale of Facebook, Twitter, or similar services, a relational database usually requires manual partitioning, also known as *sharding*. If you wish to develop for NoSQL databases such as MongoDB or Google App Engine's native datastore, try Django-nonrel so that users have the option of using either relational or non-relational databases, as opposed to just one type. (As an FYI, Google App Engine also has a relational [MySQL-compatible] database option, Google Cloud SQL.)

---

1. A Web server is not required until deployment, so you can hold off on this if you prefer. Django comes with a development server (which we'll take a look at) that aids you during the creation and testing of your application until you're ready to go live.

You can download Django-nonrel from http://www.allbuttonspressed. com/projects/django-nonrel followed by one of the adapters, https:// github.com/FlaPer87/django-mongodb-engine (Django with MongoDB), or http://www.allbuttonspressed.com/projects/djangoappengine (Django on Google App Engine's datastore). Because Django-nonrel is (at the time of this writing) a fork of Django, you can just install it instead of a stock Django package. The main reason for doing that is because you want to use the same version for both development and production. As stated at http://www.allbuttonspressed.com/projects/django-nonrel, *the modifications to Django are minimal (maybe less than 100 lines)*." Django-nonrel is available as a Zip file, so you would just unzip it, go into the folder, and issue the following command:

```
$ sudo python setup.py install
```

These are the same instructions as if you went to download the stock Django tarball (see below), so you can completely skip the next subsection (Installing Django) to the start of the tutorial.

Installing Django

There are several ways of installing Django on your system, which are listed here in increasing order of effort and/or complexity:

- Python package manager
- Operating system package manager
- Standard release tarball
- Source code repository

The simplest download and installation process takes advantage of Python package management tools like `easy_install` from Setuptools (http://packages.python.org/distribute/easy_install.html) or `pip` (http:// pip.openplans.org), both of which are available for all platforms. For Windows users with Setuptools, the `easy_install.exe` file should be installed in the `Scripts` folder in which your Python distribution is located. You only need to issue a single command; this is the command you would use from a DOS Command window:

```
C:\WINDOWS\system32>easy_install django
Searching for django
Reading http://pypi.python.org/simple/django/
Reading http://www.djangoproject.com/
Best match: Django 1.2.7
```

```
Downloading http://media.djangoproject.com/releases/1.2/Django-
1.2.7.tar.gz
Processing Django-1.2.7.tar.gz
. . .
Adding django 1.2.7 to easy-install.pth file
Installing django-admin.py script to c:\python27\Scripts

Installed c:\python27\lib\site-packages\django-1.2.7-py2.7.egg
Processing dependencies for django
Finished processing dependencies for django
```

To avoid having to type in the full path of easy_install.exe, we recommend that you add C:\Python2x\Scripts to your PATH environment variable,[2] depending on which Python 2.x you have installed. If you're on a POSIX system, easy_install will be installed in a well-known path such as /usr/bin or /usr/local/bin, so you don't have to worry about adding a new directory to your PATH, but you *will* probably need to use the sudo command to install it the typical system directories such as /usr/local. Your command will look something like

```
$ sudo easy_install django
```

or, like this:

```
$ pip install django # sudo
```

if not using virtualenv.

Using sudo is only necessary if you're installing in a location for which superuser access is required; if installing in user-land then it isn't necessary. We also encourage you to consider "container" environments such as virtualenv. Using virtualenv gives you the ability to have multiple installations with multiple versions of Python and/or Django, different databases, etc. Each environment runs in its own container and can be created, managed, executed, and destroyed at your convenience. You can find out more about virtualenv at http://pypi.python.org/pypi/virtualenv.

Another way to install Django is by using your operating system's package manager, if your system has one. These are generally confined to POSIX computers (Linux and Mac OS X). You'll issue a command similar to the following:

(Linux) $ sudo *COMMAND* install django

(Mac OS X) $ sudo port install django

---

2. Windows-based PC users can modify their PATH by right-clicking My Computer, and then selecting Properties. In the dialog box that opens, select the Advanced tab, and then click the Environment Variables button.

For Linux, *COMMAND* is your distribution's package manager, for example, apt-get, yum, aptitude, etc. You can find instructions for installing from distributions at http://docs.djangoproject.com/en/dev/misc/distributions.

In addition to the methods just described, you can simply download and install the original release tarball from the Django Web site. Once you unzip it, you can run the usual installation command:

```
$ sudo python setup.py install
```

You can find more specific instructions at http://docs.djangoproject.com/en/dev/topics/install/#installing-an-official-release

Hardcore developers might prefer to get the latest from the Subversion source tree itself. You can find the instructions at http://docs.djangoproject.com/en/dev/topics/install/#installing-the-development-version

Finally, here are the overall installation instructions:

http://docs.djangoproject.com/en/dev/topics/install/
#install-the-django-code

The next step is to bring up a server and confirm that everything installed properly and is working correctly. But first, let's talk about some basic Django concepts: projects and apps.

11.4 Projects and Apps

What are projects and apps in Django? Simply put, you can consider a *project* as the set of all files necessary to create and run an entire Web site. Within a project folder are a set of one or more subdirectories that have specific functionality; these are called *apps*, although apps don't necessarily need to be inside the project folder. Apps can be specific to the project, or they can be reusable components that you can take from project to project. Apps are the individual subcomponents of functionality, the sum of which form an entire Web experience. You can have apps that solicit and manage user/reader feedback, update real-time information, process feed data, aggregate data from other sites, etc.

One of the more well-known set of reusable Django apps can be found in a platform called Pinax. Such apps include (but are not limited to) authentication (OpenID support, password management, etc.), messaging (e-mail verification, notifications, user-to-user contact, interest groups, threaded discussions, etc.), and more stand-alone features, such as project management, blogging, tagging, and contact import. You can read more about Pinax at http://pinaxproject.com.

The concept of projects and apps makes this type of plug-n-play functionality feasible and gives the added bonus of strongly encouraging agile design and code reuse. Okay, now that you know what projects and apps are, let's create a project!

11.4.1   Creating a Project in Django

Django comes with a utility called `django-admin.py` that can streamline tasks such as the creation of the aforementioned project directories. On POSIX platforms, it will usually be installed into directories such as `/usr/local/bin`, `/usr/bin`, etc.; if you're on a Windows-based computer, it goes into the `Scripts` folder, which is directly in your Python installation folder, e.g., `C:\Python27\Scripts`. For either POSIX computers *or* Windows computers, you should make sure that `django-admin.py` is in your `PATH` environment variable so that it can be executed from the command-line (unless you like calling interpreters by using full pathnames).

For Windows computers, you will likely have to manually add `c:\python27` and `c:\python27\scripts` to your system PATH variable for everything to work well (or whatever directory you installed Python in). You do this by opening the Control Panel and then clicking System, or you can right-click My Computer, and then choose Properties. From here, select the Advanced tab, and then click the Environment Variables button. You can choose to edit the PATH entry either for a single user (the top listbox) or for all users (the bottom listbox), and then add `;c:\python27;c:\python27\scripts` after any text in the "Variable value" textbox. Some of what you see appears in Figure 11-1.

Once your PATH is set (on either type of platform), you should be able to run `python` and get an interactive interpreter and Django's `django-admin.py` command to see its usage. You can test this by opening up a Unix shell or DOS Command window and issuing those command names. Once you've confirmed that everything is working, we can proceed.

The next step is to go to a directory or folder in which you want to place your code. To create the project in the current working directory, issue the following command (we'll use a generic project name such as *mysite*, but you can call it anything you wish):

```
$ django-admin.py startproject mysite
```

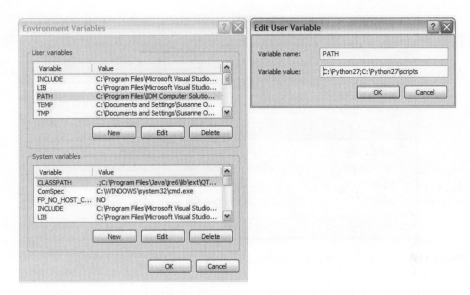

Figure 11-1 Adding Python to the Windows PATH variable.

Note that if you're on a Windows PC, you'll first need to open a DOS Command window first. Of course, your prompt will look more like `C:\WINDOWS\system32>` as a (shell) prompt instead of the POSIX dollar sign ($) or percent symbol (%) for the old-timers.

Now let's take a look at the contents of the directory to see what this command has created for you. It should look something like the following on a POSIX computer:

```
$ cd mysite
$ ls -l
total 32
-rw-r--r--  1 wesley  admin     0 Dec  7 17:13 __init__.py
-rw-r--r--  1 wesley  admin   546 Dec  7 17:13 manage.py
-rw-r--r--  1 wesley  admin  4778 Dec  7 17:13 settings.py
-rw-r--r--  1 wesley  admin   482 Dec  7 17:13 urls.py
```

If you are developing in Windows, opening an Explorer window to that folder will appear similar to Figure 11-2, if we had earlier created a folder named `C:\py\django` with the intention of putting our project there.

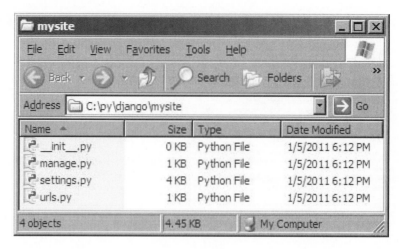

Figure 11-2 The mysite folder on a Windows-based PC.

In Django, a barebones project consists of the four files, __init__.py, manage.py, settings.py, and urls.py (you will add your applications later). Table 11-1 explains the purpose of each file.

Table 11-1 Django Project Files

Filename	Description/Purpose
__init__.py	Specifies to Python that this is a package
urls.py	Global URL configuration ("URLconf")
settings.py	Project-specific configuration
manage.py	Command-line interface for applications

You'll notice that every file created by the startproject command is Python source code—there are no .ini files, XML data, or funky configuration syntax. Django pursues a "pure Python" philosophy wherever possible. This gives you a lot of flexibility without adding complexity to the framework as well as the ability to have your settings file import additional settings from some other file, based on the current configuration, or calculate a value instead of having it hardcoded. There is no barrier, it's just Python. We're sure you've also figured out that `django-admin.py` is a Python script, too. It serves as a command-line interface between you and your project. You'll use `manage.py` in similar way to manage your apps. (Both commands have a Help option with which you can get more information on how to use each.)

11.4.2   Running the Development Server

At this point, you haven't created an app yet, but nonetheless, there are some Django conveniences in place for your use. One of the handiest is Django's built-in Web server. It's a server designed for the development phase that runs on your local computer. Note that we strongly recommend against using it for deploying public sites because it is not a production-worthy server.

Why does the development server exist? Here are some of the reasons:

1. You can use it to run your project (and apps) without requiring a full production environment just to test some code.
2. It automatically detects when you make changes to your Python source files and reloads those modules. This saves time and is convenient over systems that require you to manually restart every time you edit your code.
3. The development server knows how to find and display static media files for the Django Administration (or "admin") application so that you can get started working with that right away. (You will meet the admin soon. For now, just don't get it confused with the `django-admin.py` script.)

Running the development server is as simple as issuing the following single command from your project's `manage.py` utility:

(POSIX) `$ python ./manage.py runserver`

(PCs)   `C:\py\django\mysite> python manage.py runserver`

If you're using a POSIX system and assign your script execute permission, that is, `$ chmod 755 manage.py`, you won't need to explicitly call python, for example, `$ ./manage.py runserver`. The same is true in a DOS Command window, if Python is correctly installed in your Windows registry.

Once the server has started, you should see output similar to that in the following example (Windows uses a different quit key combination):

```
Validating models...
0 errors found.

Django version 1.2, using settings 'mysite.settings'
Development server is running at http://127.0.0.1:8000/
Quit the server with CONTROL-C.
```

Open that link (http://127.0.0.1:8000/ or http://localhost:8000/) in your browser, and you should see Django's "It Worked!" screen, as shown in Figure 11-3.

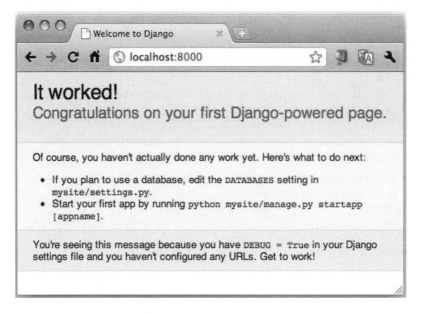

Figure 11-3 Django's initial "It worked!" screen.

Note that if you want to run your server on a different port, you can specify that on the command-line. For example, if you want to run it on port 8080, instead, issue this command: $ python ./manage.py runserver 8080. You can find all of the runserver options at http://docs.djangoproject.com/en/dev/ref/django-admin/#django-admin-runserver.

If you're seeing the "It worked!" screen in Figure 11-3, then everything is in great shape. Meanwhile, if you look in your terminal session, you'll see that the development server has logged your GET request:

```
[11/Dec/2010 14:15:51] "GET / HTTP/1.1" 200 2051
```

The four sections of the log line are, from left to right, the timestamp, request, HTTP response code, and byte count (yours might be slightly different). The "It Worked!" page is Django's friendly way of telling you that the development server is working, and that you can create applications now. If your server isn't working at this point, retrace your steps. Be ruthless! It's probably easier to delete your entire project and start from scratch than it is to debug at this point.

When the server is running successfully, we can move on to setting up your first Django application.

11.5 Your "Hello World" Application (A Blog)

Now that we have a project, we can create apps within it. To create our blog application, use manage.py again:

```
$ ./manage.py startapp blog
```

As with your project, you can call your application *blog* as we did or anything else that you prefer. It's just as simple as starting a project. Now we have a blog directory inside our project directory. Here's what's in it, first in POSIX format, then in a screenshot of the folder in Windows (Figure 11-4):

```
$ ls -l blog
total 24
-rw-r--r--  1 wesley  admin    0 Dec  8 18:08 __init__.py
-rw-r--r--  1 wesley  admin  175 Dec 10 18:30 models.py
-rw-r--r--  1 wesley  admin  514 Dec  8 18:08 tests.py
-rw-r--r--  1 wesley  admin   26 Dec  8 18:08 views.py
```

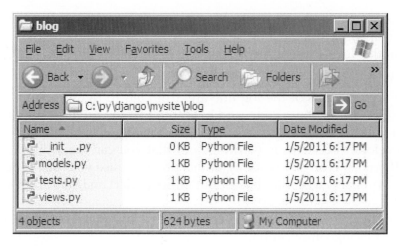

Figure 11-4 The blog folder on a Windows-based PC.

Descriptions of the app-level files are given in Table 11-2.

Table 11-2 Django App Files

Filename	Description/Purpose
__init__.py	Specifies to Python that this is a package
urls.py	The app's URL configuration ("URLconf"); this isn't automatically created such as for project URLconf (hence, why it's missing from the above)
models.py	Data models
views.py	View functions (think "controllers")
tests.py	Unit tests

As with your project, your app is a Python package, too, but in this case, the models.py and views.py files have no real code in them (yet); they're merely placeholders for you to put your stuff into. The unit tests that go into tests.py haven't been written yet and are waiting for your input there, as well. Similarly, even though you can use your project's URLconf to direct all the traffic, one for a local app isn't automatically created for you. You'll need to do it yourself, and then use the include() directive from the project's URLconf to have requests routed to an app's URLconf.

To inform Django that this new app is part of your project, you need to edit settings.py (which we can also refer to as your *settings file*). Open it in your editor and find the INSTALLED_APPS tuple near the bottom. Add your app name (blog) as a member of that tuple (usually toward the bottom), so that it looks like this:

```
INSTALLED_APPS = (
    . . .
    'blog',
)
```

Although it isn't necessary, we add a trailing comma so that if we want to add more to this tuple, we wouldn't then need to add it. Django uses INSTALLED_APPS to determine the configuration of various parts of the system, including the automatic administration application and the testing framework.

11.6 Creating a Model to Add Database Service

We've now arrived at the core of your Django-based blog application: the models.py file. This is where we'll define the data structures of the blog. Following the principle of *Don't Repeat Yourself* (DRY), Django gets a lot of mileage out of the model information you provide for your application. Let's create a basic model and then see all the stuff Django does for us using that information.

The data model represents the type of data that will be stored per record in the database. Django provides a variety of fields to help you map your data into your app. We'll use three different field types in our app (see the code sample that follows).

Open models.py in your editor and add the following model class directly after the import statement already present in the file:

```
# models.py
from django.db import models

class BlogPost(models.Model):
    title = models.CharField(max_length=150)
    body = models.TextField()
    timestamp = models.DateTimeField()
```

That's a complete model, representing a "blog post" object with three fields. (To be accurate, it has four fields—Django automatically creates an auto-incrementing, unique ID field for each model, by default). You can see that our newly minted class, `BlogPost`, is a subclass of `django.db.models.Model`. That's Django's standard base class for data models, which is the core of Django's powerful ORM. The fields are defined like regular class attributes, with each one being an instance of a particular field class, where an instance of the composite is equivalent to a single database record.

For our app, we chose the `CharField` for the blog post `title`, limiting the field to a maximum length. A `CharField` is appropriate for short, single lines of text. For larger chunks of text, such as the body of blog post, we picked the `TextField` type. Finally, the `timestamp` is a `DateTimeField`. A `DateTimeField` is represented by a Python `datetime.datetime` object.

Those field classes are also defined in `django.db.models`, and there are many more types than the three we're using here, from `BooleanField` to `XMLField`. For a comprehensive list of all that are available, read the official documentation at http://docs.djangoproject.com/en/dev/ref/models/fields/#field-types.

11.6.1   Setting Up the Database

If you don't have a database server installed and running, we recommend SQLite as the easiest way to get going. It's fast, widely available, and stores its database as a single file in the file system. Access controls are simply file permissions. If you do have a database server—MySQL, PostgreSQL, Oracle—and want to use it rather than SQLite, then use your database's administration tools to create a new database for your Django project.

Using MySQL

With your (empty) database in place, all that remains is to instruct Django on how to use it. This is where your project's `settings.py` file comes in (again). There are six potentially relevant settings here (though you might need only two): `ENGINE`, `NAME`, `HOST`, `PORT`, `USER`, and `PASSWORD`. Their names render their respective purposes pretty obvious. Just plug in the correct values corresponding to the database server you'll be using with Django. For example, settings for MySQL will look something like the following:

```
DATABASES = {
    'default': {
        'ENGINE': 'django.db.backends.mysql',
        'NAME': 'testdb',
        'USER': 'wesley',
        'PASSWORD': 's3Cr3T',
        'HOST': '',
        'PORT': '',
    }
}
```

Note that if you're using an older version of Django, then instead of everything being in a single dictionary, you'll find these as stand-alone, module-level variables.)

We haven't specified PORT because that's only needed if your database server is running on a non-standard port. For example, MySQL's server uses port 3306 by default. Unless you've changed the setup, you don't need to specify PORT. HOST was left blank to indicate that the database server is running on the current computer that runs our application. Be sure that you've already executed CREATE DATABASE testdb or whatever you named your database and that the user (and its password) already exist before you continue with Django. Using PostgreSQL is more like the setup to MySQL than is Oracle.

For details on setting up new databases, users, and your settings, see the Django documentation at http://docs.djangoproject.com/en/dev/intro/tutorial01/#database-setup and http://docs.djangoproject.com/en/dev/ref/settings/#std:setting-DATABASES as well as Appendix B of *Python Web Development with Django*, if you have the book.

Using SQLite

SQLite is a popular choice for testing. It's even a good candidate for deployment in scenarios for which there isn't a great deal of simultaneous writing going on. No host, port, user, or password information is needed because SQLite uses the local file system for storage and the native file system permissions for access control—you can also choose a pure in-memory database. This is why our DATABASES configuration in settings.py shown in the following code only has ENGINE and NAME when directing Django to use your SQLite database.

```
DATABASES = {
    'default': {
        'ENGINE': 'django.db.backends.sqlite3',
        'NAME': '/tmp/mysite.db',  # use full pathname to avoid confusion
    }
}
```

When using SQLite with a real Web server like Apache, you'll need to ensure that the account that owns the Web server process has write access both for the database file itself and the directory containing that database file. When working with the development server as we are here, permissions are typically not an issue because the user running the development server (you) also owns the project files and directories.

SQLite is also one of the most popular choices on Windows-based PCs because it comes included with the Python distribution (starting with version 2.5). Given that we have already created a `C:\py\django` folder with our project (and application), let's create a `db` directory, as well, and specify the name of the database file that will be created later:

```
DATABASES = {
    'default': {
        'ENGINE': 'django.db.backends.sqlite3',
        'NAME': r'C:\py\django\db\mysite.db',  # full pathname
    }
}
```

If you've been working with Python for some time, you're probably aware that the r before the folder name designates this is a Python raw string. This just means to take each string character verbatim and to not translate special characters, meaning that "\n" should be interpreted as a backslash (\) followed by the letter "n" instead of a single NEWLINE character. DOS file pathnames and regular expressions are two of the most common use cases for Python raw strings because they often include the backslash character, which in Python is a special escape character. See the section on strings in the Sequences chapter of *Core Python Programming* or *Core Python Language Fundamentals* for more details.

11.6.2   Creating the Tables

Now we need to instruct Django to use the connection information you've given it to connect to the database and set up the tables that your application needs. You'll use `manage.py` and its `syncdb` command, as demonstrated in the following sample execution:

```
$ ./manage.py syncdb
Creating tables ...
Creating table auth_permission
Creating table auth_group_permissions
Creating table auth_group
Creating table auth_user_user_permissions
Creating table auth_user_groups
Creating table auth_user
Creating table auth_message
Creating table django_content_type
Creating table django_session
Creating table django_site
Creating table blog_blogpost
```

When you issue the syncdb command, Django looks for a models.py file in each of your INSTALLED_APPS. For each model it finds, it creates a database table. (There are exceptions to this rule but it's true for the most part.) If you are using SQLite, you will also notice that the mysite.db database file is created exactly where you specified in your settings.

The other items in INSTALLED_APPS—the items that were there by default—all have models, too. The output from manage.py syncdb confirms this; you can see Django is creating one or more tables for each of those apps. That's not all the output from the syncdb command, though. There are also some interactive queries related to the django.contrib.auth app (see the following example). We recommend you create a superuser, because we'll need one soon. Here's how this process works from the tail end of the syncdb command:

```
You just installed Django's auth system, which means you don't have
any superusers defined.
Would you like to create one now? (yes/no): yes
Username (Leave blank to use 'wesley'):
E-mail address: ****@****.com
Password:
Password (again):
Superuser created successfully.
Installing custom SQL ...
Installing indexes ...
No fixtures found.
```

Now you have one superuser (hopefully yourself) in the auth system. This will come in handy in a moment, when we add in Django's automatic admin application.

Finally, the setup process wraps up with a line relating to a feature called *fixtures*, which represent serialized, pre-existing contents of a database. You can use fixtures to pre-load this type of data in any newly created applications. Your initial database setup is now complete. The next time you run the syncdb command on this project (which you'll do any time you add an application or model), you'll see a bit less output, because it doesn't need to set up any of those tables a second time or prompt you to create a superuser.

At this point we've completed the data model portion of our app. It's ready to accept user input; however, we don't have any way of doing this, yet. If you subscribe to the model-view controller (MVC) pattern of Web application design, you'll recognize that only the model is done. There is no view (user-facing HTML, templating, etc.) or controller (application logic) yet.

 CORE TIP: MVC vs. MTV

The Django community uses an alternate representation of the MVC pattern. In Django, it's called model-template-view or MTV. The data model remains the same, but the view is known as the template in Django because templates are used to define what the users see. Finally, the "view" in Django represents view functions, the sum of which form all of the logic of the controller. It's all the same, but just a different interpretation of the roles. To read more about Django's philosophy with regard to this matter, check out the FAQ answer at http://docs.djangoproject.com/en/dev/faq/general/#django-appears-to-be-a-mvc-framework-but-you-call-the-controller-the-view-and-the-view-the-template-how-come-you-don-t-use-the-standard-names.

11.7   The Python Application Shell

Python programmers know how useful the interactive interpreter is. The creators of Django know this as well, and have integrated it to aid in everyday Django development. In these subsections, we'll explore how to use the Python shell to perform low-level data introspection and manipulation when such things are not so easily accomplished with Web application development.

11.7.1   Using the Python Shell in Django

Even without the template (view) or view (controller), we can still test out our data model by adding some `BlogPost` entries. If your app is backed by an RDBMS, as most Django apps are, you would be adding rows to a table per blog entry. If you end up using a NoSQL database such as MongoDB or Google App Engine's datastore, you would be adding objects, documents, or entities into the database, instead.

How do we do this? Django provides a Python application shell that you can use to instantiate your models and otherwise interact with your app. Python users will recognize the familiar interactive interpreter start-up and prompt when using the `shell` command of the `manage.py` script:

```
$ python2.5 ./manage.py shell
Python 2.5.1 (r251:54863, Feb  9 2009, 18:49:36)
[GCC 4.0.1 (Apple Inc. build 5465)] on darwin
Type "help", "copyright", "credits" or "license" for more information.
(InteractiveConsole)
>>>
```

The difference between this Django shell and the standard Python interactive interpreter is that in addition to the latter, the shell is much more aware of your Django project's environment. You can interact with your view functions and your data models because the shell automatically sets up environment variables, including your `sys.path`, that give it access to the modules and packages in both Django and your project that you would otherwise need to manually configure. In addition to the standard shell, there are a couple of alternative interactive interpreters that you can consider, some of which we cover in Chapter 1 of *Core Python Programming* or *Core Python Language Fundamentals*.

Rich shells such as IPython and `bpython` are actually preferred by Django because they provide extremely useful functionality on top of the vanilla interpreter. When you run the `shell` command, Django searches first for a rich shell, employing the first one it finds or reverting to the standard interpreter if none are available.

In the previous example, we used a Python 2.5 interpreter without a rich shell; hence, the reason the standard interpreter came up. Now when we execute `manage.py shell`, in which one (IPython) *is* available, it comes up, instead:

```
$ ./manage.py shell
Python 2.7.1 (r271:86882M, Nov 30 2010, 09:39:13)
[GCC 4.0.1 (Apple Inc. build 5494)] on darwin
Type "copyright", "credits" or "license" for more information.

IPython 0.10.1 -- An enhanced Interactive Python.
?         -> Introduction and overview of IPython's features.
%quickref -> Quick reference.
help      -> Python's own help system.
object?   -> Details about 'object'. ?object also works, ?? prints
more.

In [1]:
```

You can also use the `--plain` option to force a vanilla interpreter:

```
$ ./manage.py shell --plain
Python 2.7.1 (r271:86882M, Nov 30 2010, 09:39:13)
[GCC 4.0.1 (Apple Inc. build 5494)] on darwin
Type "help", "copyright", "credits" or "license" for more information.
(InteractiveConsole)
>>>
```

Note that having a rich shell or not has nothing to do with the version of Python you have installed, as in the preceding example; it just so happens I have IPython available only for the version 2.7 installation on my computer but not for version 2.5.

If you want to install a rich shell, just use `easy_install` or `pip`, as explained earlier when we described the different methods for installing Django. Here's what it looks like for Windows PC users to install IPython on their system:

```
C:\WINDOWS\system32>\python27\Scripts\easy_install ipython
Searching for ipython
Reading http://pypi.python.org/simple/ipython/
Reading http://ipython.scipy.org
Reading http://ipython.scipy.org/dist/0.10
Reading http://ipython.scipy.org/dist/0.9.1
    . . .
Installing ipengine-script.py script to c:\python27\Scripts
Installing ipengine.exe script to c:\python27\Scripts
Installed c:\python27\lib\site-packages\ipython-0.10.1-py2.7.egg
Processing dependencies for ipython
Finished processing dependencies for ipython
```

11.7.2   Experimenting with Our Data Model

Now that we know how to start a Python shell, let's play around with our application and its data model by starting IPython and giving a few Python or IPython commands:

```
In [1]: from datetime import datetime
In [2]: from blog.models import BlogPost
In [3]: BlogPost.objects.all()  # no objects saved yet!
Out[3]: []
In [4]: bp = BlogPost(title='test cmd-line entry', body='''
   ....: yo, my 1st blog post...
   ....: it's even multilined!''',
   ....: timestamp=datetime.now())
In [5]: bp
Out[5]: <BlogPost: BlogPost object>
In [6]: bp.save()
```

```
In [7]: BlogPost.objects.count()
Out[7]: 1
In [8]: exec _i3  # repeat cmd #3; should have 1 object now
Out[8]: [<BlogPost: BlogPost object>]
In [9]: bp = BlogPost.objects.all()[0]
In [10]: print bp.title
test cmd-line entry
In [11]: print bp.body  # yes an extra \n in front, see above

yo, my 1st blog post...
it's even multilined!
In [12]: bp.timestamp.ctime()
Out[12]: 'Sat Dec 11 16:38:37 2010'
```

The first couple of commands just bring in the objects we need. Step #3 queries the database for `BlogPost` objects, of which there are none, so in step #4, we add the first one to our database by instantiating a `BlogPost` object, passing in its attributes that were defined earlier (`title`, `body`, and `timestamp`). Once our object is created, we need to write it to the database (step #6) with the `BlogPost.save()` method.

When that's done, we can confirm the object count in the database has gone from 0 to 1 by using `BlogPost.objects.count()` method (step #7). In step #8, we take advantage of the IPython command to repeat step #3 to get a list of all the `BlogPost` objects stored in the database—we could have just retyped `BlogPost.objects.all()`, but we wanted to demonstrate a rich shell feature. The last steps involve grabbing the first (and only) element of the list of all `BlogPost` objects (step #9) and dumping out all the data to show that we were able to successfully retrieve the data we just stored moments ago.

The preceding is just a sampling of what you can do with an interactive interpreter tied to your app. You can read more about the shell's features at http://docs.djangoproject.com/en/dev/intro/tutorial01/#playing-with-the-api. These Python shells are great developer tools. In addition to the standard command-line tool you get bundled with Python, you'll find them incorporated into integrated development environments (IDEs) as well as augmented with even more functionality in third-party developed interactive interpreters such as IPython and bpython.

Almost all users and many developers prefer a web-based create, read, update, delete (CRUD) tool instead, and this is true for every web app that's developed. But do developers really want to create such an administration Web console for every single app they create? Seems like you'd always want to have one, and that's where the Django admin app comes in.

11.8   The Django Administration App

The automatic back-end administration application, or *admin* for short, has been described as Django's crown jewel. For anyone who has tired of creating simple CRUD interfaces for Web applications, it's a godsend. Admin is an app that every Web site needs. Why? Well, you might want to confirm your app's ability to insert a new record as well as update or delete it. You understand that, but if your app hasn't been completed yet, that makes this a bit more difficult. The admin app solves this problem for you by giving developers the ability to validate their data manipulation code before the full UI has been completed.

11.8.1   Setting Up the Admin

Although the admin app comes free with Django, it's still optional, so you'll need to explicitly enable it by specifying this in your configuration settings, just like you did with your own blog application. Open `settings.py` and let's zoom down to the `INSTALLED_APPS` tuple again. You added `'blog'`, earlier, but you probably overlooked the four lines right above it:

```
INSTALLED_APPS = (
    . . .
    # Uncomment the next line to enable the admin:
    # 'django.contrib.admin',
    # Uncomment the next line to enable admin documentation:
    # 'django.contrib.admindocs',
    'blog',
)
```

The one we care about is the first commented-out entry, `'django.contrib.admin'`. Remove the hash character (#)—a.k.a. the octothorpe, pound sign, or comment symbol—at the beginning of the line to enable it. The second one is optional, representing the Django admin documentation generator. The `admindocs` app auto-generates documents for your project by extracting Python documentation strings ("docstrings") and makes those available to the admin. If you want to enable it, that's fine, but we won't be using it in our example here.

Every time you add a new application to your project, you should perform a `syncdb` to ensure that the tables it needs have been created in your database. Here we can see that adding the admin app to `INSTALLED_APPS` and running `syncdb` triggers the creation of one more table in our database:

```
$ ./manage.py syncdb
Creating tables ...
Creating table django_admin_log
Installing custom SQL ...
Installing indexes ...
No fixtures found.
```

Now that the app is set up, all we need to do is give it a URL so that we can get to it. In the automatically generated (project) urls.py, you'll notice these lines near the top:

```
# Uncomment the next two lines to enable the admin:
# from django.contrib import admin
# admin.autodiscover()
```

You'll also see this 2-tuple commented out near the bottom of the urlpatterns global variable:

```
# Uncomment the next line to enable the admin:
# (r'^admin/', include(admin.site.urls)),
```

Uncomment all three real lines of code and save the file. You've just directed Django to load up the default admin site when visitors to the Web site hit the URL http://localhost:8000/admin.

Finally, your applications need to specify to Django which models should show up for editing in the admin screens. To do so, you simply need to register your BlogPost model with it. Create blog/admin.py with the following lines:

```
# admin.py
from django.contrib import admin
from blog import models

admin.site.register(models.BlogPost)
```

The first two lines import the admin and our data model(s). They are followed by the line that registers our BlogPost class with the admin. This enables the admin to manage objects of this type in the database (in addition to the others already registered).

11.8.2   Trying Out the Admin

Now that we've registered our model with the admin, let's take it out for a spin. Issue the manage.py runserver command again, and then go to the same link as earlier (either http://127.0.0.1:8000 or http://localhost:8000). What do you get? Hopefully, you actually get an error. Specifically, you should get a 404 error that looks similar to the one depicted in Figure 11-5.

Figure 11-5 The admin login screen.

Why do you get this error? It's because you haven't defined an action for the '/' URL yet. The only one that you've enabled for your app is /admin, so you need to go directly to *that* URL, instead; that is, you need to go to http://127.0.0.1:8000/admin, or http://localhost:8000/admin, or just add /admin to the existing path in your browser.

In fact, if you look carefully at the error screen, Django itself informs you that only /admin is available because it tries them all before it gives up. Note that the "It Worked!" page is a special case for which you have *no* URLs set for your app. (If it weren't for that special case, you would've received a 404 error, as well.)

When you do arrive at the admin safely, you'll be prompted to login with a nice, friendly screen, as shown in Figure 11-6.

Type in the superuser username and password that you created earlier. Once you've logged in, you'll see the admin home page, as shown in Figure 11-7.

What you'll see is the set of all classes that have registered with the admin app. Because the admin allows you to manipulate all of these classes which live in the database, including Users, this means that you can add standard, "staff," or other superusers (and from a friendly Web interface, not a command-line or a shell environment).

Figure 11-6 The admin login screen.

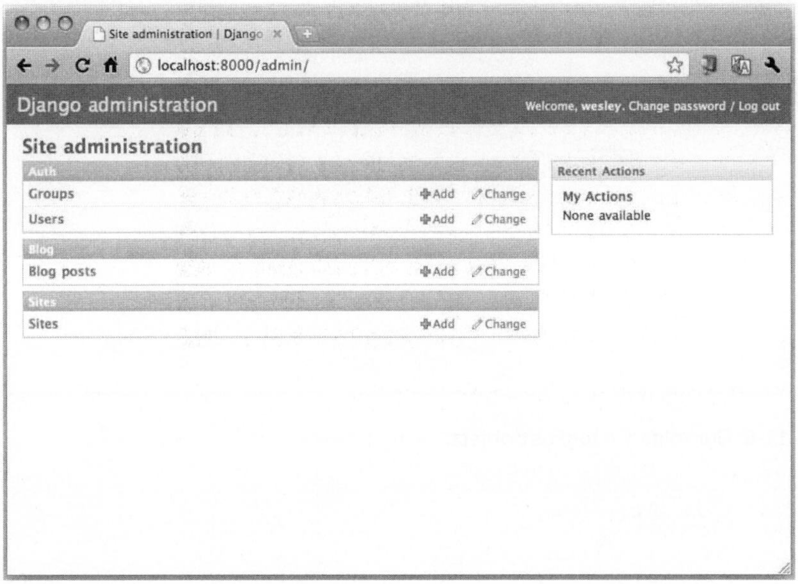

Figure 11-7 The admin home page.

CORE TIP: My class isn't there!

Sometimes, your class might not appear in the list. The three most common causes for "my app's data doesn't show up in the admin" issues include:

1. Forgetting to register your model class with `admin.site.register()`
2. Errors in the app's `models.py` file
3. Forgetting to add the app to the `INSTALLED_APPS` tuple in your `settings.py` file.

Now, let's explore the real power of the admin: the ability to manipulate your data. If you click the "Blog posts" link, you'll go to a page listing all of the `BlogPost` objects in the database (see Figure 11-8)—so far, we only have the one that we entered from the shell, earlier.

Figure 11-8 Our solitary `BlogPost` object.

Notice in the figure that it's identified with a very generic tag of "Blog-Post object." Why is the post given such an awkward name? Django is designed to flexibly handle an infinite variety of content types, so it doesn't take guesses about what field might be the best handle for a given piece of content. As a result, it's direct and not so interesting.

Because you are fairly certain that this post represents the data you entered earlier, and you're not going to confuse this entry with other Blog-Post objects, no additional information about this object is needed. Go ahead and click it to enter the edit screen shown in Figure 11-9.

Figure 11-9 Web view of our command-line BlogPost entry.

Feel free to make any changes you desire (or none at all), and then click **Save and add another** so that we can experiment with adding an entry from a Web form (instead of from the shell). Figure 11-10 illustrates how the form is identical to that in which you edited the previous post a moment ago.

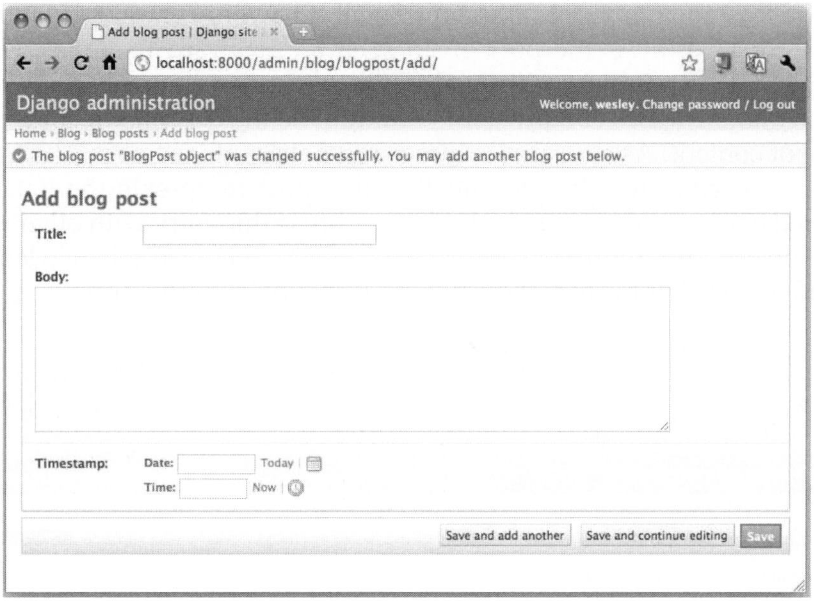

Figure 11-10 With the previous post saved, we're ready to add a new one.

What's a new `BlogPost` without content? Give your post a title and some scintillating content, perhaps similar to what you see in Figure 11-11. For the timestamp, you can click the **Today** and **Now** shortcut links to fill in the current date and time. You can also click the calendar and clock icons to pull up handy date and time pickers. When you're done writing your masterpiece, click the **Save** button.

After your post has been saved to the database, a screen pops up that displays a confirmation message (The blog post "BlogPost object" was added successfully.) along with a list of all your blog posts, as shown in Figure 11-12.

Note that this output has *not* improved any—in fact, it has become worse because we now have two `BlogPost` objects, but there's no way to distinguish between them. You just aren't going to feel satisfied seeing all the entries generically labeled as "`BlogPost` object." You're certainly not alone if you're thinking, "There has got to be a way to make it look more useful!" Well, Django gives you the power to do just that.

Earlier, we enabled the admin tool with the bare minimum configuration, namely registering our model with the admin app all by itself. However, with an extra two lines of code and a modification of the registration

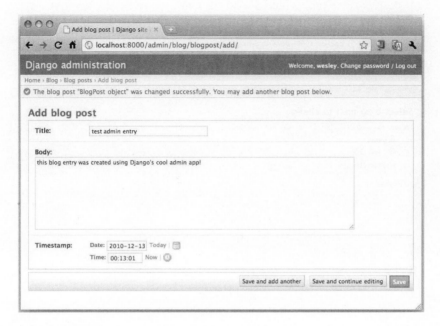

Figure 11-11 Adding a new post directly from the admin.

call, we can make the presentation of the listing much nicer and more useful. Update your `blog/admin.py` file with a new `BlogPostAdmin` class, and add it to the registration line so that it now looks like this:

```
# admin.py
from django.contrib import admin
from blog import models

class BlogPostAdmin(admin.ModelAdmin):
    list_display = ('title', 'timestamp')

admin.site.register(models.BlogPost, BlogPostAdmin)
```

Note that because we define `BlogPostAdmin` here, we do *not* prepend it as an attribute of our `blog/models.py` module; that is, we don't register `models.BlogPostAdmin`. If you refresh the admin page for `BlogPost` objects (see Figure 11-13), you will now see much more useful output, based on the new `list_display` variable you added to your `BlogPostAdmin` class:

The image in Figure 11-13 must seem like a breath of fresh air as we're no longer looking at a pair of BlogPost objects. To a developer new to Django, it might surprise you that adding two lines and editing a third is all it takes to change the output to something much more relevant.

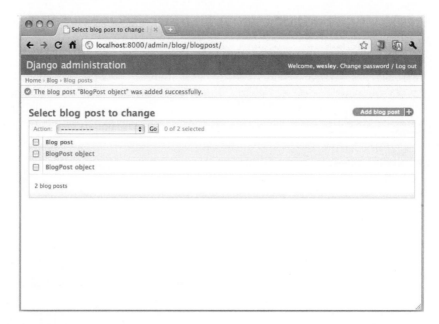

Figure 11-12 The new BlogPost has been saved. Now we have a pair of posts , but there's no way to tell them apart.

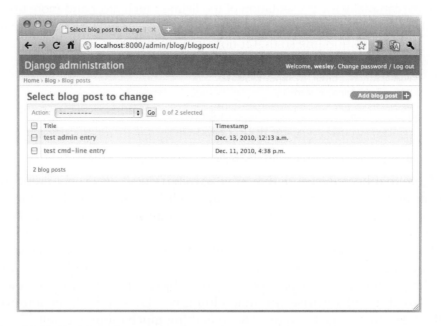

Figure 11-13 Much better!

Try clicking the **Title** and **Timestamp** column headers that have appeared—each one affects how your items are sorted. For example, click the **Title** column head once to sort in ascending order by title; click it a second time to change to descending order. Also try sorting by timestamp order. Yes, these features are already built-in to the admin! You didn't have to roll your own like in the good 'ol days.

The admin has many other useful features that can be activated with just a line or two of code: searching, custom ordering, filters, and more. We've barely touched the features in the admin, but hopefully, we've given you enough of a taste to whet your appetite.

11.9   Creating the Blog's User Interface

Everything that we have just done was strictly for you, the developer, right? Users of your app will not be using the Django shell and probably not the admin tool either. We now need to build the public-facing side of your app. From Django's perspective, a Web page has the following three typical components:

- A *template* that displays information passed to it (via a Python dictionary-like object).

- A *view function* or "view" that performs the core logic for a request. It will likely fetch (and format) the information to be displayed, typically from a database.

- A *URL pattern* that matches an incoming request with the corresponding view, optionally passing parameters to the view, as well.

When you think about it, you can see how when Django processes a request, it processes the request bottom-up: it starts by finding the matching URL pattern. It then calls the corresponding view function which then returns the data rendered into a template back to the user.

We're going to build our app in a slightly different order:

1. A basic template comes first because we need to be able to *see* stuff.
2. Design a quick URL pattern so that Django can access our app right away.
3. Prototype and then iterate as we develop the view function.

The main reason for this order is that your template and URL pattern aren't going to change very much. The heart and soul of your application will be in the view, so we want to employ an agile way of building it. By creating the view steps at a time, we're more in-line with the *test-driven development* (TDD) model.

11.9.1   Creating a Template

Django's template language is easy enough to read that we can jump right in to example code. This is a simple template for displaying a single blog post (based on the attributes of our `BlogPost` object):

```
<h2>{{ post.title }}</h2>
<p>{{ post.timestamp }}</p>
<p>{{ post.body }}</p>
```

You probably noticed that's it's just HTML (though Django templates can be used for any kind of textual output) plus special tags in curly braces: `{{ ... }}`. These tags are called *variable tags.* They display the contents of the object within the braces. Inside a variable tag, you can use Python-style dot-notation to access attributes of these variables. The values can be pure data or callables—if they're the latter, they will automatically be called without requiring you to include "()" to indicate a function/method call.

There are also special functions that you can use in variable tags called *filters*. These are functions that you can apply immediately to a variable while inside the tag. All you need to do is to insert a pipe symbol (|) right after the variable, followed by the filter name. For example, if we wanted to titlecase the `BlogPost` title, you would simply call the `title()` filter like this:

```
<h2>{{ post.title|title }}</h2>
```

This means that when the template encounters our `post.title` of "test admin entry," the final HTML output will be `<h2>Test Admin Entry</h2>`.

Variables are passed to the template in the form of a special Python dictionary called a *context*. In the preceding example, we're assuming a `Blog-Post` object called "post" has been passed in via the context. The three lines of the template fetch the `BlogPost` object's title, body, and timestamp fields, respectively. Now let's enhance the template a bit to make it a bit more useful, such as passing in all blog posts via the context so that we can loop through and display them:

```
<!-- archive.html -->
{% for post in posts %}
    <h2>{{ post.title }}</h2>
    <p>{{ post.timestamp }}</p>
    <p>{{ post.body }}</p>
    <hr>
{% endfor %}
```

The original three lines are unchanged; we've simply wrapped this core functionality with a loop over all posts. In doing so, we've introduced another construct of Django's templating language: *block tags*. Whereas variable tags are delimited by using pairs of curly braces, block tags use braces and percent symbols as enclosing pairs: {% ... %}. They are used to embed logic such as loops and conditionals into your HTML template.

Save the HTML template code above into a simple template in a file called `archive.html` and put it in a directory called `templates`, inside your app's folder; thus, the path to your template file should be `mysite/blog/templates/archive.html`. The name of the template itself is arbitrary (we could have called it `foo.html`), but the `templates` directory name is mandatory. By default, when searching for templates, Django will look for a `templates` directory inside each of your installed applications.

To learn more about templates and tags, check out the official documents page at http://docs.djangoproject.com/en/dev/ref/templates/api/#basics.

The next step is to prepare for the creation of the view function that users are eventually going to execute to see the output from our brand new template. Before we create the view, let's approach this from the user's point of view.

11.9.2 Creating a URL Pattern

In this next section, we're going to discuss how the pathnames of URLs in your users' browsers are mapped to various parts of your app. When users issue a client request from their browsers, the Internet magic of mapping hostnames to IP addresses happens, followed by the client making a connection to the server's address and at port 80 or other designated port (the Django development server uses 8000 by default).

The Project's URLconf

The server, through the magic of WSGI, will end up calling the endpoint of Django, which passes the request down the line. The type of request (GET,

POST, etc.) and path (the remainder of the URL beyond the protocol, host, and port) are accepted and arrives at the project URLconf (`mysite/urls.py`) file. Here, there must be a valid (regular expression) match on the path that resolves the request; otherwise, the server will return a 404 error just like the one we encountered earlier in the "Trying Out the Admin" subsection, because we did not define a handler for `'/'`.

We *could* create the needed URL pattern directly inside `mysite/urls.py`, but that makes for a messy coupling between our project and our app. However, we might want to use our blog app somewhere else, so it would be nice if it were responsible for its own URLs. This falls in line with code reuse principles, DRY, debugging the same code in one place, etc. To keep our project and app appropriately compartmentalized, we'll define the URL mapping in two simple steps and create two URLconfs: one for the project, and one for the app.

The first step is much like enabling the admin that you saw earlier. In `mysite/urls.py`, there's an autogenerated, commented-out example line that is almost what we need. It appears near the top of your `urlpatterns` variable:

```
urlpatterns = patterns('',
    # Example:
    # (r'^mysite/', include('mysite.foo.urls')),
    . . .
```

Edit out the comment and make the necessary name changes so that it points to our app's URLconf:

```
(r'^blog/', include('blog.urls')),
```

The `include()` function defers taking action here to another URLconf (the app's URLconf, naturally). In our example here, we're catching requests that begin with `blog/` and passing them on to the `mysite/blog/urls.py` that we're about to create. (More on `include()` coming up soon.)

Along with setting up the admin app that we did earlier, now your entire project URLconf should look like this:

```
# mysite/urls.py
from django.conf.urls.defaults import *

from django.contrib import admin
admin.autodiscover()

urlpatterns = patterns('',
    (r'^blog/', include('blog.urls')),
    (r'^admin/', include(admin.site.urls)),
)
```

The `patterns()` function takes a group of 2-tuples (URL regular expression, destination). The regex is straightforward, but what is the destination? It's either directly a view function that's called for URLs that match the pattern, or it's a call to `include()` another URLconf file.

When `include()` is used, the current URL path head is removed, and the remainder of the path is passed to the `patterns()` function of the downwind URLconf. For example, when the URL http://localhost:8000/blog/foo/bar is entered into the client browser, the project's URLconf receives `blog/foo/bar`. It matches the `'^blog'` regex and finds an `include()` function (as opposed to a view function), so it passes `foo/bar` down to the matching URL handler in `mysite/blog/urls.py`.

You can see this in the parameter to `include()`: `'blog.urls'`. A similar scenario exists for http://localhost:8000/admin/xxx/yyy/zzz; the `xxx/yyy/zzz` would be passed to `admin/site/urls.py` as specified by `include` (`admin.site.urls`). Now, if your eyes are sharp enough, you might notice something odd in the code snippet—something small and perhaps missing? It is nearly an optical illusion. Take a careful look at the calls to the `include()` function.

Do you see how the reference to `blog.urls` is in quotes, but not `admin.site.urls`? Nope, it's not a typo. Both `patterns()` and `include()` accept strings *or* objects. Generally strings are used, but some developers prefer the more concrete use of passing in objects. The only thing you need to remember when passing in objects is to ensure that they are imported. In the preceding example, the import of `django.contrib.admin` does the job.

Another example of this usage is coming up in the next subsection. To read more about strings versus objects, take a look at the documents page on this topic at http://docs.djangoproject.com/en/dev/topics/http/urls/#passing-callable-objects-instead-of-strings.

The App's URLconf

With the `include()` of `blog.urls`, we're on the hook to define URLs to match remaining path elements inside the blog application package itself. Create a new file, `mysite/blog/urls.py`, that contains these lines:

```
# urls.py
from django.conf.urls.defaults import *
import blog.views

urlpatterns = patterns('',
    (r'^$', blog.views.archive),
)
```

It looks quite similar to our project URLconf. First, let's remind you that the head (blog/) part of the request URL on which our root URLconf was matching, has been stripped, so we only need to match the empty string, which is handled by the regex ^$. Our blog application is now reusable and shouldn't care if it's mounted at blog/ or news/ or what/i/had/for/lunch/. The only mystery here is the archive() view function to which our request is sent.

Incorporating new view functions as part of your app is as simple as adding individual lines to your URLconf, not adding ten lines here, editing another five lines of some complex XML file there, etc. In other words, if you were to add view functions foo() and bar(), your updated urlpatterns would just have to be changed to the following (but don't really make these changes to yours):

```
urlpatterns = patterns('',
    (r'^$', blog.views.archive),
    (r'foo/', blog.views.foo),
    (r'bar/', blog.views.bar),
)
```

So that's great, but if you continue to develop in Django and come back to look at this file again and again, you'll begin to notice a lot of repetition here, violating DRY, of course. Do you see all the references to blog.views to get to the view functions? This is a good indicator that we should use a feature in patterns(), namely the first argument, which has been an empty string all this time.

That parameter is a prefix for the views, so we can move blog.views up there, remove the repetition, and tweak the import so that it doesn't NameError-out. Here's what the modified URLconf would look like:

```
from django.conf.urls.defaults import *
from blog.views import *
urlpatterns = patterns('blog.views',
    (r'^$', archive),
    (r'foo/', foo),
    (r'bar/', bar),
)
```

Based on the **import** statement, all three functions are expected to be in blog.views, meaning mysite/blog/views.py. From the earlier discussion, you know that because we imported it, we can pass in the objects as we just did in the preceding example (archive, foo, bar). But, would it be so bad of us to be even lazier and just not even *have* that **import** statement?

As described in the previous subsection, Django supports strings in addition to objects so that you don't even need that import. If you remove it and put quotes around your view names, that's fine, too:

```
from django.conf.urls.defaults import *

urlpatterns = patterns('blog.views',
    (r'^$', 'archive'),
    (r'foo/', 'foo'),
    (r'bar/', 'bar'),
)
```

Okay, we know that foo() and bar() don't exist in our example application, but you can expect that real projects will have multiple views in your app's URLconf. We were just showing you how to do to basic cleanup. You can find more information on reducing the clutter in URLconf files in the Django documentation at http://docs.djangoproject.com/en/dev/intro/tutorial03/#simplifying-the-urlconfs.

The final piece of our puzzle is the controller, the view function, which is called upon seeing a matching URL path.

11.9.3   Creating a View Function

In this section, we focus on the view function, the core functionality of your app. The development process can take some time, so we'll first show you how to get started quickly for those who are impatient, and then go into more detail so that you know how to do it right in practice.

"Hello World" Fake View

So, you want to debug your HTML template and URLconf right away without having to create your complete and entire view at this early stage of development? Let's do this! Blow up a fake BlogPost and render it into the template immediately. Create this "Hello World" mysite/blog/views.py six-statement file now:

```
# views.py
from datetime import datetime
from django.shortcuts import render_to_response
from blog.models import BlogPost

def archive(request):
    post = BlogPost(title='mocktitle', body='mockbody',
        timestamp=datetime.now())
    return render_to_response('archive.html', {'posts': [post]})
```

We know the view needs to be called `archive()` because of its designation in the URLconf, so that's easy. The code creates a fake blog post and passes it to the template as a single-element posts list. (Don't call `post.save()` because... well, guess why not?!?)

We'll come back to `render_to_response()` shortly, but if you just use your imagination and guess that it takes a template (`archive.html`, found in `mysite/blog/templates`) and a context dictionary, merges them together, and spits back the generated HTML to the user, then your imagination would be correct.

Bring up your development server (or run it live by using a real Web server). Work through any errors you have in your URLconf or template, and then when you've got it working, you'll see something similar to that shown in Figure 11-14.

Figure 11-14 The output from our fake "view."

Coming up with a fake view with semi-mocked data is the fastest way to get instant gratification and validation that your basic setup is okay. This iterative process is agile, and when things are good, it signals to you that it's safe to begin the real work.

The Real View

Now we're going to create the real thing, a simple view function (actually twice) that will fetch all of our blog posts from the database and display them to users by employing our template. First, we're going to do it the "formal" way, which means strict adherence to the following steps, from obtaining the data to returning the HTTP response back to the client:

- Query the database for all blog entries

- Load the template file

- Create the context dictionary for the template

- Pass the context to the template

- Render the template into HTML

- Return the HTML via the HTTP response

Open `blog/views.py` and enter the following lines of code, exactly as shown. This will execute our preceding recipe—it pretty much replaces all of your earlier fake `views.py` file:

```
# views.py
from django.http import HttpResponse
from django.template import loader, Context
from blog.models import BlogPost

def archive(request):
    posts = BlogPost.objects.all()
    t = loader.get_template("archive.html")
    c = Context({'posts': posts})
    return HttpResponse(t.render(c))
```

Check the development (or real Web) server, then go to the app again in your browser. You should see a simple, bare-bones rendering (with real data) of any blog posts that you have entered, complete with title, time-stamp, and post body, separated by a horizontal rule (<hr>), similar to what you see in Figure 11-15 (if you created the first and only pair of posts that we made earlier).

That's great! But in keeping with the tradition of not repeating yourself, the developers of Django noticed that this was an extremely common pattern (get data, render in template, return response), so they created a shortcut when rendering a template from a simple view function. This is where we run into our friend, `render_to_response()`, once again.

Figure 11-15 The user's view of blogposts.

We saw render_to_response() earlier in our fake view, but let's roll that into our real view now. Add its import from django.shortcuts, remove the now-superfluous imports of loader, Context, and HttpResponse, and replace those last three lines of your view. You should be left with this:

```
# views.py
from django.shortcuts import render_to_response
from blog.models import BlogPost

def archive(request):
    posts = BlogPost.objects.all()
    return render_to_response('archive.html', {'posts': posts})
```

If you refresh your browser, nothing will change because you've only shortened your code and haven't changed any real functionality. To read more about using render_to_response(), check out these pages from the official documentation:

- http://docs.djangoproject.com/en/dev/intro/tutorial03/#a-shortcut-render-to-response

- http://docs.djangoproject.com/en/dev/topics/http/shortcuts/#render-to-response

Shortcuts are just the beginning. There are other, special types of view functions that we'll discuss later called *generic views,* which are even more hands-off than `render_to_response()`. With a generic view, for example, you wouldn't even *need* to write a view function—you'd just use a pre-made generic view that Django provides and map to it directly from the URLconf. That is one of the main goals of generic views if you can believe it: not having to write any code at all!

11.10 Improving the Output

That's it! You did the three steps it takes to get a working app to the point where we now have a user-facing interface (and don't have to rely on the Admin for CRUD of data). So now what? We've got a simple blog working. It responds to client requests, extracts the information from the database, and displays all posts to the user. This is good but we can certainly make some useful improvements to exhibit more realistic behavior.

One logical direction to take is to show the posts in reverse chronological order; it makes sense to see the most recent posts first. Another is to limit the output. If you have any more than 10 (or even 5) posts showing on the page, it is certainly too long for users. First, let's tackle reverse-chronological order.

It's easy for us to tell Django to do that. In fact, we have a choice as to where we want to tell it to do so. We can either add a default ordering to our model, or we can add it to the query in our view code. We'll do the latter first because it's the simplest to explain.

11.10.1 Query Change

Taking a quick step back, `BlogPost` is your data model class. The `objects` attribute is a model `Manager` class, and it has an `all()` method to give you a `QuerySet`. You can think of a `QuerySet` as objects that represent the rows of data returned from the database. That's about as far as you should go because they're not the actual rows because `QuerySets` perform "lazy iteration."

The database isn't actually hit until the `QuerySet` is evaluated. In other words, you can do all kinds of `QuerySet` manipulation without touching the data at all. To find out when a `QuerySet` is evaluated, check out the official documentation at http://docs.djangoproject.com/en/dev/ref/models/querysets/.

Now we have the background out of the way. We could have simply told you to add a call to the `order_by()` method and provide a sort parameter. In our case, we want to sort newest first, which means reverse order by timestamp. It's as simple as changing your query statement to the following:

```
posts = BlogPost.objects.all().order_by('-timestamp')
```

By prepending the minus sign (–) to `timestamp`, we are specifying a descending chronological sort. For normal ascending order, remove the minus sign.

To test reading in the top ten posts, we need more than just two `BlogPost` entries in the database, so here's a great place to whip up a few lines of code using the Django shell (plain one this time; we don't need the power of IPython or bpython) and auto-generate a bunch of records in the database:

```
$ ./manage.py shell --plain
Python 2.7.1 (r271:86882M, Nov 30 2010, 09:39:13)
[GCC 4.0.1 (Apple Inc. build 5494)] on darwin
Type "help", "copyright", "credits" or "license" for more information.
(InteractiveConsole)
>>> from datetime import datetime as dt
>>> from blog.models import BlogPost
>>> for i in range(10):
...     bp = BlogPost(title='post #%d' % i,
...         body='body of post #%d' % i, timestamp=dt.now())
...     bp.save()
...
```

Figure 11-16 shows the change reflected in the browser when you perform a refresh.

The shell can also be used to test the change that we just made as well as the new query we want to use:

```
>>> posts = BlogPost.objects.all().order_by('-timestamp')
>>> for p in posts:
...     print p.timestamp.ctime(), p.title
...
Fri Dec 17 15:59:37 2010 post #9
Fri Dec 17 15:59:37 2010 post #8
Fri Dec 17 15:59:37 2010 post #7
Fri Dec 17 15:59:37 2010 post #6
Fri Dec 17 15:59:37 2010 post #5
Fri Dec 17 15:59:37 2010 post #4
Fri Dec 17 15:59:37 2010 post #3
Fri Dec 17 15:59:37 2010 post #2
Fri Dec 17 15:59:37 2010 post #1
Fri Dec 17 15:59:37 2010 post #0
Mon Dec 13 00:13:01 2010 test admin entry
Sat Dec 11 16:38:37 2010 test cmd-line entry
```

Figure 11-16 The original pair of blog entries, plus ten more.

This gives us some degree of certainty that when the core bits are copied to the view function, things should pretty much work right away.

Furthermore, the output can be limited to only the top 10 by using Python's friendly slice syntax ([:10]), so add that, too. Take these changes and update your blog/views.py file so that it looks like the following:

```
# views.py
from django.shortcuts import render_to_response
from blog.models import BlogPost

def archive(request):
    posts = BlogPost.objects.all().order_by('-timestamp')[:10]
    return render_to_response('archive.html', {'posts': posts})
```

Save the change and refresh your browser again. You should see two changes: the blogs post in reverse-chronological order, and only the ten most recent posts show up—in other words, of 12 total entries, you should no longer see either of the two original posts, as demonstrated in Figure 11-17.

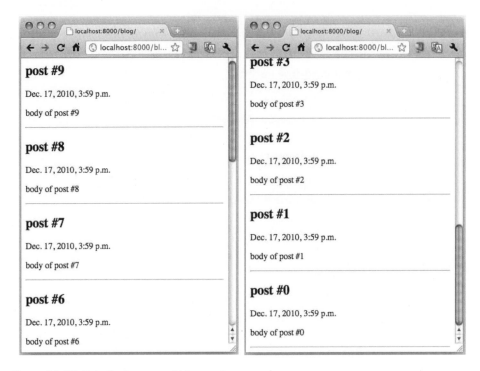

Figure 11-17 Only the ten newest blog posts appear here.

So changing the query is fairly straightforward, but for our particular case, setting a default ordering in the model is a more logical option because this (most recent, top N posts) is pretty much the only type of ordering that makes sense for a blog.

Setting the Model Default Ordering

If we set our preferred ordering in the model, any other Django-based app or project that accesses our data will use that ordering. To set default ordering for your model, give it an inner class called `Meta` and set the ordering attribute in that class:

```
class Meta:
    ordering = ('-timestamp',)
```

This effectively moves `order_by('-timestamp')` from the query to the model. Make these changes to both files, and you should be left with code shown in the following:

```
# models.py
from django.db import models

class BlogPost(models.Model):
    title = models.CharField(max_length=150)
    body = models.TextField()
    timestamp = models.DateTimeField()

    class Meta:
        ordering = ('-timestamp',)

# views.py
from django.shortcuts import render_to_response
from blog.models import BlogPost

def archive(request):
    posts = BlogPost.objects.all()[:10]
    return render_to_response('archive.html', {'posts': posts})
```

 CORE TIP (HACKER'S CORNER): Reducing archive() down to one (long) line of Python

It's possible to reduce archive() down to a single line if you feel comfortable using **lambda**:

```
archive = lambda req: render_to_response('archive.html',
    {'posts': BlogPost.objects.all()[:10]})
```

Readability is one of the hallmarks of having a Pythonic piece of code. Another goal of expressive languages such as Python, is to help reduce the number of lines of code to attain such readability. Although this does reduce the number of lines, I can't say that it helps with making it easier to read; hence, why it's in this Hacker's Corner.

Other differences to the original: the request variable was reduced to just req, and we do save a tiny bit of memory without having the posts variable. If you're new to Python, we recommend you check out the Functions chapter of *Core Python Programming* or *Core Python Language Fundamentals* which covers **lambda**.

If you refresh your Web browser, you should see no changes at all, as it should be. Now that we've spent some time improving data retrieval from the database, we're going to suggest that you minimize database interaction.

11.11 Working with User Input

So now our app is complete, right? You're able to add blog posts via the shell or admin… check. You can view the data with our user-facing data dumper… check. Are we *really* done? Not so fast!

Maybe *you* will be satisfied entering data by creating objects in the shell or through the more user-friendly admin, but your users probably don't know what a Python shell is, much less how to use it, and do you really want to give people access to your project's admin app? No way!

If you've understood the material in Chapter 10 pretty well, and include what you've learned so far in this chapter, you might be wise enough to realize that it's still the same three-step process:

- Add an HTML form in which the user can enter data

- Insert the (URL, view) URLconf entry

- Create the view to handle the user input

We'll take these on in the same order as our first view, earlier.

11.11.1 The Template: Adding an HTML Form

The first step is pretty simple: create a form for users. To make it easier for us during development, just add the following HTML to the top of `blog/templates/archive.html` (above the `BlogPost` object display) for now; we can split it off to another file later.

```
<!-- archive.html -->
<form action="/blog/create/" method="post">
    Title:
    <input type=text name=title><br>
    Body:
    <textarea name=body rows=3 cols=60></textarea><br>
    <input type=submit>
</form>
<hr>

{% for post in posts %}
. . .
```

The reason why we're putting in the same template during development is that it's helpful to have both the user input and the blog post(s) display on a single page. In other words, you won't need to click and flip back-and-forth between a separate form entry page and the `BlogPost` listing display.

11.11.2 Adding the URLconf Entry

The next step is to add our URLconf entry. Using the preceding HTML, we're going to use a path of /blog/create/, so we need to hook that up to a view function we're going to write that will save the entry to the database. Let's call our view create_blogpost(); add the appropriate 2-tuple to urlpatterns in your app's URLconf so that it looks like this:

```
# urls.py
from django.conf.urls.defaults import *

urlpatterns = patterns('blog.views',
    (r'^$', 'archive'),
    (r'^create/', 'create_blogpost'),
)
```

The remaining task is to come up with the code for create_blogpost().

11.11.3 The View: Processing User Input

Processing Web forms in Django looks quite similar to handling the common gateway interface (CGI) variables that you saw in Chapter 10: you just need to do the Django equivalent. You can do a casual flip-through of the Django documentation to get enough knowledge to whip up the snippets of code to add to blog/views.py. First you'll need some new imports, as shown in the following:

```
from datetime import datetime
from django.http import HttpResponseRedirect
```

The actual view function then would look something like this:

```
def create_blogpost(request):
    if request.method == 'POST':
        BlogPost(
            title=request.POST.get('title'),
            body=request.POST.get('body'),
            timestamp=datetime.now(),
        ).save()
    return HttpResponseRedirect('/blog/')
```

Like the archive() view function, the request is automatically passed in. The form input is coming in via a POST, so we need to check for that. Next, we create a new BlogPost entry with the form data plus the current time as the timestamp, and then save() it to the database. Then we're going to redirect back to /blog to see our newest post (as well as another blank form at the top for the next blog entry).

Again, double-check either your development or real Web server and visit your app's page. You'll now see the form on top of the data dump (see Figure 11-18), enabling us to test drive your new feature.

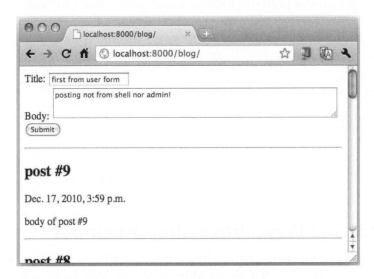

Figure 11-18 Our first user form (followed by previous entries).

11.11.4 Cross-Site Request Forgery

Not so fast! If you were able to debug your app so that you get a form and submit, you'll see that your browser does try to access the /blog/create/ URL, but it's getting stopped by the error shown in Figure 11-19.

Django comes with a data-preserving feature that disallows POSTs which are not secure against *cross-site request forgery* (CSRF) attacks. Explanations of CSRF are beyond the scope of this book, but you can read more about them here:

- http://docs.djangoproject.com/en/dev/intro/tutorial04/#write-a-simple-form

- http://docs.djangoproject.com/en/dev/ref/contrib/csrf/

For your simple app, there are two fixes, both of which involve adding minor snippets of code to what you already have:

1. Add a CSRF token ({% csrf_token %}) to forms that POST back to your site

2. Send the *request context instance* to the token via the template

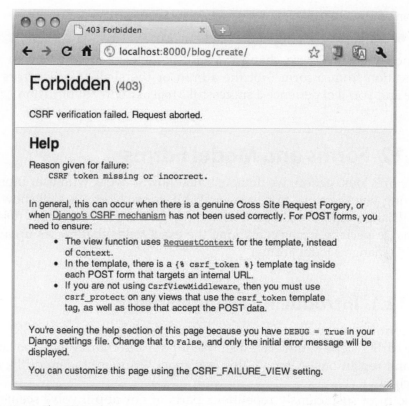

Figure 11-19 The CSRF error screen.

A request context is exactly what it sounds like: a dictionary that contains information about the request. If you go to the CSRF documentation sites that we just provided, you'll find out that `django.template.Request Context` is always processed in a way that includes built-in CSRF protection.

The first step is accomplished by adding the token to the form. Edit the <FORM> header line in `mysite/blog/templates/archive.html`, adding the CSRF token inside the form so that it looks like this:

```
<form action="/blog/create/" method=post>{% csrf_token %}
```

The second part involves editing `mysite/blog/views.py`. Alter the **return** line in your `archive()` view function by adding the `RequestContext` instance, as shown here:

```
return render_to_response('archive.html', {'posts': posts,},
    RequestContext(request))
```

Don't forget to import `django.template.RequestContext`:

```
from django.template import RequestContext
```

Once you save these changes, you'll be able to submit data to your application from a form (not the admin or the shell). CSRF errors will cease and you'll experience a successful `BlogPost` entry submission.

11.12 Forms and Model Forms

In the previous section, we demonstrated how to work with user input by showing you the steps to create an HTML form. Now, we will show you how Django simplifies the effort required to accept user data (Django Forms), especially forms containing the exact fields that makes up a data model (Django Model Forms).

11.12.1 Introducing Django Forms

Discounting the one-time additional work required to handle CSRFs, the three earlier steps to integrate a simple input form frankly look too laborious and repetitious. After all, this *is* Django, virtuous student of the DRY principle.

The most suspiciously repetitious parts of our app involve seeing our data model embedded everywhere. In the form, we see the name and title:

```
Title: <input type=text name=title><br>
Body: <textarea name=body rows=3 cols=60></textarea><br>
```

And in the `create_blogpost()` view, we see pretty much the same:

```
BlogPost(
    title=request.POST.get('title'),
    body=request.POST.get('body'),
    timestamp=datetime.now(),
).save()
```

The point is that once you've defined the data model, it should be the only place where you see title, body, and perhaps timestamp (although the last is a special case because we do not ask the user to input this value). Based on the data model alone, isn't it straightforward to expect the Web framework to come up with the form fields? Why should the developer have to write this in addition to the data model? This is where Django forms come in.

First, let's create a Django form for our input data:

```
from django import forms

class BlogPostForm(forms.Form):
    title = forms.CharField(max_length=150)
    body = forms.CharField(widget=forms.Textarea)
    timestamp = forms.DateTimeField()
```

Okay, that's not quite complete. In our HTML form, we specified the HTML textarea element to have three rows and a width of sixty characters. Because we're replacing the raw HTML by writing code that automatically generates it, we need to find a way to specify these requirements, and in this case, the solution is to pass these attributes directly:

```
body = forms.CharField(
    widget=forms.Textarea(attrs={'rows':3, 'cols':60})
)
```

11.12.2 The Case for Model Forms

Aside from the minor blip regarding specifying attributes, did you do a double-take when looking at the BlogPostForm definition? I mean, wasn't *it* repetitious too? As you can see in the following, it looks nearly identical to the data model:

```
class BlogPost(models.Model):
    title = models.CharField(max_length=150)
    body = models.TextField()
    timestamp = models.DateTimeField()
```

Yes, you would be correct: they look almost like fraternal twins. This is far too much duplication for any self-respecting Django script. What we did previously by creating a stand-alone Form object is fine if we wanted to create a form for a Web page from scratch without a data model backing it.

However, if the form fields are an exact match with a data model, then a Form isn't what we're looking for; instead, you would really do better with a Django ModelForm, as demonstrated here:

```
class BlogPostForm(forms.ModelForm):
    class Meta:
        model = BlogPost
```

Much better—now that's the laziness we're looking for. By switching from a Form to a ModelForm, we can define a Meta class that designates on which data model the form should be based. When the HTML form is generated, it will have fields for all attributes of the data model.

In our case though, we don't trust the user to enter the correct timestamp, and instead, we want our app to add that content programmatically, per post entry. Not a problem, we only need to add one more attribute named `exclude` to remove form items from the generated HTML. Integrate the import as well as the full `BlogPostForm` class presented in the following example to the bottom of your `blog/models.py` file, following your definition of `BlogPost`:

```
# blog/models.py
from django.db import models
from django import forms

class BlogPost(models.Model):
. . .

class BlogPostForm(forms.ModelForm):
    class Meta:
        model = BlogPost
        exclude = ('timestamp',)
```

11.12.3 Using the Model Form to Generate the HTML Form

What does this buy us? Well, right off the bat we can just cut out the fields in our form. Thus, change the code at the top of `mysite/blog/templates/archive.html` to:

```
<form action="/blog/create/" method=post>{% csrf_token %}
    <table>{{ form }}</table><br>
    <input type=submit>
</form>
```

Yeah, you need to leave the submit button in there. Also, as you can see, the form defaults to the innards of a table. Want some proof? Just go into the Django shell, make a `BlogPostForm`, and then mess around with it a little. It's as easy as this:

```
>>> from blog.models import BlogPostForm
>>> form = BlogPostForm()
>>> form
<blog.models.BlogPostForm object at 0x12d32d0>
>>> str(form)
'<tr><th><label for="id_title">Title:</label></th><td><input
id="id_title" type="text" name="title" maxlength="150" /></td></
tr>\n<tr><th><label for="id_body">Body:</label></th><td><textarea
id="id_body" rows="10" cols="40" name="body"></textarea></td></tr>'
```

That's all the HTML that you *didn't* have to write. (Again, note that due to our `exclude`, the timestamp is left out of the form. For fun, you can temporarily comment it out and see the additional timestamp field in the generated HTML.)

If you want output different from HTML table rows and cells, you can request it by using the `as_*()` methods: `{{ form.as_p }}` for `<p>...</p>` delimited text, `{{ form.as_ul }}` for a bulleted list with `<li>` elements, etc.

The URLconf stays the same, so the last modification necessary is updating the view function to send the `ModelForm` over to the template. To do this, you instantiate it and pass it as an additional key-value pair of the context dictionary. So, change the final line of `archive()` in `blog/views.py` to the following:

```
return render_to_response('archive.html', {'posts': posts,
    'form': BlogPostForm()}, RequestContext(request))
```

Don't forget to add the import for both your data *and* form models at the top of `views.py`:

```
from blog.models import BlogPost, BlogPostForm
```

11.12.4 Processing the `ModelForm` Data

The changes we just made were to create the `ModelForm` and have it generate the HTML to present to the user. What about after the user has submitted her information? We still see duplication in the `create_blogpost()` view which, as you know, is also in `blog/views.py`. Similar to how we defined the `Meta` class for `BlogPostForm` to instruct it to take its fields from `BlogPost`, we shouldn't have to create our object like this in `create_blogpost()`:

```
def create_blogpost(request):
    if request.method == 'POST':
        BlogPost(
            title=request.POST.get('title'),
            body=request.POST.get('body'),
            timestamp=datetime.now(),
        ).save()
    return HttpResponseRedirect('/blog/')
```

There should be no need to mention title, body, etc., because they're in the data model. We should be able to shorten this view to the following:

```
def create_blogpost(request):
    if request.method == 'POST':
        form = BlogPostForm(request.POST)
        if form.is_valid():
            form.save()
    return HttpResponseRedirect('/blog/')
```

Unfortunately, we can't do this because of the timestamp. We had to make an exception in the preceding HTML form generation, so we need to do likewise here. Here is the `if` clause that we need to use:

```
if form.is_valid():
    post = form.save(commit=False)
    post.timestamp=datetime.now()
    post.save()
```

As you can see, we have to add the timestamp to our data and then manually save the object to get our desired result. Note that this is the form save(), not the model save(), which returns an instance of the Blog model, but because commit=False, no data is written to the database until post.save() is called. Once these changes are in place, you can start using the form normally, as illustrated in Figure 11-20.

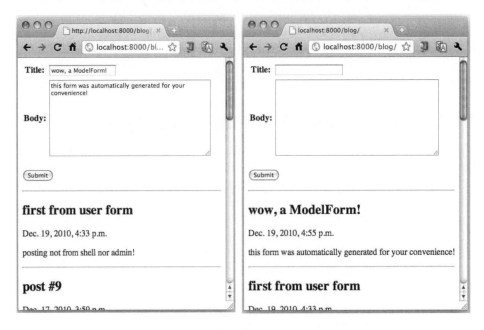

Figure 11-20 The automatically generated user form.

11.13 More About Views

The final most important thing that we need to discuss is a topic that no Django book should omit: *generic views*. So far, when you've needed a controller or logic for your app, you've rolled your own *custom view*. However, you know that Django likes to stick with DRY, hence the reason why you were exposed to shortcuts such as `render_to_response()`.

Generic views are so powerful yet so simple of an abstraction, that when you're able to employ them, you won't have to write a view at all. You'll just link to them directly from your URLconf, pass in a few pieces of required data, and not even need to edit/create any code in `views.py`. We just need to give you enough background to lead you there. We'll begin our journey by going back to a short discussion about CSRF without really talking about it. What do I mean by this?

11.13.1 Semi-Generic Views

Since CSRF is something for which you need to be vigilante in any application that posts back to your app, this renders passing the request context instance extremely repetitious. It's also not very user-friendly to beginners. This is where we can start to play with a generic view without really using it as such. We're going to tweak our custom view to use a generic view to do the heavy lifting. This is called a *semi-generic view*.

Bring up `mysite/blog/views.py` in your editor, and then replace this final line of `archive()`:

```
return render_to_response('archive.html', {'posts': posts,
    'form': BlogPostForm()}, RequestContext(request))
```

Add the new import that follows (and remove the one for `render_to_response()`):

```
from django.views.generic.simple import direct_to_template
```

Modify the final line to match the following:

```
return direct_to_template(request, 'archive.html',
    {'posts': posts, 'form': BlogPostForm()})
```

Wait... what was that all about? Yes, Django does make your life easier by reducing the amount of code you need to write, but we only dropped the request context instance. Are there any other gains to be had here? Not yet. This was just seed-planting. Because we didn't really use `direct_to_template()` as a generic view in this example, we did convert our custom view to a semi-generic view now, because of its use.

Again, pure generic view usage means we call it directly from the URL-conf and wouldn't need any code here in `view.py`. Generic views are often-reused views that are fairly basic but that you still wouldn't want to create or re-create each time you needed the same functionality. Examples include directing users to static pages, providing a generic output for objects, etc.

Really Using a Generic View

Although we employed a generic view function in the previous subsection, we didn't really use it as a pure generic view. Let's do the real thing now. Go to your project URLconf (`mysite/urls.py`). Do you remember the 404 error we got when going to http://localhost:8000/ in the "Trying Out the Admin" subsection earlier in the chapter?

We explained that Django could only handle paths for which there is a matching regular expression. Well, `'/'` matches neither `'/blog/'` nor `/admin/`, so we forced users to visit only those links to get access to your app. This is a disappointment if you want to provide your users some convenience by letting them visit the top-level `'/'` path and then have your app automatically redirect to `'/blog/'`.

Here is the perfect opportunity to use the `redirect_to()` generic view in the proper environment. All you need to do is add a single line to your `urlpatterns`, as shown in the following:

```
urlpatterns = patterns('',
    (r'^$', 'django.views.generic.simple.redirect_to',
        {'url': '/blog/'}),
    (r'^blog/', include('blog.urls')),
    (r'^admin/', include(admin.site.urls)),
)
```

Okay, maybe it's two lines, but it's all part of a single statement. Also, no import is necessary here as we've used a string instead of an object. Now when users visit `'/'`, they'll be redirected to `'/blog/'`, which is exactly what you want. No modifications were needed in `view.py`, and all you did was call it from an URLconf file (project or app). That's a generic view! (If you're looking for something more substantial, we understand—you'll have a more complex generic view exercise at the end of the chapter to get you fully up to speed.)

So far, we've seen `direct_to_template()` and `redirect_to()` generic views, but there are others that you'll likely use fairly often. These include `object_list()` and `object_detail()` as well as time-oriented generic views such as `archive_{day,week,month,year,today,index}()`. And finally, there are CRUD generic views such as `{create,update,delete}_object()`.

Finally, we would be remiss if we didn't inform that the trend is moving toward *class-based generic views*, a new feature introduced in Django 1.3. As powerful as generic views are, converting them to class-based generic views makes them even more so. (The reasons are similar to why exceptions switched from plain strings to classes back in Python 1.5.)

You can read more about plain 'ol generic views as well as class-based generic views from the official documentation at http://docs.django-project.com/en/dev/topics/generic-views/ and http://docs.djangoproject.com/en/dev/topics/class-based-views.

The remaining subsections aren't as critical but they do contain useful information that you can come back to at a later time. If you want to move further ahead, either skip to the intermediate Django app or jump all the way to Chapter 12.

11.14 *Look-and-Feel Improvements

From this point, there are a couple of things you can do to improve the way your app works and to give your site a more consistent look-and-feel:

1. Create a Cascading Style Sheets (CSS) file
2. Create a base template and use template inheritance

The CSS is fairly straightforward, so we won't go over it here, but let's take a look at a really short example of template inheritance:

```
<!-- base.html -->
Generic welcome to your web page [Login - Help - FAQ]
<h1>Blog Central</h1>
{% block content %}
{% endblock %}
&copy; 2011 your company [About - Contact]
</body>
</html>
```

It's not very fancy, but it'll do. Put the common header material, such as corporate logo, sign-in/sign-out and other links, etc., at the top; at the bottom, you'll have items such as a copyright notice, some links, etc. However, the detail to notice is the `{% block ... %}` tag in the middle. This defines a named area that subtemplates will control.

To use this new base template, you must extend it and define the block that is dropped into the base template. For example, if we wanted to have our user-facing blog app page use this template, just add the appropriate boilerplate, and you're good to go. To avoid confusion with `archive.html`, we'll call it `index.html`, generically:

```
<!-- index.html -->
{% extends "base.html" %}
{% block content %}
    {% for post in posts %}
        <h2>{{ post.title }}</h2>
        <p>{{ post.timestamp }}</p>
        <p>{{ post.body }}</p>
        <hr>
    {% endfor %}
{% endblock %}
```

The `{% extends ... %}` tag instructs Django to look for a template named `base.html` and plug the content of any named blocks in this template into the corresponding blocks in that template. If you do decide to try template inheritance, be sure to change your view to use `index.html` as the template file instead of the original `archive.html`.

11.15 *Unit Testing

Testing is something that we shouldn't even need to remind developers to do. You should eat, live, and breathe testing for every app you write. Like so many other aspects of programming, Django offers testing in the form of extending the Python stock unit-testing module that comes with the version of Python you're using. Django can also test documentation strings (or *docstrings* for short). Perhaps not a surprise, these are called *doctests*, and you can read about them in the Django documents page on testing, so we won't cover them here. More important are unit tests.

Unit tests can be simple to create. Django attempts to motivate you by auto-generating a `tests.py` file for you when you create your application. Replace `mysite/blog/tests.py` with the contents of Example 11-1.

Example 11-1   The `blog` Application Unit-Testing Module (`tests.py`)

```
1  # tests.py
2  from datetime import datetime
3  from django.test import TestCase
4  from django.test.client import Client
```

```
5      from blog.models import BlogPost
6
7      class BlogPostTest(TestCase):
8          def test_obj_create(self):
9              BlogPost.objects.create(title='raw title',
10                 body='raw body', timestamp=datetime.now())
11             self.assertEqual(1, BlogPost.objects.count())
12             self.assertEqual('raw title',
13                 BlogPost.objects.get(id=1).title)
14
15         def test_home(self):
16             response = self.client.get('/blog/')
17             self.failUnlessEqual(response.status_code, 200)
18
19         def test_slash(self):
20             response = self.client.get('/')
21             self.assertIn(response.status_code, (301, 302))
22
23         def test_empty_create(self):
24             response = self.client.get('/blog/create/')
25             self.assertIn(response.status_code, (301, 302))
26
27         def test_post_create(self):
28             response = self.client.post('/blog/create/', {
29                 'title': 'post title',
30                 'body': 'post body',
31             })
32             self.assertIn(response.status_code, (301, 302))
33             self.assertEqual(1, BlogPost.objects.count())
34             self.assertEqual('post title',
35                 BlogPost.objects.get(id=1).title)
```

Line-by-Line Explanation

Lines 1–5

Here we're importing datetime for post timestamps, the main test class, django.test.TestCase, the test Web client django.test.client.Client, and finally, our BlogPost class.

Lines 8–13

There are no naming restrictions for your test methods other than they must begin with test_. The test_obj_create() method does nothing more than test to ensure that the object was created successfully and affirms the title. The assertEqual() method ensures that both arguments equate or it fails this test. Here, we assert both the object count as well as the data entered. This is a very basic test, and with a bit of imagination, we can probably make it more useful than it stands. You might also consider testing the ModelForm, too.

Lines 15–21

The next pair of test methods checks the user interface—they make Web calls, as opposed to the first method, which just tests object creation. The `test_home()` method calls the main page for our app at `'/blog/'` and ensures an HTTP "error" code of 200 is received; `test_slash()` is practically the same, but confirms that our URLconf redirection that uses the `redirect_to()` generic view does work. The assertion here is slightly different because we're expecting a redirect response code such as 301 or 302. We're really expecting a 301 here, but don't fail the test if it returns a 302 as a demonstration of the `assertIn()` test method as well as reusing this assertion for the final two test methods, both of which *should* result in 302 responses. In lines 16 and 20, you might be wondering where `self.client` came from. If you subclass from `django.test.TestCase`, you get an instance of a Django test client automatically for free by referring to it directly as `self.client`.

Lines 23–35

These last two methods both test the view for `'/blog/create/'`, `create_blogpost()`. The first, `test_empty_create()`, tests for the situation in which someone erroneously makes a GET request without any data. Our code should ignore the request and redirect to `'/blog/'`. The second, `test_post_create()`, simulates a true user request for which real data is sent via POST, the entry created, and the user redirected to `'/blog/'`. We assert all three: 302 redirect, adding of the new post, and data validation.

Okay, let's try it out by running the following command and observing the output:

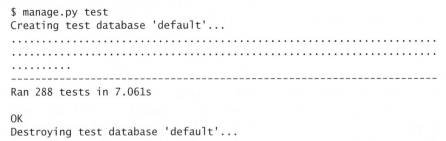

```
$ manage.py test
Creating test database 'default'...
..........................................................
..........................................................
..........
----------------------------------------------------------
Ran 288 tests in 7.061s

OK
Destroying test database 'default'...
```

By default, the system creates a separate in-memory database (called `default`) just for testing. This is so you don't panic that you're going to damage your production data. Each dot (.) means a passing test. Unsuccessful tests are denoted by "E" for error and "F" for failure. To learn more about testing in Django, check out the documentation at http://docs. djangoproject. com/en/dev/topics/testing.

11.15.1 Blog Application Code Review

Let's take a look at all the final versions of our application code at the same time (plus __init__.py [empty] and tests.py [see Example 11-1]). The comments have been left out here, but you can download either these stripped versions or versions with more documentation on this book's Web site.

Although not officially part of our blog application, the first file we look at in Example 11-2 is the project-level URLconf file, mysite/urls.py.

Example 11-2   The mysite Project URLconf (urls.py)

```
1   # urls.py
2   from django.conf.urls.defaults import *
3   from django.contrib import admin
4   admin.autodiscover()
5
6   urlpatterns = patterns('',
7       (r'^$', 'django.views.generic.simple.redirect_to',
8           {'url': '/blog/'}),
9       (r'^blog/', include('blog.urls')),
10      (r'^admin/', include(admin.site.urls)),
11  )
```

Line-by-Line Explanation

Lines 1–4

The setup lines import the stuff necessary for the project URLconf plus the admin-enabling code. Not all apps will employ the admin, so the second and third lines can be omitted if you're not using it.

Lines 6–11

The urlpatterns designate actions and directives to either generic views or any of your project's apps. The first pattern is for '/', which redirects to the handler for '/blog/' by using the redirect_to() generic view; the second pattern, for '/blog/', sends all requests to the blog app's URLconf (coming up next); and the last one is for admin requests.

The next file we look at in Example 11-3 is the app's URLconf, `mysite/blog/urls.py`.

Example 11-3   The `blog` App's URLconf (`urls.py`)

The `blog` app's URLconf file. URLs should be processed here calling view functions (or **class** methods).

```
1    # urls.py
2    from django.conf.urls.defaults import *
3
4    urlpatterns = patterns('blog.views',
5        (r'^$', 'archive'),
6        (r'^create/', 'create_blogpost'),
7    )
```

Line-by-Line Explanation

Lines 4–7

The core of `urls.py` is the definition of the URL mappings (`urlpatterns`). When users visit `'/blog/'`, they are handled by the `blog.views.archive()`. Recall that the `'/blog'` is stripped off by the project URLconf, so by the time we get here, the URL path is only `'/'`. A call to `'/blog/create/'` should only come from POSTing the form and its data; this request is handled by the `blog.views.create_blogpost()` view function.

In Example 11-4, we take a look at the data model for the blog app, `mysite/blog/models.py`. It also contains the form class, as well.

Example 11-4   The `blog` App Data and Form Models File (`models.py`)

The data models live here, but the latter group can be split off into their own file.

```
1    # models.py
2    from django.db import models
3    from django import forms
4
5    class BlogPost(models.Model):
6        title = models.CharField(max_length=150)
7        body = models.TextField()
8        timestamp = models.DateTimeField()
9        class Meta:
10           ordering = ('-timestamp',)
11
```

```
12   class BlogPostForm(forms.ModelForm):
13       class Meta:
14           model = BlogPost
15           exclude = ('timestamp',)
```

Line-by-Line Explanation

Lines 1–3

We import the classes required to define models and forms. We include both classes together in this simple app. If you had more models and/or forms, you might want to split out the forms into a separate forms.py file.

Lines 5–10

This is the definition of our BlogPost model. It includes its data attributes as well as requests that all database queries sort the objects in reverse order according to each row's timestamp field (via the Meta inner class).

Lines 12–15

Here, we create the BlogPostForm object, a form version of the data model. The Meta.model attribute specifies on which data model it should be based, and the Meta.exclude variable requests that this data field be absent from the automatically generated forms. It is expected that the developer fills in this field (if required) before the BlogPost instance is saved to the database.

The mysite/blog/admin.py file in Example 11-5 is only used if you enable the admin for your application. This file contains the classes you're registering for use in the admin as well as any specific admin classes.

Example 11-5   The blog Application Admin Configuration File (admin.py)

```
1   # admin.py
2   from django.contrib import admin
3   from blog import models
4
5   class BlogPostAdmin(admin.ModelAdmin):
6       list_display = ('title', 'timestamp')
7
8   admin.site.register(models.BlogPost, BlogPostAdmin)
```

Line-by-Line Explanation

Lines 5–8

Purely for the optional Django admin, the `list_display` attribute of the `BlogPostAdmin` class gives the admin direction as to which fields to display in the admin console to help viewers differentiate each data record. There are many other attributes we didn't get a chance to cover; however, we encourage you to read the documentation at http://docs.djangoproject.com/en/dev/ref/contrib/admin/#modeladmin-options. Without this designation, you'll just see the generic object names for every row, making it nearly impossible to differentiate instances from one another. The last thing we do (on line 8) is to register both the data and admin models with the admin app.

Example 11-6 presents the core of our app, which is in `mysite/blog/views.py`. This is where all of our views go; it is the equivalent of the controller code for most Web apps. The ironic thing about Django, its adherence to DRY, and the power of generic views is that the goal is to have an empty views file. (However, there are those who feel that they hide *too* much, making the source code harder to read and understand.) Hopefully any custom or semi-generic views you *do* create in this file are short, easy-to-read, maximize code reuse, etc.—in other words, as Pythonic as possible. Creating good tests and documentation also goes without saying.

Example 11-6   The `blog` Views File (`views.py`)

All of your app's logic lives in the `views.py` file, its components called via URLconf.

```
1    # views.py
2    from datetime import datetime
3    from django.http import HttpResponseRedirect
4    from django.views.generic.simple import direct_to_template
5    from blog.models import BlogPost, BlogPostForm
6
7    def archive(request):
8        posts = BlogPost.objects.all()[:10]
9        return direct_to_template(request, 'archive.html',
10           {'posts': posts, 'form': BlogPostForm()})
11
```

```
12  def create_blogpost(request):
13      if request.method == 'POST':
14          form = BlogPostForm(request.POST)
15          if form.is_valid():
16              post = form.save(commit=False)
17              post.timestamp=datetime.now()
18              post.save()
19      return HttpResponseRedirect('/blog/')
```

Line-by-Line Explanation

Lines 1–5

There are many imports here, so it's time to share another best practice: organize your imports by order of proximity to your app. That means access all standard library modules (`datetime`) and packages first. Those are likely to be dependencies of your framework modules and packages—these are the second set (`django.*`). Finally, your app's own imports come last (`blog.models`). Doing your imports in this order avoids the most obvious dependency issues.

Lines 7–11

The `blog.views.archive()` function is the primary view of our app. It extracts the ten most recent `BlogPost` objects from the database, and then bundles that data as well as creates an input form for users. It then passes both as the context to give to the `archive.html` template. The shortcut function `render_to_response()` was replaced by the `direct_to_template()` generic view (turning `archive()` into a semi-generic view in the process).

Originally, `render_to_response()` not only took the template name and context, but it also passed the `RequestContext` object required for the CSRF verification and the resulting response is returned back to the client. When we converted to using `direct_to_template()`, we didn't need to pass in the request context instance because all of this stuff was pushed down to the generic view to handle, leaving only core app matters for the developer to deal with, a shortcut to the (original) shortcut, if you will.

Lines 12–19

The `blog.views.create_blogpost()` function is intimately tied to the form action in `template/archive.html` because the URLconf directs all POSTs to this view. If the request was indeed a POST, then the `BlogPostForm` object is created to extract the form fields filled in by the user. After successful validation on line 16, we call the `form.save()` method to return the instance of `BlogPost` that was created.

As mentioned earlier, the `commit=False` flag instructs `save()` to not store the instance in the database yet (because we need to fill in the timestamp). This requires us to explicitly call the instance's `post.save()` method to actually persist it. If `is_valid()` comes back `False`, we skip saving the data; the same applies if the request was a GET, which is what happens when a user enters this URL directly into the address bar.

The last file we'll look at the template file `myblog/apps/templates/archive.html`, which we present in Example 11-7.

Example 11-7   The `blog` App's Main Page Template File (`archive.html`)

The template file features HTML plus logic to programmatically control the output.

```
1    <!-- archive.html -->
2    <form action="/blog/create/" method=post>{% csrf_token %}
3        <table>{{ form }}</table><br>
4        <input type=submit>
5    </form>
6    <hr>
7
8    {% for post in posts %}
9        <h2>{{ post.title }}</h2>
10       <p>{{ post.timestamp }}</p>
11       <p>{{ post.body }}</p>
12       <hr>
13   {% endfor %}
```

Line-by-Line Explanation

Lines 1–6

The first half of our template represents the user input form. Upon submission, the server executes your `create_blogpost()` view function we discussed a moment ago to create a new `BlogPost` entry in the database. The form variable in line 2 comes from an instance of `BlogPostForm`, which is the form that is based on your data model (in a tabular format). As we mentioned earlier, you can choose from other options. We also explained that the `csrf_token` on line 1 is used to protect against CSRF—it is also the reason that you must provide the `RequestContext` in the `archive()` view function so that the template can use it here.

Lines 8–13

The latter half of the template simply takes the set of (at most) ten (most recent) `BlogPost` objects and loops through them, emitting individual post details for the user. In between each (as well as just prior to this loop) are horizontal rules to visually segregate the data.

11.15.2 Blog App Summary

Of course, we could continue adding features to our blog app ad nauseam (many people do), but hopefully we've given you enough of a taste of the power of Django. (Check the exercises at the end of the chapter for additional challenges.) In the course of building this skeletal blog app, you've seen a number of Django's elegant, labor-saving features. These include the following:

- The built-in development server, which makes your development work more self-contained, and which automatically reloads your code if you edit it.

- The pure-Python approach to data model creation, which saves you from having to write or maintain SQL code or XML description files.

- The automatic admin application, which provides full-fledged content-editing features even for non-technical users.

- The template system, which can be used to produce HTML, CSS, JavaScript, or any textual output format.

- Template filters, which can alter the presentation of your data (such as dates) without interfering with your application's business logic.

- The URLconf system, which gives you great flexibility in URL design while keeping application-specific portions of URLs in the application, where they belong.

- `ModelForm` objects give you a simple way of creating form data based on your data model with little effort on your part.

Finally, we encourage you to stage your app on a real server connected to the Internet and stop using the development server. By getting off of localhost/127.0.0.1, you can really confirm that your app will work in a production environment.

If you enjoyed this example, you'll find an extended version of it along with four other similar training apps of differing variety in *Python Web Development with Django*. Now that you've got your feet wet, let's do a larger, more ambitious real-world project: a Django app that handles e-mail, talks to Twitter, performs OAuth, and is a launch point for something even bigger.

11.16 *An Intermediate Django App: The TweetApprover

Now that you have seen the basics of Django, let's create a more realistic application that does something *useful*. This second half of our treatment on Django will show you how to perform the following tasks:

1. Segment a larger Web app (project) in Django
2. Use third-party libraries
3. Use Django's permissions system
4. Send e-mails from Django

This application will solve an increasingly common use case: a company has a Twitter account and wants regular employees to post updates to it about sales, new products, etc. However, there is some business logic involved, too, and a manager must approve all tweets before they are posted.

When a reviewer approves a tweet, it is then automatically posted to the company's Twitter account, but when the reviewer rejects a tweet, it is sent back to the author with a note indicating why and/or suggestions to improve if resubmission is desired or intended. You can see this workflow illustrated in Figure 11-21.

It would take considerable effort to write this app from scratch. We'd have to build the data model, write code to connect to the database to read and write data, map data entities to Python classes, write code to handle Web requests, dress up the data in HTML before it's returned to the user, and so on. With Django, all of this become easy. And even though Django doesn't have built-in functionality for communicating with Twitter, there are Python libraries available that can do the job.

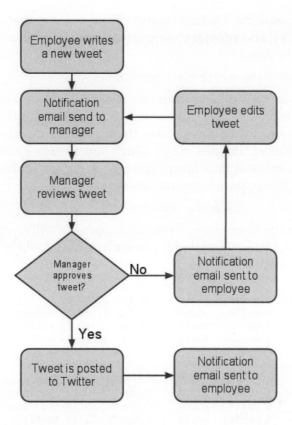

Figure 11-21 A target TweetApprover workflow.

11.16.1 Creating the Project File Structure

When designing a new Django application, the app structure is a good place to start. With Django, you can split up a project into separate applications. In our blog example, we only had one app (blog) in our project, but as we mentioned early on in the chapter, you're not restricted to just one. Whenever you are writing a non-trivial application, it is easier to manage multiple small applications as opposed to a large, single, monolithic application.

"TweetApprover" has two faces: one for regular employees (who post tweets), and one for managers (who approve tweets). We will build one Django app for each within the TweetApprover project; the apps will be called poster and approver.

First, let's create the Django project. From the command-line, run the `django-admin.py startproject` command, similar to what we did earlier with our `mysite` project.

```
$ django-admin.py startproject myproject
```

To distinguish this project from our `mysite` project earlier, we'll call it "myproject," instead—yeah... we're not exactly pushing the limits of creativity here. :-) Anyway, this creates the `myproject` directory along with the standard boilerplate files, about which you already know.

From the command line, jump into the `myproject` folder, in which we can create the two apps, `poster` and `approver`:

```
$ manage.py startapp poster approver
```

This creates the directories `poster` and `approver` within `myproject`, with those standard app boilerplate files in each. Your barebones file structure should now look like this:

```
$ ls -l *
-rw-r--r--  1 wesley  admin     0 Jan 11 10:13 __init__.py
-rwxr-xr-x  1 wesley  admin   546 Jan 11 10:13 manage.py
-rw-r--r--  1 wesley  admin  4790 Jan 11 10:13 settings.py
-rw-r--r--  1 wesley  admin   494 Jan 11 10:13 urls.py

approver:
total 24
-rw-r--r--  1 wesley  admin     0 Jan 11 10:14 __init__.py
-rw-r--r--  1 wesley  admin    57 Jan 11 10:14 models.py
-rw-r--r--  1 wesley  admin   514 Jan 11 10:14 tests.py
-rw-r--r--  1 wesley  admin    26 Jan 11 10:14 views.py

poster:
total 24
-rw-r--r--  1 wesley  admin     0 Jan 11 10:14 __init__.py
-rw-r--r--  1 wesley  admin    57 Jan 11 10:14 models.py
-rw-r--r--  1 wesley  admin   514 Jan 11 10:14 tests.py
-rw-r--r--  1 wesley  admin    26 Jan 11 10:14 views.py
```

The Settings File

After you have created a new Django project, you usually open the `settings.py` file and edit it for your installation. For TweetApprover, we need to add a few settings that aren't in the file by default. First, add a new setting to specify who should be notified when new tweets are submitted and need to be reviewed.

```
TWEET_APPROVER_EMAIL = 'someone@mydomain.com'
```

Note that this is not a standard Django setting, but something only our app needs. As the settings file is a standard Python file, we are free to add our own settings. However, rather than putting this information in each of the two apps, it's simpler to have a single place for this setting at the project level. Be sure to replace the example value above with the *real* e-mail address of the manager assigned to review tweets.

Similarly, we need to instruct Django how to send e-mail. These settings are read by Django, but they are not included in the settings file by default, so we need to add them.

```
EMAIL_HOST = 'smtp.mydomain.com'
EMAIL_HOST_USER = 'username'
EMAIL_HOST_PASSWORD = 'password'
DEFAULT_FROM_EMAIL = 'username@mydomain.com'
SERVER_EMAIL = 'username@mydomain.com'
```

Replace the example values above with valid ones for your e-mail server. If you don't have access to a mail server, feel free to skip these five e-mail settings and comment out the code in TweetApprover that sends e-mails. I'll remind you when we get to that part. For details on all of Django's settings, visit http://docs.djangoproject.com/en/dev/ref/settings.

TweetApprover will publish tweets by using Twitter's public API. To do that, the application needs to supply *OAuth* credentials. (We'll explain more about OAuth in the sidebar that's coming up.) OAuth credentials are similar to regular usernames and passwords, except that one pair of credentials is needed for the application (called "consumer" in OAuth) and one pair is needed for the user.

All four pieces of data must be sent to Twitter for the API calls to work. Just like `TWEET_APPROVER_EMAIL` in our first example in this subsection, these settings are not standard Django settings but are custom to the TweetApprover application.

```
TWITTER_CONSUMER_KEY = '. . .'
TWITTER_CONSUMER_SECRET = '. . .'
TWITTER_OAUTH_TOKEN = '. . .'
TWITTER_OAUTH_TOKEN_SECRET = '. . .'
```

Fortunately Twitter makes it easy to obtain these four values. Go to http://dev.twitter.com, sign in, and then click **Your Apps**. Next, click **Register New App** if you don't have an app yet, or select the app if you have one. For creating a new app, fill out the form to match that shown in Figure 11-22. It does not matter what you put in the **Application Website** field. Note that in our illustrations for this chapter, we are using the Tweet-Approver name, which is obviously taken already, so you will need to create your own application name.

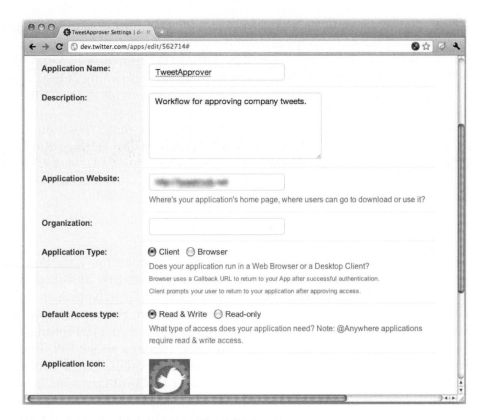

Figure 11-22 Registering a new application with Twitter.

After you have filled out the form and clicked **Save Application**, click the **Application Details** button. On the details page, look for the **OAuth 1.0a Settings**. From that section, copy the **Consumer Key** and **Consumer Secret** values into the variables TWITTER_CONSUMER_KEY and TWITTER_CONSUMER_SECRET variables, respectively, in your settings file.

Finally, we need the values for TWITTER_OAUTH_TOKEN and TWITTER_OAUTH_TOKEN_SECRET. Click the **My Access Token** button and you will see a page similar to that depicted in Figure 11-23 that has these values.

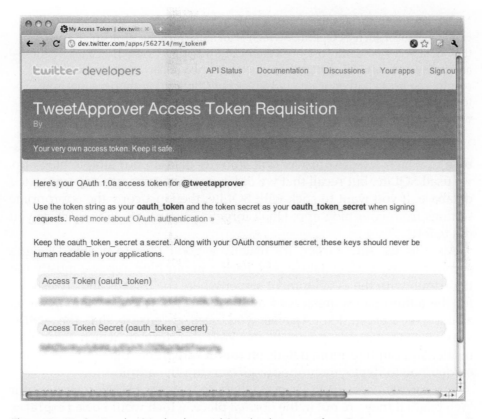

Figure 11-23 Getting the OAuth token and OAuth token secret from Twitter.

 CORE NOTE: OAuth and Authorization vs. Authentication

OAuth is an open *authorization* protocol that provides for a safe and secure way of letting applications access data on your behalf via an API. Not only does it allow you to grant access to applications without revealing your username and password, it also allows you to revoke access easily. An increasing number of Web APIs are using OAuth, just like Twitter. You can read more about how OAuth works at the following locations:

http://hueniverse.com/oauth

http://oauth.net

http://en.wikipedia.org/wiki/Oauth

Note that OAuth is an example of an authorization protocol, which is different from a protocol such as OpenID, which is an *authentication* protocol. Rather than data access, the purpose of authentication is identity, such as a username and password pair. An example in which both play a part is an app that requires a user to authenticate via Twitter but (the user) authorizes that app to (be able to) post a status update to his Twitter stream.

As usual, you should edit the DATABASES variable to point to the database in which TweetApprover will store its data. In our simple blog app, we used SQLite, but recall that we did suggest you can use any supported database. If you want to stick with SQLite, then just copy the appropriate settings from your blog app. Don't forget to run manage.py syncdb as you did before.

Also, as we saw earlier, it's usually a good idea to enable Django's admin for easy CRUD data access. Earlier in our blog app, we mostly ran the admin with the development server where the images and stylesheets for the admin pages are served automatically. If you are running on an actual Web server, like Apache, you need to ensure that the ADMIN_MEDIA_PREFIX variable points to the Web directory in which these files reside. You can find more details on this at http://docs.djangoproject.com/en/dev/howto/deployment/modwsgi/#serving-the-admin-files

You can also specify to Django where to look for HTML templates for Web pages if they are not in the normal place, which would be a templates directory under each app. For example, if you want to create a single unified place for them like we would for this app, then you need to explicitly call this out in your settings.py file.

For TweetApprover, we want to consolidate to a single templates folder in the myproject directory. To do this, edit settings.py and ensure that the TEMPLATE_DIRS variable points to that physical directory. On a POSIX computer, it would look similar to this:

```
TEMPLATES_DIRS = (
     '/home/username/myproject/templates',
)
```

On a Windows-based PC, your directory path would look a little different because of the DOS filepath names. If we were to add the project to our existing C:\py\django folder, the path would look like this:

```
r'c:\py\django\myproject\templates',
```

Recall that the leading "r" is to indicate a Python raw string, which is preferable here over requiring multiple backslashes.

Finally, you need to inform Django about the two apps (poster and approver) you created. You do this by adding 'myproject.approver' and 'myproject.poster' to the INSTALLED_APPS variable in the settings file.

11.16.2 Installing the Twython Library

The TweetApprove app will publish tweets to the world by using Twitter's public API. Fortunately, there are a couple of good libraries that make it really easy to call this API. Twitter maintains a list of the most popular ones at http://dev.twitter.com/pages/libraries#python. The upcoming Web Services chapter features both the Twython and Tweepy libraries.

For this application, we will use the Twython library to facilitate communication between our app and Twitter. We'll get it by using easy_install. (You can also install it by using pip.) easy_install will install twython as well as its dependencies, oauth2, httplib2, and simplejson. Unfortunately, due to naming conventions, although Python 2.6 and newer come with simplejson, it's named as json, so easy_install will still install all three of these libraries, which twython is dependent on, as you can see from the following output:

2.6

```
$ sudo easy_install twython
Password: ***********
Searching for twython
. . .
Processing twython-1.3.4.tar.gz
Running twython-1.3.4/setup.py -q bdist_egg --dist-dir /tmp/
easy_install-QrkR6M/twython-1.3.4/egg-dist-tmp-PpJhMK
. . .
Adding twython 1.3.4 to easy-install.pth file
. . .
Processing dependencies for twython
Searching for oauth2
. . .
Processing oauth2-1.2.0.tar.gz
Running oauth2-1.2.0/setup.py -q bdist_egg --dist-dir /tmp/
easy_install-br8On8/oauth2-1.2.0/egg-dist-tmp-cx3yEm
Adding oauth2 1.2.0 to easy-install.pth file
. . .
Searching for simplejson
. . .
Processing simplejson-2.1.2.tar.gz
Running simplejson-2.1.2/setup.py -q bdist_egg --dist-dir /tmp/
easy_install-ZiTOri/simplejson-2.1.2/egg-dist-tmp-FWOza6
Adding simplejson 2.1.2 to easy-install.pth file
. . .
Searching for httplib2
. . .
```

```
Processing httplib2-0.6.0.zip
Running httplib2-0.6.0/setup.py -q bdist_egg --dist-dir /tmp/
easy_install-rafDWd/httplib2-0.6.0/egg-dist-tmp-zqPmmT
Adding httplib2 0.6.0 to easy-install.pth file
. . .
Finished processing dependencies for twython
```

 CORE TIP: Troubleshooting your installation

Your installation of version 2.6 might not go as smoothly as we portray. Here are a couple of examples of what can go wrong:

1. I ran into a situation installing `simplejson` on Python 2.5 on a Mac in which `easy_install` just could not get it right, complained, and quit, leaving me hanging. In this case, I resorted to doing it the old-fashioned way:

    •   Find and downloaded the tarball (in my case, `simplejson`)

    •   Untar/unzip the distribution and go into the top-level directory

    •   Run python `setup.py install`

2. Another reader discovered a problem when compiling the optional `simplejson` speedups component. In this case, because it is a Python extension, it requires you to have all the necessary tools to build Python extensions, which includes `Python.h`, etc., accessible by your compiler. On a Linux system, you would just install the python-dev package.

We're sure that there are other caveats out there, but if you run into similar issues, hopefully this helps. Small incompatibilities are everywhere; don't get discouraged if it affects you. There is plenty of help out there!

Once everything has been successfully installed, it's time to decide which URLs TweetApprover will use and how they will map to different user actions.

11.16.3 URL Structure

To create a consistent URI strategy, we're going to name all functionality for the `poster` app with URLs that start with /post, and for the `approver` app, URLs that start with /approve. This means that if your copy of Tweet-Approver runs in your domain `example.com`, the `poster` URLs would start with `http://example.com/post`, and the `approver` URLs would start with `http://example.com/approve`.

Now let's go into more detail about the pages under /post that are used to propose new tweets. We will need a page for submitting a brand new tweet; let's take the user to that page when we receive the URL /post without anything after it. Once the user has submitted a tweet, we'll need a page that acknowledges the submission; let's put that at /post/thankyou. Finally, we will need a URL that takes the user to an existing tweet that needs to be edited; let's put that under /post/edit/X, where X is the ID of the tweet that should be edited.

The pages for the manager are under /approve; let's display a list of pending and published tweets when the user accesses that URL. We will also need a page for reviewing one particular tweet and leaving feedback on it; let's put that under /approve/review/X, where X is the ID of the tweet.

Finally, we have to decide what page is displayed when the user goes to the bare URL (example.com/). As most users of TweetApprover will be employees proposing new tweets, let's make the bare URL point to the same page as /post.

We have seen that Django uses configuration files to map URLs to code. At the project level, in the myproject directory, you will find the urls.py file that directs Django to which application in the project to route requests. Example 11-8 presents the file that implements the preceding URL structure:

Example 11-8   The Project URLconf file (myproject/urls.py)

As with the previous example, this project URLconf also goes to either our app or the admin site.

```
1   # urls.py
2   from django.conf.urls.defaults import *
3   from django.contrib import admin
4   admin.autodiscover()
5
6   urlpatterns = patterns('',
7       (r'^post/', include('myproject.poster.urls')),
8       (r'^$', include('myproject.poster.urls')),
9       (r'^approve/', include('myproject.approver.urls')),
10      (r'^admin/', include(admin.site.urls)),
11      (r'^login', 'django.contrib.auth.views.login',
12          {'template_name': 'login.html'}),
13      (r'^logout', 'django.contrib.auth.views.logout'),
14  )
```

Line-by-Line Explanation

Lines 1–4

The first few lines represent boilerplate that always seem to show up in URLconf files: the proper imports as well as the admin for development. (When you're done with development and/or don't want the admin, it's easy to get rid of it.)

Lines 6–14

Things become interesting when we get to the `urlpatterns` variable. Line 7 instructs Django that for any URL that starts with `post/` (after the domain name) it should consult the URL configuration `myproject.poster.urls`. This configuration is in the file `myproject/poster/urls.py`. The next line (line 8) says that any empty URL (after the domain name) should also be handled per the `poster` application's configuration. Line 9 directs Django to route URLs starting with `approve/` to the `approver` application.

Finally, the file includes directives for URLs leading to the admin (line 10) and login and logout pages (lines 11 and 12). A lot of this functionality is part of Django, so you will not need to write code for it. As yet, we haven't discussed authentication, but here it is as simple as including a few more 2-tuples in your URLconf. Django provides its own authentication system, but you can create your own, as well. In Chapter 12, you'll find that Google App Engine offers two authentication options: Google Accounts, or federated login using OpenID.

To recap, the complete URL dispatching looks like what you see in Table 11-3.

Table 11-3 The URLs Handled by This Project and Corresponding Actions

URL	Action
/post	Propose new tweet or post
/post/edit/X	Edit post X
/post/thankyou	Show acknowledgement after the user has submitted a post
/	Same as /post

URL	Action
/approve	List all pending and published tweets
/approve/review/X	Review tweet X
/admin	Go to the admin site for our project
/login	Log the user in
/logout	Log the user out

As you can see in Table 11-3, the main purpose of a project's URLconf is to route requests to the appropriate apps and their handlers, so we're going to continue our journey by looking at the app-level urls.py files. We will start with the poster application.

As we just saw in the project's URLconf, the URLs that match /post/ or "/" will be redirected to the poster application's URLconf, myproject/poster/urls.py. The job of this file in Example 11-9 is to map the rest of the URL to actual code that will be executed within the poster application.

Example 11-9   The poster Application's urls.py URLconf file

The URLconf for the poster app processes a poster's actions.

```
1    from django.conf.urls.defaults import *
2
3    urlpatterns = patterns('myproject.poster.views',
4        (r'^$', 'post_tweet'),
5        (r'^thankyou', 'thank_you'),
6        (r'^edit/(?P<tweet_id>\d+)', 'post_tweet'),
7    )
```

The regular expressions in this file only see the part of the URL that follows after /post/, and based on the first parameter to patterns(), you can see that all view functions will be in myproject/poster/views.py. For the first URL pattern, if it's empty (meaning the original request was either /post/ or "/"), the post_tweet() view is called. If that part is thankyou, then thank_you() is called. Finally, if that part of the URL is edit/X, where X is a number, then post_tweet() is called and X is passed as the tweet_id parameter to the method. Pretty nifty, isn't it? If you're unfamiliar with this regular expression syntax assigning matches to variable names instead of integers (the default), flip back to Chapter 1, "Regular Expressions," for more information.

Because we've segregated our project into two distinct applications, the URLconf and view function files are kept to a minimum. They are also simpler to digest and easier to reuse. Now that we're done looking at the setup for the `poster` application, let's do the same for the `approver` application.

By the same token as our analysis of the `poster` URLconf, the file `myproject/approver/urls.py` shown in Example 11-10 is consulted when Django sees a request for a URL that starts with /approve/. It calls `list_tweets()` if the path doesn't continue beyond /approve/, and `review_tweet(tweet_id=X)` if the URL path matches /approve/review/X.

Example 11-10 The approver Application's `urls.py` URLconf file

The URLconf for the approver app processes an approver's actions

```
1    from django.conf.urls.defaults import *
2
3    urlpatterns = patterns('myproject.approver.views',
4        (r'^$', 'list_tweets'),
5        (r'^review/(?P<tweet_id>\d+)$', 'review_tweet'),
6    )
```

This URLconf is shorter because the `approver` app consists of fewer actions. At this point, we know exactly where to direct users based on the inbound URL path. Now we need to cover the details about the data model used for our project.

11.16.4 The Data Model

TweetApprover needs to store tweets in the database. When managers review tweets, they need to be able to annotate them, so each tweet can have multiple comments. Both tweets and comments need some data fields, as illustrated in Figure 11-24.

The state field will be used to store where in the life cycle each tweet is. Figure 11-25 demonstrates that there are three different states, and Django can help us to ensure that no tweets end up in any other states.

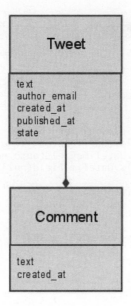

Figure 11-24 The data model for TweetApprover.

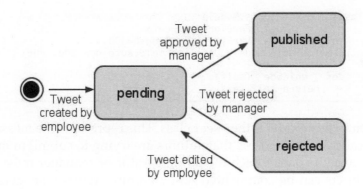

Figure 11-25 The state model for tweets in TweetApprover.

As we have seen, Django makes it really easy to create the right tables in the database and to read and write Tweet and Comment objects. In this case, the data model can go in either myproject/poster/models.py or in myproject/approver/models.py. As shown in Example 11-11, we chose, somewhat arbitrarily, to put it in the first place. Not to worry, the approver app will still be able to access the data model.

Example 11-11 The `models.py` Data Models File for the `poster` app

The data model's file for the `poster` app contains classes for posts (Tweet) as well as feedback (Comment).

```
1   from django.db import models
2
3   class Tweet(models.Model):
4       text = models.CharField(max_length=140)
5       author_email = models.CharField(max_length=200)
6       created_at = models.DateTimeField(auto_now_add=True)
7       published_at = models.DateTimeField(null=True)
8       STATE_CHOICES = (
9           ('pending',     'pending'),
10          ('published',   'published'),
11          ('rejected',    'rejected'),
12      )
13      state = models.CharField(max_length=15, choices=STATE_CHOICES)
14
15      def __unicode__(self):
16          return self.text
17
18      class Meta:
19          permissions = (
20              ("can_approve_or_reject_tweet",
21              "Can approve or reject tweets"),
22          )
23
24  class Comment(models.Model):
25      tweet = models.ForeignKey(Tweet)
26      text = models.CharField(max_length=300)
27      created_at = models.DateTimeField(auto_now_add=True)
28
29      def __unicode__(self):
30          return self.text
```

The first data model is the `Tweet` class. This represents the message, commonly called a *post* or *tweet*, that authors are trying to submit to the Twitter service, and the ones which the administrator or manager must approve. Tweet objects can be commented on by administrators/managers, so `Comment` objects are meant to represent the zero or more comments a `Tweet` can have. Let's go into some detail about these classes and their attributes.

The `text` field and `author_email` field of the `Tweet` class are limited to 140 and 200 characters, respectively. Tweets are limited to the maximum length of short message service [SMS] or text messages on mobile phones, and most regular e-mail addresses are shorter than 200 characters long.

For the `created_at` field, we use Django's handy `auto_now_add` feature. This means that whenever we create a new tweet and save it to the database, the `created_at` field will contain the current date and time, unless we explicitly set it. Another `DateTimeField`, `published_at`, is allowed to have a null value. This will be used for tweets that haven't been published to Twitter yet.

After that, we see an enumeration of states and a definition of the `state` field. By calling out the states like this and binding the state variable to them, Django will not allow `Tweet` objects to have any other but one of the three allowed states. The definition of the `__unicode__()` method instructs Django to display each `Tweet` object's `text` attribute in the administration Web site—remember earlier in this chapter how `BlogPost` object wasn't very useful? Well, neither is `Tweet` object, especially when there are more than one listed with the exact same label.

We were introduced to the `Meta` inner class earlier, but as a reminder, you can use it to inform Django about other special requirements on a data entity. In this case, it is used to alert Django about a new permission flag. By default, Django creates permission flags for adding, changing, and deleting all entities in the data model. The application can check if the currently logged-in user has permission to add a `Tweet` object; with the Django admin, the site administrator can assign permissions to registered users.

This is all fine, but the TweetApprover app needs a special permission flag for publishing a tweet to Twitter. This is slightly different from adding, changing, or deleting `Tweet` objects. By adding this flag to the `Meta` class, Django will create the appropriate flags in the database. We will see later how to read this flag to ensure that only managers can approve or reject tweets.

The `Comment` class is secondary but worth discussing anyway. It has a `ForeignKey` field that points to the `Tweet` class. This directs Django to create a one-to-many relationship between `Tweet` and `Comment` objects in the database. Like `Tweet` objects, `Comment` records also have `text` and `created_at` fields, which have identical meanings as their `Tweet` brethren.

Once the model file is in place, we can run the `syncdb` command to create the tables in the database and create a super-user login:

```
$ ./manage.py syncdb
```

Finally, as presented in Example 11-12, we need to add the `myproject/poster/admin.py` file to instruct Django to allow editing of `Tweet` and `Comment` objects within the admin.

Example 11-12 Register Models with the Admin (`admin.py`)

The URLconf for the `poster` app processes a poster's actions

```
1    from django.contrib import admin
2    from models import *
3
4    admin.site.register(Tweet, Comment)
```

All the pieces are now in place for Django to auto-generate an administration Web site for this application. If you want to try the admin Web site right now, before you have written the approver and poster views, you need to temporarily comment out lines 6–8 in Example 11-13 (`myproject/urls.py`) that reference these views. Then you can access the admin Web site (see Figure 11-26) with the `/admin` URL. Remember to uncomment these lines again once you have created `poster/views.py` and `approver/views.py`.

Example 11-13 The (Temporary) Project URLconf File (`myproject/urls.py`)

References to views we haven't written yet have been taken out, so we can try out Django's admin Web site.

```
1    from django.conf.urls.defaults import *
2    from django.contrib import admin
3    admin.autodiscover()
4
5    urlpatterns = patterns('',
6        #(r'^post/', include('myproject.poster.urls')),
7        #(r'^$', include('myproject.poster.urls')),
8        #(r'^approve/', include('myproject.approver.urls')),
9        (r'^admin/', include(admin.site.urls)),
10       (r'^login', 'django.contrib.auth.views.login',
11           {'template_name': 'login.html'}),
12       (r'^logout', 'django.contrib.auth.views.logout'),
13   )
```

Figure 11-27 shows that when you create a new user, you see the custom permission flag for **Can approve or reject tweets**. Create a user and grant the new user this permission; you will need it when testing out Tweet-Approver later. After you create a new user, you will be able to edit the user's profile and set custom permissions. (You won't be able to set those permissions while you're creating the new user.)

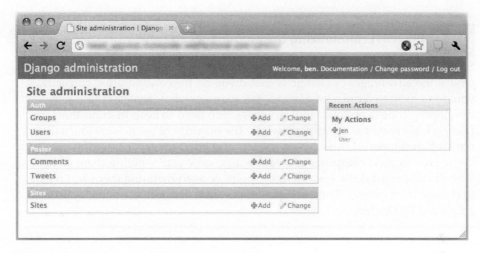

Figure 11-26 The built-in Django administration site.

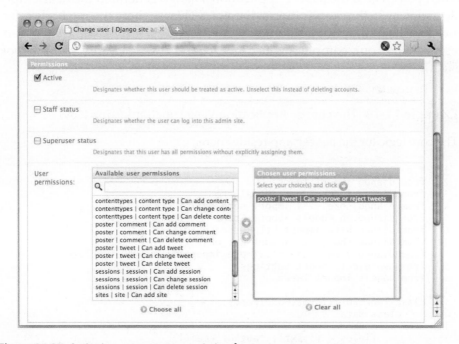

Figure 11-27 Assigning our custom permission for a new user.

CORE NOTE: Minimizing the amount of code

So far we've done a lot of configuration and very little actual programming. One of the advantages of Django is that if you do the configuration correctly, you don't have to write a lot of code. Yes, it's somewhat ironic to think that developing code is discouraged. However, you need to keep in mind that Django was created at a company where the majority of users were journalists, not Web developers. Empowering writers and other newspaper staff who know how to use a computer is great because now you're giving them some Web development skills, but not to the point of overwhelming them and trying to change their careers. This (non-developer) user-friendliness is the approach employed by Django.

11.16.5 Submitting New Tweets for Review

When you created the `poster` application, Django generated the near-empty file `views.py` in that application's directory. This is where the methods referenced in the URL configuration files should be defined. Example 11-14 represents what our complete `myproject/poster/views.py` file should look like.

Example 11-14 The `poster` Application View Functions (`views.py`)

The core logic for the `poster` app resides here.

```
1    # poster/views.py
2    from django import forms
3    from django.forms import ModelForm
4    from django.core.mail import send_mail
5    from django.db.models import Count
6    from django.http import HttpResponseRedirect
7    from django.shortcuts import get_object_or_404
8    from django.views.generic.simple import direct_to_template
9    from myproject import settings
10   from models import Tweet
11
12   class TweetForm(forms.ModelForm):
13       class Meta:
14           model = Tweet
15           fields = ('text', 'author_email')
16           widgets = {
17               'text': forms.Textarea(attrs={'cols': 50, 'rows': 3}),
18           }
```

```
19
20   def post_tweet(request, tweet_id=None):
21       tweet = None
22       if tweet_id:
23           tweet = get_object_or_404(Tweet, id=tweet_id)
24       if request.method == 'POST':
25           form = TweetForm(request.POST, instance=tweet)
26           if form.is_valid():
27               new_tweet = form.save(commit=False)
28               new_tweet.state = 'pending'
29               new_tweet.save()
30               send_review_email()
31               return HttpResponseRedirect('/post/thankyou')
32       else:
33           form = TweetForm(instance=tweet)
34       return direct_to_template(request, 'post_tweet.html',
35           {'form': form})
36
37   def send_review_email():
38       subject = 'Action required: review tweet'
39       body = ('A new tweet has been submitted for approval. '
40           'Please review it as soon as possible.')
41       send_mail(subject, body, settings.DEFAULT_FROM_EMAIL,
42           [settings.TWEET_APPROVER_EMAIL])
43
44   def thank_you(request):
45       tweets_in_queue = Tweet.objects.filter(
46           state='pending').aggregate(Count('id')).values()[0]
47       return direct_to_template(request, 'thank_you.html',
48           {'tweets_in_queue': tweets_in_queue})
```

Line-by-Line Explanation

Lines 1–10

These are nothing more than the normal import statements with which we bring in the needed Django functionality.

Lines 12–18

After all the import statements, a TweetForm is defined, based on the Tweet entity. The TweetForm is defined as containing only the fields text and author_email, as the rest are not visible to users. It also specifies that the text field should be displayed as an HTML textarea (multi-line text box) widget instead of a long, single text field. This form definition will be used in the post_tweet() method.

Lines 20–36

The `post_tweet()` method is called when the URL /post or /post/edit/X is accessed. This behavior was defined in the previous URL configuration files. The method does one of four things, as is depicted in Figure 11-28.

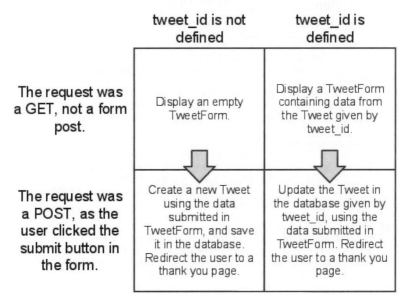

	tweet_id is not defined	tweet_id is defined
The request was a GET, not a form post.	Display an empty TweetForm.	Display a TweetForm containing data from the Tweet given by tweet_id.
The request was a POST, as the user clicked the submit button in the form.	Create a new Tweet using the data submitted in TweetForm, and save it in the database. Redirect the user to a thank you page.	Update the Tweet in the database given by tweet_id, using the data submitted in TweetForm. Redirect the user to a thank you page.

Figure 11-28 The behavior of the `post_tweet()` method.

The user starts in one of the top boxes and then moves to the box below by clicking the form's submit button. This use case and this pattern of **if** statements is common in Django view methods that deal with forms. When all the main processing is done in this method, it calls the `post_tweet.html` template and passes it a TweetForm instance. Also, note that an e-mail is sent to the reviewer by calling the `send_review_email()` method. Remove this line if you don't have access to a mail server and didn't enter any mail server details in the settings file.

This block of code also features a new function that we haven't seen before, the `get_object_or_404()` shortcut. There are some who might think there's too much magic going on here, but it really is a convenience that developers often need. It takes a data model class and a primary key and attempts to fetch an object of that type with the given ID. If the object is found, it's assigned to the `tweet` variable. Otherwise, an HTTP 404 error (not found) is thrown. We want this behavior to control unruly users who manipulate the URL by hand—users should get this error in the browser in such cases, whether malicious or otherwise.

Lines 37–42

The send_review_email() method is a simple helper that's used to send an e-mail to the manager when a new tweet has been submitted for review or if an existing tweet has been updated. It uses Django's send_mail() method, which sends e-mail by using the server and credentials you provided in the settings files.

Lines 44–48

The thank_you() method is called when the user is redirected to /post/thankyou/ after submitting the TweetForm. The method uses Django's built-in data access functionality to query the database for the number of Tweet objects that are currently in the pending state. Those of you who come from a relational database background will no doubt recognize that the Django ORM will issue SQL a command that might look something like: **SELECT** COUNT(id) **FROM** Tweet **WHERE** state= "pending". The great thing about an ORM is that those who do not know SQL can just come up with object-flavored chained method calls such as the code you see here; the ORM magically issues the SQL on the developer's behalf.

Once the number of pending posts is obtained, the app then calls up the thank_you.html template and sends that total to it. As shown in Figure 11-30, this template displays one message if there are several pending tweets, and another if there is only one. Example 11-15 and 11-16 display the template files used by the poster app.

Example 11-15 Template with the Submission Form (post_tweet.html)

The submission form for the poster app seems bare because all of the goods are handled by the TweetForm model.

```
1    <html>
2        <body>
3            <form action="" method="post">{% csrf_token %}
4                <table>{{ form }}</table>
5                <input type="submit" value="Submit" />
6            </form>
7        </body>
8    </html>
```

Example 11-16   The `thank_you()` Template After Submission
(`thank_you.html`)

The "thank you" form for the `poster` app features logic to tell the user where
they stand.

```
1    <html>
2        <body>
3            Thank you for your tweet submission. An email has been sent
4            to the assigned approver.
5            <hr>
6            {% if tweets_in_queue > 1 %}
7                There are currently {{ tweets_in_queue }} tweets waiting
8                 for approval.
9            {% else %}
10               Your tweet is the only one waiting for approval.
11           {% endif %}
12       </body>
13   </html>
```

The `post_tweet.html` template is simple: it only displays the form in an
HTML table and adds a submit button below it. Compare the template in
Example 11-15 to the form we used in our blog application earlier; you
could *almost* reuse this. I know we're always encouraging code reuse, but
sharing HTML goes above and beyond the call of duty.

Figure 11-29 shows the template output, which presents the input form
for users intending on making a post/tweet. Now we'll look at the template generating the "thanks for your submission" page that the users sees
afterward, which is depicted in Figure 11-30.

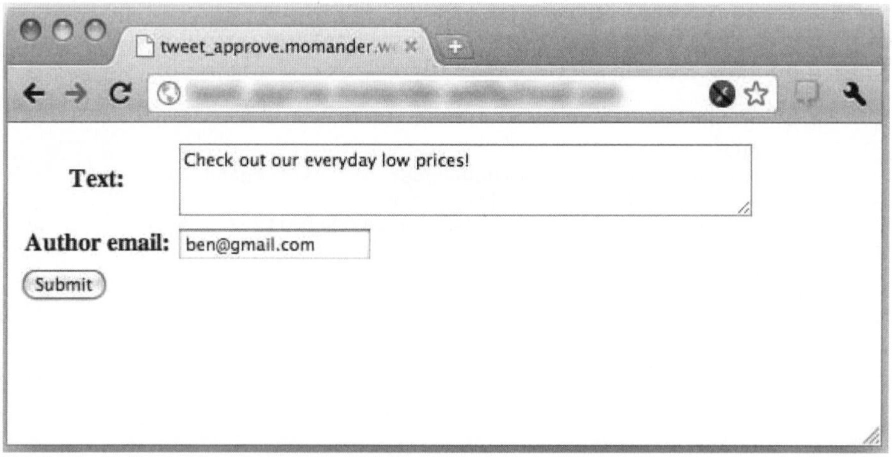

Figure 11-29   The form for submitting new tweets, available at `/post`.

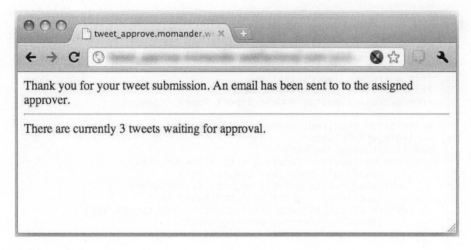

Figure 11-30 The thank you page, as seen after submitting a new tweet.

11.16.6 Reviewing Tweets

Now that we have gone through the `poster` application, it's time for the approver application. The file `myproject/approver/urls.py` calls the methods `list_tweets()` and `review_tweet()` in `myproject/approver/views.py`. You can see the entire file in Example 11-17.

Example 11-17 The `approver` App View Functions (`views.py`)

The core functionality for the `approver` app includes the form, displays posts pending review, and helps process decisions.

```
1   # approver/views.py
2   from datetime import datetime
3   from django import forms
4   from django.core.mail import send_mail
5   from django.core.urlresolvers import reverse
6   from django.contrib.auth.decorators import permission_required
7   from django.http import HttpResponseRedirect
8   from django.shortcuts import get_object_or_404
```

(Continued)

Example 11-17 The approver App View Functions (`views.py`) *(Continued)*

```
9   from django.views.generic.simple import direct_to_template
10  from twython import Twython
11  from myproject import settings
12  from myproject.poster.views import *
13  from myproject.poster.models import Tweet, Comment
14
15  @permission_required('poster.can_approve_or_reject_tweet',
16      login_url='/login')
17  def list_tweets(request):
18      pending_tweets = Tweet.objects.filter(state=
19          'pending').order_by('created_at')
20      published_tweets = Tweet.objects.filter(state=
21          'published').order_by('-published_at')
22      return direct_to_template(request, 'list_tweets.html',
23          {'pending_tweets': pending_tweets,
24           'published_tweets': published_tweets})
25
26  class ReviewForm(forms.Form):
27      new_comment = forms.CharField(max_length=300,
28          widget=forms.Textarea(attrs={'cols': 50, 'rows': 6}),
29          required=False)
30      APPROVAL_CHOICES = (
31          ('approve', 'Approve this tweet and post it to Twitter'),
32          ('reject',
33          'Reject this tweet and send it back to the author with your
    comment'),
34      )
35      approval = forms.ChoiceField(
36          choices=APPROVAL_CHOICES, widget=forms.RadioSelect)
37
38  @permission_required('poster.can_approve_or_reject_tweet',
39      login_url='/login')
40  def review_tweet(request, tweet_id):
41      reviewed_tweet = get_object_or_404(Tweet, id=tweet_id)
42      if request.method == 'POST':
43          form = ReviewForm(request.POST)
44          if form.is_valid():
45              new_comment = form.cleaned_data['new_comment']
46              if form.cleaned_data['approval'] == 'approve':
47                  publish_tweet(reviewed_tweet)
48                  send_approval_email(reviewed_tweet, new_comment)
49                  reviewed_tweet.published_at = datetime.now()
50                  reviewed_tweet.state = 'published'
51              else:
52                  link = request.build_absolute_uri(
53                      reverse(post_tweet, args=[reviewed_tweet.id]))
54                  send_rejection_email(reviewed_tweet, new_comment,
55                      link)
56                  reviewed_tweet.state = 'rejected'
57              reviewed_tweet.save()
58              if new_comment:
59                  c = Comment(tweet=reviewed_tweet, text=new_comment)
60                  c.save()
61              return HttpResponseRedirect('/approve/')
```

```
62              else:
63                  form = ReviewForm()
64              return direct_to_template(request, 'review_tweet.html', {
65                  'form': form, 'tweet': reviewed_tweet,
66                  'comments': reviewed_tweet.comment_set.all()})
67
68      def send_approval_email(tweet, new_comment):
69          body = ['Your tweet (%r) was approved & published on Twitter.'\
70              % tweet.text]
71          if new_comment:
72              body.append(
73                  'The reviewer gave this feedback: %r.' % new_comment)
74          send_mail('Tweet published', '%s\r\n' % ' '.join(
75              body), settings.DEFAULT_FROM_EMAIL, [tweet.author_email])
76
77      def send_rejection_email(tweet, new_comment, link):
78          body = ['Your tweet (%r) was rejected.' % tweet.text]
79          if new_comment:
80              body.append(
81                  'The reviewer gave this feedback: %r.' % new_comment)
82          body.append('To edit your proposed tweet, go to %s.' % link)
83          send_mail('Tweet rejected', '%s\r\n' % (' '.join(
84              body), settings.DEFAULT_FROM_EMAIL, [tweet.author_email]))
85
86      def publish_tweet(tweet):
87          twitter = Twython(
88              twitter_token=settings.TWITTER_CONSUMER_KEY,
89              twitter_secret=settings.TWITTER_CONSUMER_SECRET,
90              oauth_token=settings.TWITTER_OAUTH_TOKEN,
91              oauth_token_secret=settings.TWITTER_OAUTH_TOKEN_SECRET,
92          )
93          twitter.updateStatus(status=tweet.text.encode("utf-8"))
```

Line-by-Line Explanation

Lines 1–24

After all the imports, the first method we come across is list_tweet(). Its job is to return a list of pending and published tweets to the user. Right above the method header is the decorator @permission_required. This informs Django that only logged-in users with the permission poster.can_approve_ or_reject_tweet are allowed to access the method. This is the custom permission we declared in myproject/poster/models.py. Users who are not logged in or who are logged in but don't have the correct permission are sent to /login. (If you've forgotten what decorators are, you can review them in the Functions chapter of *Core Python Programming* or *Core Python Language Fundamentals*.)

If the user has the proper permission, the method executes. It uses Django data access functionality to pull out a list of all tweets pending approval and a list of all published tweets. Then it hands off those two lists to the `list_tweets.html` template and lets that template render the result. See the following for more details on this template file.

Lines 26–36

Next, in `myproject/approver/views.py`, we notice the definition of Review-Form. There are two ways to define forms in Django. In `myproject/poster/views.py`, a `TweetForm` was defined on the basis of the `Tweet` entity. Here, a form is defined as a collection of fields, instead, without any underlying data entity. The form will be used by managers to approve or reject pending tweets, and there is no data entity that represents a review decision. The form uses a choice collection to define the approve/reject choice that the reviewer needs to make and represents it as a list of radio buttons.

Line 38–66

After that comes the `review_tweet()` method (see Figure 11-31 for the flow). It is similar to the form-handling method in `myproject/poster/views.py`, but it assumes `tweet_id` is always defined. There is no use case that involves reviewing a non-existing tweet.

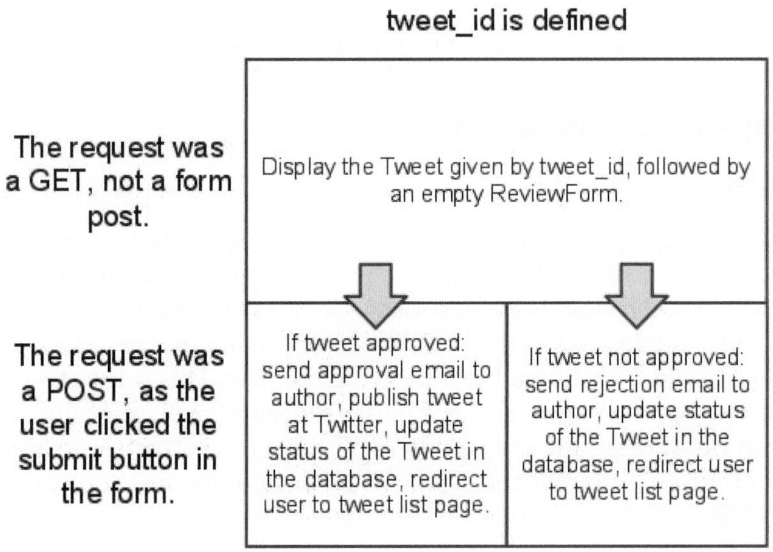

Figure 11-31 Form handling in the `review_tweet()` method.

The code needs to read what data the user submitted in the form. With Django, you can do that by using the `form.cleaned_data[]` array, which will contain the values submitted through the form by the user, converted to Python data types.

Notice how the `build_absolute_uri()` method is called on the `request` object in the `review_tweet()` view function. This method is called to get the link to the form for editing the tweet. This link will be sent in the rejection e-mail to the author so that he can take note of the manager's feedback and reword the tweet. The `build_absolute_uri()` method returns the URL that corresponds to a specific method, in this case, `post_tweet()`. We know this URL is `/poster/edit/X`, where X is the tweet's ID. Why not simply use a string containing that URL?

Well, if we ever decide that this URL should change to `/poster/change/X`, we would have to remember all the places where we hardcoded the URL pattern `/poster/edit/X` and update them to the new URL. This breaks the DRY principle behind Django. You can read more about DRY and other Django design principles at http://docs.djangoproject.com/en/dev/misc/design-philosophies.

This situation just described is different from hardcoding a flat URL without any variable component, as in `/post/thankyou`, where 1) there aren't many of them, 2) they aren't likely to change, and 3) there's no view function necessarily associated with it. To help us *not* hardcode a URL for our situation, we use another tool, `django.core.urlresolvers.reverse()` in place of a hardcoded URL. What does this do? Well, we usually start off with a URL and find a view function to which to dispatch the request. In this case, we know what view function we want but desire to build a URL from it, hence the tool's name. A view function is passed to `reverse()` along with any arguments, and a URL is returned. You can find another example by using `reverse()` in the Django tutorial at https://docs.djangoproject.com/en/dev/intro/tutorial04/#write-a-simple-form.

Lines 68–84

The two helper methods, `send_approval_email()` and `send_rejection_email()`, send e-mails to the tweet's author by using Django's `send_mail()` function. Again, remove the calls to these methods from `review_tweet()` if you are running this example without access to a mail server.

Lines 86–93

The method `publish_tweet()` is also a helper. It calls the `updateStatus()` method found in the Twython package to publish a new tweet to Twitter. Note that it uses the four Twitter credentials you added earlier in the `settings.py` file. Also, note that it encodes the tweet by using the UTF-8 character encoding, because that is the way Twitter wants it.

Now we can look at the template files. We'll start with the status page first, followed by the login because the former is surely more interesting than the latter. Example 11-18 shows the template used for the status page. The output page itself is divided into two main sections for the user: the set of posts that are awaiting a decision as well as those which have been approved and published.

Example 11-18 Template Used to Display Post Status (`list_tweets.html`)

The template for the `poster` app's status page features two main sections: pending and published posts.

```
1     <html>
2       <head>
3         <title>
4           Pending and published tweets
5         </title>
6         <style type=text/css>
7           tr.evenrow {
8             background: #FFFFFF;
9       }
10    tr.oddrow {
11          background: #DDDDDD;
12      }
13    </style>
14    </head>
15    <table>
16      <tr>
17        <td colspan=2 align=center>
18          <b>Pending tweets</b>
19        </td>
20      </tr>
21      <tr>
22        <td>
23          Tweet text
24        </td>
25        <td>
26          Submitted
27        </td>
28      </tr>
```

```
29    {% for tweet in pending_tweets %}
30      <tr class="{% cycle 'oddrow' 'evenrow' %}">
31        <td>
32          <a href="/approve/review/{{ tweet.id }}">{{ tweet.text }}</a>
33        </td>
34        <td>
35          {{ tweet.created_at|timesince }} ago
36        </td>
37      </tr>
38    {% endfor %}
39  </table>
40  <hr>
41  <table>
42    <tr>
43      <td colspan=2 align=center>
44        <b>Published tweets</b>
45      </td>
46    </tr>
47    <tr>
48      <td>
49        Tweet text
50      </td>
51      <td>
52        Published
53      </td>
54    </tr>
55    {% for tweet in published_tweets %}
56      <tr class="{% cycle 'oddrow' 'evenrow' %}">
57        <td>
58          {{ tweet.text }}
59        </td>
60        <td>
61          {{ tweet.published_at|timesince }} ago
62        </td>
63      </tr>
64    {% endfor %}
65  </table>
66  </html>
```

This template is interesting in that it is the first one we have seen that contains a loop. It iterates over the collection `pending_tweets` and then `published_tweets`. It then renders a table row for each tweet, using the `cycle` construct to give every other row a gray background, as illustrated in Figure 11-32. It also makes the text of each pending tweet a link to the page `/approve/review/X`, where X is the tweet's ID. Finally, it uses Django's `timesince` filter to display the time elapsed since the tweet was created, rather than displaying the raw date and time. This makes the list a little easier to read and it makes more sense for users who might be spread out over multiple time zones.

Once the approver selects a potential post on which to make a decision, they'll see an isolated view of that post in question, as shown in Figure 11-33.

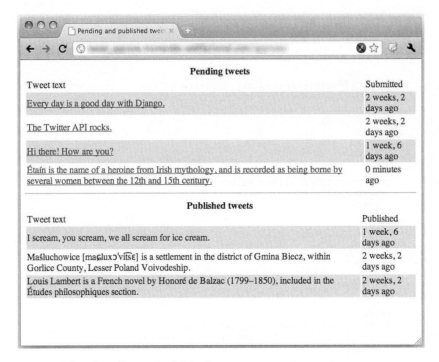

Figure 11-32 A list of pending and published tweets.

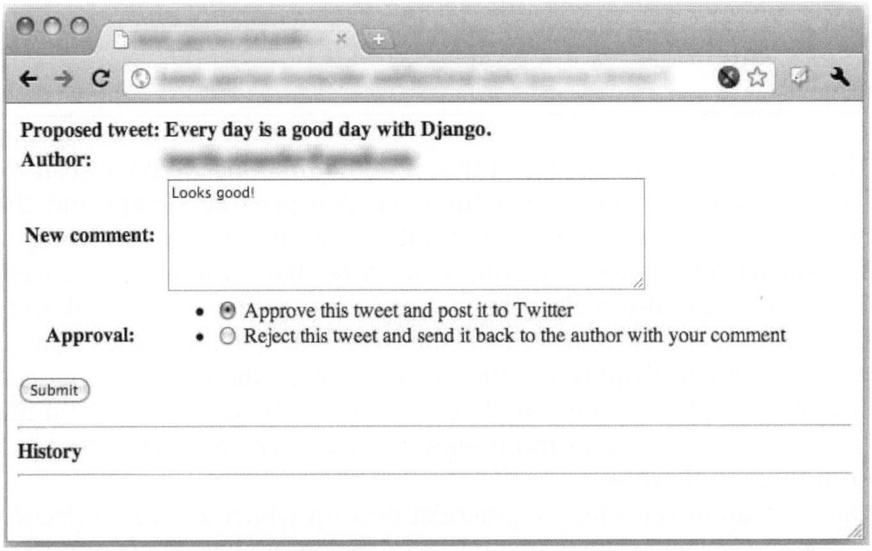

Figure 11-33 Approving a pending tweet.

The template that renders the pending tweet form is `review_tweet.html`, which is presented in Example 11-19.

Example 11-19 `myproject/templates/review_tweet.html`

The template for the `poster` app's tweet review page.

```
 1   <html>
 2       <body>
 3           <form action="" method="post">{% csrf_token %}
 4               <table>
 5                   <tr>
 6                       <td>
 7                           <b>Proposed tweet:</b>
 8                       </td>
 9                       <td>
10                           <b>{{ tweet.text }}</b>
11                       </td>
12                   </tr>
13                   <tr>
14                       <td>
15                           <b>Author:</b>
16                       </td>
17                       <td>
18                           <b>{{ tweet.author_email }}</b>
19                       </td>
20                   </tr>
21                   {{ form.as_table }}
22               </table>
23               <input type="submit" value="Submit" />
24           </form>
25           <hr>
26           <b>History</b>
27           <hr>
28           {% for comment in comments %}
29               <i>{{ comment.created_at|timesince }} ago:</i>
30               {{ comment.text }}
31               <hr>
32           {% endfor %}
33       </body>
34   </html>
```

What about the `login/` URL that users are sent to if they aren't logged in or don't have the appropriate permission? In `myproject/urls.py`, Django was instructed to run the code in the method `django.contrib.auth.views.login`, which comes with Django and handles logging in so that we don't have to. All we have to do is write the `login.html` template. Example 11-20 presents the simple one used in this application. To find out more about Django's authentication system, check the documentation at https://docs.djangoproject.com/en/dev/topics/auth/.

Example 11-20 `myproject/templates/login.html`

The template for the `poster` app's login page takes advantage of Django's authentication system.

```
1    <html>
2      {% if form.errors %}
3        Your username and password didn't match. Please try again.
4      {% endif %}
5
6      <form method="post"
7        action="{% url django.contrib.auth.views.login %}">
8      {% csrf_token %}
9      <table>
10     <tr>
11       <td>{{ form.username.label_tag }}</td>
12       <td>{{ form.username }}</td>
13     </tr>
14     <tr>
15       <td>{{ form.password.label_tag }}</td>
16       <td>{{ form.password }}</td>
17     </tr>
18     </table>
19
20     <input type="submit" value="login" />
21     <input type="hidden" name="next" value="{{ next }}" />
22     </form>
23   </html>
```

Take TweetApprover for a Spin

Now that all the pieces are in place, go back to your URLconf and uncomment all the action you just added. If you haven't created a user with permission "Can approve or reject tweets" yet, do so now. Go to /post (within your domain) with your Web browser, and then enter a new tweet. Finally, go to /approve and reject or accept the tweet. After you have accepted a tweet, go to Twitter's Web site and verify that the tweet was published.

You can download the complete project source code at this book's Web site at http://corepython.com.

11.17 Resources

Table 11-4 presents a variety of resources for topics and projects covered in this chapter.

Table 11-4 Additional Web Framework Resources

Django	http://djangoproject.com
Pyramid & Pylons	http://pylonsproject.org
TurboGears	http://turbogears.org
Pinax	http://pinaxproject.com
Python Web Frameworks	http://wiki.python.org/moin/WebFrameworks
Django-nonrel	http://www.allbuttonspressed.com
virtualenv	http://pypi.python.org/pypi/virtualenv
Twitter Developers	http://dev.twitter.com
OAuth	http://oauth.net

11.18 Conclusion

You've just touched the tip of the Django iceberg. The Web development universe is quite large when paired with Python. There is plenty to explore, so we recommend that you read the excellent Django documentation—especially the tutorial—found at http://docs.djangoproject.com/en/dev/intro/tutorial01. You can also start exploring those reusable plug-in apps that come with Pinax.

In addition, you can benefit from a more in-depth treatment of the framework in *Python Web Development with Django*. You're also now able to explore other Python Web frameworks, such as Pyramid, TurboGears, web2py, or more minimal frameworks, such as Bottle, Flask, and Tipfy. Another direction you can take is to begin exploring cloud computing. We take this journey with you in Chapter 12.

11.19 Exercises

Web Frameworks

11-1. *Review Terminology.* What do *CGI* and *WSGI* mean?

11-2. *Review Terminology.* What is the main problem with pure CGI, and why isn't it used more for production Web services today?

11-3. *Review Terminology.* What problem(s) do(es) WSGI solve?

11-4. *Web Frameworks.* What is the purpose of a Web framework?

11-5. *Web Frameworks.* Web development using frameworks typically follows the model-view controller (MVC) pattern. Describe each of these components.

11-6. *Web Frameworks.* Name some of Python's full-stack Web frameworks. Create a simple "Hello World" application by using each of them. Write down any development and execution differences between each of them.

11-7. *Web Frameworks.* Do some research on the various available Python templating systems. Create a grid or spreadsheet that compares and contrasts them. Be sure to have syntax entries for (at least) the directives to: a) display data variables, b) call functions or methods, c) embed pure Python code, d) perform loops, e) if-elseif-else conditionals, and f) template inheritance.

Django

11-8. *Background.* When and where was the Django framework created? What are some of the main goals of its existence?

11-9. *Terminology.* What is the difference between a Django project and a Django app?

11-10. *Terminology.* Instead of MVC, Django uses model-template-view (MTV). Compare and contrast MTV with MVC.

11-11. *Configuration.* Where do Django developers create their database settings?

11-12. *Configuration.* Django can run on top of:

   a) relational databases

   b) non-relational databases

   c) both a and b

   d) neither, it runs on the power of ponies

11-13. *Configuration.* Go to http://djangoproject.com then download and install the Django Web framework (and SQLite if you are not using a Windows-based PC, because it comes for free with Python 2.5+ for Windows).

a) Execute 'django-admin.py startproject helloworld' to start your project, and then 'cd helloworld; python ./manage.py startapp hello' to start your app.

b) Edit helloworld/hello/views.py to include this code:

```
from django.http import HttpResponse
def index(request):
    return HttpResponse('Hello world!')
```

c) In helloworld/settings.py, add 'hello', to the INSTALLED_APPS variable (in any position of the tuple).

d) In helloworld/urls.py, replace the commented-out line

```
# (r'helloworld/', include('helloworld.foo.urls')),
```

with this (uncommented) line:

```
# (r'^$', 'hello.views.index'),
```

e) Execute 'python ./manage.py runserver' and visit http://localhost:8000 to confirm that your code works and "Hello world!" does show up on your browser. Change the output to something other than "Hello world!".

11-14. *Configuration.* What is a *URLconf*, and where would you typically find one?

11-15. *Tutorial.* Do all four parts of the Django tutorial found starting at http://docs.djangoproject.com/en/dev/intro/tutorial01. Warning: do not merely copy the code you find there. I expect to see you modify the app to do something slightly different than what's offered, and/or add new functionality that isn't present.

11-16. *Tools.* What is the Django admin app? How do you enable it? Why is the admin useful?

11-17. *Tools.* Is there a way to test your app's code without bringing up the admin or even a Web server?

11-18. *Terminology.* What does *CSRF* mean, and why does Django contain security mechanisms to thwart such attempts?

11-19. *Models.* Name the top five model types you think you'll be using and what type of data would typically be used with those models.

11-20. *Templates*. In Django templates, what is a tag? Furthermore, what is the difference between a block tag and a variable tag? How can you distinguish between the two types of tags?

11-21. *Templates*. Describe how you would implement template inheritance by using Django.

11-22. *Templates*. In Django templates, what is a filter?

11-23. *Views*. What are generic views? Why would you want to use them? Are there any situations in which you *don't* want to have a generic view?

11-24. *Forms*. Describe forms in Django, how they work, where they live in code (from the data model to the HTML template).

11-25. *Forms*. Discuss model forms and what their benefits are.

Django Blog App

11-26. *Templates*. In the `archive.html` template of your `BlogPost` application, it loops through each post and displays them to the user. Add a test for the special case where no posts have been added yet and display a special message in such cases.

11-27. *Models*. In our application, we're still doing too much extra work for the timestamp. There is a way to instruct Django to automatically add the timestamp upon creation of our `Blog-Post` object. Find out what that is and make the necessary changes to make that happen and remove the explicit setting of the timestamp in `blog.views.create_blogpost()` and `blog.tests.BlogPostTest.test_obj_create()`. Do we also need to change `blog.tests.BlogPostTest.test_post_create()` in a similar way? Hint: You can take a peek of how Google App Engine does it elsewhere in this chapter.

11-28. *Generic views*. Deprecate your `archive()` view function and its use of `render_to_response()` and convert your app to use a generic view. You will just remove `archive()` completely from blog/views.py and also move blog/templates/ `archive.html` into blog/templates/blogpost/blogpost_ list.html. Read up on the `list_detail.object_list()` generic view and call it directly from your app's URLconf. You will need to create a dictionary with a 'queryset' as well as 'extra_context' to pass your automatically generated `BlogPostForm()` object plus all the blog entries to the template via the generic view.

11-29. *Templates*. Earlier we introduced you to Django template filters (and gave an example using `upper()`). Take the archive.html (or `blogpost_list.html`) template for your `BlogPost` app and add another line to display the total number of blog posts in the database using a filter before showing the ten most recent ones.

11-30. *Forms*. By having the form object created automatically using `ModelForm`, we've lost the ability to specify the rows and cols attributes of the body textarea (rows = 3, cols = 60), as we did with just the `Form` and specifying the HTML widget for `forms.CharField`. Instead, it defaulted to rows = 10 and cols = 40, as shown in Figure 11-20. How can we specify 3 rows and 60 cols? Hint: See the docs at http://docs.djangoproject. com/en/ dev/topics/forms/modelforms/#overriding-the-default-field-types-or-widgets

11-31. *Templates*. Create a base template for your blog app, and modify all existing templates to use template inheritance.

11-32. *Templates*. Read the Django documentation on using static files (HTML, CSS, JS, etc.) and improve the look of your blog app. If it's hard for you to get started, try these minor settings until you can think of something more contemporary:

```
<style type="text/css">
body { color: #efd; background: #453; padding: 0 5em; margin: 0 }
h1 { padding: 2em 1em; background: #675 }
h2 { color: #bf8; border-top: 1px dotted #fff; margin-top: 2em }
p { margin: 1em 0 }
</style>
```

11-33. *CRUD*. Give users the ability to edit and delete posts. You can consider adding an additional timestamp field for time edited if you wish the existing timestamp to remain representing creation time. If not, then change the existing timestamp when a post has been edited or deleted.

11-34. *Cursors and Pagination*. Showing the ten most recent posts is good, but letting users paginate through older posts is even better. Use cursors and add pagination to your app.

11-35. *Caching*. In the Google App Engine blog, we employed the use of Memcache to cache objects so that we don't have to go to the datastore again for similar requests. Do we need to do this with our Django app? Why or why not?

11-36. *Users*. Support multiple blogs on your site. Each individual user should get a set of blog pages.

11-37. *Communication*. Add another feature to your app such that whenever a new blog entry is made, both the admin of the Web site as well as the owner of the blog receive an e-mail message with the details.

11-38. *Business Logic*. In addition to the previous exercise where an e-mail message is sent, take a page from the Twitter app, and require admin approval of a blog entry before it is actually posted to the blog itself.

Django Twitter App

11-39. *Templates*. The `build_absolute_uri()` method was used to eliminate hardcoded URLs outside the URL configuration files. But there are still some hardcoded URL paths in the HTML templates. Where are they? How can these hardcoded URLs be removed? Hint: Read up on http://docs.djangoproject.com/en/dev/ref/templates/builtins/#std:templatetag-url.

11-40. *Templates*. Make the TweetApprover application pretty by adding a CSS file and referencing it from the HTML templates.

11-41. *Users*. Right now, any user can post new tweets without logging in. Modify the app so that users can't post new tweets without logging in and having the permission "add tweet" set for their user account.

11-42. *Users*. After forcing users to log in to propose new tweets, pre-populate the **Author email** field with the logged-in user's e-mail address, if the user's profile has one. Hint: Read http://docs.djangoproject.com/en/1.2/topics/auth.

11-43. *Caching*. Cache the list of tweets shown when the user visits /approve. Once a user has approved or rejected a tweet, she is sent back to that page again; when she arrives there, ensure that she sees a fresh, non-cached version of the page.

11-44. *Logging and Reporting.* Create an audit trail for tweets by adding new Comments to a post whenever it changes state. For example, when a tweet is rejected, add a Comment to it indicating that it was rejected and at what time. Whenever the text is updated, add another Comment. Whenever it is published, add another Comment saying when it was published and who approved it.

11-45. *CRUD.* Add a third option on the tweet review page that lets the reviewer delete a submitted tweet, besides accepting or rejecting it. You can delete an object from the database by calling the delete() method on it, like so:
reviewed_tweet.delete()

11-46. *Communication.* When an employee proposes a new tweet, an e-mail is sent to the manager. But the e-mail just says there is a tweet to approve. Make that e-mail friendlier by adding the text of the new tweet to it, as well as a link that the manager can click to go directly to the Web page for approving or rejecting that tweet. You can compare with how e-mails are sent in myproject/approver/views.py.

Cloud Computing: Google App Engine

Our industry is going through quite a wave of invention and it has been powered by... one major phenomenon... the Cloud. And nobody knows what this is or what it means, exactly.
—Steve Ballmer, October 2010

In this chapter...

- Introduction
- What Is Cloud Computing?
- The Sandbox and the App Engine SDK
- Choosing an App Engine Framework
- Python 2.7 Support
- Comparisons to Django?
- Morphing "Hello World" into a Simple Blog
- Adding Memcache Service
- Static Files
- Adding Users Service
- Remote API Shell

- Lightning Round (with Python Code)
- Sending Instant Messages by Using XMPP
- Processing Images
- Task Queues (Unscheduled Tasks)

- Profiling with Appstats
- The URLfetch Service
- Lightning Round (without Python Code)
- Vendor Lock-In
- Resources

12.1 Introduction

The next development system we'll explore is Google App Engine. While App Engine does not provide a full-stack framework like Django (although you can run Django on App Engine as we'll find out later in this chapter), it is a development platform, initially focused for Web applications (it comes with its own micro framework, webapp, or its replacement, the new webapp2), but it can and is certainly used for building general applications and services, as well.

In using the term "general," we don't mean *any* application can be created for or ported to App Engine; rather, we mean networked applications that need only an HTTP endpoint to be reached. This includes, but is not limited to, Web applications. One popular non-Web use case is a back-end service for user-facing mobile clients. App Engine belongs to the category of *cloud computing* focused on providing a platform for developers to build and host applications or service back-ends. Before we actually go into the platform's details, we first need to introduce the cloud computing ecosphere so that we can better define where App Engine fits into this picture.

12.2 What Is Cloud Computing?

Whereas Django, Pyramid, or Turbogears applications are served by your favorite provider or even on your own computers, Google App Engine applications are hosted by Google and are a part of a larger class of services, collectively bundled under the cloud computing umbrella. The main premise behind these services is for its users to offload or outsource part of a company's (or an individual's) computing infrastructure, whether it is actual hardware, application development and execution, or software hosting. If you are using cloud computing, you're delegating the computing, hosting, and/or serving of your application to a corporate entity other than your own.

Such services are only available on the Internet, and their exact physical location might or might not be known. This includes everything from the raw hardware[1] all the way to applications, and all other possible services in between, such as operating systems, databases, files and raw disk storage, computation, messaging, e-mail, instant messaging, virtual machines, caching (multiple levels, from Memcached to content delivery networks [CDNs]), etc. There is a lot of activity in this industry, and new services are continually being introduced by providers. Payment for services usually comes under some sort of subscription or pay-per-usage model.

Cost is usually one of the main reasons why companies deploy cloud computing services. However, the requirements differ enough that every firm needs to do their own research to determine whether it's the right decision for them. Do you own a startup company and are unable to afford all that hardware (nor do you want to lease a data center or co-location facility for those computers)? No problem, rent one computer or a thousand from Amazon or use a very large disk from Google. Gone are the days when founders of small startups would have to bootstrap their operations by investing in infrastructure like this—usually on their credit cards. Now, they can focus on their applications and the problem(s) they're trying to solve.

The situation is slightly different when looking at large enterprises or Fortune 500 companies that have enough horsepower but discover it's not being utilized to its fullest potential. You don't have to create a cloud business the likes of which Amazon did (more about this in the next section), but you can create an in-house or *private cloud* to provide cloud services internally, or perhaps you can form a *hybrid cloud* and host some of your infrastructure internally, perhaps the part that handles sensitive data, and then outsource other parts (computing, applications, storage, etc.) to a *public cloud* such as Google or Amazon.

Firms that employ cloud services are often concerned with physical location, security, a service-level agreement (SLA), and compliance; depending on their industry or governing jurisdiction, they might be compelled to do so. Obviously when outsourcing applications, data, etc., companies want

---

1. The term hardware includes physical devices (which can also include disk and memory) plus power, cooling, and networking.

guarantees that their intellectual property is safe and secure, is available from a physical location that is geographically permitted by their governing bodies (if any), and that access to such resources is available at any time. Once these requirements are met, the next decision would be to determine the appropriate level(s) of cloud computing they need.

12.2.1   Levels of Cloud Computing Service

Cloud computing is available in three levels of service. Figure 12-1 presents a view of each service layer as well as some representative products at each respective level. The lowest layer, known as *Infrastructure-as-a-Service* (IaaS), provides bare computing power such as the computers themselves (physical or virtual), storage (usually disk), and compute or computation. Amazon Web Services (AWS) provides their Elastic Compute Cloud (EC2) and Simple Storage System (S3) services at the IaaS level. Google also provides an IaaS storage service called Google Cloud Storage.

Google App Engine operates at the middle level of cloud computing known as *Platform-as-a-Service,* or PaaS. This level provides users with an execution platform for their applications. The highest layer is *Software-as-a-Service* (SaaS). At this level, users simply access applications that are native to and only accessible via the Internet. Examples of SaaS include web-based e-mail services such as Gmail, Yahoo! Mail, and Hotmail.

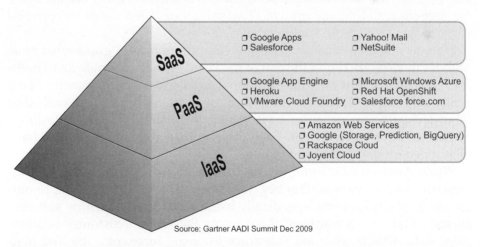

Source: Gartner AADI Summit Dec 2009

Figure 12-1 The three cloud computing service levels.

Of these three levels, IaaS and SaaS are the most well-known while PaaS doesn't bask in the limelight as often as its brethren. This might be changing, however, as PaaS is perhaps the most powerful of them all. With PaaS, you get IaaS for free, but it includes many services that are extremely costly and the most cumbersome to maintain yourself. These can include anything at the IaaS level and beyond, such as the operating system, databases, software licensing, networking and load-balancing, servers (Web and otherwise), software patches and upgrades, monitoring, alerting, security fixes, system administration, etc. A key benefit to using this service level versus maintaining your own equipment is there won't be "idle capacity" because you bought more computer firepower than you actually needed, based on the Web traffic you originally forecast. There is nothing more frustrating than sitting on an expensive investment that you know is not being properly utilized or amortized.

Although the concept of cloud computing has been around for a long time—John Gage of Sun Microsystems coined the memorable slogan, *The Network is the Computer*, in 1984—it has only been commercialized in the mid-2000s, specifically in early 2006 when Amazon introduced AWS. It was the issue of idle capacity that led them down this path. Amazon had to purchase enough computing resources to power their online retail business to withstand the traffic and demand of the holiday shopping season.

According to their whitepaper,[2] Amazon claims that *"[by] 2005, [they] had spent over a decade and hundreds of millions of dollars building and managing the large-scale, reliable, and efficient IT infrastructure that powered the operation of one of the world's largest online retail platforms."*

However, with all that capacity and computing power, guess what most of those devices are doing the rest of the year? Frankly, a whole lot of nothing, so why not rent out this additional CPU and storage capacity like a utility service? And that's exactly what they did. Since then, several other large technology companies have joined this trend: Google, Salesforce, Microsoft, RackSpace, Joyent, VMware, and many, many others who have all jumped on the cloud bandwagon.

While Amazon's EC2 and S3 services are clearly situated at the infrastructure level, a new market began to open up for those desiring to outsource their applications, specifically being able to write custom software systems that take advantage of corporate Salesforce (customer relationship) data. This is what led Salesforce to create force.com, the first platform service to do just that. Of course, not everyone wants a Salesforce

---

2. http://media.amazonwebservices.com/AWS_Overview.pdf

application written in yet another proprietary programming language, so Google developed a more general PaaS service called App Engine, which burst onto the scene in April 2008.

12.2.2 What Is App Engine?

What is App Engine doing in a Python book? Is it a core part of the language or a core third-party package? Although not really either, its release and existence have had a profound impact in the Python community and in the market; so much so, in fact, that there was strong encouragement from multiple sources to add a section on Google App Engine here. (The same thing happened with *Python Web Development with Django*, the book I wrote with my esteemed colleagues, Jeff Forcier and Paul Bissex.)

While the various web frameworks have the expected similarities and differences, App Engine is a remarkable departure from them all because not only is it a development platform but it also comes with application hosting services, which is the main reason why you would even *want* to create applications with App Engine. Users now have a much simpler alternative to developing an application and finding somewhere to host it—or worse, building their own infrastructure to support their application. All this additional work involves much more than just designing, coding, and testing an application.

Instead of having to deal with an ISP or self-hosting, developers upload their applications to Google, which will take care of all the logistics of maintaining them online. The regular Web developer now shares the same resources as all of Google, running in the same data centers and on the same hardware that powers the Internet giant itself. In fact, through App Engine and its other cloud services, Google is actually providing a public API to the stack it uses to run itself. This includes App Engine APIs, such as Datastore (Megastore, Bigtable), Blobstore, Image (Picasa), Email (GMail), Channel (GTalk), etc. In addition, now the developer no longer has to worry about computers, networking, operating systems, power, cooling, load-balancing, etc.

That's all well and good, but where does Python fit into this picture?

When App Engine originally launched in 2008, the only language runtime supported was Python. Java eventually came a year later, but Python holds a special place because it was App Engine's first supported runtime. Current Python programmers already know that it's the ease-of-use king, encourages group collaboration, allows for extremely rapid development, and does not require its users to necessarily have a computer science degree in order to use it as an effective tool. This approach is more welcoming of developers of all backgrounds and persuasions. The creator of Python himself is an engineer on the App Engine team, not to mention yours truly. Because of its ground-breaking nature and close ties to the Python community, I'm excited to help you get started with it!

There are four main components of App Engine that make up the entire system: the language runtimes, the scalable hardware infrastructure, the web-based administration console, and the software development kit (SDK) which gives users the tools they need: a development server and access to App Engine's APIs.

Language Runtimes

With regard to language runtimes, we're (obviously) going to spend the rest of the time on Python, but please be aware that at the time of this writing, Java, PHP, and Go are also available. Also, due to the Java support, developers can code in languages that have an appropriate interpreter capable of running in a Java virtual machine (JVM), such as Ruby, JavaScript, and Python, executed by JRuby, Rhino, and Jython, respectively, plus Scala and Groovy. Python via Jython is the most intriguing; some people are perplexed as to why users would want to run a Jython application when they can just use the native Python support. The primary reason involves users who want to develop new projects in Python but already have existing Java packages. Understandably, they want to take advantage of their existing packages but cannot afford or want to port those libraries to Python.

Hardware Infrastructure

The hardware infrastructure is really a black box for users: you don't know much about any of the hardware on which your code runs. You'll likely conclude it has some flavor of Linux and that the boxes sit in data centers attached to the global network. You might have even heard of *Bigtable*, the non-relational database system that App Engine uses for its datastore. For most people, this is as much as they actually need to know: remember, with cloud computing, it's not your headache anymore. The extremely difficult work and details to maintain and make such infrastructure available for users to take advantage of is pushed behind the curtains, out of sight.

Web-Based Administration and System Status

In the remaining sections of this chapter, we'll look at various features of the Python application programming interface (API). Be aware that in production, your applications are not going to be running the full version of the Python interpreter. Because your application shares resources with other users' applications, it makes sense that for security reasons, all applications must execute in a *sandbox*, which is a restricted environment. Yes, you're losing some level of control in exchange for extremely difficult-to-build components and scalability.

In exchange, App Engine provides a web-based administration console (called *admin console* for short) that gives developers an insight into their application, its traffic, data, logging, billing, settings, usage, quotas, etc. Figure 12-2, presents a screenshot of an application's admin console.

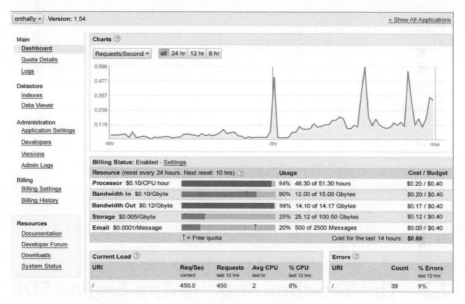

Figure 12-2 The Google App Engine application's administration console. (Image courtesy of Google)

There is also a system-wide status page (see Figure 12-3) with which you can monitor how App Engine is doing as a whole across all applications.

Keep in mind that "across all applications" really means just that. As of winter 2010, Google App Engine serves more than one billion Web pages daily. Once you create and deploy your application, you'll be adding to this total. Although that's exciting to think about, again, keep in mind that because App Engine is shared among all developers, you need to learn how to live in the sandbox. It's not as bad as it sounds because App Engine provides many services and APIs for developers.

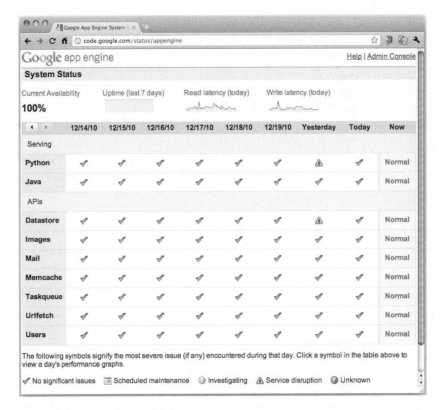

Figure 12-3 Google App Engine application's System Status page. (Image courtesy of Google)

12.3   The Sandbox and the App Engine SDK

It is a no-brainer that developers would not want other applications to be able to access their own applications' source code nor their data, so it's only fair that you respect other applications and the associated data, as well. There are certain restrictions from within the sandbox that cannot be circumvented. (From time to time, Google will lift such restrictions if and when it is safe to do so.) Verboten actions include (but are not limited to) the following:

- You cannot create a local disk file, but you *can* create a distributed one using the Files API.

- You cannot open an inbound network socket connection.

- You cannot fork new processes.

- You cannot make (operating) system calls.

- You cannot upload any non-Python source code.

Because of these limitations, the App Engine SDK comes with higher-level APIs to make up for any loss functionality due to the restrictions.

Furthermore, because the version of Python that App Engine executes (currently 2.7; the 2.5 runtime is officially deprecated) is a subset of the full distribution, you don't have access to all of Python's features, especially those which are compiled in C. Some of the C-compiled Python modules and packages are available. Version 2.7 does support significantly more C libraries, however, including some of the more well-known external packages, such as NumPy, lxml, and PIL. In fact, while the version 2.5 support for C libraries is in the form of a "whitelist," version 2.7 has made available so many more of these, that the list there is actually a "blacklist."

The Python 2.5 allowed/whitelisted and the Python 2.7 disallowed/blacklisted C-libraries are outlined at http://developers.google.com/appengine/docs/python/tools—there is a similar list for Java classes. However, if you want to use any third-party Python packages, you're welcome to bundle them with your source as long as they are pure Python (For instance, no executables, .so or .dll files, etc.) and don't use modules/packages that are not in the whitelist.

Keep in mind that there is limit to the total number of files (currently 10,000) that you can upload, another limit on the total size of all files uploaded (currently 1GB)—this includes application files or static assets such as HTML, CSS, JavaScript, etc.—as well as a per-file size limit (currently 32MB). To see the list of current size limitations, go to http://developers.google.com/appengine/docs/python/runtime.#Quotas_and_Limits as the team tries hard to raise limits wherever and whenever possible. Still, there are several workarounds that help ease the pain of these restrictions.

If your application serves media files that exceed the per-file size limit, you can store them in the App Engine Blobstore (see Table 12-1) where you can store a file that's arbitrary in size, that is, there is no size limitation for each file (blob). If you're concerned about the total number of .py files, you can store them in a Zip file and upload that, instead. Regardless of how many .py files you've archived, you only pay the penalty of a single Zip file. Of course that Zip file must also be below the per-file size limit, but at least you don't have to worry as much about the *number* of files. You can read more about using Zip files in the article located at http://docs.djangoproject.com/en/dev/ref/settings (pay attention to the note at the top of the article).

File limitations aside, let's go back to the execution restrictions (no sockets, files, processes, or system calls). Without these building blocks, it doesn't sound like you can have a very useful application. Don't despair; help is available!

12.3.1   Services and APIs

To help you get your work done, Google gives you an ever-increasing number of building blocks to work with that make up for those core restrictions. For example, *why* would you want to open a network socket? Do you want to communicate with other servers? In that case, use the URLfetch API. What about sending or receiving e-mail? The Email API was created just for that purpose. Similarly, use the XMPP (eXtensible Messaging and Presence Protocol, or simply: Jabber) API for sending or receiving instant messages (IMs). The stories are similar for accessing a network-based secondary cache (Memcache API), employing reverse AJAX or browser push (Channel API), accessing a database (Datastore API), etc. Table 12-1 lists all the services and APIs that are available to App Engine developers at the time of this writing.

Table 12-1 Google App Engine Services and APIs (Some Experimental)

Service/API	Description
App Identity	Use this when your application contains code that needs to identify itself or other APIs which demand such information.
Appstats	An event-based framework that helps you to measure the performance of your application.
Backends	If the standard request/response or task queue deadlines are not long enough for your requirements, you can use Backends to App Engine code to run indefinitely.
Blobstore	Using Blobstore, you can use applications to serve data objects ("blobs") that are too large for the Datastore (e.g., media files).
Capabilities	Gives applications the ability to detect when the App Engine datastore or memcache are unavailable in order to provide graceful downtime service to users.
Channel	This is a service with which your application can push data directly to the browser; a.k.a. Reverse Ajax, browser push, Comet.

Service/API	Description
Cloud Endpoints	Implement RESTful APIs for a backend service for your mobile apps.
Cloud SQL	Use a relational database (instead of the default scalable non-distributed datastore).
Cloud Storage	Read or write files directly to the Google Cloud Storage service by using the familiar Files API (see the description later in this table).
Cron	Cron gives you the ability to schedule tasks to run at specific dates, times, or intervals.
Datastore	A distributed, scalable, non-relational persistent storage for your data.
Denial-of-Service	Use this to set up filters to block IP addresses/families that issue Denial of Service (DoS) attacks on your application.
Download	In the event of a catastrophe, developers can download the code they uploaded to Google.
Files	Create distributed (blobstore or Cloud Storage) files using the common Python file interface.
(Full-text) Search	Perform searches for text, timestamps, lat/long, etc. in your datastore entities.
Images	Manipulate image data; for example, create thumbnails, crop, resize, and rotate images.
Logs	Allows users to access application and request logs, and even purge at runtime for long-running requests.
Mail	This API gives your application the ability to send and/or receive e-mail
MapReduce	Used to perform distributed computing over significantly large datasets. This API includes the map, shuffle, and reduce phases.
Matcher	Highly scalable real-time matching infrastructure: register queries to match against an object stream.
Memcache	Standard distributed in-memory data cache (like Memcached) between your application and persistent storage.

(Continued)

Table 12-1 Google App Engine Services and APIs (Some Experimental) *(Continued)*

Service/API	Description
Namespaces (Multitenancy)	With Namespaces, you can create multitenant applications by compartmentalizing your Google App Engine data.
NDB (new database)	New, experimental Python-App Engine higher-level datastore interface.
OAuth	Provide a secure way for third-parties to access data on a user's behalf without requiring authorization (logins/passwords, etc.).
OpenID	A Federated authentication service with which users can login from Google Accounts *and* OpenID accounts.
Pipeline	Manage multiple long-running tasks/workflows and collate their results.
Prospective Search	Somewhat in contrast to the full-text search API that allows users to search existing data, Prospective Search allows users to query for data that has *not* been created yet: set up your queries, and when matching data is stored, the API is called (think of a combination of a database trigger plus a task queue task).
Socket	Allow users to create and communicate via outbound socket connections.
Task Queue	Users can perform background tasks (concurrently if desired) away from user interaction.
URLfetch	Communicate with other applications online via HTTP/S requests/responses.
Users	App Engine's authentication service manages the user sign-in process.
WarmUp	Loads applications on instances before traffic arrives to reduce request service time.
XMPP	Gives your application the ability to chat (send and/or receive instant messages) via Jabber/XMPP protocol.

Okay, sounds exciting, but enough talk already—let's get started! The first thing you need to do is to select a framework with which to build your applications.

12.4 Choosing an App Engine Framework

If you're writing an application that's *not* user-facing—meaning other applications will just make calls to your application for service—choosing a framework is less important. Currently there are several options from which to choose, which we present in Table 12-2.

Table 12-2 Frameworks for Development with Google App Engine

Framework	Description
webapp, webapp2	A default lightweight Web framework that comes with the App Engine SDK.
bottle	A lightweight WSGI micro Web framework in Python; ships with App Engine adapter (gae).
Django	Django is a popular Python full-stack Web framework (not all features are available).
Django-nonrel	Bridges the gap between running Django applications on non-relational datastores such as App Engine.
Flask	Another microframework (like "bottle" above) based on Werkzeug & Jinja2 (like Kay below) and focused on ease of customization, and without a native data abstraction layer, you use App Engine's Datastore directly.
GAE Framework	Based on Django, but simplified. Use this framework to reuse existing infrastructure "apps" such as users, blog, admin, etc. Think simplified (Django+Pinax) for App Engine.
Google App Engine Oil (GAEO)	If Webapp is too simplistic and Django is too complex, this model-view-template framework, like Django, is also inspired by Ruby's Rails and Zend frameworks.
Kay	Also similar to Django, but uses the Werkzeug lower-level framework, the Jinja2 templating engine, and babel for doing language translations.
MVCEngine	Framework inspired by Rails and ASP.NET.
Pyramid	Another popular full-stack Web framework based on Pylons and repoze.bfg.
tipfy	More powerful lightweight framework than webapp, created just for App Engine. This also led to the creation of webapp2, meaning its original creator no longer maintains it.

(Continued)

Table 12-2 Frameworks for Development with Google App Engine
        (Continued)

Framework	Description
web2py	Another Python full-stack Web framework that has a higher-level of abstraction, meaning it's easier to use than others but hides more details (seen as both good and bad).

Most beginners to App Engine will just start with webapp or webapp2 to see how far they can get because that's the one you get with App Engine. That's a great approach, because although webapp is fairly simplistic, it provides the basic tools you need to create useful applications. However, there is a class of veteran Python Web developers who have used Django for a long time and prefer that approach, instead. Because of App Engine's restricted environment, by default you don't have access to all of Django's features. However, App Engine does have somewhat of a relationship with Django.

Some components of Django have been integrated into App Engine, and Google provides some versions of Django (albeit somewhat older) on App Engine servers so that users do not have to upload the entire Django installation along with their applications. These include the 1.2, 1.3, and 1.4 releases of Django (at the time of this writing; new versions could have been added by the time you read this). However, there several critical pieces of Django that have not been brought over to App Engine, the most important being its Object-Relational Mapper (ORM) which has traditionally relied on having a SQL relational database foundation.

I use the word traditionally because there are multiple ongoing efforts to get Django to support non-relational (NoSQL) databases, too. However, at the time of this writing, none of those projects have been integrated into the Django distribution yet. Perhaps by the time you read this, the world will have changed to the point where Django can do either relational or non-relational.

One of the other well-known projects is called Django-nonrel. This is a branch of Django that comes with adapters for Google App Engine as well as MongoDB (plus several more on the way). There is also some work to bring JOINs to the NoSQL adapters, but that is also in development at this time. If there is any material relevant for Django non-relational developers, we'll mention them along our journey.

Tipfy is a lightweight framework developed specifically for App Engine. You can think of it as a webapp++ or "webapp 2.0" as it consists of features representing functionality that is notably absent from webapp. The feature-set includes (but is not limited to) internationalization, session management, alternative forms of authentication (Facebook, FriendFeed, Twitter, etc.), access to Adobe Flash (AMF protocol access plus Flash messages), ACLs (access control lists), and additional templating engines (Jinja2, Mako, Genshi). It is based on WSGI and hooks into the Werkzeug utility set that form the foundation of any WSGI-compliant application. You can find out more about Tipfy from its Web page and wiki at http://tipfy.org.

web2py is one of the four well-known full-stack Web frameworks for Python (in addition to Django, TurboGears, and Pyramid). It is the second that is compatible with Google App Engine. web2py focuses on letting developers create fast, scalable, secure, and portable Web applications that rely on a database system, whether it be relational or Google App Engine's non-relational datastore, and it works with a wide variety of databases. A database abstraction layer (DAL) transposes ORM requests in SQL in real time and uses that as its interface to database. Naturally, for App Engine applications, you're still restricted to the relational limitations presented by the Datastore (i.e., no JOINs). It also supports a variety of Web servers such as Apache, ligHTTPD, or any WSGI-compliant server. Using web2py is a natural route for existing web2py developers who want to migrate their applications to App Engine.

You can choose any one of these frameworks to develop your applications. Alternatively, any WSGI-compliant framework will work. Here, we use the lowest common denominator (webapp); we encourage you to at least move forward and do all the examples by using webapp2.

A bit of history: one passionate App Engine developer wasn't satisfied with his framework selection, which motivated him to create tipfy. He then wanted to improve webapp, dropped tipfy, and built webapp2, which turned out so good that Google integrated it as part of the version 2.7 runtime SDK (thus, the quote at the beginning of Chapter 11, "Web Frameworks: Django").

12.4.1   Frameworks: webapp then Django

In Chapter 11, we covered Django and how to create a blog by using that framework. Here, we're going to do the same thing but use the webapp default, instead. We'll show you how to build almost the same thing by using App Engine, running it by using the App Engine development environment, just like in our Django example. Users can also optionally create a Google Account or other OpenID identification (or use an existing one) and set up an application to run on the live App Engine production environment.

We'll show you how to do that, as well, but it's not necessary nor is there any obligation to do so. No credit card is required to set up an application online, but you will need a mobile phone with text messaging or short message service (SMS) capability.

To wrap up this chapter, we'll port this application to Django and run *that* on App Engine, too (development or production environments). The concepts and features of App Engine are enough to warrant a book on its own, so although we won't be giving it a full treatment here, our material should be able to get you started and comfortable with multiple aspects of the App Engine product.

Downloading and Installing the App Engine SDK

To get started, you need to get the App Engine SDK for your development platform. There are a variety of files available to download, so you need to be aware of the correct ones for your system. Visit the Google App Engine home page located at http://code.google.com/appengine, and then click the **Downloads** link. From there, you can find the appropriate files for your system. Files are also available for Java developers, but for our purposes here, we'll focus only on Python.

Linux or *BSD users should download the Zip file, unzip the archive, and install that folder (google_appengine) in your favorite place, such as `/usr/local`, and drop a link to the `dev_appserver.py` and `appcfg.py` commands in a place similar to `/usr/local/bin`. Alternatively, you can just add `/usr/local/google_appengine` to your path. (You can skip the rest of this section as well as the next one on using the Launcher and go straight to the section, "Creating 'Hello World' manually.")

Windows PC users should download the .msi file; Mac users should grab the .dmg file. Once you've located the appropriate file, double-click or launch it to install the App Engine SDK. This process will also install the Google App Engine Launcher. The Launcher can be used to manage your App Engine applications you have on your development computer as well as to help you upload them to Google for running live in production.

Using the Launcher to Create "Hello World" (Windows and Mac Users Only)

Once you start up the Launcher, you'll see a control panel similar to those depicted in Figure 12-4 and Figure 12-5.

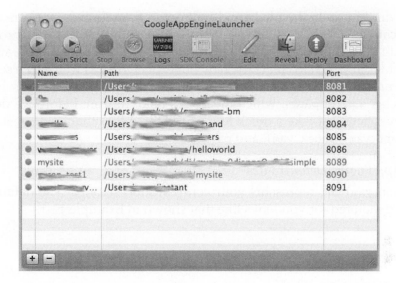

Figure 12-4 The App Engine Launcher for Mac.

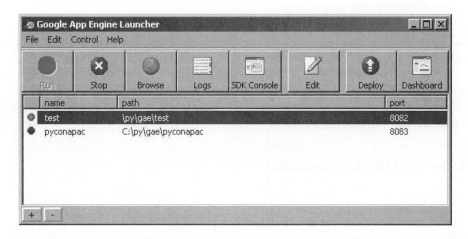

Figure 12-5 The App Engine Launcher for Windows.

There are various buttons that will bring up (and take down) your development server (**Run**); view your logs (**Logs**); browse your development admin console (**SDK console**); edit configuration settings (**Edit**); upload your application to App Engine production servers (**Deploy**); or go to your live application's admin console (**Dashboard**). Let's get started and create a new application. We'll visit several of the Launcher buttons throughout the course of developing our application.

To do this, go to the menu and pull down the selection to create a new application. Give it some sort of unique name; "helloworld" has probably already been taken. You can provide a few other options, as well, such as the folder in which to create the new boilerplate files as well as the server's port number. Once that's done, you'll see your application in the Launcher's main panel, which means it's ready to run. Before we do that however, let's just take a quick look at the three files that were created for you, app.yaml, index.yaml, and main.py.

The App Engine Default Files

The app.yaml file represents your configuration settings. The default file that's generated for you looks like that shown in Example 12-1.

Example 12-1   A Default Configuration File (app.yaml)

```
1    application: APP_ID
2    version: 1
3    runtime: python
4    api_version: 1
5
6    handlers:
7    - url: .*
8      script: main.py
```

You'll get the idea that a YAML (yet another markup language) file is made up of mappings (key-value pairs) and sequences. For more information on this file type, you can go to both http://yaml.org and http://en.wikipedia.org/wiki/Yaml.

Line-by-Line Explanation

Lines 1–4

The first section is pure configuration, assigning a name to your App Engine application (APP_ID) followed by its version number. For development, you can pick any name you like, for example, *blog*. If you intend to upload to the App Engine live production environment, you'll need to be more creative and come up with a name that hasn't been chosen yet. A quick note about names, about which you should be aware: names cannot be transferred, and names are never recycled; once a name is taken it's gone, even if an application is deleted, so choose carefully.

The version number is a unique string that you can set. It's up to you to determine how you want to implement versioning. You can go with the traditional 0.8, 1.0, 1.1, 1.1.2, 1.2, etc., or you can use another naming convention such as v1.6 or 1.3beta. It's just a string, but you're restricted to alphanumeric characters plus hyphens. You can create up to ten versions of your application (major or minor makes no difference). After that, you won't be able to upload any more until you delete at least one version.

Below the version number is the runtime type. Here, it's Python and version 1 of that API. You can also use `app.yaml` for Java and JRuby by inserting "Go," between Java and JRuby, and other runtimes for the JVM; the `app.yaml` file is used in turn to generate the `web.xml` and `appengine-web.xml` files that are actually needed for your servlet(s).

Lines 6–8

The final few lines specify your *handlers*. Just as with a Django URLconf file, you need to specify a regular expression to match against client requests as well as provide a corresponding handler. In Django, these handler url-script pairs correspond to the project-level URLconf file, which forwards requests to an application-level URLconf. Similarly in `app.yaml`, the script directive sends the request to the given Python script, which contains more specific URLs and maps them to handler classes, in the same way that a Django app's URLconf points to a view function.

To learn more about configuring your application, read the documentation at http://code.google.com/appengine/docs/python/config/appconfig.html.

Now let's look at the `index.yaml` file:

```
indexes:

# AUTOGENERATED
# This index.yaml is automatically updated whenever the dev_appserver
. . .
```

The `index.yaml` file is needed when you need to create custom indexes for your application. To make App Engine query the datastore faster, you need to have a corresponding index for each query. (Indexes for simple queries are created automatically—you don't need to do so.) You generally won't need to consider this until your queries become more complex. To read more about using indexes, view the official documentation at http://code.google.com/appengine/docs/python/config/indexconfig.html.

The last file that is automatically generated by the Launcher on your behalf is the main application file (`main.py`), as shown in Example 12-2.

Example 12-2   The Main Application File (`main.py`)

```
1   from google.appengine.ext import webapp
2   from google.appengine.ext.webapp import util
3
4   class MainHandler(webapp.RequestHandler):
5       def get(self):
6           self.response.out.write('Hello world!')
7
8   def main():
9       application = webapp.WSGIApplication([('/', MainHandler)],
10                                           debug=True)
11      util.run_wsgi_app(application)
12
13  if __name__ == '__main__':
14      main()
```

Line-by-Line Explanation

Lines 1–2

The first two lines import the `webapp` framework as well as bring in its `run_wsgi_app()` utility function.

Lines 4–6

After these introductory lines, you'll find the `MainHandler` class. This is the core functionality of this example. It defines a `get()` method to process HTTP GET requests; hence its name. A handler instance will have attributes for both the request and the response. In our example, we're only writing out the HTML/text to return to the user via the `response.out` file.

Lines 8–11

Next comes the `main()` function, which spawns an instance of an application and then runs it. Within the call to instantiate `webapp.WSGIApplication`, you'll find pairs (or 2-tuples)—well, just one so far, that determine which handler(s) process which requests. In our case, the only URL our application handles at the moment is `'/'`, and these requests will be handled by the `MainHandler` class that we just described.

Lines 13–14

Finally, we have the familiar lines for determining execution based on whether this Python source file was imported or executed directly as a script. If you're not familiar with this code, we recommend you flip back and review Chapter 3, "Internet Client Programming," and Chapter 12, in *Core Python*.

All of the code should be fairly straightforward, even if you're seeing some of this for the very first time. From this point forward, we're going to make continuous changes to the application—iterating as it were—to improve it or add new functionality.

Minor Code Cleanup

Before we start adding to the application, let's make a few cosmetic changes to main.py that don't affect execution at all, as shown in Example 12-3.

Example 12-3 Housekeeping and Cleanup of the Main Application File (main.py)

```
1   from google.appengine.ext import webapp
2   from google.appengine.ext.webapp.util import run_wsgi_app
3
4   class MainHandler(webapp.RequestHandler):
5       def get(self):
6           self.response.out.write('Hello world!')
7
8   application = webapp.WSGIApplication([
9       ('/', MainHandler),
10  ], debug=True)
11
12  def main():
13      run_wsgi_app(application)
14
15  if __name__ == '__main__':
16      main()
```

What We Did and Why

1. We don't want WSGIApplication to be instantiated each time this application is run. By moving it out of main() into the global code block, we instantiate this class only once instead of on a per-request basis. We get a minor performance benefit—it's not very big, but this is just a simple optimization that you would do in any similar Python application, regardless of whether it's App Engine or not. The only (minor) penalty is that application is now a global variable versus a local.

2. Because we're only using one function from `webapp.util`, we can simplify the import by just bringing in that one name to (barely) speed up (lookup to) the call to `run_wsgi_app()`. Calling `util.run_wsgi_app()` versus `run_wsgi_app()` doesn't matter if you're doing it once or twice, but it can add up over millions of requests to your application.

3. Having the handlers pairs on separate line(s) makes it easier to add new handlers; for example:

```
('/', MainHandler),
('/this', DoThis),
('/that', DoThat),
. . .
```

Okay, that's all we could think of at this time. It gives it more of "Djangish" kind of feel, if there's such a word.

12.5   Python 2.7 Support

2.7 The original release of Google App Engine supported Python 2.5. In 2013, the 2.5 runtime was deprecated, and new 2.5 applications cannot be created starting in 2014. At the time of this writing, the code in this chapter was primarily created using 2.5, however they should work with the 2.7 runtime with no changes. However, we recommend that you learn how to develop using 2.7 "style" anyway, as there is slightly less code to write and it may be easier to debug. That is the purpose of the remaining parts of this section.

12.5.1   General Differences

The first and one of the more critical of the differences is that the version 2.7 runtime supports concurrency. With App Engine's pricing model, you're charged based on the number of instances of your application that are serving traffic. Because the version 2.5 runtime is not concurrent, new instances must be spawned if your running instances aren't able to cope with the traffic that you're getting. This can lead to increased costs. With concurrency, your application can respond in an asynchronous manner and significantly reduce the need for additional instances.

Next, highly desired and previously forbidden C libraries are now available. These include PIL, `lxml`, NumPy, and `simplejson` (named as `json`). Version 2.7 support also comes with Jinja2 templating system along with Django templates. To see all of the differences between the version 2.5 and 2.7 runtimes, check out the official documentation at http://developers.google.com/appengine/docs/python/python27/diff27.

12.5.2   Variations in the Code

There are also some slight code differences, so let's take a look at them because these are the changes you'll be making with your code in this chapter to execute your application on the version 2.7 runtime. The `app.yaml` file sees a change to the `runtime` field. In addition, you will probably want to turn on concurrency via the `threadsafe` directive. The other major change is moving to pure WSGI—rather than specifying a script to execute, you'll point to an object (the application object), instead. All the necessary differences are shown in *italics* in Example 12-4.

Example 12-4   Sample Python 2.7 Configuration file (`app.yaml`)

```
1    application: APP_ID
2    version: 1
3    runtime: python27
4    api_version: 1
5    threadsafe: true
6
7    handlers:
8    - url: .*
9      script: main.application
```

The version 2.7 runtime features a new and improved webapp framework named `webapp2`. Because we're using WSGI instead of CGI, we can remove the previously superfluous "main()" at the bottom. All changes to `main.py` are reflected in Example 12-5, which, as you can see, is shorter and easier to read.

Example 12-5   Sample Python 2.7 Main Application file (`main.py`)

```
1    import webapp2
2
3    class MainHandler(webapp2.RequestHandler):
4        def get(self):
5            self.response.out.write('Hello world!')
6
7    application = webapp2.WSGIApplication([
8        ('/', MainHandler),
9    ])
```

Note that the `application` object in `main.py` is the `main.application` that is referred to in the `app.yaml` file. You can find more about the 2.7 `main.py` and using `webapp2` at http://developers.google.com/appengine/docs/python/tools/webapp2.

To read more about using the version 2.7 runtime time and see more information about the changes just shown, check the documentation at http://developers.google.com/appengine/docs/python/python25/migrate27.

12.6   Comparisons to Django

App Engine does not structure a Web site as a project made up of one or more applications. Instead, everything combined is a single application. We mentioned that the `app.yaml` file bears some similarity to Django's project-level `urls.py` because it maps URLs to handlers. It also has elements of `settings.py` because it is a configuration file.

The `main.py` file serves as a combination of a Django app's `urls.py` plus `views.py`. When creating the WSGI application, you have one or more handlers that designate the class whose instance will handle those requests. The class definitions as well as their corresponding `get()` or `post()` handlers are created in this file, as well. Those handlers would be the closest thing to a view function.

Throughout Chapter 11, we were able to test our application by using the development server. App Engine has its own development server, and we'll be using it as we progress.

12.7   Starting "Hello World"

There are two ways to start up an application on the development server. If you're in the Launcher, select the application's row, and then click the

Run button. After a few seconds, you'll see the icon turn green. You can then click the **Browse** button to start a Web browser that opens to your application.

To start your application via the command-line, ensure that the `dev_appserver.py` file is in your path, and then issue the following command:

```
$ dev_appserver.py DIR
```

`DIR` is the application's folder name (that contains the `app.yaml` and `main.py` files). And yes, if you're in the same directory as both files, you can just use the following:

```
$ dev_appserver.py .
```

It's a little bit different from Django, which uses a project-based command-line tool (`manage.py`) versus a common command installed for all App Engine applications. Another minor difference is that Django's development server starts on port 8080, whereas App Engine uses 8000. This just means your URL must change to http://localhost:8080/ or http://127.0.0.1:8080. If using one of the Launchers, when you create a new application, it will automatically assign it a unique port number, so you might need to use that, as well, or you can change it.

12.8 Creating "Hello World" Manually (Zip File Users)

If you aren't using the Launcher, then you probably do not need any assistance in typing in the code shown earlier. Because the `index.yaml` file is optional at this time, you really only need a skeletal `app.yaml` and `main.py` file. You can type them in manually or go to this book's Web site and download them from the Chapter 12 folder. Once you have both files there, you can start up the development server by using the same command that was just described (`dev_appserver.py`).

12.9 Uploading Your Application to Google

It might be somewhat premature, but if you want, you can choose to go beyond running your application on the development server. You can also upload it to Google and run it live in production, making your simple "Hello World" application available to… well, the world (except for places in which Google service is not available). This is completely optional, so if this isn't of interest to you, then skip to the next section to continue building your blog.

App Engine provides a free service tier, in which you can develop simple low-trafficked applications without any cost to you. You'll need a mobile phone that supports SMS as well as a Google Account, but a credit card isn't necessary unless you plan on exceeding the free quota available to all applications. Visit http://appengine.google.com and sign-in to create your App Engine account.

To upload your application (and its static files, if any), you can either use one of the Launchers (Windows or Mac only), or you can use the command-line tool, appcfg.py. You'll send the update command as well as pass in the top-level directory where your app.yaml file is located. The following is an example execution of appcfg.py in the current directory. Note that you'll need to enter the credentials (valid e-mail address and password) of a developer for that application, as demonstrated in the following:

```
$ appcfg.py update .
Application: APP_ID; version: 1.
Server: appengine.google.com.
Scanning files on local disk.
Initiating update.
Email: YOUR_EMAIL
Password for YOUR_EMAIL: *****
Cloning 2 static files.
Cloning 3 application files.
Uploading 2 files and blobs.
Uploaded 2 files and blobs
Precompilation starting.
Precompilation completed.
Deploying new version.
Checking if new version is ready to serve.
Will check again in 1 seconds.
Checking if new version is ready to serve.
Will check again in 2 seconds.
Checking if new version is ready to serve.
Closing update: new version is ready to start serving.
Uploading index definitions.
```

It can take up to a minute to upload your application (generally not more than that). The preceding example uploaded in just over 3 seconds.

Give it another few seconds after the upload has completed, and then you (and everyone else on the planet) should be able to visit http:// APP_ID.appspot.com to see your "Hello World!" output—how exciting!

CORE TIP: Choose your application name carefully

Before you upload the source and static files for your application, be sure
to choose a unique name (specified in app.yaml) that hasn't already been
used—application names are permanent and cannot be reused or transferred,
even if the application is disabled and/or deleted.

12.10 Morphing "Hello World" into a Simple Blog

Now that you've been able to successfully create and run a simple "Hello
World" application, you should be able to bring up a browser and go to
your Web site. From the Launcher, you can just click the **Browse** button,
and if you're not using it, just point any Web browser at http://localhost:8080.
You should see something similar to that shown in Figure 12-6.

Figure 12-6 Hello World from Google App Engine.

The next step is to start modifying the application into something more desirable. We're going to replicate our Django example by turning this simple "Hello World" into a blog. The reason why we're doing this is to give you the opportunity to compare and contrast developing in Django and App Engine's webapp framework.

12.10.1 Seeing Changes Quickly: Plain Text to HTML in 30 Seconds

First, confirm that you only need to update your code to see the changes reflected in the application on the development server. To do so, add an <H1> tag to the output line and close it off. Change the text to something like "The Greatest Blog" if you have no better ideas; thus, <h1>The Greatest Blog</h1>. Again, you save your change (or after *any* modifications to your source), confirm that you can go back to your browser, refresh the page, and then confirm the changes, which are displayed in Figure 12-7.

Figure 12-7 The changes to "Hello World 2," reflected immediately in the updated browser page.

12.10.2 Adding a Form

Now let's take a more significant step in your application's development: add the ability to accept user input. We'll insert a form with fields with which users can create new blog posts. The two fields are the post title and the post contents or body. Your modified `MainHandler.get()` method should now look similar to this:

```
class MainHandler(webapp.RequestHandler):
    def get(self):
        self.response.out.write('''
            <h1>The Greatest Blog</h1>
            <form action="/post" method=post>
            Title:
            <br><input type=text name=title>
            <br>Body:
            <br><textarea name=body rows=3 cols=60></textarea>
            <br><input type=submit value="Post">
            </form>
            <hr>
        ''')
```

The entire method consists of the Web form. Yes, if this were a real application, all of the HTML would be in a template.

Figure 12-8 shows the refreshed screen and the new input fields.

Figure 12-8 Adding form fields to the Blog application.

Now you can fill in the fields as desired, as illustrated in Figure 12-9.

Figure 12-9 Filling in the blog application form fields.

Like our Django example earlier, we're not quite able to process this data yet. When the user fills out and submits the form at this point, our controller has no way of handling that data, so if you to try to submit, you'll either prompt an error or see a blank screen. We need to add a POST handler to deal with new blog posts, so let's do that now by creating a new BlogEntry class and a post() method:

```
class BlogEntry(webapp.RequestHandler):
    def post(self):
        self.response.out.write('<b>%s</b><br><hr>%s' % (
            self.request.get('title'),
            self.request.get('body'))
        )
```

Note that the name of our method is post() (as opposed to get()). This is because the form submits a POST request. If you also want to support GET, you'll need another method named get(). So the class and its method are great, but your application cannot reach the handler if it (the URL-class pair) has not been specified when creating the application object. Here is what it should look like:

```
application = webapp.WSGIApplication([
    ('/', MainHandler),
    ('/post', BlogEntry),
], debug=True)
```

With this addition, you are now able to fill in the form fields and submit it to your application. The output you see (Figure 12-10) matches exactly what our post() handler specifies; it displays the BlogPost title followed by its contents:

Figure 12-10 The form submission results.

12.10.3 Adding Datastore Service

Seeing output is great, but this application is totally useless as a blog—you're not saving anything. This is one place where we've taken a departure from Django. In Django, we *had* to set up a database, and the first bit of code we wrote was the data model. App Engine takes more of an application approach—we started creating our application before we even *had* a data model. In fact, you don't even *need* a database; you can just use a cache, store your data in the Blobstore, or somewhere else in the cloud.

App Engine's data storage mechanism is its datastore. Google clearly wanted to distinguish it from a database, which explains the slightly different terminology. It's to help drive the point that this is no relational database management system (RDBMS); it is built on top of Google's Bigtable[3] and provides distributed, scalable, non-relational persistent data

---

3. http://labs.google.com/papers/bigtable.html

storage. It also uses Google's Megastore[4] technology to provide strong consistency and high availability.

Keep in mind that this datastore is only used when you deploy your application live to App Engine's production environment. When running the development server, you can store your data in a binary format (the default) or request storage in SQLite by using the `--use_sqlite` flag when running `dev_appserver.py`.

Now it's time to create our data model. Analyze and compare the model class in Django versus App Engine and notice the extreme similarities here:

```
# Django
class BlogPost(models.Model):
    title = models.CharField(max_length=150)
    body = models.TextField()
    timestamp = models.DateTimeField()

# App Engine
class BlogPost(db.Model):
    title = db.StringProperty()
    body = db.TextProperty()
    timestamp = db.DateTimeProperty(auto_now_add=True)
```

For App Engine applications, you would add this model to your existing `main.py` file: there's no equivalent `models.py` file unless you create it explicitly for yourself. Don't forget to add the datastore service by using the following import:

```
from google.appengine.ext import db
```

If you are a Django-nonrel user, meaning that you prefer to run your Django app on App Engine, you would leave your class the way it was defined originally (for Django) instead of using the App Engine data models.

Regardless of which classes you choose or whether live or in development, you can now request to persist your data with the underlying persistent storage mechanism. Creating the class is the first step. Storing actual data requires the same steps as those we did in Django: create instances, fill in the user data, and then save. For our application, we'll need to replace the code in the `post()` method. The way it stands now, all it does is output the input, which is neither very useful nor persistent.

The title and body are simple: after creating the instance, extract them from the submitted form data and assign them as attributes. The timestamp is optional because we selected to have it be set automatically when

---

4. http://research.google.com/pubs/pub36971.html

the instance was created. Once the object is "complete," we save it to the App Engine Datastore by calling the data instance's put() method, and then redirect the user to the main page for our application, just like in the Django version we did earlier.

The following is the new BlogEntry.post() method, which embodies all of the changes just discussed:

```
class BlogEntry(webapp.RequestHandler):
    def post(self):
        post = BlogPost()
        post.title = self.request.get('title')
        post.body = self.request.get('body')
        post.put()
        self.redirect('/')
```

Note that we have completely replaced our original post() method which just regurgitated what the user entered. In that earlier example, no data was saved to persistent storage. This completely changed with the preceding modifications, saving all post information to the datastore. Likewise, we need to make a similar corresponding change to our GET handler.

Specifically, we should display earlier blog posts to show that yes, we have started to persist user data. In our simple example, we'll choose to display the form followed by a dump of any existing BlogPost objects. Make the following changes to our MainHandler.get() method:

```
class MainHandler(webapp.RequestHandler):
    def get(self):
        self.response.out.write('''
            <h1>The Greatest Blog</h1>
            <form action="/post" method=post>
            Title:
            <br><input type=text name=title>
            <br>Body:
            <br><textarea name=body rows=3 cols=60></textarea>
            <br><input type=submit value="Post">
            </form>
            <hr>
        ''')

        #posts = db.GqlQuery("SELECT * FROM BlogEntry")
        posts = BlogPost.all()
        for post in posts:
            self.response.out.write('''<hr>
                <strong>%s</strong><br>%s
                <blockquote>%s</blockquote>''' % (
                post.title, post.timestamp, post.body)
            )
```

The code emitting the HTML form to the client stays as is. Below it, we add the code to fetch the results from the datastore to display to the user. App Engine provides two ways to query your data.

Doing things the "object" way is the closest to Django's query mechanism, requesting BlogPost.all() (as opposed to Django's BlogPost.objects.all()). App Engine also provides an alternative to those more comfortable with SQL: a stripped down query-language syntax known as *GQL*.

Because you don't have all of SQL at your disposal (nor JOINs) *and* it's less Pythonic, we strongly recommend that you use the native object approach. However, if you absolutely can't live without it, the commented out line right above our BlogPost.all() call provides the equivalent in GQL. Finally, the loop at the end just cycles through each entity and displays the appropriate data per post.

With these changes made, re-entering the same blog entry, we now see something different, as depicted in Figure 12-11.

Figure 12-11 Form submission results (saved to datastore).

Figure 12-12 and Figure 12-13 demonstrate that we can continue to add blog entries now that we're confident we're storing user data.

Figure 12-12 Filling out the form for a second BlogPost.

Figure 12-13 Second BlogPost object, saved and displayed.

12.10.4 Iterative Improvements

Similar to our Django example, let's make our blog more useful by reversing all the entries chronologically and also only show the 10 most recent of them. Here are the changes we need to make to the query line (and the equivalent GQL tweaks):

```
#post = db.GqlQuery("SELECT * FROM BlogPost ORDER BY timestamp
    DESC LIMIT 10")
posts = BlogPost.all().order('-timestamp').fetch(10)
```

Compare the query to Django's to see the similarities:

```
posts = BlogPost.objects.all().order_by('-timestamp')[:10]
```

Everything else remains the same. To read more about making queries in Google App Engine, go to the documentation page at http://developers. google. com/appengine/docs/python/datastore/queries.

12.10.5 The Development/SDK Console

The Datastore Viewer

While it pales in comparison to Django's admin application, App Engine does come with a development console. You can bring it up in the Launcher by clicking the **SDK Console** button. If you don't have the Launcher, you will need to manually enter the special URL, http://localhost:8080/_ah/admin/datastore. When you arrive, you'll be at the Datastore Viewer, as shown in Figure 12-14.

Here you can create a new instance of any of the entities that you've defined for your application. In our case, we only have BlogPost. You can also view the contents of objects in the datastore, as well. Figure 12-15 shows the original two posts that we created earlier.

The Interactive Console

We saw earlier how Django provides access to a Python shell during development. Although App Engine doesn't have this exact feature, you do get similar access. Click the **Interactive Console** link located on the left in the navigation links in the SDK Console; you'll be brought to a Web page that has a coding pane to the left and output to the right. From here, you can enter arbitrary Python commands and watch them execute. An example execution is provided in Figure 12-16.

Figure 12-14 The Datastore Viewer in App Engine's SDK Console.

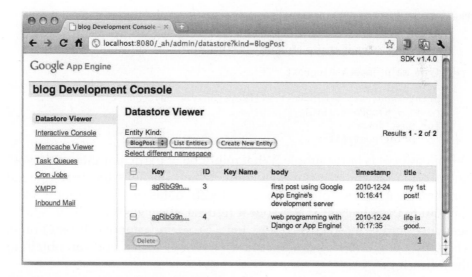

Figure 12-15 Viewing the existing BlogPost objects.

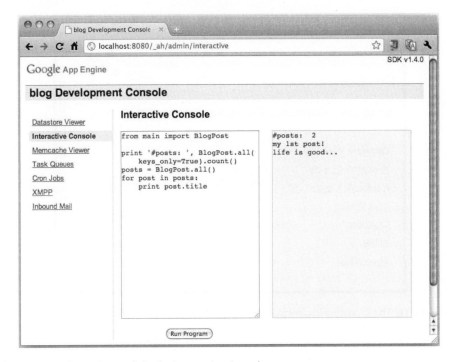

Figure 12-16 Executing code in the Interactive Console.

The code it runs is quite simple, as shown in the following script:

```python
from main import BlogPost

print '#posts: ', BlogPost.all(keys_only=True).count()
posts = BlogPost.all()
for post in posts:
    print post.title
```

This snippet is fairly simple. What might be of particular interest to you, however, is the initial print statement, which displays the current total number of BlogPost objects in the (local) datastore. You might have thought to use BlogPost.all(), but it returns a Query object which is not a sequence, and it doesn't override __len__(), so you cannot call len() on it. The only option for you is the count() method, which you can obtain at the following:

http://developers.google.com/appengine/docs/python/datastore/ queryclass#Query_count.

A simple click of the **Run Program** button is all it takes to get some instant gratification.

CORE NOTE: Counting (or the lack thereof)

Even though counting using Django and a relational database is fairly straightforward, App Engine admittedly doesn't count well because it's really meant for large-scale distributed storage. There aren't any tables, and there is no SQL, which means that you can't execute a command like, `SELECT COUNT(*) from BlogPost`. Many developers who do require a count for their application create a transactional counter, or if you have many transactions, you can create a "sharded counter." For more information, go to the following sites:

http://developers.google.com/appengine/articles/sharding_counters

http://developers.google.com/appengine/docs/python/datastore/queries#Queries_Cursors

http://googleappengine.blogspot.com/2010/08/multi-tenancy-support-high-performance_17.html

Counting has been worse in the past than it is today, so be happy with that. There used to be a 1,000 entity limit on fetches and counting, which was restrictive. With the addition of cursors in the 1.3.1 release, this limitation was removed so that whether you're performing a fetch, iterating, or using a cursor, there are no limits on the number of results. However, that restriction was still in effect for counting and offsets, meaning that you still had to use cursors to iterate through your dataset in order to count your entities. It wasn't until release 1.3.6 that this barrier was removed.

Now, a call to `count()` on Query objects will either give you the exact number of entities or time out doing so. As specified in the documentation for `count()`, you shouldn't be using it to count a large number of entities: "It's best to only use `count()` in cases where the count is expected to be small, or specify a limit. `count()` has no maximum limit. If you don't specify a limit, the datastore continues counting until it finishes counting or times out." Again, it might not be everything that you want, but it is certainly a remarkable improvement over what was available to App Engine developers before early 2010.

Again, as far as best practices go, don't get into the habit of wanting to count things, and if you do, maintain a counter. You just have to tweak your way of thinking when it comes to the App Engine datastore. In exchange for some functionality which you might have been used to, you're getting replication and scalability, two very expensive features to build.

One additional tip if you do need to count: go for "keys-only" counting. In other words, when you create your query object, pass in the `key_only` flag set to True so that you're not having to fetch full entities from the datastore, such as *BlogPost.all(keys_only=True)*. The following are some links to help you with this:

http://developers.google.com/appengine/docs/python/datastore/queryclass#Query

http://developers.google.com/appengine/docs/python/datastore/modelclass#Model_all

http://developers.google.com/appengine/docs/python/datastore/queries#Keys_Only_Queries

Finally, the App Engine team has created a series of articles to help you master the datastore. You can find them at:

http://developers.google.com/appengine/articles/datastore/overview

Another thing to be aware of is that the code you execute within the interactive console has direct access to your local datastore. Like our Django blog example, you can use a snippet of Python to autogenerate more entities, as you can see in the following code for Figure 12-17:

```
from datetime import datetime
from main import BlogPost

for i in xrange(10):
    BlogPost(
        title='post #%d' % i,
        body='body of post #%d' % i,
        timestamp=datetime.now()
    ).put()
    print 'created post #%d' % i
```

Figure 12-18 demonstrates that now we can sort in reverse order by timestamp and see the original two BlogPost objects as well as the ten we just generated in Figure 12-17.

```
from main import BlogPost

print '#posts: ', BlogPost.all(
    keys_only=True).count()
posts = BlogPost.all().order(
    '-timestamp')
for post in posts:
    print post.title
```

You can even flip back to the Datastore Viewer to see more specifics about each entity, as shown in Figure 12-19.

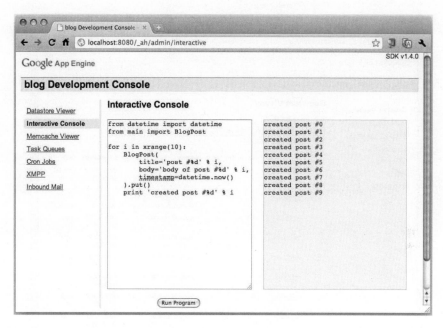

Figure 12-17 Creating more entities by using Python.

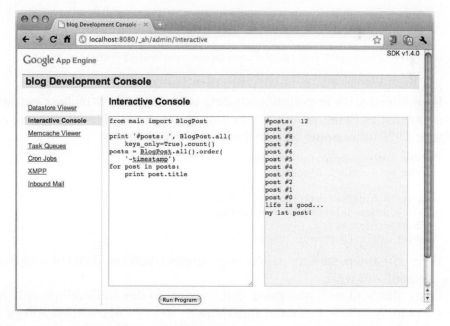

Figure 12-18 The new and old entities together.

Figure 12-19 Changing the entity display order by using the interactive console.

If you don't wish to pollute your data with these fake `BlogPost` entries, you can just as easily remove them with this snippet, shown executed in Figure 12-20 (after going back to the Interactive Console):

```
from google.appengine.ext import db
from main import BlogPost

posts = BlogPost.all(keys_only=True
    ).order('-timestamp').fetch(10)
db.delete(posts)
print 'DELETED newest 10 posts'
```

If you cut and paste the "data dump" snippet, you can then confirm that the deletion did work.

Okay, that's all well and good that we can do this in development. At some point, you'll want similar functionality in a live application and production datastore. There are two similar tools you can use there.

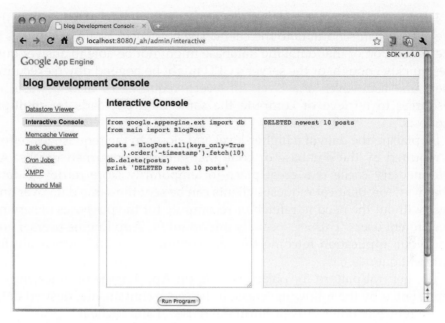

Figure 12-20 Deleting BlogPosts.

In the live production environment, you can get a shell to your application by using the remote API (you'll find out more in the section "Remote API Shell"). You can also achieve bulk deletes or bulk copying of entities to another App Engine application if you enable the Datastore Admin for your Admin Console.

Okay, so that was a quick introduction to the SDK console. It's certainly not as fully-featured as its cousin the (live) Admin Console, but it is a useful development tool. We'll come back to it again soon. First, let's add another service to our application: caching.

12.11 Adding Memcache Service

New users to App Engine often remark that its database access is slow. Well, that is a relative term, but you will contend that you're experiencing a decline in performance compared to using a standard relational database. However, keep in mind that you're making a significant trade off: in exchange for distributed, scalable, replicated storage in the cloud, you take a slight hit because as we all know, you can't get something for nothing. One of the ways to improve the speed of queries is to bring the data "closer" to your application by caching instead of going to the datastore.

High-traffic sites are rarely limited in their performance by how fast the Web server can send data to the client. The bottleneck is almost always in the generation of that data; the database might not be able to answer queries quickly enough, or the server's CPU might be bogged down executing the same code over and over for every request. It's also a waste of resources to retrieve or compute the same data payloads for multiple requests.

By placing the data at a higher-level and closer to the request, less effort is required by the database or code that generates returned results. An intermediary cache is a great place to temporarily store retrieved data. That way, for identical requests, clients can be sent the same data over and over without the need to refetch or recompute for the purposes of serving to different users. This is especially important for App Engine users if you find your application fetching the same entities over and over again for different queries.

The general pattern for object caching (in App Engine or otherwise) is represented by the following: check if the cache contains the desired data. If yes, return it; otherwise, perform the retrieval and cache it

If you were to write the above in pseudocode, it would look something like the following snippet for some constant KEY which we use to store the cached data:

```
data = cache.get(KEY)
if not data:
    data = QUERY()
    cache.set(KEY, data)
return data
```

Not surprisingly, this is pretty much the solution in Python. We're only missing a value for the KEY, a database QUERY, and this import of App Engine's low-level Memcache-compatible API:

```
from google.appengine.api import memcache
```

In our application code, we add a few lines to our `MainHandler.get()` method that surrounds the fetching of the data, only going to the datastore if we have not cached the dataset:

Before:

```
. . .
posts = BlogPost.all().order('-timestamp').fetch(10)
for post in posts:
    . . .
```

After:

```
. . .
posts = memcache.get(KEY) # check cache first
if not posts:
    posts = BlogPost.all().order('-timestamp').fetch(10)
    memcache.add(KEY, posts)  # cache this object
for post in posts:
. . .
```

Don't forget to set the key for your cache, that is, KEY = 'posts'.

With the add() call, we've effectively cached the object until we either explicitly delete it (see below), or it is evicted to make room for more recently-accessed data Just as a point of interest, the Memcache API employs an LRU (least recently used) algorithm. A third alternative is to cache an object with an expiration. For example, if we wanted to cache this object for one minute, we'd change our call to:

```
memcache.add(KEY, posts, 60)
```

The final piece of the puzzle is to invalidate the cache when a new blog post entry comes in. To make this happen, we flush the cache whenever a new entry is sent to the datastore in our code for BlogEntry.post():

```
. . .
post.put()
memcache.delete(KEY)
self.redirect('/')
```

Once these changes are made, you are certainly welcome to try it out in your browser, but because of our small dataset, it's difficult to determine whether you're getting your data from memcache or the datastore. The easiest way to do it is to take a look at the Memcache Viewer in the SDK Console (see Figure 12-21).

To see it in action, you'll need a pair of browser windows, one open to your application, and the other to the Memcache Viewer in the SDK Console. Ensure that you have some BlogPost objects in your application, and then refresh the main page of the application several times. Now refresh the Memcache Viewer page to see memcache utilization. I did this myself so you can see my usage results, which are shown in Figure 12-22.

You should have registered one cache miss but an increasing number of hits each successive pass, meaning that the datastore was only accessed the first time, helping to improve the performance for users after the initial data acquisition. To read more about using App Engine's Memcache API, read the documentation page at http://developers.google.com/appengine/docs/python/memcache.

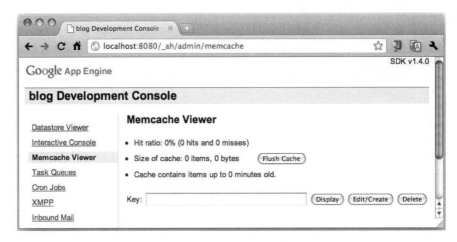

Figure 12-21   The Memcache Viewer, which here is showing empty.

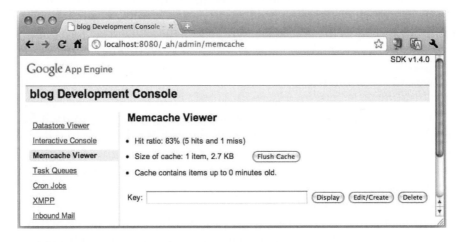

Figure 12-22   The Memcache Viewer now registers some usage.

In Chapter 11, we did not get a chance to talk about caching. Django has many levels of caching service, including object caching, as we've just done here, plus QuerySet caching, which helps push lower-level object caching further under the covers. You can find out more about the various types of caching Django has to offer in Chapter 12 of *Python Web Development with Django*.

Object-level caching is just one way to prevent the server from having to do extra work to get your data to you. Data doesn't always come from the database, however. Serving Web pages usually includes many static files, as well. App Engine provides various optimizations for developers there, too, such as requesting upstream caching by using HTTP `Cache-Control` headers in appropriate places. If you can cache on the edge or via proxies, this will allow some of your assets to be served directly to clients without even using your App Engine application.

12.12 Static Files

Web pages often include static elements that go along with any dynamic data. This includes images, CSS, text (XML, JSON, or other markup), and JavaScript files. Rather than requiring that the developer come up with handlers to serve that data, you can specify a static file directory in your `app.yaml` configuration to direct App Engine to return that data as is. What you need to do is to add a specific handler in the `handlers` section of your `app.yaml`. It will look something like this:

```
handlers:
- url: /static
  static_dir: static

- url: .*
  script: main.py
```

We place our static handler first so that matches of `/static` path requests will be processed first. All other paths will be taken care of by the handlers in `main.py`. This means that you don't need to execute application code in order to serve up static files.

In fact, why don't you just find some random `.js`, `.css`, or whatever static content you have, let's say it's `main.css`, create a folder named "static" right at the top-level directory (where your `app.yaml` and `main.py` file are located), update your `app.yaml` as described above, start your development server, and then point a browser to http://localhost:8080/static/main.css. This will work in production in the same way it does in development. App Engine serves your static data without requiring assistance from your application's handlers.

12.13 Adding Users Service

In Chapter 11, for our Django blog, we didn't add any authentication (users, passwords, accounts, etc.), but we did use Django's own authentication system in the TweetApprove application. Similarly, let's do authentication in this blog by using Google Accounts. This sure beats giving *any* user who visits your page the ability to add new blog posts; if we did, it would then be a guestbook right? Having authentication here shouldn't be a shocker. Let's assume that you wanted to create the next industry blog, like TechCrunch, Engadget, etc. The blog needs to support multiple authors, and you want them to be the only ones who can post to the blog, not just any 'ol John or Jane.

12.13.1 Google Accounts Authentication

When you create your App Engine application, the authentication that's used by default is Google Accounts. However, if you don't add any authentication mechanism, either in the configuration settings or in the actual application code, it's the same as not having authentication at all: anyone can post to your blog. Let's add in authentication checking by inserting a couple of lines at the very beginning of `MainHandler.get()` so that it looks like this:

```
. . .
from google.appengine.api import users
. . .
class MainHandler(webapp.RequestHandler):
    def get(self):
        user = users.get_current_user()
        if user:
            self.response.out.write('Hello %s' % user.nickname())
        else:
            self.response.out.write('Hello World! [<a href=%s>sign
in</a>]' % (
                users.create_login_url(self.request.uri)))
        self.response.out.write('<h1>The Greatest Blog</h1>')

        if user:
            self.response.out.write('''
                <form action="/post" method=post>
                Title:
                <br><input type=text name=title>
                <br>Body:
                <br><textarea name=body rows=3 cols=60></textarea>
```

```
        <br><input type=submit value="Post">
        </form>
        <hr>
''')

posts = memcache.get(KEY)
if not posts:
    posts = BlogPost.all().order('-timestamp').fetch(10)
    memcache.add(KEY, posts)
for post in posts:
    self.response.out.write(
        '<hr><strong>%s</strong><br>%s
            <blockquote>%s</blockquote>' % (
                post.title, post.timestamp, post.body
    ))
```

If you don't want to add specific code to ask users to login like we've just done, you can force it at the app.yaml configuration level. Just add a login: required directive; any URL that accesses that handler will force the user to login before she can access your application or its content. Here's an example of how to use that directive to block out all access to our main handler without a valid Google accounts login:

```
- url: .*
  script: main.py
  login: required
```

Another alternative is login: admin which requires a logged-in administrator of the application to access this handler, such as for critical user, app, or data access or manipulation. Users who are not administrators will get an error page which states that administrator access is required. You can read more about these directives at http://developers.google.com/appengine/docs/python/config/appconfig#Requiring_Login_or_Administrator_Status.

12.13.2 Federated Authentication

If you're uncomfortable with either creating your own authentication or do not wish to require that all of your users have a Google Account, you will probably want federated login with OpenID. With OpenID, you can allow users to sign in to your application by using accounts they created at a variety of providers, including (but not limited to) Yahoo!, Flickr, Word-Press, Blogger, LiveJournal, AOL, MyOpenID, MySpace, and even Google.

If you're using federated login, you'll need to make a minor adjustment to your call that creates login links by adding a `federated_identity` parameter such as `users.create_login_url(federated_identity=URL)`, where *URL* is any of the OpenID vendors (gmail.com [Google], yahoo.com, myspace.com, aol.com, etc). Future support for federated authentication will be integrated with the new Google Identity Toolkit (GIT).

For more on users, the GIT, and OpenID, go to the following links:

- http://developers.google.com/appengine/docs/python/users/overview

- http://developers.google.com/appengine/articles/openid

- http://openid.net

- http://developers.google.com/apis/identitytoolkit

12.14 Remote API Shell

To use the remote API shell, you need to add the following entry into your `app.yaml` file, just above the handlers to your application, as shown in the following:

```
- url: /remote_api
  script: $PYTHON_LIB/google/appengine/ext/remote_api/handler.py
  login: admin

- url: .*
      script: main.py
```

If you have another section in there for static files as we did in the previous section, it doesn't matter what the ordering is when creating the handler setup for the remote API. The important thing is that they're both above the main handler. In the preceding example, we've left out the static file stuff and added an explicit administrator login, because we're pretty sure you wouldn't want any other user to access your production datastore.

You'll need a local version of your application's data model(s). When you're in the right directory, issue the following command (substituting in the ID for your live production application) and provide the proper credentials:

```
$ remote_api_shell.py APP_ID
Email: YOUR_EMAIL
Password: *****
App Engine remote_api shell
Python 2.5.1 (r251:54863, Feb  9 2009, 18:49:36)
[GCC 4.0.1 (Apple Inc. build 5465)]
```

```
The db, users, urlfetch, and memcache modules are imported.
APP_ID> import sys
APP_ID> sys.path.append('.')
APP_ID> from main import *
APP_ID> print Greeting.all(keys_only=True).count()
24
```

The remote API shell just gives you a Python interactive interpreter to your live running application. There are many other uses of the remote API itself, most notably, the mass uploading and downloading of data to and from your application's datastore. For more on using the remote API, check out the official documentation at http://developers.google.com/appengine/articles/remote_api.

12.14.1 The Datastore Admin

The datastore admin is a recent feature that adds a component to your live application's administration console (not the SDK development server console). It gives you the ability to mass delete specific types of entities (or all of them) as well as the ability to copy entities to another live application. The one caveat is that your application must be in read-only mode during the copy. To enable the datastore admin, add the following section to your app.yaml file:

```
builtins:
- datastore_admin: on
```

You don't have to necessarily memorize this because all you need to do is to click the **Datastore Admin** link in your Admin Console. If you haven't enabled it yet, it'll alert you that you're missing this configuration in your app.yaml file.

Once you turn it on, clicking it will prompt you with a login screen (or two), and then you should see something such as that illustrated in Figure 12-23.

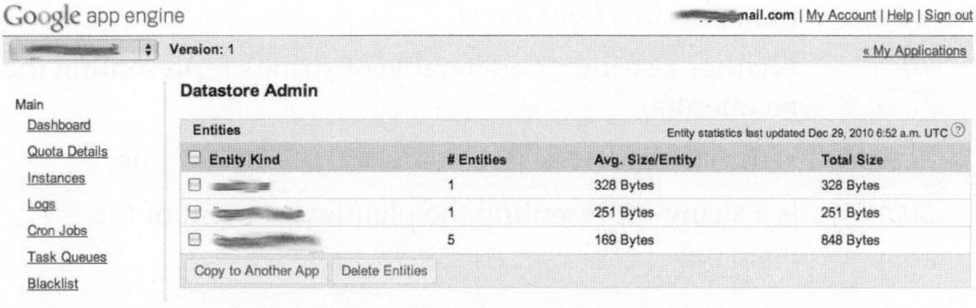

Figure 12-23 An example of an App Engine Datastore Admin screen.

To see an example `app.yaml` file with the datastore admin turned on as well as the `appengine_config.py` file necessary to allow another application to copy entities to the current application, visit the code sample repository at http://code.google.com/p/google-app-engine-samples/source/browse/#svn%2Ftrunk%2Fdatastore_admin.

You can read more about the datastore admin and its features at:

- http://developers.google.com/appengine/docs/adminconsole/datastoreadmin

- http://googleappengine.blogspot.com/2010/10/new-app-engine-sdk-138-includes-new.html

12.15 Lightning Round (with Python Code)

Given all the features and scope of the entire App Engine platform, it's not a surprise that you can write an entire book on the subject. But as our goal is to give you a high-level introduction and then let you take the wheel, we'll end it here. Before we leave, though, the "lightning round" that follows is meant to give you some quick code samples that you can use right away without necessarily integrating those features into our blog application. Of course, these will be featured in the chapter exercises coming up.

12.15.1 Sending E-Mail

In our Twitter/Django application from Chapter 11, you saw how to use Django's e-mail service. Sending e-mail in App Engine is just as easy. All you need to do is import the `mail.send_mail()` function and use it. Its basic usage is very straightforward: `mail.send_mail(FROM, TO, SUBJECT, BODY)` where:

FROM   is a string representing the e-mail address of the sender (more on this field later).

TO   is either a string or an iterable of strings representing the recipient(s).

SUBJECT   is the string that is set as part of the `Subject:` line.

BODY   is a string representing the plaintext content of the message.

There are other message fields that you can pass to `send_mail()`; you can find out more about them at http://developers.google.com/appengine/docs/python/mail/emailmessagefields.

To continue discouraging the sending of unsolicited e-mail, the `From:` address is restricted. It *must* be one of the following:

- The e-mail address of a registered administrator (developer) of the application

- The current user, if they are logged in

- Any valid receiving e-mail address for the application (of the form xxx@*APP_ID*.`appspotmail.com`)

Following is a snippet of code that includes the import and one possible call to `send_mail()`:

```
from google.appengine.api import mail
. . .
mail.send_mail(
    user and user.email() or 'admin@APP_ID.appspotmail.com', # from
    'corepython@yahoo.com', # to
    'Erratum for Core Python 3rd edition!'  # subject
    "Hi, I found a typo recently. It's...",  # body
)
```

The mail API also features additional functions to send e-mail only to the administrator(s) of the application, to validate e-mail addresses, etc., plus an `EmailMessage` class. You can also have attachments in outbound e-mail, but the attachment file types are limited to only the most popular formats that are recognized as not insecure, these include .doc, .pdf, .rss, .css, .xls, .ppt, .mp3/.mp4/.m4a, .gif, .jpg/.jpeg, .png, .tif/.tiff, .htm/.html, .txt, etc. You can find the latest group of valid attachment types at http://developers.google.com/appengine/docs/python/mail/overview#Attachments.

Finally, inbound or outbound messages have a size limitation (at the time of this writing) of 10MB. You can read the latest about the quotas and limitations of the e-mail service at:

http://developers.google.com/appengine/docs/quotas#Mail

http://developers.google.com/appengine/docs/python/mail/overview#Quotas_and_Limits

More general information about sending e-mail at:

http://developers.google.com/appengine/docs/python/mail/overview#Sending_Mail_in_Python

http://developers.google.com/appengine/docs/python/mail/
overview#Sending_Mail

http://developers.google.com/appengine/docs/python/mail/
sendingmail

12.15.2 Receiving E-Mail

What's sending without receiving? Yes, your application can handle incoming e-mail, as well. It's slightly more complicated than sending e-mail but it's not that much additional work.

Setup

In addition to writing code to handle inbound e-mail, you need to add a couple of things to your app.yaml configuration file, with the most important being *enabling* the service. By default, the receipt of inbound e-mail is disabled. To turn it on, you'll need to enable it in the inbound_services: section of the app.yaml (or add one if that section doesn't exist).

Also, earlier we mentioned that one of the valid addresses from which you can send email is a valid receiving e-mail address for the application, meaning of the form *xxx@APP_ID*.appspotmail.com. You can have one handler for all possible e-mail addresses or different handlers for specific ones. This is done by creating one or more additional handlers in your app.yaml file. To figure out how to create the handlers, we need to tell you that all inbound e-mail will be POSTed to a URL of this form: /_ah/mail/
EMAIL_ADDRESS.

Here are the relevant sections of the app.yaml that we need to add:

```
inbound_services:
- mail

handlers:
. . .
- url: /_ah/mail/.+
  script: handle_incoming_email.py
  login: admin
. . .
```

The first two lines enable incoming e-mail. The inbound_services: section is also the place to enable receiving XMPP messages (more on this in Section 12.16), Warming Requests, and other future services that you can read about in the official documents page for application configuration and the app.yaml file at http://developers.google.com/appengine/docs/python/config/appconfig#Inbound_Services.

The second set of lines comprise an inbound e-mail handler that goes in the `handlers:` section. The regular expression `/_ah/mail/.+` matches all e-mail addresses; however, there's nothing wrong with creating separate handlers for different e-mail addresses:

```
- url: /_ah/mail/sales@.+
  script: handle_sales_email.py
  login: admin
- url: /_ah/mail/support@.+
  script: handle_support_email.py
  login: admin
- url: /_ah/mail/.+
  script: handle_other_email.py
  login: admin
```

You can block malicious applications and users from accessing your e-mail handler by using the `login: admin` directive. When App Engine receives an e-mail message, it generates requests and `POST`s them to your application, resulting in a call to your handler as an "admin."

Handling Inbound E-Mail

You can handle e-mail by using the default method, which involves writing your handler in much the same way you create a standard Web handler and have an instance of `mail.InboundEmailMessage`:

```
from google.appengine.api import mail
. . .
class EmailHandler(webapp.RequestHandler):
    def post(self):
        . . .
        message = mail.InboundEmailMessage(self.request.body)
        . . .
```

Of course, you would still have to install this handler when creating your `WSGIApplication`:

```
application = webapp.WSGIApplication([
    . . .
    ('/_ah/email/+.', EmailHandler),
    . . .
], debug=True)
```

An alternative is to use the predefined helper class, `InboundMailHandler`, found in `google.appengine.ext.webapp.mail_handlers`:

```
from google.appengine.ext.webapp import mail_handlers
. . .
class EmailHandler(mail_handlers.InboundMailHandler):
    def receive(self, msg):
        . . .
```

Instead of having to extract the e-mail message from the request, this is handled automatically, so all you need to do is implement a `receive()` method which is called with the message. You also get a shortcut `mapping()` class method that autogenerates the 2-tuple which directs mail to your handler. You would use it like this:

```
application = webapp.WSGIApplication([
    . . .
    EmailHandler.mapping(),
    . . .
], debug=True)
```

Once you have the message, you're welcome to check out the main body of the e-mail, whether it is in plain text or HTML (or both), and you can also access any attachments or other message fields, such as the sender, subject, etc. You can find more general information about receiving e-mail found at:

http://developers.google.com/appengine/docs/python/mail/overview#Receiving_Mail_in_Python

http://developers.google.com/appengine/docs/python/mail/overview#Receiving_Mail

http://developers.google.com/appengine/docs/python/mail/receivingmail

12.16 Sending Instant Messages by Using XMPP

Similar to sending e-mail, your application can also send instant messages (IMs) with App Engine's XMPP API. XMPP stands for eXtensible Messaging and Presence Protocol, but it was originally called the *Jabber protocol*, named after its open-source community and created in the late 1990s. With App Engine's XMPP API, in addition to sending, you can also receive an IM, check to see if a user is available to chat, or you can send a user a chat invitation. Your application cannot communicate with a user unless she has received and accepted an invitation from it.

Below is a snippet of pseudocode that sends a chat invitation to a user, assuming that you've correctly filled in a valid IM username (or Jabber ID) for *USER_JID*:

```
from google.appengine.api import xmpp
    . . .
```

```
xmpp.send_invite(USER_JID)
self.response.out.write('invite sent')
. . .
```

Here's another piece of sample code that sends an IM (the *MESSAGE* string) to a user once he has accepted your invitation. Again, replace *USER_JID* with the user's Jabber ID:

```
. . .
if xmpp.get_presence(USER_JID):
    xmpp.send_message(USER_JID, MESSAGE)
    self.response.out.write('IM sent')
. . .
```

The third XMPP function is get_presence(), function which returns True if the user is online and available, and False if the user is away, not online, or she has not accepted your application's invitation yet. You can read more about these three functions as well as the XMPP API at:

http://developers.google.com/appengine/docs/python/xmpp/overview

http://developers.google.com/appengine/docs/python/xmpp/functions

12.16.1 Receiving Instant Messages

Receiving IMs is set up just like e-mail, that is, in the inbound_services: section of your app.yaml file:

```
inbound_services:
- xmpp_message
```

Also like receiving e-mail, messages that come to the system are POSTed by App Engine to your application. The URL path used is /_ah/xmpp/message/chat. Here is an example of how to receive chat messages in your application:

```
class XMPPHandler(webapp.RequestHandler):
    def post(self):
        . . .
        msg_obj = xmpp.Message(self.request.POST)
        msg_obj.reply("Thanks for your msg: '%s'" % msg_obj.body)
        . . .
```

Of course, we have to register our handler:

```
application = webapp.WSGIApplication([
    . . .
    ('/_ah/xmpp/message/chat/', XMPPHandler),
    . . .
], debug=True)
```

12.17 Processing Images

App Engine has an Images API with which you can manipulate an image by performing simple transformations such as rotate, flip, resize, and crop. The images can be POSTed by a user or extracted from the datastore or Blobstore.

Here's a snippet of HTML with which users can upload an image file:

```
<form action="/pic" method=post enctype="multipart/form-data">
Upload an image:
<input type=file name=pic>
<input type=submit>
</form>
```

The following sample piece of code creates a thumbnail for the image by calling the Image API's resize() function and returns it back to the browser:

```
from google.appengine.api import images

class Thumbnailer(webapp.RequestHandler):
    def post(self):
        thumb = images.resize(self.request.get('pic'), width=100)
        self.response.headers['Content-Type'] = 'image/png'
        self.response.out.write(thumb)
```

Here is the corresponding handler entry:

```
application = webapp.WSGIApplication([
    . . .
    ('/pic', Thumbnailer),
    . . .
], debug=True)
```

You can read all about the images API at http://developers.google.com/appengine/docs/python/images/usingimages.

12.18 Task Queues (Unscheduled Tasks)

Tasks in App Engine are used for additional work which might need to be done as part of your application but that is not required in generating the response that is sent back to the user. This ancillary work can include actions such as logging, creating or updating datastore entities, sending notifications, etc.

App Engine supports two different types of tasks. The first are called *Push Queues*, which are jobs that your application creates to be executed as quickly and concurrently as possible. They do not allow for external influence. The second type are *Pull Queues*, which are a bit more flexible. They're created by your App Engine application, as well; however, they can be consumed or "leased" by your App Engine or an external application via a representational state transfer application programmers interface (REST API). We'll spend most of the upcoming section discussing Push Queues, and then conclude with a brief word on Pull Queues.

12.18.1 Creating Tasks

Tasks can be started by the handler of a user-facing request, or they can be created by another task. An example of the latter is when all the work managed by the first task was not able to be completed in a timely fashion (think of a 30-second or 10-minute deadline), so the work the first task was created to do has not been completed yet.

Tasks are added to task queues. Queues are named and can have different execution rates, *replenishment* or *burstiness* rates, and retry parameters. Users get one default queue but must specify others if more are desired (more on this later). Adding a task to the default queue is straightforward and requires only one simple call once you've imported the taskqueue API:

```
from google.appengine.api import taskqueue
taskqueue.add()
```

All queue requests will be POSTed to URL, and thus a handler. If a custom URL is not created by the user, requests will go to a default URL based on the name of the queue: /_ah/queue/QUEUE_NAME. So for the default queue, that would be /_ah/queue/default. This means that you should provide a handler setting for it when creating your WSGIApplication:

```
def main():
    run_wsgi_app(webapp.WSGIApplication([
        . . .
        ('/_ah/queue/default', DoSomething),
        . . .
    ]))
```

Of course, you need the code for the actual task, too; for example, the DoSomething handler we just defined:

```
class DoSomething(webapp.RequestHandler):
    def post(self):
        # do the task here
        . . .
        logging.info('completed task')
```

We added a quick log entry at the end to confirm the task had actually executed. Obviously, you don't have to log anything if you don't want to, but it can also be a great way to confirm that the task did complete. In fact, you can even use the log entry as a placeholder if you haven't completed the code to perform the actual task's work. (Of course, if you *do* choose to log something, ensure that you have an import logging statement somewhere up above.)

12.18.2 Configuring app.yaml

With regard to configuration, you *could* leave your app.yaml alone with a default handler for all URLs:

```
handlers:
- url: .*
  script: main.py
```

This setting will direct normal application URLs to main.py but the pattern also matches /_ah/queue/default, meaning task queue requests will be sent there, as well, which might be what you want. However, the problem with this setup is that anyone can go to your /_ah/queue/default URL externally, even if they were not created as a task.

The best practice is to lock down this URL to task-only requests by adding a login: admin directive as we did earlier when configuring your application to receive e-mail. You will have to split off this special URL from all the others, like this modified app.yaml:

```
handlers:
- url: /_ah/queue/default
  script: main.py
```

```
      login: admin

    - url: .*
      script: main.py
```

12.18.3 Additional Task Creation and Configuration Options

Earlier we showed you the simplest way of creating a task by using `taskqueue.add()`. Of course, there are plenty more options to let you create a task destined for a different (not default) queue, time delay till execution desired, the ability to pass in parameters to the task, etc. The list that follows shows a few of these options, of which a user can choose one or more:

1. `taskqueue.add(url='/task')`
2. `taskqueue.add(countdown=300)`
3. `taskqueue.add(url='/send_email', params={'groupID': 1})`
4. `taskqueue.add(url='/send_email?groupID=1', method='GET')`
5. `taskqueue.add(queue_name='send-newsletter')`

In the first call, a specific URL is passed in. This is for times when you prefer to use a custom URL, as opposed to the default one. In the second case, a countdown parameter is given to delay execution of the task until at least a certain number of seconds have passed. The third call shows an example of both a custom URL as well as passing in task handler parameters. The fourth example is the same as the third, except that the user has asked for a GET request rather than the default POST. The final example we're going to look at is when you've defined a custom task queue instead of using the default.

These are just a few of the parameters that `taskqueue.add()` supports. You can read about the rest at http://developers.google.com/appengine/docs/python/taskqueue/functions.

So far, all of our previous examples have been using the default queue. You can create other queues, too; as of this writing, you can have up to ten additional queues for free applications and a hundred for those with billing enabled (subject to change, however). To do so, you'll configure them in a file named `queue.yaml` in a format that looks like the following:

```
    queue:
    - name: default
      rate: 1/s
      bucket_size: 10

    - name: send-newsletter
      rate: 1/d
```

The default is normally created on its own, but if you want to choose different parameters for it, you can specify those in queue.yaml, as we just did, overriding the default rate of 5/s and bucket_size of 5. (The rate is how fast tasks are processed, and the bucket_size controls how quickly a queue can process succeeding tasks.) The send-newsletter queue is for a once-a-day, opt-in e-mail newsletter. You can read more about all the configuration parameters for queues at http://developers.google.com/appengine/docs/python/config/queue.

The final word on tasks is that there is another kind of queue that gives developers more flexibility in terms of how and when tasks are created as well as consumed and completed. The types of task queues discussed in this section are Push Queues, which means that your application generates tasks on demand, pushing the work to queues as necessary.

We mentioned that App Engine has an alternative task interface by which jobs can be created in Pull Queues. These queues can be accessed directly by App Engine (creating or consuming work) or accessed from external applications via a REST interface. This means that work can originate from an App Engine application and be executed or processed elsewhere, if desired. Because of this, there is a more flexible execution timeline. More information on pull queues is available in the documentation at http://developers.google.com/appengine/docs/python/taskqueue/overviewpull.

12.18.4 Sending E-Mail as a Task

In an earlier example, we presented an example of how to send e-mail from your application. If you're only sending a single message, perhaps to the administrator of your application whenever someone makes a blog post entry, it's not that big of a deal to also send the e-mail as part of the handling of that request. However, if you need to send e-mail to thousands of customers, it's probably less of a good idea.

Instead, the work of sending all this e-mail is a great candidate for a task. Rather than sending the e-mail, the handler will create the task, pass in the parameters (such as all the e-mail addresses or a group ID of the group of users to receive the message), and then return the response back to the user while the task sends the e-mail on its own time (not that of the users).

Suppose that we have a Web template that lets a user configure an e-mail message and recipient group. When users submit the form to the /submit URL, it's handled by the FormHandler class, for which part of it might look like this:

```
class FormHandler(webapp.RequestHandler):
    def post(self): # should run at most 1/s
        groupID = self.request.get('group')
        taskqueue.add(params={'groupID': groupID})
        . . .
```

The `FormHandler.post()` method makes a call to `taskqueue.add()`, which adds a task on the default queue, passing in the ID of the group that will be receiving the e-mail newsletter. When the task is executed by App Engine, it issues a `POST` to `/_ah/queue/default` for which we need to define another handler class for the task.

Because we're using the default queue here, we'll take the `app.yaml` as defined in the previous subsection with the additional security lock of `login: admin`. Now our main handler (`main.py`), can specify the handlers for the form (in the previous example) as well as for the upcoming task handler we're going to create:

```
def main():
    run_wsgi_app(webapp.WSGIApplication([
        . . .
        ('/submit', FormHandler),
        ('/_ah/queue/default', SendNewsletter),
        . . .
    ]))
```

Now let's define the task handler, `SendNewsletter`, which will receive an inbound request along with the group ID, as sent from form handler. We'll then forward it to a generalized function to carry out the distribution of the newsletter e-mail messages. Here's one way you can create the `SendNewsletter` class:

```
class SendNewsletter(webapp.RequestHandler):
    def post(self): # should run at most 1/s
        groupID = self.request.get('group')
        send_group_email(groupID)
        . . .
```

This, of course, presumes that you've created a nice `send_group_email()` function to handle the task of taking a group ID, pulling in all the member e-mail addresses (possibly extracting them from the datastore), constructing the message body (from the datastore, auto-generated, pulled from another server, etc.), and of course, making the actual call to `mail.send_mail()`. Here's what some of that code might look like:

```
from datetime import date
from google.appengine.api import mail
. . .

def send_group_email(groupID):
```

```
group_emails = . . . # get addresses for groupID members
msg_body = . . . # get custom msg for groupID members
mail.send_mail('noreply@APP_ID.appspotmail.com', group_emails,
    '%s Newsletter' % date.today().strftime("%B %Y"), msg_body)
```

Why did we create a separate send_group_email() function? Couldn't we have just rolled these lines of code into our handler to avoid an additional function call? This is a valid argument; however, we feel that code reuse is an even nobler goal. A separate function gives you the option to use the same function elsewhere, perhaps a command-line tool, a special administrator screen/function, or even another application. If you roll this code into our handler here, you'd have to cut and paste it out or eventually split it up into two functions anyway, so we might as well do it now.

It's clear that it's not too difficult to create tasks to perform non-user-facing application work. Tasks are very popular with App Engine users; we invite you to give them a try. But before you do, we also recommend that you consider a convenience package if your needs are simpler than those of others: the deferred library.

12.18.5 The deferred Package

As you read in the previous subsection, App Engine's tasks queues are a great way to delegate additional work. This work is typically not user-facing, and typically, developers don't want such activities to impact the time it takes to respond back to their users. However, although tasks offer the App Engine developer flexibility in terms of customizing the creation and execution of tasks, it still seems like a bit of work required to just run some simple tasks. This is where deferred comes in.

The deferred package is a convenience tool that hides much of the effort in setting up and executing tasks: you have to adjust your form handler to create tasks, you have to extract and provide the appropriate task parameters and execution guidelines, you have to create and configure separate task handlers, etc. Why can't I just *delegate that to a task*? That's pretty much *exactly* what deferred offers.

You're only presented with a single function, deferred.defer(), that you'll use to create a deferred task. It can be as simple as a logging call, such as the following:

```
from google.appengine.ext import deferred
deferred.defer(logging.info, "Called a deferred task")
```

Other than configuring your application to use the deferred library, there's nothing else for you to do. Deferred tasks run (by default) on the default queue, and as you read earlier, you don't need to do anything special to set that up, unless you want to change the default characteristics of the default queue. You also don't need to specify a handler in your application to handle the deferred task—the deferred library implements all of this. As you can see from the preceding short example, you only need to pass deferred.defer() a Python callable and any arguments and/ or keyword arguments.

In addition, you can also pass in task arguments, too (such as the ones described in the last section), but you need to disguise them somewhat to prevent them from being mixed up with the arguments to your deferred callable. To do so, you need to prepend them with a single underscore, which precludes mistaking them for the parameters for your executable. For example, to make the same call as above, but delayed by (at least) 5 seconds, you would use this, instead:

```
deferred.defer(logging.info,
    "Called a delayed deferred task", _countdown=5)
```

We can easily convert out e-mail distribution example to this equivalent code:

```
class SendNewsletter(webapp.RequestHandler):
    def post(self):
        groupID = self.request.get('group')
        deferred.defer(send_group_email, groupID)
        . . .
```

Deferred tasks can call functions, methods, and generally any object that is callable or that have __call__ defined. From the documentation in the code, these are the callables that can be used as deferred tasks:

1. Functions defined in the top level of a module
2. Classes defined in the top level of a module
   a. Instances of those classes that implement __call__
   b. Instance methods of objects of those classes
   c. Class methods of those classes
3. Built-in functions
4. Built-in methods

However, the following are not permitted (also documented in the code):

- Nested functions or closures

- Nested classes or objects of them

- Lambda functions

- Static methods

Furthermore, all the parameters of the callable used must be "pickle-able," meaning just your basic Python objects, such as constants, numbers, strings, sequences, and hashing types. For a full list, you can consult the official Python documentation at http://docs.python.org/release/2.5.4/lib/node317.html (Python 2.5) or http://docs.python.org/library/pickle.html#what-can-be-pickled-and-unpickled (latest Python version).

The only other restriction with our example is that `send_group_email()` needs to be in a different module and an import added to our main handler. The reason for this is because at the time you "defer" your task and it's "serialized," it records that your code belongs to the __main__ module, but when the `deferred` package executes your callable after receiving it from the `POST` request that is created by the task, the `deferred` module is what is executing (hence it's [also] __main__, which means it won't be able to find your code). You'll receive an error that looks like the following if your `deferred` function were called `foo()`:

```
Traceback (most recent call last):
  File "/usr/local/google_appengine/google/appengine/ext/deferred/
deferred.py", line 258, in post
    run(self.request.body)
  File "/usr/local/google_appengine/google/appengine/ext/deferred/
deferred.py", line 122, in run
    raise PermanentTaskFailure(e)
PermanentTaskFailure: 'module' object has no attribute 'foo'
```

However, by placing it outside of `main.py` (or whatever Python module contains your main handler), you will avoid this confusion and have your code be imported and execute properly. If you would like a quick refresher on __main__, read the chapter on modules in *Core Python Programming* or *Core Python Language Fundamentals*. To find more about `deferred`, check out the original article at http://developers.google.com/appengine/articles/deferred.

12.19 Profiling with Appstats

Being able to profile how well your application performs is important in App Engine. To help you do that, you can use *Appstats*, which is a tool in the SDK with which users can optimize the performance of their applications. Beyond just a normal "code profiler," Appstats traces the various API calls made by your application, measures the time it takes to complete roundtrips to back-end services via remote procedure calls (RPCs), and provides a web-based interface for you to observe your application's behavior.

Configuring Appstats to record events is straightforward. You simply create an `appengine_config.py` file in the root directory of your application (or append to it if it already exists) by using the following function:

```
def webapp_add_wsgi_middleware(app):
    from google.appengine.ext.appstats import recording
    app = recording.appstats_wsgi_middleware(app)
    return app
```

There are additional features that you can install here, which you can read about in the documentation. Once you've installed this code, App-stats will begin to record events from your application's activity. The recorder is fairly lightweight, so you should not experience any appreciable degradation in performance.

The final step is to set up the administrative interface through which you can access the metrics that Appstats records. You can you do this in one of three ways:

1. Add a standard handler in app.yaml
2. Add a custom Admin Console page
3. Enable the interface as a built-in

12.19.1 Adding a Standard Handler in app.yaml

To add a standard handler in app.yaml (in the `handlers:` section naturally), use the following:

```
- url: /stats.*
  script: $PYTHON_LIB/google/appengine/ext/appstats/ui.py
```

12.19.2 Adding a Custom Admin Console page

If you want to add the Appstats UI as a custom Admin Console page, you can do so in the `admin_console:` section of app.yaml, as shown here:

```
admin_console:
 pages:
 - name: Appstats UI
   url: /stats
```

12.19.3 Enabling the Interface as a Built-In

You can enable the Appstats UI as a built-in by turning it on in the `builtins:` section of `app.yaml`, as demonstrated here:

```
builtins:
- appstats: on
```

Enabling it this way configures the UI to default to the `/_ah/stats` path. You can see all the magic that Appstats provides for you at the following links:

http://developers.google.com/appengine/docs/python/tools/appstats

http://googleappengine.blogspot.com/2010/03/easy-performance-profiling-with.html

http://www.youtube.com/watch?v=bvp7CuBWVgA

12.20 The URLfetch Service

One restriction that you need to take into consideration when working with App Engine is that you cannot create network sockets. This can practically render most applications useless; however, the SDK does provide for higher-level functionality as a proxy. One of the main use cases of being able to create and use sockets is to communicate with other applications on the Internet. To this end, App Engine provides a *URLfetch* service whereby your application can make HTTP requests (GET, POST, HEAD, PUT, DELETE) to other servers online. Here's a short example of how to use it:

```
from google.appengine.api import urlfetch
. . .
    res = urlfetch.fetch('http://google.com')
    if res.status_code == 200:
        self.response.out.write(
            'First 100 bytes of google.com:<p>%s</p>' %
res.content[:100])
. . .
```

In addition to App Engine's `urlfetch` module, you can also use the standard library `urllib`, `urllib2`, and `httplib` modules, modified to communicate through App Engine's URL fetch service (which naturally runs on Google's scalable infrastructure).

There are some caveats about which you should be aware, however, such as communicating to servers via HTTPS as well as request headers that cannot be modified or set. You can read more about these restrictions as well as find an overview of how to use the URLfetch service in the documentation at http://developers.google.com/appengine/docs/python/urlfetch/overview.

Finally, because some payloads have a high latency, an asynchronous URLfetch service is also available. You also have the option of polling to see if the request has completed or provide a callback. You can read more about asynchronous URLfetch at http://developers.google.com/appengine/docs/python/urlfetch/asynchronousrequests.

12.21 Lightning Round (without Python Code)

This is another "lightning round" section in which we will introduce features that are configured. This section does not feature source code.

12.21.1 Cron Service (Scheduled Tasks/Jobs)

A *cronjob* is a task that is executed at scheduled times and originated on POSIX computers. App Engine provides a cron-type service for its users. There is actually no Python code involved, except for the handler that is executed at the appropriate time.

To use the cron service, you need to create a cron.yaml file that contains contents such as the following:

```
cron:
- url: /task/roll_logs
  schedule: every day
- url: /task/weekly_report
  schedule: every friday 17:00
```

You can also specify description: and timezone: fields, as appropriate. The schedule format is fairly flexible. You can read more about cron jobs in App Engine from the documentation at http://developers.google.com/appengine/docs/python/config/cron.

12.21.2 Warming Requests

The goal of warming requests is to reduce the latency that users of your application experience when new instances need to be "spun up" to serve yet more users. Let's assume that you're doing a good job of serving your application from a single instance. But if it is suddenly *Slashdotted* or Tweeted, it can experience a sudden rush of traffic. When the running instance can no longer support this load, new instances must be brought online to serve all the requests.

Without the warming feature, the first user to access your application on the new instance would have to wait longer for a response than it would if he accessed the already-running instance. The additional delay is caused by the need to wait for the new instance to be loaded before it can service the user's request. Now if we could just "warm up" the new instance by pre-loading your application *before* it gets any traffic, then users wouldn't have to suffer this delay. That's exactly what warming requests do.

Similar to other App Engine features, warming requests are not enabled by default. To turn them on, add a line in the `inbound_services:` section of your `app.yaml` file:

```
inbound_services:
- warmup
```

Furthermore, when a new instance comes online, App Engine will issue a GET request to `/_ah/warmup`. If you create a handler for this, you can pre-load any data in your application, as well. Just keep in mind that if your application isn't getting any traffic and all, and there are no instances of it running, the very first request will still trigger a loading request for that unfortunate user (even if warming is enabled).

If you think about it, the reason is quite obvious: a warming request won't do any good, and in fact, would actually add to the latency because the loading request must already happen. You don't want to pay the penalty of issuing a warming request in addition to the loading request before your application can respond to this first user. Warming requests are really only useful if there are already servers handling traffic to your application so that App Engine can warm up new instances.

This feature is a configuration which also doesn't require any Python code. You can read more about warming requests at:

http://developers.google.com/appengine/docs/adminconsole/instances#Warmup_Requests

http://developers.google.com/appengine/docs/python/config/appconfig#Inbound_Services

12.21.3 Denial-of-Service Protection

App Engine offers a simplistic form of protection against systematic Denial-of-Service (DoS) abuse against your application. It requires you to create a dos.yaml file with a blacklist: section, as in this short example:

```
blacklist:
- subnet: 89.212.115.11
  description: block DoS offender
- subnet: 72.14.194.1/15
  description: block offending subnet
```

You can blacklist individual IP addresses or subnets for both IPv4 and IPv6. Once you upload the dos.yaml file, requests coming from the specified addresses and subnets will be filtered from reaching your application code. You will not be charged for any resources incurred from blocking computers sending traffic from these blacklisted addresses and networks.

The official documentation for the DoS protect can be found at http://developers.google.com/appengine/docs/python/config/dos.

12.22 Vendor Lock-In

The last discussion we'll have before we let you take flight to the clouds is about *vendor lock-in*. Lock-in generally refers to systems that inherently make it *very difficult or impossible to migrate* data and/or logic to other similar or competitive systems. Throughout its short lifetime, App Engine has been consistently dogged by the reputation that it "forces users" to use Google's API to access App Engine with no easy way to port applications away from the platform.

While Google does strongly recommend you use their APIs to take full advantage of the system, users must understand that there is a tradeoff. It seems to be fair that in exchange for being able to take advantage of Google's scalable infrastructure (whose management is solely the company's), that you should be using their APIs to write your code. Again, you can't get something for nothing, right? And building such scalability is one of the most difficult and expensive things to do. However, Google does try to fight lock-in as much as it can while still allowing users to take advantage of App Engine.

For example, while App Engine does come with the webapp (or webapp2) framework, you're free to use others that are open source and compatible with App Engine. Some of these include Django, web2py, Tipfy, Flask, or Bottle. With regard to the Datastore API, you can completely bypass it if you use the Django-nonrel system along with djangoappengine. These libraries allow you to run pure Django apps directly on top of App Engine, so you're free to move your apps between App Engine and any traditional hosting that supports Django. Furthermore, this isn't limited to Python as on the Java side; the App Engine team has tried hard to make its APIs as compliant with the Java Specification Request (JSR) standards as possible. If you know how to write a Java servlet, your knowledge is easily transferred to App Engine.

Finally, there are two open-source back-end systems that claim to be compatible with the App Engine client: AppScale and TyphoonAE. The latter is maintained as a more traditional open-source project, whereas the former is actively developed at the University of California, Santa Barbara. You can find out more about both projects at their respective home pages at http://appscale.cs.ucsb.edu and http://code.google.com/p/typhoonae. If you want full control of your application and don't want to run it within a Google datacenter, you can host your own platform with either of these systems.

12.23 Resources

You can write an entire book on App Engine (and people have); unfortunately, we have no choice but to leave many details out of this chapter. However, if you would like to delve deeper into it, the following are some features and references that you might find useful.

- Blobstore   Lets users serve data objects (blobs) which are too large for the Datastore, (e.g., media files)

  http://developers.google.com/appengine/docs/python/blobstore/overview

- Capabilities

  http://developers.google.com/appengine/docs/python/capabilities/overview

  http://www.slideshare.net/jasonacooper/strategies-for-maintaining-app-engine-availability-during-read-only-periods

  http://developers.google.com/appengine/docs/python/howto/maintenance

- Channel   Service that lets your application push data directly to the browser, a.k.a. Reverse Ajax, browser push, Comet

  http://googleappengine.blogspot.com/2010/12/happy-holidays-from-app-engine-team-140.html

  http://blog.myblive.com/2010/12/multiuser-chatroom-with-app-engine.html

  http://code.google.com/p/channel-tac-toe/

  http://arstechnica.com/web/news/2010/12/app-engine-gets-streaming-api-and-longer-background-tasks.ars

- High-replication datastore

  http://googleappengine.blogspot.com/2011/01/announcing-high-replication-datastore.html

  http://developers.google.com/appengine/docs/python/datastore/structuring_for_strong_consistency

- Matcher   Highly scalable real-time matching infrastructure: register queries to match against an object stream

  http://www.onebigfluke.com/2010/10/magical-api-from-future-app-engines.html

  http://groups.google.com/group/google-appengine/browse_thread/thread/5462e14c31f44bef

  http://code.google.com/p/google-app-engine-samples/wiki/AppEngineMatcherService

- Namespaces   Lets you create multi-tenant applications by compartmentalizing your Google App Engine data

  http://googleappengine.blogspot.com/2010/08/multi-tenancy-support-high-performance_17.html

http://developers.google.com/appengine/docs/python/
multitenancy/overview

http://developers.google.com/appengine/docs/python/
multitenancy/multitenancy

- OAuth   Federated authorization service that allows third-party access to applications and data without credential exchange

http://developers.google.com/appengine/docs/python/oauth/
overview

http://oauth.net

- Pipeline   Manage multiple long-running tasks/workflows and collate their results (*See also* Fantasm, another simpler workflow manager written by a third-party)

http://code.google.com/p/appengine-pipeline/wiki/
GettingStarted

http://code.google.com/p/appengine-pipeline/

http://news.ycombinator.com/item?id=2013133

http://googleappengine.blogspot.com/2011/03/implementing-workflows-on-app-engine.html

Table 12-3 lists Web addresses for many of the development frameworks presented in this chapter.

Table 12-3 Frameworks for Development with Google App Engine

Project	URL(s)
Google App Engine	http://developers.google.com/appengine
Bigtable	http://labs.google.com/papers/bigtable.html
Megastore	http://research.google.com/pubs/pub36971.html
webapp	http://developers.google.com/appengine/docs/python/gettingstarted/usingwebapp
	http://developers.google.com/appengine/docs/python/tools/webapp

Project	URL(s)
webapp2	http://developers.google.com/appengine/docs/python/gettingstartedpython27/usingwebapp
	http://developers.google.com/appengine/docs/python/tools/webapp2
	http://webapp-improved.appspot.com/
Django	http://djangoproject.com
Django-nonrel	http://www.allbuttonspressed.com/projects/django-nonrel
djangoappengine	http://www.allbuttonspressed.com/projects/djangoappengine
Bottle	http://bottlepy.org
Flask	http://flask.pocoo.org/
tipfy	http://tipfy.org
web2py	http://web2py.com
AppScale	http://appscale.cs.ucsb.edu
TyphoonAE	http://code.google.com/p/typhoonae

12.24 Conclusion

As we've seen from all the rich material in this chapter and Chapter 11, Django and Google App Engine are two of the most powerful and flexible Web frameworks in the Python community today. Add in all the others (TurboGears, Pyramid, web2py, web.py, etc.), which are quite formidable themselves, and you've got a great ecosphere of frameworks and an ample number of choices for anyone writing Web applications in Python. Even more important, all of the Python Web frameworks have a dedicated set of developers and devoted followers.

Programmers who are jacks-of-all-trades might even switch between frameworks from time-to-time, depending on whether they're the right tool for the job. It's good that the community has rallied around some of these larger, more well-known frameworks, because although the quote at the beginning of the chapter is a bit tongue-in-cheek, there is a grain of truth behind it, and the world would be much worse off if *everyone* had to write their own Web framework.

One final note: none of the examples in this chapter are available in Python 3 because neither framework supports it yet. Rest assured that when that time arrives, we'll provide that source for you online as well as in future editions of this book.

12.25 Exercises

Google App Engine

12-1. *Background.* What does Python have to do with Google App Engine?

12-2. *Background.* What makes Google App Engine different from other development environments?

12-3. *Configuration.* What are some differences between Django and App Engine configuration files?

12-4. *Configuration.* Name the places where Django applications perform URL-to-handler mapping. Do the same for App Engine applications.

12-5. *Configuration.* How do you get Django applications to run (mostly) unmodified on Google App Engine?

12-6. *Configuration.* For this exercise, go to http://code.google.com/appengine, and then download and install the latest Google App Engine SDK for your platform.

   a) Use the Launcher application if on a Windows-based PC or Mac and create an application called "helloworld." On other platforms, create the following pair of files, with the following content:

```
i. The first file is: app.yaml
application: helloworld
version: 1
runtime: python
api_version: 1

handlers:
  - url: .*
    script: main.py
ii. The second file is: main.py

from google.appengine.ext import webapp
from google.appengine.ext.webapp.util import run_wsgi_app
```

```
class MainHandler(webapp.RequestHandler):
    def get(self):
        self.response.out.write('Hello world!')

application = webapp.WSGIApplication([
    ('/', MainHandler),
], debug=True)

def main():
    run_wsgi_app(application)

if __name__ == '__main__':
    main()
```

b) Start your application by using the Launcher or executing 'dev_appserver.py *DIR*', where *DIR* is the directory in which both app.yaml and main.py are located, and then visit http://localhost:8080 (or the appropriate port number) to confirm your code works and "Hello world!" does show up on your browser. Change the output to something other than "Hello world!".

12-7. *Tutorial.* Complete the entire *Getting Started* tutorial found at http://code.google.com/appengine/docs/python/ gettingstarted. Warning: do not simply copy the code you find there. I expect to see you modify the application to do something slightly different than what's offered, and/or add new functionality that isn't present.

12-8. *Communication.* E-mail is a critical application feature. In an earlier exercise, you added e-mail distribution when a new blog entry is made. Do the same with your App Engine blog application.

12-9. *Images.* Allow users to submit one photo or picture per blog entry and create a suitably tasteful display of blog posts.

12-10. *Cursors and Pagination.* Like the Django blog application, showing the ten most recent posts is good, but letting users paginate through older posts is even better. Use cursors and add pagination to your application.

12-11. *Communication.* Allow users to communicate with your application by using IMs. Create a menu of commands to post blog entries, retrieve the most recent entries and any other feature that you think would be "cool."

Development with Django or App Engine

12-12.   *User Cloud Data Management System.* Build a weather monitoring system. Allow multiple users in your system, using
         whichever form of authentication you prefer. Every user
         should have a set of locations (postal or ZIP code, airport
         code, [city, state], [city, country], etc.). The user should be
         presented a grid of all the locations they're interested in,
         along with the current forecast and an extended
         3–5 day forecast. There are various online weather APIs
         you can use.

12-13.   *Financial Management System.* Create a stock/equity portfolio
         management system. This includes normal stocks (on any
         exchange), mutual funds, exchange-traded funds (ETFs),
         American depositary receipts (ADRs), stock exchange indices, or anything that has a ticker symbol by which you can
         perform lookups. If you do not live in the United States,
         adopt your solution to the trading vehicles used in your
         country.

12-14.   *Sports Statistics Application.* You're an avid participant in the
         global sport of bowling. Sure, it's easy to make an application
         that manages your scores, gives you averages, etc., but you
         should do more than that. Show trending, moving-day averages, and also allow users to enter the number of open
         frames along with the scores. This way they can verify
         whether they really had a good game or whether they got
         lucky by hitting *Brooklyns* all evening long. Also, include a
         check box that can be selected to indicate whether a game is
         sanctioned or not, and allow links to video clips be tied to
         specific games. Live and breathe your sport—away from
         your bowling alley. Create a network server that allows you
         to access this data over the Internet when you're out of town
         or from your mobile phone.

12-15.   *Course Logistics and Social Management System.* Implement a
         secondary or collegiate course management system. It
         should support users being able to login, have a chat room
         for live conversation, forums for offline Out-of-Band (OoB)
         communication, and a place to submit homework and get
         grades. Similarly for teachers, they should be able to add
         new and grade existing assignments, participate in chats and
         forums along with students, post course announcements,

static files, and send messages to students. Choose either Django or Google App Engine to implement your solution, or better yet, use Django-nonrel to create a Django app that can run in a traditional hosted environment or by Google on App Engine.

12-16. *Recipe Manager*. Develop an application to manage a virtual collection of cooking recipes. This is slightly different from managing, for instance, a music collection for which you have all your MP3 or other sound files locally. These food recipes only exist online. When users enter recipe URLs, your application should allow them to be placed in multiple categories (but the actual URL should only be saved once). Also, the user should be alerted when a link no longer works by e-mail, IM/XMPP, or even by SMS if you can find an appropriate e-mail-to-SMS gateway (see http://en.wikipedia.org/wiki/List_of_SMS_gateways) if you are not running your own SMS service. Create a mini-crawler so that when listing recipes, you'll also display a thumbnail of an image found on the same page as the recipe URL (if one is available). You should also allow your users to browse by category/cuisine.

CHAPTER 13

Web Services

I'm not addicted to Twitter. I only tweet when I have time:
lunch time, break time, off time, this time, that time,
any time, all the time.
          —(unknown), earlier than May 2010

In this chapter...

- Introduction
- The Yahoo! Finance Stock Quote Server
- Microblogging with Twitter

In this chapter, we give brief introductions on how to use a couple of Web services available today; an "old" service, Yahoo's stock quote server, and a new one, Twitter.

13.1   Introduction

There are many Web services and applications on the Internet, providing a wide variety of services. You will find application programming interfaces (APIs) from most of the big players, such as Yahoo!, Google, Twitter, and Amazon, to name just a few. In the past, APIs have been used just to access data by using these services; however, today's APIs are different. They are rich and fully featured, and you are able to actually integrate services into your own personal Web sites and Web pages, commonly known as *mash-ups*.

This is an area of active interest that we will continue to explore (REST, XML, JSON, RSS, Atom, etc.), but for now, we are going to take a trip back in time to play around with an older interface that is still useful and has displayed tremendous longevity: the stock quote server from Yahoo! at http://finance.yahoo.com.

13.2   The Yahoo! Finance Stock Quote Server

If you visit the Yahoo! Finance Web site and pull up a quotation for any stock, you will find a URL link under the basic quote data labeled **Download Data** in the Toolbox section, toward the page bottom. This lets users download a .csv file suitable for importing into Microsoft Excel or Intuit Quicken. The URL would look similar to the following if you were on the page for GOOG:

http://quote.yahoo.com/d/quotes.csv?s=GOOG&f=sl1d1t1c1ohgv&e=.csv

If your browser's MIME settings are set correctly, it will actually launch software on your system configured to handle CSV data, usually spreadsheet applications such as Excel or LibreOffice Calc. This is due primarily to the final variable (key-value) pair found in the link, e=.csv. This variable is actually not used by the server because it always sends back data in CSV format, anyway.

If we use our friend `urllib2.urlopen()`, we see that for any stock ticker symbol, one CSV string is returned:

```
>>> from urllib2 import urlopen
>>> url = 'http://quote.yahoo.com/d/quotes.csv?s=goog&f=s11d1c1p2'
>>> u = urlopen(url, 'r')
>>> for row in u:
...     print row
...
"GOOG",600.14,"10/28/2011",+1.47,"+0.25%"

>>> u.close()
```

The string would then need to be manually parsed (by stripping the trailing whitespace and splitting on the comma delimiter). As an alternative to parsing the data string ourselves, we can use the `csv` module, introduced in Python 2.3, which does both the string split and the whitespace strip. Using `csv`, we can replace the **for** loop in the previous example with the following, assuming that all other lines are left intact:

```
>>> import csv
>>> for row in csv.reader(u):
...     print row
...
['GOOG', '600.14', '10/28/2011', '+1.47', '+0.25%']
```

By analyzing the argument field `f` passed to the server via the URL string and from reading Yahoo!'s online help for this service, you will see that the symbols (`s11d1c1p2`) correspond to: ticker symbol, last price, date, change, and percentage change.

You can get more information by checking the Yahoo! Finance Help pages—just search for "download data" or "download spreadsheet format." Further analysis of the API reveals a few more options such as the previous closing price, the percentage change of the current price to the previous close, the 52-week high and low, etc. The options are summarized in Table 13-1 along with the formats of the returned components. (Don't be shocked at the stock price of Yahoo! from the last decade; that's what it really was back then.)

Table 13-1 Yahoo! Finance Stock Quote Server Parameters

Stock Quotation Data	Field Name[a]	Format Returned[b]
Stock ticker symbol	s	"YHOO"
Price of last trade	l1	328
Last trade date	d1	"2/2/2000"
Time of last trade	t1	"4:00pm"
Change from previous close	c1	+10.625
Percentage change from previous close	p2	"+3.35%"
Previous closing price	p	317.375
Last opening price	o	321.484375
Daily high price	h	337
Daily low price	g	317
52-week range	w	"110 - 500.125"
Volume for the day	v	6703300
Market capitalization	j1	86.343B
Earnings per share	e	0.20
Price-to-earnings ratio	r	1586.88
Company name	n	"YAHOO INC"

a. The first character of the field name is alphabetic; the second, if any, is numeric.
b. Some values come back (additionally) quoted, although all are returned as part of a single CSV string from the server.

The server presents the field names in the order that you specify. Just concatenate them as a single argument to the field parameter f, as part of the requesting URL. As mentioned in the footnote b., of Table 13-1, some of the components returned are quoted separately. It's up to the parser to properly extract the data. Observe the resulting (sub)strings when parsed manually versus using the csv module in our previous example. If a value is not available, the quote server returns "N/A" as shown in the code that follows.

For example, if we give the server a field request of f=s1ld1c1p2, we get back a string such as the following for a valid stock ticker (back in 2000 when I really ran this query):

```
"YHOO",166.203125,"2/23/2000",+12.390625,"+8.06%"
```

For cases for which the stock is no longer publicly traded, we get something like this, instead (note again how fields that come back quoted still do, even if N/A):

```
"PBLS.OB",0.00,"N/A",N/A,"N/A"
```

You can also specify multiple stock ticker symbols, such as s=YHOO,GOOG,EBAY,AMZN. You will get back one row of data such as the preceding for each company. Just keep in mind that *"[any] redistribution of quotes data displayed on Yahoo! is strictly prohibited,"* as quoted in the Yahoo! Finance Help pages, so you should use this data for your personal use only. Also be aware that all of the quotes you download are delayed.

Using what we know now, let's build an example application that reads and displays some stock quote data for some of our favorite Internet companies, as shown in Example 13-1.

Example 13-1   Yahoo! Finance Stock Quote Example (`stock.py`)

This script downloads and displays stock prices from the Yahoo! quote server.

```
1   #!/usr/bin/env python
2
3   from time import ctime
4   from urllib2 import urlopen
5
6   TICKs = ('yhoo', 'dell', 'cost', 'adbe', 'intc')
7   URL = 'http://quote.yahoo.com/d/quotes.csv?s=%s&f=s1lc1p2'
8
9   print '\nPrices quoted as of:%s PDT\n' % ctime()
10  print 'TICKER', 'PRICE', 'CHANGE', '%AGE'
11  print '------', '-----', '------', '----'
12  u = urlopen(URL % ','.join(TICKs))
13
14  for row in u:
15      tick, price, chg, per = row.split(',')
16      print tick, '%.2f' % float(price), chg, per,
17
18  u.close()
```

When we run this script, we see the following output:

```
$ stock.py

Prices quoted as of: Sat Oct 29 02:06:24 2011 PDT

TICKER PRICE CHANGE %AGE
------ ----- ------ ----
"YHOO" 16.56 -0.07 "-0.42%"
"DELL" 16.31 -0.01 "-0.06%"
"COST" 84.93 -0.29 "-0.34%"
"ADBE" 29.02 +0.68 "+2.40%"
"INTC" 24.98 -0.15 "-0.60%"
```

Line-by-Line Explanation

Lines 1–7

This Python 2 script uses `time.ctime()` to display the current time at which stock information was downloaded from Yahoo!, and `urllib2.urlopen()` to connect to Yahoo!'s service to get the stock data. Following the import statements are the stock ticker symbols as well as the fixed URL that retrieves all the data.

Lines 9–12

This short block of code displays the stock information download time-stamp as well as uses `urllib2.urlopen()` to request the data. (If you read earlier editions of this book, you will note that we've simplified output code quite a bit, thanks to the sharp-eyed readers out there!)

Lines 14–18

Once we have an open file-like object to the data downloaded from the Web, we iterate through each returned row, split the comma-delimited list, and then display them to the screen.

Similar to reading lines in from a text file, the trailing line termination character is also retained, so we need to add a trailing comma to the end of the **print** statement to suppress its NEWLINE; otherwise, the output will all be double-spaced.

Lastly, note that some of the fields returned come enclosed in quotes. There are several exercises at the end of this chapter that will give you the opportunity to improve upon the default output.

13.3   Microblogging with Twitter

In this section, we will explore the world of microblogging with the Twitter service. We'll start with a brief introduction to social networking, describe where Twitter fits in, introduce the various interfaces available in Python, and finally, show you both a simple and an intermediate example.

13.3.1   Social Networking

Social media has developed significantly in the past five-plus years. It started with a very simple concept, such as *Web logging*, or *blogging* for short. This type of service hosts user accounts on which you can post essays or some other form of written communication. Think of it as a public online journal or diary whereby people can report on current events, give some opinion or diatribe, or anything else you would like to communicate to others.

However, being online means that you are sharing your communications with entire world. Users could not target specific individuals or organizations, much less their friends or family. Thus came the social networks, with MySpace, Facebook, Twitter, and Google+ being the most well-known brand names. With these systems, users can connect with their friends, family, colleagues, and other people in their social circles. Although each of these services let users approach the same audience from the user's perspective, they're unique in their own way. Their methods of interaction differ; thus, they generally do not compete directly with each other. Let's briefly describe each, and then dive deeper into Twitter.

MySpace is mostly for young people (junior high and high school level) with a focus on music; Facebook originally targeted college students but is now open to all. It is more of a general platform than MySpace, offering the ability to host applications on its network—this was widely seen as one of the features that brought it mainstream. Twitter is a *microblogging* service, through which users set a status, usually an opinion, thus the comparison to blogging. Google+ is the Internet giant's recent foray into the field, attempting to provide features similar to the others, but it also includes new features to differentiate it from the others.

Of the common social media applications, the most basic is Twitter. You use Twitter to publish short status messages called *tweets*. Others can "follow" you; that is, they can subscribe to your tweets. By the same token, you can follow the tweets of other users you find interesting.

Twitter is referred to as a microblogging service because, unlike a standard blog that allows users to create posts of any length, tweets are limited to a maximum of 140 characters per update. The size restriction is due mainly to the fact that the service originally targeted the web *and* text messages on mobile phones via the Short Message Service (SMS), which themselves have a cap of 160 ASCII characters. Users benefit by not being flooded with too much to read, plus it forces posters to be expressive enough to capture their thoughts in 140 characters or less.

13.3.2 Twitter and Python

There are several Twitter API libraries for Python. They are posted on Twitter's developer documentation at https://dev.twitter.com/docs/twitter-libraries#python. They are all similar and different in their own way, so we recommend that you try several to find one that suits your style. So that we don't limit ourselves *too* much, we'll use Twython and Tweepy in this chapter. You can find them at http://github.com/ryanmcgrath/twython and http://tweepy.github.com, respectively.

As with most Python packages, you can use either `easy_install` or `pip` to get either or both of these Twitter libraries on your system. If you want to play with the code more, the source trees for both are available on GitHub. Alternatively, you can just download the latest `.tgz` or `.zip` from GitHub and call the typical `setup.py` install command:

```
$ sudo python setup.py install
Password:
running install
running bdist_egg
running egg_info
creating twython.egg-info
. . .
Finished processing dependencies for twython==1.4.4
```

Libraries like Twython will need some additional help to be able to communicate with Twitter. It depends on `httplib2`, `oauth2`, and `simplejson`. (The last is the external version of the `json` library that is available in the standard library starting with version 2.6.)

Getting Started

To get you going, here's a quick example of how to use the Tweepy library to do a search on Twitter:

```
# tweepy-example.py
import tweepy
results = tweepy.api.search(q='twython3k')
for tweet in results:
    print '    User: @%s' % tweet.from_user
    print '    Date: %s' % tweet.created_at
    print '    Tweet: %s' % tweet.text
```

If you execute this Python 2 snippet—at the time of this writing, Tweepy is not available for Python 3—with the exact query shown, you'll notice that the search term was specifically chosen for its few results, meaning you'll see just a couple of tweets (mostly from yours truly at this time) returned by Twitter regarding the Python 3 version of the Twython library:

```
$ python twython-example.py
    User: @wescpy
    Date: Tue, 04 Oct 2011 21:09:41 +0000
    Tweet: Testing posting to Twitter using Twython3k (another story of
life on the bleeding edge)

    User: @wescpy
    Date: Tue, 04 Oct 2011 17:18:38 +0000
    Tweet: @ryanmcgrath cool... thx! i also have a &quot;real&quot;
twython3k bug i need to file... will do it officially on github. just
giving you a heads-up!

    User: @wescpy
    Date: Tue, 04 Oct 2011 08:01:09 +0000
    Tweet: @ryanmcgrath Hey ryan, good work on Twython thus far!
Can you pls drop twitter_endpoints.py into twython3k? It's out-of-
date. .. thx! :-)
```

The Tweepy library's `search()` call retrieves the results in a list. The code iterates over the tweets and displays the various attributes of interest. Twython is a similar Python library to the Twitter API.

Twython is similar yet different from Tweepy. It's available for both Python 2 and 3, but it also uses pure Python dictionaries instead of objects to hold resulting data. Contrast `tweepy-example.py` with this script, `twython-example.py`, which also happens to be compatible with Python 2 and 3:

```
# twython-example.py
from distutils.log import warn as printf
try:
    import twython
except ImportError:
    import twython3k as twython

TMPL = '''\
    User: @%(from_user)s
    Date: %(created_at)s
    Tweet: %(text)s
'''

twitter = twython.Twython()
data = twitter.searchTwitter(q='twython3k')
for tweet in data['results']:
    printf(TMPL % tweet)
```

The `distutils.log.warn()` function serves as our proxy for the **print** statement (in Python 2) and function (in Python 3). We also attempt imports of both (Python 2 and 3) Twython libraries, hoping that one will succeed.

In terms of output, yes, `Twython.searchTwitter()` results in a dictionary, and the object located at the `results` key is a list of dicts, each of which represent a resulting tweet. This lets us simplify the display because results are dictionaries—a simpler call indeed. (The penalty is paid in the string template where we need to expand the key variables within.)

The other change made here is that instead of pure single-lines of output, we put all the strings together into one larger string template, and then passed in the output dictionary to it. The reason for this is that in practice, it's more likely that you would be using some sort of template (whether string or Web), anyway.

The output, as you would expect, is identical to that of the Tweepy version, so we won't duplicate it here.

13.3.3   A Longer Combination API Example

Those simple little snippets are great in terms of getting a quick introduction that you can use right away. However, in practice, you're more likely to come across a scenario in which using or integrating with multiple, similar APIs might be necessary. Let's go for a longer example that helps us practice this. We'll write a compatibility library that supports a set of basic Twitter commands by using *both* Tweepy and Twython. This exercise will help you learn both libraries as well as familiarize you more with Twitter's API.

Authentication

To move forward with this exercise, you'll need a Twitter account. Go to http://twitter.com and register if you haven't already. *Authentication* comes in the form of a username and password. (More modern solutions also include biometric authentication via fingerprinting or retina-scanning.) These credentials serve the purpose of authenticating who you are. Data access is another matter.

Authorization

Just because you're authenticated doesn't mean you have access to the data (yours or anyone else's). You need to have the correct *authorization* for that. You need to be authorized to be able to access your data or that of others, or you must authorize a third party to access data on your behalf, such as allowing an external application to download your Twitter stream or to post a status update to your Twitter account.

To obtain your authorization credentials with Twitter, you need to create an application. You can accomplish this at http://dev.twitter.com. Once you have at least one application, click the one whose credentials you want to use. The URL will look similar to https://dev.twitter.com/apps/APP-ID/show. Here you'll find four important pieces that you'll need to access data on Twitter: your OAuth settings include your *consumer key* and *consumer secret*. It will also give you your *access token* and *access token secret*, giving you access to your Twitter data.

Grab those four valuable pieces of data and stick them somewhere safe—which means *not* your source code! In this example, I stored them as four global variables in a module called `tweet_auth.py`, which I will import from our eventual application. In practice, you'd likely either only distribute a bytecode-compiled `.pyc` (not plain text!) or have it available via a database or elsewhere on the network, probably encrypted. Now that we're all set up, let me describe the application before showing you the code.

A Hybrid Twitter API Application

This application performs four operations: first it runs a search on Twitter and prints out the results; next, it retrieves some details about the current user and prints them out; it then acquires the current user's timeline of status messages and prints them out; and then finally it posts a tweet on behalf of the current user. All four of these operations are performed twice: once using the Tweepy library, and once using the Twython library. To carry this out, we're going to support four Twitter API commands, as shown in Table 13-2.

Table 13-2 The Four Commands of the Hybrid Twitter API Application

Command	Description
search	Take a search query and perform a search on Twitter for the most recent tweets that match. This is an unauthenticated call (the only one in our application), meaning anyone can do it at any time.
verify_credentials	Ask Twitter for the current information on the authenticated user.
user_timeline	Get the most recent tweets from the authenticated user.
update_status	Perform a status update from the authenticated user—yes, this will create a new tweet on your behalf.

Next, this application will support both Twython and Tweepy. Finally, it will run under both Python 2 and 3. The code will consist of the supported commands, steps to initiate both libraries, and then contain code that supports each of the commands. Ready? Let's take a look at twapi.py in Example 13-2:

Example 13-2   Twitter API Combination Library Example (twapi.py)

A demonstration of interfacing with Twitter by using the Twython and Tweepy libraries.

```
1   #!/usr/bin/env python
2
3   from distutils.log import warn as printf
4   from unittest import TestCase, main
5   from tweet_auth import *
6
7   # set up supported APIs
8   CMDs = {
9       'twython': {
10          'search':              'searchTwitter',
11          'verify_credentials':  None,
12          'user_timeline':       'getUserTimeline',
13          'update_status':       None,
14      },
15      'tweepy': dict.fromkeys((
16          'search',
17          'verify_credentials',
18          'user_timeline',
19          'update_status',
20      )),
```

(Continued)

Example 13-2   Twitter API Combination Library Example (twapi.py)
(Continued)

```
21  }
22  APIs = set(CMDs)
23
24  # remove unavailable APIs
25  remove = set()
26  for api in APIs:
27      try:
28          __import__(api)
29      except ImportError:
30          try:
31              __import__('%s3k' % api)
32          except ImportError:
33              remove.add(api)
34
35  APIs.difference_update(remove)
36  if not APIs:
37      raise NotImplementedError(
38          'No Twitter API found; install one & add to CMDs!')
39
40  class Twitter(object):
41      'Twitter -- Use available APIs to talk to Twitter'
42      def __init__(self, api, auth=True):
43          if api not in APIs:
44              raise NotImplementedError(
45                  '%r unsupported; try one of: %r' % (api, APIs))
46
47          self.api = api
48          if api == 'twython':
49              try:
50                  import twython
51              except ImportError:
52                  import twython3k as twython
53              if auth:
54                  self.twitter = twython.Twython(
55                      twitter_token=consumer_key,
56                      twitter_secret=consumer_secret,
57                      oauth_token=access_token,
58                      oauth_token_secret=access_token_secret,
59                  )
60              else:
61                  self.twitter = twython.Twython()
62          elif api == 'tweepy':
63              import tweepy
64              if auth:
65                  auth = tweepy.OAuthHandler(consumer_key,
66                      consumer_secret)
67                  auth.set_access_token(access_token,
68                      access_token_secret)
```

```
69                   self.twitter = tweepy.API(auth)
70             else:
71                   self.twitter = tweepy.api
72
73       def _get_meth(self, cmd):
74           api = self.api
75           meth_name = CMDs[api][cmd]
76           if not meth_name:
77               meth_name = cmd
78               if api == 'twython' and '_' in meth_name:
79                   cmds = cmd.split('_')
80                   meth_name = '%s%s' % (cmds[0], cmds[1].title())
81           return getattr(self.twitter, meth_name)
82
83       def search(self, q):
84           api = self.api
85           if api == 'twython':
86               res = self._get_meth('search')(q=q)['results']
87               return (ResultsWrapper(tweet) for tweet in res)
88           elif api == 'tweepy':
89               return (ResultsWrapper(tweet)
90                   for tweet in self._get_meth('search')(q=q))
91
92       def verify_credentials(self):
93           return ResultsWrapper(
94               self._get_meth('verify_credentials')())
95
96       def user_timeline(self):
97           return (ResultsWrapper(tweet)
98               for tweet in self._get_meth('user_timeline')())
99
100      def update_status(self, s):
101          return ResultsWrapper(
102              self._get_meth('update_status')( status=s))
103
104  class ResultsWrapper(object):
105      "ResultsWrapper -- makes foo.bar the same as foo['bar']"
106      def __init__(self, obj):
107          self.obj = obj
108
109      def __str__(self):
110          return str(self.obj)
111
112      def __repr__(self):
113          return repr(self.obj)
114
115      def __getattr__(self, attr):
116          if hasattr(self.obj, attr):
117              return getattr(self.obj, attr)
```

(Continued)

Example 13-2   Twitter API Combination Library Example (`twapi.py`)
(Continued)

```python
118            elif hasattr(self.obj, '__contains__') and attr in self.obj:
119                return self.obj[attr]
120            else:
121                raise AttributeError(
122                    '%r has no attribute %r' % (self.obj, attr))
123
124        __getitem__ = __getattr__
125
126 def _demo_search():
127     for api in APIs:
128         printf(api.upper())
129         t = Twitter(api, auth=False)
130         tweets = t.search('twython3k')
131         for tweet in tweets:
132             printf('----' * 10)
133             printf('@%s' % tweet.from_user)
134             printf('Status: %s' % tweet.text)
135             printf('Posted at: %s' % tweet.created_at)
136         printf('----' * 10)
137
138 def _demo_ver_creds():
139     for api in APIs:
140         t = Twitter(api)
141         res = t.verify_credentials()
142         status = ResultsWrapper(res.status)
143         printf('@%s' % res.screen_name)
144         printf('Status: %s' % status.text)
145         printf('Posted at: %s' % status.created_at)
146         printf('----' * 10)
147
148 def _demo_user_timeline():
149     for api in APIs:
150         printf(api.upper())
151         t = Twitter(api)
152         tweets = t.user_timeline()
153         for tweet in tweets:
154             printf('----' * 10)
155             printf('Status: %s' % tweet.text)
156             printf('Posted at: %s' % tweet.created_at)
157         printf('----' * 10)
158
159 def _demo_update_status():
160     for api in APIs:
161         t = Twitter(api)
162         res = t.update_status(
163             'Test tweet posted to Twitter using %s' % api.title())
164         printf('Posted at: %s' % res.created_at)
165         printf('----' * 10)
166
```

```
167 # object wrapper unit tests
168 def _unit_dict_wrap():
169     d = {'foo': 'bar'}
170     wrapped = ResultsWrapper(d)
171     return wrapped['foo'], wrapped.foo
172
173 def _unit_attr_wrap():
174     class C(object):
175         foo = 'bar'
176     wrapped = ResultsWrapper(C)
177     return wrapped['foo'], wrapped.foo
178
179 class TestSequenceFunctions(TestCase):
180     def test_dict_wrap(self):
181         self.assertEqual(_unit_dict_wrap(), ('bar', 'bar'))
182
183     def test_attr_wrap(self):
184         self.assertEqual(_unit_attr_wrap(), ('bar', 'bar'))
185
186 if __name__ == '__main__':
187     printf('\n*** SEARCH')
188     _demo_search()
189     printf('\n*** VERIFY CREDENTIALS')
190     _demo_ver_creds()
191     printf('\n*** USER TIMELINE')
192     _demo_user_timeline()
193     printf('\n*** UPDATE STATUS')
194     _demo_update_status()
195     printf('\n*** RESULTS WRAPPER')
196     main()
```

Before we take this script apart, let's run it and see the output. Be sure to first create a `tweet_auth.py` file with these variables (and correct corresponding values for your Twitter application):

```
# tweet_auth.py
consumer_key = 'SOME_CONSUMER_KEY'
consumer_secret = 'SOME_CONSUMER_SECRET'
access_token = 'SOME_ACCESS_TOKEN'
access_token_secret = 'SOME_ACCESS_TOKEN_SECRET'
```

Now you're ready to go. Naturally, the following output was produced during this one execution performed at the time of this writing. Yours will definitely differ from mine. Here's what happened when we ran it (the "..." means we truncated the output to keep it shorter):

```
$ twapi.py

*** SEARCH
TWYTHON
----------------------------------------
```

```
@ryanmcgrath
Status: #twython is now version 1.4.4; should fix some utf-8 decoding
issues, twython3k should be caught up, etc: http://t.co/s6fTVhOP /cc
@wescpy
Posted at: Thu, 06 Oct 2011 20:25:17 +0000
----------------------------------------
@wescpy
Status: Testing posting to Twitter using Twython3k (another story of
life on the bleeding edge)
Posted at: Tue, 04 Oct 2011 21:09:41 +0000
----------------------------------------
@wescpy
Status: @ryanmcgrath cool... thx! i also have a &quot;real&quot;
twython3k bug i need to file... will do it officially on github. just
giving you a heads-up!
Posted at: Tue, 04 Oct 2011 17:18:38 +0000
----------------------------------------
@wescpy
Status: @ryanmcgrath Hey ryan, good work on Twython thus far! Can you
pls drop twitter_endpoints.py into twython3k? It's out-of-date. ..
thx! :-)
Posted at: Tue, 04 Oct 2011 08:01:09 +0000
----------------------------------------
TWEEPY
----------------------------------------
@ryanmcgrath
Status: #twython is now version 1.4.4; should fix some utf-8 decoding
issues, twython3k should be caught up, etc: http://t.co/s6fTVhOP /cc
@wescpy
Posted at: 2011-10-06 20:25:17

. . .


----------------------------------------


*** VERIFY CREDENTIALS
@wescpy
Status: .@imusicmash That's great that you're enjoying corepython.com!
Note: there will be lots of cookies at #SVCC: yfrog.com/kh1azqznj
Posted at: Fri Oct 07 22:37:37 +0000 2011
----------------------------------------
@wescpy
Status: .@imusicmash That's great that you're enjoying corepython.com!
Note: there will be lots of cookies at #SVCC: yfrog.com/kh1azqznj
Posted at: 2011-10-07 22:37:37
----------------------------------------


*** USER TIMELINE
TWYTHON
----------------------------------------
Status: .@imusicmash That's great that you're enjoying corepython.com!
Note: there will be lots of cookies at #SVCC: yfrog.com/kh1azqznj
Posted at: Fri Oct 07 22:37:37 +0000 2011
----------------------------------------
```

```
Status: SFBayArea: free technical conference w/free
food+drinks+parking this wknd! I'm doing #Python & @App_Engine http://
t.co/spvVjYUA
Posted at: Fri Oct 07 15:20:46 +0000 2011
-----------------------------------------
Status: RT @GoogleCode @Google Cloud SQL: your database in the cloud
http://t.co/4wt2cjpH @app_engine #mysql
Posted at: Thu Oct 06 20:12:26 +0000 2011
-----------------------------------------
. . .
Status: Watch this: http://t.co/pm2QCLtW Read this: http://t.co/
Om5TtLZP  Note the 2 paragraphs that start w/"No one wants to die"
Posted at: Thu Oct 06 00:36:27 +0000 2011
-----------------------------------------
Status: I'm wondering: will future Apple products visually be designed
as well & have as much impact on the market? What do you think?
Posted at: Thu Oct 06 00:02:16 +0000 2011
-----------------------------------------
. . .
-----------------------------------------
TWEEPY
-----------------------------------------
Status: .@imusicmash That's great that you're enjoying corepython.com!
Note: there will be lots of cookies at #SVCC: yfrog.com/kh1azqznj
Posted at: 2011-10-07 22:37:37
. . .
-----------------------------------------

*** UPDATE STATUS
Posted at: Sat Oct 08 05:18:51 +0000 2011
-----------------------------------------
Posted at: 2011-10-08 05:18:51
-----------------------------------------

*** RESULTS WRAPPER
..
----------------------------------------------------------------
-
Ran 2 tests in 0.000s

OK
$
```

You can see that we run through all four functions, executing them with each library. Executing this script on Windows-based PCs has the same results if everything is installed correctly. Because our code is also compatible with Python 3, you should also achieve similar output; however, you should only see output from Twython because Tweepy has not been ported (at the time of this writing). Now let's take a closer look at the source.

Line-by-Line Explanation

Lines 1–5

The set of imports includes a pair from the standard library (using `distutils.log.warn()` as a proxy for the **print** statement or function, depending on whether you're running in Python 2 or 3, plus the basic attributes to run unit tests in Python) and our Twitter authorization credentials.

We also want to remind you that in general, the use of **from** `module` **import** * (line 5) is discouraged because standard library or third-party packages might use the same variable names as your modules, thus potentially being an issue. In this case, we have full control over `tweet_auth.py` and know about all (four) of its variables. Its sole purpose is to hide user credentials. In practice, such a file would only be installed in production as a byte-compiled (`.pyc`) or optimized (`.pyo`) file, which are not human-readable, or they will come from a database or otherwise be a network call away.

Lines 7–38

The first real body of code does exactly one thing: it determines what Twitter client libraries are available for the Python interpreter that's running your code. That's really it.

`CMDs` is a dictionary that has one entry per supported library. In our case, we have Twython (`twython`) and Tweepy (`tweepy`). In one of the exercises at the end of the chapter, you'll add support for a third library.

For each library, we provide the method names representing the corresponding Twitter API commands that should be called for the four functions mentioned earlier that we want to support. If the value is `None`, this means that the method name is an exact match; thus, any "real" (meaning *not* `None`) value represents an exception to the rule.

Tweepy makes things easy for us because its method names match the commands. Because of this, we use `dict.fromkeys()` to create a dictionary with all `None` values for its keys. Twython is trickier because it uses names that employ camel capitalization *and* there are exceptions to the rule. See lines 71–80 for a description of how the names are derived and methods chosen.

On line 22, we collate all supported APIs into a set. This data structure is the fastest membership check in the language. We will also loop over each of the APIs using this variable. So far, we've only created the possible APIs; now we need to see what is really available and remove those which are not.

The code on lines 25–33 attempts to import each of the libraries and removes those that cannot be found by collecting the non-existent APIs in another set called `remove`. After this loop is complete, we know what we don't have and subtract them all (on line 35) from the overall set of APIs. If there are no reachable libraries, we raise a `NotImplementedError` on lines 36–38.

Lines 40–71

The Twitter class is the primary object in this application. We define the initializer, which takes the `api` (in our case, either "twython" or "tweepy"), and an optional `auth` flag. This flag defaults to `True` because most of the time, we need (authenticated and) authorized access to a user's data. (Search is the only function that does not require authentication.) We cache the chosen API into `self.api`.

The remainder of this section (lines 48–71) instantiates the Twitter endpoint based on the chosen API and the authentication setting. The instance is then assigned to `self.twitter`. That object is our handle to executing Twitter API commands.

Lines 73–81

The `_get_meth()` method handles the magic in putting together the correct method name to call for each API. Note that we prepended the single underscore character (_) to the function name. This notation indicates that this routine should not be called by users. Instead, it is an internal method that should be called by one of the other methods in our class.

We could use `self.api` through this method, but a well-known best practice is to assign frequently-used instance attributes to a local variable for quick access. The use of `self.api` requires two lookups, whereas "api" needs only one. One extra lookup doesn't cost much in terms of CPU time, but if this were in a type loop and/or executed with frequency, all that time does add up. This is pretty much the reason for the local assignment on line 74.

On the next line, the appropriate command from the requested API is looked up and assigned to `meth_name`. If it is `None`, the default action is that the method name is the same as the command name. For Tweepy, it's easy; we already mentioned that its methods are named the exact same as the commands. The next set of lines handle special cases for which we have to derive the correct name.

As mentioned earlier, Twython uses camel capitalization for its "words" instead of being divided by an underscore (_). This means that we must break up each word on the underscore, capitalize the second word, then append it to the first word (lines 79–80). The final act is to use that name and retrieve the method object from the requested API; it is a first-class object and returned directly to the caller.

Lines 83–102

The four supported Twitter commands are realized in these four functions: `search()`, `verify_credentials()`, `user_timeline()`, `update_status()`. Aside from `search()`, the others are fairly simplistic and nearly identical between the pair of supported libraries. Let's look at these first, and then wrap up with a closer look at `search()`.

Verifying an authenticated user's credentials is just one thing you can do with the `verify_credentials` command. It's also the quickest way for you to programmatically access your most recent tweet. Your user information comes back and is wrapped by using the `ResultsWrapper` (more on this soon), and then returned back to the caller. You can find more information on using this command in the Twitter documentation at http://dev.twitter.com/docs/api/1/get/account/verify_credentials.

A user's timeline is made up of his most recent tweets (and retweets). The `user_timeline` Twitter command by default returns the most recent 20, but you can request up to 200 by using the `count` parameter, which we don't use in this example, but you'll be adding it in another exercise at the end of the chapter. You can find more information on this function at http://dev.twitter.com/docs/api/1/get/statuses/user_timeline. Unlike `verify_credentials()`, we wrap each individual tweet returned rather than the entire result coming from Twitter and return a generator expression iterable of tweets.

Twitter's most basic functionality comes in the form of users updating their statuses, a.k.a. tweeting. You can argue that without this functionality, there would be no Twitter. You can see the `update_status()` takes an additional parameter, `s`, which is the text of the tweet. The returned value is the tweet itself (also wrapped by `ResultsWrapper`), with the most important characteristic being the `created_at` field, which acknowledges that the tweet was indeed created and now flowing to the masses. You'll see `created_at` in the following code, which demonstrates this functionality. You can find more information on using it at http://dev.twitter.com/docs/api/1/post/statuses/update.

Now back to search. The two APIs differ here, which is why there's more code than normal. Twython tries to be honest and interpret the results from Twitter nearly verbatim, turning the JavaScript Object Notation (JSON) into a Python dictionary, a close cousin. This data structure contains various metadata as well as the "real goods" you're looking for under the `results` key (which is why we need to do that lookup on line 86).

Tweepy, on the other hand, is more realistic and returns those search results directly in a list-like object—actually, `ResultsSet` is a subclass of list—because its developer knows that's really what you want. This makes it more convenient and saves you from any further lookup. What about all that extra metadata? They're just attributes of the returned `ResultsSet`.

Lines 104–124

This next chunk of code is a general-purpose class that you can use anywhere, outside of this application. There is no relationship to the Twitter libraries or anything because it's only used as a convenience for our users in that it provides a common interface to the objects returned from those libraries.

Have you ever been frustrated by objects that are either dictionary-like or object-like? What I mean is that with the first, you need to do the equivalent of a `__getitem__()` call in order to retrieve a value, i.e. `foo['bar']`, and with the second, you have to deal with objects that have an attribute interface, i.e., `foo.bar`? Wouldn't it be great to be able to use either for all objects and not have to worry about it again? That's exactly what the `ResultsWrapper` class does.

I just came up with this while writing, so it might not be perfect yet, but the idea is to take any Python object and wrap it up in an object that delegates the lookup (via `__getitem__()` or `__getattr__()`) to the wrapped object. (For a review on delegation, see the Object-Oriented Programming chapter of *Core Python Programming* or *Core Python Language Fundamentals*.)

In the initializer (lines 106–107), we wrap the object. All its string representations come next (lines 109–113). Most of the magic happens in `__getattr__()`. When a request for an attribute comes in that's not recognized, `__getattr__()` checks to see if that attribute exists in the wrapped object (lines 116–117). If it's not available there, perhaps it's a dictionary-like object, so let's check if it's a "key" (lines 118–119). Naturally, before using the **in** operator, we need to check whether the object supports that type of check or access—this is done by seeing if the object has a `__contains__` attribute first. If all else fails, just give the bad news to the user (lines 120–122).

The last line to look at (124) is for when a user tries to access an attribute in a dictionary-like way, by using the attribute name as a key. Because of this, we want the exact same behavior as __getattr__(). This way, no matter what type of object is wrapped, we're able to pull out and return what the user wants.

Lines 126–165

The purpose of the _demo_*() functions is to do exactly what they're named: _demo_search() demonstrates searching for the term "twython3k" using all available APIs, and then displays the resulting tweets' data; _demo_ver_creds() executes the verify_credentials command and displays the authenticated user's most recent tweet; _demo_user_timeline() brings up the 20 most recent tweets, displaying each tweet's text and timestamp. Finally, _demo_update_status() posts new tweets, describing the API that was used to do so.

Lines 167–184

This section of code is dedicated to testing the ResultsWrapper class. The _unit_*_wrap() functions each test wrapping dictionaries (or dictionary-like objects) as well as objects with an attribute interface. Both forms of attribute access, whether by obj['foo'] or obj.foo should result in the same result: "bar". This validation is carried out by the unittest class, TestSequenceFunctions (lines 179–184).

Lines 186–196

The lines of main() display which function is being tested and calls the specific _demo_*() functions, which display their own output. The final call, is to the unittest.main() function, which executes the unit tests.

13.3.4 Summary

With the material in this section, we hope that you've received a solid introduction to interfacing with a couple of services currently available on the Web: Yahoo!'s stock quote server, and Twitter. It's important to realize that Yahoo's interface is completely URL-driven and unauthenticated, whereas Twitter provides a full REST API and OAuth authorization for secure data access. We were able to take advantage of the power of both by using Python code that was digestable and got the job done.

We just looked at a pair of Web services; there are plenty more out there. We will revisit both of these in Chapter 14, "Text Processing."

13.3.5   Additional Online Resources

Yahoo! Finance

- http://gummy-stuff.org/Yahoo-data.htm
- http://gummy-stuff.org/forex.htm

Twitter

- http://dev.twitter.com/docs/twitter-libraries#python.
- http://github.com/ryanmcgrath/twython
- http://tweepy.github.com

13.4   Exercises

Web Services

13-1.   *Web Services.* In your own words, describe what Web services are. Find some of these services online and describe how they work. What is their API and how do you access such data? Is authentication or authorization required?

13-2.   *REST and Web Services.* Study how REST and XML or JSON are used in more contemporary Web services APIs and applications. Describe the additional functionality they afford you over older systems such as the Yahoo! quote server, which uses URL parameters.

13-3.   *REST and Web Services.* Build an application framework by using Python's support for REST and XML that will allow you to share and reuse this code when writing applications that use any of the newer Web services and APIs available today. Display your code by using APIs from Yahoo!, Google, eBay, and/or Amazon.

Exercises 13-4 to 13-11 involve updating the Yahoo! stock quote example (stock.py) presented earlier in the chapter.

13-4.   *Web Services*. Update stock.py to download other stock quote data, given the additional parameters listed in Table 13-1. You can just take stock.py as shown earlier in the chapter and add the new functionality.

13-5.   *String Processing*. You've noticed that some of the fields that are returned contain quotes, cluttering the output. Remove the quotes. Is there another way to remove the quotes besides the solution you chose?

13-6.   *String Processing*. Not all stock tickers are four letters in length. Similarly, not all stock prices (per share) are between ten dollars and $99.99. The same goes for the daily change in price and change percentage. Make the necessary changes to your script so that even if the output fields are strings of different lengths, the output is still formatted evenly, justified, and consistent for all stocks. Here's an example:

```
C:\py>python stock.py

Prices quoted as of: Sat Oct 29 02:38:53 2011

TICKER   PRICE   CHANGE    %AGE
------   -----   ------    ----
YHOO      16.56   -0.07   -0.42%
GOOG     600.14   +1.47   +0.25%
T         29.74   +0.60   +2.06%
AMZN     217.32  +10.54   +5.10%
BAC        7.35   +0.30   +4.26%
BRK-B     79.96  +0.065   +0.08%
```

13-7.   *Files*. Update the application to save the quote data to a file instead of displaying it to the screen. Extra Credit: You can change the script so that users can choose to display the quote data or save it to a file.

13-8.   *Web Services and the csv Module*. Convert stock.py from using a normal **for** loop and parsing the data manually to using the csv module to parse the incoming data, like we did in the example code snippet.

13-9.   *Robustness*. Yahoo! tends to change the download hostname from time to time. It might be quote.yahoo.com one day then finance.yahoo.com the next. Today's "hostname du jour" is download.finance.yahoo.com. Sometimes the names revert to older ones. Build robustness into your application(s) by maintaining a list of these hostnames and ping the Web servers at those hosts to see if they are good before fetching quotes. You can also periodically screenscrape any Yahoo! quote page and grab the hostname from the **Download Data** link in the **Toolbox** section at the bottom of the page.

13-10. *Extending the API*. There are plenty more commands available in the Yahoo! quote server. To see a more comprehensive list, go to http://gummy-stuff.org/Yahoo-data.htm. Select several new data points and integrate them into your `stock.py` script.

13-11. *Python 3*. Port `stock.py` to Python 3 and call it `stock3.py`. Extra Credit: Create a solution that runs on both versions 2.x and 3.x and describe any special technique(s) you used.

13-12. *Foreign Exchange*. The Yahoo! quote server can also pull up foreign currency exchange rates. Take a peek at http://gummy-stuff.org/forex.htm and create a new `forex.py` script that performs these lookups.

13-13. *Stock Charts*. Yahoo! also provides a way to autogenerate charts. Here are some example URLs to give you an idea of the service:

Small chart:

1 day: http://chart.yahoo.com/t?s=GOOG

5 days: http://chart.yahoo.com/v?s=GOOG

1 year: http://chart.yahoo.com/c/bb/m/GOOG

Large chart:

1 day: http://chart.yahoo.com/b?s=GOOG

5 days: http://chart.yahoo.com/w?s=GOOG

3 months: http://chart.yahoo.com/c/3m/GOOG

6 months: http://chart.yahoo.com/c/6m/GOOG

1 year: http://chart.yahoo.com/c/1y/GOOG

2 years: http://chart.yahoo.com/c/2y/GOOG

5 years: http://chart.yahoo.com/c/5y/GOOG

Max: http://chart.yahoo.com/c/my/GOOG

Similar to our robustness Exercise 13-9, chart.yahoo.com, ichart.yahoo.com, and ichart.finance.yahoo.com are currently all interchangeable, so use them all to check for data. Create an application to allow users to generate graphs for their stock portfolio. Also offer the ability to launch a Web browser directly to a page showing the chart. Hint: See the `webbrowser` module.

13-14. *Historical Data.* It appears that ichart.financial.yahoo.com also provides historical lookups. Use this example URL to find out how it works and create an application that performs historical stock price queries: http://chart.yahoo.com/table.csv?s=GOOG&a=06&b=12&c=2006&d=10&e=2&f=2007.

Twitter

13-15. *Twitter Service.* Describe the Twitter service in your own words. Define what tweets are, and point out some of its limitations.

13-16. *Twitter Libraries.* Discuss the similarities and differences between Twython and Tweepy Python libraries.

13-17. *Twitter Libraries.* Take a look at other Python libraries you know which among them you would use to access Twitter's API. How do they compare with the ones we looked at in this chapter?

13-18. *Twitter Libraries.* You don't like either Twython and Tweepy Python libraries; write one of your own that communicates with Twitter in a safe and RESTful way. Start by going to https://dev.twitter.com/docs.

The following exercises require that you augment the `twapi.py` example from this chapter.

13-19. *User Queries.* Add functionality to query a user's Twitter screen name and return her corresponding ID. Note that some user screen names are actually integers, so ensure that you allow users to enter them as potential screen names. Use that ID to fetch that user's most recent tweet.

13-20. *Retweeting.* Augment the search functionality by not only letting users query for tweets, but also give them the ability to retweet selected tweets. You can provide either a command-line, Web, or GUI interface to support this functionality.

13-21. *Tweet Deletion.* Similar to Exercise 13-20, provide the user with a way to delete his own posts. Be aware that this just removes those tweets from Twitter. The contents of the tweets contents might already have been distributed elsewhere.

13-22. *Follows.* Add support that lets you look up a user's followers (IDs) as well as the IDs of users whom a user is following.

13-23. *Twitter Libraries.* Add support for a different Python/Twitter client library to twapi.py. For example, you can try doing this exercise with python-twitter, found at http://code. google.com/p/python-twitter. Other libraries can be found at http://dev.twitter.com/docs/twitter-libraries#python.

13-24. *Profile Editing.* Configure so that a user can update his profile and/or to upload a new profile picture. Extra Credit: Allow users to update their profile colors or background image.

13-25. *Count.* The user_timeline() Twitter function also supports a count variable. By default, Twitter returns the most recent 20 tweets in a user's timeline, but users can request up to 200. Add support for count and other optional parameters to twapi.py.

13-26. *Direct Messages.* Support direct messages (DMs), sending them to a specific user, getting a list of DMs sent, retrieving a list of current DMs, and removing DMs.

In our twapi.py example, we were able to examine and modify our Twitter stream because we had all the credentials necessary from Twitter for our application. However, it's another matter when you want to write an application that tweets on your behalf or that of your registered users. In these cases, you'll need to go through the entire OAuth flow in order to get the access token and secret so that your application can act upon the behalf of that user.

This next exercise will be time consuming because you have to learn all about OAuth. Start by reading these two documents: https://dev.twitter.com/docs/auth/oauth and https://dev.twitter.com/docs/auth/moving-from-basic-auth-to-oauth.

13-27. *Tweet Archive.* Create a Twitter archival service for yourself (or others). Since Twitter saves only up to the 200 most recent tweets, you start losing your history fairly quickly. Build a Twitter archival service that preserves a registered users' tweets. If you search the Web for "twitter archive" or "twitter research tools," you'll come up with a slew of them. Hopefully with this exercise, you'll be breaking ground for the next generation Twitter analysis tool!

13-28. *Shortlinking, Feed Polling.* Augment your blogging career. Create a periodic scanner (RSS or other) of your personal or work blog. When a new blogpost is made, autotweet a short link and the first N words from the blogpost title.

13-29. *Other Web Services.* Read about Google's Prediction API at http://code.google.com/apis/predict and try its "Hello World" tutorial. Once you're up to speed, develop your own model that scans various Tweets (yours or tweets from the public timeline). Create and train a prediction model that determines whether the contents of a tweet are positive, negative, or neutral. Once trained, use your tool to determine the sentiments of new tweets by using the same query. To do this exercise, you'll need to create a project at Google's API console—http://code.google.com/apis/console—and enable both Google Prediction and Google Storage. If you don't want to create a Google account, you're welcome to use any similar API.

Supplemental/
Experimental

Text Processing

As a developer, I prefer editing in plain text. XML doesn't count.
—Wesley Chun, July 2009
(verbally at OSCON conference)

In this chapter...

- Comma-Separated Values
- JavaScript Object Notation
- Extensible Markup Language
- Related Modules

R egardless of what type of applications you create, inevitably, you will need to process human-readable data, which is referred to generally as *text*. Python's standard library provides three text processing modules and packages to help you get this job done: csv, json, and xml. We'll explore these briefly in that order in this chapter.

At the end, we'll merge together XML along with some of the client-server knowledge you acquired from Chapter 2, "Network Programming," and show you how to create XML-RPC services using Python. Because this style of programming isn't considered text processing, and you're not manipulating the XML itself, which is just the data transport format, just consider this last section as bonus material.

14.1 Comma-Separated Values

In the first section of this chapter, we'll look at comma-separated values (CSV). We begin with a quick introduction then move to a code sample of how to use Python to read and write CSV files. Finally we revisit an old friend.

14.1.1 Introduction to Comma-Separated Values

Using CSVs is a common way to move data into and out of spreadsheet applications in plain text, as opposed to a proprietary binary file format. In fact, CSV doesn't even represent true structured data; the contents of CSV files are just rows of string values delimited by commas. There are some subtleties with CSV formats, but in general, they're fairly minor. In many cases, you actually don't need the power of a CSV-oriented module.

Sounds pretty easy to parse, doesn't it? Offhand, I'd say just do a str.split(',') and call it a day. However, we can't do that because individual field values might contain embedded commas, hence the need for CSV-parsing and generating a library like Python's csv module.

Let's look at a quick example of taking data, writing CSV out to a file, and then reading the same data back. We'll also have individual fields that include commas, as well, just to make things a bit more difficult. Example 14-1 presents csvex.py, a script that takes 3-tuples and writes each corresponding record to disk as a CSV file. Then, it reads and parses the previously-written CSV data.

Example 14-1   CSV Python 2 and Python 3-Compatible Example (`csvex.py`)

This simple script demonstrates writing out CSV data and reading it back in.

```
1   #!/usr/bin/env python
2
3   import csv
4   from distutils.log import warn as printf
5
6   DATA = (
7       (9, 'Web Clients and Servers', 'base64, urllib'),
8       (10, 'Web Programming: CGI & WSGI', 'cgi, time, wsgiref'),
9       (13, 'Web Services', 'urllib, twython'),
10  )
11
12  printf('*** WRITING CSV DATA')
13  f = open('bookdata.csv', 'w')
14  writer = csv.writer(f)
15  for record in DATA:
16      writer.writerow(record)
17  f.close()
18
19  printf('*** REVIEW OF SAVED DATA')
20  f = open('bookdata.csv', 'r')
21  reader = csv.reader(f)
22  for chap, title, modpkgs in reader:
23      printf('Chapter %s: %r (featuring %s)' % (
24          chap, title, modpkgs))
25  f.close()
```

Following is another example of writing scripts that are compatible with both Python 2 and 3. Regardless of which version you use, you get the following identical output:

```
$ python csvex.py
*** WRITING CSV DATA
*** REVIEW OF SAVED DATA
Chapter 9: 'Web Clients and Servers' (featuring base64, urllib)
Chapter 10: 'Web Programming: CGI & WSGI' (featuring cgi, time, wsgiref)
Chapter 13: 'Web Services' (featuring urllib, twython)
```

Line-by-Line Explanation

Lines 1–10

We first import the csv module as well as `distutils.log.warn()` as a proxy for the **print** statement or function. (It's not really compatible except for a single string, but it gets the job done, provided you can work with its limitation.) Following the import statements is our data set. This is made up of 3-tuples that have columns representing chapter numbers, chapter titles, and modules and packages that are used in the code samples of their respective chapters.

Lines 12–17

These six lines are fairly self-explanatory. `csv.writer()` is a function that takes an open file (or file-like) object and returns a writer object. The writer features a `writerow()` method, which you use to output lines or rows of comma-separated data to the open file. After it has done its job, the file is closed.

Lines 19–25

In this section, `csv.reader()` is the opposing function which returns an iterable object that you can use to read in and parse each row of CSV data. Like `csv.writer()`, `csv.reader()` also takes an open file handle and returns a reader object. When you iterate through each row of data, the CSVs are automatically parsed and returned to you (line 22). We display the output then close the file when all rows have been processed.

In addition to `csv.reader()` and `csv.writer()`, the `csv` module also features the `csv.DictReader` and `csv.DictWriter` classes which read CSV data into a dictionary (with given field names provided or the first row if not) and write dictionary fields to a CSV file.

14.1.2   Stock Portfolio Example Reprise

Before moving on to another text processing format, take a look at another example. We'll rewind a bit and re-examine the stock portfolio script, `stock.py`, from Chapter 13, "Web Services." Rather than doing a `str.split(',')`, we'll port that application so that it uses the `csv` module, instead.

Also, instead of showing you *all* of the code, most of which is identical to `stock.py`, we're going to focus only on the differences, or *diffs*, as engineers abbreviate it. Below is a quick review of the entire (Python 2) `stock.py` script (feel free to flip back to Chapter 13 for the line-by-line explanation):

```
#!/usr/bin/env python

from time import ctime
from urllib2 import urlopen
```

```
TICKs = ('yhoo', 'dell', 'cost', 'adbe', 'intc')
URL = 'http://quote.yahoo.com/d/quotes.csv?s=%s&f=sl1c1p2'

print '\nPrices quoted as of: %s PDT\n' % ctime()
print 'TICKER', 'PRICE', 'CHANGE', '%AGE'
print '------', '-----', '------', '----'
u = urlopen(URL % ','.join(TICKs))

for row in u:
    tick, price, chg, per = row.split(',')
    print tick, '%.2f' % float(price), chg, per,

u.close()
```

The output of both the original version as well as our modified version will be similar. Here's one example execution as a reminder:

```
Prices quoted as of: Sat Oct 29 02:06:24 2011 PDT

TICKER PRICE CHANGE %AGE
------ ----- ------ ----
"YHOO" 16.56 -0.07 "-0.42%"
"DELL" 16.31 -0.01 "-0.06%"
"COST" 84.93 -0.29 "-0.34%"
"ADBE" 29.02 +0.68 "+2.40%"
"INTC" 24.98 -0.15 "-0.60%"
```

All we're going to do is to copy the code from stock.py into a new script named stockcsv.py and make the changes necessary to use csv instead. Let's see what the differences are, focusing on the code that follows the call to urlopen(). As soon as we have this open file, we assign it to csv.reader(), as shown here:

```
reader = csv.reader(u)
for tick, price, chg, pct in reader:
    print tick.ljust(7), ('%.2f' % round(float(price), 2)).rjust(6), \
        chg.rjust(6), pct.rstrip().rjust(6)

u.close()
```

The **for** loop is mostly still the same, except that now we do not read in an entire row and split it on the comma. Instead, the csv module parses the data naturally for us and lets users specify the target field names as loop variables. Note the output is close but isn't an exact match. Can you tell the difference (other than the timestamp)? Take a look:

```
Prices quoted as of: Sun Oct 30 23:19:04 2011 PDT

TICKER PRICE CHANGE %AGE
------ ----- ------ ----
YHOO 16.56 -0.07 -0.42%
DELL 16.31 -0.01 -0.06%
```

```
COST 84.93 -0.29 -0.34%
ADBE 29.02 +0.68 +2.40%
INTC 24.98 -0.15 -0.60%
```

The difference is subtle. There appears to be quotes around some of the fields in the `str.split()` version but not in the `csv`-processed version. Why is this happening? Recall from Chapter 13 that some values come back quoted and that there is an exercise at the end of that chapter for you to manually remove the extra quotes.

This isn't an issue here as the `csv` module helps us process the CSV data, including finding and scrubbing the superfluous quotes that come from the Yahoo! server. Here's a code snippet and output to confirm those extra quotes:

```
>>> from urllib2 import urlopen
>>> URL = 'http://quote.yahoo.com/d/quotes.csv?s=goog&f=sl1c1p2'
>>> u = urlopen(URL, 'r')
>>> line = u.read()
>>> u.close()
>>> line
'"GOOG",598.67,+12.36,"+2.11%"\r\n'
```

The quotes are an extra hassle that developers don't need to deal with; `csv` takes care of that for us, making the code a bit easier to read without the required extra string processing.

To improve on the data management, it would be even nicer if the data was structured in a more hierarchical fashion. For example, it would be good to have each row that comes back be part of a single object where the price, change, and percentage are attributes of that object. With a 4-value CSV row, there's no indication which is the "primary key," as it were, unless you use the first value or similar convention. This is where JSON might be a more appropriate tool for your applications.

14.2   JavaScript Object Notation

As you can gather from its name, JavaScript Object Notation, or JSON, comes from the world of JavaScript—it's a subset of the language used specifically to pass around structured data. It is based on the ECMA-262 standard and is meant to be a lightweight data interchange alternative to the Extensible Markup Language (XML) which we'll look at in the final section of this chapter. JSON is considered to be a more human-readable way of transporting structured data. You can learn more about JSON at http://json.org.

2.5-2.6   Support for JSON was officially added to the standard library in Python 2.6 via the `json` module. It is basically the now-integrated version of the external `simplejson` library, whose developers have maintained backward compatibility to 2.5. For more information, go to http://github.com/simplejson/simplejson.

Furthermore, `json` (thus also `simplejson`) provides an interface similar to those found in `pickle` and `marshal`, that is, `dump()`/`load()` and `dumps()`/`loads()`. In addition to the basic parameters, those functions also include various JSON-only options. The module also includes encoder and decoder classes, from which you can derive or use directly.

A *JSON object* is extremely similar to a Python dictionary, as demonstrated in the following code snippets, in which we use a `dict` to transfer data to a JSON object and then back again:

```
>>> dict(zip('abcde', range(5)))
{'a': 0, 'c': 2, 'b': 1, 'e': 4, 'd': 3}
>>> json.dumps(dict(zip('abcde', range(5))))
'{"a": 0, "c": 2, "b": 1, "e": 4, "d": 3}'
>>> json.loads(json.dumps(dict(zip('abcde', range(5)))))
{u'a': 0, u'c': 2, u'b': 1, u'e': 4, u'd': 3}
```

Notice that JSON only understands Unicode strings, so when translating back to Python, the last of the preceding examples (all Python 2) turns the keys into Unicode strings. Running the exact same line of code in Python 3 appears more normal without the Unicode string operator (the u designator in that precedes the opening quote):

```
>>> json.loads(json.dumps(dict(zip('abcde', range(5)))))
{'a': 0, 'c': 2, 'b': 1, 'e': 4, 'd': 3}
```

Python `dict`s are converted to JSON objects. Similarly, Python `list`s or `tuple`s are considered *JSON arrays*:

```
>>> list('abcde')
['a', 'b', 'c', 'd', 'e']
>>> json.dumps(list('abcde'))
'["a", "b", "c", "d", "e"]'
>>> json.loads(json.dumps(list('abcde')))
[u'a', u'b', u'c', u'd', u'e']
>>> # ['a', 'b', 'c', 'd', 'e'] in Python 3
>>> json.loads(json.dumps(range(5)))
[0, 1, 2, 3, 4]
```

What are the other differences between Python and JSON data types and values? Table 14-1 highlights some of the key differences.

Table 14-1 Differences Between JSON and Python Types

JSON	Python 2	Python 3
object	dict	dict
array	list, tuple	list, tuple
string	unicode	str
number (int)	int, long	int
number (real)	float	float
true	True	True
false	False	False
null	None	None

Another subtle difference not shown in Table 14-1 is that JSON does not use single quotes/apostrophes; every string is delimited by using double quotes. Also, there are no extra trailing commas that Python programmers casually place at the end of each sequence or mapping element for convenience.

To helps us further visualize some of these differences, Example 14-2 presents dict2json.py, which is a script that is compatible with Python 2 and 3 that dumps the content of a dictionary out in four different ways, twice as a Python dict and twice as a JSON object.

Example 14-2 Python dict to JSON Example (dict2json.py)

This script converts a Python dict to JSON and displays it in multiple formats.

```
1  #!/usr/bin/env python
2
3  from distutils.log import warn as printf
4  from json import dumps
5  from pprint import pprint
6
```

(Continued)

Example 14-2   Python `dict` to JSON Example (`dict2json.py`) *(Continued)*

```
7   BOOKs = {
8       '0132269937': {
9           'title': 'Core Python Programming',
10          'edition': 2,
11          'year': 2007,
12      },
13      '0132356139': {
14          'title': 'Python Web Development with Django',
15          'authors': ['Jeff Forcier', 'Paul Bissex', 'Wesley Chun'],
16          'year': 2009,
17      },
18      '0137143419': {
19          'title': 'Python Fundamentals',
20          'year': 2009,
21      },
22  }
23
24  printf('*** RAW DICT ***')
25  printf(BOOKs)
26
27  printf('\n*** PRETTY_PRINTED DICT ***')
28  pprint(BOOKs)
29
30  printf('\n*** RAW JSON ***')
31  printf(dumps(BOOKs))
32
33  printf('\n*** PRETTY_PRINTED JSON ***')
34  printf(dumps(BOOKs, indent=4))
```

Line-by-Line Explanation

Lines 1–5

We import three functions to use in this script: 1) `distutils.log.warn()` as a substitute for the **print** statement in Python 2 and `print()` function in Python 3; 2) `json.dumps()` to return a JSON string representation of a Python object; and 3) `pprint.pprint()` that does simple pretty-printing of Python objects.

Lines 7–22

The `BOOKs` data structure is a Python dictionary representing books identified by their International Standard Book Numbers (ISBNs). Each book can have additional information such as title, author, publication year, etc. Instead of using a more "flat" data structure such as a list, we chose a `dict` because it lets us build a structured hierarchy of attributes. Note all the extra commas that will be removed in its equivalent JSON representation.

Lines 24–34

The remainder of this script performs all the output. The first is just a dump of the Python `dict`; nothing special here. Note our extra commas are also removed here. It's mostly for human convenience that we use them in the source code. The second example is the same Python `dict` but seen through the eyes of a pretty-printer.

The last two outputs are in JSON format. The first is a plain JSON dump after conversion. The second is the additional pretty-printing functionality built into `json.dumps()`. You only need to pass in the indentation level to turn on this feature.

Executing this script in either Python 2 or 3 results in the following output:

```
$ python dict2json.py
*** RAW DICT ***
{'0132269937': {'edition': 2, 'year': 2007, 'title': 'Core Python
    Programming'}, '0137143419': {'year': 2009, 'title': 'Python
    Fundamentals'}, '0132356139': {'authors': ['Jeff Forcier',
    'Paul Bissex', 'Wesley Chun'], 'year': 2009, 'title': 'Python
    Web Development with Django'}}

*** PRETTY_PRINTED DICT ***
{'0132269937': {'edition': 2,
                'title': 'Core Python Programming',
                'year': 2007},
 '0132356139': {'authors': ['Jeff Forcier', 'Paul Bissex', 'Wesley
    Chun'],
                'title': 'Python Web Development with Django',
                'year': 2009},
 '0137143419': {'title': 'Python Fundamentals', 'year': 2009}}

*** RAW JSON ***
{"0132269937": {"edition": 2, "year": 2007, "title": "Core Python
    Programming"}, "0137143419": {"year": 2009, "title": "Python
    Fundamentals"}, "0132356139": {"authors": ["Jeff Forcier",
    "Paul Bissex", "Wesley Chun"], "year": 2009, "title": "Python
    Web Development with Django"}}

*** PRETTY_PRINTED JSON ***
{
    "0132269937": {
        "edition": 2,
        "year": 2007,
        "title": "Core Python Programming"
    },
    "0137143419": {
        "year": 2009,
        "title": "Python Fundamentals"
    },
```

```
    "0132356139": {
        "authors": [
            "Jeff Forcier",
            "Paul Bissex",
            "Wesley Chun"
        ],
        "year": 2009,
        "title": "Python Web Development with Django"
    }
}
```

This example demonstrates moving from `dicts` to JSON. You can also move data between `lists` or `tuples` and JSON arrays. The `json` module also provides classes for encoding and decoding of other Python data types to and from JSON. While we don't cover all of these here, you can see that there is plenty to explore with JSON, other than the light introduction provided here.

Now let's take a look at the 800-pound text formatting gorilla in the room, XML.

14.3   Extensible Markup Language

The third topic in data processing that we're covering in this chapter is Extensible Markup Language (XML). Similar to our earlier exploration of CSV, we'll have a brief introduction followed by a tutorial of how to process XML data by using Python. After a short code sample, we'll parse some real data coming from the Google News service.

14.3.1   Introduction to XML

In the final section of this chapter, we'll take a look at XML, an older structured data format which also claims to be a "plain text" format used to represent structured data. Although XML data is plain text, many argue that XML is not human-readable—and for good reason. It can be near illegible without the assistance of a parser. However, XML has been around longer and is still more widespread than JSON. There are XML parsers in nearly every programming language today.

XML is a restricted form of Standard Generalized Markup Language (SGML), itself an ISO standard (ISO 8879). XML traces its origins back to 1996, when the World Wide Web Consortium (W3C) formed a working group to design it. The first XML specification was published in 1998; the most recent update was released in 2008. You can think of XML as a subset of SGML. You can also consider HTML as an even *smaller* subset of SGML.

14.3.2   Python and XML

Python's original support for XML occurred with the release of version 1.5 and the `xmllib` module. Since then, it has evolved into the `xml` package, which provides a variety of ways to both parse as well as construct XML documents.

Python supports both document object model (DOM) tree-structured as well as event-based Simple API for XML (SAX) processing of XML documents. The current version of the SAX specification is 2.0.1, so Python's support generally refers to this as SAX2. The DOM standard is older and has been around for almost as long as XML itself. Both SAX and DOM support was added to Python in the 2.0 release.

2.0

SAX is a streaming interface, meaning that the documents are parsed and processed one line at a time via a continuous bytestream. This means that you can neither backtrack nor perform random access within an XML document. You can guess the tradeoff is event-based processors that are faster and more memory efficient, whereas tree-based parsers give you full access to the entire document in memory at any time.

We note for you here that the `xml` package depends on the availability of at least one SAX-compliant XML parser. At that time, this meant that users needed to find and download third-party modules or packages to help them meet this requirement. Fortunately starting in version 2.3, the Expat streaming parser became bundled in the standard library under the `xml.parsers.expat` name.

2.3

Expat came before SAX and is SAX-incompliant. However, you can use Expat to create SAX or DOM parsers. Also note that Expat exists for speed. It is quick because it is *non-validating*, meaning that it does not check for fully-compliant markup. As you can imagine, *validating* parsers are slower because of the required additional processing.

Python support for XML matured further in version 2.5 with the addition of ElementTree—a highly-popular, quick, and Pythonic XML document parser and generator—added to the standard library as `xml.etree.ElementTree`. We'll be using ElementTree for all of our raw XML examples (with a bit of help from `xml.dom.minidom`) then show you some examples of writing client/server applications using Python's XML-RPC support.

2.5

In Example 14-3 (`dict2xml.py`), we take structured data in a Python dictionary, use `ElementTree` to build up a valid XML document representing that data structure, use `xml.dom.minidom` to pretty-print it, and then finally, utilize various `ElementTree` iterators to parse and display relevant content from it.

Example 14-3   Converting a Python `dict` to XML (`dict2xml.py`)

This Python 2 script converts a `dict` to XML and displays it in multiple formats.

```python
1   #!/usr/bin/env python
2
3   from xml.etree.ElementTree import Element, SubElement, tostring
4   from xml.dom.minidom import parseString
5
6   BOOKs = {
7       '0132269937': {
8           'title': 'Core Python Programming',
9           'edition': 2,
10          'year': 2006,
11      },
12      '0132356139': {
13          'title': 'Python Web Development with Django',
14          'authors': 'Jeff Forcier:Paul Bissex:Wesley Chun',
15          'year': 2009,
16      },
17      '0137143419': {
18          'title': 'Python Fundamentals',
19          'year': 2009,
20      },
21  }
22
23  books = Element('books')
24  for isbn, info in BOOKs.iteritems():
25      book = SubElement(books, 'book')
26      info.setdefault('authors', 'Wesley Chun')
27      info.setdefault('edition', 1)
28      for key, val in info.iteritems():
29          SubElement(book, key).text = ', '.join(str(val) .split(':'))
30
31  xml = tostring(books)
32  print '*** RAW XML ***'
33  print xml
34
35  print '\n*** PRETTY-PRINTED XML ***'
36  dom = parseString(xml)
37  print dom.toprettyxml('    ')
38
39  print '*** FLAT STRUCTURE ***'
40  for elmt in books.getiterator():
41      print elmt.tag, '-', elmt.text
42
43  print '\n*** TITLES ONLY ***'
44  for book in books.findall('.//title'):
45      print book.text
```

Running this script, which is easily portable to Python 3, results in the following output:

```
$ dict2xml.py
*** RAW XML ***
<books><book><edition>2</edition><authors>Wesley Chun</
authors><year>2006</year><title>Core Python Programming</title></
book><book><edition>1</edition><authors>Wesley Chun</
authors><year>2009</year><title>Python Fundamentals</title></
book><book><edition>1</edition><authors>Jeff Forcier, Paul Bissex,
Wesley Chun</authors><year>2009</year><title>Python Web Development
with Django</title></book></books>

*** PRETTY-PRINTED XML ***
<?xml version="1.0" ?>
<books>
    <book>
        <edition>
            2
        </edition>
        <authors>
            Wesley Chun
        </authors>
        <year>
            2006
        </year>
        <title>
            Core Python Programming
        </title>
    </book>
    <book>
        <edition>
            1
        </edition>
        <authors>
            Wesley Chun
        </authors>
        <year>
            2009
        </year>
        <title>
            Python Fundamentals
        </title>
    </book>
    <book>
        <edition>
            1
        </edition>
        <authors>
            Jeff Forcier, Paul Bissex, Wesley Chun
        </authors>
```

```
            <year>
                2009
            </year>
            <title>
                Python Web Development with Django
            </title>
        </book>
</books>

*** FLAT STRUCTURE ***
books - None
book - None
edition - 2
authors - Wesley Chun
year - 2006
title - Core Python Programming
book - None
edition - 1
authors - Wesley Chun
year - 2009
title - Python Fundamentals
book - None
edition - 1
authors - Jeff Forcier, Paul Bissex, Wesley Chun
year - 2009
title - Python Web Development with Django

*** TITLES ONLY ***
Core Python Programming
Python Fundamentals
Python Web Development with Django
```

Line-by-Line Explanation

Lines 1–21

The first half of this script is quite similar to that of `dict2json.py` that we presented in the previous section. Obvious changes include the imports of `ElementTree` and `minidom`. We are aware that you know what you need to do to make your code work for both Python 2 and 3, so we'll leave out all the complexity and focus solely on a Python 2 solution.

Finally, the most subtle difference is that rather than being a list as it was in `dict2json.py`, the `'authors'` field is a single colon-delimited string. This change is optional, however, and it can remain a list if desired.

The reason for changing it is to help simplify the data processing. One of the key places this is evident is in line 29. Another difference is that in the JSON example, we did not set a default author value if one was not provided and here we do. It's easier to check for a colon (:) and not have to do an additional check if our data value is a string or a list.

Lines 23–29

The real work of this script happens here. We create a top-level object, `books`, and then attach everything else under that node. For each book, a book subnode is added, taking default values of `authors` and `edition` if not provided for in the original dictionary definition above. That's followed by iterating over all key-value pairs and adding them as further subnodes of each book.

Lines 31–45

The final block of code dumps out the data in a variety of formats: raw XML, pretty-printed XML (with the help of the MiniDOM), iterating over all nodes as one large flat structure, and finally, demonstrating a simple search over an XML document.

14.3.3   XML In Practice

While the previous example shows the various things you can do to create and parse XML documents, it's without a doubt that most applications are trying to do the latter rather than the former, so let's look at another short application that parses data to produce useful information.

In Example 14-4, `goognewsrss.py` grabs the "Top Stories" feed from the Google News service and extracts the titles of the top five (by default) news stories as well as referral links to the actual stories themselves. The solution, `goognewsrss.topnews()` is a generator, easily identified by a **yield** expression. This means that individual pairs of (title, link) are emitted by the generator in an iterative fashion. Take a look at the code and see if you can figure out what is going on and guess the output (because as we won't show any here). Why? That's coming up next after the source.

Example 14-4　Parsing an Actual XML Stream (goognewsrss.py)

This script, which is compatible with Python 2 and 3, displays the top news stories (default is five) and their corresponding links from the Google News service.

```python
1    #!/usr/bin/env python
2
3    try:
4        from io import BytesIO as StringIO
5    except ImportError:
6        try:
7            from cStringIO import StringIO
8        except ImportError:
9            from StringIO import StringIO
10
11   try:
12       from itertools import izip as zip
13   except ImportError:
14       pass
15
16   try:
17       from urllib2 import urlopen
18   except ImportError:
19       from urllib.request import urlopen
20
21   from pprint import pprint
22   from xml.etree import ElementTree
23
24   g = urlopen('http://news.google.com/news?topic=h&output=rss')
25   f = StringIO(g.read())
26   g.close()
27   tree = ElementTree.parse(f)
28   f.close()
29
30   def topnews(count=5):
31       pair = [None, None]
32       for elmt in tree.getiterator():
33           if elmt.tag == 'title':
34               skip = elmt.text.startswith('Top Stories')
35               if skip:
36                   continue
37               pair[0] = elmt.text
38           if elmt.tag == 'link':
39               if skip:
40                   continue
41               pair[1] = elmt.text
42               if pair[0] and pair[1]:
43                   count -= 1
44                   yield(tuple(pair))
45                   if not count:
46                       return
47                   pair = [None, None]
48
49   for news in topnews():
50       pprint(news)
```

Before you execute the code, be sure to review the *Terms of Service* (ToS) found at the following page: http://news.google.com/intl/en_us/terms_ google_news.html. It outlines the conditions under which you can use this Google service. The key is this phrase, "*You may only display the content of the Service for your own personal use (i.e., non-commercial use) and may not otherwise copy, reproduce, alter, modify, create derivative works, or publicly display any content.*"

What this means, of course, is that because this book is available to the public, I can't actually paste a sample execution here, nor can I try to mask actual output as this would be modifying the contents, but you can do it privately on your own.

You will see a set of the top five news story titles and their links as 2-tuples. Note that because this is a live service with ever-changing content, running the script again at another time will most likely yield different results.

Line-by-Line Explanation

Lines 1–22

Yes, we're aware that purists will note this is some ugly chunk of code due to the imports that make the code difficult to read, and I'd agree they have a point. However, in practice, when you have multiple versions of a language around executing production code, especially with Python 3 getting into the picture, there are going to be those "ifdef"-type of statements, and this is no exception. Let's take them apart so that you can at least see what's going on.

We are going to need a large string buffer with the interface of a file. In other words, this is one large string in-memory that supports the file interface; that is, it has file methods like `write()`. This would be the `StringIO` class. Data that comes off the network is usually in ASCII or pure bytes, not Unicode. So if we're running Python 3, we need to use the `io.BytesIO` class as `StringIO`.

If we are using Python 2, Unicode isn't part of the picture, so we would want to try to use the faster C-compiled `cStringIO.StringIO` class, if available. If not, our fallback is the original `StringIO.StringIO` class.

Next, we want this to be good for memory; thus, we would prefer the iterator version of the built-in `zip()` function, `itertools.izip()`. If `izip()` is available in the `itertools` module, we know we're in Python 2; therefore, import it as `zip()`. Otherwise, we know we're in Python 3 because `izip()` replaces and is renamed to `zip()`, meaning that we should just ignore the `ImportError` if not found. Note this code doesn't use either `zip()` or `izip()`; for more information on this, see the Hacker's Corner sidebar that's coming up in just a bit.

The final special case is for the Python 2 `urllib2` module, which has merged with a few others into Python 3's `urllib.request` submodule. Whichever one comes back donates its `urlopen()` function for us to use.

Lastly, we'll be using `ElementTree` as well as the pretty-printing `pprint.pprint()` function. The output generally wraps in this example, so we prefer this as an alternative to `disutils.log.warn()` for our output.

Lines 24–28

The data gathering in this application happens here. We start by opening up a connection to the Google News server and requesting the RSS output, which is in XML format. We read the entire feed and write that directly to our in-memory `StringIO`-equivalent file.

The topic requested is the headlining top stories, which is specified via the `topic=h` key-value pair. Other options include: `ir` for spotlight stories, `w` for world stories, `n` for USA stories, `b` for business, `tc` for technology, `e` for entertainment, `s` for sports, `snc` for science, and `m` for health.

The file to the Web connection is closed, and we pass the file-like object to the `ElementTree.parse()` function, which parses the XML document and returns an instance of the `ElementTree` class. Note that you can instantiate it yourself, because calling `ElementTree.parse(f)` is equivalent to `ElementTree.ElementTree(file=f)` in this example. Finally, we close the in-memory file.

Lines 30–50

The `topnews()` function does all the work in collating the output for the caller. We only want to return properly formatted news items, so we create a 2-tuple in the form of the pair list, with the first element for the title and the second, the link. Only when we have both do we yield the data item, at which point we either quit if we've returned the count requested (or the default of 5 if not provided) or just reset this 2-tuple.

We need special code for the first title, which isn't really a story title as it is the news-type title. In our case, because we requested the headlines, we get back in the "title" field something that's not a title to a news story, but rather, a title "category" with its contents as the exact string of "Top Stories". We ignore these.

The final pair of lines in this script output the 2-tuples emitted by `topnews()`.

⚠ CORE TIP (HACKER'S CORNER): Reducing `topnews()` down to one (long) line of Python

It is possible to reduce `topnews()` to just a nasty-looking one-liner:

```
topnews = lambda count=5: [(x.text, y.text) for x, y in zip
(tree.getiterator('title'), tree.getiterator('link')) if not
x.text.startswith('Top Stories')][:count]
```

Hope that doesn't hurt your eyes too much. The secret sauce to making this possible is the `ElementTree.getiterator()` function and the assumption that all story data is formatted properly. Neither `zip()` nor `itertools.izip()` are used at all in the standard version of `topnews()`, but it is used here to pair up the titles and their corresponding links.

Text processing isn't the only thing that XML can do. While the next section is clearly XML-related, you'll find little or no XML at all. XML is a building block with which developers who provide online services can code at a higher-level of client/server computing. To put it simply, you're not creating a service as much as you're giving clients the ability to call functions, or more specifically, remote procedure calls (RPCs).

14.3.4 *Client-Server Services Using XML-RPC

XML-RPC was created in the late 1990s as a way to give developers a means to create a remote procedure call (RPC) service by using the Hyper-Text Transfer Protocol (HTTP) as the transport mechanism, with the payload being an XML document.

This document contains both the name of the RPC as well as any parameters being sent to it for execution. XML-RPC then led to the creation of SOAP but is certainly not as complex as SOAP is. Since JSON is more human-readable than XML, it's no surprise that there is a JSON-RPC as well, including a SOAP version named SOAPjr.

Python's XML-RPC support comes in three packages: `xmlrpclib` on the client side, plus `SimpleXMLRPCServer` and `DocXMLRPCServer` on the server side. Logically, these three are reorganized into `xmlrpc.client` and `xmlrpc.server` in Python 3.x.

Example 14-5 presents is `xmlrpcsrvr.py`, which is a Python 2 script containing a single XML-RPC service with a wide variety of RPC calls. We'll first show you the code then describe each of the services provided by the RPCs.

Example 14-5   XML-RPC Server Code (xmlrpcsrvr.py)

This is an example XML-RPC server that contains a variety of RPC functions.

```
1    #!/usr/bin/env python
2
3    import SimpleXMLRPCServer
4    import csv
5    import operator
6    import time
7    import urllib2
8    import twapi # twapi.py from the "Web Services" chapter
9
10   server = SimpleXMLRPCServer.SimpleXMLRPCServer(("localhost", 8888))
11   server.register_introspection_functions()
12
13   FUNCs = ('add', 'sub', 'mul', 'div', 'mod')
14   for f in FUNCs:
15       server.register_function(getattr(operator, f))
16   server.register_function(pow)
17
18   class SpecialServices(object):
19       def now_int(self):
20           return time.time()
21
22       def now_str(self):
23           return time.ctime()
24
25       def timestamp(self, s):
26           return '[%s] %s' % (time.ctime(), s)
27
28       def stock(self, s):
29           url = 'http://quote.yahoo.com/d/quotes.csv?s=%s&f=l1c1p2d1t1'
30           u = urllib2.urlopen(url % s)
31           res = csv.reader(u).next()
32           u.close()
33           return res
34
35       def forex(self, s='usd', t='eur'):
36           url = 'http://quote.yahoo.com/d/quotes.csv?s=%s%s=X&f=nl1d1t1'
37           u = urllib2.urlopen(url % (s, t))
38           res = csv.reader(u).next()
39           u.close()
40           return res
41
```

```
42          def status(self):
43              t = twapi.Twitter('twython')
44              res = t.verify_credentials()
45              status = twapi.ResultsWrapper(res.status)
46              return status.text
47
48          def tweet(self, s):
49              t = twapi.Twitter('twython')
50              res = t.update_status(s)
51              return res.created_at
52
53      server.register_instance(SpecialServices())
54
55      try:
56          print 'Welcome to PotpourriServ v0.1\n(Use ^C to exit)'
57          server.serve_forever()
58      except KeyboardInterrupt:
59          print 'Exiting'
```

Line-by-Line Explanation

Lines 1–8

The various `import` statements include the most important one first, `SimpleXMLRPCServer`, as well as auxiliary statements that are used for the services provided. The services even include use of the Yahoo! stock quote server and Twitter code that is covered in Chapter 13.

We import all the standard library modules/packages first, followed by a user-level module, `twapi`, which we wrote to talk to the Twitter service. The order of the import statements follows the best practice guidelines: standard library, third-party, and then user-defined.

Lines 10–11

Once all the imports are out of the way, `SimpleXMLRPCServer`, establishes our service with the given hostname or IP address and port number. In this case, we just use *localhost* or *127.0.0.1*. That is followed by the registration of the generally accepted XML-RPC introspection functions.

These functions allow clients to query the server to determine its capabilities. They assist the client in establishing what methods the server supports, how it can call a specific RPC, and whether there is any documentation for a specific RPC. The calls which resolve those questions are named `system.listMethods`, `system.methodSignature`, and `system.methodHelp`.

You can find the specifications for these introspection functions at http://scripts.incutio.com/xmlrpc/introspection.html. For an example of how to implement these explicitly, go to http://www.doughellmann.com/PyMOTW/SimpleXMLRPCServer/#introspection-api.

Lines 13–16

These four lines of code represent standard arithmetic functions that we want to make available via RPC. We use the pow() built-in function (BIF) and grab the others from the operator module. The server.register_func-tion() function just makes them available for RPC client requests.

Lines 18–26

The next set of functions we want to add to our service are time-related. They also come in the form of a SpecialServices() class that we made up. There's no real difference having the code outside or inside of a class, and we wanted to demonstrate that with the arithmetic functions and these three: now_int(), which returns the current time in seconds after the epoch; now_str(), which returns a Unix-friendly timestamp representing the current time in the local time zone; and the timestamp() utility function, which takes a string as input and returns a timestamp prepended to it.

Lines 28–40

Here, we borrow code liberally from Chapter 13, starting with the code that interfaces with the Yahoo! quote server. The stock() function takes the ticket symbol of a company, and then fetches the latest price, last change, change percentage, and the date and time of last trade. The forex() function does something similar but for currency exchange rates.

Using the code from Chapter 13 is optional, so if you haven't covered that material yet, you can skip implementing either of these functions, as neither are necessary for learning XML-RPC concepts.

Lines 42–53

The last RPCs we'll register utilize the Twitter code that we developed in Chapter 13 by using the Twython library. The status() function retrieves the current status of the current user, and tweet() posts a status update on behalf of that user. In the final line of this block, we register all functions in the SpecialServices class by using the register_-instance() function.

Lines 55–59

The final five lines launch the service (via its infinite loop) as well as detect when the user wants to quit (via Ctrl+C from the keyboard).

Now that we have a server, what good does it do us if there's no client code to take advantage of this functionality? In Example 14-6, we take a look at one possible client application, xmlrpcclnt.py. Naturally, you can execute this on any computer that can reach the server with the appropriate host/port address pair.

Example 14-6   Python 2 XML-RPC Client Code (xmlrpcclnt.py)

This is one possible client that makes calls to our XML-RPC server.

```
1    #!/usr/bin/env python
2
3    from math import pi
4    import xmlrpclib
5
6    server = xmlrpclib.ServerProxy('http://localhost:8888')
7    print 'Current time in seconds after epoch:', server.now_int()
8    print 'Current time as a string:', server.now_str()
9    print 'Area of circle of radius 5:', server.mul(pi, server.pow(5, 2))
10   stock = server.stock('goog')
11   print 'Latest Google stock price: %s (%s / %s) as of %s at %s' %
     tuple(stock)
12   forex = server.forex()
13   print 'Latest foreign exchange rate from %s: %s as of %s at %s' %
     tuple(forex)
14   forex = server.forex('eur', 'usd')
15   print 'Latest foreign exchange rate from %s: %s as of %s at %s' %
     tuple(forex)
16   print 'Latest Twitter status:', server.status()
```

There isn't much to the client piece here, but let's take a look anyway.

Line-by-Line Explanation

Lines 1–6

To reach an XML-RPC server, you need the xmlrpclib module in Python 2. As mentioned earlier, in Python 3 you would use xmlrpc.client, instead. We also grab the π constant from the math module. In the first line of real code, we connect to the XML-RPC server, passing in our host/port pair as a URL.

Lines 7–16

Each of the remaining lines of code make one RPC request out to the XML-RPC server which returns the desired results. The only function not tested by this client is the `tweet()` function, which we'll leave as an exercise for the reader. Making this many calls to the server might seem redundant, and it is, so that's why at the end of the chapter you'll find an exercise to address this issue.

With the server up, we can now run the client and see some input (your output will differ):

```
$ python xmlrpcclnt.py
Current time in seconds after epoch: 1322167988.29
Current time as a string: Thu Nov 24 12:53:08 2011
Area of circle of radius 5: 78.5398163397
Latest Google stock price: 570.11 (-9.89 / -1.71%) as of 11/23/2011 at
4:00pm
Latest foreign exchange rate from USD to EUR: 0.7491 as of 11/24/2011
at 3:51pm
Latest foreign exchange rate from EUR to USD: 1.3349 as of 11/24/2011
at 3:51pm
Latest Twitter status: @KatEller same to you!!! :-) we need a
celebration meal... this coming monday or friday? have a great
thanksgiving!!
```

Although we have reached the end of this chapter, we have only just scratched the surface of XML-RPC and JSON-RPC programming. For further reading, we suggest you take a look at self-documenting XML-RPC servers via the `DocXMLRPCServer` class, the various types of data structures you can return from an XML-RPC server (see the `xmlrpclib/xmlrpc.client` documentation), etc.

14.4 References

There are plenty of online documents pertaining to all the material covered in this chapter. The following list, although not exhaustive, provides a considerable number of resources for you to explore:

- http://docs.python.org/library/csv
- http://json.org/
- http://simplejson.readthedocs.org/en/latest/
- http://pypi.python.org/pypi/simplejson

- http://github.com/simplejson/simplejson
- http://docs.python.org/library/json
- http://en.wikipedia.org/wiki/JSON
- http://en.wikipedia.org/wiki/XML
- http://docs.python.org/library/xmlrpclib
- http://docs.python.org/library/simplexmlrpcserver
- http://docs.python.org/library/docxmlrpcserver
- http://www.saxproject.org
- http://en.wikipedia.org/wiki/Expat_(XML)
- http://en.wikipedia.org/wiki/Xml-rpc
- http://scripts.incutio.com/xmlrpc/introspection.html
- http://en.wikipedia.org/wiki/JSON-RPC
- http://json-rpc.org/
- http://www.doughellmann.com/PyMOTW/ SimpleXMLRPCServer/#introspection-api

For a deeper treatment on this subject, we recommend that you take a look at *Text Processing in Python* (Addison-Wesley, 2003), the classic Python treatise on this topic. There is another book on text processing called *Python 2.6 Text Processing* (Packt, 2010). Despite the title, the information found there can be used with most current Python releases.

14.5   Related Modules

Table 14-2 Text-Processing-Related Modules

Module/Package	Description
csv[a]	Comma-separated values processing
SimpleXMLRPCServer	XML-RPC server (merged into xmlrpc.server in Python 3)
DocXMLRPCServer	Self-documenting XML-RPC server (merged into xmlrpc.server in Python 3)
xmlrpclib	XML-RPC client (renamed to xmlrpc.client in Python 3)
json[b]	JSON encoding and decoding (externally known as simplejson, usually pre-version 2.6)
xml.parsers.expat[c]	Fast, non-validating XML parser
xml.dom[b]	Tree/DOM-based XML parsing
xml.sax[b]	Event/Stream-based XML parsing
xml.etree.ElementTree[c]	ElementTree XML parser and tree-builder

a. New in Python 2.3.
b. New in Python 2.6.
c. New in Python 2.0.
d. New in Python 2.5

14.6   Exercises

CSV

14-1. *CSV.* What is the CSV format, and for what types of applications is it usually suited?

14-2. *CSV vs. str.split().* Come up with some examples of data for which str.split(',') does not suffice, and where use of the csv module is really the only way to go.

14-3. *CSV vs. str.split().* In Chapter 13, for Exercise 13-16, you were asked to make the output of stock.py more flexible, making all columns line up as much as possible, despite the varying length of stock ticker symbols, different stock prices and change in prices. Further update that modified script by switching from using `str.split(',')` to `csv.reader()`.

14-4. *Alternative CSV Formats.* There are alternative delimiters used besides commas. For example, POSIX-compliant password files are colon (`:`) delimited, whereas e-mail addresses in Outlook are semi-colon (`;`) delimited. Create functions that can read or write documents using these alternative delimiters.

JSON

14-5. *JSON.* What are the differences in syntax between JSON format and Python dictionaries and lists?

14-6. *JSON Arrays.* The `dict2json.py` example only demonstrates converting from Python `dict`s to JSON objects. Create a sister script named `lort2json.py` to show moving from lists or tuples to JSON arrays.

14-7. *Backward Compatibility.* Running Example 14-2, `dict2json.py`, using Python 2.5 and older fails:

```
$ python2.5 dict2json.py
Traceback (most recent call last):
  File "dict2json.py", line 12, in <module>
    from json import dumps
ImportError: No module named json
```

a) What do you need to do to get this to run in older Python releases?

b) Modify the code in `dict2json.py` that imports JSON functionality to work with older versions of Python (for example, versions 2.4 and 2.5) as well as version 2.6 and newer.

14-8. *JSON.* Add new code to your `stock.py` example from Chapter 13 that retrieves stock quotes from Yahoo! Finance Service so that it returns a JSON string representing all of the stock data in a hierarchical data structure format, as opposed to just dumping the results on-screen.

14-9. *JSON and Types/Classes.* Write some script that encodes and decodes any type of Python object, such as numbers, classes, instances, etc.

XML and XML-RPC

14-10. *Web Programming.* Enhance the `goognewsrss.py` script to output formatted HTML representing anchors/links that can be piped directly to a flat `.html` file for browser rendering. The links should be correct/valid and ready for users to click and launch the corresponding Web pages.

14-11. *Robustness.* In `xmlrpcsrvr.py`, add support for the >, >=, <, <=, ==, != operations as well as true and floor division.

14-12. *Twitter.* In `xmlrpcclnt.py`, we did not test the `SpecialServices.tweet()` method. Add this functionality to your script.

14-13. *CGIXMLRPCRequestHandler.* By default, `SimpleXMLRPCServer` uses the `SimpleXMLRPCRequestHandler` handler class. What's the difference between this handler and `CGIXMLRPCRequestHandler`? Create a new server that uses the `CGIXMLRPCRequestHandler`, instead.

14-14. *DocXMLRPCServer.* Investigate self-documenting XML-RPC servers, and then answer the following:

a) What are the differences between the `SimpleXMLRPCServer` and `DocXMLRPCServer` objects? Beyond that, what are the lower-level differences (over the network)?

b) Convert both your standard XML-RPC client and server to be self-documenting.

c) Also convert your CGI version from the previous problem to using the `DocCGIXMLRPCRequestHandler` class.

14-15. *XML-RPC Multicalls.* In `xmlrpcclnt.py`, we make individual requests to the server. Clients making multiple calls to the server will experience a performance improvement by being able to make a *multicall,* meaning multiple RPC calls with one service request to the server. Investigate the `register_multicall_functions()` function, and then add this functionality to your server. Finally, modify your client to use multicall.

14-16. *XML and XML-RPC.* How is any of the XML-RPC material covered in this chapter related to XML at all? The material in the last section was quite different from the rest of the chapter; how does it tie together?

14-17. *JSON-RPC vs. XML-RPC.* What is JSON-RPC and how does it relate to XML-RPC?

14-18. *JSON-RPC.* Port both your XML-RPC client and server code to their equivalent `jsonrpcsrvr.py` and `jsonrpcclnt.py`.

## CHAPTER 15

Miscellaneous

*At Google, Python is one of the three "official languages"
alongside with C++ and Java.*
—Greg Stein, March 2005
(verbally at SDForum meeting)

In this chapter...

- Jython
- Google+

A s with Chapter 14, "Text Processing," this chapter provides brief preview introductions to miscellaneous areas of Python programming that we did not have time to explore more fully. We hope to eventually develop these into full chapters for future editions of this book. We start with Java and Jython programming, followed by a discussion of the Google+ API, afterwards.

15.1   Jython

In the first part of this chapter, we'll take a look at how to run Python on the JVM using Jython. We'll first introduce what Jython is and describe how it works like Python (or perhaps doesn't). This is followed by a GUI code sample using Swing. While this is not usually what people use Java for, it does make for a nice example where we show you the Java code followed by its equivalent in Python and executed by Jython. We hope to develop more Java examples in future editions.

15.1.1   Introduction to Jython

Jython is one of those tools that has the ability to unite two diverse programming populations. For one, it caters to Python programmers embedded in a Java development environment and gives them the ability to rapidly prototype solutions that seamlessly integrate into an existing Java platform. Another reason is that it helps simplify the lives of millions of Java programmers by giving Java a scripting language environment. No longer do Java programmers have to write a test harness or driver application to simply test a class they wrote.

Jython gives you most of what Python has to offer along with the ability to instantiate and interact with Java classes, too! Jython code is dynamically compiled into Java bytecode, plus you can extend Java classes in Jython. You can also extend Python by using Java. It is quite easy to write a class in Python and then use it as a Java class. You can always statically compile a Jython script into Java bytecode.

Jython can be downloaded from the book's Web site or at http://jython.org. When you run the Jython interactive interpreter for the first time, it displays notices informing you that new .jar files are being processed, as shown in the following:

```
$ jython
*sys-package-mgr*: processing new jar, '/usr/local/jython2.5.2/
jython.jar'
*sys-package-mgr*: processing new jar, '/System/Library/Java/
JavaVirtualMachines/1.6.0.jdk/Contents/Classes/classes.jar'
        . . .
*sys-package-mgr*: processing new jar, '/System/Library/Java/
JavaVirtualMachines/1.6.0.jdk/Contents/Home/lib/ext/sunpkcs11.jar'
Jython 2.5.2 (Release_2_5_2:7206, Mar 2 2011, 23:12:06)
[Java HotSpot(TM) 64-Bit Server VM (Apple Inc.)] on java1.6.0_26
Type "help", "copyright", "credits" or "license" for more information.
>>>
```

Each successive invocation looks eerily like you're using Python. And yes, Virginia, you can still do the same old "Hello World!" in Python:

```
$ jython
Jython 2.5.2 (Release_2_5_2:7206, Mar 2 2011, 23:12:06)
[Java HotSpot(TM) 64-Bit Server VM (Apple Inc.)] on java1.6.0_26
Type "help", "copyright", "credits" or "license" for more information.
>>> print 'Hello World!'
Hello World!
```

The more interesting thing about the Jython interactive interpreter is that now you can do "Hello World!" by using Java:

```
>>> from java.lang import System
>>> System.out.write('Hello World!\n')
Hello World!
```

Java gives Python users the added bonuses of native exception handling (not available in standard Python, or *CPython* as it is called, when being referred to among other implementations) and the use of Java's own garbage collector (so Python's did not have to be [re]implemented for Java).

15.1.2   GUI Example with Swing

By having access to all Java classes, we have a much broader universe of what is possible. One example is GUI development. In Python, we have the default GUI of Tk via the Tkinter module, but Tk is not a native Python toolkit. However, Java does have Swing, and it is native. With Jython, we can actually write a GUI application by using Swing components; not with Java, but using Python.

Example 15-1 presents a simple "Hello World!" GUI written in Java followed by Example 15-2, which shows its equivalent in Python, both of which mimic the Tk examples tkhello3.py found in Chapter 5, "GUI Programming." These programs are called swhello.java and swhello.py, respectively.

Example 15-1   Swing "Hello World" in Java (`swhello.java`)

This program creates a GUI just like `tkhello3.py` but uses Swing instead of Tk.
It is written in Java.

```java
1    import java.awt.*;
2    import java.awt.event.*;
3    import javax.swing.*;
4    import java.lang.*;
5
6    public class swhello extends JFrame {
7        JPanel box;
8        JLabel hello;
9        JButton quit;
10
11       public swhello() {
12           super("JSwing");
13           JPanel box = new JPanel(new BorderLayout());
14           JLabel hello = new JLabel("Hello World!");
15           JButton quit = new JButton("QUIT");
16
17           ActionListener quitAction = new ActionListener() {
18               public void actionPerformed(ActionEvent e) {
19                   System.exit(0);
20               }
21           };
22           quit.setBackground(Color.red);
23           quit.setForeground(Color.white);
24           quit.addActionListener(quitAction);
25           box.add(hello, BorderLayout.NORTH);
26           box.add(quit, BorderLayout.SOUTH);
27
28           addWindowListener(new WindowAdapter() {
29               public void windowClosing(WindowEvent e) {
30                   System.exit(0);
31               }
32           });
33           getContentPane().add(box);
34           pack();
35           setVisible(true);
36       }
37
38       public static void main(String args[]) {
39           swhello app = new swhello();
40       }
41   }
```

Example 15-2   Swing "Hello World" in Python (`swhello.py`)

This is an equivalent Python script to the previous Java program and executed with the Jython interpreter.

```
1    #!/usr/bin/env jython
2
3    from pawt import swing
4    import sys
5    from java.awt import Color, BorderLayout
6
7    def quit(e):
8        sys.exit()
9
10   top = swing.JFrame("PySwing")
11   box = swing.JPanel()
12   hello = swing.JLabel("Hello World!")
13   quit = swing.JButton("QUIT", actionPerformed=quit,
14       background=Color.red, foreground=Color.white)
15
16   box.add("North", hello)
17   box.add("South", quit)
18   top.contentPane.add(box)
19   top.pack()
20   top.visible = 1     # or True for Jython 2.2+
```

The code for both matches that of `tkhello3.py`, except that they use Swing instead of Tk. We will describe both at the same time.

Block-by-Block Combined Code Explanation

Both `swhello.java` and `swhello.py` start by importing the proper modules, libraries, and packages. The next blocks of code in each script use the Swing primitives. The quit callback is done within the Java block of code, whereas the Python code defines this function before getting into the core part of the application.

After the widgets are defined, the next blocks of code place them in their proper locations in the overall UI. The final action places everything into the content pane, packs all the widgets, and then makes the entire interface user-visible.

The hallmark of the Python version is the significant reduction in the number of lines of code necessary to do the same thing in Java. The Python code is more expressive, with each line of code having more significance. In short, there is less "white noise." Java code tends to have a lot more boilerplate code to get work done; with Python, you can concentrate on the important parts of your application: the solution to the problem you are trying to solve.

Whereas both applications are compiled to Java bytecode, it is no surprise that they look exactly alike when executing on the same platform (see Figure 15-1).

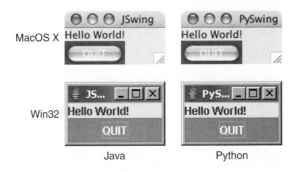

Figure 15-1 The Swing Hello World demonstration scripts. (swhello.{java,py})

Jython is a great development tool because you get the expressiveness of Python plus the rich API in the Java libraries. If you are a Java developer, we hope that we have whet your appetite for what you can now do with the power of Python behind you. If you are new to Java, Jython can ease you in gently. You can prototype in Jython, and then easily port your work to Java, as necessary. It's also a great scripting environment to complement everyday Java development.

15.2   Google+

The second half of this experimental chapter pertains to Google's social platform, Google+. We first introduce what it is, and then discuss how to connect to it from Python. Finally, we have a brief code sample to show a few things that you can do with it. Since the product is always adding new features, we hope to have more to show you in the future.

15.2.1   Introduction to the Google+ Platform

One way of looking at Google+ is that it's another social platform with an API. Another way of looking at it, from more of the corporate perspective, is that it weaves in a Google+ interface for most of its products, serving as an augmentation of its existing feature set, hence the name, Google+.

Regardless of your take on what it is, there is definitely a social aspect, and as with most things Google, there's an API for it. With Google+, users can post messages and pictures. They can also follow the activity of others as well as show that they like a message by clicking the "+1" button associated with it. Users can comment on a message and/or reshare it to one or more *circles*, Google+'s reference to subgroups in your networks, or publicly with the world.

As just mentioned, Google+ has an API. At the time of this writing, developers can use the API to access and search for Google+ users and Google+ users' activity streams, including comments to those activities. Developers can also write applications integrating Google+ Hangouts because it has an API, as well. Such APIs enable developers to write applications that can search public posts and pull up user's profiles. Let's look at an example.

15.2.2   Python and the Google+ API

Accessing this functionality from Python is simple. However, in this brief overview, we're not even going to touch the authenticated stuff (there is plenty more you can do once your application has proper authorization to access Google+ data), so bear in mind that this example is going to be even easier than normal.

Before we get started, you must first install Google's APIs Client Library for Python, if you haven't done so already. You can do this easily with a tool like `pip` or `easy_install`. (You need Python 2.4 or newer because the library isn't available for version 3.x yet.) If using `easy_install`, the update/install command would look like this:

2.4

```
$ sudo easy_install --upgrade google-api-python-client
```

Note that this library can be used to access many Google services, not just the Google+ API. You can find a complete list of supported APIs at http://code.google.com/p/google-api-python-client/wiki/SupportedApis

Next we need an access key. Go to http://code.google.com/apis/console and create a new project. Select to the **Services** tab in the newly created project, and then enable **Google+ API**. Next, select the **API Access** tab, copy the API key, and then paste it into the following code; or better yet, refactor privileged data such as credentials out to a separate file. With that, we're ready to begin.

15.2.3   A Simple Social Media Analysis Tool

In Example 15-3, we've created a simple social media analysis tool. Using this tool, you can see what people are saying on Google+ about a particular topic. But not all posts are created equal. Some are seen by very few people, but others are commented on and reshared many times.

In this application, we focus on these popular posts. It ranks the posts by popularity and lists the top five posts over the past week, either on Python or a search term of the user's choice. The other minor piece of functionality in this script is the ability to look up and display the profile of a Google+ user.

Our script is named `plus_top_posts.py`, but before we look at the code, let's look at the following sample execution of this menu-driven program so that you can get an idea of how it works:

```
$ python plus_top_posts.py

----------------------------------------
      Google+ Command-Line Tool v0.3
----------------------------------------
(p) Top 5 Python posts in past 7 days
(u) Fetch user profile (by ID)
(t) Top 5 posts in past 7 days query

Enter choice [QUIT]: p

*** Searching for the top 5 posts matching 'python' over the past 7
days...

From: Gretta Bartels (110414482530984269464)
Date: Fri Nov 25 02:01:16 2011
Chatter score: 19
Post: Seven years old. Time to learn python. And maybe spelling.
Link: https://plus.google.com/110414482530984269464/posts/MHSdkdxEyE7


----------------------------------------

From: Steven Van Bael (106898588952511738977)
Date: Fri Nov 25 11:00:50 2011
Chatter score: 14
Post: Everytime I open a file in python I realize how awesome the
language actually is for doing utility scripts. f =
open('test.txt','w') f.write('hello world') f.close() Try doing that
in java
Link: https://plus.google.com/106898588952511738977/posts/cBRko81uYX2


----------------------------------------
```

From: Estevan Carlos Benson (115832511083802586044)
Date: Fri Nov 25 20:02:11 2011
Chatter score: 11
Post: Can anyone recommend some online Python resources for a
beginner. Also, for any python developers, your thoughts on the
language?
Link: https://plus.google.com/115832511083802586044/posts/9GNWa9TXHzt

----

From: Michael Dorsey Jr (103222958721998092839)
Date: Tue Nov 22 11:31:56 2011
Chatter score: 11
Post: I slowly but surely see python becoming my language of choice.
Programming language talk at the gym. Must be cardio time.
Link: https://plus.google.com/103222958721998092839/posts/jRuPPDpfndv

----

From: Gabor Szabo (102810219707784087582)
Date: Fri Nov 25 17:59:14 2011
Chatter score: 9
Post: In http://learnpythonthehardway.org/ Zed A. Shaw suggest to read
code backwards. Any idea why would that help? Anyone practicing
anything like that?
Link: https://plus.google.com/102810219707784087582/posts/QEC5TQ1qoQU

      Google+ Command-Line Tool v0.3

(p) Top 5 Python posts in past 7 days
(u) Fetch user profile (by ID)
(t) Top 5 posts in past 7 days query

Enter choice [QUIT]: u
Enter user ID [102108625619739868700]:
Name: wesley chun
URL: https://plus.google.com/102108625619739868700
Pic: https://lh3.googleusercontent.com/-T_wVWLlmg7w/AAAAAAAAAAI/
AAAAAAAAAAA/zeVf2azgGYI/photo.jpg?sz=50
About: WESLEY J. CHUN, MSCS, is the author of Prentice Hall's
bestseller, <a href="http://corepython.com">Core Python
Programming</a>, its video
    . . .

```
----------------------------------------
      Google+ Command-Line Tool v0.3
----------------------------------------
(p) Top 5 Python posts in past 7 days
(u) Fetch user profile (by ID)
(t) Top 5 posts in past 7 days query

Enter choice [QUIT]:
$
```

Now let's check out the source.

Example 15-3   Simple Social Media Tool (`plus_top_posts.py`)

This Python 2 script searches Google+ for matching queries and user profiles.

```python
1   #!/usr/bin/env python
2
3   import datetime as dt
4   from apiclient.discovery import build
5
6   WIDTH = 40
7   MAX_DEF = 5
8   MAX_RES = 20
9   MAX_TOT = 60
10  UID = '102108625619739868700'
11  HR = '\n%s' % ('-' * WIDTH)
12  API_KEY = 'YOUR_KEY_FROM_CONSOLE_API_ACCESS_PAGE'
13
14  class PlusService(object):
15      def __init__(self):
16          self.service = build("plus", "v1",
17              developerKey=API_KEY)
18
19      def get_posts(self, q, oldest, maxp=MAX_TOT):
20          posts = []
21          cap = min(maxp, MAX_RES)
22          cxn = self.service.activities()
23          handle = cxn.search(maxResults=cap, query=q)
24          while handle:
25              feed = handle.execute()
26              if 'items' in feed:
27                  for activity in feed['items']:
28                      if oldest > activity['published']:
29                          return posts
30                      if q not in activity['title']:
31                          continue
32                      posts.append(PlusPost(activity))
33                      if len(posts) >= maxp:
34                          return posts
35                  handle = cxn.search_next(handle, feed)
36              else:
37                  return posts
38          else:
39              return posts
40
```

```
41        def get_user(self, uid):
42            return self.service.people().get(userId=uid).execute()
43
44  scrub = lambda x: ' '.join(x.strip().split())
45
46  class PlusPost(object):
47      def __init__(self, record):
48          self.title = scrub(record['title'])
49          self.post = scrub(record['object'].get(
50              'originalContent', ''))
51          self.link = record['url']
52          self.when = dt.datetime.strptime(
53              record['published'],
54              "%Y-%m-%dT%H:%M:%S.%fZ")
55          actor = record['actor']
56          self.author = '%s (%s)' % (
57              actor['displayName'], actor['id'])
58          obj = record['object']
59          cols = ('replies', 'plusoners', 'resharers')
60          self.chatter = \
61              sum(obj[col]['totalItems'] for col in cols)
62
63  def top_posts(query, maxp=MAX_DEF, ndays=7):
64      print '''
65  *** Searching for the top %d posts matching \
66  %r over the past %d days...''' % (maxp, query, ndays)
67      oldest = (dt.datetime.now()-dt.timedelta(ndays)).isoformat()
68      posts = service.get_posts(query, oldest, maxp)
69      if not posts:
70          print '*** no results found... try again ***'
71          return
72      sorted_posts = sorted(posts, reverse=True,
73          key=lambda post: post.chatter)
74      for i, post in enumerate(sorted_posts):
75          print '\n%d)' % (i+1)
76          print 'From:', post.author
77          print 'Date:', post.when.ctime()
78          print 'Chatter score:', post.chatter
79          print 'Post:', post.post if len(post.post) > \
80              len(post.title) else post.title
81          print 'Link:', post.link
82          print HR
83
84  def find_top_posts(query=None, maxp=MAX_DEF):
85      if not query:
86          query = raw_input('Enter search term [python]: ')
87      if not query:
88          query = 'python'
89      top_posts(query, maxp)
90  py_top_posts = lambda: find_top_posts('python')
91
```

(Continued)

Example 15-3   Simple Social Media Tool (`plus_top_posts.py`) *(Continued)*

```
 92  def find_user():
 93      uid = raw_input('Enter user ID [%s]: ' % UID).strip()
 94      if not uid:
 95          uid = UID
 96      if not uid.isdigit():
 97          print '*** ERROR: Must enter a numeric user ID'
 98          return
 99      user = service.get_user(uid)
100      print 'Name:', user['displayName']
101      print 'URL:', user['url']
102      print 'Pic:', user['image']['url']
103      print 'About:', user.get('aboutMe', '')
104
105  def _main():
106      menu = {
107          't': ('Top 5 posts in past 7 days query', find_top_posts),
108          'p': ('Top 5 Python posts in past 7 days', py_top_posts),
109          'u': ('Fetch user profile (by ID)', find_user),
110      }
111      prompt = ['(%s) %s' % (item, menu[item][0]) for item in menu]
112      prompt.insert(0, '%s\n%s%s' % (HR,
113          'Google+ Command-Line Tool v0.3'.center(WIDTH), HR))
114      prompt.append('\nEnter choice [QUIT]: ')
115      prompt = '\n'.join(prompt)
116      while True:
117          ch = raw_input(prompt).strip().lower()
118          if not ch or ch not in menu:
119              break
120          menu[ch][1]()
121
122  if __name__ == '__main__':
123      service = PlusService()
124      _main()
```

Line-by-Line Explanation

Lines 1–12

Interestingly enough, even though this script is one of the longer ones in this book, there are only two imports. One is the standard library `datetime` package; the other is from the Google APIs Client Library for Python. With respect to the latter, we're only interested in the `build()` function. Actually, one of the reasons why this part is so simple is that we're leaving out security (authorization). You'll have your chance at it in one of the exercises at the end of the chapter.

In the last part of this code block are the constants we're going to use. The `WIDTH` and `HR` variables are only relevant for the user display. The

API_KEY is how you authenticate to Google and gain access to the Google+ (public data) API. We strongly recommend that you move this value outside of your logic to another file such as secret.py to keep it more secure; you should only provide a secret.pyc if your files are accessible by other users. (A .pyc isn't foolproof, but it does require that intruders know the Python VM internals in order to reverse engineer it.) If you missed it, you can find instructions on how to get the API key earlier in the chapter.

MAX_DEF is the default number of results to display, MAX_RES is the maximum number of search results that you can (currently) request from the Google+ API, MAX_TOT is the current maximum we're allowing users of this script to be able to request, and UID is the default user ID (which is that of yours truly).

Lines 14–17

The PlusService class provides the main interface of our tool to the Google+ API. In the __init__() initializer, we connect to the API by calling apiclient.discovery.build(), passing in the desired API (Google+ is represented by "plus" and its version number) and your API key.

Lines 19–39

The get_posts() method does the heavy lifting. It does the setup and filtering, plus makes the primary call to get the data from Google. It starts with initialization of the results list (posts), setting the maximum number of results to request from Google (which must be less than or equal to MAX_RES), caching the API connection, and making the initial call to the Google+ API, returning a handle if the request succeeded. The while loop ensures that we run indefinitely until there are no more results coming back from the API. There are additional ways to get out of this loop, as we'll soon see.

Using the connection handle, we execute the query and receive a feed from Google+. It comes over the wire as a JSON structure and is converted into a Python dictionary. If there are items in the feed (meaning there is a key named 'items'), we loop through it, grabbing and saving data; otherwise there is no more data, so we break out and return any intermediate results. Within the loop, we can also exit due to age. Because the API returns results in reverse chronological order, once we've passed one week's time, we know all remaining posts will be older; hence, we can safely exit and return the dataset.

The age comparison is made by comparing the ISO 8601/RFC 3339 time-stamps directly. All Google+ posts are sent to us natively in this format, whereas our timestamp had to be converted from a `datetime.datetime` object to its ISO-equivalent—see this conversion in the description for `top_posts()`, which is coming up in a little bit.

The next filter skips all posts that do not feature the search term in the post title. This is probably not the most accurate search because the search term might appear in an attachment or in the full content body. You will have the chance to fix this in the exercises at the end of the chapter. This is the last test or filter featured in our solution; any others you develop can be added here.

Once we've passed these tests, we create a new `PlusPost` object, passing its initializer the entire post's object and have it filter out only those fields that are relevant to us.

Next, we check to see if we've achieved the maximum number of results. If so, we exit. Otherwise, we call the Google+ API's `search_next()` method passing in the current connection `handle` and `feed` so it knows where we last left off (yes, acting like a cursor).

The final **else** clause returns if the search itself came up empty to begin with.

Lines 41–44

The final method in our class is `get_user()`. Because this is considered "people" functionality and not an "activity," we use `self.service.people()` instead of `self.service.activity()`. The specific action we want is for `get()` to retrieve information on a specific Google+ user by ID.

The final line of code in this section features a utility function (`scrub()`), which takes a multiline body of text and reduces it to a single-line string by replacing all whitespace (even consecutive) with a single space character. This helps control the output in a command-line script but isn't as necessary for equivalent Web applications.

Lines 46–61

The purpose of the `PlusPost` object is to create a stripped down and sanitized equivalent of a post's data that contains only the stuff we care about. This object represents a single Google+ post made by a user. The Google+ API returns a highly nested data structure of JavaScript Object Notation (JSON) objects and arrays converted to Python `dicts` and `lists`, which can be tricky to navigate. This class transforms that data structure to a flat object with the most important properties exposed as instance variables.

The title and post contents are scrubbed, the URL is taken verbatim, and a more human-readable timestamp is employed. The original poster's saved information includes the display name and the ID, the latter of which you can use to look up more information for that user. The post's timestamp is parsed then converted from ISO 8601/RFC 3339 to a native Python `datetime.datetime` object, and then assigned.

The "chatter score" helps measure a post's impact and relevancy. *Chatter* is defined here as the sum of "+1"s, comments, and reshares of a post. The higher the chatter score is, the more important the post is for our (and any other) social media analysis tool. All of these signals are delivered in the `'object'` data structure and filed under the `totalItems` field for each of these metrics. The code uses `sum()` to tally all these columnar values via a generator expression to arrive at the assigned chatter score.

A more obvious way of writing this summation code if you're newer to Python is the following:

```
self.chatter = api_record['object']['replies']['totalItems']\
             + api_record['object']['plusoners']['totalItems']\
             + api_record['object']['resharers']['totalItems']
```

We made a variety of changes to code like this to arrive at the preceding source. What changes did we make and why?

1. There is a repeated lookup of `api_record['object']`. If we only ran this code several times, this isn't a big deal. However if we're executing searches millions of times daily in a server, it eventually eats into performance. A common Python best practice is to assign a local variable to cache such references, as in `obj = record['object']`.

2. We seem to be fetching a column of the same name (`totalItems`), so why not reuse that too?

3. Instead of adding the values manually by using plus (+), I often like to defer to BIFs such as `sum()` because they're usually written in C, which performs faster than pure Python.

4. If we can enhance our chatter score with additional metrics, this involves adding another long line of code such as "`+api_record['object'][SOMETHING_ELSE]['totalItems']`" when we could just add a single word to our columns field such as `cols = ('replies', 'plusoners', 'resharers', SOMETHING_ELSE)`.

Given that one of the most important goals in making code Pythonic is to keep things readable, simple, and elegant, either solution would work fine in this case. However, this is different matter if the chatter score required the summation of, say, ten values.

Getting back on topic again, while similar to Google+ Ripples, chatter is not exactly the same because Ripples is more of a tool that provides *visual insight* of a post's chatter score. (You can find out more about Ripples at http://googleblog.blogspot.com/2011/10/google-popular-posts-eye-catching.html and http://google.com/support/plus/bin/answer.py?answer=1713320.)

Lines 63–82

The `top_posts()` function represents the user interface for searching posts. It displays a message indicating the start of the query, collates and sorts the results, and then displays them one at a time to the user. The function sorts in descending order of the chatter score, as per the call to the `sorted()` BIF.

By default, the application displays the top five matching and most relevant posts. This can be altered by the caller, and the final **if** statement ensures this. Another point of control is the overall set of posts that make up the entire dataset.

Lines 84–90

The `find_top_posts()` function is the user interface that prompts the user for the search term, and then calls `top_posts()` with that query, defaulting to `'python'` if the user doesn't provide one. `py_top_posts()` is a customization that calls `find_top_posts()` directly with the `python` search term.

Lines 92–103

The `find_user()` function works similar to `find_top_posts()`, except that its job is to get a user ID and call `get_user()` to do its work. It will also ensure that the user entered a numeric ID and displays the results to the screen.

Lines 105–124

The final code block features `_main()`, which displays a menu of options to the user. It first parses the functionality `dict`, menu, and then inserts the boilerplate text around it. The user is prompted for her choice, which if valid, is then executed. Otherwise, the script quits by default.

Google+ is still a fairly new system at this time, and many things are likely to be changed or enhanced during the lifetime of this text, so be prepared for changes. Like the previous section in this chapter, we've just barely touched upon the potential of the entire Google+ platform and its API. As with Jython, we hope that this bit of dialog along with some sample code has you excited about both technologies and given you an idea as to what is possible. I look forward to expanding both of these sections in future editions of this book!

15.3 Exercises

Java, Python, Jython

15-1. *Jython.* What is the difference between Jython and CPython?

15-2. *Java and Python.* Take an existing Java application and port it to Python. Write down your experience in a journal. When complete, give an executive summary of what has to be accomplished, what some of the important steps are, and what common operations you have to perform to make it happen.

15-3. *Java and Python.* Study the Jython source code. Describe how some of Python standard types are implemented in Java.

15-4. *Java and Python.* Extend Python by writing an extension in Java. What are the necessary steps? Demonstrate your working solution by showing how it works with the Jython interactive interpreter.

15-5. *Jython and Databases.* Find an interesting exercise in Chapter 6, "Database Programming," and port it to Jython. One of the best things about Jython is that starting in version 2.1, it comes with a JDBC database module called zxJDBC that is nearly Python DB-API 2.0-compliant.

15-6. *Python and Jython.* Find a Python module not available in Jython (yet) and port it. Consider submitting it as a patch to the Jython distribution.

Google+

15-7. *Number of Results.* In `plus_top_posts.py`, we limited the number of results displayed to the "top 5" while clearly the code supports plenty more. Add another menu option that lets users choose how many results to return (up to a reasonable number).

15-8. *Timeline.* In `top_posts()`, there is a `ndays` variable which defaults the script to retrieving the most popular posts within the past seven days. Broaden the scope by supporting a variable timeline (any number of days).

15-9. *Object-Oriented Programming and Global Variables.* In `plus_top_posts.py`, we put all the core functionality into the `PlusService` class. All of the user-facing code (`raw_input()`s and **print** statements) are in functions outside of the class.

    a) This forced us to make `service` a global variable. Why are those bad again?

    b) Refactor the code so that `service` is no longer used as a global variable access from those external functions. You can consider the following: integrate external functions as methods of `PlusService` (including `_main()`), pass it around as a local variable, etc.

15-10. *Python 3.* The Google APIs Client Library for Python isn't available in Python 3 yet, but in anticipation, port `plus_top_posts.py` to an equivalent in Python 3 or create a hybrid that runs under both Python 2 or 3. You'll be able to test it once Python 3 availability occurs, but it's good to practice anyway.

15-11. *Progress "Bar."* While the "Searching for..." message is helpful so that users can see and prepare to wait momentarily while their results are being collated, it's more informative to get clues as this is happening. To do this, add an import of the `sys` module to `plus_top_posts.py`. Then, in `PlusService.get_posts()`, add a call that writes out a single dot or period to the screen—right after a new `PlusPost` object is appended to the results set.

We recommend that you use stderr instead of stdout because the former is unbuffered and will flush immediately to the screen. When you execute another search, you'll get a better idea of the intermediate work required to pull together the results before you see them.

15-12. *Google+.* Users can respond to posts by making comments. In plus_top_posts.py, we only list the posts. Augment its functionality to also show the comments for each post. You can find out more at https://developers.google.com/+/api/latest/comments.

15-13. *Authorization.* None of the searches performed in plus_top_posts.py were authorized, meaning that the application can only search public data. Add support for OAuth2 to gain access to user and private data. You can learn more at https://developers.google.com/+/api/oauth and http://code.google.com/p/google-api-python-client/wiki/OAuth2Client.

15-14. *Accuracy.* In the search code, our plus_top_posts.py script, specifically the get_posts() method, we filter out irrelevant content. We do this by ensuring that the search term appears in the title of the post. This is somewhat of a blunt measure because the title is only part of an overall message. Improve the accuracy of our filtering by also checking if the *content* contains the search term as well, and if either one is a match for any particular post, we should save it. To see how to get the content, take a look at the initializer for PlusPost objects. Try to minimize duplication of code where possible. Extra Credit: Also check attachment content for the search term.

15-15. *Time vs. Relevance.* The default Google+ search order is by the most recent posts first. In the call to self.service.activities().search(), there is an implied orderBy='recent' parameter. More on orderBy can be found in the developer documentation at https://developers.google.com/+/api/latest/activities/search.

   a) This ordering can be altered from the most recent to the most relevant posts by changing that parameter to 'best', instead. Make this change.

   b) How does this affect the code in the `get_posts()` method,
       which returns once we've reached a post older than our
       threshold?

   c) What should be done to address this (if anything)? If so,
       make that change.

15-16. *People Search*. Add support for people search via the Google+
        API by creating a function called `find_people()`. The current
        activity search uses the `self.service.activities().search()`
        method. You will use the equivalent for user search, that is,
        `self.service.people().search()`. For more information, go
        to http://developers. google.com/+/api/latest/people/search.

15-17. *Attachments*. Our `plus_top_posts.py` script does not do any-
        thing about attachments, which are sometimes the key rea-
        son behind posts. In the sample output executing this script
        showing the top five Python-related posts (at the time of this
        writing), at least one post featured a link to the relevant Web
        page, and at least another featured a picture. Add support
        for attachments to your version of this script.

15-18. *Command-line Arguments*. The version of `plus_top_posts.py`
        featured in this chapter is a command-line menu-driven pro-
        gram. However in reality, you might prefer a non-interactive
        interface, especially for scripting, cron jobs, etc. Augment the
        application by integrating a command-line argument pars-
        ing interface (and equivalent functionality). We recommend
        that you use `argparse`,[1] but `optparse`[2] or even the old `getopt`
        module will suffice.

15-19. *Web Programming*. The `plus_top_posts.py` script works fine
        as a command-line tool, however you might not always be in
        front of a terminal and possibly in a place where online
        access might be the only option. Develop a completely sepa-
        rate Web application version of this tool. Use any tools at
        your disposal.

---

1. New in Python 2.7.
2. New in Python 2.3.

APPENDIX A

Answers to Selected Exercises

*The Answer to the Great Question... Of Life, the Universe
and Everything... Is... Forty-two, said Deep Thought,
with infinite majesty and calm.*
—Douglas Adams, October 1979
(from *The Hitchhiker's Guide to the
Galaxy,* 1979, Pan Books)

Chapter 1

Regular Expressions

1-1.   Matching strings

bat, hat, bit, etc.

`[bh][aiu]t`

1-2.   First name last

`[A-Za-z-]+ [A-Za-z-]+`

(Any pair of words separated by a single space, that is, first
and last names, hyphens allowed)

1-3.   Last name first

[A-Za-z-]+, [A-Za-z]

(Any word and single letter separated by a comma and single space, as in, last name, first initial)

[A-Za-z-]+, [A-Za-z-]+

(Any pair of words separated by a comma and single space, such as, last, first names, hyphens allowed)

1-8.   Python longs

\d+[lL]

(Decimal [base 10] integers only)

1-9.   Python floats

[0-9]+(\.[0-9]*)?

(Describes a simple floating-point number, that is, any number of digits followed optionally by a single decimal point and zero or more numeric digits, as in "0.004," "2," "75.," etc.)

Chapter 2

2-3.   Sockets

 TCP

2-6.   Daytime service

```
>>> import socket
>>> socket.getservbyname('daytime', 'udp')
13
```

Chapter 3

3-20. Identifiers

pass is a keyword, so it cannot be used as an identifier. The common idiom in all such cases is to append an underscore (_) to the name of the offending variable.

Chapter 4

4-2.   Python threads

I/O-bound... why?

Chapter 5

5-1. Client/server architecture

Window(ing) clients are GUI events generated usually by users which must be processed by the window(ing) system that acts as the server; it is responsible for making timely updates to the display as to be apparent to the user.

Chapter 6

6-1. Extending Python

- Performance improvement

- Protecting source code

- New or desired change of functionality

- And more!

Chapter 7

7-16. Improving title slide designation. (*partial solution*)

The main problem in our code is that it calls `str.title()` for both a talk title as well as individual slide titles. Line 43 really needs to be improved:

```
s.Shapes[0].TextFrame.TextRange.Text = line.title()
```

We can make a quick change so that the code only applies title case to the title (which is currently in all capital letters), leaving non-title slide titles alone:

```
s.Shapes[0].TextFrame.TextRange.Text = title and
line.title() or line
```

We can do better, however. This exercises asks what to do with TCP/IP and how to avoid changing it to "Tcp/Ip." Suppose that we make a new `eachWord` variable. My suggestion there is to check if `eachWord == eachWord.upper()`. If it's an acronym, then leave it alone; otherwise, we can apply title case. Yes, there are exceptions, but if we cover for the 80 percent, then that's good enough for now.

Chapter 8

8-1.   DB-API

The DB-API is a common interface specification for all Python database adapters. It is good in that it forces all adapter writers to code to the same specification so that end-user programmers can write consistent code that can be (more) easily ported to other databases with the minimum amount of effort.

Chapter 10

10-6.   CGI errors

The Web server returns either no data or error text, which results in an HTTP 500 or Internal Server Error in your browser because that (returned data) is not valid HTTP or HTML data. The cgitb module captures the Python traceback and returns it as valid data through CGI, which is displayed to the user—a great debugging tool.

Chapter 13

13-8.   Web services and the csv module

Replace the **for** loop in stock.py with the following:

```
import csv
for tick, price, chg, per in csv.reader(f):
    print tick.ljust(7), ('%.2f' % round(float(price),
        2)).rjust(6), chg.rjust(6), per.rjust(6)
```

Chapter 14

14-2.   CSV versus str.split().

Obviously, the comma is really not the best delimiter to use when parsing data that uses a different delimiter; that goes without saying. Beyond that, using commas is also fraught with danger if the fields (individual "column" values) can contain quotes. Complications can also manifest if fields can contain quotes, not just because commas can go inside as string values, but also parsing literature in which commas can appear either to the left or right of a quotation mark.

Quotes themselves cause problems—how would you parse a string that contains quoted strings when you want all words of that quoted string to be treated as a single entity? (Hint: see http://docs.python.org/library/shlex)

14-11. Robustness.

In `xmlrpcsrvr.py`, change line 13

```
FUNCs = ('add', 'sub', 'mul', 'div', 'mod')
```

by adding all the required functions:

```
FUNCs = ('add', 'sub', 'mul', 'div', 'mod',
    'gt', 'ge', 'lt', 'le', 'eq', 'ne',
     truediv', 'floordiv',
)
```

These are all available in the `operator` module, so no additional work beyond this change is necessary. Now you should have enough knowledge to be able to add unary -, **, and the bitwise operators &, |, ^, and ~.

Chapter 15

15-1. Jython.

Jython is the Java implementation of (most of) the standard Python interpreter, which is written in C, hence it's name, CPython. It's byte-compiled to run on a Java Virtual Machine (JVM). Rather than a direct port, the creator of Jython recognized that Java had its own memory management and exception handling frameworks, so those language features did not require porting. The Jython versions are numbered to specific compatibility, that is, Jython 2.5 is compatible to CPython 2.5. The original version of Jython was named JPython, but it was superseded by Jython. You can find more information in the Jython online FAQ at http://wiki.python.org/jython/JythonFaq/GeneralInfo.

Reference Tables

Anybody else on the list got an opinion?
Should I change the language or not?
—Guido van Rossum, December 1991

Python Keywords

Table B.1 lists Python's keywords.

Table B-1   Python Reserved Words[a]

and	as[b]	assert[c]	break
class	continue	def	del
elif	else	except	exec[d]
finally	for	from	global
if	import	in	is
lambda	nonlocal[e]	not	or

| pass | print[d] | raise | return |
| try | while | with[b] | yield[f] |

a. **None** became a constant in Python 2.4; None, **True**, **False** became keywords in version 3.0.
b. New in Python 2.6.
c. New in Python 1.5.
d. Became built-in function and removed as keyword in Python 3.0.
e. New in Python 3.0.
f. New in Python 2.3.

Python Standard Operators and Functions

Table B-2 represents the operators and functions (built-in and factory) that can be used with most standard Python objects as well as user-defined objects in which you have implemented their corresponding special methods.

Table B-2 Standard Type Operators and Functions

Operator/function	Description	Result[a]
String representation		
` `[b]	A string representation that can be evaluated	str
Built-in and factory functions		
cmp(*obj1*, *obj2*)	Compares two objects	int
repr(*obj*)	A string representation that can be evaluated	str
str(*obj*)	Printable string representation	str
type(*obj*)	Object type	type
Value comparisons		
<	Less than	bool
>	Greater than	bool

(Continued)

Table B-2   Standard Type Operators and Functions *(Continued)*

Operator/function	Description	Result[a]
Value comparisons		
<=	Less than or equal to	bool
>=	Greater than or equal to	bool
==	Equal to	bool
!=	Not equal to	bool
<>[b]	Not equal to	bool
Object comparisons		
is	The same as	bool
is not	Not the same as	bool
Boolean operators		
not	Logical negation	bool
and	Logical conjunction	bool
or	Logical disjunction	bool

a. Boolean comparisons return either **True** or **False**.
b. Removed in Python 3.0; use !=, instead.

Numeric Type Operators and Functions

Table B-3 represents the operators and functions (built-in and factory) that apply to Python's numeric objects.

Table B-3   Operators and Built-In Functions for All Numeric Types

Operator/ Built-In	Description	int	long[a]	float	complex	Result[a]
abs()	Absolute value	•	•	•	•	number[a]
bin()	Binary string	•	•	•	•	str
chr()	Character	•	•			str

Operator/built-in	Description	int	long[a]	float	complex	Result[a]
coerce()	Numeric coercion	•	•	•	•	tuple
complex()	Complex factory function	•	•	•	•	complex
divmod()	Division/modulo	•	•	•	•	tuple
float()	Float factory function	•	•	•	•	float
hex()	Hexadecimal string	•	•			str
int()	Int factory function	•	•	•	•	int
long()[a]	Long factory function	•	•	•	•	long
oct()	Octal string	•	•			str
ord()	Ordinal		(string)			int
pow()	Exponentiation	•	•	•	•	number
round()	Float rounding			•		float
sum()[c]	Summation	•	•	•		float
**[d]	Exponentiation	•	•	•	•	number
+[e]	No change	•	•	•	•	number
-[d]	Negation	•	•	•	•	number
~[d]	Bit inversion	•	•			int/long
**[c]	Exponentiation	•	•	•	•	number
*	Multiplication	•	•	•	•	number
/	Classic or true division	•	•	•	•	number

(Continued)

Table B-3   Operators and Built-In Functions for All Numeric Types *(Continued)*

Operator/ Built-In	Description	int	long[a]	float	complex	Result[a]
//	Floor division	•	•	•	•	number
%	Modulo/ remainder	•	•	•	•	number
+	Addition	•	•	•	•	number
–	Subtraction	•	•	•	•	number
<<	Bit left shift	•	•			int/long
>>	Bit right shift	•	•			int/long
&	Bitwise AND	•	•			int/long
^	Bitwise XOR	•	•			int/long
|	Bitwise OR	•	•			int/long

a. The long type was removed in Python 3.0; use int, instead.
b. A result of "number" indicates any of the numeric types, perhaps the same as the operands.
c. New in Python 2.3.
d. ** has a unique relationship with unary operators.
e. Unary operator.

Sequence Type Operators and Functions

Table B-4 contains the set of operators, functions (built-in and factory), and built-in methods that can be used with sequence types.

Table B-4   Sequence Type Operators, Functions, and Built-In Methods

Operator, Built-In Function or Method	str	list	tuple
[] (list creation)		•	
()			•
""	•		
append()		•	

Operator, Built-In Function or Method	str	list	tuple
capitalize()	•		
center()	•		
chr()	•		
cmp()	•	•	•
count()	•	•	•[a]
decode()	•		
encode()	•		
endswith()	•		
expandtabs()	•		
extend()		•	
find()	•		
format()	•[a]		
hex()	•		
index()	•	•	•[a]
insert()		•	
isalnum()	•		
isalpha()	•		
isdecimal()	•[b]		
isdigit()	•		
islower()	•		
isnumeric()	•[b]		
isspace()	•		
istitle()	•		

(Continued)

Table B-4   Sequence Type Operators, Built-in Functions, and Methods
(Continued)

Operator, Built-In Function or Method	str	list	tuple
isupper()	•		
join()	•		
len()	•	•	•
list()	•	•	•
ljust()	•		
lower()	•		
lstrip()	•		
max()	•	•	•
min()	•	•	•
oct()	•		
ord()	•		
partition()	•[c]		
pop()		•	
raw_input()	•		
remove()		•	
replace()	•		
repr()	•	•	•
reverse()		•	
rfind()	•		
rindex()	•		
rjust()	•		
rpartition()	•[c]		

Operator, Built-In Function or Method	str	list	tuple
rsplit()	•[d]		
rstrip()	•		
sort()		•	
split()	•		
splitlines()	•		
startswith()	•		
str()	•	•	•
strip()	•		
swapcase()	•		
title()	•		
translate()	•		
tuple()	•	•	•
type()	•	•	•
upper()	•		
zfill()	•[e]		
. (attributes)	•	•	
[] (slice)	•	•	•
[:]	•	•	•
*	•	•	•
%	•		
+	•	•	•

(Continued)

Table B-4 Sequence Type Operators, Built-in Functions, and Methods
(Continued)

Operator, Built-In Function or Method	str	list	tuple
in	•	•	•
not in	•	•	•

a. New in Python 2.6 (first methods for tuples ever).
b. Only for Unicode strings in Python 2.x; "new" in Python 3.0.
c. New in Python 2.5.
d. New in Python 2.4.
e. New in Python 2.2.2.

String Format Operator Conversion Symbols

Table B-5 lists the formatting symbols that can be used with the string format operator (%).

Table B-5 String Format Operator Conversion Symbols

Format Symbol	Conversion
%c	Character (integer [ASCII value] or string of length 1)
%r[a]	String conversion via repr() prior to formatting
%s	String conversion via str() prior to formatting
%d / %i	Signed decimal integer
%u[b]	Unsigned decimal integer
%o[b]	(Unsigned) octal integer
%x[b] / %X[b]	(Unsigned) hexadecimal integer (lower/UPPERcase letters)
%e / %E	Exponential notation (with lowercase e/UPPERcase E)

Format Symbol	Conversion
%f / %F	Floating point real number (fraction truncates naturally)
%g / %G	The shorter of %e and %f/%E% and %F%
%%	Percent character (%) unescaped

a. New in Python 2.0; likely unique only to Python.
b. %u/%o/%x/%X of negative int will return a signed string in Python 2.4+.

String Format Operator Directives

When using the string format operator (see Table B-5), you can enhance or fine-tune the object display with the directives shown in Table B-6.

Table B-6   Format Operator Auxiliary Directives

Symbol	Functionality
*	Argument specifies width or precision
–	Use left justification
+	Use a plus sign (+) for positive numbers
<sp>	Use space-padding for positive numbers
#	Add the octal leading zero (0) or hexadecimal leading 0x or 0X, depending on whether x or X was used
0	Use zero-padding (instead of spaces) when formatting numbers
%	%% leaves you with a single literal %
(var)	Mapping variable (dictionary arguments)
m.n	*m* is the minimum total width and *n* is the number of digits to display after the decimal point (if applicable)

String Type Built-In Methods

The descriptions for the string built-in methods in Table B-4 are given in Table B-7.

Table B-7 String Type Built-In Methods

Method Name	Description
string.capitalize()	Capitalizes first letter of string
string.center(*width*)	Returns a space-padded *string* with the original *string* centered to a total of *width* columns
string.count(*str*, *beg*=0, *end*=len(*string*))	Counts how many times *str* occurs in *string*, or in a substring of *string* if starting index *beg* and ending index *end* are given
string.decode(*encoding*= 'UTF-8', *errors*='strict')[e]	Returns decoded string version of string; on error, default is to raise a ValueError unless *errors* is given with ignore or replace
string.encode(*encoding*= 'UTF-8', *errors*='strict')[a]	Returns encoded string version of string; on error, default is to raise a ValueError unless *errors* is given with ignore or replace
string.endswith(*str*, *beg*=0, *end*=len(*string*))[b]	Determines if *string* or a substring of *string* (if starting index *beg* and ending index *end* are given) ends with *str*; returns True if so, and False otherwise
string.expandtabs(*tabsize*=8)	Expands tabs in *string* to multiple spaces; defaults to eight spaces per tab if *tabsize* not provided
string.find(*str*, *beg*=0 *end*=len(*string*))	Determines if *str* occurs in *string*, or in a substring of *string* if starting index *beg* and ending index *end* are given; returns index if found, and –1 otherwise
string.format(**args*, ***kwargs*)	Perform string formatting based on *args* and/or *kwargs* passed in
string.index(*str*, *beg*=0, *end*=len(*string*))	Same as find(), but raises an exception if *str* not found

Method Name	Description
string.isalnum()[a,b,c]	Returns True if *string* has at least 1 character and all characters are alphanumeric, and False otherwise
string.isalpha()[a,b,c]	Returns True if *string* has at least 1 character and all characters are alphabetic, and False otherwise
string.isdecimal()[a,b,d]	Returns True if *string* contains only decimal digits, and False otherwise
string.isdigit()[b,c]	Returns True if *string* contains only digits, and False otherwise
string.islower()[b,c]	Returns True if *string* has at least 1 cased character and all cased characters are in lowercase, and False otherwise
string.isnumeric()[b,c,d]	Returns True if *string* contains only numeric characters and, False otherwise
string.isspace()[b,c]	Returns True if *string* contains only whitespace characters, and False otherwise
string.istitle()[b,c]	Returns True if *string* is properly "title-cased" (see title()), and False otherwise
string.isupper()[b,c]	Returns True if *string* has at least one cased character and all cased characters are in uppercase, and False otherwise
string.join(*seq*)	Merges (concatenates) the string representations of elements in sequence *seq* into a string, with separator *string*
string.ljust(*width*)	Returns a space-padded *string* with the original string left-justified to a total of *width* columns
string.lower()	Converts all uppercase letters in *string* to lowercase
string.lstrip()	Removes all leading whitespace in *string*

(Continued)

Table B-7   String Type Built-In Methods *(Continued)*

Method Name	Description
string.replace(*str1*, *str2*, *num*=*string*.count(*str1*))	Replaces all occurrences of *str1* in *string* with *str2*, or at most *num* occurrences if *num* given
string.rfind(*str*, *beg*=0, *end*=len(*string*))	Same as find(), but search backwards in *string*
string.rindex(*str*, *beg*=0, *end*=len(*string*))	Same as index(), but search backwards in *string*
string.rjust(*width*)	Returns a space-padded *string* with the original string right-justified to a total of *width* columns
string.rstrip()	Removes all trailing whitespace of *string*
string.split(*str*="", *num*=*string*.count(*str*))	Splits *string* according to delimiter *str* (space if not provided) and returns list of substrings; split into at most *num* substrings if given
string.splitlines(*num*=string.count('\n'))[b,c]	Splits *string* at all (or *num*) NEWLINEs and returns a list of each line with NEWLINEs removed
string.startswith(*str*, *beg*=0, *end*=len(*string*))[b]	Determines if *string* or a substring of *string* (if starting index *beg* and ending index *end* are given) starts with substring *str*; returns *True* if so, and False otherwise
string.strip([*obj*])	Performs both lstrip() and rstrip() on *string*
string.swapcase()	Inverts case for all letters in *string*
string.title()[b,c]	Returns "titlecased" version of *string*, that is, all words begin with uppercase, and the rest are lowercase (also see istitle())

Method Name	Description
string.*translate*(*str*, *del*="")	Translates *string* according to translation table *str* (256 chars), removing those in the *del* string
string.upper()	Converts lowercase letters in *string* to uppercase
string.zfill(*width*)	Returns original *string* left-padded with zeros to a total of *width* characters; intended for numbers, zfill() retains any sign given (less one zero)

a. Applicable to Unicode strings only in version 1.6, but to all string types in version 2.0.
b. Not available as a string module function in version 1.5.2.
c. New in Python 2.1.
d. Applicable to Unicode strings only.
e. New in Python 2.2.

List Type Built-In Methods

In Table B-8, we present full descriptions and usage syntax for the list built-in methods given in Table B-4.

Table B-8   List Type Built-In Methods

List Method	Operation
list.append(*obj*)	Adds obj to the end of *list*
list.count(*obj*)	Returns count of how many times *obj* occurs in *list*
list.extend(seq)[a]	Appends contents of *seq* to *list*
list.index(*obj*, *i=0*, *j=len*(*list*))	Returns lowest index k where *list*[k] == *obj* and $i <= k < j$; otherwise ValueError raised
list.insert(*index*, *obj*)	Inserts *obj* into *list* at offset *index*

(Continued)

Table B-8   List Type Built-In Methods *(Continued)*

List Method	Operation
`list.pop(index=-1)`[a]	Removes and returns *obj* at given or last *index* from *list*
`list.remove(obj)`	Removes object *obj* from *list*
`list.reverse()`	Reverses objects of *list* in place
`list.sort(func=None,` `key=None, reverse=False)`	Sorts list members with optional comparison *function*; *key* is a callback when extracting elements for sorting, and if *reverse* flag is True, then list is sorted in reverse order

a.   New in Python 1.5.2.

Dictionary Type Built-In Methods

In Table B-9, we list the full description and usage syntax for the dictionary built-in methods.

Table B-9   Dictionary Type Methods

Method Name	Operation
`dict.clear`[a]`()`	Removes all elements of `dict`
`dict.copy`[a]`()`	Returns a (shallow[b]) copy of `dict`
`dict.fromkeys`[b]`(seq,` `val=None)`	Creates and returns a new dictionary with the elements of `seq` as the keys and `val` as the initial value (defaults to None if not given) for all keys
`dict.get(key,` `default=None)`[a]	For key *key*, returns value or *default* if *key* not in `dict` (note that default's default is None)
`dict.has_key(key)`[e]	Returns True if *key* is in `dict`, False otherwise; partially deprecated by the **in** and **not in** operators in version 2.2 but still provides a functional interface
`dict.items()`	Returns an iterable[g] of the (key, value) tuple pairs of `dict`

Method Name	Operation
dict.iter*[c]()	iteritems(), iterkeys(), itervalues() are all methods that behave the same as their non-iterator counterparts but return an iterator instead of a list
dict.keys()	Returns an iterable[f] of the keys of *dict*
dict.pop[b](*key*[, *default*])	Similar to get() but removes and returns dict[*key*] if key present and raises KeyError if key not in *dict* and *default* not given
dict.setdefault(*key*, *default*=None)[d]	Similar to get() but sets dict[*key*]=*default* if key is not already in dict
dict.update(*dict2*)[a]	Adds the key-value pairs of *dict2* to *dict*
dict.values()	Returns an iterable[f] of the values of *dict*

a. New in Python 1.5.
b. New in Python 2.3.
c. New in Python 2.2.
d. New in Python 2.0.
e. Deprecated in Python 2.2 and removed in Python 3.0; use in, instead.
f. The iterable is a set view starting in Python 3.0 and a list in all previous versions.

Set Types Operators and Built-In Functions

Table B-10 outlines the various operators, functions (built-in and factory), and built-in methods that apply to both set types (set [mutable] and frozenset [immutable]).

Table B-10 Set Type Operators, Functions, and Built-In Methods

Function/Method Name	Operator Equivalent	Description
All Set Types		
len(s)		Set cardinality: number of elements in s
set([*obj*])		Mutable set factory function; if obj given, it must be iterable, new set elements taken from obj; if not, creates an empty set

(Continued)

Table B-10 Set Type Operators, Functions, and Methods *(Continued)*

Function/Method Name	Operator Equivalent	Description
All Set Types		
`frozenset ([`*obj*`])`		Immutable set factory function; operates the same as `set()` except returns immutable set
	obj **in** *s*	Membership test: is *obj* an element of *s*?
	obj **not in** s	Non-membership test: is *obj* not an element of *s*?
	s == *t*	Equality test: do *s* and *t* have exactly the same elements?
	s != *t*	Inequality test: opposite of ==
	s < *t*	(Strict) subset test; s != *t* and all elements of *s* are members of *t*
`s.issubset(`*t*`)`	*s* <= *t*	Subset test (allows improper subsets): all elements of s are members of t
	s > *t*	(Strict) superset test: s != **t** and all elements of *t* are members of *s*
`s.issuperset(`*t*`)`	*s* >= *t*	Superset test (allows improper supersets): all elements of t are members of *s*
`s.union(`*t*`)`	*s* | *t*	Union operation: elements in *s* or *t*
`s.intersection(`*t*`)`	**s** & *t*	Intersection operation: elements in *s* and *t*
`s.difference(`*t*`)`	*s* - *t*	Difference operation: elements in *s* that are not elements of *t*
`s.symmetric_difference(`*t*`)`	*s* ∧ *t*	Symmetric difference operation: elements of either *s* or *t* but not both
`s.copy()`		Copy operation: return (shallow) copy of *s*

Function/Method Name	Operator Equivalent	Description
Mutable Sets Only		
`s.update(t)`	`s |= t`	(Union) update operation: members of *t* added to *s*
`s.intersection_update(t)`	`s &= t`	Intersection update operation: *s* only contains members of the original *s* and *t*
`s.difference_update(t)`	`s -= t`	Difference update operation: *s* only contains original members who are not in *t*
`s.symmetric_difference_update(t)`	`s ^= t`	Symmetric difference update operation: *s* only contains members of *s* or *t* but not both
`s.add(obj)`		Add operation: add *obj* to *s*
`s.remove(obj)`		Remove operation: remove *obj* from *s*; Key-Error raised if *obj* not in *s*
`s.discard(obj)`		Discard operation: friendlier version of remove()—remove *obj* from s if *obj* in *s*
`s.pop()`		Pop operation: remove and return an arbitrary element of *s*
`s.clear()`		Clear operation: remove all elements of *s*

File Object Methods and Data Attributes

Table B-11 lists the built-in methods and data attributes of file objects.

Table B-11 Methods for File Objects

File Object Attribute	Description
`file.close()`	Closes *file*
`file.fileno()`	Returns integer file descriptor (FD) for *file*
`file.flush()`	Flushes internal buffer for *file*
`file.isatty()`	Returns True if *file* is a tty-like device, and False otherwise
`file.next`[a]`()`	Returns the next line in the file [similar to `file.readline()`] or raises `StopIteration` if no more lines are available
`file.read(size=-1)`	Reads *size* bytes of file, or all remaining bytes if *size* not given or is negative, as a string and return it
`file.readinto`[b]`(buf, size)`	Reads *size* bytes from *file* into buffer *buf* (unsupported)
`file.readline(size=-1)`	Reads and returns one line from *file* (includes line-ending characters), either one full line or a maximum of *size* characters
`file.readlines(sizhint=0)`	Reads and returns all lines from *file* as a list (includes all line termination characters); if *sizhint* given and > 0, whole lines are returned consisting of approximately *sizhint* bytes (could be rounded up to next buffer's worth)
`file.xreadlines`[c]`()`	Meant for iteration, returns lines in *file* read as chunks in a more efficient way than `readlines()`

File Object Attribute	Description
`file.seek(off, whence=0)`	Moves to a location within *file*, *off* bytes offset from *whence* (0 == beginning of file, 1 == current location, or 2 == end of file)
`file.tell()`	Returns current location within *file*
`file.truncate(size=file.tell())`	Truncates *file* to at most *size* bytes, the default being the current file location
`file.write(str)`	Writes string *str* to *file*
`file.writelines(seq)`	Writes *seq* of strings to *file*; *seq* should be an iterable producing strings; prior to version 2.2, it was just a list of strings
`file.closed`	True if *file* is closed, and False otherwise
`file.encoding`[d]	Encoding that this file uses—when Unicode strings are written to file, they will be converted to byte strings using `file.encoding`; a value of None indicates that the system default encoding for converting Unicode strings should be used
`file.mode`	Access mode with which *file* was opened
`file.name`	Name of *file*
`file.newlines`[d]	None if no line separators have been read, a string consisting of one type of line separator, or a tuple containing all types of line termination characters read so far
`file.softspace`	0 if space explicitly required with print, 1 otherwise; rarely used by the programmer—generally for internal use only

a. New in Python 2.2.
b. New in Python 1.5.2 but unsupported.
c. New in Python 2.1 but deprecated in Python 2.3.
d. New in Python 2.3.

Python Exceptions

Table B-12 lists exceptions in Python.

Table B-12 Python Built-In Exceptions

Exception Name	Description
BaseException[a]	Root class for all exceptions
SystemExit[b]	Request termination of Python interpreter
KeyboardInterrupt[c]	User interrupted execution (usually by pressing Ctrl+C)
Exception[d]	Root class for regular exceptions
StopIteration[e]	Iteration has no further values
GeneratorExit[a]	Exception sent to generator to tell it to quit
SystemExit[f]	Request termination of Python interpreter
StandardError[d]	Base class for all standard built-in exceptions
ArithmeticError[d]	Base class for all numeric calculation errors
FloatingPointError[d]	Error in floating point calculation
OverflowError	Calculation exceeded maximum limit for numerical type
ZeroDivisionError	Division (or modulus) by zero error (all numeric types)
AssertionError[d]	Failure of **assert** statement
AttributeError	No such object attribute
EOFError	End-of-file marker reached without input from built-in
EnvironmentError	Base class for operating system environment errors

Exception Name	Description
IOError	Failure of input/output operation
OSError	Operating system error
WindowsError	MS Windows system call failure
ImportError	Failure to import module or object
KeyboardInterrupt[f]	User interrupted execution (usually by pressing Ctrl+C)
LookupError[d]	Base class for invalid data lookup errors
IndexError	No such index in sequence
KeyError	No such key in mapping
MemoryError	Out-of-memory error (non-fatal to Python interpreter)
NameError	Undeclared/uninitialized object (non-attribute)
UnboundLocalError	Access of an uninitialized local variable
ReferenceError	Weak reference tried to access a garbage-collected object
RuntimeError	Generic default error during execution
NotImplementedError	Unimplemented method
SyntaxError	Error in Python syntax
IndentationError	Improper indentation
TabError[g]	Improper mixture of TABs and spaces
SystemError	Generic interpreter system error
TypeError	Invalid operation for type

(Continued)

Table B-12 Python Built-In Exceptions *(Continued)*

Exception Name	Description
ValueError	Invalid argument given
UnicodeErrorh	Unicode-related error
UnicodeDecodeError	Unicode error during decoding
UnicodeEncodeError	Unicode error during encoding
UnicodeTranslate Errori	Unicode error during translation
Warningj	Root class for all warnings
DeprecationWarningj	Warning about deprecated features
FutureWarningi	Warning about constructs that will change semantically in the future
OverflowWarningk	Old warning for auto-long upgrade
PendingDeprecation Warningi	Warning about features that will be deprecated in the future
RuntimeWarningj	Warning about dubious runtime behavior
SyntaxWarningj	Warning about dubious syntax
UserWarningj	Warning generated by user code

a. New in Python 2.5.
b. Prior to Python 2.5, SystemExit subclassed Exception.
c. Prior to Python 2.5, KeyboardInterrupt subclassed StandardError.
d. New in Python 1.5, the release when class-based exceptions replaced strings.
e. New in Python 2.2.
f. Only for Python 1.5 through 2.4.x.
g. New in Python 2.0.
h. New in Python 1.6.
i. New in Python 2.3.
j. New in Python 2.1.
k. New in Python 2.2 but removed in Python 2.4.

Special Methods for Classes

Table B-13 represents the set of special methods that can be implemented to allow user-defined objects to take on behaviors and functionality of Python standard types.

Table B-13 Special Methods for Customizing Classes

Special Method	Description
Basic Customization	
`C.__init__(self[, arg1, ...])`	Constructor (with any optional arguments)
`C.__new__(self[, arg1, ...])`[a]	Constructor (with any optional arguments); usually used for setting up subclassing of immutable data types
`C.__del__(self)`	Destructor
`C.__str__(self)`	Printable string representation; `str()` built-in and **print** statement
`C.__repr__(self)`	Evaluatable string representation; `repr()` built-in and `''` operator
`C.__unicode__(self)`[b]	Unicode string representation; `unicode()` built-in
`C.__call__(self, *args)`	Denote callable instances
`C.__nonzero__(self)`	Define `False` value for object; `bool()` built-in (as of version 2.2)
`C.__len__(self)`	"Length" (appropriate for class); `len()` built-in

(Continued)

Table B-13 Special Methods for Customizing Classes *(Continued)*

Special Method	Description
***Object (Value) Comparison*[c]**	
*C.*__cmp__*(self, obj)*	Object comparison; cmp() built-in
*C.*__lt__*(self, obj)* and *C.*__le__*(self, obj)*	Less than/less than or equal to; < and <= operators
*C.*__gt__*(self, obj)* and *C.*__ge__*(self, obj)*	Greater than/greater than or equal to; > and >= operators
*C.*__eq__*(self, obj)* and *C.*__ne__*(self, obj)*	Equal/not equal to; ==, != and <> operators
Attributes	
*C.*__getattr__*(self, attr)*	Get attribute; getattr() built-in
*C.*__setattr__*(self, attr, val)*	Set attribute; setattr() built-in
*C.*__delattr__*(self, attr)*	Delete attribute; **del** statement
*C.*__getattribute__*(self, attr)*[a]	Get attribute; getattr() built-in
*C.*__get__*(self, attr)*	Get attribute; getattr() built-in
*C.*__set__*(self, attr, val)*	Set attribute; setattr() built-in
*C.*__delete__*(self, attr)*	Delete attribute; **del** statement
Customizing Classes/Emulating Types	
Numeric Types: binary operators[d]	
*C.*__*add__*(self, obj)*	Addition; + operator
*C.*__*sub__*(self, obj)*	Subtraction; - operator
*C.*__*mul__*(self, obj)*	Multiplication; * operator
*C.*__*div__*(self, obj)*	Division; / operator
*C.*__*truediv__*(self, obj)*[f]	True division; / operator
*C.*__*floordiv__*(self, obj)*[e]	Floor division; // operator

Special Method	Description
Customizing Classes/Emulating Types	
Numeric Types: binary operators[d]	
`C.__*mod__(self, obj)`	Modulo/remainder; % operator
`C.__*divmod__(self, obj)`	Division and modulo; `divmod()` built-in
`C.__*pow__(self, obj[, mod])`	Exponentiation; `pow()` built-in; ** operator
`C.__*lshift__(self, obj)`	Left shift; << operator
`C.__*rshift__(self, obj)`	Right shift; >> operator
`C.__*and__(self, obj)`	Bitwise AND; & operator
`C.__*or__(self, obj)`	Bitwise OR; | operator
`C.__*xor__(self, obj)`	Bitwise XOR; ^ operator
Numeric Types: unary operators	
`C.__neg__(self)`	Unary negation
`C.__pos__(self)`	Unary no-change
Numeric Types: unary operators	
`C.__abs__(self)`	Absolute value; `abs()` built-in
`C.__invert__(self)`	Bit inversion; ~ operator
Numeric Types: numeric conversion	
`C.__complex__(self, com)`	Convert to complex; `complex()` built-in
`C.__int__(self)`	Convert to int; `int()` built-in
`C.__long__(self)`	Convert to long; `long()` built-in
`C.__float__(self)`	Convert to float; `float()` built-in

(Continued)

Table B-13 Special Methods for Customizing Classes *(Continued)*

Special Method	Description
Customizing Classes/Emulating Types	
Numeric Types: base representation (string)	
`C.__oct__(`*self*`)`	Octal representation; `oct()` built-in
`C.__hex__(`*self*`)`	Hexadecimal representation; `hex()` built-in
Numeric Types: numeric coercion	
`C.__coerce__(`*self, num*`)`	Coerce to same numeric type; `coerce()` built-in
Sequence Types[d]	
`C.__len__(`*self*`)`	Number of items in sequence
`C.__getitem__(`*self, ind*`)`	Get single sequence element
`C.__setitem__(self, `*ind*`, val)`	Set single sequence element
`C.__delitem__(`*self, ind*`)`	Delete single sequence element
`C.__getslice__(`*self, ind1, ind2*`)`	Get sequence slice
`C.__setslice__(`*self, i1, i2, val*`)`	Get sequence slice
`C.__delslice__(`*self, ind1, ind2*`)`	Delete sequence slice
`C.__contains__(`*self, val*`)`[f]	Test sequence membership; **in** keyword
`C.__*add__(`*self, obj*`)`	Concatenation; + operator
`C.__*mul__(`*self, obj*`)`	Repetition; * operator
`C.__iter__(`*self*`)`[e]	Create iterator class; `iter()` built-in
Mapping Types	
`C.__len__(`*self*`)`	Number of items in mapping
`C.__hash__(`*self*`)`	Hash function value

Special Method	Description
Customizing Classes/Emulating Types	
Mapping Types	
C.__getitem__(*self, key*)	Get value with given key
C.__setitem__(*self, key, val*)	Set value with given key
C.__delitem__(*self, key*)	Delete value with given key

a. New in Python 2.2; for use with new-style classes only.
b. New in Python 2.3.
c. All except cmp() new in Python 2.1.
d. "*" either nothing (self OP obj), "r" (obj OP self), or "i" for in-place operation (new in Python 2.0), i.e., __add__, __radd__, or __iadd__.
e. New in Python 2.2.
f. New in Python 1.6.

Python Operator Summary

Table B-14 represents the complete set of Python operators and to which standard types they apply. The operators are sorted from highest-to-lowest precedence, with those sharing the same shaded group having the same priority.

Table B-14 Python Operators († - unary)

Operator[a]	int[b]	long	float	complex	str	list	tuple	dict	set, frozenset[c]
[]					•	•	•		
[:]					•	•	•		
**	•	•	•	•					
+†	•	•	•	•					
-†	•	•	•	•					

(Continued)

Table B-14 Python Operators († - unary) *(Continued)*

Operator[a]	int[b]	long	float	complex	str	list	tuple	dict	set, frozenset[c]
~†	•	•							
*	•	•	•	•	•	•	•		
/	•	•	•	•					
//	•	•	•	•					
%	•	•	•	•	•				
+	•	•	•	•	•	•	•		
-	•	•	•	•					•
<<	•	•							
>>	•	•							
&	•	•							•
^	•	•							•
|	•	•							•
<	•	•	•	•	•	•	•	•	•
>	•	•	•	•	•	•	•	•	•
<=	•	•	•	•	•	•	•	•	•
>=	•	•	•	•	•	•	•	•	•
==	•	•	•	•	•	•	•	•	•
!=	•	•	•	•	•	•	•	•	•
<>	•	•	•	•	•	•	•	•	•
is	•	•	•	•	•	•	•	•	•
is not	•	•	•	•	•	•	•	•	•
in					•	•	•		•

Operator[a]	int[b]	long	float	complex	str	list	tuple	dict	set, frozenset[c]
not in					•	•	•		•
not†	•	•	•	•	•	•	•	•	•
and	•	•	•	•	•	•	•	•	•
or	•	•	•	•	•	•	•	•	•

a. Can also include corresponding augmented assignment operators.
b. Operations involving Boolean types will be performed on the operands as ints.f.
c. (Both) set types new in Python 2.4.

APPENDIX C

Python 3: The Evolution of a Programming Language

Matz (the author of Ruby) has a great quote,
"Open Source needs to move or die."
—Guido van Rossum, March 2008
(verbally at PyCon conference)

P ython 3 represents an evolution of the language such that it will not execute most older code that was written against the version 2.x interpreters. This doesn't mean that you won't recognize the old code any more, or that extensive porting is required to make old code work under version 3.x. In fact, the new syntax is quite similar to that of the past. However, when the **print** statement no longer exists, it makes it easy to disrupt the old code. In this appendix, we discuss **print** and other version 3.x changes, and we shed some light on the required evolution that Python must undergo to be better than it was before. Finally, we present a few migration tools that might help you to make this transition.

C.1   Why Is Python Changing?

Python is currently undergoing its most significant transformation since it was released in the early 1990s. Even the revision change from 1.x to 2.x in 2000 was relatively mild—Python 2.0 ran 1.5.2 software just fine. One of the main reasons for Python's stability over the years has been the steadfast determination of the core development team to preserve backward compatibility. Over the years, however, certain "sticky" flaws (issues that hang around from release to release) were identified by creator Guido van Rossum, Andrew Kuchling, and other users (refer to the references section at the end of this appendix for links to relevant articles). Their persistence made it clear that a release with hard changes was needed to ensure that the language evolved. The 3.0 release in 2008 marked the first time that a Python interpreter has been released that deliberately breaks the tenets of backward compatibility.

C.2   What Has Changed?

The changes in Python 3 are not mind-boggling—it's not as if you'll no longer recognize Python. The remainder of this appendix provides an overview of some of the major changes:

- `print` becomes `print()`.
- Strings are cast into Unicode by default.
- There is a single class type.
- The syntax for exceptions has been updated.
- Integers have been updated.
- Iterables are used everywhere.

C.2.1   `print` Becomes `print()`

The switch to `print()` is the change that breaks the greatest amount of existing Python code. Why is Python changing from a statement to a built-in function (BIF)? Having `print` as a statement is limiting in many regards, as detailed by Guido in his "Python Regrets" talk, in which he outlined what he feels are shortcomings of the language. In addition, having `print` as a statement limits improvements to it. However, when `print()` is available as a function, new keyword parameters can be added, certain standard behaviors can be overridden with keyword parameters, and `print()` can be replaced if desired, just like any other BIF. Here are before-and-after examples:

Python 2.x

```
>>> i = 1
>>> print 'Python' 'is', 'number', i
Pythonis number 1
```

Python 3.x

```
>>> i = 1
>>> print('Python' 'is', 'number', i)
Pythonis number 1
```

The omission of a comma between `'Python'` and `'is'` is deliberate; it was done to show you that direct string literal concatenation has not changed. You can see more examples in the "What's New in Python 3.0" document (refer to the references section at the end of this appendix). You can find additional information about this change in PEP 3105.

C.2.2   Strings: Unicode by Default

The next "gotcha" that current Python users face is that strings are now Unicode by default. This change couldn't have come soon enough. Not a day goes by that countless Python developers don't run into a problem when dealing with Unicode and regular ASCII strings that looks something like this:

```
UnicodeEncodeError: 'ascii' codec can't encode character
u'\xae' in position 0: ordinal not in range(128)
```

These types of errors will no longer be an everyday occurrence in 3.x. For more information on using Unicode in Python, see the Unicode HOWTO document (refer to the References section at the end of this appendix for the Web address). With the model adopted by the new version of Python, users shouldn't even use the terms Unicode and ASCII/non-Unicode strings anymore. The "What's New in Python 3.0" document sums up this new model pretty explicitly.

Python 3 uses the concepts of *text* and (binary) *data* instead of Unicode strings and 8-bit strings. All text is Unicode; however, encoded Unicode is represented as binary data. The type used to hold text is `str`, and the type used to hold data is `bytes`.

With regard to syntax, because Unicode is now the default, the leading u or U is deprecated. Similarly, the new `bytes` objects require a leading b or B for *its* literals (more information can be found in PEP 3112).

Table C-1 compares the various string types, showing how they will change from version 2.x to 3.x. The table also includes a mention of the new mutable `bytearray` type.

Table C-1   Strings in Python 2 and 3

Python 2	Python 3	Mutable?
`str ("")`	`bytes (b"")`	no
`unicode (u"")`	`str ("")`	no
N/A	`bytearray`	yes

C.2.3   Single Class Type

Prior to Python 2.2, Python's objects didn't behave like classes in other languages: classes were "class" objects and instances were "instance" objects. This is in stark contrast to what people perceive as normal: classes are types and instances are objects of such types. Because of this "flaw," you could not subclass data types and modify them. In Python 2.2, the core development team came up with *new-style classes*, which act more like what people expect. Furthermore, this change meant that regular Python types could be subclassed—a change described in Guido's "Unifying Types and Classes in Python 2.2" essay. Python 3 supports only new-style classes.

C.2.4   Updated Syntax for Exceptions

Exception Handling

In the past, the syntax to catch an exception and the exception argument/instance had the following form:

```
except ValueError, e:
```

To catch multiple exceptions with the same handler, the following syntax was used:

```
except (ValueError, TypeError), e:
```

The required parentheses confused some users, who often attempted to write invalid code looking like this:

```
except ValueError, TypeError, e:
```

The (new) **as** keyword is intended to ensure that you do not become confused by the comma in the original syntax; however, the parentheses are still required when you're trying to catch more than one type of exception using the same handler. Here are two equivalent examples of the new syntax that demonstrate this change:

```
except ValueError as e:
```

```
except (ValueError, TypeError) as e:
```

The remaining version 2.x releases beginning with 2.6 accept both forms when creating exception handlers, thereby facilitating the porting process. You can find more information about this change in PEP 3110.

Raising Exceptions

The most popular syntax for raising exceptions in Python 2.x is as follows:

```
raise ValueError, e
```

To truly emphasize that you are creating an instance of an exception, the only syntax supported in Python 3.x is the following:

```
raise ValueError(e)
```

This syntax really isn't new at all. It was introduced over a decade ago in Python 1.5 (yes, you read that correctly) when exceptions changed from strings to classes, and we're sure you'll agree that the syntax for class instantiation looks a lot more like the latter than the former.

C.2.5   Updates to Integers

Single Integer Type

Python's two different integer types, int and long, began their unification in Python 2.2. That change is now almost complete, with the new int behaving like a long. As a consequence, OverflowError exceptions no longer occur when you exceed the native integer size, and the trailing L has been dropped. This change is outlined in PEP 237. long still exists in Python 2.x but has disappeared in Python 3.0.

Changes to Division

The current division operator (/) doesn't give the expected answer for those users who are new to programming, so it has been changed to do so. If this change has brought any controversy, it is simply that programmers are used to the floor division functionality. To see how the confusion arises, try to convince a programming newbie that 1 divided by 2 is 0 (1 / 2 == 0). The simplest way to describe this change is with examples. Following are some excerpted from "Keeping Up with Python: The 2.2 Release," found in the July 2002 issue of *Linux Journal.* You can also find out more about this update in PEP 238.

Classic Division

The default Python 2.x division operation works this way: given two integer operands, / performs integer floor division (truncates the fraction as in the earlier example). If there is at least one float involved, true division occurs:

```
>>> 1 / 2          # floor
0
>>> 1.0 / 2.0      # true
0.5
```

True Division

In Python 3.x, given any two numeric operands, / will always return a float:

```
>>> 1 / 2          # true
0.5
>>> 1.0 / 2.0      # true
0.5
```

To try true division starting in Python 2.2, you can either import `division` from __future__ or use the -Qnew switch.

Floor Division

The double-slash division operator (//) was added in Python 2.2 to always perform floor division, regardless of operand type, and to begin the transition process:

```
>>> 1 // 2        # floor
0
>>> 1.0 // 2.0    # floor
0.0
```

Binary and Octal Literals

The minor integer literal changes were added in Python 2.6+ to make literal nondecimal (hexadecimal, octal, and new binary) formats consistent. Hex representation stayed the same, with its leading 0x or 0X (where the octal had formerly led with a single 0). This format proved confusing to some users, so it has been changed to 0o for consistency. Instead of 0177, you must now use 0o177. Finally, the new binary literal lets you provide the bits of an integer value, prefixed with a leading 0b, as in 0b0110. Python 3 does not accept 0177. You can find more information on integer literals updates in PEP 3127.

C.2.6   Iterables Everywhere

Another theme inherent to version 3.x is memory conservation. Using iterators is much more efficient than maintaining entire lists in memory, especially when the target action on the objects in question is iteration. There's no need to waste memory when it's not necessary. Thus, in Python 3, code that returned lists in earlier versions of the language no longer does so.

For example, the functions map(), filter(), range(), and zip(), plus the dictionary methods keys(), items(), and values(), all return some sort of iterator. Yes, this syntax can be more inconvenient if you want to glance at your data, but it's better in terms of resource consumption. The changes are mostly under the hood—if you only use the functions' return values to iterate over, you won't notice a thing.

C.3   Migration Tools

As you have seen, most of the Python 3.x changes do not represent some wild mutation of the familiar Python syntax. Instead, the changes are just enough to break the old code base. Of course, the changes affect users, so a good transition plan is clearly needed—and most good plans come with good tools or aids to smooth the way. Such tools include (but are not limited to) the following: the 2to3 code converter, the latest Python 2.x release (at least 2.6), and the external (non-standard library) 3to2 tool and six library. We'll cover the first two here and let you investigate the latter pair on your own.

C.3.1   The 2to3 Tool

The 2to3 tool will take Python 2.x code and attempt to generate a working equivalent in Python 3.x. Here are some of the actions it performs:

- Converts a **print** statement to a print() function
- Removes the L long suffix
- Replaces <> with !=
- Changes single backquoted strings ('...') to repr(...)

This tool does a lot of the manual labor—but not everything; the rest is up to you. You can read more about porting suggestions and the 2to3 tool in the "What's New in Python 3.0" document as well as at the tool's Web page (http://docs.python.org/3.0/library/2to3.html). In Appendix D, "Python 3 Migration with 2.6+," we'll also briefly mention a companion tool named 3to2.

C.3.2   Python 2.6+

Because of the compatibility issue, the releases of Python that lead up to 3.0 play a much more significant role in the transition. Of particular note is Python 2.6, the first and most pivotal of such releases. For users, it represents the first time that they can start coding against the version 3.x family of releases, because many 3.x features have been backported to version 2.x.

Whenever possible, the final version 2.x releases (2.6 and newer) incorporate new features and syntax from version 3.x, while remaining compatible with existing code by not removing older features or syntax. Such features are described in the "What's New in Python 2.x" document for all such releases. We detail some of these migration features in Appendix D.

C.4   Conclusion

Overall, the changes outlined in this appendix do have a high impact in terms of updates required to the interpreter, but they should not radically change the way programmers write their Python code. It's simply a matter of changing old habits, such as using parentheses with print—thus, print(). Once you've gotten these changes under your belt, you're well on your way to being able to effectively jump to the new platform. It can be a bit startling at first, but these changes have been coming for some time. Don't panic: Python 2.x will live on for a long time to come. The transition will be slow, deliberate, pain resistant, and even-keeled. Welcome to the dawn of the next generation!

C.5   References

Andrew Kuchling, "Python Warts," July 2003, http://web.archive.org/web/20070607112039, http://www.amk.ca/python/writing/warts.html

A. M. Kuchling, "What's New in Python 2.6," June 2011 (for 2.6.7), http://docs.python.org/whatsnew/2.6.html.

A. M. Kuchling, "What's New in Python 2.7," December 2011 (for 2.7.2), http://docs.python.org/whatsnew/2.7.html.

Wesley J. Chun, "Keeping Up with Python: The 2.2 Release," July 2002, http://www.linuxjournal.com/article/5597.

PEP Index, http://www.python.org/dev/peps.

"Unicode HOWTO," December 2008, http://docs.python.org/3.0/howto/unicode.html.

Guido van Rossum, "Python Regrets," July 2002, http://www.python.org/doc/essays/ppt/regrets/PythonRegrets.pdf.

Guido van Rossum, "Unifying Types and Classes in Python 2.2," April 2002, http://www.python.org/2.2.3/descrintro.html.

Guido van Rossum, "What's New in Python 3.0," December 2008, http://docs.python.org/3.0/whatsnew/3.0.html.

APPENDIX D

Python 3 Migration with 2.6+

We keep the language evolving... [we] need to move forward or die.
—Yukihiro "Matz" Matsumoto
(まつもとゆきひろ), September 2008
(verbally at Lone Star Ruby conference;
the actual quote Guido was referring to)

D.1 Python 3: The Next Generation

Python is currently undergoing its most significant transformation since it was first released back in the winter of 1991. Python 3 is backward incompatible with all older versions, so porting will be a more significant issue than in the past.

Unlike other end-of-life efforts, however, Python 2.x will not disappear anytime soon. In fact, the remainder of the version 2.x series will be developed in parallel with 3.x, thereby ensuring a smooth transition from the current to next generation. Python 2.6 is the first of these final version 2.x releases.

807

This document reinforces material covered Appendix C, "Python 3: The Evolution of a Programming Language," but goes into more detail when appropriate.

D.1.1   Hybrid 2.6+ as Transition Tool

Python 2.6 and remaining 2.x releases are hybrid interpreters. This means that they can run a considerable amount of version 1.x code, all version 2.x software, and can even run a limited amount of 3.x (code that is native version 3.x but made available in 2.6+). Some will argue that Python releases dating back to version 2.2 have already been mixed interpreters because they support creation of both classic classes as well as new-style classes, but that is as far as they go.

The version 2.6 release is the first version with specific version 3.x features backported to it. The most significant of these features are summarized here:

- Integers
  - Single integer type
  - New binary and modified octal literals
  - Classic or true division
  - The -Q division switch
- Built-in functions
  - **print** or print()
  - reduce()
  - Other updates
- Object-oriented programming
  - Two different class objects
- Strings
  - bytes literals
  - bytes type
- Exceptions
  - Handling exceptions
  - Raising exceptions

- Other transition tools and tips
  - Warnings: the -3 switch
  - 2to3 tool

This appendix does not discuss other new version 2.x features that are stand-alone, meaning they do not have any consequences for porting applications to version 3.x. Thus, without further ado, let's jump right in.

D.2 Integers

Python integers face several changes in version 3.x and beyond, relating to their types, literals, and the integer division operation. We describe each of these changes next, highlighting the role that version 2.6 and newer versions play in terms of migration.

D.2.1   Single Integer Type

Previous versions of Python featured two integer types, int and long. The original ints were limited in size to the architecture of the platform on which the code ran (i.e., 32-bit, 64-bit), whereas longs were unlimited in size except in terms of how much virtual memory the operating system provided. The process of unifying these two types into a single int type began in Python 2.2 and will be complete in version 3.0.[1] The new single int type will be unlimited in size, and the previous L or l designation for longs is removed. You can read more about this change in PEP 237.

As of version 2.6, there is little trace of long integers, save for the support of the trailing L. It is included for backward-compatibility purposes, to support all code that uses longs. Nevertheless, users should be actively purging long integers from their existing code and should no longer use longs in any new code written against Python 2.6+.

---

1. The bool type also might be considered part of this equation, because bools behave like 0 and 1 in numerical situations rather than having their natural values of False and True, respectively.

D.2.2   New Binary and Modified Octal Literals

Python 3 features a minor revision to the alternative base format for integers. It has basically streamlined the syntax to make it consistent with the existing hexadecimal format, prefixed with a leading 0x (or 0X for capital letters)—for example, 0x80, 0xffff, 0xDEADBEEF.

A new binary literal lets you provide the bits to an integer number, prefixed with a leading 0b (e.g., 0b0110). The original octal representation began with a single 0, but this format proved confusing to some users, so it has been changed to 0o to bring it in line with hexadecimal and binary literals, as just described. In other words, 0177 is no longer allowed; you must use 0o177, instead. Here are some examples:

Python 2.x

```
>>> 0177
127
```

Python 3 (including 2.6+)

```
>>> 0o177
127
>>> 0b0110
6
```

Both the new binary and modified octal literal formats have been backported to version 2.6 to help with migration. In fact, version 2.6 and newer, in their role as transition tools, accept *both* octal formats, whereas no version 3.x release accepts the old 0177 format. You can find more information on the updates to integer literals in PEP 3127.

D.2.3   Classic or True Division

A change that has been a long time coming, yet remains controversial to many, is the change to the division operator (/). The traditional division operation works in the following way: given two integer operands, / performs integer floor division. If there is at least one float involved, true division occurs:

Python 2.x: Classic Division

```
>>> 1 / 2           # floor
0
>>> 1.0 / 2.0       # true
0.5
>>> 1.0 / 2         # true (2 is internally coerced to float)
0.5
```

In Python 3, the / operator will always return a float, regardless of operand type.

Python 3.x: True Division

```
>>> 1 / 2          # true
0.5
>>> 1.0 / 2        # true
0.5
```

The double-slash division operator (//) was added as a proxy in Python 2.2 to always perform floor division, regardless of the operand type and to begin the transition process.

Python 2.2+ and 3.x: Floor Division

```
>>> 1 // 2         # floor
0
>>> 1.0 // 2       # floor
0.0
```

Using // will be the only way to obtain floor division functionality in version 3.x. To try true division in Python 2.2+, you can add the line from __future__ import division to your code, or use the -Q command-line option (discussed next).

Python 2.2+: Division Command-Line Option

If you do not wish to import division from __future__ module in your code, but you want true division to always prevail, you can use the -Qnew switch. There are also other options for using -Q, as summarized in Table D-1.

Table D-1 Division Operation -Q Command-Line Options

Option	Description
old	Always perform classic division
new	Always perform true division
warn	Warn against int/int and long/long operations
warnall	Warn against all use of /

For example, the -Qwarnall option is used in the Tools/scripts/fixdiv.py script found in the Python source distribution.

As you might have guessed by now, all of the transition efforts have already been implemented in Python 2.2, and no specific additional functionality as far as this command-line has been added to versions 2.6 or 2.7 with respect to Python 3 migration. Table D-2 summarizes the division operators and their functionality in the various Python releases.

Table D-2 Python Default Division Operator Functionality by Release

Operator	2.1-	2.2+	3.x[a]
/	Classic	Classic	True
//	Not applicable	Floor	Floor

a. The "3.x" column also applies to Python 2.2+ with -Qnew or the __future__.division import.

You can read more about the change to the division operator in PEP 238 as well as in an article titled "Keeping Up with Python: The 2.2 Release" that I wrote for *Linux Journal* in July 2002.

D.3 Built-In Functions

D.3.1   The print Statement or print() Function

It's no secret that one of the most common causes of breakage between Python 2.x and 3.x applications is the change in the **print** statement, which becomes a built-in function (BIF) in version 3.x. This change allows print() to be more flexible, upgradeable, and swappable, if desired.

Python 2.6 and newer support either the **print** statement or the print() BIF. The default is the former usage, as it should be in a version 2.x language. To discard the **print** statement and go with only the function in a "Python 3 mode" application, you would simply import print_function from __future__:

```
>>> print 'foo', 'bar'
foo bar
>>>
>>> from __future__ import print_function
```

```
>>> print
<built-in function print>
>>> print('foo', 'bar')
foo bar
>>> print('foo', 'bar', sep='-')
foo-bar
```

The preceding example demonstrates the power of print() as a function. Using the **print** statement, we display the strings foo and bar to the user, but we cannot change the default delimiter or separator between strings, which is a space. In contrast, print() makes this functionality available in its call as the argument sep, which replaces the default—and allows **print** to evolve and progress.

Note that this is a one-way import, meaning that there is no way to revert print() to a statement. Even issuing a "del print_function" will not have any effect. This major change is detailed in PEP 3105.

D.3.2   reduce() Moved to functools Module

In Python 3.x, the reduce() function has been demoted (much to the chagrin of many Python functional programmers) from being a BIF to functools module function, beginning in version 2.6.

```
>>> from operator import add
>>> reduce(add, range(5))
10
>>>
>>> import functools
>>> functools.reduce(add, range(5))
10
```

D.3.3   Other Updates

One key theme in Python 3.x is the migration to greater use of iterators, especially for BIF and methods that have historically returned lists. Still other iterators are changing because of the updates to integers. The following are the most high-profile BIFs, changed in Python 3.x:

- range()
- zip()
- map()
- filter()
- hex()
- oct()

Starting in Python 2.6, programmers can access the new and updated functions by importing the `future_builtins` module. Here is an example that demonstrates both the old and new `oct()` and `zip()` functions:

```
>>> oct(87)
'0127'
>>>
>>> zip(range(4), 'abcd')
[(0, 'a'), (1, 'b'), (2, 'c'), (3, 'd')]
>>> dict(zip(range(4), 'abcd'))
{0: 'a', 1: 'b', 2: 'c', 3: 'd'}
>>>
>>> import future_builtins
>>> future_builtins.oct(87)
'0o127'
>>>
>>> future_builtins.zip(range(4), 'abcd')
<itertools.izip object at 0x374080>
>>> dict(future_builtins.zip(range(4), 'abcd'))
{0: 'a', 1: 'b', 2: 'c', 3: 'd'}
```

If you want to use only the Python 3.x versions of these functions in your current Python 2.x environment, you can override the old ones by importing all the new functions into your namespace. The following example demonstrates this process with `oct()`:

```
>>> from future_builtins import *
>>> oct(87)
'0o127'
```

D.4 Object-Oriented Programming: Two Different Class Objects

Python's original classes are now called *classic classes*. They had many flaws and were eventually replaced by *new-style* classes. The transition began in Python 2.2 and continues today.

Classic classes use the following syntax:

```
class ClassicClass:
    pass
```

New-style classes use this syntax:

```
class NewStyleClass(object):
    pass
```

New-style classes feature so many more advantages than classic classes that the latter have been preserved only for backward-compatibility purposes and are eliminated entirely in Python 3. With new-style classes, types and classes are finally unified (see Guido's "Unifying Types and Classes in Python 2.2" essay as well as PEP 252 and PEP 253).

There are no other changes added in Python 2.6 or newer for migration purposes, unless you count class decorators as a version 3.x feature. Just be aware that all 2.2+ versions serve as hybrid interpreters, allowing for both class objects and instances of those classes. In Python 3, both syntaxes shown in the preceding examples result only in new-style classes being created. This behavior does not pose a serious porting issue, but you do need to be aware that classic classes don't exist in Python 3.

D.5 Strings

One especially notable change in Python 3.x is that the default string type is changing. Python 2.x supports both ASCII and Unicode strings, with ASCII being the default. This support is swapped in Python 3: Unicode becomes the default, and ASCII strings are now called `bytes`. The `bytes` data structure contains byte values and really shouldn't be considered a string (anymore) as much as it is an immutable byte array that contains data.

Current string literals will now require a leading `b` or `B` in Python 3.x, and current Unicode string literals will drop their leading `u` or `U`. The type and BIF names will change from `str` to `bytes` and from `unicode` to `str`. In addition, there is a new mutable "string" type called `bytearray` that, like `bytes`, is also a byte array, only mutable.

You can find out more about using Unicode strings in the HOWTO and learn about the changes coming to string types in PEP 3137. Refer to Table C-1 for a chart on the various string types in both Python 2 and Python 3.

D.5.1 `bytes` Literals

To smooth the way for using `bytes` objects in Python 3.x, you can optionally prepend a regular ASCII/binary string in Python 2.6 with a leading `b` or `B`, thereby creating `bytes` literals (`b''` or `B''`) as synonyms for `str` literals (`''`). The leading indicator has no bearing on any `str` object itself or any of the object's operations (it is purely decorative), but it does prepare you for situations in Python 3 for which you need to create such a literal. You can find out more about `bytes` literals in PEP 3112.

bytes is str

It should not require much of a stretch of the imagination to recognize that if `bytes` literals are supported, then `bytes` objects themselves need to exist in Python 2.6+. Indeed, the `bytes` type is synonymous with `str`, as demonstrated in the following:

```
>>> bytes is str
True
```

Thus, you can use `bytes` or `bytes()` in Python 2.6+ wherever you use `str` or `str()`. Further information on `bytes` objects can be found in PEP 358.

D.6 Exceptions

Python 2.6 and newer version 2.x releases have several features that you can use to port exception handling and raise exceptions in Python 3.x.

D.6.1   Handling Exceptions (Using as)

The syntax in Python 3 for catching and handling a single exception looks like this:

```
except ValueError as e:
```

The e variable contains the instance of the exception that provides the reason why the error was thrown. It is optional, as is the entire **as** e phrase. Thus, this change really applies only to those users who save this value.

The equivalent Python 2 syntax uses a comma instead of the as keyword:

```
except ValueError, e:
```

This change was made in Python 3.x because of the confusion that occurs when programmers attempt to handle more than one exception with the same handler.

To catch multiple exceptions with the same handler, beginners often write this (invalid) code:

```
except ValueError, TypeError, e:
```

In fact, if you are trying to catch more than one exception, you need to use a tuple that contains the exceptions:

```
except (ValueError, TypeError), e:
```

The **as** keyword in Python 3.x (and version 2.6+) is intended to ensure that the comma in the original syntax is no longer a source of confusion. However, the parentheses are still required when you are trying to catch more than one type of exception using the same handler:

```
except (ValueError, TypeError) as e:
```

For porting efforts, Python 2.6 and newer accept either the comma or as when defining exception handlers that save the instance. In contrast; only the idiom with as is permitted in Python 3. You can find more information about this change in PEP 3110.

D.6.2 Raising Exceptions

The change in raising exceptions found in Python 3.x really isn't a change at all; in fact, it doesn't even have anything to do with the transition efforts associated with Python 2.6. The Python 3 syntax for raising exceptions (providing the optional reason for the exception) looks like this:

```
raise ValueError('Invalid value')
```

Long-time Python users have probably been using the following idiom (although both approaches are supported in all version 2.x releases):

```
raise ValueError, 'Invalid value'
```

To emphasize that raising exceptions is equivalent to instantiating an exception class *and* to provide some additional flexibility, Python 3 supports only the first idiom. The good news is that you don't have to wait until you adopt version 2.6 to start using this technique—as we mentioned in Appendix C, this syntax has actually been valid since the Python 1.x days.

D.7 Other Transition Tools and Tips

In addition to Python 2.6, developers have access to an array of tools that can make the transition to Python 3.x go more smoothly—in particular, the -3 switch (which provides obsolescence warnings) and the 2to3 tool (you can read more about it at http://docs.python.org/3.0/library/2to3.html). However, the most important tool that you can "write" is a good transition plan. In fact, there's no substitute for planning.

Clearly, the Python 3.x changes do not represent some wild mutation of the familiar Python syntax. Instead, the variations are just enough to break

the old code base. Of course, the changes will affect users, so a good transition plan is essential. Most good plans come with tools or aids to help you
out in this regard. The porting recommendations in the "What's New in
Python 3.0" document specifically state that good testing of code is critical,
in addition to the use of key tools. Without mincing words, here is *exactly*
what is suggested at http://docs.python.org/3.0/whatsnew/3.0.html#porting-
to-python-3-0:

1. (Prerequisite) Start with excellent test coverage.
2. Port to Python 2.6. This should involve no more work than the
   average port from Python 2.x to Python 2.(x+1). Ensure that
   all your tests pass.
3. (Still using 2.6) Turn on the -3 command-line switch. It
   enables warnings about features that have been removed
   (or changed) in Python 3.0. Run your test suite again, and fix
   any code that generates warnings. Ensure that all your tests
   still pass.
4. Run the 2to3 source-to-source translator over your source
   code tree. Run the result of the translation under Python 3.0.
   Manually fix any remaining issues, and continue fixing problems until all tests pass again.

Another alternative to consider is the 3to2 tool. As you can guess from
its name, it does the opposite of 2to3: it takes Python 3 code and attempts
to deliver a working Python 2 equivalent. This library is maintained by an
external developer and isn't part of the standard library; however, it's an
interesting alternative because it encourages people to code in Python 3 as
their main development tool, and that can't be a bad thing. You can learn
more about 3to2 at http://pypi.python.org/pypi/3to2.

The third alternative is to not port at all; instead, write code that runs on
both 2.x and 3.x (with no changes to the source) to begin with. Is this possible?

D.8 Writing Code That is Compatible in Both Versions 2.x and 3.x

While we're in the crossroads transitioning from Python 2 to 3, you might
wonder whether it is possible to write code that runs without modification
in both Python 2 and 3. It seems like a reasonable request, but how would
you get started? What breaks the most Python 2 code when executed by a
version 3.x interpreter?

D.8.1   print vs. print()

If you think like me, you'd say that the answer to the preceding question is the **print** statement. That's as good a place to start as any, so let's give it a shot. The tricky part is that in version 2.x, it's a statement, thus a keyword or reserved word, whereas in version 3.x, it's just a BIF. In other words, because language syntax is involved, you cannot use **if** statements, and no, Python still doesn't have #ifdef macros!

Let's try just putting parentheses around the arguments to **print**:

```
>>> print('Hello World!')
Hello World!
```

Cool! That works in both Python 2 and Python 3! Are we done? Sorry, not quite.

```
>>> print(10, 20) # Python 2
(10, 20)
```

You're not going to be as lucky this time because the former is a tuple, whereas in Python 3, you're passing in multiple arguments to print():

```
>>> print(10, 20) # Python 3
10 20
```

If you think a bit more, perhaps we can check if **print** is a keyword. You might recall that there is a keyword module that contains a list of keywords. Because **print** won't be a keyword in version 3.x, you might think that it can be as simple as this:

```
>>> import keyword
>>> 'print' in keyword.kwlist
False
```

As a smart programmer, you'd probably try it in version 2.x, expecting a **True** for a response. Although you would be correct, you'd still fail for a different reason:

```
>>> import keyword
>>> if 'print' in keyword.kwlist:
...     from __future__ import print_function
...
  File "<stdin>", line 2
SyntaxError: from __future__ imports must occur at the beginning of
the file
```

One workable solution requires that you use a function that has similar capabilities as **print**. One of them is sys.stdout.write(); another solution is distutils.log.warn(). For whatever reason, we decided to use the latter in many of this book's chapters. I suppose sys.stderr.write() will also work, if unbuffered output is your thing.

The "Hello World!" example would then look like this:

```
# Python 2.x
print 'Hello World!'
# Python 3.x
print('Hello World!')
```

The following line would work in both versions:

```
# Python 2.x & 3.x compatible
from distutils.log import warn as printf
printf('Hello World!')
```

That reminds me of why we didn't use `sys.stdout.write()`; we would need to add a NEWLINE character at the end of the string to match the behavior:

```
# Python 2.x & 3.x compatible
import sys
sys.stdout.write('Hello World!\n')
```

The one real problem isn't this little minor annoyance, but that these functions are no true proxy for **print** or print() for that matter; they only work when you've come up with a single string representing your output. Anything more complex requires more effort on your part.

D.8.2   Import Your Way to a Solution

In other situations, life is a bit easier, and you can just import the correct solution. In the code that follows, we want to import the `urlopen()` function. In Python 2, it resides in `urllib` and `urllib2` (we'll use the latter), and in Python 3, it's been integrated into `urllib.request`. Your solution, which works for both versions 2.x and 3.x, is neat and simple in this case:

```
try:
    from urllib2 import urlopen
except ImportError:
    from urllib.request import urlopen
```

For memory conservation, perhaps you're interested in the iterator (Python 3) version of a well-known built-in such as `zip()`. In Python 2, the iterator version is `itertools.izip()`. This function is renamed to and replaces `zip()` in Python 3. In other words, `itertools.izip()` replaces `zip()` and takes on its name. If you insist on this iterator version, your import statement is also fairly straightforward:

```
try:
    from itertools import izip as zip
except ImportError:
    pass
```

One example, which isn't as elegant looking, is the `StringIO` class. In Python 2, the pure Python version is in the `StringIO` module, meaning you access it via `StringIO.StringIO`. There is also a C version for speed, and that's located at `cStringIO.StringIO`. Depending on your Python installation, you might prefer `cStringIO` first and fallback to `StringIO` if `cStringIO` is not available.

In Python 3, Unicode is the default string type, but if you're doing any kind of networking, it's likely that you'll have to manipulate ASCII/bytes strings instead, so instead of `StringIO`, you'd want `io.BytesIO`. To get what you want, the import is slightly uglier:

```python
try:
    from io import BytesIO as StringIO
except ImportError:
    try:
        from cStringIO import StringIO
    except ImportError:
        from StringIO import StringIO
```

D.8.3 Putting It All Together

If you're lucky, these are all the changes you need to make, and the rest of your code is simpler than the setup at the beginning. If you install the imports of `distutils.log.warn()` [as `printf()`], `url*.urlopen()`, `*.StringIO`, and a normal import of `xml.etree.ElementTree` (2.5 and newer), you can write a very short parser to display the top headline stories from the Google News service with just these roughly eight lines of code:

```python
g = urlopen('http://news.google.com/news?topic=h&output=rss')
f = StringIO(g.read())
g.close()
tree = xml.etree.ElementTree.parse(f)
f.close()
for elmt in tree.getiterator():
    if elmt.tag == 'title' and not \
            elmt.text.startswith('Top Stories'):
        printf('- %s' % elmt.text)
```

This script runs exactly the same under version 2.x and 3.x with no changes to the code whatsoever. Of course, if you're using version 2.4 and older, you'll need to download `ElementTree` separately.

The code snippets in this subsection come from Chapter 14, "Text Processing," so take a look at the `goognewsrss.py` file to see the full version in action.

Some will feel that these changes really start to mess up the elegance of your Python source. After all, readability counts! If you prefer to keep your code cleaner yet still write code that runs in both versions 2.x and 3.x without changes, take a look at the six package.

six is a compatibility library who's primary role is to provide an interface to keep *your* application code the same while hiding the complexities described in this appendix subsection from the developer. To find out more about six, go to http://packages.python.org/six.

Whether you use a library like six or choose to roll your own, we hoped to show in this short narrative that it is possible to write code that runs in both versions 2.x and 3.x. The bottom line is that you might need to sacrifice some of the elegance and simplicity of Python, trading it off for true 2-to-3 portability. I'm sure we'll be revisiting this issue for the next few years until the whole world has completed the transition to the next generation.

D.9 Conclusion

We know big changes are happening in the next generation of Python, simply because version 3.x code is backward incompatible with older releases. The changes, although significant, won't require entirely new ways of thinking for programmers—though there is obvious code breakage. To ease the transition period, current and future releases of the remainder of the version 2.x interpreters will contain version 3.x-backported features.

Python 2.6 is the first of the "dual-mode" interpreters with which you can start programming against the version 3.x code base. Python 2.6 and newer run all version 2.x software as well as understand some version 3.x code. (The current goal is for version 2.7 to be the final 2.x release. To find more information on the fictional Python 2.8 release, go to PEP 404 at http://www.python.org/dev/peps/pep-0404.) In this way, these final version 2.x releases help simplify the porting and migration process and will ease you gently into the next generation of Python programming.

INDEX

Symbols

∧ (carat) symbol
  for matching from start of string, 6, 10
  for negation, 12
? (question mark), in regex, 6, 12–13, 24, 47
. (dot) symbol, in regex, 6, 9, 23
(?:...) notation, 32
(?!...) notation, 33
(?=...) notation, 33
{ } (brace operators), 12
{% %} (percent signs and braces), for Django
    block tags, 529
{% block ... %} tag, 553
{% extends ... %} tag, 554
* (asterisk), in regex, 6, 12–13
** (exponentiation), 771
/ (division operator), 771, 810
  Python 3 changes, 803–804
// (double-slash division operator), 804, 811
// (floor division), 772, 803, 804, 810, 811
\ (backslash) to escape characters to include in
    search, 23
\s special character, for whitespace characters,
    14
& (ampersand), for key-value pairs, 403
# (hash symbol)
  for comment, 32
  for Django comments, 518
% (percent sign)
  for hexadecimal ordinal equivalents, 403
  for modulo, 772
  in string format operator conversion
    symbols, 776
+ (plus sign)
  for encoding, 403
  in regex, 6, 12–13

| (pipe symbol)
  for Django variable tag filters, 528
  in regex, 9
~ (bit inversion), 771
$ (dollar sign), for matching end of string, 6, 10

Numerics

2to3 tool, 187, 407, 805, 817
-3 switch, for Python 3 transition, 817
3to2 tool, 805, 818
500 HTTP error, 445

A

\A special character, for matching start of
    string, 10
abs() function, 770
__abs__() method, 793
AbstractFormatter object, 415
accept() method, 62, 65
access key, for Google+ API, 749
access token secret, for Twitter, 694
access token, for Twitter, 694
acquire() method (lock object), 165, 169, 190,
    193
Active FTP mode, 98, 103
Active Record pattern, 295
active sheet in Excel, 329
activeCount() function (threading module),
    179
active_count() function (threading module),
    179
ActiveMapper, 295
ActiveX, 326
    See also COM (Component Object Model)
      programming
adapter for database. See database adapters
add() function (set types), 785

823

__*add__() method, 792, 794
addition sign (+). *See* + (plus sign)
address families, 58
Admin Console page, adding Appstats UI
   as custom, 671
admin.py file, 559
  to register data models, 580
administration app in Django, 518–527
  setup, 518–519
ADMIN_MEDIA_PREFIX variable, 570
adodbapi, 317
AdvCGI class, 476
advcgi.py CGI application, 468–478
advertising on cloud services, 135
AF_INET sockets, 58
AF_INET6 sockets, 58
AF_LOCAL sockets, 58
AF_NETLINK sockets, 59
AF_TIPC sockets, 59
AF_UNIX sockets, 58
all() method, 298
allocate_lock() function, 165
alphabet, for regular expressions, 5
alphanumeric character class, \w special class
   for, 14
alphanumeric character, matching in regex, 7
alternation (|) operation, in regex, 9
Amazon, 608
  "Conditions of Use" guidelines, 182
Amazon Web Services (AWS), 607
ampersand (&), for key-value pairs, 403
anchors, parsing, 418
and operator, 770
__*and__() method, 793
animalGtk.pyw application, 242–244
animalTtk.pyw application, 245
animalTtk3.pyw application, 246
anonymous FTP login, 96, 102
Apache web server, 428, 446, 479
  Django and, 497
apiclient.discovery.build() function, 755
API_KEY variable for Google+, 755
apilevel attribute (DB-API), 260
APIs (application programming interfaces),
   685
  Google App Engine and, 614–616
  Twitter libraries, 691
App Engine Blobstore, 613
App Engine. *See* Google App Engine
App Identity API, 614
app.yaml file, 628
  for handling inbound e-mail, 658
  for tasks queues, 664
  handler for Appstats, 671
  inbound_services: section, 661
  for remote API shell, 654
append() function, 772
append() method (list), 781
appengine_config.py file, 671

"application/x-www-form-urlencoded", 466
applications
  event-driven, 80
  Google hosting of, 605
  recording events from, 671
  uploading to Google, 629
  visibility on desktop, 330
apps in Django, 501
  creating, 566
AppScale back-end system, 676
Appstats, 614, 670
  handler for, 671
APSW, 317
archive() view function, 543
arguments, default for widgets, 221
ArithmeticError, 788
arraysize attribute (DB-API Cursor object), 265
article() method (NNTP object), 107
as keyword, 802, 816
ASCII strings
  regular expression with, 188
  vs. Unicode, 800–801, 815
ASCII symbols, vs. regular expression special
   characters, 34
assertEqual() method, 555
AssertionError, 788
asterisk (*), in regex, 6, 12–13
async* module, 88
asynchat module, 88
asyncore module, 88
atexit.register() function, 183, 185, 195
_atexit() function, registering, 195
attachment to e-mail, 131
AttributeError exceptions, 21, 788
authentication, 487
  in Django, 574, 595
  federated, 653
  in Google, 755
  with Google Accounts, 652
  in Google App Engine, 574
  SMTP, 118
  for Twitter account, 694
  urllib2 HTTP example, 405–407
  vs. authorization, 569
authentication header, base64-encoded, in
   HTTP request, 406
authorization
  vs. authentication, 569
  with Twitter, 694
auto_now_add feature, in Django, 578

B
\B special character, for word boundary
   matches, 10
\b special character, for word boundary
   matches, 10
backbone, 395
backend server, 394
Backends service/API, 614

background color of button, argument for, 227
backslash (\) to escape characters to include in
        search, 23
backward compatibility, 799
Barrier object (threading module), 170
base (Web) server, 429
base representation, 794
base64 module, 147
base64-encoded authentication header, in
        HTTP request, 406
BaseException, 788
BaseHTTPRequestHandler class, 429, 430, 447
BaseHTTPServer class, 430, 432, 489
BaseHTTPServer module, 429, 435
BaseRequestHandler class (SocketServer
        module), 79
BaseServer class (SocketServer module), 79
BeautifulSoup package, 185, 418, 421, 422, 424,
        435, 489
BeautifulSoup.BeautifulSoup class
        importing, 427
Beazley, David, 384
beginning of string, matching from, 10
Berkeley sockets, 58
Bigtable, 610, 635
bin() function, 770
binary literals, 804, 810
binary operators, 792, 793
BINARY type object (DB-API), 267
Binary type object (DB-API), 267
binascii module, 147
bind() method, 62, 67, 74
binding, 233
binhex module, 147
Bissex, Paul, *Python Web Development with
        Django*, 496
bit inversion (~), 771
bitwise operators, 772
blacklist section, in dos.yaml file, 675
blank lines, in newsgroup article, 113
Blobstore, 614
    resources, 676
block tags in Django, 529
blocking-oriented socket methods, 63
blog application
    admin.py file, 559
    code review, 557–563
    from Google App Engine, 631–647
        adding datastore service, 635–638
        adding form, 633–635
        iterative improvements, 640
        plain text conversion to HTML, 632
    manage.py to create, 507
    models.py file, 558
    reverse-chronological order for, 537
    summary, 563
    template file, 562
    URL pattern creation, 529–533
    urls.py file, 557

user interface, 527–537
    view function creation, 533–537
    views.py file, 560
blog.views.archive() function, 561
blog.views.create_blogpost() function, 561
blog/admin.py file, updating with
        BlogPostAdmin class, 525
BlogEntry.post() method, 637
blogging, 690
BlogPostAdmin class, 525
BlogPostForm object, 559
Boa Constructor module, 248
body() method (NNTP object), 107
boilerplate code, 370–377
    include Python header file, 371
    initModule() modules, initializer function,
        376
    PyMethodDef ModuleMethods[] array, 376
    PyObject* Module_func() wrappers,
        371–376
    SWIG and, 384
boilerplate, base server as, 429
bookrank.py script, 182–189
    adding threading, 186–187
    non-threaded version, 182–185
    porting to Python 3, 187–189
bookrank3CF.py script, 208–209
bool type, 809
Boolean operators, 770
borrowed reference, 383
bot, 410
bottle framework, App Engine and, 617, 676
BoundedSemaphore class, 199
BoundedSemaphore object (threading module),
        170
    context manager, 196
BoxSizer widget, 241
bpython, 515
brace operators ({ }), 12
BSD Unix, 58
*BSD, Zip files for App Engine SDK, 620
BSON format, 311
buffer size, for timestamp server, 67
build() function, 754
build_absolute_uri() method, 591
built-in functions in Python 3, 813
__builtins__ module, 285
burstiness rates, for task queues, 663
Button widget, 220, 222
    Label and Scale widgets with, 224–225
    Label widget with, 223
buy() function, 200
bytecode, 19
bytes literals, 815
bytes objects, and string format operator, 409
bytes type, 800, 815

C
C language
    converting data between Python and, 372

C language *(continued)*
    creating application for extension, 368–370
    extensions in, 365
    memory leak, 375
    Python-wrapped version of library, 380–382
caching, 647
    key for, 649
    Memcache in App Engine for, 647–651
    on proxy server, 394
    __call__() method, 791
callable classes, for threads, 175–176
callables
    as deferred tasks, 669
    in Django templates, 528
    WSGI applications defined as, 481
callbacks, 217
    binding event to, 233
callproc() method (DB-API Cursor object), 265
camel capitalization in Twython, 703
candy.py script, 198–200
    porting to Python 3, 201
Canvas widget, 220
Capabilities service/API, 614
capitalize() function, 773
capitalize() method (string), 778
capitalizing name in form, 460
carat (^) symbol
    for matching from start of string, 6, 10
    for negation, 12
Cascading Style Sheets (CSS), 553
C-compiled modules/packages, whitelist, 613
center() method (string), 773, 778
cformat() function, 285, 288
CGI (common gateway interface)
    alternatives, 479–487
        external processes, 480
        server integration, 479
        See also WSGI (Web Server Gateway
            Interface)
    basics, 442–444
    errors, exercise answer, 766
    form encodings specifications, 466
    scalability limitations, 494
CGI applications, 444
    cookies, 466–478
    form and results page generation, 452–456
    form page creation, 448–450
    fully interactive Web sites, 457–463
    multivalued fields, 467
    results page, 450–452
    Unicode with, 464–465
    Web server setup, 446–448
cgi module/package, 433, 445, 488
CGI-capable development server, 432
CGIHTTPRequestHandler class, 429, 447
CGIHTTPServer class, 430, 489
CGIHTTPServer module, 432, 435
    handlers in, 430
cgitb module, 433, 445–446, 488

Channel service/API, 614
    resources, 677
character classes, creating, 24
character sets
    negation of matches, 14
    special characters for, 14
characters
    escaping to include in search, 23
    hexadecimal ordinal equivalents of
        disallowed, 403
    matching any single, 6, 23
    non-ASCII, 464
    See also special characters
chat invitation, 660
chatter score, for Google+ posts, 757
Checkbutton widget, 220
checkUserCookie() method, 476
Cheeseshop, 311, 418
CherryPy, 494
child threads, main thread need to wait for, 166
child widget, 217
chr() function, 770, 773
CIL (Common Intermediate Language), 387
class type in Python 3, 801
class wrapper, 486
class-based generic views, 553
classes, special methods for, 791–795
classic classes, 814
clear() function (set types), 785
clear() method (dictionary), 782
client/server architecture
    exercise answer, 765
    hardware, 55
    network programming, 56–57
    software, 55–56
    Web surfing and, 391–392
    window system, 216
    XML-RPC and, 733–738
clientConnectionFailed() method, 87
clientConnectionLost() method, 87
clients, 54
    awareness of server, 57
    for NNTP, 108–114
    for UDP
        creating, 74–76
        executing, 76
    FTP
        example program, 100–102
        list of typical, 103
    Internet, 95
    location on Internet, 394–395
    socket methods, 62–63
    spawning threads to handle requests, 65
    TCP
        creating, 68–71
        executing, 71–73
        executing Twisted, 87
        SocketServer execution, 83

SocketServer for creating, 82–83
Twisted for creating, 85–87
client-side COM programming, 326–327
with Excel, 328–330, 338–340
with Outlook, 334–337, 340–347
with PowerPoint, 332–334, 347–356
with Word, 331
close() method, 63, 66
for server, 72
for UDP server, 73
close() method (DB-API Connection object),
264
close() method (DB-API Cursor object), 265
close() method (file object), 786
close() method (IMAP4 object), 129
close() method (urlopen object), 401
closed() method (file object), 787
closing spreadsheet without saving, 330
cloud computing, 605–611
levels of service, 607–609
Web-based SaaS, 135
Cloud SQL service/API, 615
Cloud Storage service/API, 615
clrDir() method, 235
CMDs dictionary, 702
cmp() function, 769, 773
__cmp__() method, 792
coerce() function, 771
__coerce__() method, 794
co-location, 395
columns in database tables, 255
column-stores, 310
COM (Component Object Model) programming, client-side, 326–327
basics, 325
with Excel, 328–330, 338–340
with Outlook, 334–337, 340–347
with PowerPoint, 332–334, 347–356
with Word, 331
ComboBox widget, 236, 238, 241
ComboBoxEntry widget, position of labels, 244
command shell, executing http.server
module from, 447
command-line
FTP clients, 103
to start App Engine application, 629
comma-separated values (CSV), 715–719
Yahoo! Stock Quotes example, 717–719
Comment class, 579
Comment objects, for TweetApprover, 578
comments
hash symbol (#) for, 32
in regex, 8, 16
commit() method (DB-API Connection object),
264, 271
common gateway interface. See CGI (common
gateway interface)
Common Intermediate Language (CIL), 387

communication endpoint, 58
See also sockets
comparisons, 769
compatibility library, for Tweepy and
Twython, 693–706
compilation of regex, decision process, 19
compile() function, 17
compiled languages, vs. interpreted, 367
compiling extensions, 377–379
complex() function, 771
__complex__() method, 793
Concurrence networking framework, 89
concurrency, 626
concurrent.futures module, 207, 210
concurrent.futures.ProcessPoolExecutor, 207
concurrent.futures.ThreadPoolExecutor, 207
Condition object (threading module), 170
context manager, 196
conditional expressions, 288
conditional regular expression matching, 34
connect() attribute (DB-API), 260
connect() function, 286
for database access, 261–262
connect() method, 62
connect_ex() method, 62
connection attribute (DB-API Cursor object),
265
Connection objects (DB-API), 263–264
database adapters with, 271
connectionless socket, 60
connectionMade() method, 86
connection-oriented sockets, 60
constants
in Outlook, 336
in PowerPoint, 334
constructors (DB-API), 266–268
consumer key, for OAuth, 694
consumer secret, for OAuth, 694
consumer() function, 200
container environments, and Django install,
500
containers, widgets as, 217
__contains__() method, 794
context, for Django template variables, 528
continue statement, 113
Control widget, 236, 238
Conversion package/API, 615
converting data between Python and C/C++,
372
cookie jar, 476
Cookie module/package, 433, 476, 488
cookielib module/package, 433, 476, 488
cookies, 392, 487
CGI for, 466–478
expiration date, 467
copy() function (set types), 784
copy() method (dictionary), 782
costs, cloud computing services and, 606

CouchDB, 318
couchdb-python, 318
count() function, 773
count() method (list), 781
count() method (string), 778
counters
    semaphores as, 197, 199
    value display for debugging, 201
counting, by App Engine, 643
crawl.py script, 411–418
    sample invocation, 417–418
crawler, 410
Crawler class, 416
CREATE DATABASE statement (SQL), 256
CREATE TABLE statement (MySQL), 271
CREATE TABLE statement (SQL), 256
create() function, for database table, 287
create_blogpost() view function, 562
create_connection() function, 77
cron job, 101
cron service, 615, 673
cron.yaml file, 673
cross-site request forgery, 544
cStringIO module/package, 413
cStringIO.StringIO class, 731
CSV (comma-separated values), 715–719
    downloading files for importing into Excel
        or Quicken, 685
csv module, 740
    exercise answer, 766
    importing, 716
csv.DictReader class, 717
csv.DictWriter class, 717
csv.reader() function, 717
csv.reader() script, 718
csv.writer() function, 717
csvex.py script, 715–717
current_thread function (threading module),
    179
currentThread() function (threading
        module), 179
cursor for databases, 255
cursor objects (DB-API), 265–266
cursor() method (DB-API Connection object),
    264
custom views, 551
customization of classes, special methods for,
    791
cwd Tk string variable, 235
cwd() method (FTP objects), 99
cx_Oracle, 318
Cython, 385

D
\d special character, for decimal digit, 14
daemon attribute (Thread object), 172
daemon threads, 171
data
    converting between Python and C/C++, 372
    in Python 3, 800
    manipulation, 3
data attributes (DB-API), 260–261
"Data Mapper" pattern, 295
data models
    admin.py file to register, 580
    BlogPostForm object for, 559
    file for TweetApprover poster app, 578
    for blog application, 558
    for TweetApprover, 576–582
    in Django, experimenting with, 516–517
    repetition vs. DRY, 546
data set, script to generate, 41–43
data strings. See strings
data types, 267
database adapters, 258
    basics, 270
    example application, 275–288
        porting to Python 3, 279–288
    examples, 270–275
        MySQL, 271–272
        PostgreSQL, 272–274
        SQLite, 274–275
database application programmer's interface
        (DB-API), 259–288
    changes between versions, 268
    Connection objects, 263–264
    cursor objects, 265–266
    exceptions, 263
    exercise answer, 766
    module attributes, 260–263
        data attributes, 260–261
        function attributes, 261–262
    relational databases, available interfaces,
        269–270
    type objects and constructors, 266–268
    web resources, 268
database servers, 55
Database Source Names (DSNs), 294
DatabaseError exception (DB-API), 263
databases
    auto-generating records for testing, 538
    basics, 254–257
    create() function for tables, 287
    creating engine to, 296
    Django model for, 509–514
        table creation, 512–514
        using MySQL, 510–511
        using SQLite, 511–512
    for Django, 498
    list of supported, 270
    non-relational, 309–315
        MongoDB, 310
        PyMongo, 311–315
    NoSQL, 498
    Python and, 257–258
    row insertion, update, and deletion, 297
    SQL, 256–257
    testing, 556

user interface, 255
Web resources on modules/packages, 316
See also object relational managers (ORMs)
DATABASES variable, for TweetApprover, 570
DataError exception (DB-API), 263
datagram type of socket, 60
DatagramRequest-Handler class (SocketServer module), 79
dataReceived() method, 86
datastore admin, for App Engine, 655
Datastore service/API, 614, 615
date
    converting American style to world format, 29
    converting integer to, 43
Date type object (DB-API), 267
DateFromTicks type object (DB-API), 267
datetime package, 754
DATETIME type object (DB-API), 267
days of the week, extracting from timestamp, 44
DB-API. *See* database application programmer's interface (DB-API)
dbDump() function, 288
dbDump() method, 298, 307, 315
DB_EXC, 285
DCOracle2, 318
debugging, counter value display and, 201
decode() function, 773
decode() method (string), 778
default arguments, widgets with, 221
default radio button, 454
deferred package, in Google App Engine, 668–670
deferred.defer() function, 668
Dejavu, 289
__del__() method, 791
__delattr__() method, 792
dele() method (POP3 object), 125
delegation, for database operations, 298
DELETE FROM statement (MySQL), 272
DELETE FROM statement (SQL), 257
delete() function, for database adapter, 288
__delete__() method, 792
delete() method, 297, 298
delete() method (FTP objects), 99
__delitem__() method, 794, 795
__delslice__() method, 794
_demo_search() function, 706
denial-of-service protection, 675
Denial-of-Service service/API, 615
DeprecationWarning, 790
description attribute (DB-API Cursor object), 265
desktop, application visibility on, 330
detach() method, 63
developer servers, 446–448
development server in Django, 505–507

dict.fromkeys() function, 702
dict() factory function, 314
dict2json.py script, 722–724
dict2xml.py script, 725–729
dictionary type built-in methods, 782–783
Diesel, 496
difference_update() function (set types), 785
difference() function (set types), 784
digits
    \d special character for, 14
    matching single in regex, 7
dir() method (FTP objects), 99
directory tree traversal tool, 230–236
direct_to_template() generic view, 561
DirList class, defining constructor for, 232
discard() function (set types), 785
dispatch, static vs. dynamic, 329
Dispatch() function, 329
displayFirst20() function, 113
displaying sets, 192
Distribute, 290
distutils package, 377
distutils.log.warn() function, 279, 285, 693, 716, 722, 819, 821
__*div__() method, 792
division from __future__ module, 811
division operator (/), 771, 810
    Python 3 changes, 803–804
divmod() function, 771
__*divmod__() method, 793
Django, 428, 494
    administration app, 518–527
        data manipulation, 522–527
        setup, 518–519
        trying out, 519–527
    App Engine and, 617, 676
    authentication in, 574, 595
    auto_now_add feature, 578
    basics, 496
    caching, 650
    data model experimenting, 516–517
    development server in, 505–507
    fixtures, 513
    forms, 546–550
        defining, 590
        model forms, 547
        ModelForm data processing, 549
        ModelForm to generate HTML form, 548
    "Hello World" application, 507
    installation, 499–501
        prerequisites, 497–499
    labor-saving features, 563
    look-and-feel improvements, 553
    model for database service, 509–514
        table creation, 512–514
        using MySQL, 510–511
        using SQLite, 511–512
    non-relational databases and, 618
    output improvement, 537–541

Django *(continued)*
    model default ordering, 540
    query change, 537–540
    projects and apps, 501
        basic files, 504
        project creation, 502–505
    Python application shell, 514–517
    resources, 597
    sending e-mail from, 567
    templates
        directory for, 529
        specifying location for Web pages, 570
    testing blog application code review, 557–563
    tutorial, 597
    unit testing, 554–557, ??–563
    user input, 542–546
        cross-site request forgery, 544
        template for, 542
        URLconf entry, 543
        view, 543
    user interface for blog, 527–537
        template creation, 528–529
        URL pattern creation, 529–533
        view function creation, 533–537
    views, 551–553
        generic views, 552–553
        semi-generic views, 551
    vs. App Engine, 628–630
    See also TweetApprover
Django's Database API, 289
django-admin.py startproject command, 566
django-admin.py utility, 502, 505
Django-nonrel, 498
    App Engine and, 617
    resources, 597
.dmg file, for App Engine SDK, 620
document object model (DOM) tree-structure, 725
document stores, 310
documentation strings (docstrings), 518
    testing, 554
DocXMLRPCServer module/package, 434, 733, 740
do_GET() method, 430, 432
do_HEAD() method, 432
dollar sign ($), for matching end of string, 6, 10
doLS() method, 235
do_POST() method, 432
doResults() method, 477, 478
DOS Command window
    Django project creation in, 503
    for installing Django, 499
dos.yaml file, blacklist section, 675
dot (.) symbol, in regex, 6, 9, 23
double-slash division operator (//), 804, 811
Download service/API, 615
download() method, 415

downloading
    CSV files for importing into Excel or Quicken, 685
    e-mail, Yahoo! Mail Plus account for, 139
    file from Web site, 101
    Google App Engine SDK, 620
    HTML, urlretrieve() for, 402
    stock quotes into Excel, 338–340
downloadStatusHook function, 402
DP-API *See* database application programmer's interface (DB-API)
DROP DATABASE statement (SQL), 256
DROP TABLE statement (SQL), 256
DRY principle, 530, 532, 551, 560
    resources on, 591
    vs. repetition, 546
DSNs (Database Source Names), 294
Durus, 289
dynamic dispatch, 329, 346

E

East Asian fonts, 464
EasyGUI module, 248
easy_install (Setuptools), for Django, 499
ECMA-262 standard, 719
ehlo() method (SMTP object), 119
Elastic Compute Cloud (EC2), 607
electronic mail. *See* e-mail
ElementTree XML document parser, 725
ElementTree.getiterator() function, 733
Elixir, 295
e-mail, 114–146
    attachment, 131
    best practices in security and refactoring, 136–138
    composition, 131–134
    definition of message, 114
    Google App Engine for receiving, 658–660
    Google App Engine for sending, 656
    Google Gmail service, 144–146
    handler for inbound, 659
    IMAP, 121–122
        Python and, 128
    instructing Django to send, 567
    multipart alternative messages, 133
    parsing, 134
    POP, 121–122
        interactive example, 123–124
        methods, 124–125
        Python and, 122
    Python modules, 146–147
    receiving, 121
    sending, 116–117
    sending, as task, 666–668
    system components and protocols, 115–116
    Web-based SaaS cloud computing, 135
    Yahoo! Mail, 138–144

Yahoo! Mail Plus account for downloading, 139
  See also Outlook
e-mail addresses, regex for, 24–26
Email API, 614
email module/package, 131, 147
email.message_from_string() function, 134
email.mime.multiple.MIMEMultipart class, 133
email.mime.text.MIMEText class, 133
email-examples.py script, 132–134
embedding, extensions vs., 387
employee role database example, 291–309
  SQLAlchemy for, 291–304
Empty exception (Queue/queue module), 202
empty() method (queue object), 203
encode() function, 773
encode() method, 464
encode() method (string), 778
encoding() method (file object), 787
end of string, matching from, 6, 10
endswith() function, 773
endswith() method (string), 778
ENGINE setting, for Django database, 510
Entry widget, 220
enumerate() function (threading module), 179
environment variables, 481
  Django project shell command setup of, 515
  wsgi.*, 483
EnvironmentError, 788
EOFError, 72, 788, 789
__eq__() method, 792
eric module, 249
Error exception (DB-API), 263
error exception (socket module), 77
error page, for Advcgi script, 477
error submodule, 400
errorhandler() method (DB-API Connection object), 264
escaping characters, in regex, 9
ESMTP, 116
estock.pyw script, 338–340
/etc/services file, 59
Event object (threading module), 170
event-based processors for XML, 725
event-driven applications, 80
event-driven processing, 218
events, 217
Excel
  COM programming with, 328–330, 338–340
  downloading CSV files for importing into, 685
excel.pyw script, 328–330
Exception, 788
exceptions, 788–790
  DB-API, 263
  in Python 3, 816–817
  Python 3 changes, 801–802

for socket module, 77
syntax for handling in database adapters, 280
exc_info, and start_response(), 482
execute() method (DB-API Cursor object), 265
execute*() method (DB-API Cursor object), 266
executemany() function, 287
executemany() method (DB-API Cursor object), 265
execution rates, for task queues, 663
executor.map(), 208
executor.submit(), 208
exit() function (thread module), 165
exiting threads, 161
expandtabs() method (string), 773, 778
Expat streaming parser, 725
expiration date of cookies, 467
exponentiation (**), 771
extend() method (list), 773, 781
Extended Passive Mode (FTP), 98
eXtensible Markup Language. *See* XML (eXtensible Markup Langauge)
extension notations, for regex, 16, 31–34
extensions
  basics, 365
  creating
    boilerplate wrapper for, 370–377
    C application code, 368–370
    compilation, 377–379
  creating on different platforms, 365–366
  disadvantages, 367–368
  Global Interpreter Lock and, 384
  importing, 379
  reasons for, 366–367
  reference counting and, 382–383
  testing, 379–382
  threading and, 384
  vs. embedding, 387
external processes, as CGI alternative, 480
Extest2.c C library, 380–382
ExtJS, 495

F

fac() function, 368–370
Facebook, 690
  scalability issues, 310
factorial function, thread for, 180–182
fake views, 533
family attribute, for socket object, 64
FastCGI, 480
fasterBS() function, 421, 422
federated authentication, 653
fetch() method (IMAP4 object), 129, 130
fetch*() method (DB-API Cursor object), 266
fetchall() method (DB-API Cursor object), 266, 288
fetching database rows, 255
fetchone() method (DB-API Cursor object), 266
Fibonacci function, 180–182

fields, multivalued in CGI, 467
FieldStorage class (cgi module), 445
    instance, 451
file input type, 466
file objects, methods and data attributes,
    786–787
file servers, 55
File Transfer Protocol (FTP), 96–98
    client example, 100–102
    interactive example, 100
    miscellaneous notes, 103–104
fileno() method (file object), 786
fileno() method (socket object), 64
fileno() method (urlopen object), 401
file-oriented socket methods, 63
files, 254
    uploading, 478
Files service/API, 615
fill parameter, for packer, 224
filter() function, 804
filter() method, 297
filter_by() method, 297
filters, in Django variable tags, 528
find() method (string), 778
findall() function, 33–34
findall() function/method, 17, 27
findAll() method, 421
finditer() function, 17, 28, 33–34
find_top_posts() function, 758
find_user() function, 758
finish() method, 299, 307
Firebird (InterBase), 317
firewalls, 394
first() method, 298
fixtures, 513
flags
    for speciallzed regex compilation, 19
    in regex, 8, 18
Flask framework, App Engine and, 617
Flask, App Engine and, 676
float type, division and, 810
float() function, 771
__float__() method, 793
FloatingPointError, 788
floor division (//), 772, 803, 804, 810, 811
__*floordiv__() method, 792
flush() method (file object), 786
Foord, Michael, Python Cookbook, 407
Forcier, Jeff, Python Web Development with
    Django, 496
foreground color of button, argument for, 227
forex() function, 736
ForgetSQL, 289
ForkingMixIn class (SocketServer module), 79
ForkingTCPServerclass (SocketServer
    module), 79
ForkingUDPServer class (SocketServer
    module), 79

form variable, 451
format parameter style, for database parame-
    ters, 261
format() function, 773
format() method (string), 778
formatter module/package, 413
formatter object, 415
FormHandler class, 666
forms
    CGI specifications on encodings, 466
    classes to define, 559
    "hidden" variable in, 454
    hidden variable in, 467
    in Django, 546–550
        defining, 590
forward proxies, 394
Frame class, 241
Frame object, 224
Frame widget, 220, 233
Friedl, Jeffrey E.F., Mastering Regular
    Expressions, 48
friendsA.py script, 450
friendsB.py script, 453–456
friendsC.py script, 457–462
friendsC3.py script, 462–463
from module import *, 702
fromfd() function, 77
from-import module, 42
fromkeys() method (dictionary), 782
frozenset() function (set types), 784
FTP (File Transfer Protocol)
    creating client, 98
    support for, 399
ftplib module, 98, 148, 400
ftplib.FTP class
    instantiating, 98
    methods, 99–100
Full exception (Queue/queue module), 202
full() method (queue object), 203
full-stack systems, 494
function attributes (DB-API), 261–262
functions
    PFAs for, 226
    standard, 769
    vs. methods, 19
functools module, reduced() moved to in
    Python 3, 813
functools.partial() method, 229
future_builtins module, 814
FutureWarning, 790
FXPy module, 249

G

Gadfly, 275, 286, 316
    database, 258
GAE Framework, App Engine and, 617
Gage, John, 608
gaierror exception, for socket module, 77
__ge__() method, 792

gendata.py script, 41–43
GeneratorExit, 788
generic views, 537, 551, 552–553
    direct_to_template(), 561
Genshi, 495
geometry managers, 218
GET method,decison to use, 448
GET request
    Django development server logging of, 507
    for HTTP requests, 400
    reading, 430
    variables and values in URL, 452
__get__() method, 792
get() method (dictionary), 782
get() method (queue object), 203
get() method, for HTTP GET requests, 624
getaddrinfo() function, 77
__getattr__() method, 299, 705, 792
__getattribute__() method, 792
getCPPCookies() method, 476, 478
get_file() method, 414
getFirstNNTP.py script, 109–114
getfqdn() function, 78
gethostbyaddr() function, 78
gethostbyname() function, 78
gethostbyname_ex() function, 78
gethostname() function, 78
__getitem__() method, 794, 795
getLatestFTP.py script, 101–102
_get_meth() method, 703
getName() method (Thread object), 172
get_nowait() method (queue object), 203
get_object_or_404() shortcut, 584
get_page() method, 416
getpeername() method, 63
get_posts() method, 755
get_presence() function (XMPP), 661
getprotobyname() function, 78
getRanking() function, 182, 184
    with statement use by, 208
getResult() method, 178
getservbyname() function, 78
getservbyport() function, 78
__getslice__() method, 794
getsockname() method, 63
getsockopt() method, 63
getSubject() function, 137, 143
gettimeout() method, 63
geturl() method (urlopen object), 401
get_user() method, 756
GIF (Graphics Interchange Format), 401
GitHub, 691
Glade module, 249
Global Interpreter Lock (GIL), 160–163
    extensions and, 384
gmail.py script, 144–146
GNOME-Python module, 249
go() method, 416, 477

Google
    Account authentication, 652
    APIs Client Library for Python, 749
    applications hosted by, 605
    Terms of Service, 731
    uploading application to, 629
Google App Engine, 495
    adding users service, 652–654
    administration console, 611
    authentication options, 574
    basics, 605, 609–611
    counting by, 643
    cron service, 673
    datastore admin, 655
    Datastore viewer, 640
    deferred package, 668–670
    denial-of-service protection, 675
    documentation, 640
    frameworks
        choices, 617–626
        resources, 678
    free service tier, 629
    hardware infrastructure, 610
    "Hello World" application, 620–626
        app.yaml file for configuration settings,
            622–624
        creating manually, 629–630
        index.yaml file, 623
        starting, 628
    "Hello World" application morphed to blog,
        631–647
        adding datastore service, 635–638
        adding form, 633–635
        iterative improvements, 640
        plain text conversion to HTML, 632
    Images API, 662
    interactive console, 640–647
    language runtimes, 610
    limit to file uploads, 613
    Memcache API, 647–651
    native datastore, 498
    pricing model, 626
    Python 2.7 support, 626–628
    receiving e-mail, 658–660
    remote API shell, 654
    resources, 676
    sandbox restrictions, 612–616
    sending e-mail, 656
    sending instant messages, 660
    services and APIs, 614–616
    static files, 651
    System Status page, 612
    task queues, 663
    URLfetch service, 672
    vendor lock-in, 675
    vs. Django, 628–630
    warming requests, 673
    Web-based administration and system
        status, 610–611

Google App Engine development servers, 428
Google App Engine Oil (GAEO), 617
Google App Engine SDK, 613
   downloading and installing, 620
Google Cloud SQL, 498
Google Gmail service, 135, 144–146
Google News server, connection to, 732
Google Web crawlers, 418
Google+ platform, 690, 748–759
   basics, 748
   chatter score for posts, 757
   Python and, 749
   social media analysis tool, 750–759
Google+ Ripples, 758
goognewsrss.py script, 730–733, 821
Gopher, support for, 399
gopherlib module, 400
GQL, 638
greediness, 13, 46
Grid (geometry manager), 219
Groovy, 610
group() method, 18, 20, 25–26, 106
group() method (NNTP objects), 107
groupdict() method, 18
groups in regex, parentheses for, 14–15, 45
groups() method, 18, 20, 25–26
__gt__() method, 792
GTK, importing, 243
GTKapp class, 243
guest downloads with FTP, 96
GUI programming, 216
   basics, 217–219
      event-driven processing, 218
      geometry managers, 218
   default arguments, 221
   FTP client, 103
   related modules, 247–250
   Swing example, 745–748
   toolkit alternatives, 236–246
      GTK+ and PyGTK, 242–244
      PMW (Python MegaWidgets), 239
      Tile/TtK, 244–246
      Tix (Tk Interface eXtensions), 238
      wxWidgets and wxPython, 240–242
GUI scripts
   Button widget, 222
   Label and Button widgets, 223
   Label widget, 221–222
   Label, Button and Scale widgets, 224–225

H
hacking, 394
Hammond, Mark, 326
handle() method, 81
handler class, 406
handlers, 430
   for inbound e-mail, 659
   for Google App Engine configuration, 623
handles, for urlopen() function, 400

handle_starttag() method, 423
hardware client/server architecture, 55
Harr, Lee, *Python Cookbook*, 407
hash symbol (#)
   for Django comments, 518
   for regex comment, 32
__hash__() method, 794
has_key() method (dictionary), 782
head() method (NNTP object), 107
headers, extracting from newsgroup articles, 112
heavyweight process, 159
"Hello World" application
   in Google App Engine, 620–626
      morphed to blog, 631–647
   in Django, 507
   in Java, 746
   print statement vs. print() function, 820
   in Python, 747
helo() method (SMTP object), 119
herror exception, for socket module, 77
hex() function, 771, 773
__hex__() method, 794
hexadecimal format, 810
hexadecimal ordinal equivalents, of disallowed characters, 403
hidden variable in form, 454, 467
hops, 115
HOST setting, for Django database, 510
HOST variable, 67
   for timestamp client, 70
host-port pairs for socket addresses, 59
howmany variable (Python), 451
HR variable for Google+ program, 754
HSC tool, 462
.htaccess file, 405
HTML (HyperText Markup Language), 401, 442
   3rd-party tools for generating, 462
   parsing tree format, 423
   separating HTTP headers from, 451
   separating HTTP MIME header from, 454
   urlretrieve() to download, 402
HTML forms
   in Django for user input, 542
   ModelForm to generate, 548
   processing ModelForm data, 549
html5lib package, 185, 418, 423, 489
htmlentitydefs module/package, 433, 488
HTMLgen package, 435, 462
htmllib module/package, 413, 433, 488
HTMLParser class, 415, 418
HTMLparser module/package, 185, 433, 488
htmlparser() function, 422
htonl() function, 78
htons() function, 78
htpasswd command, 405
HTTP (HyperText Transfer Protocol), 96, 392

separating headers from HTML, 451
separating MIME header from HTML body, 454
support for, 399
XML-RPC and, 733
http.cookiejar module, 476
http.cookies module, 476
http.server class, 430, 489
http.server module, 435, 447
HTTP_COOKIE environment variable, 468
httplib module, 148, 400, 404, 414, 433, 489
httplib2 library, 571
HTTPServer server class, 429
hybrid cloud, 606
hypertext, 442
Hyves social network, 89

I

IaaS (Infrastructure-as-a-Service), 607
ident attribute (Thread object), 172
if statement, 819
IIS (Internet Information Server), 428
Images API, 615, 662
IMAP (Internet Message Access Protocol), 121–122
    interactive example, 128
    Python and, 128
    Yahoo! Mail example, 142–144
IMAP4 class, 128
IMAP4_SSL class, 128
IMAP4_stream class, 128
imaplib module, 128, 148
imaplib.IMAP4 class, methods, 129–131
import statement, 532
ImportError exception, 16, 789
importing
    csv module, 716
    extensions, 379
    ordering guidelines for, 421, 561, 735
    PyGTK, GTK, and Pango, 243
    Tkinter module, 215
    to create compatible code for Python 2.x and 3.x, 820–821
inbound e-mail, handler for, 659
InboundMailHandler class, 659
include Python header file, in boilerplate code, 371
include() directive, in Django project, 508
include() function, 530
IndentationError, 789
index() function, 773
index() method (list), 781
index() method (string), 778
IndexError, 789
inet_aton() function, 78
inet_ntoa() function, 78
inet_ntop() function, 78
inet_pton() function, 78
info() method (urlopen object), 401

Infrastructure-as-a-Service (IaaS), 607
ingmod, 318
Ingres, 318
Ingres DBI, 318
__init__ method (Thread object), 172
__init__.py file in Django project, 504, 508
__init__() method, 176, 414, 791
initModule() module initializer function, 376
input() function, 280
INSERT INTO statement (MySQL), 271
INSERT INTO statement (SQL), 257
insert() function, 287, 773
insert() method (list), 781
insert() method, for MongoDB collection, 314
inserting database rows, 255
INSTALLED_APPS variable, 571
installing
    Django, 499–501
        prerequisites, 497–499
    Google App Engine SDK, 620
    Tkinter, 215
    Twython library, 571–572
instance attributes, local variable for, 703
instant messages
    Google App Engine for sending, 660
    receiving, 661
int type, 802, 809
int() function, 771
__int__() method, 793
integers
    converting to date, 43
    Python 3 changes, 802–804
    Python 3 migration and, 809–812
IntegrityError exception (DB-API), 263
InterfaceError exception (DB-API), 263
"Internal Server Error" messages, 446
InternalError exception (DB-API), 263
International Standard Book Number (ISBN), 184
Internet, 392–395
    protocols, related modules, 148
    See also cloud computing
Internet addresses, 59
    formatting, 121
Internet clients, 95
    and servers location, 394–395
    See also e-mail
Internet Protocol (IP), 60
Internet Server Application Programming Interface (ISAPI), 479
interpreted languages, vs. compiled, 367
intersection() function (set types), 784
intersection_update() function (set types), 785
__invert__() method, 793
io.BytesIO class, 731
ioctl() method, 63
IOError, 789
IP (Internet Protocol), 60

IP address, binding, 62
IPv6 TCP client, creating, 71
IPython, 515
    starting and using commands, 516
IronPython, 325
is not operator, 770
is operator, 770
isAlive method (Thread object), 172
is_alive() method (Thread object), 172
isalnum() method (string), 773, 779
isalpha() method (string), 773, 779
isatty() method (file object), 786
ISBN (International Standard Book Number),
    184
isDaemon() method (Thread object), 172
isdecimal() method (string), 773, 779
isdigit() method (string), 773, 779
islower() method (string), 773, 779
isnumeric() method (string), 773, 779
ISP (Internet Service Provider), 394
isspace() method (string), 773, 779
issubset() function (set types), 784
issuperset() function (set types), 784
istitle() method (string), 773, 779
isupper() method (string), 774, 779
items() function, 804
items() method (dictionary), 782
__iter__() method, 794
__iter__() method (DB-API Cursor object), 266
iter*() method (dictionary), 783
iterables, Python 3 changes, 804
itertools.izip() function, 731, 820

J
Jabber protocol, 614, 660
Java, 610
    "Hello World" application, 746
    Jython and, 744
    vs. Python, 747
JavaScript, 610
JavaScript Object Notation (JSON), 719–724
join() function, 774
join() method, 298
join() method (queue object), 203
join() method (string), 779
join() method (thread object), 172, 174, 186
JOINs, Web resources on, 298
JPEG (Joint Photographic Experts Group), 401
jQuery, 495
JRuby, 610
JSON (JavaScript Object Notation), 719–724
    converting Python dict to, 722–724
    objects, 311
        Python dists conversion to, 720
JSON arrays, 720
json package, 740
json.dumps() function, 722
Jython, 610, 744–748
    basics, 744
    GUI example with Swing, 745–748

K
Kantor, Brian, 105
Kay framework, App Engine and, 617
key for cache, 649
KeyboardInterrupt, 72, 788, 789
KeyError, 789
keys() function, 804
keys() method (dictionary), 783
keys-only counting, 643
key-value pairs
    in CGI, 445
    urlencode() encoding of, 403
key-value stores, 310
keyword module, 819
keywords, 768
KInterbasDB, 317
Klassa, John, 341
Kleene Closure, 12
Kuchling, Andrew, 799

L
Label widget, 220, 238, 241
    Button and Scale widgets with, 224–225
    Button widget with, 223
LabelFrame widget, 220, 247
LAN (Local Area Network), 394
language runtimes of App Engine, 610
Lapsley, Phil, 105
last() method (NNTP object), 107
lastrowid attribute (DB-API Cursor object), 265
Launcher, 628
__le__() method, 792
len() function, 774
len() function (set types), 783
__len__() method, 791, 794
libevent, 89
LibreOffice, 357
LibreOffice Calc, 685
LifoQueue class, 202
ligHTTPD, 428, 446, 494
lightweight processes, 159
limit() method, 297
line termination characters, 346
    for Word documents, 331
links, parsing, 418
Linux
    package manager for Django install, 501
    Zip file for App Engine SDK, 620
list type built-in methods, 781–782
list() function, 774
list() method (POP3 object), 125
Listbox bind() method, 233
Listbox widget, 220
listdir.py script, 230–236
listen() method, 62, 67
list_tweet() method, 589
list_tweets() method, 587
literals
    binary and octal, 804
    bytes, 815

LiteSpeed, 428
`ljust()` function, 774
`ljust()` method (string), 779
LMTP (Local Mail Transfer Protocol), 117
`LMTP` class, 118
load-balancing, 394
`loc.close()` method, 102
Local Mail Transfer Protocol (LMTP), 117
local variables
    assigning to cache, 757
    for instance attributes, 703
localhost, 64
Lock object (`threading` module), 164–169
    context manager, 196
`locked()` method, 165
locks for threads, vs. sleep, 167
logical OR, 9
    brackets for, 11
login
    admin directive, for Google App Engine, 653
    anonymous FTP, 96, 102
    avoiding plaintext, 136, 142
    for database creation, 271
    for FTP access, 96
    registering password, 405
    required directive, 653
    for SMTP servers, 133
`login.html` template, 595
`login()` method (FTP objects), 99
`login()` method (IMAP4 object), 129
`login()` method (SMTP object), 119
`logout()` method (IMAP4 object), 129
Logs, 615
long type, 802, 809
`long()` function, 771
`__long__()` method, 793
lookahead assertions, 8, 33
`LookupError`, 789
`loop()` function, 168, 195
    lock use in, 193
`loseConnection()` method, 87
`lower()` function, 774
`lower()` method (string), 779
LRU (least recently used) algorithm,
        Memcache API use of, 649
`__*lshift__()` method, 793
`lstrip()` method (string), 774, 779
`__lt__()` method, 792
lxml package, 185, 489

M
Mail service/API, 615
`mail.send_mail()` function, 656
`_main()` function, 185
`mailbox` module, 147
`mailcap` module, 147
`mainloop()`, starting GUI app, 222, 235
`makedirs()` function, 414
`makefile()` method, 64

makefiles, 377
`make_img_msg()` function, 131, 133
`make_mpa_msg()` function, 131
Makepy utility, 329
`make_server()` function, 483
`manage.py` file in Django project, 504
    shell command, 515
`manage.py runserver` command, 519
`map()` function, 804
`map()` method, 207
Mapper, resources, 677
MapReduce service/API, 615
markup parser, 185
Mastering Regular Expressions (Friedl), 48
match objects, 20
`match()` function/method, 4, 17, 20–21, 26
Matcher service/API, 615
    resources, 677
matching
    conditional, 34
    strings, 44–45
    vs. searching, 4, 21–22, 46–48
`max()` function, 774
MaxDB (SAP), 317
`mech.py` script, 425–428
Mechanize module, 424, 435
Mechanize.Browser class
    importing, 427
Megastore, 636
Memcache API, 614, 615, 647–651
    documentation, 649
memory conservation in Python 3, 804
memory leak, 383
    in C code, 375
`MemoryError`, 789
Menu widget, 220
Menubutton widget, 220
message transport agents (MTA), 115–116
    well-known, 117
message transport system (MTS), 116
Message widget, 220
`message.get_payload()` method, 134
`message.walk()` method, 134
messages attribute (DB-API `Cursor` object), 266
Meta class, 579
metacharacters, 6
methods
    permission to access, 589
    vs. functions, 19
`mhlib` module, 147
microblogging with Twitter, 690–707
Microsoft
    Exchange, 122
    Internet Server Application Programming
        Interface (ISAPI), 479
    MFC, 249
middleware onion, 485
middleware, for WSGI, 485

migration to Python 3, 807–822
    built-in functions, 813
migration to Python *(continued)*
    exceptions, 816–817
    integers and, 809–812
    object-oriented programming, 814
    print statement vs. print() function, 812
    reduced() moved to functools module, 813
    strings, 815
migration tools for Python 3, 805
MIME (Mail Interchange Message Extension), 131
MIME (Multipurpose Internet Mail Extension), headers, 401
mimetools module, 147
mimetypes module, 147
MimeWriter module, 147
mimify module, 147
min() function, 774
MiniFieldStorage, 445
mkd() method (FTP objects), 99
__*mod__() method, 793
mode() method (file object), 787
model forms, in Django, 547
ModelForm
    data processing, 549
    HTML form generation with, 548
models
    classes to define, 559
    in Django, setting default ordering, 540
models.py file, 558
    for Django app, 508
model-template view (MTV) pattern, 514
model-view controller (MVC) pattern, 514
module initializer function, 376
modules, order for importing, 421
Modules/Setup file, Tkinter and, 215
mod_wsgi Apache module, Django and, 497
MongoDB, 310, 318, 498
mouse move event, 218
msg.get_payload() method, 134
msg.walk() method, 134
.msi file, for App Engine SDK, 620
mtfacfib.py script, 180–182
mtsleepA.py script, 165
mtsleepB.py script, 167–169, 173
mtsleepC.py script, 173
mtsleepD.py script, 175
mtsleepE.py script, 177–178
mtsleepF.py script, 191, 194–196
    porting to Python 3, 196–197
__*mul__() method, 792, 794
multipart encoding, 468
"multipart/form-data", 466
multiprocessing module, 207, 209
multithreaded (MT) programming
    basics, 157–158
    Python Virtual Machine, 160–163
    related modules, 209

thread module, 164–169
    threads and processes, 158–159
multivalued fields in CGI, 467
mutex module, 209
MVCEngine, 617
myhttpd.py script, 430
myMail.py script, 126–128
MySpace, 690
MySQL, 255, 271–272, 316, 498
MySQL Connector/Python, 280, 316
MySQL for Django database, 510–511
MySQLdb package, 280, 286, 316
myThread.py script, 178

N
name attribute (Thread object), 172
name identifier, for saving matches, 32
NAME setting, for Django database, 510
name() method (file object), 787
named matches, 20
named parameter style, for database parameters, 261
NameError, 789
names
    for Django projects, 502
    for Google App Engine application, 631
    strategy for Python 2 to Python 3, 408
namespaces for App Engine, resources, 677
Namespaces service/API, 616
NDB (new database) service/API, 616
__ne__() method, 792
__neg__() method, 793
negation
    in regex, 12
    of character set matches, 14
negative lookahead assertion, 8, 33
.NET, 325
Netscape Server Application Programming Interface (NSAPI), 479
Netscape, cookies specification, 468
Network News Transfer Protocol (NNTP)
    additional resources, 114
    basics, 105
    client program example, 108–114
    interactive example, 108
    Python and, 105
network programming
    for client/server architecture, 56–57
    related modules, 88–89
    socket module for, 61–62
    sockets, 58–61
    TCP server creation, 64–68
    Twisted framework, 84–87
networks, location components, 397
__new__() method, 791
NEWLINE characters, to separate HTTP header from HTML, 451
newlines() method (file object), 787
newsgroups, 104–114

new-style classes, 814
next() method (DB-API Cursor object), 266
next() method (file object), 786
next() method (NNTP object), 107
nextset() method (DB-API Cursor object), 266
nlst() method (FTP objects), 99
NNTP. *See* Network News Transfer Protocol
    (NNTP)
nntplib class, 105
nntplib module, 148
nntplib.NNTP class, 105
    methods, 107
non-ASCII characters, \u escape for, 464
non-blocking sockets, 65
nondeterministic activity, 157
non-relational databases, 309–315, 498
    Django and, 618
    MongoDB, 310
    PyMongo, 311–315
    Web resources, 319
non-validating, Expat parser as, 725
__nonzero__() method, 791
noop() method (IMAP4 object), 130
NoSQL, 310
not operator, 770
NotImplementedError, 789
NotSupportedError exception (DB-API), 263
now_int() function, 736
now_str() function, 736
ntohl() function, 78
ntohs() function, 78
NULL objects, 267
    check for, 383
NUMBER type object (DB-API), 267
numeric conversion, 793
numeric parameter style, for database
    parameters, 261
numeric type operators, 770–772

O
OAuth, 494, 569
    credentials for Twitter's public API, 567
    resources, 597, 678
    Twitter and, 694
oauth2 library, 571
object comparisons, 770
object-level caching, 651
object-oriented programming, 814
object-relational managers (ORMs), 289–309
    employee role database example, 291–309
        SQLAlchemy for, 291–304
        SQLObject for, 304–309
    explicit/"classical" access, 301–304
    setup and installation, 290–291
Object-Relational Mapper (ORM)
    App Engine and, 618
objects
    comparison, 792
    creating and caching, 329

oct() function, 771, 774
__oct__() method, 794
octal literals, 804
octothorpe. *See* hash symbol (#)
offset() method, 298
olook.pyw script, 335–337
one() method, 298
onethr.py script, 162–163
OpenDocument text (ODT) format, 357
OpenID service/API, 616, 653
OpenOffice, 356
OperationalError exception (DB-API), 263
operators, 769
    numeric type, 770–772
    sequence type, 772–776
    summary, 795–797
OR
    logical, 9
    logical, brackets for, 11
or operator, 770
__*or__() method, 793
Oracle, 317, 498
Oracle Open Office, 357
ord() function, 771, 774
order_by() method, 297, 538
os module, 414
    importing, 232
os.makedirs() function, 414
os.popen() command, 37
os.spawnv() function, 346
OSError, 789
Outlook
    address book protection in, 336
    COM programming with, 334–337, 340–347
outlook_edit.pyw script, 341–347
output() function, 421
OverflowError exception, 788, 802
OverflowWarning, 790
owned reference, 382

P
PaaS (Platform-as-a-Service), 607
package manager, for Django install, 500
packer, 224
    fill parameter, 224
Packer (geometry manager), 218
page views, persistent state across multiple,
    467
PanedWindow widget, 220, 247
Panel widget, 241
Pango, importing, 243
parallel processing, 157
paramstyle attribute (DB-API), 260, 261
parent widget, 217
parentheses, for regex groups, 14–15
parse() function, 423
parse_links.py script, 419–424
parse_links() method, 415

parsing
  data string, csv module for, 686
  e-mail, 134
parsing *(continued)*
  tree format for HTML documents, 423
  Web content, 418–424
part.get_content_type() method, 134
Partial Function Application (PFA), 226–229
partition() function, 774
pass_() method (POP3 object), 125
Passive FTP mode, 98, 103
PASSWORD setting, for Django database, 510
passwords
  for anonymous FTP, 97
  See also login
PATH environment variable
  django-admin.py in, 502
  easy_install and, 500
pattern-matching, 4
patterns() function, 531
PC COM client programming, 325
P_DETACH flag, 346
PDO, 289
PendingDeprecation Warning, 790
PEP 333, 496
PEP 3333, 487
PEP 444, 487
percent sign (%)
  for hexadecimal ordinal equivalents, 403
  for modulo, 772
  in string format operator (%)
    conversion symbols, 776
performance, interpreted vs. compiled
    languages, 367
period (.) symbol, in regex, 6, 9, 23
permission flags, in Django, 579
@permission_required decorator, 589
permissions, to access method, 589
persistence, in state across multiple page
    views, 467
persistent storage, 254, 488
  databases and, 255
  scalability issues, 310
pfaGUI2.py script, 227–229
PHP, 610
Pinax platform, 501
  resources, 597
pip, for Django install, 499
pipe symbol (|)
  for Django variable tag filters, 528
  in regex, 9
Pipeline, 616
  resources, 678
Placer (geometry manager), 218
plaintext
  avoiding for login, 136, 142
  See also comma-separated values (CSV)
planning for transition to Python 3, 817

platform.python_version() function, 142
Platform-as-a-Service (PaaS), 607
plus sign (+)
  for encoding, 403
  in regex, 6, 12–13
PlusService class, 755
plus_top_posts.py script, 752–759
  sample execution, 750
PMW (Python MegaWidgets), 239, 248
PNG (Portable Network Graphics), 401
P_NOWAIT flag, 346
pop() function, 774
pop() function (set types), 785
pop() method (dictionary), 783
pop() method (list), 782
poplib class, 122
poplib module, 148
poplib.POP3 class, 122
  methods, 124–125
poplib.POP3_SSL class, 123
PoPy, 272
PORT setting, for Django database, 510
PORT variable, for timestamp client, 70
port, for Web server, 447
porting Python version 2 to version 3, 408
ports, 397
  for Django development server, 506
  for SMTP, 118
  reserved numbers, 59
  well-known numbers, 59
__pos__() method, 793
Positive Closure, 12
positive lookahead assertion, 8, 33
POSIX systems
  http.server module on, 447
POSIX-compliant threads, 161
POST handler, for blog posts, 634
Post Office Protocol (POP), 121–122
  example, 126–128
  interactive example, 123–124
  poplib.POP3 class methods, 124–125
  Python and, 122
  Yahoo! Mail example, 142–144
POST request method, for HTTP requests, 400
post() method (FormHandler), 667
post() method (NNTP object), 107
Postel, Jonathan, 96, 116
PostgreSQL, 272–274, 317, 498
postings on newsgroups, 104
post-processing, 485
post_tweet.html template, 586
post_tweet() method, 584
pound sign (#) *See* hash character (#)
P_OVERLAY flag, 346
pow() function, 736, 771
__*pow__() method, 793
PowerPoint, COM programming with,
    332–334, 347–356

ppoint.pyw script, 333
pprint.pprint() function, 732
precompiled code objects, performance, 19
preprocessing, 485
prettyprinting, 732
print servers, 55
print statement, 196
    proxy for, 716
    Python 2 vs. 3 versions, 279
    vs. print() function, 799–800, 812, 819
print() function, 38
PriorityQueue class, 202
private cloud, 606
process() function, 424, 455
processes
    synchronization, 190
    threads and, 158–159
prodcons.py script, 204–206
producer() function, 200
production servers, 446
    Apache as, 498
profiling with Appstats, 670
ProgrammingError exception (DB-API), 263
programs, vs. processes, 158
projects
    file structure for TweetApprover, 565–571
    in Django, 501
        basic files, 504
        creating, 502–505
proprietary source code, extensions to protect,
    367
Prospective Search service/API, 616
proto attribute, for socket object, 64
proxy servers, 394
Psycho, 386
psycopg, 272, 317
    Connection object setup code, 273
    output, 273
pthreads, 161
public cloud, 606
publish_tweet() method, 592
pull queues, 663, 666
purge() function/method, 18, 19
push queues, 663, 666
put() method (queue object), 203
put_nowait() method (queue object), 203
P_WAIT flag, 346
pwd() method (FTP objects), 99
Py_ Build Value() function, 372
PyArg_Parse*() functions, 372
PyArg_ParseTuple() function, 374
PyCon conference Web site, 425
Py_DECREF() function, 383
PyDO/PyDO2, 289, 318
pyFLTK module, 249
pyformat parameter style, for database
        parameters, 261
PyGreSQL, 272, 317
    Connection object setup code, 273
    output, 273

PyGTK, 242–244
PyGTK module, 248
    importing, 243
PyGUI module, 249
Py_INCREF() function, 383
Py_InitModule() function, 376
PyKDE module, 249
Pylons, 494, 495
    resources, 597
PyMethodDef ModuleMethods[] array, 376
PyMongo, 311–315, 318
PyMongo3, 318
pymssql, 317
PyObject* Module_func() wrappers, 371–376
PyOpenGL module, 249
PyPgSQL, 272, 317
    Connection object setup code, 273
    output, 273
PyPy, 386
PyQt module, 249
PyQtGPL module, 249
Pyramid, 495
    resources, 597
Pyramid framework, App Engine and, 617
Pyrex, 385
pysqlite, 274, 317
Python, 610
    and App Engine, 609
    converting data between C/C++ and, 372
    "Hello World" application with Swing, 747
    obtaining release number as string, 142
    supported client libraries, 98
    vs. Java, 747
    Web servers with, 446
    writing code compatible with versions 2.x
            and 3.x, 818–822
        importing for, 820–821
Python 2.6+, 805
Python 3 changes, 798–806, 807–809
    class type, 801
    division, 803–804
    exceptions, 801–802
    integers, 802–804
    iterables, 804
    migration tools, 805
    print statement vs. print() function, 799–800
    reasons for, 799
    Unicode vs. ASCII, 800–801
    See also migration to Python 3
Python application shell in Django, 514–517,
        407
Python dict
    conversion to JSON, 722–724
    converting to XML, 725–729
Python Extensions for Windows, 327
Python interpreter, 655
    compilation, enabled threads and, 162
Python MegaWidgets (PMW), 239
Python objects, wrapping in object to delegate
        lookup, 705

Python types, vs. JSON types, 721
Python Virtual Machine (PVM), 160–163
    extensions and, 384
Python/ceval.c file, 161
PythonCard module, 248
.pyw extension, 237, 327

Q
QLime, 289
qmark parameter style, for database
        parameters, 261
-Qnew switch, 811
qsize() method (Queue object), 203
Quercus, 610
queries, 255
    change to reverse output order, 537–540
    in Google App Engine, documentation, 640
    speed of, caching and, 647
Query methods, Web resources on, 298
QuerySet, 537
question mark (?), in regex, 6, 12–13, 24, 47
Queue data structure, 158
Queue module, 163
queue.yaml file, 665
Queue/queue module, 202–206, 209
queues for tasks, 663
Quicken, downloading CSV files for importing
        into, 685
quit Button, 238, 241
quit() method (FTP objects), 99
quit() method (NNTP object), 107
quit() method (POP3 object), 125
quit() method (SMTP object), 118, 119
quopri module, 147
quote() function, 404
quote*() functions, 402
quote_plus() function, 404

R
race conditions, 159, 190
radio buttons
    default, 454
    string to build list, 454
Radiobutton widget, 220
raising exceptions
    in Python 3, 817
    Python 3 changes, 802
randName() function, 287
random data, script to generate, 41
random.choice() function, 43
random.randint() method, 205
random.randrange() function, 43
range() function, 804
ranges (-) in regex, 12
raw strings, 27, 34, 36, 512
    note on use, 35
raw_input() function, 280, 774
rcp command (Unix), 96

RDBMS (relational database management
        system), 255
re module, 3, 16–35
    character classes creation, 24
    core functions and methods, 17–18
    match objects, 20
    match() function/method, 20–21
    matching any single character, 23
    matching multiple strings, 22
    search() function, 21–22
re.compile() function, 183, 189
re.I/IGNORECASE, 31
re.L/LOCALE flag, 34
re.M/MULTILINE, 31
re.S/DOTALL, 31
re.split() function, 39
re.U/UNICODE flag, 34
re.X/VERBOSE flag, 32
read() method (file object), 786
read() method (urlopen object), 401
reader() function, 205
readinto() method (file object), 786
readline() method, 81
readline() method (file object), 786
readline() method (urlopen object), 401
readlines() method (file object), 786
readlines() method (urlopen object), 401
readQ() function, 205
realm, 405
receiving e-mail, 121
    Google App Engine for, 658–660
recording events from application activity, 671
records in database, autogenerating for
        testing, 538
recv() method, 63
recvfrom() method, 63
recvfrom_into() method, 63
recv_into() method, 63
redirect_to() generic view, 552
reduced() function, Python 3 move to
        functools module, 813
refactoring, 136
reference counting, extensions and, 382–383
reference server, WSGI, 483
ReferenceError, 789
refill() function, 200
regex module, 16
regex. See regular expressions
registering password for login, 405
regsub module, 16
regular expressions, 3, 4
    alternation (|) operation, 9
    characters, escaping to include, 9
    comments, 8, 16
    compilation decision, 19
    conditional matching, 34
    creating first, 5

escaping characters to include, 23
examples, 36–41
    in-depth, 41–48
exercise answers, 763
extension notations, 16, 31–34
for e-mail addresses, 24–26
grouping parts without saving, 32
groups, 14–15
matching from start or end of strings or
    word boundaries, 10, 26–27
for obtaining current book ranking, 182
ranges (-) and negation (^), 12
repetition, 12–13, 24–26
special characters for character sets, 14
special symbols and characters, 6–16
splitting string based on, 30–31
Unicode string vs. ASCII/bytes string, 188
See also re module
relational databases, available interfaces,
    269–270
release() method (lock object), 165, 190, 193
remote API shell, 654
remote procedure calls (RPCs), XML and,
    733–738
remove() function, 774
remove() function (set types), 785
remove() method (list), 782
ren command, 188
rename() method (FTP objects), 99
render_to_response() method, 534, 536, 561
repetition, in regex, 12–13
replace() function, 774
replace() method (string), 780
replacing, searching and, 29
replenishment rates, for task queues, 663
ReplyThread, 158
repr() function, 769, 774
__repr__() method, 791
request context instance, 544
Request for Comments (RFCs), for cookies, 468
request in CGI, 444
RequestProcessor, 158
reserved port numbers, 59
reserved words, 768
reshtml variable, 451
resize() function, 225
response in CGI, 444
response submodule, 400
ResultsWrapper class, 705
    for Twitter, 704
    testing, 706
retasklist.py script, 40
retr() method (POP3 object), 125, 127
retrbinary() method (FTP objects), 99, 102
Retriever class, 414
retrlines() method (FTP objects), 99
retry parameters, for task queues, 663
reverse proxy, 394

reverse() function, 368–370, 375, 774
reverse() method (list), 782
reverse-chronological order
    for blog, 537
    query change for, 537–540
review_tweet() method, 587, 590
rewho.py script, 38
Reynolds, Joyce, 96
rfind() function, 774
rfind() method (string), 780
Rhino, 610
rich shells for Django, 515
rindex() function, 774
rindex() method (string), 780
rjust() function, 774
rjust() method (string), 780
RLock object (threading module), 170
    context manager, 196
rmd() method (FTP objects), 99
road signs, PFA GUI application, 227–229
robotparser module, 400, 433, 489
rollback() method (DB-API Connection ob-
    ject), 264
root window, 217
round() function, 771
rowcount attribute (DB-API Cursor object), 265
ROWID type object (DB-API), 267
rownumber attribute (DB-API Cursor object),
    266
rows in database table, 255
    inserting, 257
    insertion, update, and deletion, 297
rpartition() function, 774
RPython, 387
__*rshift__() method, 793
rsplit() function, 775
rstrip() function, 775
rstrip() method, 113, 780
rsync command (Unix), 96
Ruby, 610
run() method (Thread object), 172
run_bare_wsgi_app() function, 484
RuntimeError, 789
RuntimeWarning, 790
run_wsgi_app() function, 624
run_wsgi_app() method, 483

S
SaaS (Software-as-a-Service), 135, 607
Salesforce, 608
sandbox, 611
    restrictions, 612–616
sapdb, 317
saving
    matches from regex, 32
    subgroup from regex, 7
SAX (Simple API for XML), 725
Scala, 610
scalability issues for storage, 310

Scale widget, 220
    Label and Button widget with, 224–225
scanf() function, 280, 285
scp command (Unix), 96
scripts, standalone, 102
Scrollbar widget, 220, 233
Scrollbar.config() method, 233
sdb.dbapi, 317
search command (Twitter API), 695
search on Twitter, Tweepy library for, 692
Search service/API, 615
search() function (Twitter), 704
search() function/method, 4, 17, 21–22, 26–27
search() method (IMAP4 object), 130
searching
    and replacing, 29
    subgroups from, 27
    vs. matching, 4, 21–22, 46–48
secret.pyc file, 136
Secure Socket Layer (SSL), 393, 404
security
    e-mail and, 136
    for Outlook address book, 337
seek() method (file object), 787
SELECT * FROM statement (MySQL), 272
select module, 88
select() function, 88
select() method (IMAP4 object), 130
self.api, 703
self.error variable, 477
self.service.people() function, 756
Semaphore class, 199
Semaphore object (threading module), 170
    context manager, 196
semi-generic views in Django, 551
send() method, 63
sendall() method, 63
send_approval_email() method, 591
sendData() method, 86
send_group_email() function, 667
sending e-mail, 116–117
    Google App Engine for, 656
sendmail() method (SMTP object), 118, 119
sendMsg() method, 133
SendNewsletter class, 667
send_rejection_email() method, 591
send_review_email() method, 585
sendto() method, 63
sequence type operators, 772–776
sequential program, 157
server integration, as CGI alternative, 479
server.py module, 429
server.register_function() function, 736
servers, 54, 56
    for UDP, 76
    implementing exit scheme, 66, 72
    as Internet providers, 95
    location on Internet, 394–395

socket methods, 62
TCP
    creating, 64–68
    creating Twisted Reactor, 84–85
    executing, 71–73
    executing Twisted, 87
    SocketServer execution, 83
    timestamp from, 73
    WSGI, 482
session management, 488
set types, operators and functions, 783–785
set() function, 783
__set__() method, 792
__setattr__() method, 792
setblocking() method, 63
"Set-Cookie" header, 468
setCPPCookies() method, 476, 477, 478
setDaemon() method (Thread object), 172
set_debuglevel() method (SMTP object), 119
setdefault() method (dictionary), 783
setDirAndGo() method, 235
setinputsizes() method (DB-API Cursor
        object), 266
__setitem__() method, 794, 795
setName() method (Thread object), 172
setoutputsize() method (DB-API Cursor
        object), 266
setprofile() function (threading module), 179
sets
    displaying, 192
    for names of running threads, 192
__setslice__() method, 794
setsockopt() method, 63
settimeout() method, 63
settings file, for TweetApprover, 566–571
settings.py file
    in Django project, 504
settings.py file in Django project
    INSTALLED_APPS tuple in, 509
settrace() function (threading module), 179
setup.py script, creating, 377–378
SGML (Standard Generalized Markup
        Language), 724
sgmllib module/package, 418, 433, 489
sharded counter, 643
sharding, 498
Short Message Service (SMS), 691
showError() function, 459
showForm() function, 454
showForm() method, 477
_showRanking() function, 184, 186
showRanking() function, 182
showResults() method, 478
showwarning message box, 329
shutdown() method, 63
Simple API for XML (SAX), 725
Simple Mail Transfer Protocol (SMTP), 116
    authentication, 118

example, 126–128
interactive example, 119–120
Python and, 118
web resources, 120
Yahoo! Mail example, 142–144
Simple Storage System (S3), 607
simpleBS() function, 421, 422
SimpleHTTPRequestHandler class, 429, 447
SimpleHTTPServer class, 430, 489
SimpleHTTPServer module, 432, 435
handlers in, 430
simplejson library, 571, 720
simpletree format, for HTML documents, 423
simple_wsgi_app() app, 483
simple_wsgi_app(), wrapping, 485
SimpleXMLRPCServer package, 434, 733, 740
single-threaded process, 157
six package, 822
Slashdot, and traffic, 674
sleep, 159
vs. thread locks, 167
sleep() function, 166, 181, 354
SMS (Short Message Service), 691
smtpd module, 147
smtplib class, 118
smtplib module, 148
smtplib.SMTP class, 118
methods, 118–119
SMTP_SSL class, 118, 139
SOAP, 733
social media analysis tool, 750–759
social networking, 690
See also Twitter
SOCK_DGRAM socket, 61
Socket, 616
socket module, 61–62, 88, 404
attributes, 76–78
socket.error, 143
socket.socket() function, 61–62, 65, 74, 77
socketpair() function, 77
sockets, 58–61
addresses with host-port pairs, 59
built-in methods, 62–64
connection-oriented vs. connectionless, 60–61
data attributes, 64
for FTP, 97
related modules, 88–89
SocketServer class
TCP client creation, 82–83
TCP server and client execution, 83
TCP server creation, 80–82
SocketServer module, 65, 79–83, 88, 210
classes, 79
SOCK_STREAM socket, 60
softspace() method (file object), 787
software client/server architecture, 55–56
Software-as-a-Service (SaaS), 135, 607

sort() function, 775
sort() method (list), 782
sorted() function, 758
SoupStrainer class, 419, 422
spaces, plus sign (+) for encoding, 403
spam e-mail, 127
special characters
for character sets, 14
regular expressions with, 5, 7
vs. ASCII symbols, 34
spider, 410
spin locks, 174
Spinbox widget, 220, 247
SpinButton widget, 236
position of labels, 244
SpinCtrl widget, 241, 242
split() function, 775
split() function/method, 17
split() method, 30–31
split() method (string), 780
splitlines() function, 775
splitlines() method (string), 780
spreadsheets
closing without saving, 330
processing data from, 328
See also Excel
SQL, 256–257
viewing ORM-generated, 296
SQL Server, 317
SQLAlchemy, 289, 291–304, 318, 495
setup and install, 290
SQLite, 274–275, 317, 498, 510
for Django database, 511–??
loading database adapter and, 286
SQLite for Django database, ??–512
sqlite3 package, 290
sqlite3a, 317
SQLObject, 289, 304–309, 318
setup and install, 290
SQLObject2, 318
ssl() function, 77
standalone script, 102
standalone widgets, 217
Standard Generalized Markup Language (SGML), 724
StandardError, 788
StarOffice, 357
start of string, matching, 6, 10
_start() function, 356
start() method (Thread object), 172, 174
start_new_thread() function, 165, 166
startproject command, 502, 504
start_response() callable, 481
startswith() function, 775
startswith() method (string), 780
starttls() method (SMTP object), 119
stat() method (NNTP object), 107
stat() method (POP3 object), 125, 127

stateless protocol
   HTTP as, 392
states, enumeration and definition, 579
static dispatch, 329
static PyObject* function, 371
status() function, 736
stock quotes
   downloading into Excel, 338–340
   Yahoo! server for, 685–689
stock.py script, 688
   csv module for, 717
stockcsv.py script, 718
StopIteration, 788
storage mechanisms, 254
storbinary() method (FTP objects), 99
storlines() method (FTP objects), 99
Storm, 289, 318
str type, 800
str.format() method, 196, 207
str.__getslice__() method, 138
str.join() method, 137
str.startswith() method, 138
str.title() method, 460
str() function, 769, 775
__str__() method, 192, 296, 306, 791
strdup() function, 375
stream socket, 60
StreamRequestHandler class, 79, 81
string format operator (%)
   bytes objects and, 409
   directives, 777
STRING type object (DB-API), 267
StringIO class, 475, 731
strings
   built-in methods, 778–781
   converting to Unicode, 189
   in Python 3, 815
   in regular expressions, Unicode vs. ASCII/
      bytes, 188
   matching, 44–45
      from start or end, 10
      multiple, 22
   obtaining Python release number as, 142
   parsing, csv module for, 686
   raw, 512
   script to generate, 41–43
   searching for pattern in middle, 21
   splitting based on regex, 30–31
   "title-case formatter", 285
   Unicode vs. ASCII, 800–801, 815
strip() function, 775
strip() method (string), 780
sub() function/method, 18, 29
__*sub__() method, 792
subclassing Thread(), 177–178
subgroup from regex
   matching saved, 7
   saving, 7
   searches, 27

subn() function/method, 29
subprocess module, 206, 209
sudo command, 500
sum() function, 771
summation function, thread for, 180–182
Sun Microsystems Java/Swing, 249
superuser
   creating, 513
   login as, 520
swapcase() function, 775
swapcase() method (string), 780
swhello.java program, 746, 747
swhello.py program, 747
SWIG (Simplified Wrapper and Interface
      Generator), 384
swing module, 249
Swing, GUI development and, 745–748
sybase, 317
symmetric_ difference_ update() function
      (set types), 785
symmetric_difference() function (set types),
      784
syncdb command, 512, 579
   and database table creation, 518
   superuser creation, 513
synchronization of threads, 166, 170
synchronization primitives, 201
   shared resources and, 261
synchronization primitives for threads,
      190–201
   context management, 196
   locking example, 190–196
   semaphore example, 197–201
SyntaxError, 789
SyntaxWarning, 790
sys module/package, 414
sys.stdout.write() function, 819
SystemError, 789
SystemExit, 161, 788

T
t.timeit() method, 138
TabError, 789
__tablename__ attribute, 296
tables in database, 255
   create() function for, 287
   creation with Django, 512–514
Task Queue service/API, 616
task queues, 663
task_done() method (queue object), 203
tasklist command, 38, 39
   parsing output, 40
taskqueue.add() method, 665
tasks
   callables as deferred, 669
   in App Engine, creating, 663–666
   sending e-mail as, 666–668
Tcl (Tool Command Language), 214
TCP (Transmission Control Protocol), 60
   client creation, 68–71

executing server and clients, 71–73
listener setup and start, 62
server creation, 64–68
    SocketServer class for, 80–82
SocketServer class for client creation, 82–83
timestamp server, 66–68
Twisted server creation, 84–85
TCP client socket (tcpCliSock), 70
TCP/IP socket, creating, 61
TCPServer class (SocketServer module), 79
tell() method (file object), 787
tempfile module, 345
templates
    for blog application, 562
    in Django
        cross-site request forgery, 544
        directory, 529
        for user input, 542
        for user interface, 528–529
        for Web page, 527
        for Web pages, 570
        inheritance, 553
    for TweetApprover
        to display post status, 592
        login.html, 595
        pending tweet form, 595
Terms of Service (ToS)
    for Google service, 731
ternary/conditional operator, 229
test-driven development (TDD) model, 528
test_home() method, 556
testing
    auto-generating database records for, 538
    database, 556
    Django blog application code review,
        557–563
    extensions, 379–382
    in Django, 554–557
    ResultsWrapper class, 706
    user interface, 556
    when porting code to Python 3, 818
test_obj_create() method, 555
tests.py file for Django app, 508
    auto-generation, 554–557
text editors, for email editing in Outlook, 341
text file, converting to PowerPoint, 347–356
text font size on Label widget, 224
text in Python 3, 800
text processing, 3
    comma-separated values (CSV), 715–719
    JavaScript Object Notation (JSON), 719–724
    related modules, 740
    resources, 738
    XML (eXtensible Markup Langauge),
        724–738
Text widget, 221
tformat() function, 285, 288
thank_you() method, 585

themed widget sets, 244
thread module, 161, 163, 164–169, 209
    avoiding use, 164
    functions and methods, 165
Thread object (threading module), 170
thread.al-locate_lock() function, 169
ThreadFunc class, 176
ThreadFunc object, 176
Threading MixIn class (SocketServer module),
    79
threading module, 161, 163, 169, 209
    bookrank.py script, 182–189
    functions, 179
    synchronization primitives, 201
    Thread class, 171–179
    vs. thread module, 164
threading.activeCount() method, 196
threading.currentThread() method, 195
threading.current_thread() method, 195
threading.enumerate() method, 195
ThreadingTCPServer class (SocketServer
    module), 79
ThreadingUDPServer class (SocketServer
    module), 79
threads, 159
    alternatives, 206–209
    app to spawn random number, 191
    creating object instance
        passing in callable class instance, 175–176
        passing in function, 173–175
        subclass instance, 177–178
    example without, 162–163
    execution of single, 160
    exiting, 161
    extensions and, 384
    for Fibonacci, factorial, summation func-
        tions, 180–182
    loops executed by single, 162–163
    modules supporting, 163
    processes and, 158–159
    Python access to, 161
    set for names of running, 192
    spawning to handle client requests, 65
    synchronization primitives, 190–201
        context management, 196
        locking example, 190–196
        semaphore example, 197–201
threadsafety attribute (DB-API), 260
thttpd, 428, 446
TIDE + module, 248
Tile/Ttk module, 244–246, 248
time module, 168
Time type object (DB-API), 267
time.ctime() function, 43, 689
time.sleep() function, 162, 232, 354
TimeFromTicks type object (DB-API), 267
timeout exception, for socket module, 77
timeout, for FTP connections, 97

Timer object (`threading` module), 170
timestamp
   extracting days of week from, 44
   from server, 73
`Timestamp` type object (DB-API), 267
`timestamp()` function, 736
`TimestampFromTicks` type object (DB-API), 267
TIPC (Transparent Interprocess Communication) protocol, 59
Tipfy, 617, 618
   App Engine and, 676
`title()` function, 775
`title()` method (string), 460, 780
"title-case formatter", 285
Tix (Tk Interface eXtensions), 238
Tix module, 248
Tk GUI toolkit, 214
   geometry managers, 218
   widgets, 219–221
Tk Interface eXtensions (Tix), 238
Tk library, 244–246
`tkhello1.py` script, 221–222
`tkhello2.py` script, 222
`tkhello3.py` script, 223
`tkhello4.py` script, 224–225
Tkinter module, 214–215, 248
   demo code, 235
   examples
      `Button` widget, 222
      directory tree traversal tool, 230–236
      `Label` and `Button` widgets, 223
      `Label` widget, 221–222
      `Label`, `Button`, and `Scale` widgets, 224–225
   importing, 215
   installing, 215
   Python programming and, 216–221
   Tk for GUI, 745
TkZinc module, 248
TLS (Transport Layer Security), 144, 146
Tool Command Language (Tcl), 214
`Toplevel` widget, 221
`topnews()` function, 732
`top_posts()` function, 758
Tornado, 496
ToscaWidgets, 495
traceback, 445
transactional counter, 643
transition plan, 817
`translate()` function, 775
`translate()` method (string), 781
Transmission Control Protocol (TCP), 60
   client creation, 68–71
   `SocketServer` server and client execution, 83
   timestamp server, 66–68
Transparent Interprocess Communication (TIPC) protocol, 59
tree format, for HTML documents, parsing, 423

tree-based parsers for XML, 725
troubleshooting Twython library install, 572
`__*truediv__()` method, 792
`truncate()` method (file object), 787
try-except statement, while loop inside **except** clause, 72
`Ts_ci_wrapp` class, 486
`ts_simple_wsgi_app()`, for wrapping apps, 485
`tsTcIntV6.py` script, 71
`tsTclnt.py` script, 69–71
`tsTclntTW.py` script, 85, 86
`tsTserv.py` script, 66–68
`tsTserv3.py` script, 67, 68
`tsTservSS.py` script, 80
`tsTservTW.py` script, 84
`tsUclnt.py` script, 75
`tsUserv.py` script, 73, 74
`tuple()` function, 775
`TurboEntity`, 295
TurboGears, 495
   resources, 597
`twapi` module, 735
`twapi.py` script, 695–696, 698–706
Tweepy, 691
   compatibility library for Twython and, 693–706
`Tweet` class, for TweetApprover, 578
TweetApprover, 564–596
   approver app
      `urls.py` URLconf file, 576
      `views.py` file, 587–592
   data model, 576–582
   `DATABASES` variable, 570
   installing Twython library for, 571–572
   poster and approver apps, 565
   poster app
      data models file, 578
      `urls.py` URLconf file, 575
      `views.py` file, 582
   project file structure, 565–571
   Project URLconf file, 573–575
   reviewing tweets, 587–596
   settings file, 566–571
   submitting tweets for review, 582–586
   templates
      for pending tweet form, 595
      `login.html`, 595
      to display post status, 592
   URL structure, 572–576
   user creation, 580
   workflow, 565
`tweet_auth.py` file, 699
`TweetForm`, definition, 583
tweets, 690
Twisted framework, 84–87
   executing TCP server and client, 87
   TCP client creation, 85–87
   TCP server creation, 84–85
   Web site, 89

Twitter, 690–707
    authorization with, 694
    documentation, 704
    hybrid app, 694–706
    OAuth credentials for public API, 567
    Python and, 691–693
    resources, 707
    scalability issues, 310
    and traffic, 674
    Tweepy library for search, 692
Twitter account, authentication, 694
Twitter developers, resources, 597
TWITTER_CONSUMER_KEY setting, 567
TWITTER_CONSUMER_SECRET setting, 567
TWITTER_OAUTH_TOKEN setting, 567
TWITTER_OAUTH_TOKEN_SECRET setting, 567
Twython, 691
    camel capitalization, 703
    compatibility library for Tweepy and,
        693–706
Twython library, 736
    installing, 571–572
twython-example.py script, 692
txt2ppt.pyw script, 351–356
txt2ppt() function, 354
type attribute,for socket object, 64
type objects (DB-API), 266–268
type() function, 769, 775
TypeError, 789
types, JSON vs. Python, 721
TyphoonAE back-end system, 676

U
\u escape, for non-ASCII characters, 464
UDP (User Datagram Protocol), 61
    client creation, 74–76
    executing server and client, 76
    server creation, 73–74
UDP/IP socket, creating, 61
UDPServer class (SocketServer module), 79
unary operators, 793
UnboundLocalError, 789
uniCGI.py script, 465
Unicode strings
    converting to, 189
    in CGI applications, 464–465
    regular expression with, 188
    vs. ASCII strings, 800–801, 815
__unicode__() method, 579, 791
UnicodeDecodeError, 790
UnicodeEncodeError, 790
UnicodeError, 790
UnicodeTranslateError, 790
union OR, 9
union() function (set types), 784
unit testing in Django, 554–557, ??–563
_unit_*_wrap() functions, 706
Universal Network Objects (UNO), 357
University of California, Berkeley version of
    Unix, 58

Unix sockets, 58
UnixDatagramServer class (SocketServer
    module), 79
UnixStreamServer class (SocketServer
    module), 79
Unix-to-Unix Copy Protocol (UUCP), 96
unquote() function, 403, 404
unquote_plus() function, 403, 404
UPDATE statement (MySQL), 272
UPDATE statement (SQL), 257
update() function (set types), 785
update() function, for database adapter, 288
update() method, 297, 298, 314
update() method (dictionary), 783
update_status command (Twitter API), 695
update_status() function, 704
updateStatus() method, 592
updating database table rows, 255
uploaded file, retrieving, 468
uploading files, 478
    application to Google, 629
upper() function, 775
upper() method (string), 781
URIs (Uniform Resource Identifiers), 396
URL mappings, in urls.py file, 558
URL patterns, for Web pages from Django, 527
URLconf file, 543
    for Django app, 531–533
    for Django project, 529–531
    for TweetApprover, 573–575, 576
    for TweetApprover poster app, 575
urlencode() function, 403, 404
URLfetch service/API, 614, 616, 672
urljoin() function, 399, 422
urllib module/package, 103, 396, 399, 414, 434
urllib.error module/package, 434
urllib.parse module/package, 434
urllib.quote() function, 402, 476
urllib.quote_plus() function, 402
urllib.requestg module/package, 434
urllib.unquote() function, 476
urllib2 module, 401, 434, 732
    authentication example, 405–407
        porting, 407–410
urllib2.urlopen() function, 689
urllib2.urlopen() method, 184, 686
urlopen() function, 400–402, 732
    importing, 820
urlopen_auth.py script, 405, 406
urlopen_auth3.py script, 409, 410
urlparse module/package, 398–404, 414, 434
urlparse() function, 398, 399
urlpatterns global variable, 519
urlretrieve() function, 402, 404, 415
URLs (Uniform Resource Locators), 396–398
    avoiding hardcoding, 591
    breaking into components, 398
    encoding data for inclusion in URL string,
        402

URLs (Uniform Resource Locators) *(continued)*
  GET request variables and values in, 452
  structure for TweetApprover, 572–576
  variables in, 392
URLs variable, 421
urls.py file, 531
  for Django app, 504, 508
urlunparse() function, 398, 399
URNs (Uniform Resource Names), 396
USE statement (SQL), 256
Usenet News System, 104–114
User Datagram Protocol (UDP), 61
user input
  Django and, 542–546
    cross-site request forgery, 544
    templates, 542
    URLconf entry, 543
    views, 543
  Web services processing of, 442
user interface
  for blog, 527–533
  for databases, 255
  for searching posts, 758
  testing, 556
user profile in Google+, 750
USER setting, for Django database, 510
user() method (POP3 object), 125
username for anonymous FTP, 97
UserRequestThread, 158
Users service, 616
  adding in App Engine, 652–654
users, creating in TweetApprover, 580
user_timeline command (Twitter API), 695
user_timeline() function, 704
UserWarning, 790
ushuffle_*.py application, porting to use
    MongoDB, 312
ushuffle_db.py application, 276–279
ushuffle_mongo.py application, 312–315
ushuffle_sad.py application, 292–301
  output, 299–301
  vs. ushuffle_sae.py application, 304
ushuffle_sae.py application, 301–304
ushuffle_so.py application, 304–309
UTF-8 encoding, 464

V
validating parsers, 725
value comparisons, 769
ValueError, 790
values() function, 804
values() method (dictionary), 783
van Rossum, Guido, 799
variables
  hidden, in form, 454, 467
  in URLs, 392
  tags in Django templates, 528
vendor lock-in, 675

verify_credentials command (Twitter API),
  695
verify_credentials() function (Twitter), 704
view functions, 543
  create_blogpost(), 562
  for blog application, 533–537
  for Web page from Django, 527
  in Django app, 532
views
  fake, 533
  for TweetApprover approver app, 587–592
  for TweetApprover poster app, 582
  generic, 537
  in Django, 551–553
    for user input, 543
    generic views, 552–553
    semi-generic views, 551
views.py file
  for blog application, 560
  for Django app, 508
virtual circuit, 60
virtualenv, 500
  resources, 597
VSTO, 325

W
\W alphanumeric character set, 34
\w alphanumeric character set, 34
\w special character, for alphanumeric charac-
    ter class, 14
warming requests, in Google App Engine, 673
WarmUp service/API, 616
Warning, 790
Warning exception (DB-API), 263
Watters, Aaron, 258
Web addresses. *See* URLs (Uniform Resource
    Locators)
Web applications
  Google App Engine and, 605
  model-view controller (MVC) pattern, 514
Web browsers
  as FTP client, 103
  cookie management, 476
Web clients, 391–392, 394
  parsing Web content, 418–424
  programmatic browsing, 424–428
  Python tools, 396–410
    porting urllib2 HTTP authentication
      example, 407–410
    urllib module/package, 399
    urllib2 HTTP authentication example,
      405–407
    urlparse module/package, 398–404
  simple Web crawler/spider/bot, 410–418
Web connection, opening, 400
Web forms, adding database entry from, 523

Web frameworks, 487, 494–496
  App Engine vs., 609
  resources on, 597
Web page templates in Django, 527
Web programming
  real world development, 487
  related modules, 433, 488–489
Web resources
  concurrent.futures module, 209
  DB-API, 268
  list of supported databases, 270
  on App Engine, 676
  on Appstats, 672
  on building extensions, 366
  on Cython, 385
  on database-related modules/packages, 316
  on DRY, 591
  on extensions, 387
  on FTP, 104
  on GUIs, 250
  on JOINs, 298
  on JSON, 719
  on Jython, 744
  on MongoDB, 311
  on NNTP, 114
  on non-relational databases, 319
  on NoSQL, 310
  on Office applications, 357
  on Psyco, 386
  on PyPy, 387
  on Pyrex, 385
  on Python versions, 806
  on Query methods, 298
  on receiving e-mail, 660
  on SMTP, 120
  on SWIG, 384
  on text processing, 738
  on Twitter, 704, 707
  on Twitter API libraries, 691
  on Web frameworks, 597
  on XML-RPC, 736
  on Yahoo! Finance Server, 707
  on race conditions, 190
  on urllib2, 407
Web server farm, 395
Web Server Gateway Interface (WSGI), 480–482
  reference server, 483
Web servers, 55, 391–392, 428–433
  implementing simple base, 430–431
  in Django, 505
  scaling, 487
  setup for CGI, 446–448
  typical modern-day components, 444
Web services
  basics, 685

microblogging with Twitter, 690–707
Yahoo! Finance Stock Quotes Server, 685–689
Web sites
  CGI for fully interactive, 457–463
  downloading latest version of file, 101
Web surfing, 391–392
web.py, 496
web2py, 496, 618
  App Engine and, 676
web2py framework, 619
webapp framework, 617, 619
webapp2 framework, 617, 627
Web-based SaaS cloud services, 135
webbrowser module/package, 433, 489
WebWare MiddleKit, 289
well-known port numbers, 59
whitespace characters
  \s in regex for, 14
  matching in regex, 7
  removing, 113
who command (POSIX), regular expression for output, 36–38
who variable (Python), 451
widgets, 217
  default arguments, 221
  in top-level window object, 219
WIDTH variable for Google+ program, 754
win32com.client module, 327
win32ui module, 249
windowing object, 216
  top-level, 217
    defining size, 225
    widgets in, 219
Windows Extensions for Python, 326
windows servers, 55
WindowsError, 789
with statement, 38
  context manager and, 196
  getRanking() use of, 208
withdraw() function, 329
word boundaries
  matching and, 7, 10, 26
  matching from start or end, 10
Word, COM programming with, 331
word.pyw script, 331
workbook in Excel, 329
wrappers, listing for Python interpreter, 376
wrapping apps, 485
write() function, WSGI standard and, 481
write() method, 81, 102
write() method (file object), 787
writelines() method (file object), 787
writeQ() function, 205
writer() function, 205
writerow() method, 717

WSGI (Web Server Gateway Interface), 496
    middleware and wrapping apps, 485
    sample apps, 484
    servers, 482
    updates in Python 3, 486
wsgi.* environment variables, 483
wsgiref module, 435, 489
    demonstration app, 484
wsgiref.sim ple_server.demo_app(), 484
wsgiref.simple_server.WSGIServer, 483
wxGlade module, 248
wxPython module, 248
wxWidgets, animalWx.pyw application, 240–242

X

xhdr() method (NNTP object), 107, 112
xist tool, 462
XML (eXtensible Markup Language), 724–738
    converting Python dict to, 725–729
    vs. JSON, 719
    in practice, 729–733
xml package, 434, 725
xml.dom module/package, 434, 740
xml.dom.minidom, 725
xml.etree module/package, 434
xml.etree.ElementTree module/package, 740
    importing, 821
xml.parsers.expat package, 434, 740
xml.sax module/package, 434, 740
xmllib module, 434, 725
XML-RPC, 733–738
    client code, 737–738
    resources, 736
xmlrpc.client package, 733
xmlrpc.server package, 733

xmlrpcclnt.py script, 737–738
xmlrpclib module, 148, 434, 733, 737, 740
xmlrpcsrvr.py script, 734–737
XMPP (eXtensible Messaging and Presence
    Protocol), 614
XMPP (eXtensible Messaging and Presence
    Protocol) API, 616, 660
__*xor__() method, 793
xreadlines() method (file object), 786

Y

Yahoo! Finance Stock Quotes Server, 685–689
    code interface with, 736
    csv module for, 717–719
    parameters, 687, 695
    resources, 707
Yahoo! Mail, 135, 138–144
Yahoo! Mail Plus, 135, 139
YAML (yet another markup language), 622
yielding, 159
ymail.py script, 140–144

Z

\Z special character, for matching from end of
    string, 10
ZeroDivisionError, 788
zfill() function, 775
zfill() method (string), 781
Zip files
    for App Engine SKD, 620
    Google App Engine and, 613
zip() function, 731, 804
    iterator version, 820
Zope, 496

PRENTICE HALL

REGISTER
THIS PRODUCT

informit.com/register

Register the Addison-Wesley, Exam Cram, Prentice Hall, Que, and Sams products you own to unlock great benefits.

To begin the registration process, simply go to **informit.com/register** to sign in or create an account. You will then be prompted to enter the 10- or 13-digit ISBN that appears on the back cover of your product.

Registering your products can unlock the following benefits:

- Access to supplemental content, including bonus chapters, source code, or project files.
- A coupon to be used on your next purchase.

Registration benefits vary by product. Benefits will be listed on your Account page under Registered Products.

About InformIT — THE TRUSTED TECHNOLOGY LEARNING SOURCE

INFORMIT IS HOME TO THE LEADING TECHNOLOGY PUBLISHING IMPRINTS Addison-Wesley Professional, Cisco Press, Exam Cram, IBM Press, Prentice Hall Professional, Que, and Sams. Here you will gain access to quality and trusted content and resources from the authors, creators, innovators, and leaders of technology. Whether you're looking for a book on a new technology, a helpful article, timely newsletters, or access to the Safari Books Online digital library, InformIT has a solution for you.

THE TRUSTED TECHNOLOGY LEARNING SOURCE

Addison-Wesley | Cisco Press | Exam Cram
IBM Press | Que | Prentice Hall | Sams

SAFARI BOOKS ONLINE